BEHAVIORAL FINANCE

Psychology, Decision-Making, and Markets

BEHAVIORAL FINANCE

Psychology, Decision-Making, and Markets

Lucy F. Ackert
Michael J. Coles College of Business
Kennesaw State University

Richard Deaves
DeGroote School of Business
McMaster University

SOUTH-WESTERN
CENGAGE Learning

Australia • Brazil • Japan • Korea • Mexico • Singapore • Spain • United Kingdom • United States

SOUTH-WESTERN
CENGAGE Learning

Behavioral Finance: Psychology, Decision-Making and Markets
Lucy F. Ackert, Richard Deaves

Vice President of Editorial, Business:
Jack W. Calhoun

Publisher: Joe Sabatino

Executive Editor: Mike Reynolds

Sr. Developmental Editor:
Laura Bofinger Ansara

Marketing Manager: Nathan Anderson

Sr. Content Project Manager:
Tamborah Moore

Production Technology Analyst: Jeff Weaver

Media Editor: Scott Fidler

Sr. Frontlist Buyer, Manufacturing: Kevin Kluck

Production Service: Cadmus

Compositor: Cadmus/KGL

Sr. Rights Acquisitions Manager/Text:
Margaret Chamberlain-Gaston

Sr. Permissions Acquisitions Manager/Images:
Dean Dauphinais

Sr. Editorial Assistant: Adele Scholtz

Sr. Art Director: Michelle Kunkler

Internal Designer: Juli Cook

Cover Designer: Rokusek Design

Cover Image: © Loke Yek Mang / Shutterstock

For product information and technology assistance, contact us at
Cengage Learning Customer & Sales Support, 1-800-354-9706

For permission to use material from this text or product, submit all requests online at **www.cengage.com/permissions**

Further permissions questions can be emailed to
permissionrequest@cengage.com

Library of Congress Control Number: 2009932742

ISBN-13: 978-0-324-66117-0

ISBN-10: 0-324-66117-7

South-Western Cengage Learning
5191 Natorp Boulevard
Mason, OH 45040
USA

Cengage Learning products are represented in Canada by Nelson Education, Ltd.

For your course and learning solutions, visit **www.cengage.com**
Purchase any of our products at your local college store or at our preferred online store **www.ichapters.com**

Printed in the United States of America
PRINT NUMBER: 04   PRINT YEAR: 2015

To Bryan, Moira, William, and Rory
    —Lucy Ackert
To Karen and André
    —Richard Deaves

Brief Contents

Preface   **xx**

About the Authors   **xxiv**

Introduction   **xxvi**

PART I   Conventional Finance, Prospect Theory, and Market Efficiency   1

CHAPTER 1   Foundations of Finance I: Expected Utility Theory   3

CHAPTER 2   Foundations of Finance II: Asset Pricing, Market Efficiency, and Agency Relationships   19

CHAPTER 3   Prospect Theory, Framing, and Mental Accounting   37

CHAPTER 4   Challenges to Market Efficiency   60

PART II   Behavioral Science Foundations   81

CHAPTER 5   Heuristics and Biases   83

CHAPTER 6   Overconfidence   106

CHAPTER 7   Emotional Foundations   120

PART III   Investor Behavior   135

CHAPTER 8   Implications of Heuristics and Biases for Financial Decision-Making   137

CHAPTER 9   Implications of Overconfidence for Financial Decision-Making   151

CHAPTER 10   Individual Investors and the Force of Emotion   168

PART IV   SOCIAL FORCES   183

CHAPTER 11   Social Forces: Selfishness or Altruism?   185

CHAPTER 12   Social Forces at Work: The Collapse of an American Corporation   202

PART V   MARKET OUTCOMES   217

CHAPTER 13   Behavioral Explanations for Anomalies   219

CHAPTER 14   Do Behavioral Factors Explain Stock Market Puzzles?   237

PART VI   CORPORATE FINANCE   263

CHAPTER 15   Rational Managers and Irrational Investors   265

CHAPTER 16   Behavioral Corporate Finance and Managerial Decision-Making   279

PART VII   RETIREMENT, PENSIONS, EDUCATION, DEBIASING, AND CLIENT MANAGEMENT   293

CHAPTER 17   Understanding Retirement Saving Behavior and Improving DC Pensions   295

CHAPTER 18   Debiasing, Education, and Client Management   319

PART VIII   MONEY MANAGEMENT   333

CHAPTER 19   Behavioral Investing   335

CHAPTER 20   Neurofinance and the Trader's Brain   351

GLOSSARY   359
REFERENCES   367
INDEX   383

Contents

Preface **xx**

About the Authors **xxiv**

Introduction **xxvi**

PART I — Conventional Finance, Prospect Theory, and Market Efficiency 1

CHAPTER 1 — **Foundations of Finance I: Expected Utility Theory** 3

Introduction 3

Neoclassical Economics 4
Rational Preferences 4
Utility Maximization 4
Relevant Information 6

Expected Utility Theory 6

Risk Attitude 8

Allais Paradox 11

Framing 14

Looking Forward 14

Chapter Highlights 14

Discussion Questions and Problems 15

Appendix: More on Expected Utility Theory   16
  Definitions   16
  Axioms Required to Derive Expected Utility   17
  Sketch of a Proof   17
  Characteristics of Utility Functions   18
Endnotes   18

CHAPTER 2   **Foundations of Finance II: Asset Pricing, Market Efficiency, and Agency Relationships**   19

Introduction   19
The Pricing of Risk   20
  Risk and Return for Individual Assets   20
  Risk and Return for Portfolios of Assets   21
  The Optimal Portfolio   22
  Capital Asset Pricing Model   26
  Operationalizing the CAPM   27
Market Efficiency   28
  Efficiency and Information   28
  What Does Market Efficiency Imply?   29
  Misconceptions about Market Efficiency   30
  Joint Hypothesis Problem   30
Agency Theory   31
From Rationality to Psychology   33
Chapter Highlights   33
Discussion Questions and Problems   34
Endnotes   35

CHAPTER 3   **Prospect Theory, Framing, and Mental Accounting**   37

Introduction   37
Prospect Theory   38
  Key Aspects of Observed Behavior   38
  Value Function   40
  Lottery Tickets and Insurance   41
  Weighting Function   42
  Hypothetical Value and Weighting Functions   44
  Some Examples   45
  Other Issues   45
    Riskless Loss Aversion   45
    Origins of Prospect Theory   46
    Prospect Theory and Psychology   47
    Competing Alternative Theories   47

Framing   47
   Does Prospect Theory Work with Nonmonetary Outcomes?   48
   Integration vs. Segregation   48

Mental Accounting   50
   Opening and Closing Accounts   50
   Evaluating Accounts and Choosing When to Close Them   51
   Closure, Integration, and Segregation   52

From Theory to Practice   52

Chapter Highlights   53

Discussion Questions and Problems   53

Appendix: Conditions Required for the Prospect Theory Weighting
Function   55
   Conditions   55

Endnotes   56

CHAPTER 4   **Challenges to Market Efficiency**   60

Introduction   60

Some Key Anomalies   61
   Lagged Reactions to Earnings Announcements   61
   Small-Firm Effect   62
   Value vs. Growth   63
   Momentum and Reversal   65

Noise-Trading and Limits to Arbitrage   67
   Theoretical Requirements for Market Efficiency   67
      Support 1: All Investors Are Always Rational   67
      Support 2: Investor Errors Are Uncorrelated   68
      Shiller's Model   68
      Support 3: There are no Limits to Arbitrage   71
   What Limits Arbitrage?   72
      Fundamental Risk   72
      Noise-Trader Risk   72
      Implementation Costs   73

Looking Forward   75

Chapter Highlights   75

Discussion Questions and Problems   76

Appendix: Proofs for Shiller Model   77

Endnotes   78

PART II   BEHAVIORAL SCIENCE FOUNDATIONS   81

CHAPTER 5   **Heuristics and Biases**   83

Introduction   83

Perception, Memory, and Heuristics   84
Perception   84
Memory   84
Framing Effects   85
Ease of Processing and Information Overload   86
Heuristics   86
Examples of Heuristics   87

Familiarity and Related Heuristics   87
Familiarity   87
Ambiguity Aversion   88
Diversification Heuristic   89
Status Quo Bias and Endowment Effect   89
Heuristics and Biases, Prospect Theory, and Emotion   90

Representativeness and Related Biases   90
Conjunction Fallacy   91
Base Rate Neglect   91
  Bayesian updating   92
  Hot Hand Phenomenon   93
Gambler's Fallacy vs. Hot Hand   95
Overestimating Predictability   95
Availability, Recency, and Salience   96

Anchoring   97
What Explains Anchoring?   98
Anchoring vs. Representativeness   99

Irrationality and Adaptation   99
Fast and Frugal Heuristics   99
Response to Critique   100

Looking Ahead   100
Heuristics and Biases and Financial Decision-Making   100
Do Heuristic-Induced Errors Cancel Out?   101

Chapter Highlights   101

Discussion Questions and Problems   102

Endnotes   103

CHAPTER 6   **Overconfidence**   106

Introduction   106

Miscalibration   106
What Is It?   106
Example of a Calibration Test   107

Other Strains of Overconfidence   110
  Better-Than-Average Effect   110
  Illusion of Control   111
  Excessive Optimism   111
  Being Overconfident in More than One Sense   112
  Are People Equally Overconfident?   112
  Are People Consistently Overconfident?   113
Factors Impeding Correction   114
  Biases Interfering with Learning   114
  Is Overconfidence an Unmitigated Flaw?   114
Looking Ahead to Financial Applications   115
Chapter Highlights   116
Discussion Questions and Problems   116
Endnotes   117

CHAPTER 7   **Emotional Foundations**   120

Introduction   120
The Substance of Emotion   120
A Short History of Emotion Theory   122
Evolutionary Theory   124
The Brain   126
Emotion and Reasoning   128
Our Minds, Bodies, and Emotion   130
Looking Ahead   130
Chapter Highlights   132
Discussion Questions and Problems   132
Endnotes   133

PART III   INVESTOR BEHAVIOR   135

CHAPTER 8   **Implications of Heuristics and Biases for Financial Decision-Making**   137

Introduction   137
Financial Behaviors Stemming from Familiarity   138
  Home Bias   138
  Distance, Culture and Language   139
  Local Investing and Informational Advantages   140
  Investing in Your Employer or Brands that You Know   141
Financial Behaviors Stemming from Representativeness   141
  Good Companies vs. Good Investments   142

Chasing Winners   143
Availability and Attention-Grabbing   145
Anchoring to Available Economic Cues   145
An Experimental Study of Real Estate Appraisals   145
Anchoring vs. Herding and Analysts   147
Chapter Highlights   147
Discussion Questions and Problems   148
Endnotes   148

CHAPTER 9   **Implications of Overconfidence for Financial Decision-Making**   151

Introduction   151
Overconfidence and Excessive Trading   151
Overconfident Traders: A Simple Model   152
Evidence from the Field   157
Evidence from Surveys and the Lab   159
Demographics and Dynamics   161
Gender and Overconfidence in the Financial Realm   161
Dynamics of Overconfidence among Market Practitioners   161
Underdiversification and Excessive Risk Taking   162
Excessive Optimism and Analysts   163
Chapter Highlights   164
Discussion Questions and Problems   164
Endnotes   165

CHAPTER 10   **Individual Investors and the Force of Emotion**   168

Introduction   168
Is the Mood of the Investor the Mood of the Market?   169
Pride and Regret   170
The Disposition Effect   171
Empirical Evidence   171
Prospect Theory as an Explanation for the Disposition Effect   172
Another Possible Explanation   174
Experimental Evidence   174
House Money   175
Evidence of a House Money Effect on a Large Scale   175
Prospect Theory and Sequential Decisions   176
Affect   177
Chapter Highlights   178
Discussion Questions and Problems   179
Endnotes   179

PART IV   SOCIAL FORCES   183

CHAPTER 11   **Social Forces: Selfishness or Altruism?**   185

Introduction   185
Homo Economicus   186
Fairness, Reciprocity, and Trust   186
  Ultimatum and Dictator Games   187
  The Trust Game   189
  Who Is More Fair?   191
Social Influences Matter   192
  Competition in Markets   193
  Incentives and Contract Design   194
Conformity   196
  Testing Conformity   196
  Obedience to Authority   197
Social Behavior and Emotion   198
Social Behavior and Evolution   198
Chapter Highlights   199
Discussion Questions and Problems   199
Endnotes   200

CHAPTER 12   **Social Forces at Work: The Collapse of an American Corporation**   202

Introduction   202
Corporate Boards   203
  Benefits of a Corporate Board   203
  Outside Directors   204
  It's a Small World   205
  Directors, Compensation, and Self-Interest   205
  Directors and Loyalty   206
Analysts   206
  What Do Professional Security Analysts Do?   207
  The Performance of Security Analysts   207
  Do Analysts Herd?   208
Enron   209
  The Performance and Business of Enron   209
  The Directors   211
  The Analysts   212
  Other Players in Enron's Downfall   213
  Organizational Culture and Personal Identity   213

Chapter Highlights   214
Discussion Questions and Problems   214
Endnotes   215

PART V   MARKET OUTCOMES   217

CHAPTER 13   **Behavioral Explanations for Anomalies**   219

Introduction   219
Earnings Announcements and Value vs. Growth   220
   What is Behind Lagged Reactions to Earnings Announcements?   219
   What Is Behind the Value Advantage?   220
What is Behind Momentum and Reversal?   221
   Daniel-Hirshleifer-Subrahmanyam Model and Explaining Reversal   222
   Grinblatt-Han Model and Explaining Momentum   224
   Barberis-Shleifer-Vishny Model and Explaining Momentum and Reversal   227
Rational Explanations   230
   Inappropriate Risk Adjustment   230
   Fama-French Three-Factor Model   232
   Explaining Momentum   232
   Temporary Deviations from Efficiency and the Adaptive Markets Hypothesis   233
Chapter Highlights   233
Discussion Questions and Problems   234
Endnotes   234

CHAPTER 14   **Do Behavioral Factors Explain Stock Market Puzzles?**   237

Introduction   237
The Equity Premium Puzzle   238
   The Equity Premium   238
   Why Is the Equity Premium a Puzzle?   238
   What Can Explain This Puzzle?   240
Real-World Bubbles   243
   Tulip Mania   244
   The Tech/Internet Bubble   245
Experimental Bubbles Markets   247
   Design of Bubbles Markets   248
   What Can We Learn From These Experiments?   249
Behavioral Finance and Market Valuations   251
Excessive Volatility   251
   Do Prices Move Too Much?   251
   Demonstrating Excessive Volatility   252

Explaining Excessive Volatility 253
Volatility Forecasts and the Spike of 2008 253

Markets in 2008 254

Chapter Highlights 258

Discussion Questions and Problems 259

Endnotes 259

PART VI CORPORATE FINANCE 263

CHAPTER 15 **Rational Managers and Irrational Investors** 265

Introduction 265

Mispricing and the Goals of Managers 266
A Simple Heuristic Model 266
First Order Conditions 267

Examples of Managerial Actions Taking Advantage of Mispricing 268
Company Name Changes 268
Explaining Dividend Patterns 269
Share Issues and Repurchases 272
Mergers and Acquisitions 272

Irrational Managers or Irrational Investors? 274

Chapter Highlights 275

Discussion Questions and Problems 275

Endnotes 276

CHAPTER 16 **Behavioral Corporate Finance and Managerial Decision-Making** 279

Introduction 279

Capital Budgeting: Ease of Processing, Loss Aversion, and Affect 279
Payback and Ease of Processing 280
Allowing Sunk Costs to Influence the Abandonment Decision 280
Allowing Affect to Influence Choices 280

Managerial Overconfidence 282

Investment and Overconfidence 282
Overinvestment 282
Investment Sensitivity to Cash Flows 283
Mergers and Acquisitions 284
Start-ups 285

Can Managerial Overconfidence Have a Positive Side? 288

Chapter Highlights 288

Discussion Questions and Problems 289

Endnotes 289

PART VII   RETIREMENT, PENSIONS, EDUCATION, DEBIASING,
AND CLIENT MANAGEMENT   293

CHAPTER 17   **Understanding Retirement Saving Behavior and
Improving DC Pensions**   295

Introduction   295

The World-Wide Move to DC Pensions and its Consequences   296
  DBs vs. DCs   296
  Problems Faced by Employee-Investors   298

Saving with Limited Self-Control and Procrastination   298
  How Much Needs to be Saved?   298
  Limited Self-Control   300
  Exponential and Hyperbolic Discount Functions   301
  Procrastination   302
  Evidence on Retirement Preparedness   303

Asset Allocation Confusion   303
  Documenting the Problem   303
  Are There "Correct" Asset Allocations?   305
  Moving toward a Solution   306
  Is Education the Answer?   307

Improvements in DC Pension Design   307
  Automatic Enrollment   308
  Scheduled Deferral Increase Programs   310
  Asset Allocation Funds   311
  Moving toward the Ideal 401(k)   313

Chapter Highlights   313

Discussion Questions and Problems   314

Endnotes   315

CHAPTER 18   **Debiasing, Education, and Client Management**   319

Introduction   319

Can Bias be Eliminated?   319
  Steps Required to Eliminate Bias   319
  Strategies for Helping Those Affected by Bias   321

Debiasing Through Education   322
  Psychographic Profiling, Personality Types, and Money Attitudes   323
  Optimizing Education   325

Client Management Using Behavioral Finance   326
  Traditional Process of Asset Allocation Determination   326
  Using Behavioral Finance to Refine Process   328

Chapter Highlights   330

Discussion Questions and Problems   330

Endnotes   331

PART VIII   MONEY MANAGEMENT   333

CHAPTER 19   **Behavioral Investing**   335

Introduction   335
Anomaly Attenuation, Style Peer Groups, and Style Investing   335
Refining Anomaly Capture   337
Refining Value Investing Using Accounting Data   337
Refining Momentum-Investing Using Volume   337
Momentum and Reversal   339
Momentum and Value   341
Multivariate Approaches   342
Style Rotation   345
Is it Possible to Enhance Portfolio Performance Using Behavioral Finance?   346
Early Evidence   346
What is Behavioral Investing?   347
Chapter Highlights   348
Discussion Questions and Problems   348
Endnotes   348

CHAPTER 20   **Neurofinance and the Trader's Brain**   351

Introduction   351
Expertise and Implicit Learning   351
Neurofinance   353
Insights from Neurofinance   354
Expertise and Emotion   355
Chapter Highlights   356
Discussion Questions and Problems   356
Endnotes   357

GLOSSARY   359
REFERENCES   367
INDEX   383

Preface

Writing an overview of a burgeoning field is a daunting task. When we started our project, existing research in behavioral finance was already abundant. Since then, new work has appeared virtually daily. The only reasonable approach was to be selective. While we hope this book is a comprehensive treatment of the more important contributions in the field of behavioral finance, worthy research has certainly been excluded.

In writing this book, the students we have taught and the professional audiences we have addressed were a driving force. It is our hope that the material covered in this book will allow readers to consider financial decision-making in a new light. While a number of useful books that cover topics in behavioral finance are available to the interested reader, our goal was to write a book that would provide an accessible overview of the field, while at the same time illustrating how behavioral finance can be applied in real-world settings. With this in mind, the level of rigor has been kept low and theory has been kept to a minimum.

It is our belief that this book is suitable for undergraduate and graduate students in business and economics, as well as interested practitioners. The book can be used for a dedicated elective course or as a supplement to a more traditional corporate or managerial finance course.

To support the instructor and promote student learning an Instructor's Manual (IM) accompanies this book. The IM includes three parts: Solutions to Discussion Questions and Problems; Teaching Exercises; and Lecture Slides. Each of the 20 chapters in the book contains a number of Discussion Questions and Problems and the first part of the IM provides suggested solutions to each exercise. The second part of this manual presents Teaching Exercises that are designed to promote hands-on learning including experiments, cases and other items, running the gamut from Trading Simulators to Star Trek, from a price prediction game to a dice game, from a risk-taking survey to the Super Bowl, from Barings Bank to Royal

Dutch Shell, and so on. Finally, to give the instructor a head-start in the classroom, we have assembled a series of Lecture Slides.

ACKNOWLEDGEMENTS

We are particularly indebted to those early researchers who provided a path for the growing numbers of scholars who have built upon their work, including Werner De Bondt, Robert Dreman, Daniel Kahneman, Robert Shiller, Hersh Shefrin, Andrei Shleifer, Vernon Smith, Meir Statman, Richard Thaler, and Amos Tversky.

Though we are certainly forgetting numerous names, some of the researchers whose work has been influential and who appear prominently in these pages are: Maurice Allais, Marc Alpert, Solomon Asch, Clifford Asness, Malcolm Baker, Nardin Baker, Guido Baltussen, Brad Barber, Nicholas Barberis, Sanjoy Basu, Max Bazerman, Shlomo Benartzi, Itzhak Ben-David, Douglas Bernheim, Bruno Biais, Fischer Black, Robert Bloomfield, Nancy Brekke, Stephen Brown, Colin Camerer, Walter Cannon, David Centerbar, Louis Chan, John Conlisk, Michael Cooper, Joshua Coval, David Cutler, Antonio Damasio, Kent Daniel, Bradford De Long, Stéphanie Desrosiers, John Dickhaut, Orlin Dimitrov, John Doukas, Darren Duxbury, Jon Elster, Richard Fairchild, Eugene Fama, Ernst Fehr, Urs Fischbacher, Baruch Fischhoff, Christina Fong, Kenneth French, Laura Frieder, Simon Gächter, Simon Gervais, Gerd Gigerenzer, Thomas Gilovich, Markus Glaser, William Goetzmann, John Graham, David Grether, Dale Griffin, Mark Grinblatt, Dirk Hackbarth, Jeffrey Hales, Bing Han, Campbell Harvey, Robert Haugen, Chip Heath, Denis Hilton, David Hirshleifer, Charles Holt, Harrison Hong, Christopher Hsee, Ming Huang, Gur Huberman, William James, Narasimhan Jegadeesh, Wei Jiang, Eric Johnson, Charles Jones, Matti Keloharju, Thomas Kida, Alok Kumar, Josef Lakonishok, Owen Lamont, Rafael La Porta, Henry Latane, Susan Laury, Charles Lee, Jonathan Lewellen, Jean-François L'Her, Andrew Lo, George Loewenstein, Dan Lovallo, Brigitte Madrian, Ulrike Malmendier, Karine Mazurier, Rajinish Mehra, Stanley Milgram, Olivia Mitchell, Kimberly Moreno, Tobias Moskowitz, Margaret Neale, John Nofsinger, Gregory Northcraft, Terrance Odean, Dimitris Petmezas, Joseph Piotroski, Jean-François Plante, Michael Pompian, Thierry Post, James Poterba, Sébastien Pouget, Edward Prescott, Howard Raiffa, Raghavendra Rau, Marc Reinganum, Richard Rendleman, Mark Riepe, Stephen Ross, Yuval Rottenstreich, Richard Ruback, William Samuelson, Tano Santos, Stanley Schachter, Myron Scholes, William Schwert, Dennis Shea, Jeremy Siegel, Herbert Simon, Jerome Singer, James Smith, Brett Steenbarger, Avanidhar Subrahmanyam, Gerry Suchanek, Barbara Summers, Larry Summers, Bhaskaran Swaminathan, Geoffrey Tate, Robert Vallone, Martijn van den Assem, Robert Vishny, Robert Waldmann, Martin Weber, Arlington Williams, Timothy Wilson, Jeffrey Wurgler, Wei Xiong, Robert Zajonc, and Ganggang Zhang. While a number of these researchers are not overly sympathetic to the behavioral perspective, it is fair to say that all have contributed to the debate.

We also appreciate the support of Cengage Learning and their excellent team, led by Laura Ansara and Mike Reynolds, with the able support of Tamborah Moore and Andrea Clemente. Finally, we thank colleagues and students who have provided input: George Athanassakos, Gokul Bhandari, Narat Charupat, Bryan Church, Aey Chatupromwong, Shawn Davis, Travis Derouin, Jerry Dwyer, Ann Gillette, Rongbing Huang, Marcelo Klotzle, Brian Kluger, Swetlana Ljubicic, Erik Lüders, Matt Miller, Peter Miu, Budina Naydenova, Oksana Ogrodnik, Melissa Parlar, Li Qi, Gabriel Ramirez, Mark Rider, Michael Schröder, Paula Tkac, Ted Veit, Barry White, and Ao Yang.

In addition, we wish to thank the numerous reviewers of drafts of the book:

Brandon Adams
Harvard University

Bulent Aybar
Southern New Hampshire University

Brad M. Barber
UC Davis

Candy A. Bianco
Bentley College

Deanne Butchey
Florida International University

Haiwei Chen
California State, San Bernardino

Jing Chen
University of Northern British Columbia

Hsiang-Hsuan Chih
National Dong Hwa University

David Enke
University of Tulsa

Richard John Fairchild
University of Bath, UK

James Felton
Central Michigan University

Merlyn Foo
Athabasca University

Laura Frieder
Purdue University

Satyananda Gabriel
Mount Holyoke College

Nancy R. Jay
Mercer University

Steven T. Jones
Samford University

Shimon Kogan
Carnegie Mellon University

Alok Kumar
University of Texas, Austin

Henry Pruden
Golden Gate University

Li Qi
Agnes Scott College

Raghavendra Rau
Purdue University

Thomas A. Rietz
University of Iowa

Scott Smart
Indiana University

Bijesh Tolia
Chicago State University

P.V. Viswanath
Pace University

Lucy Ackert (in Atlanta) and Richard Deaves (in Burlington), May 22, 2009

About the Authors

Lucy F. Ackert is Professor of Finance in the Michael J. Coles College of Business at Kennesaw State University and Visiting Scholar at the Federal Reserve Bank of Atlanta. Dr. Ackert holds a Ph.D. in financial economics from Emory University. Her research interests include individual's use of information and financial market reaction to information. Dr. Ackert has published numerous articles in refereed journals including the *American Economic Review*, *Journal of Accounting Research*, and *Journal of Finance*.

In 1993 Dr. Ackert received a Smith Breeden Prize for Distinguished Paper in the *Journal of Finance*. Her research has received funding from various organizations including the Center for the Study of Futures Markets at Columbia University, the Chicago Board of Trade, the Canadian Investment Review, and the Social Sciences and Humanities Research Council of Canada. In 2008 Dr. Ackert received the Kennesaw State University Distinguished Graduate Scholarship Award.

Dr. Ackert has previously taught at Emory University, Berry College, and Wilfrid Laurier University. She has taught a range of courses for graduate as well as undergraduate students, including Behavioral Finance, Corporate Finance, Futures and Options Markets, Financial Institutions, Cases in Finance, Introduction to Statistical Methods, and Microeconomics.

Richard Deaves earned his Ph.D. from the University of Toronto and currently teaches at the DeGroote School of Business, McMaster University in Hamilton, Canada. In addition to McMaster, Dr. Deaves has been a visiting professor at the University of Toronto, Concordia University, and Rollins College. He has taught a variety of courses, including Behavioral Finance, Security Analysis, Portfolio Management, Derivatives and Applied Investment Management.

Dr. Deaves's research publications have appeared in numerous journals, such as the *Journal of Financial and Quantitative Analysis*, the *Journal of Banking and Finance*, and the *Journal of Monetary Economics*. He has conducted research in such areas as investor knowledge and pension fund design, experimental asset markets, investment fund performance, fixed-income return enhancement, modeling and predicting interest rates, pricing and hedging futures contracts, and the relationship between financial markets and the macroeconomy.

Dr. Deaves has consulted for large and small private firms and government agencies, and has appeared as an expert witness, in such diverse areas as market efficiency, the behavioral aspects of investment, saving and pension design, the predictability of interest rates, the design of risk management programs, and capital market performance.

INTRODUCTION

The rapidly growing field of behavioral finance uses insights from psychology to understand how human behavior influences the decisions of individual and professional investors, markets, and managers. We are all human, which means that our behavior is influenced by psychology. Some decisions are simple, day-to-day choices, such as how hard we are going to study for the next test, or what brand of soda we are going to buy, but others significantly impact our financial well-being, such as whether we should buy a particular stock, or how we should allocate our 401(k) money among various investment funds. The purpose of this book is to present what we have learned about financial decision-making from behavioral finance research, while recognizing the challenges that remain.

Looking ahead, we will see that behavioral finance is very useful in helping us understand certain puzzles at the level of the investor. For example, why do people tend to invest in local companies? Why do investors confuse a good company and a good stock? Why do people increase the amount of risk they are willing to take on if they have experienced good *or* bad portfolio performance? Why are they reluctant to eliminate poorly performing investments from their portfolios? Why do many investors trade as often as they do? Why do they insufficiently diversify their asset holdings? Why do people follow the crowd?

While it would be difficult to find anyone who would seriously question the contention that psychology impacts individual financial decisions, there is less agreement on whether market outcomes are also impacted. This is because the belief that human psychology affects markets is inconsistent with the traditional view that market forces lead to efficient outcomes. Nevertheless, if human psychology can lead to individual behavior that is not optimal and such errors are sometimes correlated, and there are limits to arbitrage, then, provided there limits to arbitrage, the traditional view of markets is likely an incomplete story.

More recently, behavioral finance has also made strides in providing insight into the behavior of managers. Given what we have learned about investor psychology, it would be surprising if behavioral factors did not play a role in managerial decision-making. On the one hand, can managers take information relating to individual psychology into account in an effort to achieve improvements in personal performance? On the other hand, do managers, being themselves human, fall prey to their own behavioral errors?

PLAN OF THE BOOK

To make sense of how human psychology impacts individuals and markets, we need to take a few steps back. We begin, in Part I of the book, by reviewing the foundations of modern finance, its inability to account for various paradoxes and anomalies, and the genesis of behavioral finance as reflected in prospect theory and the limits to arbitrage perspective. Expected utility theory, reviewed in Chapter 1, is an axiomatic, normative model that demonstrates how people *should* behave when facing decisions involving risk. In comparing prospects, which are simply probability distributions of final wealth levels, the basic procedure is to assign a utility level to each possible wealth outcome, weight each utility value by the associated probability, and choose the prospect with the highest expected utility.

Although expected utility theory has been very useful in modeling individual decision-making, financial theorists required a paradigm to describe how investors evaluated risk and determined prices in markets. Mean-variance analysis and the CAPM, reviewed in Chapter 2, were central developments, providing for the first time guidance on how risk should be measured and risky assets priced. At around the same time, the notion of market efficiency became prominent. This is the view that, because competitive markets embody all relevant information, the price of an asset should be virtually identical to its fundamental value. The realization that information was not costless, along with the impossibility theorem of Grossman and Stiglitz, caused this to be altered to the contention that nobody should be able to earn excess (risk-adjusted) returns on a consistent basis.[1] Importantly, market efficiency is inextricably linked to asset pricing models because of the joint hypothesis problem, the fact that tests of market efficiency also require the use of a particular risk-adjustment mechanism.

Despite the elegance of these foundations, it was not long before holes were found. Careful analysis of people's actual choices revealed a number of violations of expected utility theory. For example, while risk aversion was the norm for many, at times risk-seeking behavior was patently obvious, people's willingness to buy lottery tickets being a prime example. It soon became evident that a new theory of individual choice was required, one that would be grounded in actual behavior and research in psychology. Among alternative models that have been proposed, Kahneman and Tversky's prospect theory has attracted the most attention.[2] Positive rather than normative in nature, prospect theory is reviewed in Chapter 3. For some purposes, prospect theory is supplemented with mental accounting, an important thrust of which is path dependence. The key elements of these models include evaluating outcomes relative to a reference point (such as the status quo), a strong aversion to losses, and context-dependent risk attitudes.

Modern finance also came under siege as it became clear that CAPM and market efficiency were often at odds with empirical evidence using naturally occurring data. Chapter 4 begins by reviewing several anomalies, which are defined as findings inconsistent with the *simultaneous* validity of both the CAPM and efficiency. Theoretical developments also played a role. While in the past people were inclined to argue that profit opportunities could always be easily "arbitraged away" in competitive markets, some began to question whether arbitrage was as simple and risk free as the textbooks seemed to suggest. This school of thought argued that there were significant limits to arbitrage. These limits were driven by such factors as noise-trader risk (the possibility that wrong prices might get worse in the short run); fundamental risk (which exists when substitute securities do not exist); and significant implementation costs (trading costs and the potential unavailability of the security that must be short-sold).

Behavioral finance more than other branches of finance is interdisciplinary. It borrows heavily from the academic literature in accounting, economics, statistics, psychology, and sociology. The psychology literature is particularly useful in revealing how people make decisions and where biases may reveal themselves. In Part II, we provide the necessary foundations from psychology. The taxonomy we adopt slots potential psychologically based behaviors into three silos: cognitive limitations and heuristics, overconfidence, and emotion. We begin, in Chapter 5, by noting that modern economic and financial models often seem to be predicated on the existence of an emotionless decision-maker possessing virtually unlimited cerebral RAM. Such a decision-maker considers all relevant information, arriving at the optimal choice in a process known as constrained optimization. And yet a host of cognitive limitations are evident, including faulty and selective perception and memory, inattention, and frame influence. Complicated problems must be simplified, and heuristics, or rules-of-thumb, are designed for this purpose. Evolutionary survival pressures have led to the crafting of a host of such procedures. While they usually lead to judicious actions, at times man's "toolkit" may be faulty. This is particularly so when decisions must be made in a complex modern environment, when many of the procedures were first developed to find and ensure food and shelter. We look at various classes of heuristics, including those impacting preference primarily via comfort-seeking and those designed to estimate probability. While there is abundant evidence of error, some, especially those espousing the "fast and frugal" heuristics view, have argued that heuristics perform much better than they are often given credit for.

Next, in Chapter 6, we recognize people's tendency toward overconfidence. Overconfident people overestimate their knowledge, abilities, and the precision of their information, or are overly sanguine of the future and their ability to control it. Overconfidence takes on such forms as miscalibration (the tendency to believe that your knowledge is more precise than it really is), the better-than-average effect, illusion of control (an unfounded belief that you can influence matters), and excessive optimism. Overconfidence can encourage action when caution is warranted.

Finally, in Chapter 7, we consider what emotions are and how they impact decision-making. A lot of money, not to mention careers, is at stake when financial decisions are made, and high stakes can only raise the emotional thermometer.

There is certainly a presumption on the part of the media that emotions influence markets, which of course implies that they first impact individual decisions. While it is true that rampant emotion can be a bad thing, a balanced emotional state (as opposed to an emotionless state) can actually foster judicious decision-making.

Armed with this psychological background, Part III turns to an examination of how psychology impacts financial decision-making at the level of the individual. For the time being, our gaze is fixed on investors and related capital market practitioners rather than the managers of corporations. We begin, in Chapter 8, by investigating the extent to which the faulty use of heuristics leads to suboptimal financial decision-making. For example, the representativeness heuristic can persuade people that good companies are good investments, and companies with good recent stock market performance are good buys. Familiarity can lead to excessive domestic and local investment. The availability bias pushes people into concentrating investments in securities where information is freely available. Anchoring causes individuals to be excessively anchored to available cues, instead of relying on their own opinion or expertise.

In Chapter 9, we explore the extent to which overconfidence can lead to suboptimal behavior on the part of investors and capital market participants. The tendency to believe that one's analysis is more accurate than is actually so appears to cause investors to trade too much. Other documented problems linked to overconfidence are underdiversification and taking on too much risk.

The final chapter of this section, Chapter 10, examines how emotion impacts financial decisions. The evidence appears strongest for the break even effect, the house money effect, and the disposition effect. It is notable that these observed behaviors have competing explanations based on prospect theory. What they have in common is that they are all in some sense based on path dependence. In the first two cases, results worse than or better than expectations may lead to an increase in risk taking: in the first case, because people, who hate to lose, want to get back to square one; and, in the second case, because people, after a windfall, know they can take on a high amount of risk without flirting with a loss. As for the disposition effect, a losing investment may be held too long because people fear the regret that would result if their poor investment is sold off.

In Part IV, we turn to an examination of how social forces impact the choices people make. This is an important issue in behavioral finance because investors, financial practitioners, and managers do not make decisions in isolation. We begin in Chapter 11 with evidence that social forces matter for people in distinct cultures around the world and in the business realm. While conventional theory postulates that man is a rational, self-interested decision-maker, the evidence suggests that human beings sometimes choose actions that are not in their material self-interest, and that social interests influence how people make decisions, including what we call other-regarding preferences, such as fairness and reciprocity. To illustrate their importance, we show how social forces can impact competition in markets and contract design.

Next, in Chapter 12, to illustrate the importance of social forces, we show that such forces contributed to the fall of a large American corporation, Enron. Of particular focus are two important sets of participants: the corporate board and professional financial analysts. The corporate board is charged with providing internal governance to the firm, but how do social forces impact its effectiveness? Financial analysts are important information intermediaries for investors and managers, but can their opinions be shaped by the social group?

In Part V, we consider what behavioral finance can tell us about observed market outcomes. Following up on Chapters 2 and 4, where we noted that the first tests of market efficiency were largely supportive, while later tests produced evidence that was often at odds with the this theory, we return, in Chapter 13, to a discussion of these anomalies, but now the focus is on describing potential behaviorally based explanations for them. Two anomalies in particular, the value advantage and momentum, are most troubling, and for this reason receive special attention.

Chapter 14 addresses some central stock market puzzles. Over the last number of years, researchers have begun to question whether observed stock market valuation levels and price volatility are consistent with the predictions of theory. Of particular note is that in the 1990s the entire U.S. market seems to have deviated far from valuations based on economic fundamentals. In addition to considering the basis for market valuations, we review evidence regarding the level of stock market volatility. Additionally, the equity premium puzzle, the historical tendency for equities to outperform fixed-income investment by more than their differential risk would seem to require, is also addressed in this chapter.

Part VI describes how psychological biases have the potential to impact the behavior of managers. How we think about the outcomes depends on whether the behavior of markets or managers is the source of bias. Both the abilities of rational managers to take actions when markets are believed to reflect irrationality and the possibility that managers are themselves the source of bias are addressed. Chapter 15 argues that there is evidence that rational managers at times take advantage of the valuation mistakes made by irrational investors. We begin with a heuristic model, which shows that rational managers in a world with irrational investors have conflicts between short-run and long-run goals. These conflicts can lead to choices that maximize price rather than value. We also describe examples of catering to investors, including changing the company name to something more appealing to investors and responding to dividend payout preferences. Empirical evidence consistent with these tendencies is presented.

Chapter 16 focuses on the potential for suboptimal financial decisions by corporate decision-makers and entrepreneurs. We first consider possible mistakes in the capital budgeting process caused by cognitive and emotional forces. Overconfidence may also impact managerial decisions deleteriously. In this regard, we address overinvestment, investment sensitivity to cash flows, mergers and acquisitions, and start-ups. Finally, we consider whether managerial overconfidence can sometimes play a positive role.

In Part VII we turn to retirement, pensions, education, debiasing, and client management. This is a key area where the lessons of behavioral finance are increasingly being put to good use. In Chapter 17, the focus is on retirement and pensions. Around the world, as firms have moved from defined benefit to defined contribution pension plans, affected workers have been forced to deal with the challenge of trying to optimally manage retirement savings. Unfortunately, such individuals are often susceptible to self-control problems, procrastination, and confusion regarding asset allocation. Nevertheless, there is evidence that innovation in pension design can lead to better outcomes.

In Chapter 18, we look at various debiasing strategies that can improve financial decision-making. It is possible that a significant payoff can be obtained from a careful financial education program. We argue that education can be enhanced with knowledge of the psychological mindset of the investor. Finally, we provide insight for wealth managers whose clients may be subject to bias and emotion.

The book closes with Part VIII, which is designed to be of most use to investors and traders. Behavioral investing, the topic of Chapter 19, is the attempt to enhance portfolio performance by applying lessons learned from behavioral finance research. Given that empirical regularities such as momentum and the value advantage appear robust, improving portfolio performance by tilting toward stocks embodying these attributes seems to be called for. Nevertheless, matters are seldom as simple as one might initially believe. Complications and opportunities include anomaly attenuation, style peer groups, style investing, and various refinements to simplistic anomaly capture. We close this chapter by considering whether objective evidence exists that behavioral investing can lead to desirable results.

The final chapter of the book, Chapter 20, focuses on what it takes to be a highly skilled professional trader. By looking at how the brain reacts during various activities, scientists learn how the brain functions and solves problems. Neurofinance researchers use neurotechnology to examine how the brain behaves while a person is making financial decisions. Potential insights include information regarding which kinds of responses are controlled and which are automatic. It takes many hours of training for any professional to become skilled. In addition to practice, we consider the knowledge that traders can take from behavioral finance research to generate better performance.

APPROACH AND METHODOLOGY OF BEHAVIORAL FINANCE

In any science, advancements are made through the interplay of theory and empirics. Observation suggests appropriate theory, and models are tested using data. When the data are inconsistent with theory, new models are formulated. The communication between theory and evidence is the ebb and flow of science, and academic finance works in the same way. As you will see as you progress through this book, behavioral finance is rather eclectic in the tools used for observation. The data may be naturally occurring, generated from controlled experiments in the lab, or obtained through surveys. Experimental finance and economics use the laboratory method to test the validity of existing theories and examine the impact of new mechanisms. In the tradition of psychology, surveys are often conducted by researchers in behavioral finance.

Some conventional finance researchers are skeptical of behavioral finance as they see it as proposing a new theory to fit every new finding.[3] Of course, if a parsimonious model could predict human behavior, things certainly would be less complicated. But, how many of us really believe that all human actions can be summarized in a simple way? At the same time, we believe it is important to possess skepticism. We hope to present a full treatment of the evidence and let you, the reader, decide.

How does behavioral finance contribute to our knowledge of finance? In our view, behavioral finance does not replace modern finance. Instead, it is an important complement. The tools of modern finance remain extremely useful for corporate managers, investors, and others who make financial decisions. Yet, the ebb and flow of science operates here as well. When results are uncovered that are inconsistent with conventional wisdom, new theory is posited, often building on the existing knowledge. At some point in the future, the "new conventional theory" will be shaped by behavioral findings. In this sense, we look forward to future developments in behavioral finance.

ENDNOTES

1 Grossman, S. J., and J. E. Stiglitz, 1980, "On the impossibility of informationally efficient markets," *American Economic Review* 70(3), 393–408.

2 Kahneman, D., and A. Tversky, 1979, "Prospect theory: An analysis of decision under risk," *Econometrica* 47(2), 263–291.

3 Fama, E. F., 1998, "Market efficiency, long-term returns and behavioral finance," *Journal of Financial Economics* 49, 283–306.

Conventional Finance, Prospect Theory, and Market Efficiency

CHAPTER 1   Foundations of Finance I: Expected Utility Theory

CHAPTER 2   Foundations of Finance II: Asset Pricing, Market Efficiency, and Agency Relationships

CHAPTER 3   Prospect Theory, Framing, and Mental Accounting

CHAPTER 4   Challenges to Market Efficiency

FOUNDATIONS OF FINANCE I: EXPECTED UTILITY THEORY

1.1 INTRODUCTION

The behavior of individuals, practitioners, markets, and managers is sometimes characterized as "irrational," but what exactly does that mean? To answer this question, we must take several steps back and fully understand the foundations of modern finance, which are based on rational decision-making. The first two chapters of the book are designed to accomplish this goal, with the first presenting the standard theory of how individuals make decisions when confronted with uncertainty.

As background, we first consider what standard (or neoclassical) economics argues about rational behavior when economic decisions are made and there is no uncertainty about the future. In the next section, it is argued that individuals should maximize utility (or happiness) based on their preferences, the constraints they face, and the information at their disposal. In Section 1.3, we note that decisions become complicated when there is uncertainty. An extension of utility theory has been developed for this purpose and is known as expected utility maximization. The basic procedure is to ascertain the utility level generated by varying levels of wealth, and then, when choosing among prospects, which are defined to be probability distributions of different wealth levels, to calculate the expected level of utility of each of these prospects. Finally, the decision-maker chooses the prospect with the highest expected utility. In the following section, we discuss the role of risk attitude. Specifically, since people prefer to avoid risk, it is necessary to compensate them for assuming it, and the degree to which they must be compensated depends on their risk aversion. Despite the elegance of expected utility, there are a number of occasions when many people act contrary to it. The best-known instance is the Allais paradox presented in Section 1.5. The final two sections of the chapter look ahead to the importance of how a problem is presented, that is, the decision frame, and to prospect theory, the principal alternative to expected utility maximization, which will be the major focus of Chapter 3.

1.2   NEOCLASSICAL ECONOMICS

Traditional finance models have a basis in economics, and **neoclassical economics** is the dominant paradigm. In this representation, individuals and firms are self-interested agents who attempt to optimize to the best of their ability in the face of constraints on resources. The value (or price) of an asset is determined in a market, subject to the influences of supply and demand.[1] In this chapter, we focus on individual decision-making, leaving markets to the following chapter.

Neoclassical economics makes some fundamental assumptions about people:[2]

1. People have rational preferences across possible outcomes or states of nature.
2. People maximize utility and firms maximize profits.[3]
3. People make independent decisions based on all relevant information.

These assumptions seem quite reasonable upon first consideration, but let's be sure we really understand what they mean.

RATIONAL PREFERENCES

What does it mean for individuals to have **rational preferences**? Certain conditions are commonly imposed on preferences. We will introduce some notation to understand these conditions. Suppose a person is confronted with the choice between two outcomes, x and y. The symbol $>$ means that one choice is strictly preferred to another, so that the relation $x > y$ means that x is always the preferred choice when x and y are offered to some individual. The symbol $\sim$ indicates indifference, so that $x \sim y$ indicates that the person values the two outcomes the same. Finally, the symbol $\geqslant$ indicates weak preference, so that $x \geqslant y$ means that the person prefers x or is indifferent between x and y.

An important assumption is that people's **preferences** are **complete**. This means that a person can compare all possible choices and assess preference or indifference. Thus, for any pair of choices, $x \geqslant y$ or $y \geqslant x$ or both, which would mean that $x \sim y$. This assumption does not seem to cause too many problems. Surely most people know what they like and what they do not like.

A second assumption, **transitivity**, does not seem to be too strong an assumption for most people. Suppose now that a person is confronted with a choice among three outcomes: x, y, and z. According to transitivity, if $x > y$ and $y > z$, then $x > z$. If I prefer vanilla ice cream to chocolate, and chocolate to strawberry, I should also prefer vanilla to strawberry. If transitivity does not hold, we cannot determine an optimal or best choice. So, rational choices are transitive.

UTILITY MAXIMIZATION

Utility theory is used to describe preferences. With a **utility function**, denoted as u($\bullet$), we assign numbers to possible outcomes so that preferred choices receive higher numbers. We can think of utility as the satisfaction received from a particular outcome. Normally an outcome is characterized by a "bundle" of goods. For example, someone might have to choose between two loaves of bread *plus* one bottle of water and one loaf of bread *plus* two bottles of water. If this individual reveals a preference for the former, we would say that:

1.1   u(2 bread, 1 water) > u(1 bread, 2 water)

Notice that we have not specified any numerical values for u(•). This is because, while the ordering of outcomes by a utility function is important, the actual number assigned is immaterial. The utility function is ordinal (i.e., order-preserving) but not cardinal (which would mean the exact utility value matters). To arrive at her optimal choice, an individual considers all possible bundles of goods that satisfy her budget constraint (based on wealth or income), and then chooses the bundle that maximizes her utility.[4]

If there is a single good of interest, then ranking under certainty is trivial. This stems from the principle of non-satiation, which simply means the more the better. As an example of a single good, utility functions are often defined in relation to wealth. Though mathematically a utility function can be specified in different ways, we will use the example of a logarithmic function. In this case, the utility derived from wealth level w is $u(w) = \ln(w)$. Consider Table 1.1. In the table, wealth is defined in $10,000s, so that a wealth level of "1" translates to $10,000, a wealth level of 10 translates to $100,000, and so on.

Figure 1.1 graphs this utility function. Notice that the slope gets flatter as wealth increases. For a person with this utility function, added wealth at low income levels increases utility more than added wealth at high income levels. We will return to this pattern later in the chapter.

TABLE 1.1 | Logarithmic Utility of Wealth

Wealth (in $10,000s)	$u(w) = \ln(w)$
1	0
2	0.6931
5	1.6094
7	1.9459
10	2.3026
20	2.9957
30	3.4012
50	3.9120
100	4.6052

FIGURE 1.1 Logarithmic Utility Function

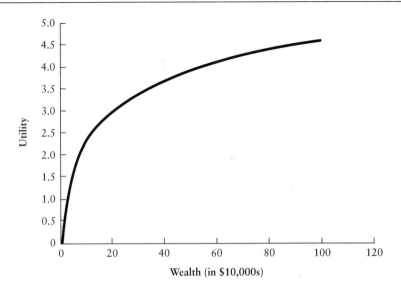

RELEVANT INFORMATION

Neoclassical economics assumes that people maximize their utility using full information of the choice set. Of course, economists recognize that information is rarely free. Not only are there costs associated with acquiring information, but there are also costs of assimilating and understanding information that is already at hand. Students who spend many hours working toward success in a challenging course are keenly aware that information is not free. In the following chapter, we will return to this topic and consider how to define what information is "relevant" when making financial decisions.

1.3   EXPECTED UTILITY THEORY

So far in this chapter, we have dodged the issue of uncertainty. In the real world, there is not much that we can count on with certainty. In financial decision-making, there is clearly a great deal of uncertainty about outcomes.

Expected utility theory was developed by John von Neumann and Oskar Morgenstern in an attempt to define rational behavior when people face uncertainty.[5] This theory contends that individuals *should* act in a particular way when confronted with decision-making under uncertainty. In this sense, the theory is "normative," which means that it describes how people should rationally behave. This is in contrast to a "positive" theory, which characterizes how people actually behave.

Expected utility theory is really set up to deal with **risk**, not **uncertainty**. A risky situation is one in which you know what the outcomes could be and can assign a probability to each outcome. Uncertainty is when you cannot assign probabilities or even come up with a list of possible outcomes. Frank Knight clarified the difference between risk and uncertainty:[6]

> But Uncertainty must be taken in a sense radically distinct from the familiar notion of Risk, from which it has never been properly separated. The term "risk," as loosely used in everyday speech and in economic discussion, really covers two things which, functionally at least, in their causal relations to the phenomena of economic organization, are categorically different.... The essential fact is that 'risk' means in some cases a quantity susceptible of measurement, while at other times it is something distinctly not of this character; and there are far-reaching and crucial differences in the bearings of the phenomena depending on which of the two is really present and operating.... It will appear that a measurable uncertainty, or "risk" proper, as we shall use the term, is so far different from an unmeasurable one that it is not in effect an uncertainty at all.

Risk is measurable using probability, but uncertainty is not. Whereas, conforming to common practice, we began by saying that we were going to address decision-making under uncertainty, the truth is that we will almost always focus on decision-making under risk.

For almost all purposes, when considering decision-making under risk, it is sufficient to think in terms of just wealth. Let's suppose, for simplicity, that there are only two states of the world: low wealth and high wealth. When it is low, your wealth is $50,000, and when it is high, your wealth is $1,000,000. And further assume that you can assign probabilities to each of these outcomes. You are fairly optimistic about your future, so you assign a probability of 40% to low wealth and 60% to high wealth. Formally, a **prospect** is a series of wealth outcomes, each of which is associated with a probability.[7] If we call the latter prospect P1, we can represent this situation using the following convenient format:

1.2   P1(0.40, $50,000, $1,000,000)

Note that with two outcomes the first number is the probability of the first outcome, and the next two numbers are the two outcomes. If only one dollar figure is given, as in P(.3, $100), the assumption is that the second outcome is "0."

It can be shown that if one makes the assumptions previously discussed along with several others that most people consider to be reasonable, a procedure allowing us to make appropriate choices under risk results. In a nutshell, this procedure involves calculating the probability-weighted expected value of the different possible utility levels (that is, the expected utility). The Appendix to this chapter outlines a set of assumptions that allow us to rank outcomes based on expected utility maximization. In addition, a proof is sketched out, and certain characteristics of utility functions are described.

Let us use the notation U(P) for the expected utility of a prospect. For P1, the expected utility, or U(P1), is:

1.3 $U(P1) = 0.40u(50,000) + 0.60u(1,000,000)$

With the logarithmic utility function previously presented, the expected utility of this prospect (using Table 1.1) is:

1.4 $U(P1) = 0.40(1.6094) + 0.60(4.6052) = 3.4069$

Expected utility can be used to rank risky alternatives because it is order-preserving (i.e., ordinal). It can be shown that for a given individual it is also cardinal, in the sense that it is unique up to a positive linear transformation. This feature will come in handy in Chapter 3 for several demonstrations.

   If one prospect is preferred to another, its expected utility will be higher. Let us consider another prospect:

1.5 $P2(.50, \$100,000, \$1,000,000)$

P2 is superior to P1 in that the low-wealth outcome is now higher ($100,000 vs. $50,000). On the other hand, it is inferior because the probability of the high-wealth outcome is now lower (.50 vs. .60). So it is not obvious which prospect would be preferred. Once again we take the expected utility of the prospect:

1.6 $U(P2) = 0.50(2.3026) + 0.50(4.6052) = 3.4539$

Therefore, if someone has logarithmic utility, then they would prefer P2 to P1. Of course we could specify another functional form for utility such that P1 is preferred to P2.

1.4   RISK ATTITUDE

There is abundant evidence that most people avoid risk in most circumstances. People are, however, willing to assume risk if they are compensated for it. For example, when choosing between two stocks with the same expected return, if you are like most people, you would invest in the one with the lower risk. If you are going to take on a riskier investment, you will demand a higher return to compensate for the risk. In the following chapter, we will talk more about the trade-off between risk and return. Now we want to focus on what we mean by risk attitude.

   The utility function is useful in defining risk preferences. Returning to P1, the expected value of wealth is:

1.7 $E(w) = 0.40(\$50,000) + 0.60(\$1,000,000) = \$620,000 = E(P1)$

Note that the expected value of wealth is synonymous with the expected value of the prospect. The utility of this expected value of wealth is:

1.8 $u(E(w)) = \ln(62) = 4.1271$

On the other hand, as we saw before, the expected utility is 3.4069, so u(E(*w*)) > U(P1). This means that a person, whose preferences can be described by a logarithmic utility function, prefers the expected value of a prospect to the prospect itself. In other words, if you have a logarithmic utility function, you would rather have wealth of $620,000 than a prospect in which you have a 40% chance of wealth of $50,000 and a 60% chance of wealth of $1,000,000. A person of this type dislikes risk, and we say this person is **risk averse**.

Figure 1.2 illustrates the situation. In the figure, we see that the utility of the expected wealth (u(E(*w*)) = u(62) = 4.1271) is greater than the expected utility of the prospect (U(P1) = 3.4069). Someone who is risk averse has a concave utility function, which means that:

1.9 $$u(E(P)) > U(P)$$

Such a person's preferences imply that the utility of the expected value of a prospect is greater than the expected utility of the prospect. This person would rather have the expected value of the prospect with *certainty* than actually take a gamble on the *uncertain* outcome. For our example, a risk-averse person would rather have wealth of $620,000 with certainty as compared to a prospect with a 40% chance of wealth of $50,000 and a 60% chance of wealth of $1,000,000.

A risk-averse person is willing to sacrifice for certainty. The **certainty equivalent** is defined as that wealth level that leads the decision-maker to be indifferent between a particular prospect and a certain wealth level. In the case of P1 and logarithmic utility, the certainty equivalent is $301,700. This is because, as Figure 1.2 shows, wealth of 30.17 (in $10,000s) leads to a utility level equal to the expected

---

FIGURE 1.2 Utility Function for a Risk-averse Individual

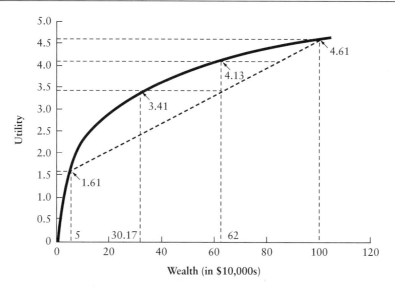

Wealth (in $10,000s)

utility of the prospect. The utility of the certainty equivalent is equal to the expected utility of the prospect or:

1.10 $u(30.17) = u(w) = U(P1) = 0.40(1.6094) + 0.60(4.6052) = 3.4069$

You would give up \$318,300 in expected value in order to exchange the prospect for certainty.

We often assume that people are risk averse, but some people actually seem to prefer, at least at times, to take on risk. Such a person is called a **risk seeker** and has a convex utility function, as in:

1.11 $$u(E(P)) < U(P)$$

For such an individual, the utility of the expected value of a prospect is *less* than the expected utility of the prospect. This person would rather gamble on the uncertain outcome than take the expected value of the prospect with certainty. Figure 1.3 shows the relationship between the utility of expected wealth and the expected utility of wealth for a risk seeker. For a risk seeker, the certainty equivalent level of wealth is greater than the expected value. Returning to our previous example, a risk seeker would rather have a prospect with a 40% chance of wealth of \$50,000 and a 60% chance of wealth of \$1,000,000 versus wealth of \$620,000 with certainty.

Finally, people who are risk neutral lie between risk averters and risk seekers. These people only care about expected values and risk does not matter at all. For someone who is **risk neutral** we have:

1.12 $$u(E(P)) = U(P)$$

FIGURE 1.3 Utility Function for a Risk Seeker

FIGURE 1.4 Utility Function for a Risk-neutral Individual

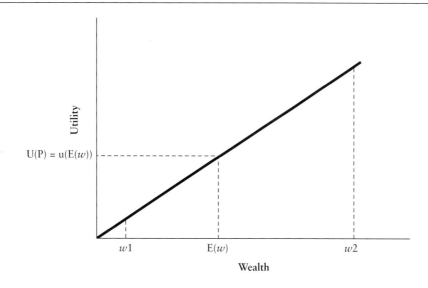

Thus the utility of the expected value of a prospect is equal to the expected utility of the prospect, as illustrated in Figure 1.4. Again, returning to our previous example, a risk-neutral individual would be indifferent between a prospect with a 40% chance of wealth of $50,000 and a 60% chance of wealth of $1,000,000 and wealth of $620,000 with certainty. For a risk-neutral person, the certainty equivalent level of wealth is equal to the expected value of the prospect.

1.5   ALLAIS PARADOX

Throughout this book we will consider a number of observed behaviors that appear to be contrary to predictions generated by conventional finance models. Now we will look at one persistently documented contradiction of expected utility theory, the so-called **Allais paradox**.[8] Alternative approaches to decision-making under uncertainty have been developed because researchers have detected this and other departures from expected utility theory. The most famous is the prospect theory of Daniel Kahneman and Amos Tversky, which will be the major focus of Chapter 3.[9]

Consider the prospect choices in Table 1.2. In the case of Question 1, people can choose between A and A*, while in the case of Question 2, people can choose between B and B*. Questions 1 and 2 have been presented to many people. Take a moment now and answer each question. For Question 1, would you prefer Prospect A or Prospect A*? For Question 2, would you prefer Prospect B or Prospect B*?

Are you like many people? A large number of people choose A over A* *and* B* over B. We now show that this violates expected utility theory. If expected utility theory can be used to rank outcomes, a preference for A over A*, that is, U(A) > U(A*), implies:

1.13 $U(A) = u(\$1,000,000) > .89u(\$1,000,000) + .1u(\$5,000,000) = U(A^*)$

Simplifying, we have:

1.14 $.11u(\$1,000,000) > .1u(\$5,000,000)$

Again, if expected utility theory holds, a preference for B* over B, that is, U(B*) > U(B), implies:

1.15 $.1u(\$5,000,000) > .11u(\$1,000,000)$

Since $.11u(\$1,000,000) > .1u(\$5,000,000)$ *and* $.1u(\$5,000,000) > .11u(\$1,000,000)$ cannot both hold, such choices are clearly contradictory.

John Conlisk carefully investigated the robustness of the Allais paradox.[10] He gave several variations of the questions in Table 1.2 to the student participants in his research study. He found that when the questions were presented in a form that better allowed the students to see how the choice between A and B is similar to the choice between A* and B*, violations of expected utility declined significantly. As an example, refer to Table 1.3. This table presents the same questions as Table 1.2, but the format is changed to illustrate the problem. Would you still make the same choices you made when you first considered Table 1.2? For Question 1, would you now prefer Prospect A or Prospect A*? For Question 2, would you now prefer Prospect B or Prospect B*?

For Question 1, both prospects offer an 89% chance to win $1,000,000, so this does not provide a basis for preference of A or A*. For Question 2, both

TABLE 1.2 | PROSPECT CHOICES

Question 1				
Prospect A			Prospect A*	
$1,000,000	100%		0	1%
			$1,000,000	89%
			$5,000,000	10%

Question 2				
Prospect B			Prospect B*	
0	89%		0	90%
$1,000,000	11%		$5,000,000	10%

TABLE 1.3   RECONSIDERING THE PROSPECT CHOICES

Question 1			
Prospect A		Prospect A*	
$1,000,000	89%	$1,000,000	89%
$1,000,000	11%	0	1%
		$5,000,000	10%

Question 2			
Prospect B		Prospect B*	
0	89%	0	89%
$1,000,000	11%	0	1%
		$5,000,000	10%

prospects offer an 89% chance of "0," which again should provide no basis for choice because it is identical for both prospects. Notice that after removing commonalities, now the choices between prospects A and A* *or* B and B* are exactly the same. Thus, people should choose A and B *or* A* and B*. Without such aids, many people do not seem to understand the structure of the decision and choose A and B*.

The Allais paradox is not the only documented violation of expected utility theory. Sometimes researchers demonstrate that people do not make choices in accordance with certain axioms on which expected utility theory rests. For example, failures in the ability to order outcomes on a consistent basis and lack of transitivity have been reported.[11] One can also show that an axiom (Axiom 5, as described in the Appendix) known as "context independence" is contradicted by the Allais paradox.

To understand this contradiction, consider the following. Suppose a person is indifferent between two prospects, A and B. If we consider another prospect, C, independence implies that this person should also be indifferent between one gamble that combines A with C and another that combines B with C with fixed probability. We can illustrate this idea as follows. Suppose you are looking for a new car and you are trying to decide between a Toyota and a BMW. The latter is a better car, but it is also more expensive. Two charities are selling lottery tickets with identical ticket prices. The prize for the first lottery is the BMW, and the prize for the second lottery is the Toyota. Now assume you believe you have a better chance of winning the Toyota, so that you are actually indifferent between these two lotteries. Suppose now you consider a third lottery with a prize of a new television. The consolation prize is a ticket for one of the car lotteries. Since you were indifferent between the two car lotteries, you should *also* be indifferent between the BMW lottery plus the television lottery and the Toyota lottery plus the television lottery.

1.6   FRAMING

Decision problems can be presented in many different ways, and some evidence suggests that people's decisions are not the same across various presentations. If I ask you if you'd rather have a glass that is half empty or a glass that is half full, virtually everyone would see through this transparent difference in decision frames and say that it doesn't matter. A decision **frame** is defined to be a decision-maker's view of the problem and possible outcomes. A frame is affected by the presentation mode and the individual's perception of the question, as well as personal characteristics. Sometimes frames are opaque, which means that they are trickier to see through. For this reason, when we present a choice problem to a person, a change in frame can lead to a change in decision, as we saw with the choices in Tables 1.2 and 1.3. This is a violation of expected utility theory, which rests on the assumption that people should have consistent choices, regardless of presentation.

Psychologists and economists have documented that the frame has significant effects on the decisions people make, including decisions of a financial nature.[12] Framing has been shown to have important implications in many areas of behavioral finance, and we will return to this important concept in Chapter 3 as well as elsewhere throughout this book.

1.7   LOOKING FORWARD

Later in this book, we will consider an important alternative model of individual behavior called prospect theory. Although prospect theory has support particularly among behavioralists, much of finance theory continues to rest on expected utility theory. Despite observed behaviors that are inconsistent with the expected utility framework, it is still very useful in modeling individual decision-making.

In addition to understanding individual behavior, we are interested in market outcomes. As we said at the beginning of this chapter, the value or price of an asset is determined in a market. For the analysis of financial assets, imagine trying to list all payoffs for every state of the world as expected utility theory expects! The following chapter describes the traditional finance framework that uses mean and variance as the choice variables.

CHAPTER HIGHLIGHTS

1. Modern finance models are based on the models of economics, and neoclassical economics is the dominant paradigm.
2. The key assumptions of neoclassical economics are that individuals and firms are self-interested and attempt to optimize to the best of their ability in the face of constraints on resources; the value (or price) of goods and assets is determined in markets, subject to the influences of supply and demand; and people have rational preferences across possible outcomes or states of nature.
3. Utility functions describe preferences and assign numbers to possible outcomes so that preferred choices receive higher numbers.
4. Expected utility theory is used to define rational behavior when people face uncertainty.

5. The expected utility function is useful in defining risk preferences. A risk-averse individual prefers the expected value of a prospect to the prospect itself. A risk seeker would rather have the prospect than the expected value of the prospect with certainty. A risk-neutral person derives the same utility from a gamble and its expected value.
6. The Allais paradox is a frequently cited example of a violation of expected utility theory.
7. How a prospect question is framed or presented sometimes impacts peoples' choices.

DISCUSSION QUESTIONS AND PROBLEMS

1. Differentiate the following terms/concepts:

   a. Prospect and probability distribution
   b. Risk and uncertainty
   c. Utility function and expected utility
   d. Risk aversion, risk seeking, and risk neutrality

2. When eating out, Rory prefers spaghetti over a hamburger. Last night, she had a choice of spaghetti or macaroni and cheese and decided on the spaghetti again. The night before, Rory had a choice of spaghetti, pizza, or a hamburger, and this time she had pizza. Then, today, she chose macaroni and cheese over a hamburger. Does her selection today indicate that Rory's choices are consistent with economic rationality? Why or why not?

3. Consider a person with the following utility function over wealth: $u(w) = e^w$, where e is the exponential function (approximately equal to 2.7183) and w = wealth in hundreds of thousands of dollars. Suppose that this person has a 40% chance of wealth of $50,000 and a 60% chance of wealth of $1,000,000 as summarized by P(0.40, $50,000, $1,000,000).

   a. What is the expected value of wealth?
   b. Construct a graph of this utility function.
   c. Is this person risk averse, risk neutral, or a risk seeker?
   d. What is this person's certainty equivalent for the prospect?

4. An individual has the following utility function: $u(w) = w^{.5}$ where w = wealth.

   a. Using expected utility, order the following prospects in terms of preference, from the most to the least preferred:

   P1(.8, 1,000, 600)
   P2(.7, 1,200, 600)
   P3(.5, 2,000, 300)

   b. What is the certainty equivalent for prospect P2?
   c. Without doing any calculations, would the certainty equivalent for prospect P1 be larger or smaller? Why?

5. Consider two problems:

   Problem 1: Choose between Prospect A and Prospect B.

Prospect A:	$2,500 with probability .33, $2,400 with probability .66, Zero with probability .01.
Prospect B:	$2,400 with certainty.

   Problem 2: Choose between Prospect C and Prospect D.

Prospect C:	$2,500 with probability .33, Zero with probability .67.
Prospect D:	$2,400 with probability .34, Zero with probability .66.

   It has been shown by Daniel Kahneman and Amos Tversky (1979, "Prospect theory: An analysis of decision under risk," *Econometrica* 47(2), 263–291) that more people choose B when presented with Problem 1, and more people choose C when presented with Problem 2. These choices violate expected utility theory. Why?

MORE ON EXPECTED UTILITY THEORY

We begin with some definitions; then present one set of axioms (i.e., assumptions) that allow us to derive expected utility model; next sketch out a non-rigorous proof; and finally consider some characteristics of the utility function. While the following prospects have at most two possible outcomes, all results can easily be generalized to the case of three or more outcomes.

DEFINITIONS

- **Prospect**, as described in the chapter, is a probability distribution of wealth outcomes, and can be written as $P(pr, w1, w2)$ where pr is the probability of the first wealth level.
- **Minimum wealth level** (w_L) and **maximum wealth level** (w_H) are those at the bottom and at the top if we order all possible wealth states of the world.
- **Standard prospect** (P_0) has w_H and w_L as its only possible wealth outcomes, as in $P_0(u, w_H, w_L)$. Here, u, later interpreted as "utility," is used in place of generic pr.
- **Equivalent standard prospect** is a standard prospect that, when compared with a certain wealth level $w_L < w^* < w_H$, is viewed with indifference by the decision-maker.
- **Compound prospect** has at least one prospect as an outcome. An example (having two prospects as outcomes) is $P_C(pr, P1, P2)$.
- **Rational equivalent prospect** (P_{RE}) is a restatement of a compound prospect. In a rational equivalent prospect, all outcomes are in terms of wealth (not prospects).
- **Standard compound prospect** is a compound prospect that has only standard prospects as outcomes.
- **Standard rational equivalent prospect** is a rational equivalent prospect associated with a standard compound prospect. Since standard prospects have only w_H and w_L as wealth levels, a standard rational equivalent prospect will also have only w_H and w_L as wealth levels, which makes it a standard prospect.
- **U** is defined in terms of the following:

A1.1 $U = pr * u1 + (1-pr) * u2$

It can be shown that U is the probability of w_H in a standard rational equivalent prospect; where pr is the probability of the first standard prospect; u1 is the probability of w_H in

16

the first standard prospect; and u2 is the probability of w_H in the second standard prospect.

- **Expected utility** is another term for U. This is natural since, if we call u1 and u2 (probabilities of w_H in standard prospects) utilities, U is an expected value of utility levels.

AXIOMS REQUIRED TO DERIVE EXPECTED UTILITY

1. **AXIOM 1 (Ordering of prospects):** Given any two prospects, a decision-maker can always say that one is preferred to the other, or that he/she is indifferent between them. Moreover, completeness and consistency must hold. Completeness means that all possible prospects can be so ranked, and consistency (transitivity) means that if A is preferred to B, and B is preferred to C, then A must be preferred to C.

2. **AXIOM 2 (Preference increasing with probability):** Given two standard prospects, $P1_0$ and $P2_0$ with associated u1 and u2, we have:

   A1.2 $\qquad P1_0 > P2_0$ implies u1 > u2

   A1.3 $\qquad P1_0 \sim P2_0$ implies u1 = u2

3. **AXIOM 3 (Equivalent standard prospects):** Given any certain income level w^* between w_L and w_H, there exists one and only one value u* such that:

A1.4 $\qquad w^* \sim P_0 (u^*, w_H, w_L)$

Note that this in effect defines a function $u(w)$ (i.e., a utility function) which is bounded by 0 and 1, such that $u(w_L) = 0$ and $u(w_H) = 1$.

4. **AXIOM 4 (Rational equivalence):** Given a standard compound prospect (P_{SC}), and given its standard rational equivalent, which is itself a standard prospect (P_0), then:

   A1.5 $\qquad P_{SC} \sim P_0$

5. **AXIOM 5 (Context independence):** A prospect P can always be expressed as a standard compound prospect (P_{SC}), where the wealth levels of the former are replaced by their equivalent standard prospects.

SKETCH OF A PROOF

- Consider a hypothetical prospect $P(p^*, w1, w2)$.
- According to Axiom 5, this prospect is equivalent to a standard compound prospect. In other words:

  A1.6 $\qquad P \sim P_{SC}$

- According to Axiom 4, a standard compound prospect is equivalent to a standard rational equivalent prospect, which is just a particular standard prospect. In other words:

  A1.7 $\qquad P_{SC} \sim P_0$

- So Axiom 5 and Axiom 4 together say that a prospect can always be expressed as a standard prospect:

  A1.8 $\qquad P \sim P_0$

- According to Axiom 2, all standard prospects (or, here, standard rational equivalent prospects) can be completely ordered by the different u values (here U values) that appear in them.
- Thus all prospects can be ordered.
- And the ordering is determined by U.
- And since U is the expected utility of a prospect, this means that all prospects can be ordered by expected utility.

CHARACTERISTICS OF UTILITY FUNCTIONS

▨ Axiom 2 implies that u(*w*) is an increasing function. Higher wealth levels are equivalent to standard prospects with higher probabilities of w_H. Or we can say that higher wealth leads to higher utility.

▨ Typically it is *assumed* that u is twice differentiable (implying continuity) and that u" < 0 (concavity). As discussed in the body of the chapter, this comes from the observation that most of us most of the time are risk averse. Risk aversion implies that the certainty equivalent, namely a certain wealth level such that you are indifferent between this wealth level and a particular prospect, is less than the expected value of wealth of the prospect.

▨ Utility functions are cardinal and unique for given values of w_H and w_L. This is in contradistinction to the mere ordinality of utility under certainty. (Think of a set of indifference curves: utility values assigned to each are irrelevant as long as higher indifference curves have higher utility values.)

▨ It can be shown that by varying w_H and w_L different (cardinal) utility functions will result. Nevertheless, all utility functions for a given individual are unique up to a positive linear transformation.

ENDNOTES

1 In the next chapter, we will discuss whether price (what a security trades at in a market) and value (its true or "intrinsic" value) are always the same.

2 E. R. Weintraub outlines the assumptions of neoclassical economics at http://www.econlib.org/library/enc/NeoclassicalEconomics.html (accessed on June 18, 2008).

3 This is for a single-period world. In a multiperiod world, people should maximize utility in an intertemporal sense (which involves trading off current for future satisfaction), and firms (through the decisions of managers) should maximize firm value.

4 Varian, H. R., 2005, *Intermediate Microeconomics: A Modern Approach*, 7th ed. (W. W. Norton, New York).

5 See von Neumann, J., and O. Morgenstern, 1944, *Theory of Games and Economic Behavior* (Princeton University Press, Princeton, New Jersey).

6 Knight, F. H., 1921, *Risk, Uncertainty, and Profit* (Houghton Mifflin Company, Boston). Reprinted 1967, quote on page 19 in Chapter 1.

7 Sometimes the term "lottery" is used in place of "prospect." We will reserve the former term for a skewed prospect, that is, a prospect with a low probability of a very good outcome.

8 The Allais paradox is a prospect choice problem first proposed by Maurice Allais in Allais, M., 1953, "L'Extension des théories de l'équilibre économique général et du rendement social au cas du risque," *Econometrica* 21(2), April, 269–290. The presentation here follows Conlisk, J., 1989, "Three variants on the Allais example," *American Economic Review* 79(3), June, 392–407.

9 See Kahneman, D., and A. Tversky, 1979, "Prospect theory: An analysis of decision under risk," *Econometrica* 47(2), 263–291.

10 Conlisk, J., 1989, "Three variants on the Allais example," *American Economic Review* 79(3), June, 392–407.

11 For a review of the axioms of expected utility theory and their violations, see Fishburn, P. C., 1988, "Expected utility: An anniversary and a new era," *Journal of Risk and Uncertainty* 1(3), September, 267–283.

12 See Tversky, A., and D. Kahneman, 1981, "The framing of decisions and the psychology of choice," *Science* 211, January, 453–458.

CHAPTER 2

FOUNDATIONS OF FINANCE II: ASSET PRICING, MARKET EFFICIENCY, AND AGENCY RELATIONSHIPS

2.1 INTRODUCTION

In finance we study how individuals and organizations acquire and allocate resources, while taking into account associated risks. Though in earlier times financial economists considered psychological influences, in more recent decades finance has moved away from the social sciences and toward the framework adopted in natural sciences. In the natural sciences the universe is viewed as adhering to rules of a natural order. In this tradition, financial decision-making is usually modeled based on assumptions about the behavior of individuals and markets.

In this chapter three central theories of modern finance are reviewed. In Section 2.2, the capital asset pricing model (CAPM) which describes how assets are priced in markets is presented. Prior to this model, while it was clear to observers that risky assets should be priced to earn, on average, higher returns than less risky assets in compensation for the risk borne, there was no rigorous model that described the trade-off between risk and return. The CAPM was the first to specify the nature of risk and the extent to which it should be priced. Next, in Section 2.3, we consider the **efficient markets hypothesis (EMH)**, or, synonymously, **market efficiency**, which posits that asset prices reflect information so that excess returns cannot be earned on a consistent basis. The validity of the EMH is hotly debated by those proponents of behavioral finance who argue that individual irrationality impacts market outcomes. Finally, in Section 2.4, we review agency theory, which suggests that conflicts of interest have important implications for corporate finance theory.

2.2   THE PRICING OF RISK

In the previous chapter we reviewed expected utility theory, which says that individuals faced with uncertainty maximize the utility expected across possible states of the world. Of course, for a financial asset with potentially innumerable possible future outcomes, this is not a manageable task. Fortunately, asset pricing theory provides a way to quantify the trade-off between risk and return. Before formally considering how assets should be priced, we will examine how the trade-off between risk and return can be measured.

RISK AND RETURN FOR INDIVIDUAL ASSETS

Modern portfolio theory provides a practical framework that assumes that investors are risk averse and preferences are defined in terms of the mean and variance of returns. This theory is based on statistics, so it is empirically based and the variables are measurable. We can think of the return on an asset as being a random variable. In other words, the return next period is not perfectly predictable, but it is determined by a probability distribution. One parameter characterizing this distribution is the **expected value** of returns, denoted as $E(R_i)$, where $E(\bullet)$ denotes expectation. The expected value is a kind of distributional average. If one sampled from this distribution a very large number of times, the average value of observations would converge to the expected value. While investors care about the likely return, we know that they also focus on risk. You would not be indifferent between two assets that have the same expected return but very different levels of risk.

With the same expected return, an investor would prefer the asset that has a more certain outcome or less uncertainty about possible returns. Although there are different ways we could measure uncertainty, for an individual asset, variance or dispersion from the mean is the most common measure. The **variance** of returns, denoted as σ_i^2, reflects squared deviations from the mean so large deviations above or below the mean count equally. The **standard deviation** of returns (σ_i) is simply the positive square root of the variance. Variance and standard deviation are proxies for risk, and both rank securities in terms of risk identically.

When considering an asset in isolation, notice that an investor really wants to know the expected future return and future variance in returns. These parameters from the distribution of returns are not observable. Therefore, in finance applications and empirical research, it is common to estimate them using historical data.[1] We often use a sample of data, gathered ex post, to accomplish this purpose. With n observations of the return for asset i, the **mean return** is computed as

$$\mathbf{2.1} \qquad \overline{R_i} = \frac{1}{n} \sum_{t=1}^{n} R_{i,t}$$

The mean return is our best estimate of the true distributional expected value of returns. The **sample variance** of returns is:

$$\mathbf{2.2} \qquad s_i^2 = \frac{1}{n-1} \sum_{t=1}^{n} (R_{i,t} - \overline{R_i})^2$$

And the **sample standard deviation** of returns is:

2.3

$$s_i = \sqrt{s_i^2}$$

This sample variance and sample standard deviation are estimates of the true (distributional) variance and sample standard deviation. With these measures for mean return and risk, the investor can make risk-return trade-off comparisons, but we will soon see that understanding risk is slightly more intricate.

RISK AND RETURN FOR PORTFOLIOS OF ASSETS

Smart investors understand that the risk of a portfolio is not simply the average risk of the assets in the portfolio. This is because by combining assets in a portfolio, investors can eliminate some, but not all, variability. Recall the old adage that advises, "don't put all your eggs in one basket." This is the principle of **diversification**. Finance theorists have shown it to be an important factor when setting an investment strategy.

How do we know how much variability can be eliminated by combining two assets in a portfolio? Consider the act of combining two assets. As long as the assets' returns do not move together in exactly the same way all the time, variability is reduced. Statistical measures of how random variables are related are **covariance** and **correlation**. When one variable tends to be above (below) its mean and at the same time the other variable tends to be above (below) its mean, the covariance and correlation are positive. If the two variables tend to move in opposite directions, the covariance and correlation are negative. The covariance of a sample including n returns for assets i and j is:

2.4

$$\hat{\sigma}(R_i, R_j) = \frac{1}{n-1} \sum_{t=1}^{n} (R_{i,t} - \overline{R_i})(R_{j,t} - \overline{R_j})$$

The sample correlation is the sample covariance divided by the product of the (sample) standard deviations of returns for each asset or:

2.5

$$\hat{\rho}_{i,j} = \frac{\hat{\sigma}(R_i, R_j)}{s_i s_j}$$

Note that true distributional parameters (covariance and correlation) are written as $\sigma(R_i, R_j)$ and $\rho_{i,j}$ (which means we merely remove the "hats"). The correlation always lies between -1.0 and $+1.0$, whereas the covariance can take any positive or negative value.

With a measure of how the returns for the two assets move together (or apart), we can compute the portfolio mean return and variance for two-asset portfolios. The mean return of the portfolio is simply the weighted average of the mean returns of each asset, with the weights (w_i) representing the percentage amount invested in each asset:

2.6

$$\overline{R_p} = w_i \overline{R_i} + w_j \overline{R_j}$$

Of course weights must sum to 1.0 (representing 100%) because our money must be invested somewhere. It can be shown that the sample variance of portfolio returns is:

2.7
$$s_p^2 = w_i^2 s_i^2 + w_j^2 s_j^2 + 2w_i w_j \hat{\rho}_{i,j} s_i s_j$$

As long as the correlation is less than 1.0, the standard deviation of returns for the portfolio will be lower than the weighted average of the standard deviations of returns for the two assets. What would these expressions look like in the case of more than two assets? For example, if we have three assets, the mean return is:

2.8
$$\overline{R_p} = w_i \overline{R_i} + w_j \overline{R_j} + w_k \overline{R_k}$$

And the variance is:

2.9
$$s_p^2 = w_i^2 s_i^2 + w_j^2 s_j^2 + w_k^2 s_k^2 + 2w_i w_j \hat{\rho}_{i,j} s_i s_j + 2w_i w_k \hat{\rho}_{i,k} s_i s_k$$
$$+ 2w_j w_k \hat{\rho}_{j,k} s_j s_k$$

As more assets are added to the portfolio, the expressions expand analogously, and additional variability is eliminated through diversification—up to a limit as we now discuss.[2]

THE OPTIMAL PORTFOLIO

We have reviewed how to compute the return and standard deviation of returns on a portfolio. Now we consider what finance theory tells us about which portfolio the investor should choose. In the preceding section, we considered sample statistics for a set of portfolio returns $(\overline{R_p}, s_p^2)$. But when choosing optimal portfolios, it is important to use distributions that generate returns in the future, and we must remember that historical sample estimates are only estimates for the true distributional parameters. Therefore we will now work in terms of true expected values rather than sample means and true distributional variances rather than sample variances $(E(R_p), \sigma_p^2)$.[3]

For simplicity, suppose there are only two stocks and a risk-free asset in a market. The stocks are ownership interests in High Tech Corporation and Low Tech Corporation, and the risk-free asset can be thought of as investing in short-term government bonds (such as U.S. Treasury bills) or depositing funds in a bank.[4] Information for the three investment opportunities is summarized in Table 2.1. High Tech has the highest expected return of 15%, but also the highest variability in returns with a standard deviation of 30%. Low Tech is in the middle with expected returns of 8% and variability of 10%. The risk-free asset provides a low, but risk-free, return (4%). The returns to High Tech and Low Tech are negatively correlated. In our example, the risk-free asset's returns are certain and uncorrelated with the other assets' returns.[5] Note that zero variability in returns is what is meant by a risk-free investment.

Suppose you are considering investing in a portfolio of our two stocks, High Tech and Low Tech. Using the formulas provided in the previous section with

TABLE 2.1 | RETURNS FOR HIGH TECH AND LOW TECH

	Expected Return	Standard Deviation of Returns
High Tech (HT)	15%	30%
Low Tech (LT)	8%	10%
Risk-free Asset (RF)	4%	0%
Correlation between HT and LT	−0.10	
Correlation between HT and RF	0	
Correlation between LT and RF	0	

distributional parameters used in place of sample estimates, we can compute the return and variability for a portfolio made up of High Tech and Low Tech. For example, suppose you put 40% of your funds in High Tech and 60% in Low Tech. The expected return for the portfolio is:

2.10 $E(R_P) = 0.40(0.15) + 0.60(0.08) = 0.108$

And the variance of portfolio returns is:

2.11 $\sigma_p^2 = 0.40^2 0.30^2 + 0.60^2 0.10^2 + 2(0.40)(0.60)(-0.10)(0.30)(0.10)$
        $= 0.0166$

Taking the square root of the variance gives a standard deviation of 0.1288 (or 12.88%). Notice that the standard deviation is less than the weighted average of the standard deviations of each stock.[6] This reflects the fact that benefits from diversification have been achieved.

While diversification benefits are evident, we still don't know how much of our money we should invest in each of the two stocks. More generally, if there are many stocks to choose from, how much should we invest in each? Here is where the efficient frontier (or efficient set) comes in.[7] We begin with Figure 2.1. In this and the next two figures, risk is proxied by standard deviation (of portfolio returns). Figure 2.1 depicts all possible risk-return combinations of High Tech and Low Tech. The curve in the figure is constructed by varying the weights for each asset and recalculating the expected return and standard deviation. The curvature of this relationship stems from the correlation between the two securities: the lower the correlation, the greater the curvature.

Investors actually have thousands of risky investment opportunities. If we consider all combinations of securities (and there are clearly an infinite number of combinations), it can be shown that a graph depicting all these combinations would show a solid curved mass, which is sometimes compared to a "bullet." Referring to Figure 2.2, notice that several individual investments (A-D) and several portfolios (E-G) are shown. In the manner of Figure 2.1, if we combine individual investments on a pairwise basis, we achieve diversification as reflected in the (interior) risk-return trade-off curves. By mixing together many assets, we can do even

FIGURE 2.1 Risk vs. Expected Return for High Tech and Low Tech

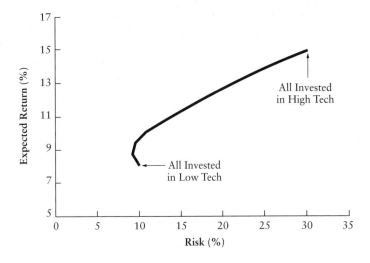

FIGURE 2.2 The Efficient Set

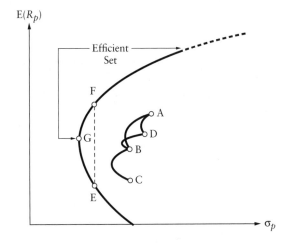

better. When we have moved as far to the left as possible (as in portfolios E-G), we have reached the "skin" of the bullet. Above and to the right of the minimum risk point (the tip of the bullet, which is portfolio G) is that portion of the curve called the **efficient frontier**.[8] The efficient frontier represents that set of portfolios that maximize expected return for a given level of risk. No investor would choose a portfolio under the curve because this would not be optimal (i.e., there exists another portfolio with the same risk, but higher return.) Thus, all rational investors would choose a portfolio on the efficient frontier.

As more assets are added to the portfolio, the investor can eliminate more risk because assets seldom move in tandem, or, synonymously, correlations are almost always less than one for pairs of risky assets. We refer to the risk that can be eliminated as **diversifiable risk** or **nonsystematic risk**. The risk that can be diversified is specific to the asset in question. For a common stock, this would reflect firm-specific events. The risk we cannot eliminate is called **nondiversifiable risk** or **systematic risk**. Systematic risk is common to all risky assets in the system, so we cannot diversify it away no matter how many stocks are added to the portfolio. If we add the assumption that all investors have the same, or homogeneous, expectations, then all investors have the same efficient frontier.

We now know that only portfolios lying along the efficient frontier should be considered. But, exactly which one do you want?[9] You might find an investor whose primary goal is to eliminate as much risk as possible, and he would locate himself right on the minimum-risk point. Most of us, however, are not that risk averse. Investors recognize the trade-off between risk and return and, depending on their risk attitude, may be willing to take on some risk to earn a higher return. An investor who is willing to take additional risk to generate a higher return will pick a spot on the efficient frontier to the right of the minimum-risk portfolio. When we introduce the risk-free asset to the mix, we see that there is just one portfolio of risky assets that will be held by investors. Adding the risk-free asset is like adding an exchange mechanism that allows investors to borrow or lend all they want at the risk-free rate. With the ability to borrow and lend, we get **two-fund separation**. Separation means that investors maximize utility by combining the risk-free asset with a fund of risky assets. Because the returns for the risk-free asset are uncorrelated with the returns of the other assets, the return *and* risk for a portfolio including the risk-free asset with any other risky asset will be a linear function of the returns and risks.[10]

Figure 2.3 shows the efficient frontier for all risky investment opportunities, along with two lines representing investment in the risk-free asset in combination with the two different portfolios of risky stocks. Consider the lower line, which

FIGURE 2.3 The Capital Market Line

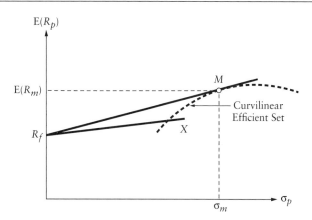

combines the risk-free security (R_f) and portfolio X located on the efficient frontier. All points on this line can be obtained by varying the weights in R_f and X. The line begins at a return of R_f and risk of zero, which represents 100% investment in the risk-free asset. Moving along the line, one increases the percentage invested in X. Points to the right of X indicate borrowing (i.e., a negative weight in R_f) along with a more than 100% weighting in X. A little thought, however, should indicate that there is a better risky portfolio than X. By choosing as our risky portfolio another portfolio (not shown) above and to the right of X, this new line would be everywhere above the first line. In fact, this argument holds true until we reach our second line, which is the unique tangency portfolio. While portfolios below this line can be achieved, they are suboptimal. Notice that any point on the line to the right of the tangency represents borrowing because more than 100% of the available funds are invested in the risky portfolio.

What exactly is the makeup of this tangency portfolio? Recall that as we add more and more risky assets to our portfolio, we diversify away firm-specific risk. The tangency portfolio is the market portfolio which includes all risky assets weighted by their value because this is the most diversified portfolio possible, and we denote it as M.[11] The line joining R_f and M is called the **capital market line** (**CML**), and represents all combinations of the risk-free asset and the market portfolio. The CML tells the investor how much more return can be earned for taking on additional risk.

CAPITAL ASSET PRICING MODEL

According to this framework, rational investors hold the market portfolio in combination with the risk-free asset because otherwise more risk could be diversified away. Investors will not be compensated for taking on diversifiable risk unrelated to market movements. This is the critical insight provided by the **capital asset pricing model** (**CAPM**).[12] Remember that we are assuming that beliefs are identical across individuals, which means that investors have the same efficient frontier, implying that all investors hold the same portfolio of risky assets, the market portfolio.

According to the CAPM, only risk related to market movements is priced in the market. The variance or standard deviation of returns for an asset is not the appropriate gauge of risk because it measures total risk, including both diversifiable, firm-specific risk, and systematic, market risk. The CAPM's measure of risk, **beta** (β), takes into account an asset's sensitivity to the market and, thus, only measures systematic, nondiversifiable risk. It can be proved that under these conditions the expected return for asset i is given by:

2.12
$$E(R_i) = R_f + \beta_i(E(R_m) - R_f)$$

where $E(R_m)$ is the expected return for the market. This relationship is depicted in Figure 2.4. The beta for stock i is calculated as:

2.13
$$\beta_i = \frac{\sigma(R_i, R_m)}{\sigma_m^2}$$

FIGURE 2.4 The Security Market Line

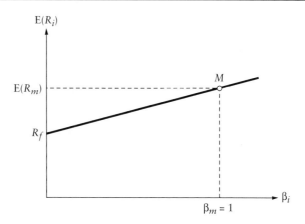

In other words, beta is the covariance of stock i's returns with the market's returns, divided by the variance of the market return. The beta for the market is one, because the market moves exactly with itself. With a positive beta, the expected return on an asset increases with increases in the market risk premium $(E(R_m) - R_f)$. The **market risk premium** (or **equity premium**) is the expected return on the market in excess of the risk-free rate. Later, in Chapter 14, we will discuss whether the market risk premium has, historically speaking, been too high, and what this implies.

OPERATIONALIZING THE CAPM

Let us provide an example using U.S. data. The return for the market is often measured using a broad-based stock index, such as the New York Stock Exchange (NYSE) Composite Index, and the risk-free rate is often proxied by the rate on short-term U.S. Treasury bills. Table 2.2 provides some historical information for the NYSE index and U.S. Treasury bills, as well as a few stocks selected for

TABLE 2.2   RISK MEASURES FOR THE NYSE COMPOSITE STOCK INDEX AND SELECTED STOCKS

Stock	Industry	Average Return (2002–2006)	Standard Deviation Of Returns	Beta
NYSE Index	Broad-based index of stocks	9.02%	11.92%	1.00
U.S. Treasury Bills	Measure of risk-free rate	1.45%	5.02%	0
ABN Amro Holdings	Foreign Bank	22.04%	29.94%	1.40
CytRx Corp.	Drug	35.58%	105.03%	0.55
JDS Uniphase	Electronics	–24.71%	77.84%	1.45
YUM! Brands	Restaurant	18.16%	21.04%	0.55

illustrative purposes. Average returns and standard deviations of returns are computed using five years of data from January 2002 through December 2006. Betas for the four firms are taken from the *Value Line Investment Survey* and are also estimated using five years of data. For the few stocks selected, there is no clear relationship between return, standard deviation, and beta. Remember that the CAPM is a theoretical relationship regarding the trade-off between risk and expected future return and predicts higher returns with higher betas. In Table 2.2, we have a firm with a low beta and high average return (CytRx Corp.) and another with a high beta and low average return (JDS Uniphase). This, in fact, is the opposite of what the CAPM predicts, but given randomness (remember the CAPM is in terms of expectations) and the fact that our sample is short, this is not overly alarming (and certainly is not sufficient evidence to call the model into question).

The first tests of the CAPM generally indicated that the model was a success. Expected returns seemed to be positively correlated with beta, and beta appeared to do a good job explaining how returns varied across firms.[13] Researchers, however, began to find evidence that beta, alone, could not satisfactorily explain returns. Perhaps most significantly, researchers found that other factors, in addition to the excess return on the market, were helpful in explaining variation in expected returns across stocks.[14] In future chapters, we will delve more deeply into the evidence that led behavioral researchers to explore psychology research and consider alternative pricing models. Some concern surrounds assumptions of the CAPM, a key one being that investors all have the same expectations about asset returns. In the following section, we will consider the efficient markets hypothesis and its predictions about behavior.

2.3   MARKET EFFICIENCY

Capital markets are crucial to the development and functioning of an economy because they perform a critical service. It is through efficient and well-performing capital markets that resources are allocated to their best use. Ideally, markets transfer funds from savers to borrowers with good investment opportunities. Borrowers may have opportunities that provide good returns based on their level of risk, but insufficient capital to proceed with such investment. With efficient capital markets, lenders are better off because they earn a higher risk-adjusted return, and borrowers are better off because they do not have to forgo profitable opportunities. Of course, well-documented "mistakes" do occur, such as the Internet bubble of the late 1990s and the recent subprime financial crisis. It is always a matter of debate (ex post) whether those supplying capital were wise to do so at the time—given what they knew at the time.

EFFICIENCY AND INFORMATION

Eugene Fama has provided a careful description of an **efficient market** that has had a lasting influence on practitioners and academics in finance.[15] According to Fama:

> The primary role of the capital market is allocation of ownership of the economy's capital stock. In general terms, the idea is a market in which prices

provide accurate signals for resource allocation: that is, a market in which firms can make production-investment decisions, and investors can choose among the securities that represent ownership of firms' activities under the assumption that security prices at any time "fully reflect" all available information. A market in which prices always "fully reflect" available information is called "efficient."

Because prices always accurately reflect information, they are good signals of value and encourage the best allocation of capital. If a market is efficient, information is fully and instantaneously reflected in prices.

Notice that the definition of an efficient market relies critically on information. Fama defined three versions of market efficiency to clarify what is intended by "all available information." In the **weak form**, prices reflect all the information contained in historical returns. In the **semi-strong form**, prices reflect *all* publicly available information, including past earnings and earnings forecasts, everything in the publicly released financial statements (past and most recent), everything relevant appearing in the business press, and anything else considered relevant. In the **strong form**, prices even reflect information that is not publicly available, such as insiders' information.

Notice that if prices *always* reflect *all* information, we must be assuming that the cost of information acquisition and generation is zero. Of course, we all know this is not reasonable. Thus, a better working definition of the EMH is that prices reflect all information such that the marginal benefit of acting on the information does not exceed the marginal cost of acquiring the information. In other words, no investor can consistently generate **excess returns**.[16]

In this context, it is important to note that *excess* means after all costs have been considered. Other than obvious trading costs, we must take into account the cost of acquiring information or undertaking analysis (or paying someone to do so on your behalf). For example, if a particular mutual fund is able to on average beat the market by 1.5% (on a gross basis), but charges a 1.5% management expense ratio (MER) to investors, which means that investors would only match the market's return, this is *not* evidence against the EMH. Further complicating the meaning of excess is the requirement to "risk-adjust," an issue which we discuss later in the context of the joint hypothesis problem.

WHAT DOES MARKET EFFICIENCY IMPLY?

In accounting, finance, and economics, an efficient market is often taken to imply that an asset's price equals its expected fundamental value.[17] For example, according to the present value model of stock prices, a stock's price equals the present value of expected future dividends.[18] Price is thus simply expressed as:

2.14
$$p_t = \sum_{i=1}^{\infty} \frac{E_t(d_{t+i})}{(1+\delta)^i}$$

where p_t is the stock price today at time t, $E_t(d_{t+i})$ is the expected value of the future dividend at time $t+i$ using information available today, and δ is the discount rate, which reflects the stock's risk. Some of the evidence against the efficient markets hypothesis discussed later in the book is based on violations of this relationship. Tests of the present value model must specify the information available to traders in forming their expectations of future dividends. The **present value model of stock prices** says that in an efficient market a stock's price is based on reasonable expectations of its fundamental value.

For most people information means knowledge, but in finance when we say "information" we mean items that are truly unanticipated.[19] If it is announced that the unemployment rate has risen to 6% and most people already expected the unemployment rate to be 6%, this is not considered to be true information. Because information arrival is by definition unpredictable, stock price changes, if they are only driven by information, must themselves be unpredictable. This is the basis for the argument that stock prices should follow a **random walk**.[20] The next step in a random walk is unpredictable, and the best forecast of where you will land on the next step is where you are today. If stock prices follow a random walk, any return on a stock in excess of the risk-adjusted expected return is random and cannot be predicted.

Proponents of the EMH argue that technical analysis based on charts of historical data and fundamental analysis based on publicly available financial information will not successfully generate excess returns. Often a passive investment strategy in which the goal is to track, rather than attempt to beat, the market is recommended. In this case, an investor avoids individually held stocks, instead investing in index mutual funds or exchange-traded index funds (ETFs), such as Standard and Poor's Depositary Receipts (SPDRs, also known as "spiders"), or the iShares MSCI EAFE Index Fund, the largest exchange-traded international equity benchmark.

MISCONCEPTIONS ABOUT MARKET EFFICIENCY

Market efficiency does not suggest that individuals are ill-advised to invest in stocks. Nor does it suggest that all stocks have the same expected return. The EMH does not suggest that any stock or portfolio is as good as any other. While a manager cannot systematically generate returns above the expected, risk-adjusted return, stocks are priced fairly in an efficient market. Because investors have different attitudes toward risk, they may have different portfolios.

In addition, while the EMH suggests that excess return opportunities are unpredictable, it does not suggest that price levels are random. Prices are fair valuations of the firm based on the information available to the market concerning the actions of management and the firm's investment and financing choices.

JOINT HYPOTHESIS PROBLEM

As stated before, an excess return is a return that exceeds the return that both nets out all costs, but also one that would be considered fair given the level of risk of the investment. Because an excess return is defined in relation to a risk-adjusted return, the measurement of excess returns requires a model of returns. For example, if the CAPM is deemed to be the best model of returns, stock i is generating an excess return when:[21]

2.15
$$R_i - (R_f + \beta_i(R_m - R_f)) > 0$$

In this case, stock i's return is higher than required based on its level of risk as reflected in its beta (β_i).

The **joint-hypothesis problem** arises because of the need to utilize a *particular* risk-adjustment model to produce required returns, that is, to risk-adjust. This is innocuous if we know with certainty what the correct risk-adjustment model is, but unfortunately we do not. If a test rejects the EMH, is it because the EMH does not hold, or because we did not properly measure excess returns? We simply do not know the answer to this question. Early empirical tests of the EMH were generally supportive of the hypothesis.[22] These tests suggested that excess returns could not be consistently generated by using mechanical trading rules, and prices reacted quickly and appropriately to new information. Moreover, money managers did not seem to be able to generate positive excess returns after all costs were considered, including transaction costs and management fees. More recent research, however, has reported a series of persistent anomalies, that is, findings that appear to be contrary to the EMH.

Consider the **value premium**. It has been found that investing in value stocks (i.e., stocks with low prices relative to book value or earnings) has historically been a winning strategy. Such a simplistic strategy seems to be evidence against the EMH, but what if value stocks are riskier, and what if their risk is insufficiently captured by the CAPM? Then we may not have an anomaly after all, just an inappropriate asset pricing model. In fact, the famous Fama-French three-factor model includes a value risk factor.[23] We will return to this debate later, principally in Chapters 4 and 14. Next we focus on a theory of the behavior of corporate management.

2.4 AGENCY THEORY

An **agency relationship** exists whenever someone (the principal) contracts with someone else (the agent) to take actions on behalf of the principal and represent the principal's interests. In an agency relationship, the agent has authority to make decisions for the principal. An **agency problem** arises when the agent's and principal's incentives are not aligned.

Consider, for example, the situation when you want to sell your home. You (the principal) contract with a realtor (the agent) to sell your home. You want to structure the contract so that the realtor has the incentive to get the best price as quickly as possible. Thus, realtors are normally compensated a fixed percentage of the selling price, rather than a flat fee. Compensation tied to the selling price gives the realtor the incentive to expend effort to get the best possible price. Even in this case where you attempted to align incentives, realtors, who are self-interested agents, do not necessarily work in your (the home seller's) best interest. For example, suppose you receive an offer to sell your home for $300,000. If the realtor's fee is 5%, she receives $15,000. Suppose you really believe your home value is closer to $320,000. If you rejected the first offer and later received an offer of $320,000, you would receive an additional $19,000 and the realtor would receive only an additional $1,000. Even if the realtor agrees that the value of the home is closer to $320,000, she might discourage you from rejecting the first offer. The additional $1,000 may not be adequate compensation for the amount of additional effort required on her behalf to attract the higher offer. So, notice that your incentive might be to get the highest price for your home, but her incentive might be to get the highest compensation per unit of effort.[24] This is a classic case of conflict of interest.

In firms, conflicts of interest often surface, particularly between owners and managers.[25] In the United States today, corporations receive a lot of attention because the corporate form of organization is prevalent. In a large corporation, we usually observe separation of ownership from the management of the firm. A corporation actually has a separate legal identity from its owners. The shareholders are the owners of the firms and they elect a board of directors who decide on the management team. Agency theory has important implications concerning the structure of a corporation because of principal-agent problems between managers and stockholders.

Agency costs that arise from principal-agent problems are both direct and indirect.[26] These costs are incurred because managers' incentives are not consistent with maximizing the value of the firm. Direct costs include expenditures that benefit the manager but not the firm, such as purchasing a luxury jet for travel. Other direct costs result from the need to monitor managers, including the cost of hiring outside auditors. Indirect costs are more difficult to measure and result from lost opportunities. For example, managers of a firm that is an acquisition target may resist the takeover attempt because of concern about keeping their jobs, even if the shareholders would benefit from the merger.

With the large size of modern corporations and possibly thousands of stockholders, day-to-day interaction between owners and managers is not realistic. Consider, for example, The Coca-Cola Company, which produces one of the most recognizable products in the world. In 2008, the market value of the company was over $100 billion and the firm had more than 300,000 shareholders. Clearly, managers cannot possibly confer with all of these owners on a regular basis. About half of the stock is held by institutional investors. Even frequent interaction between the management team and these institutions would not be possible as there are over 1,000 of them! The separation of ownership and management can allow businesses to flourish—that is, if managers act in the shareholders' best interest.

Much finance theory has focused on how to design an **optimal compensation contract** to align the interests of shareholders and managers. The best design of the contract will depend on many factors including whether the manager's actions are observable, the degree of information asymmetry between managers and shareholders, adequacy of performance measures, and differing horizons of managers and shareholders. To motivate agents, principals include rewards and penalties in compensation contracts, which are referred to as "carrots and sticks."

Good corporate governance, including optimal incentive contract design, is critical to the maximization of the value of a firm and the optimal allocation of capital in our economy. Later in this book we will see that the principal-agent problem can arise in other contexts, such as when a money manager (the agent) invests on behalf of investors (the principals). Further, we will consider how behavioral influences add to our understanding of the principal-agent problem and how its costs can be minimized.

2.5   FROM RATIONALITY TO PSYCHOLOGY

In this chapter, we have reviewed three leading theories that have shaped the practice of modern finance. Later in this book we will consider the evidence that has led some researchers to question the appropriateness of the traditional approach. In particular, in Chapter 4 we will review evidence suggesting that markets may not be quite as efficient as was once thought. Various anomalies, or empirical findings apparently inconsistent with market efficiency, have been documented. Additionally, aside from what the data tell us, there appear to be theoretical arguments that weaken the edifice of the EMH. Many of these arguments come under the rubric "limits to arbitrage." As a result of such research, in recent decades some investigators have attempted to move back to thinking about how financial decision-making is shaped by human psychology.

As in the discipline of psychology itself, researchers study many distinct behavioral phenomena. Behavioral finance is still a relatively new field and often is criticized because it lacks a unified framework. This criticism in and of itself does not invalidate the merits of recognizing the importance of psychology for understanding the decisions of individual investors, finance practitioners, markets, and managers. Some years back, the influential twentieth-century economist John Maynard Keynes noted the influence of psychology on financial decision-making. Consider this passage from his book *The General Theory of Employment, Interest, and Money*, first published in 1936:[27]

> If I may be allowed to appropriate the term *speculation* for the activity of forecasting the psychology of the markets, and the term *enterprise* for the activity of forecasting the prospective yield of assets over their whole life, it is by no means always the case that speculation predominates over enterprise. As the organisation of investment markets improves, the risk of the predominance of speculation does, however, increase. In one of the greatest investment markets in the world, namely, New York, the influence of speculation (in the above sense) is enormous. Even outside the field of finance, Americans are apt to be unduly interested in discovering what average opinion believes average opinion to be; and this national weakness finds its nemesis in the stock market.

Clearly the recognition that psychological influences are important is not new in finance or economics.

CHAPTER HIGHLIGHTS

1. Investors recognize a trade-off between return and risk. Expected return and risk are commonly proxied by the historical mean return and variance (or standard deviation) of returns.
2. Covariance and correlation are statistical measures of how random variables are related.

3. The efficient frontier represents portfolios that maximize expected return for a given level of risk. No rational investor would choose a portfolio below the curve because a portfolio with higher return and the same risk exists.

4. In a portfolio of assets, firm-specific risk can be diversified away. Systematic, market risk, however, cannot be eliminated.

5. The capital market line gives combinations of the risk-free asset and the market portfolio. Rational investors should choose a portfolio on this line in order to achieve the highest return with the lowest risk.

6. According to the capital asset pricing model, investors will not be compensated for taking on diversifiable risk.

7. Beta measures risk related to market movements. An asset's beta can be used to estimate its expected return.

8. The efficiency of markets is important because it allocates capital across firms.

9. In an efficient market, no investor can consistently earn excess returns.

10. An agency problem may exist when an agent's incentives are not aligned with the principal's.

11. Conflicts of interest between the owners and managers of large corporations are potentially costly.

12. Optimal compensation contracts align the incentives of stockholders and management.

DISCUSSION QUESTIONS AND PROBLEMS

1. Differentiate the following terms/concepts:

   a. Systematic and nonsystematic risk
   b. Beta and standard deviation
   c. Direct and indirect agency costs
   d. Weak, semi-strong, and strong form market efficiency

2. A stock has a beta of 1.2 and the standard deviation of its returns is 25%. The market risk premium is 5% and the risk-free rate is 4%.

   a. What is the expected return for the stock?
   b. What are the expected return and standard deviation for a portfolio that is equally invested in the stock and the risk-free asset?
   c. A financial analyst forecasts a return of 12% for the stock. Would you buy it? Why or why not?

3. What is the joint hypothesis problem? Why is it important?

4. Warren Buffett has been a very successful investor. In 2008, Luisa Kroll reported that Buffett topped *Forbes Magazine*'s list of the world's richest people with a fortune estimated to be worth $62 billion (March 5, 2008, "The world's billionaires," *Forbes*). Does this invalidate the EMH?

5. You are considering whether to invest in two stocks, Stock A and Stock B. Stock A has a beta of 1.15 and the standard deviation of its returns has been estimated to be 0.28. For Stock B, the beta is 0.84 and standard deviation is 0.48.

   a. Which stock is riskier?
   b. If the risk-free rate is 4% and the market risk premium is 8%, what is the expected return for a portfolio that is composed of 60% A and 40% B?
   c. If the correlation between the returns of A and B is 0.50, what is the standard deviation for the portfolio that includes 60% A and 40% B?

ENDNOTES

1 Although using realized returns to measure future expectations is common, the practice is questioned by some. See, for example, Elton, E. J., 1999, "Expected return, realized return, and asset pricing tests," *Journal of Finance* 52(4), 1199–1220. Elton argues that the historical experience poorly measures future expected returns and calls for additional work on how to better estimate future expected returns.

2 For a portfolio of m assets, the mean return is $\overline{R_p} = \sum\limits_{i=1}^{m} w_i \overline{R_i}$ and the portfolio variance is $s_p^2 = \sum\limits_{i=1}^{m} \sum\limits_{j=1}^{m} w_i w_j \hat{\sigma}(R_i, R_j)$.

3 For a portfolio of m assets, the true expected return is $E(R_p) = \sum\limits_{i=1}^{m} w_i E(R_i)$ and the true portfolio variance is $\sigma_p^2 = \sum\limits_{i=1}^{m} \sum\limits_{j=1}^{m} w_i w_j \sigma(R_i, R_j)$.

4 In our illustrations, we will assume that the risk-free asset is, in fact, risk-free. In actuality even investment in short-term U.S. government debt instruments such as T-bills is associated with some risk.

5 A constant and a random variable have by definition zero covariance and zero correlation.

6 The weighted average standard deviation is $0.40(0.30) + 0.60(0.10) = 0.18$.

7 The theory of optimal portfolio selection was pioneered by Harry Markowitz so that the efficient frontier is sometimes called the Markowitz Frontier. See Markowitz, H., 1952, "Portfolio selection," *Journal of Finance* 7(1), 77–91.

8 Notice that points below the minimum-risk point should be excluded from consideration. For example, E is obviously bettered by F, since the latter has higher expected return with identical risk.

9 For a portfolio including two risky assets, we can denote the weight of the first asset as w, so that the weight of the second asset is $(1-w)$. Then the minimum-risk portfolio for a combination of the two assets can be found by taking the derivative of the portfolio variance with respect to w. For High Tech and Low Tech, the minimum variance portfolio includes 12.26% in High Tech and 87.74% in Low Tech Stock. This minimum-risk portfolio has an expected return of 8.86% and a standard deviation of 9.17%.

10 This follows from the fact that both portfolio expected return and portfolio standard deviation are linear combinations of individual asset expected returns and standard deviations. This is true for standard deviations either when both assets are perfectly positively correlated (i.e., correlation coefficient of one) or (as here) when one of the assets is a constant.

11 Since all investors are holding the same risky portfolio, this can only be the market portfolio.

12 The model is also referred to as the Sharpe-Lintner-Black Model as it was offered independently by several researchers, building on the earlier work of Harry Markowitz on the benefits of diversification, and then later further shaped upon by others. See Treynor, J. L., 1961, "Towards a theory of the market value of risky assets," Unpublished manuscript; Sharpe, W. F., 1964, "Capital asset prices: A theory of market equilibrium under conditions of risk," *Journal of Finance* 19(3), 425–442; Lintner, J., 1965, "The valuation of risk assets and the selection of risky investments in stock portfolios and capital budgets," *Review of Economics and Statistics* 47(1), 13–37; and Black, F., 1972, "Capital market equilibrium with restricted borrowing," *Journal of Business* 45(3), 444–455.

13 See Fama, E. F., 1991, "Efficient capital markets: II," *Journal of Finance* 46(5), December, 1575–1617.

14 See the ground-breaking study by Fama, E. F., and K. R. French, 1992, "The cross-section of

expected stock returns," *Journal of Finance* 47(2), June, 427–465.

15 Fama, E. F., 1970, "Efficient capital markets: A review of theory and empirical work," *Journal of Finance* 31(1), May, 383–417.

16 The term *abnormal return* is often used in place of *excess return*.

17 See, for example, Shiller, R. J., 1981, "Do stock prices move too much to be justified by subsequent changes in dividends?" *American Economic Review* 71(3), 421–436; and Lee, C. M. C., 2001, "Market efficiency and accounting research: A discussion of 'Capital market research in accounting' by S. P. Kothari," *Journal of Accounting and Economics* 31, 233–253.

18 Of course, there are many stocks that are not currently paying dividends. In fact, many stocks have never paid any dividends. This is not problematic for the model because it assumes price is the present value of all expected future dividends. More generally, dividends can be thought of as all cash flows to stockholders, including distributions through share repurchases and mergers and acquisitions. No investor will buy a stock that is expected to never pay anything! See Ackert, L. F., and B. F. Smith, 1993, "Stock price volatility, ordinary dividends, and other cash flows to shareholders," *Journal of Finance* 48(4), 1147–1160.

19 Information-based models in finance consider how information is reflected in market prices. In this literature a common approach is to think of an item of information as a signal that arrives at the market about the value of an asset. See Easley, D., and M. O'Hara, 1987, "Price, trade, size, and information in securities markets," *Journal of Financial Economics* 19, 69–90.

20 Technically, stocks should follow a random walk "with drift," because of the fact that over time we anticipate positive returns because of time value and risk. See Malkiel, B. G., 2004, *A Random Walk down Wall Street*, 7th ed. (W.W. Norton & Company, New York).

21 This expression is the same as the CAPM relationship, with ex post values instead of expected values being used.

22 For thorough reviews of the early literature, see Fama, E. F., 1970, "Efficient capital markets: A review of theory and empirical work," *Journal of Finance* 31(1), May, 383–417; and Fama, E. F., 1991, "Efficient capital markets: II," *Journal of Finance* 46(5), December, 1575–1617.

23 See Fama, E. F., and K. R. French, 1993, "Common risk factors in the returns on stocks and bonds," *Journal of Financial Economics* 33, 3–56.

24 See Levitt, S. D. and S. J. Dubner, 2006, *Freakonomics: A Rogue Economist Exposes the Hidden Side of Everything* (William Morrow: An Imprint of HarperCollins Publishers, New York).

25 Conflicts between managers and shareholders are not the only possible principal-agent problems, though they are often of focus. For example, there are potential conflicts of interest between shareholders and bondholders. Shareholders may prefer more risky investments, but bondholders prefer lower-risk investments because the value of the debt is higher with lower risk. For other conflicts of interest between bondholders and stockholders, see Smith, C. W., and J. B. Warner, 1979, "On financial contracting: An analysis of bond covenants," *Journal of Financial Economics* 7(2), 117–161.

26 On how agency costs are defined, see Jensen, M. C., and W. H. Meckling, 1979, "Theory of the firm: Managerial behavior, agency costs, and ownership structure," *Journal of Financial Economics* 3(4), October, 305–360.

27 Keynes, J. M., 1964, *The General Theory of Employment, Interest, and Money* (Harcourt, Brace, Jovanovich, New York). (First Harbinger Edition, quote on pages 158–159, Chapter 12, Section VI.)

PROSPECT THEORY, FRAMING, AND MENTAL ACCOUNTING

CHAPTER 3

3.1 INTRODUCTION

The first two chapters of this book presented the traditional approaches to understanding individual behavior, financial decision-making, and market outcomes. This chapter will consider more recent attempts to describe behavior that incorporate observed aspects of human psychology. Throughout the remainder of the book we will return to these relatively new theories while describing empirical challenges to the traditional approaches. This chapter is central to the story of behavioral finance. The field of behavioral finance arose in response to evidence that calls into question the traditional approaches. This should not be viewed as a shortcoming of the behavioral approach. Most scientists, and not just social scientists, observe outcomes before developing a theory or model. After all, a theory is a way to explain an observation.

Much of this chapter describes prospect theory, an alternative to expected utility theory developed by Daniel Kahneman and Amos Tversky.[1] It and like-minded theories were inspired by demonstrated violations of expected utility theory, so we begin this chapter by turning to some of these violations. Three key aspects of observed behavior immediately follow, and these key aspects imply a particular shape for the prospect theory value function, which is analogous to the utility function of expected utility theory. Another key building block of prospect theory is the use of decision weights rather than probabilities. We illustrate how the value function and weighting function together allow one to assess the value of prospects in a way that is both similar and quite different from expected utility theory. Hypothetical functional forms are provided based on evidence from actual decisions. Next, Section 3.3 describes how the frame or presentation of a problem impacts the decision a person makes. Then, in Section 3.4, we describe how people use a framing approach known as mental accounting to simplify, and sometimes distort, decision-making. Finally, we consider the issue of moving from theory to practice.

3.2   PROSPECT THEORY

Normative theory says that reasonable people should act in a certain way. In contrast, **positive theory** looks at what people actually do and bases models on these observations. Expected utility theory is a normative model of economic behavior that is based on a rigorous axiomatic treatment. Although it has proven to be very useful in describing how people should behave, some have questioned how good it is at describing actual behavior. The most widely accepted and tested alternative to expected utility theory is prospect theory. Prospect theory is positive (or descriptive) because it is firmly based on how people actually behave.

Prospect theory begins with the contention that standard expected utility theory cannot fully account for observed decision-making under risk. This contention is based on empirical evidence that people often behave contrary to expected utility theory. Before presenting the central tenets of prospect theory, we will consider the evidence that stimulated Kahneman and Tversky to develop their behavioral model.

KEY ASPECTS OF OBSERVED BEHAVIOR

Psychologists routinely observe the decisions of people to provide evidence on a question of interest. Across many studies psychology researchers noted similar responses to decision problems that were not consistent with expected utility theory. This section will illustrate a few of the problems and report on the decisions of actual respondents. These problems illustrate three key aspects of observed decision-making that provide a basis for prospect theory.

In presenting prospects, we will use the same notation as in Chapter 1. Recall that a prospect $P(pr, x, y)$ is a gamble where you have a probability pr of obtaining x and a probability $1 - pr$ of obtaining y. If the second outcome is omitted, as in $P(pr, x)$, it is assumed to be zero, and if the probability is also omitted, as in $P(x)$, it is assumed to be a certain (riskless) prospect. For the first problem, consider the following pair of choices between prospects:[2]

Problem 1:[3]

Imagine that you face the following pair of concurrent decisions. First examine both decisions, and then indicate the options you prefer.

Decision (i): Choose between P1($240) and P2(.25, $1,000).

Decision (ii): Choose between P3(–$750) and P4(.75, –$1000).

In other words, the first choice is between a sure gain of $240 and a 25% chance to gain $1,000. The second choice is between a sure loss of $750 and a 75% chance to lose $1,000. For Problem 1, 84% of the respondents chose P1 in Decision (i), which is consistent with risk aversion. Yet, 87% chose P4 in Decision (ii), which is consistent with risk seeking. Expected utility theory cannot incorporate changes in risk attitude like this. Prospect theory, however, allows for changes in risk attitude depending on the nature of the prospect, as we will see next.

> *Key aspect 1:* People sometimes exhibit risk aversion and sometimes exhibit risk seeking, depending on the nature of the prospect.

Researchers also noticed that gains and losses seem to be what people care about, rather than the level of wealth. In the previous problem, for example, we witnessed risk aversion in the domain of gains and risk seeking in the domain of losses. That is to say, the status quo marked a boundary point between risk aversion and risk seeking. On the other hand, expected utility theory generally uses the *level* of wealth, not *changes* in wealth, as the variable of importance in a utility function, and allows for no boundary points between risk aversion and risk seeking—people are assumed to exhibit consistent risk preferences. How would you choose in the following problem?[4]

Problem 2:

> Decision (i): Assume yourself richer by $300 than you are today. Then choose between P5($100) and P6(.50, $200).
>
> Decision (ii): Assume yourself richer by $500 than you are today. Then choose between P7(–$100) and P8(.50, –$200).

Notice that the two decisions are effectively the same. In both cases, the decision is between $400 with certainty and a prospect with a 50% chance of $500 and a 50% chance of $300. Yet, 72% of respondents chose P5 and 64% chose P8. The choice of many indicates risk aversion for Decision (i), but risk seeking for Decision (ii). This problem illustrates that risk attitude is not the same across gains and losses, implying that it is the change in wealth, rather than the level, that matters to people. People evaluate an outcome based on the gain or loss from a **reference point,** usually taken to be current wealth. Notice that in this problem the two decisions assume different starting wealth positions. Expected utility theory assumes that people value outcomes based on the final wealth position, regardless of the person's initial wealth. This leads to the second key aspect of decision-making:

> **Key aspect 2:** Peoples' valuations of prospects depend on gains and losses relative to a reference point. This reference point is usually the status quo.

Researchers also noticed that people seemed to feel a loss more strongly than a gain of equivalent absolute value. Consider a third problem:[5]

Problem 3:

> What value of x would make you indifferent between P9(0) and P10(0.50, x, –$25)?

P9 is the status quo. The average response in one experiment was $61.[6] That is, for a fair gamble, when the loss is $25, the typical person requires a gain of $61 to be indifferent between accepting or rejecting the gamble. It is quite clear that people are quite averse to a loss. **Loss aversion** is the term that describes the observation that, for most people, losses loom larger than gains. Noting that risk neutrality implies x = $25, the upside had to be more than two times the absolute value of the downside in order to induce indifference between the two prospects. Was your choice consistent with the average, or do you require more or less? A third key observation for understanding how people make choices follows:

> **Key aspect 3:** People are averse to losses because losses loom larger than gains.

It is important to note that loss aversion is quite different from risk aversion. While people also prefer a sure thing to a gamble with only positive outcomes when the expected values are identical (e.g., $75 with certainty vs. $50 or $100 with a 50/50 probability), their aversion to such gambles is much weaker than when one of the outcomes pushes them into the loss column (as in Problem 3).

VALUE FUNCTION

The results summarized in the previous section, as well as others, encouraged many researchers to consider alternatives to expected utility theory. Prospect theory provides a model of decision-making under risk that incorporates such *observed* behaviors.[7] The **value function** in prospect theory replaces the utility function in expected utility theory. While utility is usually measured in terms of the level of wealth, value is defined by gains and losses relative to a reference point. The three key observed aspects of decision-making described previously necessitate certain characteristics for the value function: people exhibit risk aversion in the positive domain and risk seeking in the negative domain, which means the value function is concave in the positive domain and convex in the negative domain; decisions are made by focusing on gains and losses, which means that the argument for the value function is not wealth, but rather changes in wealth; and people dislike losses, so the value function is steeper for losses than for gains.

In addition, instead of using simple probabilities as in expected utility, prospect theory uses **decision weights**. These decision weights, as we will discuss, are a function of probabilities. We will use $v(z)$ to refer to the value of a wealth change, where it should be noted that z is used instead of w, which refers to a wealth level. We will also speak of the value of prospects, $V(P)$. For a prospect $P(pr, z1, z2)$ value is:

3.1
$$V(pr, z1, z2) = V(P) = \pi(pr) * v(z1) + \pi(1 - pr) * v(z2)$$

where $\pi(pr)$ is the decision weight associated with probability pr. Note that $V(P)$, the value of a prospect, is analogous to $U(P)$, the expected utility of a prospect.[8]

Figure 3.1 illustrates a typical value function. Changes in wealth from a reference point determine the value along the vertical axis, rather than terminal wealth. Also notice that the value function is concave in the positive domain, consistent with risk aversion, and convex in the negative domain, consistent with risk seeking. Finally, notice that despite risk aversion in the positive domain and risk seeking in the negative domain, losses loom larger than gains. This is evident because the value function is steeper for losses than for gains, implying that losses are felt more strongly than gains of equivalent size. In other words, people exhibit loss aversion. We will postpone saying more about the weighting function until we consider lottery tickets and insurance.

FIGURE 3.1 Typical Value Function

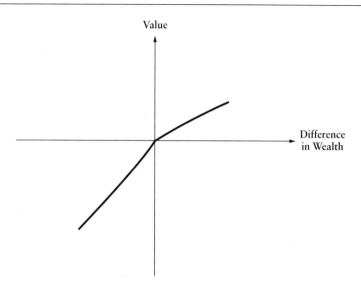

LOTTERY TICKETS AND INSURANCE

A question that has perplexed researchers for years is: Why do people who buy lottery tickets also purchase insurance?[9] In the expected utility framework, this is puzzling because with a lottery a person is seeking risk. The expected payoff from a lottery is well known to be substantially less than the price of a ticket and the odds of winning are massively stacked against the ticket holder. With insurance, the same person may pay to reduce risk, appearing to be risk averse. Prospect theory can account for the observation that some people buy lottery tickets and insurance at the same time. It does so by overweighting low-probability events. Specifically, as we describe next, prospect theory incorporates overweighting of low-probability events by using decision weights ($\pi(p_i)$), rather than event probabilities (p_i) to determine the value of a prospect.

To see why such overweighting is needed, consider the following choice:[10]

Problem 4 (Lottery):

Choose between prospects P11(0.001, $5,000) and P12(1.0, $5).

Even though the expected values of the two prospects are equal ($5) as you almost certainly have observed, many people prefer P11 to P12, consistent with risk seeking. Such a choice is indicative of risk seeking in the domain of gains. Earlier we observed another instance of risk seeking, but this was in the domain of losses. It seems that risk seeking can also occur in the domain of gains as well.

Next consider this choice:

Problem 5 (Insurance):

Choose between prospects P13(0.001, –$5,000) and P14(1.0, –$5).

In this case we often see people choosing prospect P14, consistent with risk aversion. But this implies risk aversion in the negative domain.

In sum, while we normally have risk aversion in the positive domain, when there is a quite low probability of a payoff this generally shifts to risk seeking. On the other hand, while we normally have risk seeking in the negative domain, when there is a quite low probability of a loss this generally shifts to risk aversion. This is what Kahneman and Tversky characterized as the **fourfold pattern of risk attitudes**.[11] This pattern suggests risk aversion for gains and risk seeking for losses when the outcome probability is high, and risk seeking for gains and risk aversion for losses when the outcome probability is low. In one study, they found that 92% (22 out of 25) of subjects displayed the full pattern.[12] Clearly, then, any viable theory of decision-making under risk must confront this fourfold pattern. Prospect theory does so by utilizing a nonlinear weighting function, which we turn to next.

WEIGHTING FUNCTION

While in the original version of prospect theory published in 1979 Kahneman and Tversky spoke of what conditions an appropriate **weighting function** should embody, they did not attempt to formulate such a function. This was left to their more mathematically rigorous version of prospect theory, known as **cumulative prospect theory**, published in 1992.[13] In this paper, mathematical specifications for both the value function and the weighting function are presented and estimated.

Before getting there, let us consider what sort of shape an appropriate weighting function should have. Recall the Allais paradox which was addressed in Chapter 1. In this section, we look at two additional violations of expected utility pointed to by Allais.[14] The first of them gives us insight about the difference between highly probable outcomes and *certain* outcomes. Problem 6 requires the reader to make two choices:[15]

Problem 6:

Decision (i): Choose between P15(0.80, $4,000) and P16(1.00, $3,000).

Decision (ii): Choose between P17(0.20, $4,000) and P18(0.25, $3,000).

Are you like many people? For Decision (i), did you pick P15 or P16? For Decision (ii), did you pick P17 or P18?

Kahneman and Tversky found that 80% of their respondents to Problem 6 chose P16, while 65% chose P17. Notice that Decision (ii) in Problem 6 is identical to Decision (i), except that the probabilities are multiplied by .25. It appears that lowering the probability from 100% to 25% (P16 to P18) has a larger effect than lowering the probability from 80% to 20% (P15 to P17). For obvious reasons, this problem, and the next, are said to be examples of the "common ratio effect." Kahneman and Tversky argue that the reason for this is that people value what is certain relative to that which is merely probable. Because people apparently overweight certain outcomes versus probable ones, Kahneman and Tversky refer to this phenomenon as the **certainty effect**.[16] This implies that the slope of the weighting function in the neighborhood of certainty is relatively steep (i.e., has a slope greater than one).

The next violation of expected utility theory gives us a sense of what the weighting function should look like in the neighborhood of highly unlikely events. Which of the following prospects would you choose?[17]

Problem 7:

Decision (i): Choose between P19(0.45, $6,000) and P20(0.90, $3,000).

Decision (ii): Choose between P21(0.001, $6,000) and P22(0.002, $3,000).

Notice that for a risk-neutral decision-maker P19 ~ P20 and P21 ~ P22, because their expected values are identical. Kahneman and Tversky report that 86% of their respondents picked P20 (risk aversion), yet 73% picked P21 (risk seeking). While earlier we saw that people overweight low probabilities, both the probability associated with P21 and that associated with P22 are quite low, so it must be that the overweighting is greater for .001 than for .002. This suggests that the overweighting is greatest at the lowest probabilities, which, again, implies that the weighting function is relatively steep (i.e., has a slope greater than one) in the neighborhood of zero.

So what do we have so far? We have that the weighting function is steep in the neighborhood of both $p = 0$ and $p = 1$. Using these conditions and setting $\pi(0) = 0$ and $\pi(1) = 1$, it must be that for intermediate probabilities the slope of the weighting function is relatively flat (less than one). Figure 3.2 depicts a weighting function that is consistent with all these requirements. It is sometimes described as an inverted S-curve. The Appendix to this chapter sets out more rigorously the key conditions that a reasonable weighting function should embody.

FIGURE 3.2 Typical Weighting Function

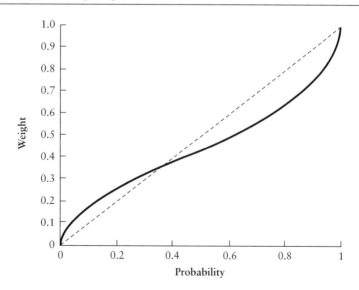

HYPOTHETICAL VALUE AND WEIGHTING FUNCTIONS

Kahneman and Tversky used an experiment to extensively examine individual choices and provide detailed information about the form that value and weighting functions might take.[18] Subjects were asked to provide certainty equivalents for a number of prospects. Recall from Chapter 1 that a certainty equivalent is the wealth level that leads the decision-maker to be indifferent between a particular prospect and a certain wealth level. Based on the experimental results, Kahneman and Tversky proposed hypothetical forms for the value and weighting functions and estimated the relevant parameters.

As we have said, a prospect theory value function should reflect concavity for gains and convexity for losses and loss aversion. A functional form that is consistent with these properties is:

3.2
$$v(z) = \begin{array}{ll} z^\alpha & 0 < \alpha < 1 \qquad \text{if } z \geq 0 \\ -\lambda(-z)^\beta & \lambda > 1,\ 0 < \beta < 1 \quad \text{if } z < 0 \end{array}$$

This functional form is called a two-part power function. Based on their empirical data, Kahneman and Tversky estimated α and β each to be approximately 0.88 and λ to be approximately 2.25. These estimates give a value function for which losses loom larger than gains, like the one illustrated in Figure 3.1. In fact, Figure 3.1 is a depiction of this particular value function. The way to view this function is that it is a *typical* decision-maker's value function. Some people will have lower/higher values for the relevant parameters.

Kahneman and Tversky also suggested a weighting function based on their estimates:[19]

3.3a
$$\pi(p_{\imath}) = \frac{p_{\imath}^\gamma}{(p_{\imath}^\gamma + (1 - p_{\imath})^\gamma)^{\frac{1}{\gamma}}} \qquad \gamma > 0, \text{if } z \geq 0$$

3.3b
$$\pi(p_{\imath}) = \frac{p_{\imath}^\chi}{(p_{\imath}^\chi + (1 - p_{\imath})^\chi)^{\frac{1}{\chi}}} \qquad \chi > 0, \text{if } z < 0$$

Figure 3.2 illustrates this weighting function. In their estimation they found that $\gamma = .61$ and $\chi = .69$. Since these magnitudes are close, we will, for simplicity, use the average value (.65) in both the gain and loss domain. Notice from the figure that low-probability outcomes are given relatively higher weights and certainty is weighted highly relative to near certainty, consistent with the evidence. For example, for an event with probability of 10%, $\pi(p_{\imath}) = 0.1152$, so that relatively low-probability events are overweighted. In the Appendix we describe a condition known as "subcertainty," which means that, while probabilities sum to one, the sum of corresponding decision weights comes in lower than one—that is, $\pi(p_{\imath}) + \pi(1 - p_{\imath}) < 1.0$, while $p_{\imath} + (1 - p_{\imath}) = 1.0$. For example, take the case of $p_{\imath} = .90$. We have that $\pi(.90) = 0.7455$ and, from above, that $\pi(.1) = 0.1152$, so that $\pi(.90) + \pi(.10) = 0.8607$.

Because of its ability to explain a wide range of behavior when people must make decisions under risk, prospect theory has been quite influential and is recognized as an important contribution to economics. In fact, in 2002 Daniel Kahneman won the Nobel Prize in Economics "for having integrated insights from psychological research into economic science, especially concerning human judgment and decision-making under uncertainty."[20] In the next section, we use the "artillery" of this section to value several of the prospects that we have considered so far.

SOME EXAMPLES

Consider Problem 4, where we saw that people like to buy lottery tickets. The value of P11 is:

3.4 $$V(P11) = \pi(.001) * v(5000) = .011 * 1799.26 = 19.864$$

Compare this to P12, the certain $5:

3.5 $$V(P12) = \pi(1) * v(5) = 1 * 4.12 = 4.12$$

So we can see that a typical decision-maker likes to buy a lottery ticket. This result is driven by the fact that the decision weight on $pr = .001$ is about 10 times higher than the probability.

As another example, consider Problem 6. The first decision is P15 vs. P16, whose prospect values are:

3.6 $$V(P15) = \pi(.80) * v(4000) = .64 * 1478.47 = 946.24$$

3.7 $$V(P16) = \pi(1) * v(3000) = 1 * 1147.80 = 1147.80$$

So the typical decision-maker prefers P16. And the second decision is P17 vs. P18, whose prospect values are:

3.8 $$V(P17) = \pi(.20) * v(4000) = .256 * 1478.47 = 384.29$$

3.9 $$V(P18) = \pi(.25) * v(3000) = .293 * 1147.80 = 336.66$$

So the typical decision-maker prefers P17. The reason for the flip-flop is the weight attached to certainty is much higher than the weight attached to the merely probable. In the more intermediate range ($pr = .20$ to $pr = .25$), decision weights rise about as much as probabilities.

OTHER ISSUES

RISKLESS LOSS AVERSION   We have seen from previous discussion that people are reluctant to expose themselves to fair gambles because they are loss averse. Typically, for a 50/50 bet the gain has to be at least twice as great as the loss. Loss aversion can also be viewed in a riskless context. Experiments have examined people's willingness to pay for a good, compared to their willingness to accept money in exchange for the same good. Here is one illustration. Students are given cash and asked how much they would be willing to pay for a mug with the university's emblem. Then another group of students is given mugs and asked how much they would accept in return. In one session the students were willing to pay only $1.34 for a mug, yet others would not accept less than $8.83 for the exact same mug.[21]

The term **endowment effect** (or **status quo bias**) is used because the value of a good seems to increase once a person owns it. This is consistent with prospect theory because losses (i.e., giving up the good) are felt much more strongly than gains (receiving the good).[22] As illustrated in Figure 3.3, if we think in terms of mugs as wealth, positive and negative changes in wealth of equal magnitude ($-x$ or $+x$) have quite different effects on value. The absolute value of $v(-x)$ is more than double the value of $v(+x)$. We will revisit the status quo bias in Chapter 5.

ORIGINS OF PROSPECT THEORY   Expected utility is about how people should act, while prospect theory is about how people actually act. Why the difference? Up to now we have not addressed the origin of prospect-theory-type preferences. Is it social, or is it more innate? Consider the following evidence. In a recent experimental study involving chimpanzees, a pronounced endowment effect was observed in the matter of food choice.[23] When allowed to choose freely between peanut butter and juice, 58% of the chimps preferred peanut butter. When endowed with peanut butter though, 79% preferred to keep it when offered a trade for juice. On the other hand, when endowed with juice, 58% preferred to keep it when offered a trade. In another recent experiment, it has been shown that capuchin monkeys exhibit reference point dependence and loss aversion when confronted with gambles.[24]

Such work suggests an evolutionary basis for prospect theory (specifically for loss aversion and the endowment effect). When primates and man share the same behaviors, it is generally believed that it is probable that such behaviors have an

---

FIGURE 3.3 Endowment Effect

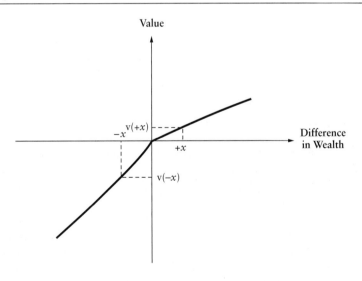

evolutionary (adaptive) rather than social basis. In what sense might loss aversion be adaptive? Consider a primitive man with barely enough to eat.[25] Being able to increase his food intake by 50% might be quite nice, but losing 50% is likely to be catastrophic—that is, losses are more painful than gains are pleasurable.

PROSPECT THEORY AND PSYCHOLOGY   In Chapters 5–7, we will step back from economics and finance and consider the psychological foundations of behavioral finance. In Chapter 5, we discuss heuristics, which are decision-making tools employed based on limited information. As will be discussed, heuristics likely have an evolutionary basis. When employed outside their natural domain, specifically in a complex financial environment, they may lead to suboptimal decision-making. The same characterization is possible for prospect theory—evolutionary in origin, but potentially suboptimal when employed in a financial context. Indeed, it is possible to argue that prospect theory is in fact a family of heuristics concerning how people make choices when confronted with risky options.

The topic of Chapter 6 is overconfidence, as can be manifested in excessive optimism and an illusion of control. The latter is a person's belief that he has a kind of "magical" control over events. Could it be that these tendencies are involved when people exhibit risk-seeking behavior?

In Chapter 7, we discuss how emotion influences decision-making. Some argue that decision-making under risk, in general, and prospect theory, in particular, has a strong emotional basis.[26] In line with this, evidence has been provided that the weighting function shifts farther away from linearity (i.e., probability-weighting) as the context of the choice becomes more emotion-laden.[27] Should it be surprising then that, as will be described in Chapter 10, certain key financial behaviors (in particular, the house money effect and disposition effect) have competing prospect theory and emotion explanations?

COMPETING ALTERNATIVE THEORIES   We do not want the reader to be left with the view that prospect theory, as it now stands, is the final word. Indeed, other alternatives to expected utility theory have been produced. As one recent review writes, "how many [readers] ... will be aware that these so-called non-expected utility models now number well into the double figures?"[28] Some of these theories are more normative in nature, while others are more positive in nature.[29]

3.3   FRAMING

In Chapter 1 we introduced the concept of framing. Recall that a decision frame is a decision-maker's view of a problem and the possible outcomes. A frame is affected by the presentation, the person's perception of the question, and personal characteristics. If a person's decision changes simply because of a change in frame, expected utility theory is violated because it assumes that people should have consistent choices, regardless of presentation. We saw an illustration of how the frame matters in Problem 2 earlier in this chapter where respondents were asked to imagine different starting wealth positions. We now turn to another problem where the frame matters. In this case, the outcomes are nonmonetary.

DOES PROSPECT THEORY WORK WITH NONMONETARY OUTCOMES?

In the following problem, would you choose Program A or Program B?[30]

Problem 8 (Survival frame):

> Imagine that the United States is preparing for the outbreak of an unusual Asian disease, which is expected to kill 600 people. Two alternative programs to combat the disease have been proposed. Assume that the exact scientific estimates of the consequences of the programs are as follows:
>
> If Program A is adopted, 200 people will be saved.
>
> If Program B is adopted, there is a ⅓ probability that 600 people will be saved, and a ⅔ probability that no people will be saved.
>
> Which of the two programs would you favor?

Of the respondents to Problem 8, 72% picked Program A. The majority seems to be risk averse. Notice what happens when the same problem is framed in a different way:

Problem 8 (Mortality frame):

> Imagine that the United States is preparing for the outbreak of an unusual Asian disease, which is expected to kill 600 people. Two alternative programs to combat the disease have been proposed. Assume that the exact scientific estimates of the consequences of the programs are as follows:
>
> If Program C is adopted, 400 people will die.
>
> If program D is adopted, there is a ⅓ probability that nobody will die, and a ⅔ probability that 600 people will die.
>
> Which of the two programs do you favor?

In this case, 78% of the respondents chose Program D. Though the problems are identical, now the majority seems to be risk seeking. Kahneman and Tversky report this change in risk attitude for students, faculty, and physicians alike. This clearly illustrates that the frame matters.

The results are consistent with prospect theory once we recognize that the two problem descriptions suggest the use of different reference points: the survival frame starts from full mortality and moves toward partial survival, while the mortality frame starts from full survival and moves toward partial mortality. Saving lives (survival frame) is a gain, while conceding casualties (mortality frame) is a loss. Since people are prone to loss aversion, the lost lives in the mortality frame loom larger than the lives saved in the survival frame.

INTEGRATION VS. SEGREGATION

In the previous two problems, the questions were posed to encourage a particular reference point (e.g., lives saved or lives lost). In many cases, the decision-maker *chooses* the reference point, and whether an outcome is perceived as positive or negative will depend on the reference point selected. For example, suppose you lost $150 at the horse track today.[31] You are considering betting another $10 in the next and final race of the day on a horse with 15:1 odds. This means that if your horse wins, your payoff for the race will be $150, but if your horse loses, you lose the $10 bet. Notice how important the bettor's reference point is here. If he includes his losses over the day, the bet will result in either a break even position if the horse wins or an overall loss of $150 if the horse loses. But if the bettor ignores his prior losses and considers his reference point to be a fresh slate, the outcome of the final bet is either a gain of $150 or a loss of $10. Prospect theory predicts that a decision-maker who adopts the latter approach of segregating outcomes will be less inclined to accept risk in this situation, both because the gamble crosses over between a loss and a gain so that loss aversion stares at her, and, to the extent that we are in the domain of gains, the value function is concave. In contrast, a decision-maker who takes the first reference point and integrates the outcomes of the bets on the day will be more risk seeking since she will be in the domain of losses. For this type of person, the last bet presents the opportunity to break even.

Figure 3.4 illustrates the difference between integration and segregation. **Integration** occurs when positions are lumped together, while **segregation** occurs when situations are viewed one at a time. Standard prospect theory mostly assumes that people segregate, though Kahneman and Tversky did recognize that sometimes people adopt the frame of integration. They note, for example, that more bets are placed on long shots at the end of a racing day, suggesting that at least some bettors are integrating the outcomes of races and taking risks they would not ordinarily take in order to try to break even.[32]

In the horse racing example, some people are willing to increase their risk in order to break even. When risk increases after losses, this is called the **break even**

FIGURE 3.4 Integration vs. Segregation

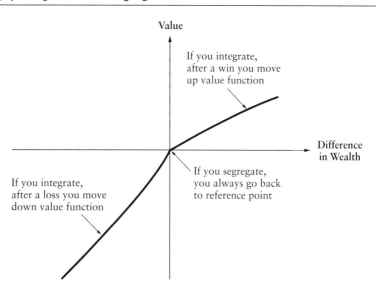

effect. How would people behave, according to prospect theory, after gains? Symmetry might suggest that risk taking would decline, but the reality is otherwise. If new decisions (e.g., whether and how much to bet on the next race) are integrated with prior gains, then, because you have moved up the value function and are some distance from the loss boundary, it is likely that you will be willing to assume *greater* risk. Using the language of the casino rather than the track, you are betting with the "house money." The **house money effect** is said to be operative when someone increases risk taking after prior gains. Both the break even effect and the house money effect are quite important in the context of financial decision-making because they may influence decisions after portfolio growth or shrinkage. For this reason, they will be revisited extensively in Chapter 10. We now turn to the related issue of mental accounting, where the issue of integration versus segregation is also critical.

3.4   MENTAL ACCOUNTING

As we have seen, the framing of outcomes has an important impact on the decisions people make. Let us turn to an example of this in a riskless context. Answer the following yes-or-no question.

Problem 9:

Imagine that you have decided to see a play where admission is $10 per ticket. As you enter the theater, you discover that you have lost a $10 bill. Would you still pay $10 for a ticket to the play?

Mentally note your response, and then answer the next yes-or-no question.[33]

Problem 10:

Imagine that you have decided to see a play and have paid the admission price of $10 per ticket. As you enter the theater, you discover that you have lost the ticket. The seat was not marked and the ticket cannot be recovered. Would you pay $10 for another ticket?

Of course nothing is really different between the questions. A certain amount of money ($10) has been irretrievably lost, and the only decision you have to make is whether or not the theater experience is worth $10 to you. Whether or not the $10 was lost in the form of cash or in the form of a theater ticket is truly irrelevant. Do people see it this way? Many do not. Of the respondents given the first question, 88% said they would buy a ticket. Yet, of the respondents given the second version of the question, the majority (54%) said they would *not* buy a ticket.

OPENING AND CLOSING ACCOUNTS

The difference in the responses is due to **mental accounting**. Mental accounting is one method people use to make decision-making manageable. According to Richard Thaler, "mental accounting is the set of cognitive operations used by individuals and households to organize, evaluate, and keep track of financial activities."[34] Key components of mental accounting are account assignment, closure, and evaluation. Consider what sorts of accounts may exist. Many people nominally place their money in silos: expenditures (food, housing, entertainment, vacation), wealth (checking account, retirement savings), and income (salary, bonus). It is important to note that often these "accounts" are mental constructs rather than actual accounts. For example, most of us have not explicitly set up a bank account (or piggy bank) for entertainment.

Traditionally, economists have assumed that funds are fungible (substitutable), but, because of the silo approach created by mental accounting, this may not be so. Actual decisions people make indicate that money is not always fungible. While distortions and otherwise odd behavior can result, mental accounting can have a beneficial side in that it may help people exert self-control, encouraging the use of rules such as "don't dip into retirement savings," and "pay for luxuries (like vacations to Cancun or Crete) out of savings."[35] People may, thus, be encouraged to economize and save more.

Returning to the ticket problem, when the ticket was originally purchased, a "ticket purchase account" was set up. If all had gone as planned, the play would have been attended using the original ticket, the pleasure of witnessing the play would have offset the cost of the ticket, and the "ticket purchase account" would have been closed. In Problem 9, the lost $10 bill is not directly linked to the ticket, so people are willing to purchase a new ticket. While not happy about losing $10, absent budget constraints, there is no reason to connect this loss to the ticket purchase decision. On the other hand, in Problem 10, the price of an additional ticket is posted to the still open "ticket purchase account," so the price of a ticket now *seems* to be $20, which many find to be too high a price.

EVALUATING ACCOUNTS AND CHOOSING WHEN TO CLOSE THEM

In the previous problem, there was a natural time to close the account. When a consumption item is paid for in advance, it is natural to close the account when the item is actually consumed (i.e., the play is attended). Other accounts may, however, be somewhat more subtle. Consider the case where there is more discretion as to when accounts should be evaluated and/or closed. Accounts set up for saving and investment fall into this category. How often are such accounts examined—every day or just once a year? And, a different question: How often and under what circumstances are they closed—whenever they are examined, or might other triggers be needed? The answer will surely depend on the type of account. Behavior with respect to retirement savings is likely to be different from behavior with respect to your "lunch money" account.

Prospect theory tells us that people feel losses more severely than gains, which implies that when there is discretion as to when to close an account, they may choose to avoid doing so if losses will result. If gains, on the other hand, will result, they may be quite ready to close an account. An example of this is in the context of a stock portfolio. Consider a stock investor who has witnessed one of his picks drop in price. As long as he holds it, he can view it as a "paper loss." Such a frame means that the account remains open. Selling the stock, which can actually be advisable from a tax perspective, necessitates closing the account—and closing the account, especially because of loss aversion, is a painful experience. On the other hand, selling a winning stock allows one to close the account in the gain territory and enjoy the associated gain. The tendency to avoid selling losers is known as the **disposition effect**.[36] It is an important investor behavior, and we will revisit it in detail in Chapter 10.

The disposition effect, along with the previously discussed break even and house money effects, suggest that decisions often have **path dependence** to them. Path dependence exists if it is important to your decision how you got where you are rather than merely focusing on your current location. It takes enormous mental discipline to simply look forward without agonizing or gloating over what has transpired. It seems that many have some way to go.

CLOSURE, INTEGRATION, AND SEGREGATION

Consider what is going on in the previous stock example. According to the prospect value function, a loss is painful, which is why the investor holds off selling the stock. In effect, his frame is to *integrate* the current decision and the past performance of the stock. What would segregation look like? Segregation would imply separating the past from decisions to be made now. So the type of investor who looks at a stock and notices that it has dropped, realizes that this event is history, and resets his new reference point to the current stock price, is segregating. Such an approach precludes a disposition effect.

What about the theater ticket purchase example? In this problem, whether the additional $10 is spent on the ticket depends on whether the prior loss of $10 is integrated with or segregated from the cost of the ticket. If the lost $10 theater ticket in Problem 10 is integrated with the cost of a new ticket, a decision-maker would view the cost of a ticket as $20, as the majority of respondents did. But, again, a proper view would be to segregate and realize that the original lost ticket is a sunk cost.[37]

3.5 FROM THEORY TO PRACTICE

Although prospect theory has been the prominent behavioral theory, it is not accepted by all. Some economists question the reliability of the challenges to expected utility theory outlined earlier in this chapter because many of the studies were based on hypothetical choice problems given to students.[38] In economics it is important that the researcher ensure that the decision-maker has adequate incentives, which means that real money is at stake rather than hypothetical outcomes.[39] Others argue that students are not representative of the general population. Later, researchers continued to document the phenomena reported by Kahneman and Tversky with diverse subject pools including game show contestants.[40] Though many experiments present results that are consistent with prospect theory, some do not.[41] Finally, it is important to remember that prospect theory is a model of *individual* behavior. Behavioral research on individual choices and market outcomes are both based on the evidence that individuals are affected in systematic ways by psychological influences. Yet, it is not entirely clear how individual behavior aggregates to predict group decisions or, of particular interest to us in finance, market outcomes.[42]

According to Nobel prize-winning economist Vernon Smith, "[w]ell-formulated theories in most sciences tend to be preceded by much observation, which in turn stimulates curiosity as to what accounts for the documented regularities."[43] Throughout the remainder of this book, many consistently observed deviations from traditional theory will be presented. It is the consistency of the behavior that has stimulated the curiosity of behavioral researchers. In addition to describing observed human behavior, we will consider how financial decision-making is affected, as well as how you, as an aware decision-maker, can make better financial decisions.

CHAPTER HIGHLIGHTS

1. Using decision-making problems, psychologists have noted violations of expected utility theory.
2. Prospect theory, developed by Daniel Kahneman and Amos Tversky, is the most accepted behavioral model of individual behavior.
3. There are three key aspects of observed behavior: risk aversion in gains and risk seeking in losses; gains and losses are defined relative to a reference point; and losses loom larger than gains (loss aversion).
4. In prospect theory, the value function replaces the idea of utility.
5. Prospect theory uses overweighting of small probabilities to explain why a person might buy a lottery ticket and insurance.
6. Cumulative prospect theory, an extension of the original model, includes more flexible decision weights that reflect overweighting of low probabilities and different weights for gains and losses of equal size.
7. The certainty effect is the finding that people overweight more certain outcomes.
8. Kahneman and Tversky used experimental evidence to propose functional forms for value and weighting functions.
9. How a problem is framed or presented can affect the choices people make.
10. People use mental accounting to organize, evaluate, and monitor financial matters.
11. Three aspects of mental accounting are important: the decision frame, assignment of accounts, and frequency of account evaluation.

DISCUSSION QUESTIONS AND PROBLEMS

1. Differentiate the following terms/concepts:

   a. Lottery and insurance
   b. Segregation and integration
   c. Risk aversion and loss aversion
   d. Weighting function and event probability

2. According to prospect theory, which is preferred?

    a. Prospect A or B?
        Decision (i). Choose between:
        A(0.80, $50, $0) and
        B(0.40, $100, $0)

    b. Prospect C or D?
        Decision (ii). Choose between:
        C(0.00002, $500,000, $0) and
        D(0.00001, $1,000,000, $0)

    c. Are these choices consistent with expected utility theory? Why or why not?

3. Consider a person with the following value function under prospect theory:

$$v(w) = w^{.5} \qquad \text{if } w \geq 0$$
$$\quad\;\; = -2(-w)^{.5} \qquad \text{if } w < 0$$

    a. Is this individual loss averse? Explain.

    b. Assume that this individual weights values by probabilities, instead of using a prospect theory weighting function. Which of the following prospects would be preferred?

        P1(.8, 1000, −800)
        P2(.7, 1200, −600)
        P3(.5, 2000, −1000)

4. Now consider a person with the following value function under prospect theory:

$$v(w) = w^{.8} \qquad \text{if } w \geq 0$$
$$\quad\;\; = -3(-w)^{.8} \qquad \text{if } w < 0$$

This individual has the following weighting function:

$$\pi(pr) = \frac{pr^{\gamma}}{\left(pr^{\gamma} + (1 - pr)^{\gamma}\right)^{1/\gamma}}$$

where we set $\gamma = .65$.

    a. Which of the following prospects would he choose?

        PA(.001, −5000)
        PB(−5)

    b. Repeat the calculation, but using probabilities instead of weights. What does this illustrate?

5. Why might some prefer a *prix fixe* (fixed price) dinner costing about the same as an *à la carte* one (where you pay individually for each item)? (Assume the food is identical.)

CONDITIONS REQUIRED FOR THE PROSPECT THEORY WEIGHTING FUNCTION

In their seminal 1979 paper first outlining prospect theory, Kahneman and Tversky set out a number of conditions that, according to the evidence, an appropriate weighting function should embody.

Below we list the conditions, show how revealed prospect choices require them, and illustrate them in terms of the hypothetical weighting function equation 3.3 (and depicted in Figure 3.2).

CONDITIONS

▦ **Low-probability overweighting: For low** pr, $\pi(pr) > pr$.

From Problems 4 and 5, we see that risk aversion/seeking in the positive/negative domain becomes risk seeking/aversion when the positive-outcome/negative-outcome event has a low probability. This suggests that the weight attached to a low-probability event is higher than its probability. Referring to the graph, we see that the weighting function is indeed above the 45% degree line (where $\pi = pr$) for low probabilities.

▦ **Subadditivity: For low** pr, $\pi(r * pr) > r\pi(pr)$, **where** $0 < r < 1$.

Intuitively, this means that the second derivative of the weighting function is negative at low probabilities. If this were not so, since for low probabilities $\pi(pr) > pr$, weights would move farther and farther away from pr with increases in pr. Recall that the P21 versus P22 typical choice (from Problem 7) is:

> **A3.1**   P21(0.001, \$6,000) ≻
> P22(0.002, \$3,000)

Subadditivity follows from this choice. We have:

> **A3.2** $\pi(.001) * v(6000) >$
> $\pi(.002) * v(3000)$

Rearranging and invoking risk aversion in the positive domain we have:

> **A3.3** $\pi(.001) / \pi(.002) >$
> $v(3000) / v(6000) > .5$

This is rewritten as:

> **A3.4** $\pi(.001) > .5\pi(.002)$

Letting r = .5 and pr = .002, we have our result. Again, graphically, we observe that the slope is declining because the second derivative of the weighting function is negative for low probabilities.

▦ **Subcertainty:** $\pi(pr) + \pi(1 - pr) < 1$, where $0 < pr < 1$.

To demonstrate subcertainty, recall the prospects that we used to demonstrate the Allais paradox in Chapter 1. Returning to those choices, but now using prospect theory instead of expected utility theory, we have for the first choice (where we are now working in millions of dollars):

A3.5 $V(A) = v(\$1) > \pi(.89)v(\$1) + \pi(.1)v(\$5) = V(A^*)$

This simplifies to:

A3.6 $[1 - \pi(.89)]v(\$1) > \pi(.1)v(\$5)$

For the second choice we have:

A3.7 $V(B^*) = \pi(.1)v(\$5) > \pi(.11)v(\$1) = V(B)$

Putting the two together we have:

A3.8 $[1 - \pi(.89)]v(\$1) > \pi(.11)v(\$1)$

This simplifies to:

A3.9 $1 > \pi(.11) + \pi(.89)$

Subcertainty is consistent with the hypothetical weighting function, as was illustrated in our discussion of hypothetical value and weighting functions earlier in the chapter. Additionally, it is quite clear from an inspection of the graph. Logically, if there is an overweighting of low probabilities and subcertainty holds, then it must be the case that after a certain point probabilities are underweighted rather than overweighted. We see this crossover in the figure where the weighting function cuts the 45% degree line from above.

- **Subproportionality:**
$\pi(pι*q)/\pi(pι)\leq\pi(pι*qr)/\pi(pι*r)$ **where r ≤ 1.** Subproportionality follows from the typical choices made in both parts of Problem 7. To review the first choice implies:

A3.10 $\pi(.90) * v(3000) > \pi(.45) * v(6000)$

Rearranging yields:

A3.11 $v(3000) / v(6000) > \pi(.45) / \pi(.90)$

And the second choice implies:

A3.12 $\pi(.001) * v(6000) > \pi(.002) * v(3000)$

Rearranging yields:

A3.13 $\pi(.001) / \pi(.002) > v(3000) / v(6000)$

The two choices together imply:

A3.14 $\pi(.001) / \pi(.002) > \pi(.45) / \pi(.90)$

This is the desired result if we let $pι = .9$, q = .5, and r = 1/450. In terms of our hypothetical function, we have: $\pi(.001) = .0110$; $\pi(.002) = .0172$; $\pi(.001)/\pi(.002) = .64$; $\pi(.45) = .4104$; $\pi(.90) = .7456$; and $\pi(.45)/\pi(.90) = .55$, which is consistent with what is required.

ENDNOTES

1 Much of this chapter is based on the following seminal article of Kahneman and Tversky: Kahneman, D., and A. Tversky, 1979, "Prospect theory: An analysis of decision under risk," *Econometrica* 47(2), 263–291. Some simplified elements of Tversky, A., and D. Kahneman, 1992, "Advances in prospect theory: Cumulative representation of uncertainty," *Journal of Risk and Uncertainty* 5, 297–323, are also incorporated into our treatment of prospect theory.

2 Problem 1 is from Tversky, A., and D. Kahneman, 1981, "The framing of decisions and the psychology of choice," *Science* 211, 453–458.

3 While our prospect choices are presented in terms of dollars, they have often been tested using other currencies and work equally well. For example, some of Kahneman and Tversky's original prospects were performed using Israeli shekels. In most cases, payouts have been hypothetical. For one exception, see Laury, S. K., and C. A. Holt, 2005,

"Further reflections on prospect theory," Working paper.

4 This problem is from Tversky, A., and D. Kahneman, 1986, "Rational choice and the framing of decisions," *Journal of Business* 59(4), pt. 2, S251–S278.

5 Tversky, A., and D. Kahneman, 1992, "Advances in prospect theory: Cumulative representation of uncertainty," *Journal of Risk and Uncertainty* 5, 297–323.

6 Tversky, A., and D. Kahneman, 1992, "Advances in prospect theory: Cumulative representation of uncertainty," *Journal of Risk and Uncertainty* 5, 297–323.

7 This is extended to uncertainty in Tversky, A., and D. Kahneman, 1992, "Advances in prospect theory: Cumulative representation of uncertainty," *Journal of Risk and Uncertainty* 5, 297–323.

8 Notice that we have not assumed that $\pi(pr) + \pi(1 - pr) = 1$. In fact, as discussed later in the chapter, the sum of the weights is less than one.

9 See, for example, Friedman, M., and L. J. Savage, 1948, "The utility analysis of choices involving risk," *Journal of Political Economy* 56(4), 279–304.

10 This problem is from Kahneman, D. and A. Tversky, 1979, "Prospect theory: An analysis of decision under risk," *Econometrica* 47(2), 263–291.

11 Tversky, A., and D. Kahneman, 1992, "Advances in prospect theory: Cumulative representation of uncertainty," *Journal of Risk and Uncertainty* 5, 297–323.

12 Tversky, A., and D. Kahneman, 1992, "Advances in prospect theory: Cumulative representation of uncertainty," *Journal of Risk and Uncertainty* 5, 297–323.

13 Tversky, A., and D. Kahneman, 1992, "Advances in prospect theory: Cumulative representation of uncertainty," *Journal of Risk and Uncertainty* 5, 297–323.

14 Allais, M., 1953, "L'extension des théories de l'équilibre économique général et du rendement social au cas du risque," *Econometrica* 21(2), April, 269–290.

15 This problem is from Kahneman, D., and A. Tversky, 1979, "Prospect theory: An analysis of decision under risk," *Econometrica* 47(2), 263–291.

16 It is also true that very near certainty is overweighted relative to the probable. If one repeats Problem 6 replacing the P16 with .99 and P18 with .2475, the same selections will be made (according to the hypothetical functions used in the next section of the chapter).

17 This problem is from Kahneman, D., and A. Tversky, 1979, "Prospect theory: An analysis of decision under risk," *Econometrica* 47(2), 263–291.

18 Tversky, A., and D. Kahneman, 1992, "Advances in prospect theory: Cumulative representation of uncertainty," *Journal of Risk and Uncertainty* 5, 297–323.

19 In their original 1979 version of prospect theory, Kahneman and Tversky conjecture that the weighting function is not well behaved at the endpoints. Though they repeat this in their 1992 paper, they still estimate it throughout the entire probability range (including the endpoints).

20 See http://nobelprize.org/nobel_prizes/economics/laureates/2002 (accessed on June 30, 2008).

21 Ackert, L. F., B. K. Church, and G. P. Dwyer, Jr., 2007, "When the shoe is on the other foot: Experimental evidence on valuation disparities," *Public Finance Review* 35 (2), 199–214.

22 Kahneman, D., J. L. Knetsch, and R. H. Thaler, 1990, "Experimental tests of the endowment effect and the Coase theorem," *Journal of Political Economy* 98(6), 1325–1348.

23 Brosnan, S. F., O. D. Jones, S. P. Lambeth, M. C. Mareno, A. S. Richardson, and S. J. Schapiro, 2007, "Endowment effects in chimpanzees," *Current Biology* 17(19), 1704–1707.

24 Chen, M. K., V. Lakshminarayanan, and L. Santos, 2005, "The evolution of our preferences: Evidence from capuchin-monkey trading behavior," Working paper.

25 McDermott, R., J. H. Fowler, and O. Smirnov, 2008, "On the evolutionary origin of prospect theory preferences," *Journal of Politics* 70(2), 335–350.

26 Loewenstein, G. F., C. K. Hsee, E. U. Weber, and N. Welch, 2001, "Risk as feelings," *Psychological Bulletin* 127, 267–286.

27 Rottenstreich, Y., and C. K. Hsee, 2001, "Money, kisses and electric shocks: On the affective psychology of risk," *Psychological Science* 12, 185–190.

28 Starmer, C., 2000, "Developments in non-expected utility theory: The hunt for a descriptive theory of choice under risk," *Journal of Economic Literature* 38, 332–382.

29 Examples of the former are Machina, M. J., 1982, "'Expected utility' theory without the independence axiom," *Econometrica* 50, 277–323; and Chew, S. H., L. G. Epstein, and U. Segal, 1991, "Mixture symmetry and quadratic utility," *Econometrica* 59, 139–163. Examples of the latter are Loomes, G., and R. Sugden, 1982, "Regret theory: An alternative theory of rational choice under uncertainty," *Economic Journal* 92, 805–824; and Gul, F., 1991, "A theory of disappointment aversion," *Econometrica* 59, 667–686.

30 This problem is from Tversky, A., and D. Kahneman, 1981, "The framing of decisions and the psychology of choice," *Science* 211, January, 453–458.

31 Tversky, A., and D. Kahneman, 1981, "The framing of decisions and the psychology of choice," *Science* 211, January, 453–458.

32 Tversky, A., and D. Kahneman, 1981, "The framing of decisions and the psychology of choice," *Science* 211, January, 453–458.

33 These problems are from Tversky, A., and D. Kahneman, 1981, "The framing of decisions and the psychology of choice," *Science* 211, January, 453–458.

34 Thaler, R. H., 1999, "Mental accounting matters," *Journal of Behavioral Decision Making* 12, 183–206. This paper provides an excellent review of mental accounting.

35 Self-control has been used to explain why some investors seem to prefer cash dividend payments over capital gains. See Shefrin, H. M., and M. Statman, 1984, "Explaining investor preference for cash dividends," *Journal of Financial Economics* 13, 253–282.

36 Shefrin, H., and M. Statman, 1985, "The disposition to sell winners too early and ride losers too long: Theory and evidence," *Journal of Finance* 40(4), 777–792.

37 Does it make you happier to integrate or segregate outcomes? This issue is known as "hedonic editing." Some rules of thumb are suggested by the shape of the value function. People are better off segregating gains because the value function is concave in the domain of gains, and integrating losses because the function is convex for losses. In addition, a small loss should be integrated with larger gain to offset loss aversion, and a small gain should be segregated from a larger loss. See Thaler, R. H., 1999, "Mental accounting matters," *Journal of Behavioral Decision Making* 12, 183–206, for a discussion.

38 See Hogarth, R. M., and M. W. Reder, 1986, "Editors' comments: Perspectives from economics and psychology," *Journal of Business* 59(4), S185–S207.

39 Davis, D. D., and C. A. Holt, 1993, *Experimental Economics* (Princeton University Press, Princeton, New Jersey) and Kagel, J. H., and A. E. Roth, eds., 1995, *Handbook of Experimental Economics* (Princeton University Press, Princeton, New Jersey).

40 See Tversky, A., and D. Kahneman, 1986, "Rational choice and the framing of decisions," *Journal of Business* 59(4), pt. 2, S251–S278; and Post, T., M. J. an den Assem, G. Baltussen, and R. H. Thaler, 2008, "Deal or no deal? Decision making under risk in a large-payoff game show," *American Economic Review* 98(1), 38–71.

41 See, for example, Battalio, R. C., J. H. Kagel, and K. Jiranyakul, 1990, "Testing between alternative models of choice under uncertainty: Some initial results," *Journal of Risk and Uncertainty* 3, 25–50; and Baltussen, G., T. Post, and P. Van Vliet, 2006, "Violations of cumulative prospect theory

in mixed gambles with moderate probabilities," *Management Science* 52(8), 1288–1290.

42 See, for example, Ackert, L. F., N. Charupat, B. K. Church, and R. Deaves, 2006, "An experimental examination of the house money effect in a multi-period setting," *Experimental Economics* 9, 5–16; and

Levy, J. S., 1997, "Prospect theory, rational choice, and international relations," *International Studies Quarterly* 41, 87–112.

43 See Smith, V. L., 1994, "Economics in the laboratory," *Journal of Economic Perspectives* 8(1), 113–131.

CHALLENGES TO MARKET EFFICIENCY

CHAPTER 4

4.1 INTRODUCTION

Since the heyday of the market efficiency hypothesis about 30 years ago, researchers have gradually, both on theoretical and empirical grounds, increasingly chipped away at its edifice. While, as discussed in Chapter 2, early tests of market efficiency were largely positive, more recent empirical evidence has uncovered a series of anomalies. **Anomalies** are empirical results that appear, until adequately explained, to run counter to market efficiency. *Appear* is the operative word since virtually all tests of market efficiency require the use of an asset pricing model to adjust for risk. The result is that efficiency tests are by their very nature joint hypothesis tests, which means that market efficiency and a particular risk-adjustment technique (CAPM until more recent tests) together constitute the maintained hypothesis. Rejection implies either inefficiency or an inappropriate risk-adjustment method (or perhaps both). Because one cannot say which, it is virtually impossible to categorically reject efficiency. The first half of this chapter reviews some of these key anomalies.

Empirical evidence notwithstanding, it has been suggested that for theoretical reasons the forces of rational valuation may be weaker than many at first believed.[1] When those investors who are on the lookout for opportunities detect mispricing, it is natural that through their trading they will try to take advantage of them. Market efficiency suggests that the collective action of such traders causes such opportunities to be arbitraged away. Technically, **arbitrage** involves the simultaneous purchase and sale (or short-sale) of securities (which are perfect substitutes) so as to lock in a risk-free profit.[2] In the second half of this chapter, we argue that because there are significant limits to arbitrage, not all mispricing need disappear quickly. These limits stem from noise-trader risk (the possibility that mispricing worsens in the short run); fundamental risk (which exists when the substitute security is an imperfect substitute); and implementation costs (trading costs and the potential nonavailability of the security that must be short-sold).

4.2   SOME KEY ANOMALIES

This section reviews a few highlights from the empirical literature on anomalies. In particular, focus is accorded to: 1) lagged reactions to earnings announcements; 2) the small-firm effect; 3) value versus growth; and 4) momentum and reversal. The last two anomalies are especially important since they appear prominently later in the book. Explanations of these anomalies, behavioral or otherwise, will for the most part be deferred until Chapter 13.

LAGGED REACTIONS TO EARNINGS ANNOUNCEMENTS

Market efficiency tests based on earnings announcements have typically used the **event study** methodology.[3] The essence of an event study is to look at a large number of similar events (e.g., earnings announcements, stock splits, dividend changes, secondary equity offerings, etc.) for a comprehensive sample of firms; work in terms of event-time rather than calendar-time; calculate excess returns on days leading up to the event, on the day of the event, and on days after the event; average these excess returns (or residuals) over all events in the sample; and then accumulate these average residuals to arrive at cumulative average residuals (*CARs*). Recall that excess returns are over and above what needs to be earned in compensation for the risk borne. If markets are efficient, we should expect to see a positive/negative reaction to good/bad news (i.e., a rising/falling *CAR* path) over a window that includes the event (along with a gradual comparable reaction on days prior to the event as the word gradually gets out), but no further reaction on days after the announcement, since an efficient market should have completely reacted to relevant information immediately after the occurrence of the event.

An important event that all firms regularly experience is an earnings announcement. Early earnings-announcement event studies generally tended to find evidence consistent with market efficiency,[4] while later (often more methodologically subtle) studies in this vein often found evidence casting doubt on efficiency. As an example of the latter, Richard Rendleman, Charles Jones, and Henry Latane examined daily return data around the quarterly earnings announcements of about 1,000 firms during 1972–1980.[5] Their procedure was to divide earnings announcements into 10 deciles, ranging from extremely positive (in decile 10) surprises to extremely negative (in decile 1) surprises. Surprises are defined to be announced earnings minus expected earnings (scaled by volatility). More specifically, for each (earnings) event, they calculated standardized unexpected earnings (*SUE*), as follows:

4.1
$$SUE = \frac{EPS - E(EPS)}{SEE}$$

where *EPS* and *E(EPS)* are actual and forecasted earnings per share, respectively. Forecasts were generated by a time-series regression, whose unexplained component was used to calculate what is known as the standard error of the estimate (or *SEE*), which is a reflection of earnings volatility. Based on these *SUE* values, each announcement was put into one of the *SUE* categories. Next, *CAR* paths were calculated over the relevant quarter for each of the *SUE* categories.

FIGURE 4.1 CAR Paths for Quarterly Earnings Announcements

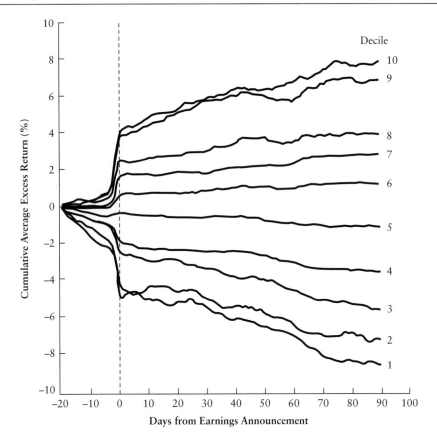

Source: Reprinted from the Journal of Financial Economics, Vol 10, Issue 3, Rendleman, R. J., C. P. Jones, and H. A. Latane, "Empirical anomalies based on unexpected earnings and the importance of risk adjustments," pp. 269–287, © November 1982. With permission from Elsevier.

Figure 4.1 tells the story. Notice that to a certain extent the market anticipates positive and negative surprises, since news comes out in a number of forms (not just in earnings announcements) and publicized earnings forecasts are changed gradually. Also, as expected, on the day of the announcement the market reacts positively to positive surprises and negatively to negative surprises. Most notable, though, from the standpoint of efficiency, is the tendency for there to be a continued drift in prices, especially after unexpected very good or unexpected very bad earnings announcements. This is inconsistent with market efficiency since it appeared that the drift was sufficiently large so that, even after covering likely transaction costs, a speculative profit would remain.

SMALL-FIRM EFFECT

The **small-firm effect** is the tendency for firms with low levels of market capitalization to earn excess returns after accounting for market risk. Using U.S. data, for example, a portfolio—long the smallest firms and short the largest firms—was able to earn 1.52% per month during 1931–1975.[6] Deepening the mystery, further research indicated that much of the small-firm effect was concentrated in January, implying that in some sense the effect was largely a "January effect."[7]

A number of different explanations were advanced. The tax-loss selling-pressure hypothesis argued that some investors sold securities at the end of each calendar year to establish short-term capital losses for income tax purposes. Selling pressure at year-end temporarily depressed prices, after which they rebounded in January. This view was reinforced by the fact that the size of a stock's rebound was directly related to how poorly the stock had performed in the prior year.[8] Even if a tax-based story is compelling, efficiency is not in the clear since the question remains why arbitrageurs did not largely eliminate the decline in prices at year-end.

Whenever puzzling results are found, for them to be taken seriously they must pass the consistency test. In other words, it is always possible to detect correlations in data merely due to randomness, but these correlations are only compelling if they hold over a number of periods. Such consistency leaves an anomaly less susceptible to the data-snooping criticism. The argument here is that the

> more scrutiny a collection of data receives, the more likely "interesting" spurious patterns will be observed. Stock prices are probably the most studied financial series and, therefore, most susceptible to data snooping.[9]

In other words, **data snooping** is the act of analyzing a dataset "to death" so as to detect "anomalies." As the previous quote makes clear, patterns in the data will often be found merely because of randomness.

In this regard, the stability of the small-firm effect has been questioned. Most troubling, the small-firm effect has declined dramatically in the last 20 years or so.[10] One possibility is that published research has revealed to arbitrageurs profitable opportunities that they have then systematically exploited. Anecdotal evidence in support of this is the fact that small-cap investing became a recognized strategy employed by specialists shortly after the publication of relevant research.

VALUE VS. GROWTH

Further problems for market efficiency appeared under the rubric "value investing." **Value stocks** are defined to be stocks with prices that are low relative to such accounting magnitudes as earnings, cash flows, and book value. Conversely, **growth stocks** (or **glamour stocks**) are stocks with prices that are high relative to earnings, cash flows and book value, at least in part because the market anticipates high future growth. **Value investing** is the tendency to overweight value stocks (relative to growth stocks) in one's portfolio.

A study by Sanjoy Basu focused on price-to-earnings (P/E) ratios.[11] Sampling an average of 500 stocks per year over 1956–1969, he grouped them into quintiles on the basis of P/E ratios: the 20% with the highest P/Es were put in one quintile, the 20% with the second-highest P/Es were put into the next quintile, and so on. Hypothetical portfolios were formed at the beginning of the year and then held for 12 months. Table 4.1 shows average returns for each quintile over the 14 years of the sample. Other than the fact that there was virtually no difference between the two highest P/E quintiles (A and B) in terms of future returns, it is apparent that high P/E firms had lower returns than did low P/E firms. Market risk did not

TABLE 4.1	STATISTICS BY P/E GROUP				
	Quintile A: High P/E	Quintile B	Quintile C	Quintile D	Quintile E: Low P/E
Median P/E	35.80	19.10	15.00	12.80	9.80
Average return	9.34%	9.28%	11.65%	13.55%	16.30%
Estimated beta	1.11	1.04	0.97	0.94	0.99

Source: Basu, S., 1977, "Investment performance of common stocks in relation to their price-earnings ratios: A test of the efficient market hypothesis," *Journal of Finance* 32, 663–682.

account for this regularity, however. From the table, it is clear that low P/E portfolios were actually *less* risky than were high P/E portfolios—at least in the sense of CAPM and beta risk.

A related anomaly is based on the book-to-market price (B/P) ratio. Research has indicated that firms with high book-to-market ratios have tended to outperform firms with low book-to-market ratios, after controlling for risk. Table 4.2 provides the relevant findings from one study.[12] The highest book-to-market decile (decile 10) earned on average 17.3%, while the lowest book-to-market decile (decile 1) earned 11.0%. Over five-year return intervals, the gap was even greater: 19.8% vs. 9.3%.

Still other research along these lines was in terms of the CF/P (cash flow-to-price) ratio, with higher/lower CF/Ps leading to higher/lower future returns.[13] Once again, note that all three anomalies considered so far in this section share a common characteristic: they are based on ratios that compare per share accounting magnitudes (earnings, book values, and cash flows) to market values per share. Holding these accounting measures constant, a lower price has an impact on all three ratios, and, according to the evidence, leads to higher *future* returns. The same holds in reverse for higher prices, with lower future returns often being on the horizon. So, it is likely that these value anomalies are related.

As mentioned earlier, mitigating the criticism of data snooping to a great extent is consistency over different markets and time periods. In Table 4.3, the returns from various value investing approaches (that is, using different price ratios as screens) are shown for the United States, Japan, the United Kingdom, France, and Germany during 1975–1995.[14] We see that in *all* 15 cases value stocks outperformed

TABLE 4.2	PORTFOLIO PERFORMANCE (%) BY B/P GROUP					
	Decile 1: Lowest B/P	Dec. 2	Dec. 5	Dec. 6	Dec. 9	Dec 10: Highest B/P
Annual return	11.0	11.7	13.1	15.4	18.3	17.3
Avg. return over 5 years	9.3	12.5	15.8	16.6	19.6	19.8

Source: Lakonishok, J., A. Shleifer, and R. Vishny, 1994, "Contrarian investment, extrapolation and risk," *Journal of Finance* 49, 1541–78.

TABLE 4.3 | PORTFOLIO PERFORMANCE (%) FOR VALUE VS. GLAMOUR STOCKS IN
VARIOUS COUNTRIES

Country	Market	B/P		E/P		CF/P	
		Value	Glamour	Value	Glamour	Value	Glamour
U.S.	9.57	14.55	7.55	14.09	7.38	13.74	7.08
Japan	11.88	16.91	7.06	14.14	6.67	14.95	5.66
U.K.	15.33	17.87	13.25	17.46	14.81	18.41	14.51
France	11.26	17.10	9.46	15.68	8.70	16.17	9.30
Germany	9.88	12.77	10.01	11.13	10.58	13.28	5.14

Source: Fama, E. F., and K. R. French, 1998, "Value vs. growth: The international evidence," *Journal of Finance* 53, 1975–99.

glamour stocks, where value/glamour portfolios were formed within each country by forming portfolios from the top/bottom 30% of stocks for each year on the basis of beginning-of-year B/P, E/P, and CF/P.[15]

MOMENTUM AND REVERSAL

As was discussed in Chapter 2, weak form efficiency stipulates that returns should not be predictable by conditioning merely on lagged returns.[16] There is abundant evidence that this does not always hold in practice. Importantly, the sign of the correlation is horizon-dependent. **Momentum** exists when returns are positively correlated with past returns, while **reversal** exists when returns are negatively correlated with past returns. For short-term (one-month) intervals, there is reliable reversal.[17] For medium-term intervals (about 3–12 months) there is well-documented momentum. And for long-term intervals (about 3–5 years) reversal is typical. The first appears to be primarily a technical issue, making medium-term momentum and long-term reversal of greater interest.[18]

We begin with the latter since this work came to light first. Werner De Bondt and Richard Thaler formed portfolios of "winner" and "loser" portfolios based on past stock market performance relative to benchmarks.[19] One way in which they operationalized this was by forming portfolios of the top/bottom 50 stocks in terms of performance net of the market over the previous three years. Then these winner and loser portfolios were tracked going forward. If markets are efficient (and we have appropriately adjusted for risk), there should be no difference between the post-formation returns of winners and losers. Figure 4.2, based on five-year formation periods and future returns being tracked five years out, indicates that there *are* substantial differences. The difference between winners and losers is stark, with past losers substantially outperforming past winners. Also salient from the figure are two other points: first, much of the difference is generated by the strong performance of losers rather than the weak performance of winners; and, second, much of the return boost/drop occurs in the month of January. A further point, not apparent from the figure, is the fact that while there are differences between winning and losing portfolios that are significant in a statistical sense, the p-values are not convincingly high.

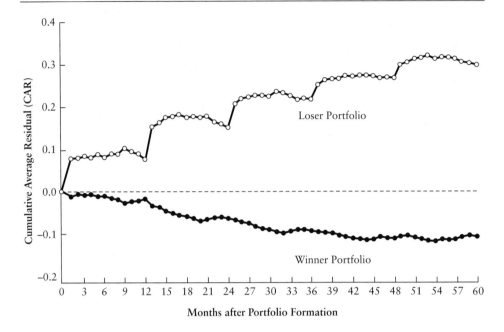

FIGURE 4.2 Cumulative Average Residuals for Winner and Loser Portfolios of 35 Stocks (1–60 months into the test period)

Source: Figure 3 from De Bondt, W. F. M., and R. Thaler, From "Does the stock market overreact?" in *Journal of Finance* 40, pp. 793–807. © 1985 Wiley Publishing, Inc. This material is used by permission of John Wiley & Sons, Inc.

Several years later, intermediate-term (3–12 month) momentum was documented by Narasimhan Jegadeesh and Sheridan Titman.[20] Their approach was similar to that of De Bondt and Thaler except that their return intervals were shorter. Table 4.4 reproduces some key results from their paper. They found, for example, that a long-short zero-cost portfolio formed on the basis of returns over the previous six months earned an average excess return of 0.95% per month over the next six months. Other research found that momentum existed not just at the level of the firm, but also at the level of the industry.[21] Nevertheless, industry momentum, though substantial, did not subsume firm-specific momentum. While transaction costs lead to some erosion of momentum profitability, they remain reliable for institutional investors.[22] Also, there is a relationship between post-earnings announcement drift and momentum—though whether momentum disappears after accounting for post-earnings announcement drift is a point of debate.[23]

As mentioned earlier, the charge of data snooping is lessened by demonstrating that anomalies operate outside the market where they are first discovered. Momentum has been found to be robust internationally. In an examination of 12 European countries, momentum profits to a long-short strategy of 1% per month were found.[24] Another study found the presence of momentum in most countries around the world, with Japan being a notable exception.[25] Additionally, though research

TABLE 4.4 | RETURNS (%)/MONTH AND T-STATS (IN PARENTHESES) FOR VARIOUS MOMENTUM STRATEGIES

		Test period (months)			
		3	6	9	12
Formation period (months)	3	0.0032 (1.10)	0.0058 (2.29)	0.0061 (2.69)	0.0069 (3.53)
	6	0.0084 (2.44)	0.0095 (3.07)	0.0102 (3.76)	0.0086 (3.36)
	9	0.0109 (3.03)	0.0121 (3.78)	0.0105 (3.47)	0.0082 (2.89)
	12	0.0131 (3.74)	0.0114 (3.40)	0.0093 (2.95)	0.0068 (2.25)

Source: Jegadeesh, N., and S. Titman, 1993, "Returns to buying winners and selling losers: Implications for stock market efficiency," *Journal of Finance* 48, 65–91.

in this regard is of a more limited nature, long-term reversals have been documented in a number of markets outside the United States.[26]

4.3   NOISE-TRADING AND LIMITS TO ARBITRAGE

THEORETICAL REQUIREMENTS FOR MARKET EFFICIENCY

Market efficiency theoretically rests on three supports: investor rationality, uncorrelated errors, and unlimited arbitrage. Only one support is required for market efficiency. If all three fail, market efficiency can be called into question.

SUPPORT 1: ALL INVESTORS ARE ALWAYS RATIONAL   The first potential support for market efficiency is investor rationality, specifically that all investors are always rational. Most would agree that this merits little discussion: its falseness is clear to all those who have had discussions with a few retail investors and have as a result observed that some investors at least some of the time execute trades on less than fully rational grounds. Even more sophisticated investors, if honest with themselves, will sometimes have to plead guilty in this regard. Fischer Black, in his 1986 American Finance Association Presidential Address, put it aptly:[27]

> People sometimes trade on information in the usual way. They are correct in expecting to make profits from these trades. On the other hand, people sometimes trade on *noise* [our italics] as if it were information. If they expect to make profits from noise trading, they are incorrect.

By the way, as we will later discuss, the accuracy of the last statement has been debated. But focusing on the heart of the quote, what did Black mean by "noise"? **Noise** exists when trades are based on misinformation, that is, information not relevant for the valuation of securities. Noise (and the trading it induces) is not necessarily an unmitigated evil as it provides liquidity to markets. In fact, without noise, there would be very little trading because the informed would lack ready counter-parties and they would only trade due to cash needs.

SUPPORT 2: INVESTOR ERRORS ARE UNCORRELATED People may trade on noise because they think they have useful information or simply because they enjoy trading. The behavior of such people may be socially driven in that they may trade based on a rumor provided by a neighbor, friend, or coworker.[28] They may even trade because they observe others trading and don't want to miss out on a good thing.

If the behavior of such traders were random, there would be no cause for concern about the efficiency of markets because their trades would cancel out. There would be negligible impact on prices. But, as will be seen in later chapters, the evidence provided by psychologists indicates that people are subject to the same kinds of judgment errors—that is, people often deviate from expectations *in the same way*. This is where problems arise. If traders' behavior is correlated, they may drive prices farther and farther from fundamental value.

Social forces may also influence many of us. The importance of the latter is stressed by Robert Shiller:[29]

> Investing in speculative assets is a social activity. Investors spend a substantial part of their leisure time discussing investments, reading about investments, or gossiping about others' successes or failures in investing. It is thus plausible that investors' behavior (and hence prices of speculative assets) would be influenced by social movements. Attitudes or fashions seem to fluctuate in many other popular topics of conversation, such as food, clothing, health, or politics. These fluctuations in attitude often occur widely in the population and often appear without any apparent logical reason. It is plausible that attitudes or fashions regarding investments would also change spontaneously or in arbitrary social reaction to some widely noted events.

Whether psychology or social forces (or some combination) are the key, when large numbers of investors simultaneously and erroneously value some or all securities in the same way, we say that **sentiment** is driving prices. One can therefore say that sentiment is noise that is correlated among many investors. A commonly used term (which we will adopt) to characterize such individuals is **noise-traders**.

SHILLER'S MODEL Shiller formulates a simple heuristic model of equilibrium in a world where one group of investors, the so-called **smart-money traders**, trade for purely rational reasons, while a second group (we will refer to them as noise-traders) estimates value based at least in part on noise, and this noise is correlated, leading to broad sentiment.[30] Note that many, though far from all, retail (or individual) investors will be in this latter category. Even some institutional investors without discernible skills may be appropriately slotted here.

In Shiller's model, there is only one risky security. This is tantamount to looking at things at the level of the stock market. When noise-traders are too optimistic about market prospects, they push up the price of this risky security too high; when they are too pessimistic, they push its price down below fundamentals. In the former case, once they realize the error of their ways—this may happen quickly or slowly—the price will decline, leading to a transitional period of lower-than-typical returns.

In the latter case, once clear thinking is restored, the price will rise, leading to a transitional period of higher-than-typical returns. This model assumes that smart-money investors want to remain invested in the market even if prices are somewhat higher than they should be (implying that lower-than-typical returns are in the offing).[31] Still, when this is so, they reduce their holdings from what is their norm. On the other hand, when prices are lower than what fundamentals dictate, they increase their holdings from what is typical. Their demand for stock is specified as:

4.2
$$q_t = \frac{E_t R_{t+1} - \rho}{\varphi}$$

where q_t is the demand at time t of smart-money investors for stock as a percentage of total demand (which is equal to the number of shares demanded, since we normalize the total number of shares at unity); ρ is the expected return such that the demand of smart-money investors equals zero; and φ is that level of the risk premium such that smart-money investors are induced to hold all the stock.[32]

In a fully rational world, the price of the risky security is the present value of future expected dividends, as follows:

4.3
$$p_t = \sum_{k=1}^{\infty} \frac{E_t d_{t+k}}{(1+\delta)^k}$$

Note that d_t is the dividend at t; and δ is the appropriate discount rate for equity cash flows.

In a world where sentiment exists, prices are affected by the erroneous views of noise-traders. Without speculating at this point on the exact source or nature of sentiment and noise (and changes thereto), we will define y_t as the total value of stock demanded per share by noise-traders, written as follows:

4.4
$$y_t = n_t * p_t$$

where n_t is the percentage of total demand for the stock on the part of noise-traders (which, again, is the same as the total number of shares demanded by this group). If y_t is at a level consistent with a rational equilibrium, we will say that there is no sentiment (or that sentiment is neutral). If, on the other hand, it is above/below this level, there is positive/negative sentiment.[33] To clear markets, total demand must equal total supply (which, as stated above, is one share):

4.5
$$q_t + n_t = 1$$

The Appendix to this chapter shows that price is a function of both expected future dividends and current and expected future sentiment, as follows:

4.6
$$p_t = \sum_{k=1}^{\infty} \frac{E_t d_{t+k} + \phi E_t y_{t-1+k}}{(1+\rho+\varphi)^k}$$

Problematically for rational investors, they must forecast both dividends *and* sentiment.

To see what occurs when sentiment moves away from fundamentals, suppose that future expected dividends are constant at $1, and the rate of discount (δ) is 10%. Under these circumstances, the "right" price (let's call it the "steady-state" price) is always $10.[34] Suppose that $\rho = 0\%$ and $\varphi = 20\%$. It can be shown that these parameter values imply that in the steady state both smart-money traders and noise-traders hold half of all stock, so from Equation 4.4 the value of y_t consistent with this steady state is $5.[35] If y_t is above/below this level, sentiment is positive/negative.

Beginning in the steady state just before $t = 0$, say that noise-traders suddenly become unduly optimistic about stocks. Suppose for illustrative purposes that y_t immediately doubles (from $5 to $10). Smart-money traders see this as temporary, though, believing that y will remain at this elevated level only for five years (i.e., to $t = 5$), after which it will drop by $1 per year until it reaches its steady state level by year 10.[36] Figure 4.3 shows what this means for the price of the risky security. It immediately jumps in response to increased current and future noise-trader demand to a little below $14. Moving forward, though, the price is anticipated to gradually decline back toward its steady-state level by year 10. Figure 4.4 shows that noise-traders hold more stock during the transitional period. This must be accommodated by smart-money traders reducing their holdings. This means that some of their wealth is shifted elsewhere. In the Shiller model, which is merely designed for illustrative purposes, smart-money investors do not contemplate arbitraging away mispricing—they merely "make space" for noise-traders who increase their demand. The next section addresses whether it might make sense to pursue arbitrage.

FIGURE 4.3 Price Path after Change in Demand from Noise-traders Based on Shiller Model

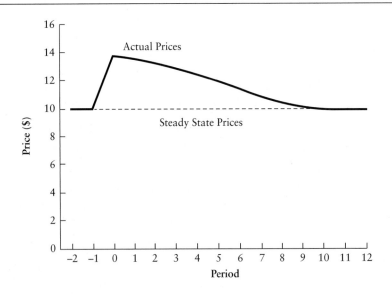

FIGURE 4.4 Ownership Shares after Change in Demand from Noise-traders
Based on Shiller Model

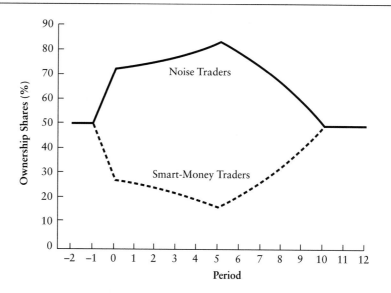

SUPPORT 3: THERE ARE NO LIMITS TO ARBITRAGE   Even if some investors sometimes act irrationally *and* their errors are correlated, provided smart-money investors are able to act in such a fashion so as to arbitrage away incorrect prices, market efficiency will remain intact. This is because any pricing gap between a relatively expensive security and a relatively cheap one will be vigorously capitalized on.

Before discussing why it is likely that there are significant limits to arbitrage, it is useful to briefly illustrate so-called "textbook arbitrage." Textbook arbitrage requires no money and entails no risk. In the real world, what might be closest is triangular arbitrage in foreign exchange markets.

To illustrate how this works, in May 2008 the following three foreign exchange rates among dollars, euros, and yen were observed (*x* will be explained):

Currency pair	Rate
¥/€	159.3403
€/$	0.6455
¥/$	*x*

There are two ways to convert dollars into yen: directly at *x*, or indirectly using euros as the bridge currency. A bridge currency works in the following way. First convert dollars to euros at 0.6455, and then convert euros to yen at 159.3403. This indirect method yields 0.6455 * 159.3403 = 102.8543. This figure has to be virtually identical to *x*.[37] Were this not so, arbitrage would be profitable. To see this, what if, counterfactually, the ¥/$ rate were 100? This would create a money machine. You could start with a borrowed $1, turn this into €0.6455, and then turn this amount into ¥102.8543. Given a ¥/$ rate of 100, you could now convert back to more than $1, repaying the loan and obtaining a profit in addition.[38] Of course all these numbers could be multiplied by millions, making us wealthy. The fact that this is not possible means that foreign exchange markets are priced so that triangular arbitrage is virtually never possible (and, if it is, occasionally, only for mere seconds).

WHAT LIMITS ARBITRAGE?

Unfortunately, arbitrage is seldom as clean as this example from the foreign exchange market. There are three main potential problems: fundamental risk, noise-trader risk, and implementation costs.

FUNDAMENTAL RISK Let us begin with **fundamental risk**, which exists because of the potential for rational revaluation as new information arrives. Suppose, for example, that an arbitrageur believes a particular stock is overvalued in the market relative to the stock's expected future dividends. This arbitrageur would naturally short-sell the stock in the expectation that the price will be lower later when he purchases the stock to close the position. Even if he is correct in this belief based on available information, he is subject to risk. For one thing, new information that no one could have anticipated might suddenly arrive. If this is of a positive nature, the price will rise and a loss will be incurred. Such losses will require margin payments. Further, if realized dividends on the stock are higher than expected, the arbitrageur could face an additional cash crunch. Note that when shares are sold-short, the arbitrageur must cover the dividends paid on the stock because he has borrowed the stock from another investor. An arbitrageur may limit trading because of fear that the firm could perform unexpectedly well, in which case losses from short-selling would be incurred.

The use of substitutes and spread trading can be used to mitigate fundamental risk. Spread trading is the simultaneous purchase and sale of similar securities (sometimes even very close substitutes). You buy the one that you consider to be relatively cheap, and sell (or short-sell) the one that you consider to be relatively expensive, in the hope that the spread will narrow.

For example, one could simultaneously short-sell the overpriced security and buy with the proceeds the "market" (say, using stock index futures). Now if market-wide information causes all stocks to rise, gains on the market offset the losses from the short position. Of course, much information is likely to be of a firm-specific or industry-specific nature. If you believe that Merck, for example, is overvalued, you could hedge by going long on a basket of pharmaceuticals (excluding Merck). Now you would be hedged against both market and industry risk. Still, it is not possible to hedge against firm-specific risk here because there is no perfect substitute for Merck. Merck might unexpectedly announce success in a drug trial. This will affect Merck, but not other pharmaceuticals. It is the fact that a perfect substitute rarely exists that makes arbitrage risky and hence less likely to eliminate mispricing.

NOISE-TRADER RISK Even if there are perfect substitutes, we are not home free. Andrei Shleifer and Robert Vishny use the example of two Bund (German bond) futures contracts trading on two different exchanges (one in London and the other in Frankfurt).[39] Assuming that these contracts are perfectly identical in all respects (that is, they are perfect substitutes), let's say that the one trading in London is priced above the one trading in Frankfurt. It is obvious that one should buy a Frankfurt contract and sell a London contract. At delivery, cash flows will cancel out, so on the surface one can simply pocket a profit *today*. The reality is a little more complex, however. The problem is that "wrong" prices might become even more wrong in the short run. This is the essence of **noise-trader risk**.[40]

In futures markets, one must contribute margin when prices move against you.[41] Suppose the London contract goes up and the Frankfurt contract goes down, implying that you must contribute cash in both markets. This is fine, *if* you are managing your own money and are not wealth-constrained.[42] But if you are managing your own money and you are wealth-constrained, you might be forced to liquidate your position at a loss because you are running out of money, even though it is clear that your arbitrage trade will eventually be profitable.

What if you are managing other people's money? Now because other people are controlling your capital, you are subject to a different sort of wealth control. Additionally, because they have the power to hire and fire, your horizon is of necessity short. In fact, many who are attempting to exploit arbitrage opportunities are subject to this reality. They are managing money for individuals (e.g., those pooling their money through mutual funds or hedge funds) or institutions (such as endowments), many of whom will not have a clear idea of the issues involved. While the Bund example is simple enough for even nonexperts to follow, many real-world arbitrage opportunities will be more subtle. What are controllers of capital with limited knowledge to think? They will naturally enough tend to base their view of ability on short-term performance. What they will see, namely short-term losses, will not be comforting.

It is the risk of such eventualities occurring that will make money managers reticent to try to exploit such opportunities through arbitrage in the first place, thus creating **limits to arbitrage**. Bradford De Long, Andrei Shleifer, Larry Summers, and Robert Waldmann show the importance of this in their model of noise-trading and what it means for prices, returns, and the likelihood that mispricing will be fully eliminated.[43] In their model, because smart-money traders know that when they choose to sell prices might still be wrong, they need to be compensated for this risk before the fact. As should be clear from our discussion of risk in Chapter 2, only nondiversifiable risk should be priced. It turns out that there is evidence that noise-trader risk is indeed systematic.[44]

One argument that is sometimes made is that noise-traders should eventually disappear because their poor trades will cause them to lose their wealth. This would serve to move the world toward efficiency. Aside from the obvious "there is a fool born every minute" argument, there are some rather more subtle issues. In the De Long-Shleifer-Summers-Waldmann model, it can be seen that noise-traders may actually perform well enough to survive if they tend toward excessive optimism and risk-taking.[45]

IMPLEMENTATION COSTS Aside from fundamental risk and noise-trader risk, transaction costs can potentially obstruct arbitrage. Transaction costs are commissions, spreads, and market impact costs that are incurred when trades are executed. For institutional traders who are likely to be performing most arbitrage, these costs are negligible. Things become much more complicated when short-selling is required. If, as discussed earlier, one recognizes a pricing imbalance between two substitute securities, one side of the required arbitrage is to short-sell the high-priced security. This leads to two problems. If one does not have access to the short-sale proceeds (so that interest cannot be earned) this adds to the cost of the transaction. Further, in some cases, the security that needs to be short-sold simply cannot be obtained. How serious are these problems? For institutional investors and highly liquid stocks, neither of these potential problems will likely be significant most of the time. This is because institutional traders will normally have little problem obtaining shares to short-sell, and the loss of short-sale proceeds is rarely significant for them.[46] Nevertheless, sometimes there can be a short squeeze. This means that those initiating a short position may have to exit it before they wish to do so. Or it is even possible that one cannot, in the case of less liquid stocks, initiate a short at all because of nonavailability of the stock to short.

Such issues are usually behind egregious cases of mispricing. Shiller points out an apparent example of mispricing that on the surface should have been amenable to short-selling.[47] The popular press, regulators, and academics alike have recognized that the late 1990s were subject to "irrational exuberance" on the part of investors, particularly for Internet stocks.[48] In 1999, the Internet toy retailer eToys.com reported sales of $30 million and losses of $28.6 million. In the same year, Toys "R" Us reported sales of $11.2 *billion* and *profits* of $376 million. Yet, eToys.com had a stock market value of $8 billion and Toys "R" Us a value of only $6 billion.

An even more striking example is the case of Palm and 3Com reported by Owen Lamont and Richard Thaler.[49] On March 2, 2000, the company 3Com carved out in an IPO 5% of its subsidiary Palm. Prior to the IPO, 3Com also announced that in the near future the remaining 95% would be distributed to current shareholders of 3Com (roughly 1.5 shares of Palm/share of 3Com). A little thought indicates that there were two ways of buying Palm: buy Palm shares directly; or buy Palm *indirectly* by buying 3Com shares. This is because a share of 3Com represented a claim to 1.5 shares of Palm. Clearly, we should have the following relationship between Palm and 3Com share prices:

4.7 $$p(3Com) \geq 1.5 * p(PALM)$$

The extent to which the price of Palm exceeded 1.5 times the price of 3Com is due to the fact that the rest of the 3Com business likely had some residual value. This is known as the "stub value."

What actually happened was quite surprising. After the first day of Palm trading, its shares were trading at $95.06. At the same time, 3Com shares were selling for $81.81. Summing over all the shares, the implied stub value was an unbelievable *negative* $22 billion. Oddly, many people understood the situation very clearly. As Lamont and Thaler write, "the nature of the mispricing was so simple that even the dimmest market participants … were able to grasp it."[50] Incredibly, the mispricing persisted for months.[51]

This situation involved negligible fundamental risk. Like in the Bund example, while noise-trader risk did exist, since the opportunity was so obvious, there would clearly be many investors with deep pockets and a long enough horizon able and willing to try to profit from it. Additionally, the existence of a terminal date (as in the Bund example) meant that arbitrageurs knew that they didn't have to hang on indefinitely. In fact, the reason for such egregious mispricing seems to have been the nonavailability of Palm stock to short-sell. This made it impossible for most smart-money traders to take advantage of the situation. Of course there really is no good reason why anybody should have held Palm shares in preference to 3Com shares in the first place at these prices. For this, the only answer appears to be investor irrationality.

4.4   LOOKING FORWARD

In the last two chapters, we have begun to explore some of the major contributions of behavioral finance. Work along these lines was pursued because of the inability of modern finance to fully account for various observed decisions made when facing uncertainty and empirical tests of market efficiency.

Before moving forward, it is appropriate to step back for a time and investigate some key findings from the psychology literature that help elucidate financial decision-making. While it is remarkable how often people come up with good decisions when forced to decide in real time based on limited information, we will see that systematic error can occur. In the next chapter, we see that rules-of-thumb known as heuristics can lead to systematic error, particularly when used outside of their natural domain. Other culprits seem to be the tendency to exaggerate one's knowledge and to wear rose-colored glasses, and unbalanced emotion.

CHAPTER HIGHLIGHTS

1. An anomaly is an empirical result apparently contrary to market efficiency.
2. Some major anomalies are lagged reactions to earnings announcements, the small-firm effect, the value advantage, and momentum and reversal.
3. Market efficiency theoretically rests on three supports. Markets are efficient if investors are rational. Failing this, if their errors are random, markets are efficient. And failing this, if arbitrage is unlimited, markets are efficient.
4. Noise exists when some traders base value on misinformation. If many make the same kind of mistake at the same time, sentiment exists.
5. Noise-trader risk is the risk that "wrong" prices will become even more wrong.
6. There are limits to arbitrage because of fundamental risk, noise-trader risk, and implementation costs.

DISCUSSION QUESTIONS AND PROBLEMS

1. Differentiate the following terms/concepts:

   a. Momentum and reversal
   b. Value and growth stocks
   c. Fundamental risk and noise-trader risk
   d. Carve-out and stub value

2. Refer back to the set of exchange rates in the "Support 3: There are no limits to arbitrage" section earlier in the chapter. Describe a profitable arbitrage strategy if $x = 105$.

3. Arbitrage is limited because the wealth of arbitrageurs is limited. Discuss this statement in the context of those who are managing their own money and those who are managing other people's money.

4. What is data snooping? What sort of empirical evidence is useful for obviating this critique?

5. What are the three supports on which market efficiency rests? Why is it that only one of them is required?

PROOFS FOR SHILLER MODEL

Proof of equation 4.6

Begin with market-clearing (supply equals demand):

4.5
$$q_t + n_t = 1$$

Substituting using equations 4.1 and 4.4 yields:

A4.1
$$\frac{E_t R_{t+1} - \rho}{\varphi} + \frac{y_t}{p_t} = 1$$

Note that returns are dividend yields plus percentage capital gains:

A4.2
$$E_t R_{t+1} = \frac{E_t p_{t+1} - p_t - E_t d_{t+1}}{p_t}$$

Substituting A4.2 into A4.1, multiplying both sides by φ, and rearranging slightly yields:

A4.3
$$\frac{1}{p_t}(E_t p_{t+1} + \varphi y_t - E_t d_{t+1}) = 1 + \varphi + \rho$$

This easily simplifies to:

A4.4
$$p_t = \frac{E_t d_{t+1} + \varphi y_t - E_t d_{t+1}}{1 + \varphi + \rho}$$

One period forward this would be:

A4.5
$$p_{t+1} = \frac{E_{t+1} p_{t+2} + \varphi y_{t+1} - E_{t+1} d_{t+2}}{1 + \varphi + \rho}$$

Similar expressions can be written for even more distant periods. A process of repeated substitution known as recursive substitution eventually takes us to equation 4.6:

4.6
$$p_t = \sum_{k=1}^{\infty} \frac{E_t d_{t+k} + \phi E_t y_{t-1+k}}{(1 + \rho + \varphi)^k}$$

Steady state for our numerical example

The steady-state parameters are $\rho = 0\%$; $\varphi = 20\%$; and $\delta = 10\%$. In the steady state (where noise-traders have neutral sentiment), fundamentals drive things, which implies:

A4.6
$$E_t R_{t+1} = \delta$$

Substituting this and our parameter values into 4.2 gives us:

A4.7
$$q_t = \frac{E_t R_{t+1} - \rho}{\varphi} = \frac{0.10-0}{0.20} = .5$$

This implies that $n_t = 0.5$ as well, since collectively all stock must be held. From 4.4, the value of y_t that is consistent with this is $5:

4.4
$$y_t = n_t * p_t = .5 * \$10 = \$5$$

ENDNOTES

1 This argument is presented well in Chapter 1 of Shleifer, A., ed., 2000, *Inefficient Markets: An Introduction to Behavioral Finance* (Clarendon Lectures in Economics–Oxford University Press, Oxford, U.K.).

2 As will be discussed later in the chapter, this is really a definition of "textbook arbitrage."

3 See Fama, E. F., L. Fisher, M. C. Jensen, and R. Roll, 1969, "The adjustment of stock prices to new information," *International Economic Review* 12, 1–21, for one of the first event studies. This event study examined stock splits.

4 The earliest earnings-announcement event study is Ball, R., and P. Brown, 1968, "An empirical evaluation of accounting income numbers," *Journal of Accounting Research* 6, 159–178.

5 Rendleman, R. J., C. P. Jones, and H. A. Latane, 1982, "Empirical anomalies based on unexpected earnings and the importance of risk adjustments," *Journal of Financial Economics* 10, 269–287.

6 Banz, R. W., 1981, "The relationship between return and market value of common stocks," *Journal of Financial Economics* 9, 3–18.

7 Keim, D. B., 1983, "Size-related anomalies and stock return seasonality: Further empirical evidence," *Journal of Financial Economics* 12, 13–32.

8 Roll, R., 1981, "A possible explanation of the small firm effect," *Journal of Finance* 36, 879–888.

9 The quote is from page 1733 of Brock, W., J. Lakonishok, and B. LeBaron, 1992, "Simple technical trading rules and the stochastic properties of stock returns," *Journal of Finance* 47, 1731–1764.

10 See Easterday, K. E., P. K. Sen, and J. A. Stephan, 2007, "The small firm/January effect: Is it disappearing in U.S. markets because of investor learning?" Working paper, for a discussion.

11 Basu, S., 1977, "Investment performance of common stocks in relation to their price-earnings ratios: A test of the efficient market hypothesis," *Journal of Finance* 32, 663–682.

12 Lakonishok, J., A. Shleifer, and R. Vishny, 1994, "Contrarian investment, extrapolation and risk," *Journal of Finance* 49, 1541–1578.

13 See, for example, Chan, L. K. C., Y. Hamao, and J. Lakonishok, 1991, "Fundamentals and stock returns in Japan," *Journal of Finance* 46, 1739–1789, which provides evidence for Japan.

14 Fama, E. F., and K. R. French, 1998, "Value vs. growth: The international evidence," *Journal of Finance* 53, 1975–1799.

15 Earlier we spoke of the P/E ratio as is conventional, but here we have expressed all ratios (including the E/P ratio, which is the reciprocal of the P/E) as accounting numbers vs. the price, for the sake of consistency.

16 More precisely, excess returns should not be predictable using any publicly available information including past returns (raw or excess).

17 Jegadeesh, N., 1990, "Evidence of predictable behavior of security returns," *Journal of Finance* 45, 881–898.

18 There is evidence that very short-term reversal is largely explained by liquidity-induced price pressure (rendering it difficult to capitalize on). See Boudoukh, J., M. P. Richardson, and R. F. Whitelaw, 1994, "A tale of three schools: Insights on autocorrelations of short-horizon stock returns," *Review of Financial Studies* 7, 539–573.

19 De Bondt, W. F. M., and R. Thaler, 1985, "Does the stock market overreact?" *Journal of Finance* 40, 793–807.

20 Jegadeesh, N., and S. Titman, 1993, "Returns to buying winners and selling losers: Implications for stock market efficiency," *Journal of Finance* 48, 65–91.

21 Moskowitz, T. J., and M. Grinblatt, 1999, "Do industries explain momentum?" *Journal of Finance* 54, 1249–1290.

22 Korajczyk, R., and R. Sadka, 2004, "Are momentum profits robust to trading costs?" *Journal of Finance* 59, 1039–1082.

23 See Chan, L. K. C., N. Jegadeesh, and J. Lakonishok, 1999, "The profitability of momentum strategies," *Financial Analysts Journal* (Special Issue on Behavioral Finance), 80–90; and Chordia, T., and L. Shivakumar, 2006, "Earnings and price momentum," *Journal of Financial Economics* 80, 627–656.

24 Rouwenhorst, K. G., 1998, "International momentum strategies," *Journal of Finance* 53, 267–284.

25 Griffin, J. M., X. Ji, and S. Martin, 2003, "Momentum investing and business cycle risk: Evidence from pole to pole," *Journal of Finance* 63, 2515–2547.

26 For Germany, see Schierek, D., W. De Bondt, and M. Weber, 1999, "Contrarian and momentum strategies in Germany," *Financial Analysts Journal* (Special Issue on Behavioral Finance), 104–116; and, for Canada, see Deaves, R., and P. Miu, 2007, "Refining momentum strategies by conditioning on prior long-term returns: Canadian evidence," *Canadian Journal of Administrative Sciences* 24, 135–145.

27 This quote is from page 529 of Black, F., 1986, "Noise," *Journal of Finance* 41(3), 529–543.

28 See Shiller, R. J., 1984, "Stock prices and social dynamics," *Brooking Papers on Economic Activity* 2, 457–498, for a discussion.

29 This quote is from page 457 of Shiller, R. J. 1984, "Stock prices and social dynamics," *Brooking Papers on Economic Activity* 2, 457–498.

30 Shiller, R. J. 1984, "Stock prices and social dynamics," *Brooking Papers on Economic Activity* 2, 457–498. The model is heuristic in the sense that it is incomplete and illustrative. For example, preferences are

not modeled. Shiller's usage is to call this second group of traders "irrational investors."

31 The noise-trader risk model touched on later incorporates compensation for bearing noise-trader risk.

32 To see this, set $E_t R_{t+1} = \rho + \varphi$ in Equation 4.2.

33 Further, if we assume unitary demand elasticity on the part of noise traders, y_t can be viewed as exogenous to the model.

34 A steady state is a kind of dynamic equilibrium.

35 See Appendix for details.

36 Specifically, y_t = 10, 9, 8, 7, 6, 5 for t = 5, 6, 7, 8, 9, 10.

37 Because of transaction costs, x can be very slightly different from the product of the other two exchange rates.

38 Since this would take mere seconds, the interest that you would have to pay would be close to zero.

39 Shleifer, A., and R. Vishny, 1997, "The limits of arbitrage," *Journal of Finance* 52, 35–55.

40 The term "resale price risk" is also used.

41 Conversely, if prices move in your favor, cash can be withdrawn.

42 At the terminal date, the situation is akin to a spot market. As in the triangular arbitrage example, it would then be straightforward to perform arbitrage.

43 De Long, J. B., A. Shleifer, L. H. Summers, and R. Waldmann, 1990, "Noise trader risk in financial markets," *Journal of Political Economy* 98, 703–738. Also see Shleifer, A., and L. H. Summers, 1990, "The noise trader approach to finance," *Journal of Finance* 4 (2), 19–33.

44 See Lee, C. M. C., A. Shleifer, and R. H. Thaler, 1988, "Closed-end mutual funds," *Journal of Economic Perspectives* 4, 153–164.

45 De Long, J. B., A. Shleifer, L. H. Summers, and R. Waldmann, 1990, "Noise trader risk in financial markets," *Journal of Political Economy* 98, 703–738. Also, see Hirshleifer, D., and G. Y. Luo, 2001, "On the survival of

overconfident traders in a competitive security market," *Journal of Financial Markets* 4, 73–84.

46 Geczy, C. C., D. K. Musto, and A. V. Reed, 2002, "Stocks are special too: An analysis of the equity lending market," *Journal of Financial Economics* 66, 241–269.

47 Shiller, R. J., 2000, *Irrational Exuberance* (Princeton University Press, Princeton, New Jersey).

48 Again, see Shiller, R. J., 2000, *Irrational Exuberance* (Princeton University Press, Princeton, New Jersey). "Irrational exuberance," the title of Shiller's book is from a famous quote of Alan Greenspan, chairman of the Federal Reserve Board, from a 1996 speech in which he was describing the behavior of investors in the stock market.

49 Lamont, O. A., and R. H. Thaler, 2003, "Can the market add and subtract? Mispricing in tech stock carve-outs," *Journal of Political Economy* 111, 227–268.

50 Again, see Lamont, O. A., and R. H. Thaler, 2003, "Can the market add and subtract? Mispricing in tech stock carve-outs," *Journal of Political Economy* 111, 227–268.

51 Other negative stub cases existed as well. See Lamont, O. A., and R. H. Thaler, 2003, "Can the market add and subtract? Mispricing in tech stock carve-outs," *Journal of Political Economy* 111, 227–268, for examples.

Behavioral Science Foundations

CHAPTER 5 Heuristics and Biases

CHAPTER 6 Overconfidence

CHAPTER 7 Emotional Foundations

HEURISTICS AND BIASES · CHAPTER 5

5.1 INTRODUCTION

One criticism that is levied against traditional models in economics and finance is that they are sometimes formulated as if the typical decision-maker were an individual with unlimited cerebral RAM. Such a decision-maker would consider all relevant information and come up with the best choice under the circumstances in a process known as constrained optimization.

Normal humans are imperfect and information requirements are for some models egregious. Are we asking too much? Take the capital asset pricing model (CAPM), a model famous and important enough that William Sharpe won the 1990 Nobel Prize for Economic Sciences for this contribution. This model assumes that investors are capable of studying the universe of securities in order to come up with all required model inputs. These inputs include expected returns and variances for all securities, as well as covariances among all securities. Only then is the investor able to make appropriate portfolio decisions.

This chapter focuses on how people make decisions with limited time and information in a world of uncertainty. It begins in the next section by discussing certain cognitive limitations that may render the expectations of some models unreasonable. Perception and memory are imprecise filters of information, and the way in which information is presented, that is, the frame, influences how it is received. Because too much information is difficult to deal with, people have developed shortcuts or heuristics in order to come up with reasonable decisions. Unfortunately, sometimes these heuristics lead to bias, especially when used outside their natural domains. A class of heuristics impacting preferences primarily via comfort-seeking is discussed in Section 5.3. In Section 5.4, we discuss several heuristics designed to estimate probability. The most important of these is representativeness in its various manifestations. In the next section, we turn to anchoring, the tendency to change one's view more slowly than is appropriate. Section 5.6 discusses a major critique of the heuristics and biases program, the so-called "fast and frugal" heuristics view that argues that heuristics actually work surprisingly well.

Finally, in the last section, we look ahead to how the heuristics and associated biases described in this chapter come into play in the context of financial decision-making.

5.2   PERCEPTION, MEMORY, AND HEURISTICS

PERCEPTION[1]

It is commonplace for an information-processing model to assume that agents are able to acquire and store costless information without difficulty. Unfortunately, **perception**, which downloads information to the "human computer," often misreads it. For example, we often "see" what we *expect* to see. In one experiment, participants were shown a hand of five playing cards, all of which were either hearts or spades.[2] One of the cards was a *black* three of hearts, but most people missed (or misinterpreted) the error. A common reaction was to be certain that one had seen a normal three of hearts or a normal three of spades. The lesson to be learned is that perception is selective, with expectations strongly conditioning perception.

It is also true that people "see" what they *desire* to see. After a particularly rough football game between Dartmouth and Princeton, a sample of students from the two universities was asked which team had precipitated the excessively physical play.[3] Of the Dartmouth students, only 36% thought that their team had done so. On the other hand, 86% of the Princeton students thought Dartmouth had initiated the bad conduct.

Sometimes perception can be distorted in a self-serving fashion. **Cognitive dissonance** creates a situation where people are motivated to reduce or avoid psychological inconsistencies, often in order to promote a positive self-image. In one experiment, voters in a Canadian election were surveyed either before or after leaving the ballot box.[4] Respondents were more likely to believe that their candidate was the best choice and would be victorious if surveyed *after* voting rather than *before*. Apparently there was an unconscious coalescence of actions and views.

MEMORY

Imprecision multiplies when one tries to recall past perceptions or views, that is, when one remembers. The common view that past experiences have somehow been written to the brain's hard drive and are then retrieved, even if at considerable effort, is not the way our brain works. In fact, **memory** is reconstructive. One way we know this is that, in an experimental context, when people witness an event and receive misleading information about it, this misinformation is often incorporated into their memory.[5]

Memory is not only reconstructive, but also variable, in intensity. Have you ever noticed how easily and quickly you can bring to mind certain very positive or negative memories (e.g., when you won the million-euro lottery, or when you realized you put the winning ticket in the wash)? While a full discussion of emotions will be reserved for Chapter 7, the reason for this seems to be that events are remembered more vividly when they arouse emotions.[6]

Since pleasant memories make you happier than unpleasant ones, it is not surprising that we are sometimes prone to "rewriting history." It also makes us feel better to think we have more control over events than we really do, or that we have a good sense of what is likely to happen in the future. The corollary to this is that in the past we also must have had a pretty good sense of what was likely to transpire. In other words, "we knew it all along." This is known as hindsight bias, a bias that will be discussed in more detail in the next chapter.[7]

FRAMING EFFECTS

Perception and memory are influenced by context, or the frame. This is an important reason why financial decisions are influenced by the frame, as we discussed in Chapter 3. A number of studies have produced corroborating evidence on the importance of the frame for perception and memory. For example, a sports announcer of average height looks short when interviewing a basketball player, but tall when interviewing a jockey. This is known as the "contrast effect."[8] Some perceptual illusions rely on this. Figure 5.1 provides a well-known example.[9] While the lines have equal length, the context of the inward or outward arrows makes the observer believe otherwise.

The importance of the frame is also clear in primacy and recency effects.[10] The **primacy effect** is based on research that shows that if subjects are asked their impressions of someone based on a series of attributes, then what comes first will often dominate. Someone described as "intelligent, industrious, impulsive, critical, stubborn, envious" generally creates more positive impressions than someone described as "envious, stubborn, critical, impulsive, industrious, intelligent." Since the second series of epithets is the exact transposition of the first series, this suggests that what comes first has greater impact.

When items are temporally sequential, rather than first impressions dominating, a **recency effect** can instead be observed. In other words, what comes last has greater impact. This begs the question: Is the primacy effect or the recency effect stronger? The answer seems to be that it depends. When events are separated by a nontrivial passage of time, recency generally dominates. For example, an event occurring last week will have more impact than one occurring last year, but the first

---

FIGURE 5.1 Which Line Is Longer?

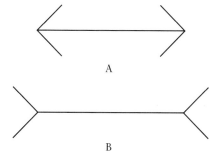

A

B

---

of two related sequential events, one following on the heels of the other (e.g., two political speeches), will often have greater impact.

A **halo effect** has also been observed.[11] Any job candidate intuitively knows that his statements and views will be taken more seriously if his grooming and attire are impeccable at the interview stage. Less fairly though, endowed physical attributes also create an impression. Research has shown that essays are viewed as being of higher quality when written by someone judged to be physically attractive.[12]

EASE OF PROCESSING AND INFORMATION OVERLOAD

The discussion up to now has suggested that people can have difficulty processing information in certain situations. Interestingly, people seem to prefer situations characterized by ease of processing. **Ease of processing** amounts to ready understanding. Information that is easier to understand is often viewed as more likely to be true.[13]

Difficulty assessing information is exacerbated by the plethora of information at our disposal. While this is obvious enough in some realms—for example, consider how much information is potentially relevant for estimating the value of Microsoft stock—even when the information set seems less cluttered, **information overload**, a state of confusion and decision avoidance, can still occur.

In one experiment, shoppers in a supermarket were presented with free samples of jams and jellies.[14] In the first treatment, a small selection was available for tasting; in the second, a large selection was available. While everyone likes the idea of abundant choice, and indeed the table with the greater selection attracted larger crowds, it was the table with fewer samples that led to the most sales. The likely reason is that the large selection led to information overload, the feeling that the decision was too complicated for immediate action. As we all know from personal experience, procrastination will probably lead to indefinite inaction.

HEURISTICS

In many cases, delay is not feasible. Decisions need to be made, even if the environment is one of limited attention, information, and processing capacity, so shortcuts, or **heuristics**, are necessary. A heuristic is a decision rule that utilizes a subset of the information set. Since in virtually all cases people must economize and cannot analyze all contingencies, we use heuristics without even realizing it.

Heuristics come in all shapes and sizes. One dichotomy is between those heuristics that are reflexive, autonomic, and noncognitive, and economize on effort (Type 1); and others, which are cognitive in nature (Type 2).[15] **Type 1 heuristics** are appropriate when a very quick decision must be made or when the stakes are low ("I choose a hamburger over a hot dog because I usually prefer them"). **Type 2 heuristics** are more effortful and are appropriate when the stakes are higher. In some cases, an initial reaction using a Type 1 heuristic can be overruled or corroborated using a Type 2 heuristic ("No, I will choose the hot dog today because it is prepared a bit differently and I like to try new things").

Where do heuristics come from? It is likely that evolutionary forces have equipped us with a good set to meet the challenges of survival.[16] This echoes our discussion in Chapter 3 where evidence was presented that prospect theory had an evolutionary foundation. The connection is not surprising because prospect theory can be viewed as a related set of rules of thumb for making decisions when facing risk, as we also argued in Chapter 3.

Has evolution equipped us with the perfect "toolkit" of heuristics? Not necessarily, because a good set of heuristics is not the same as an optimal set—evolutionary forces only really require that survivors' heuristics are better than those of their rivals. Heuristics have been part of our toolkit for centuries, while many of the problems that we must deal with in a financial realm are recent, so it should not be surprising that such tools, when used outside of their natural domain, may falter.[17]

EXAMPLES OF HEURISTICS

Next we will describe some heuristics, beginning with a couple that are clearly autonomic in nature. If you hear a loud sound while walking down the street, your tendency is to move away from it until examination and analysis can be undertaken. There is no thought here: command-and-control is entirely in the primitive emotional recesses of the brain. After a second, of course, you take a look around and ascertain whether the sound is a threat (if a gunshot, let's move even farther away) or an item of curiosity (if a human cannonball at a carnival, let's take a closer look).

Another example is in the kitchen. If you look into the refrigerator and an item of food emits an odor that you are not exactly familiar with, the obvious reaction is to dispose of the food. There is a reasonable probability that you might become sick if you eat it. The reader will likely agree that both the "move away from the loud sound" and the "avoid eating food with an unfamiliar odor" heuristics make eminently good sense, and there is no difficulty in seeing how these shortcuts have contributed to man's survival. While the heuristics we have discussed so far are autonomic, we now turn to some heuristics that are cognitive in nature.

5.3 FAMILIARITY AND RELATED HEURISTICS

In this section we explore a series of related heuristics that induce people to exhibit preferences unrelated to objective considerations. People are more comfortable with the **familiar**. They dislike ambiguity and normally look for ways to avoid unrewarded risk. People tend to stick with what they have rather than investigate other options. They put off undertaking new initiatives, even if deep down they know the effort could be worthwhile. All of these point to a tendency to seek comfort.

FAMILIARITY

People are more likely to accept a gamble if they feel they have a better understanding of the relevant context, that is, if they feel more competent. Chip Heath and Amos Tversky conducted an experiment whose first stage involved a series of general knowledge multiple choice questions (with four options).[18] Each multiple choice question had an associated confidence query, where the options ranged

FIGURE 5.2 Choice of Competence Bet vs. Random Bet as a Function of Judged Probability

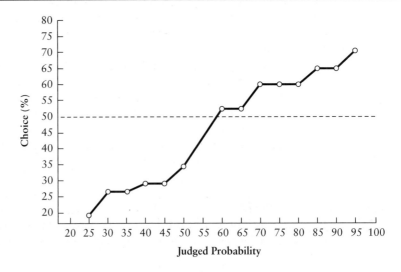

Source: With kind permission from Springer Science+Business Media: *Journal of Risk and Uncertainty*, Preference and belief: Ambiguity and competence in choice under uncertainty, Volume 4, 1991, pp. 5–28, Heath, C., and A. Tversky, figure number 2.

from 100% certainty to 25%. With four possible responses, confidence of 25% indicated pure guessing. Let's say that a particular participant had a self-assessed confidence rating of 60% (averaged over all questions). She would then be offered a choice of two gambles: one where a payoff was randomly obtained with a 60% probability, and a second where a payoff was received if one of her randomly selected answers was correct.[19]

Figure 5.2 shows the results. When people felt that they had some competence on the questions, they were more likely to choose a gamble based on this competence rather than a random lottery. This is evidenced by the positive relationship between judged probability of being right on the questions and the percentage choosing the competence bet. It is important to note that *whatever* the self-perceived level of knowledge, the probability of success on the bet was viewed by participants as identical between the two alternatives (according to their own statements). If, for example, a participant was 50% comfortable in her answers being correct, then the random lottery would have been successful with a 50% probability. If, alternatively, another participant was 75% comfortable in his answers being correct, then the random lottery would have been successful with a 75% probability.[20] The logical conclusion is that people have a preference for the familiar.

AMBIGUITY AVERSION

Consulting Figure 5.2 once again, we see that whereas when judged probability was at its highest the clear tendency was to prefer the competence bet, when judged probability was at its lowest the clear tendency was to prefer the random bet.

While familiarity seems to account for the former, the latter is likely due to **ambiguity aversion**. Take the 35% certain case. The reason the bet with the random payoff is preferred (which pays off 35% of the time) is because you know the precise distribution (you will win with 35% probability), but, when knowledge is low, you really don't know what you know or don't know (which means, while your best guess might be a 35% probability that you answered questions correctly, there is uncertainty that this is the probability of winning the bet).

In the classic demonstration of ambiguity aversion, subjects preferred to bet that a red (or black) ball could be drawn from an urn known to have 50 black balls and 50 red balls, versus the case where subjects were only informed that the urn contained 100 balls of black and red balls in unknown proportions.[21] If one thinks about it, the unconditional probability of success in either case is identical. Ambiguity aversion is driven by the fact that people prefer risk to uncertainty. In Chapter 1 we differentiated risk and uncertainty. Risk exists when we precisely know the probability distribution. In the first case, it is clear that the probability of drawing a red (or black) ball is 50%. Uncertainty exists when we don't know the probability distribution. Although our best guess in the second case is a 50% probability for either color, people are uncomfortable with the inherent uncertainty of the situation.

Some take the view that ambiguity aversion is more an emotional behavior than a heuristic. Indeed it does reflect a tendency for emotions, particularly fear, to influence choice in risky situations.[22] Despite the best intentions of experimenters, there may also be the fear that ambiguity could lend itself to manipulation.

DIVERSIFICATION HEURISTIC

The **diversification heuristic** suggests that people like to try a little bit of everything when choices are not mutually exclusive.[23] A common behavior among buffet diners is to sample most (if not all) dishes. To concentrate on one or two runs the risk of not liking your selections and/or missing out on a good thing. Such behavior is similar to that reported by Itamar Simonson, who reports shoppers are more likely to choose a variety of items (e.g., different yogurt flavors) when they must make multiple purchases for future consumption, versus the case when they make single purchases just prior to each consumption decision.[24]

Simonson argues that certain factors drive such behavior. First, many people have a hardwired preference for variety and novelty.[25] This preference is much more salient when multiple purchases are made. Second, future preferences embody some uncertainty. "I may slightly prefer raspberry yogurt to strawberry now, but how will I feel in a week?" Spreading purchases over different categories reduces risk in the same fashion that spreading your money over different stocks accomplishes the same risk-reduction goal in a well-diversified portfolio. A final motivation for variety-seeking is it makes your choice simpler, thus saving time and reducing decision conflict.

STATUS QUO BIAS AND ENDOWMENT EFFECT

A preference for the current state also follows from comfort-seeking. People are resistant to change, fearing the regret that might follow if active steps are undertaken to alter the status quo. Thus, they tend to hold on to what is currently possessed, that is, one's endowment.[26] In Chapter 3 we discussed the status quo bias (or the endowment effect) as a manifestation of loss aversion in a riskless context. The status quo bias is also mentioned here as a heuristic: "stick with what you have unless there are strong reasons for doing otherwise."

In Chapter 3 we provided the example of experimental subjects being reticent to part with endowed mugs. Here we provide an example of experimental subjects' portfolio allocation decisions. Respondents were told that they could allocate money that they had just inherited among four investment choices: a. shares in XYZ that had moderate risk; b. shares in ABC that had high risk; c. T-bills; and d. municipal bonds.[27] The average allocation was: a. 32%; b. 18%; c. 18%; and d. 32%. In addition to this base case, four additional treatments were conducted, where participants were told that one of the four investment choices (instead of money) had been left to them. They could leave their money where it was, or without cost shift it to one of the other three choices. No matter which investment option was chosen as the original endowment, it was always the most popular choice. People felt most comfortable with the current state of affairs even though it was not something that they had any part in choosing.

HEURISTICS AND BIASES, PROSPECT THEORY AND EMOTION

In the previous section, we mentioned that the status quo bias could either be viewed as an implication of prospect theory or as a heuristic with potential for bias. Earlier we argued that ambiguity aversion embodied an obvious emotional component. In fact, the same can be said of all the heuristics in this section to the extent that they stem from comfort-seeking. Indeed, it is our view that quite often the distinctions among prospect theory, heuristics and biases, and emotion are somewhat blurred.

5.4   REPRESENTATIVENESS AND RELATED BIASES

In a series of articles, Amos Tversky and Daniel Kahneman identified three key heuristics—namely representativeness, availability, and anchoring—that can potentially lead individuals astray. Representativeness and its close cousin, availability, will be the topic of this section, while anchoring will be covered in the next section. Much of this early research on these heuristics and biases is summarized in the opening chapter of *Judgment under Uncertainty: Heuristics and Biases*.[28] While these heuristics often provide reasonable answers, sometimes they are misapplied. The typical result is probability judgment error: thinking some event is more (or less) likely than it actually is based on a proper understanding of the situation.

Indeed, many financial decisions are based on probability assessment. How likely is it that a particular company will continue to post earnings increases? What is the probability that interest rates will rise by 100 basis points over the next quarter? How likely is it that some firm's current round of R&D will bear fruit? And so on. The problem is that many people have great difficulty understanding probability.

FIGURE 5.3 Venn Diagram of Events "Winning Lottery" and "Being Happy"

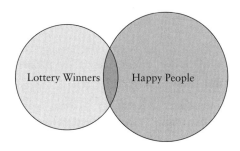

CONJUNCTION FALLACY

An example of people having difficulty with probabilities is when they have no no-tion of the difference between simple probabilities (probability of A) and joint probabilities (probability of both A *and* B). For example, they naturally feel that the probability that they will win the lottery and be overjoyed the next day is higher than the probability that they will just win the lottery. Of course, the oppo-site is true, since they might be diagnosed with cancer the day after their lottery number comes up.

It is easy to show that such a view must be wrong. Suppose that A denotes winning the lottery and B denotes being happy. The corresponding probabilities are $pr(A)$ and $pr(B)$. Figure 5.3 uses the familiar Venn diagram to show that the probability of someone being both a lottery winner *and* happy at the same time, that is, $pr(A \cap B)$, must be less than $pr(A)$, unless *all* lottery winners are happy. Those making this mistake are said to be prone to the **conjunction fallacy**.

This fallacy is one manifestation of representativeness. Under the **representative-ness heuristic**, "probabilities are evaluated by the degree to which A is representative of B, that is, by the degree to which A resembles B. For example, when A is highly representative of B, the probability that A originates from B is judged to be high. On the other hand, if A is not similar to B, the probability that A originates from B is judged to be low."[29] B can be a class and A can be a variable defined on that class, or an instance of that class, or a subset of that class. On the other hand, B can be a causal system and A can be a possible consequence or realization coming from that system.[30] In the case of the lottery, the mental picture of smiling winners and disappointed losers (the consequence) seems more representative of the class of lottery players (winners and losers) than someone (of unknown expression) who just wins, so it seems that being a happy winner is more probable than just winning.

BASE RATE NEGLECT

An important variant of representativeness is **base rate neglect**. To illustrate, sub-jects were shown personality sketches, allegedly from a group of professionals made up of engineers and lawyers.[31] In one treatment, subjects were told that 70% of the professionals were engineers and 30% were lawyers; in another, they were told that 30% were engineers and 70% were lawyers. Obviously, when no specific information is available, one should see that there is a 70% chance of randomly selecting a lawyer/engineer when this occupation is in the majority, and subjects were able to see this. Now consider the following sketch that was presented:

> *Dick is a 30-year-old man. He is married with no children. A man of high ability and high motivation, he promises to be quite successful in his field. He is well liked by his colleagues.*

This sketch was designed to be neutral and unlikely to push subjects in one direction or the other. Indeed, subjects saw this description as neutral, with about 50% saying Dick was a lawyer and 50% saying Dick was an engineer. The problem was that this was true, *regardless* of whether they had been previously told that 70% of the sample were engineers or 70% of the sample were lawyers. In other words, subjects were ignoring the base rate, hence the term *base rate neglect*. In terms of representativeness, the description appears representative of a random (50/50) process, so we believe this is indeed the process, ignoring what we know about prior probabilities.

The lawyer/engineer example is egregious, in that the base rate is ignored. It is more common that it is paid attention to, but insufficiently. At this point, it is useful to digress and investigate what probability theory tells us about the optimal use of prior and sample information.

BAYESIAN UPDATING **Bayes' rule**, a useful relationship that allows us to evaluate conditional probabilities, is:

| 5.1 |

$$pr(B|A) = pr(A|B) * [pr(B)/pr(A)]$$

Bayes' rule allows one to optimally update probabilities based on the arrival of new information. It says that the probability of event B, conditional on event A, is equal to the probability of event A, conditional on event B, times the ratio of the simple probabilities of event B to event A.[32]

To illustrate, say that you have a barometer that predicts the weather. Without looking either outside or at the barometer (that is, without accessing sample information), the probabilities of a rainy day and of a dry day (based on historical frequencies for this time of the year) are as follows: $pr(rain) = 40\%$ and $pr(dry) = 60\%$. Suppose we also know the following:

| 5.2 |

$$pr(rain\ predicted\ |\ rain) = 90\%$$

| 5.3 |

$$pr(rain\ predicted\ |\ dry) = 2.5\%$$

In other words, conditional on the fact that it did rain, rain was predicted (by the barometer) 90% of the time; and conditional on the fact that it turned out to be dry, rain was predicted 2.5% of the time. While the best prediction of tomorrow's weather without looking at the barometer is that there is a 40% chance of rain, how should this base rate be adjusted if we know that the barometer (the sample) is predicting rain? It is easy to show that the barometer predicts rain 37.5% of the time.[33] Intuitively, if the barometer points to rain, there is an increased probability of a rainy day. It is possible to be more specific. Using Bayes' rule, we have:

5.4 $pr(\text{rain} \mid \text{rain pred.}) = pr(\text{rain pred.} \mid \text{rain}) * [pr(\text{rain}) / pr(\text{rain pred.})]$
$$= .9 * (.4 / .375) = .96$$

That is to say, if we know that the barometer is predicting rain, there is a 96% chance that it will rain, versus only a 40% chance if we don't know the barometer reading.

HOT HAND PHENOMENON Let's consider an example from sports. The fictitious John Cash is a mid-level NBA basketball player. Over the year, he has successfully hit 40% of his shots from the floor. Tonight he is hot, though, as he has hit on 80% (8 of 10). The game is down to the wire. John's team is down by a single point with seconds to go, and there is time for one more shot. Should his team try to move the ball to John, or to Freddie Munny, who is only 3/10 tonight, but who over the year has hit a team-leading 60%? In other words, should we bank on the **hot hand,** or just fall back on historical frequencies that have been only negligibly impacted by the game in progress. One can think of the past percentage of successful shots as the base rate. While we can't totally discard the notion that tonight's performance is the beginning of a long-term upward/downward trend for John/Freddie, it is more natural to think that what has occurred during the game is a temporary blip that may or may not have some staying power. Let's suppose for the moment that it is logical to think that it does have *some* staying power—but only for the short term (which includes the final shot of the game, which is in the very short term).

Let's say that B is the probability that John will hit on his next shot. The unconditional probability given his record is 40%. Let's say that A is the event that John hits on 8/10 of his previous 10 shots. Based on looking at the historical record, this happened 4% of the time. We also need the probability that John has hit 80% of his last 10 shots *conditional* on his making the next shot. Let's say that based on history this value is 6%. Now we can work out the probability that John will hit on the final shot of the game:

5.5 $pr(\text{hit} \mid \text{made 8}) = pr(\text{hit}) * [pr(\text{made 8} \mid \text{hit})/pr(\text{make 8})]$
$$= .4 * (.06 / .04) = .6$$

Indeed, based on our hypothetical numbers, there is a hot hand at work. A similar exercise would have to be undertaken for everybody else on the team (maybe some players have not in the past exhibited a hot/cold hand tendency). Then the best move would be to go to the player with the highest probability of scoring *conditional* on their recent performance.

What would base rate underweighting look like here? It would imply a view that John has a higher than 60% probability of hitting. While the numbers we have assumed suggest that the data-generating process has temporarily shifted in John's favor, it would be possible to be too optimistic about John's chances.

While we have "cooked" the numbers to produce a hot hand, one might ask what the reality in basketball is. Thomas Gilovich, Robert Vallone, and Amos Tversky address this issue using both real basketball data and people's views about the data.[34] Specifically, they obtained performance data from the Philadelphia 76ers for much of the 1980–1981 season. First, these researchers established that among basketball fans the typical view is that players often have a hot (or cold) hand: 91% of respondents to a survey said they believed that a player has "a better chance of making a shot after having just made his last two or three shots than he does after having just missed his last two or three shots."

Table 5.1 shows that the evidence does not bear out this view. If anything, reversal seems more the norm (consistent with gambler's fallacy discussed later). On average, the team made 52% of its shots from the floor. After three misses, a player's success was typically higher (56%), while, after three hits, a player's success was typically lower (46%). In one case, the difference was quite stark: Darryl Dawkins, the best shooter on the team (with a 62% unconditional average), was a much stronger bet to hit (88%) after a string of misses than after a series of hits (51%). Additionally, the table presents correlation coefficients, where shot success is related to *previous* shot success. All but one of these correlations is negative. For Daryl Dawkins, it is strongly negative and statistically significant. These findings, taken together, suggest that the hot hand is an illusion in basketball (at least for this team at this time).

Are there valid reasons why reversal is a bit more likely in this context? Several suggest themselves. After success, one might get a bit too cocky and try lower-percentage shots. Moreover, the defense might pay closer attention to the hot

TABLE 5.1	PROBABILITY OF MAKING A SHOT CONDITIONAL ON PREVIOUS SHOT SUCCESS FOR PHILADELPHIA 76ER PLAYERS DURING 1980–1981

Player	pr(hit | 3 misses)	pr(hit)	pr(hit | 3 hits)	Correlation
C. Richardson	50%	50%	48%	−0.020
J. Erving	52%	52%	48%	0.160
L. Hollins	50%	46%	32%	−0.004
M. Cheeks	77%	56%	59%	−0.038
C. Jones	50%	47%	27%	−0.016
A. Toney	52%	46%	34%	−0.083
B. Jones	61%	54%	53%	−0.049
S. Mix	70%	52%	36%	−0.015
D. Dawkins	88%	62%	51%	−0.142
Weighted means	56%	52%	46%	−0.039

Source: Gilovich, T. R., R. Vallone, and A. Tversky, 1985, "The hot hand in basketball: On the misperception of random sequences," *Cognitive Psychology* 17, 592–596.

shooter. On the other hand, a player might tend to favor higher-percentage shots after a bad streak. Still, it's remarkable that the evidence flies in the face of common belief. The authors put this down to the fact that a random sequence, in the eyes of many people, looks like it has too many runs for randomness, while a sequence with too few runs for it to be consistent with randomness actually looks random to many people.

GAMBLER'S FALLACY VS. HOT HAND

While a belief in a hot hand is thinking the conditional distribution should look like the sample, sometimes it seems that people think the reverse—namely that the sample, however small, should look like the population, in the sense that essential features should be shared.[35] Of course for this to make sense, we need to have a fairly strong sense of what the distribution should look like.

To illustrate, suppose some friends have been playing poker, and Susan, who has been having lots of big hands, sees her stake growing. What are her friends thinking? Some of her friends might be thinking that she has a hot hand. While such a view may conceivably make sense in the realm of sport (it turned out not to apply for basketball), it can't make sense with cards, because the reality is that, unless Susan has been employing legerdemain with the deck, the odds of getting more good hands than bad the rest of the night are 50/50—exactly the same as is true for her up-to-now luckless friends.[36]

Others of her friends perhaps might be thinking that Susan is due for some bad hands, since, after all, in their reasoning, performance has to average out. This equally fallacious view is sometimes called **gambler's fallacy**. The friends who are subject to gambler's fallacy see chance as a self-correcting process. They know that in the long run Susan will get as many bad hands as good. This is called the law of large numbers. Their mistake is in applying it over a small sample, that is, in utilizing the incorrect "law of small numbers."

Consider an experiment where gambler's fallacy was documented.[37] A group of subjects were asked the following question:

> *All families of six children in a city were surveyed. In 72 families the exact order of births of boys and girls was GBGBBG. What is your estimate of the number of families surveyed in which the exact order of births is BGBBBB?*

If one thinks about it for a minute, it is clear that any ordering is equiprobable. Still, the majority of subjects thought that fewer families would report the second sequence because it just doesn't look random enough.

OVERESTIMATING PREDICTABILITY

It has been shown that people tend to believe that there is more predictability than is usually the case.[38] For example, when students were asked to predict college GPA on the basis of sense of humor (which is probably uninformative), they tended to believe there was a positive relationship. The mean correlation over all respondents was 0.7. Thus there seems to be a strong predilection to find predictability even when it's unlikely to be present, perhaps because it is comforting to think that we have some control. It is hard for us to accept that some things are inherently almost impossible to predict.

Intuitively, one should make forecasts of some variable by appropriately weighting both the overall population mean and the value suggested by the data at hand. If, for example, the average GPA over the relevant population is 3.0 and you believe that humor is uninformative, you should predict a GPA of 3.0 regardless of someone's sense of humor. On the other hand, if you believe there is logically a positive correlation between an input and the magnitude to be forecasted, the greater your belief in the sensitivity of GPA to this input (and the greater the perceived positive correlation), the more you should pay attention to the sample. On the other hand, the more uninformative you believe the sample to be, the closer you should move in the direction of the mean.

Nevertheless, it seems to be the case that people usually underestimate true regression to the mean, which is tantamount to exaggerating predictability. In another GPA example, subjects were asked to predict GPA in college from high school GPA of entrants to the college.[39] The high school average GPA was 3.44 (with a standard deviation of 0.36), while the GPA achieved at college was 3.08 (with a standard deviation of 0.40). Two representative students were chosen for illustration purposes: one with a high school GPA of 2.2 and another with a high school GPA of 3.8. Subjects were then asked to predict the college GPA for these two students. Again, the obvious approach is to combine sample and population data. For the lower achiever, this would mean predicting his college GPA as something below 3.08, substantially below if we believe that a student with a low high school GPA is representative of a bad student. The average response was 2.03. In reality, a student of this type had a college GPA of 2.7.[40] Regression to the mean exists because high school marks are very much imperfect predictors of college achievement. Randomness aside, people obviously can change their work habits, and weaker students have an incentive to push themselves harder in order to thrive at university.

Finally, it is worth noting that the tendency to underestimate regression to the mean is in a certain sense similar to the base rate underweighting problem that was previously discussed. The reason is that in both cases the sample data at hand are accorded too much weight versus what is known about the underlying population or distribution.

AVAILABILITY, RECENCY, AND SALIENCE

As we have seen from the previous discussion, sample data are often given undue importance relative to population parameters. This tendency is accentuated when the data are easy to obtain and process, that is, when they are "available." This is especially so when the events in question have occurred recently and are salient.

According to the **availability** heuristic, events that are called to mind easily are believed to have a greater likelihood of occurring. While frequency and ease of recall should be correlated, the reality is that ease of recall can be influenced by other factors. Do you think more words begin with a k or have a k in the third position? It has been hypothesized that since it is easier to think of words beginning with a k relative to those with a k in the third position, people will believe that more words begin with this letter. Indeed, experimental evidence indicates that this is true, even though the reality is that fewer words begin with a *k*. Many such examples have been documented, where availability influences probability assessment.[41]

Another example is based on egocentric judgments. In a survey of married couples, both spouses were asked to what extent (in percentage terms) they contributed to certain shared household chores (such as shopping for groceries or cleaning house). For 16 of the 20 surveyed tasks, the aggregate percentage was over 100% (e.g., the wife said 60% and the husband said 60%), a result that was highly statistically significant overall. Spouses were also asked to recall self- or spouse-relevant behaviors (e.g., he/she went grocery shopping yesterday). Not surprisingly, it turned out that people tended to remember their own behaviors better, since it is easier to recall what we did. Moreover, the greater the tendency to remember self-relevant versus spouse-relevant behaviors, the greater was the overestimation in perceived responsibility.[42]

Two factors abet availability. When something has occurred recently, it is likely to be called to mind more easily.[43] The term that is used here is **recency bias**. Our earlier discussion of primacy and recency effects is helpful here: recall that, provided events are temporally spaced, what comes last tends to be remembered best.[44]

Salience also enhances availability (hence the term **salience bias**). Consider a plane crash that has just occurred. This event splashed all over the news is vivid and horrifyingly easy to visualize—it is salient. The result of media coverage of this sort of event is that some people will, at least temporarily, viscerally overestimate the probability of a repeat occurrence, and as a result may even shy away from air travel. One study investigated salience in a social context.[45] When subjects were shown groups interacting in a simulated work environment, in cases where a woman (or a black) was alone in a committee of six, their actions (whether positive or negative) were remembered better by viewers than when there were two or more of the same gender (or color) on the same committee. Additionally, judgments in a solo context were more extreme (i.e., the person in question either did very well or very poorly rather than somewhat well/poorly).

5.5   ANCHORING

In many situations, people make estimates by starting from an initial value and adjusting it to generate a final estimate. Often the adjustment is insufficient. The initial value often naturally comes from the frame of the problem. As an example, quickly look at the following product of eight numbers:[46]

$$1 \times 2 \times 3 \times 4 \times 5 \times 6 \times 7 \times 8$$

Without explicitly calculating, what is your estimate of the final answer? Most people will unconsciously multiply the first few numbers in the sequence before providing the answer. The median answer when people were asked this question in an experimental setting was 512—versus the true answer of 40,320.

The situation improved somewhat when the sequence was transposed, as follows:

$$8 \times 7 \times 6 \times 5 \times 4 \times 3 \times 2 \times 1$$

In this case, the median answer was 2,250. But the use of the product of the first few numbers as an anchor—without regard to the length of the sequence—still led to insufficient adjustment.

More surprisingly, people can **anchor** on obviously irrelevant numbers that appear in the problem frame. In one demonstration of this, a wheel with numbers 1–100 (which participants were told to view as percentages) was spun.[47] Subjects were then asked whether the percentage of countries from Africa in the U.N. was higher or lower than this number coming from the wheel. The experimenters were more interested in a second question, which was: What is the percentage of countries coming from Africa in the U.N.? Obviously this percentage has nothing to do with the result of the wheel spin, yet its influence was apparent. The median answer was 25 for those seeing 10 from the wheel, while the median answer was 45 for those seeing 65 from wheel. Thus anchoring can occur with obviously meaningless numbers.

Sometimes anchors are self-generated. In one experiment, people were asked to estimate four magnitudes.[48] In two cases, the anchor was provided by the experimenter (e.g., typical length of whale, with 69 feet provided as an anchor); in two other cases, an obvious general knowledge anchor was present. One example of the latter was: "When did the second European explorer land in the West Indies?" Since most people know that Columbus was the first European explorer to land in the West Indies and he did so in 1492 (37 of 50 subjects knew this), it is natural to start to start with 1492 and adjust it upwards. Interestingly, though we have already seen the power of irrelevant anchors, when interviewed afterwards, while 64%–89% said they used the relevant anchor in their estimation, only 12%–14% claimed to do so in the case of irrelevant anchors.

WHAT EXPLAINS ANCHORING?

While the aforementioned study using relevant anchors indicates that people start with a benchmark value and adjust it in the obvious direction, this may not be the whole story. There are two views as to why adjustment tends to be insufficient, with the first working best for relevant anchors and the second working best for irrelevant anchors.[49] One view is based on uncertainty about the true value. Because of this uncertainty, decision-makers move their answer away from the anchoring value only until they enter a plausible range. The greater is their uncertainty, the greater is the plausible range, and the more insufficient will be the adjustment undertaken.

Another class of explanations focuses on lack of cognitive effort, cognitive laziness, as it were. While focusing on the anchor is easy, movement away from the anchor is effortful, so for this reason people will often stop too early. It may seem odd that obviously irrelevant anchors can have any impact. One possible explanation for this is that the anchor inherent in the problem frame acts as a kind of conscious or subconscious suggestion, leading to stored information consistent with the anchor coming more easily to kind. In this way, memory is "primed," or external search is biased.

ANCHORING VS. REPRESENTATIVENESS

Anchoring and the base rate underweighting variant of representativeness can at times appear to be in conflict. The latter normally says people are too influenced by sample information (especially, in the recency version, the latest information), while anchoring can lead to people paying insufficient attention to sample data.

The following hypothetical situation may help to reconcile the conflict. It relates to the notion that people are "coarsely calibrated," that is, they see things in black or white, and not in shades of grey. Suppose you are going to take your family on a picnic. You hear the forecast on the radio and the meteorologist predicts a rainless sunny day. Indeed, the day has started off sunny as you head for the park. Some dark clouds start to move in. Since you are anchored to your prior view, you discount these clouds, viewing them as an aberration. More dark clouds roll in. You continue to discount them, saying to yourself, "surely it will turn out to be a nice day." Now the sky is growing darker. In line with the coarse calibration view, you abruptly transition and now believe, "it's going to rain for sure, so let's head home before we get wet."

Reality is more complex. When the day began it was never certain that it would be a sunny day. In fact, if you had listened closely to the weather forecast, the meteorologist may have said that it was likely going to be a sunny day, with the P.O.P. being 20%. But you, being coarsely calibrated, only heard "sunny day." As it were, in your mind the probability of rain was 0%. You clung to this view in the face of mounting evidence to the contrary. (Note that even weather departments update forecasts given new evidence.) When the sky became too dark to ignore, you coarsely transitioned to a 100% probability of rain. But of course the dark clouds might have blown over. Perhaps the true probability had moved to 80%. Instead of heading home, maybe you should have stayed close to the car, ready for either a sudden downpour or for the clouds to pass over allowing the picnic to be resumed.

5.6   IRRATIONALITY AND ADAPTATION

Much of the previous discussion has been from the "heuristics and biases" tradition whose thrust often seems to be to elucidate cases where heuristics lead people astray and where probability misjudgment occurs. Some have argued that it is not heuristics that are flawed, but rather this particular view of them.

FAST AND FRUGAL HEURISTICS

Gerd Gigerenzer and like-minded researchers, who have coined the term **fast and frugal heuristics**, argue that the purpose of heuristics is to employ a minimum of time, knowledge, and computation in order to make adaptive choices in real-world environments.[50] This approach is in the spirit of so-called **bounded rationality**, as developed by Herbert Simon, which posits that it is unreasonable to believe that man is capable of the kind of complicated optimization problems that conventional economic models assume.[51] Instead, man "satisfices," which amounts to doing the best that he can under the circumstances. As it were, our minds have evolved and now possess a number of tricks (or heuristics) for us to make decisions that are reasonable enough.

The "fast and frugal" program of research stresses the notion of "ecological rationality," which requires that heuristics match the environment, and the "adaptive toolbox," whereby rational decision-makers seek to employ the right tool at the right time. Further, they argue against the view that complicated full-information models are necessarily better than fast-and-frugal heuristics that may only use one or two items of salient information. The former unfortunately often "overfit" in viewing all data as information rather than partly noise.[52] The latter, on the other hand, have been honed by evolution to zero in on "swamping forces." These researchers also criticize the fact that the heuristics and biases program stresses probability mistakes. But does it really matter much if people make probability errors if they are coming up with reasonable decisions given the constraints of their environment?

RESPONSE TO CRITIQUE

Thomas Gilovich and Dale Griffin in their introduction to *Heuristics and Biases: The Psychology of Intuitive Judgment* put the heuristics and biases program into historical perspective and respond to its critics.[53] They argue that sometimes people misread this research agenda in associating heuristics with irrationality and "lazy and inattentive minds." Instead, heuristics are far from inherently irrational: they often rely on sophisticated underlying processes, and are normal intuitive responses to questions of likelihood. Nevertheless, they do concede that the agenda of the heuristics and biases program is to pinpoint instances when heuristics, usually because they are used outside of their natural domains, lead to systematic bias. There is a prescriptive side to this as some research effort, as will be described in Chapter 18, has been accorded to "debiasing." Further, they argue against the view that heuristics, because they have been honed by many years of evolutionary forces, must be, for this reason, optimal.[54]

5.7   LOOKING AHEAD

HEURISTICS AND BIASES AND FINANCIAL DECISION-MAKING

In later chapters, we will revisit the heuristics and biases discussed up to now, detailing how they have been argued to influence financial decision-making. In Chapter 8, we deal with investors and other market practitioners. In Chapter 13, the contribution of some of these behaviors to explanations of anomalies will be addressed. In Chapter 16, our focus is on the decisions of corporate managers. And in Chapter 17, our stress is on decisions made in the context of retirement and self-directed pensions.

To preview, familiarity is argued to lead to excessive investment in local and domestic securities. The tendency to overestimate predictability can foster the fallacious view that "good companies are good investments." Once views (faulty or reasonable) are formed, anchoring may lead people to adhere to them too long.

Underestimating regression to the mean can cause one to extrapolate past earnings growth too far into the future. Availability induces investors to concentrate on those securities that are in the news. Recency leads them to purchase hot stocks or funds when there is little evidence that this is wise. The apparent tendency of corporate managers to utilize suboptimal capital budgeting criteria may be linked to a preference for that which is easy to process. In the context of self-directed pensions, the diversification heuristic, when used to select funds, can lead to poor asset allocation decisions. The status quo bias is also deleterious in this regard as it can cause one to be too willing to stick with an inappropriate company default allocation. Information overload may also contribute to an explanation of low pension participation rates.

DO HEURISTIC-INDUCED ERRORS CANCEL OUT?

Do heuristic-induced errors cancel out, or do they map into market outcomes? In other words, are prices wrong because of systematic investor error? This, of course, was a major discussion topic in the last chapter. What the present chapter adds is the notion of investor error occasioned by the use of heuristics. If many investors are using the same heuristic at the same time, this could be a source of systematic error.

In Chapter 13, we discuss how biases at the level of the individual may map into market outcomes. As mentioned in Chapter 4, two key anomalies are momentum and reversal. One well-known model seeks to explain these phenomena using base rate neglect and anchoring.[55] Another puzzle at the level of the market is the so-called equity premium puzzle, the finding that stocks seem to have historically earned much more relative to bonds than they should have when risk is properly factored in. One proposed explanation for this is ambiguity aversion, which matters here because stock investment entails not just risk in the standard sense, but also uncertainty as to what the true distribution of stock returns actually is.

CHAPTER HIGHLIGHTS

1. Perception sometimes distorts information gathering. Memory can be self-serving and colored by emotion. Primacy and recency effects lead to the importance of sequence.
2. Information overload and limited attention necessitate the use of heuristics, or decision-making shortcuts. Some heuristics are autonomic and reflexive (Type 1); others are cognitive and deliberative (Type 2).
3. Some heuristics influence preference through comfort-seeking. Examples are familiarity, ambiguity aversion, diversification, and reliance on the status quo.
4. Representativeness, where probabilities are evaluated by the degree to which A resembles B, is one of the most important and well-documented heuristics.
5. Often representativeness leads to the tendency to ignore the base rate and to put too much weight on sample data.
6. Bayes' rule allows one to optimally update prior probabilities as new sample information comes in.

7. Downplaying the base rate and putting too much weight on the sample is analogous to believing that the population should look like the sample. It is sometimes also believed that the sample should look like the population. To think in terms of gambling or sports, the former is associated with a hot hand view, while the latter is associated with gambler's fallacy.

8. Availability and its cousins, recency and salience, lead people to overestimate probabilities of events.

9. When unsure, people often anchor on available values and adjust their views slowly. Anchoring can even occur when the anchor is obviously immaterial.

10. It has been argued that people are coarsely calibrated: they see black and white and have more difficulty with shades of grey. This can lead to anchoring and conservative adjustment initially, followed by representativeness.

11. Gigerenzer and like-minded researchers have criticized the "heuristics and biases" approach, stressing that "fast and frugal" heuristics generally perform their tasks quite successfully.

12. One counterargument is that while heuristics have been honed by evolutionary forces, there can be an adjustment period during which heuristics, when used outside of their natural domain, lead to bias.

DISCUSSION QUESTIONS AND PROBLEMS

1. Differentiate the following terms/concepts:

   a. Primacy and recency effects
   b. Salience and availability
   c. Fast-and-frugal heuristics and bias-generating heuristics
   d. Autonomic and cognitive heuristics

2. Which description of Mary has higher probability?

   a. Mary loves to play tennis.
   b. Mary loves to play tennis and, during the summer, averages at least a game a week.

   Explain your answer. Define the conjunction fallacy. How does it apply here? Assume for the purpose of illustration that the probability that someone loves to play tennis is .2; the probability that someone plays tennis once or more a week during the summer is .1; and the probability of one or the other of these things is .22.

3. Rex is a smart fellow. He gets an A in a course 80% of the time. Still, he likes his leisure, only studying for the final exam in half of the courses he takes. Nevertheless, when he does study, he is almost sure (95% likely) to get an A. Assuming he got an A, how likely is it he studied? If someone estimates the above to be 75%, what error are they committing? Explain.

4. Why are two people who witnessed the same event last month likely to describe it differently today?

5. How do gambling fallacy and clustering illusion relate to representativeness? Provide examples from sports. In what way are they different?

ENDNOTES

1 This section (and the next two on memory and framing effects) relies extensively on Plous, S., 1993, *The Psychology of Judgment and Decision-making* (McGraw-Hill, New York).

2 Bruner, J. S., and L. J. Postman, 1949, "On the perception of incongruity: A paradigm," *Journal of Personality* 18, 206–223.

3 Hastorf, A. H., and H. Cantril, 1954, "They saw a game: A case study," *Journal of Abnormal and Social Psychology* 49, 129–134.

4 Frenkel, O. J., and A. N. Doob, 1976, "Post-decision dissonance at the polling booth," *Canadian Journal of Behavioural Science* 8, 347–350.

5 Loftus, E. F., 2003, "Make-believe memories," *American Psychologist* 58, 867–873.

6 See, for example, Thomas, D. L., and E. Diener, 1990, "Memory accuracy in the recall of emotions," *Journal of Personality and Social Psychology* 59, 291–297.

7 Hawkins, S. A, and R. Hastie, 1990, "Hindsight: Biased judgments of past events after the outcomes are known," *Psychological Bulletin* 107, 311–327.

8 Coren, S., and J. Miller, 1974, "Size contrast as a function of figural similarity," *Perception and Psychophysics* 16, 355–357.

9 Figure 5.1 is a famous representation called the Muller-Lyer illusion.

10 Miller, N., and D. T. Campbell, 1959, "Recency and primacy in persuasion as a function of the timing of speeches and measurements," *Journal of Abnormal and Social Psychology* 59, 1–9.

11 Landy, D., and H. Sigall, 1974, "Beauty is talent: Task evaluation as a function of the performer's physical attractiveness," *Journal of Personality and Social Psychology* 29, 299–304.

12 This is why some professors adopt a marking mechanism whereby the names of students are kept hidden until marks are awarded.

13 Reber, R., and N. Schwarz, 1999, "Effects of perceptual fluency on judgments of truth," *Consciousness and Cognition* 8, 338–342.

14 Iyengar, S. S., and M. Lepper, 2000, "When choice is demotivating: Can one desire too much of a good thing?" *Journal of Personality and Social Psychology* 76, 995–1006.

15 See Gilovich, T., D. Griffin, and D. Kahneman, 2002, "Heuristics and biases: Then and now," in T. Gilovich, D. Griffin, and D. Kahneman, eds., *Heuristics and Biases: The Psychology of Intuitive Judgment* (Cambridge University Press, Cambridge, U.K.), for a discussion.

16 Ibid.

17 Consider the analogy of a Swiss army knife with its manifold tools. It provides a set of tools that can solve many problems. When we confront new, unfamiliar problems, we might use a tool that is not exactly suited to the task at hand. We do the best with what we have. If we need a better tool over time, we might be able to devise one, but in the short run (which may last for some time) we may have to make do. During this time, our use of the improper tool may lead to suboptimal decisions.

18 Heath, C., and A. Tversky, 1991, "Preference and belief: Ambiguity and competence in choice under uncertainty," *Journal of Risk and Uncertainty* 4, 5–28.

19 In the example, the respondent is saying that the *average* (over all questions) certainty level is 60%. With a question being randomly selected, 60% would be the best guess of the probability of being right on any particular question. The next chapter deals with overconfidence, the tendency to think that you know more than you actually do know. Overconfidence here would entail being right less than 60% of the time.

20 Of course if one had known in advance, it would have been trivial to "game" this setup by exaggerating certainty and then taking the random bet.

21 Ellsberg, D., 1961, "Risk, ambiguity and the Savage axioms," *Quarterly Journal of Economics* 75, 643–669.

22 Indeed David Hirshleifer, in his influential review of behavioral finance, slots ambiguity aversion in his section on emotion. See Hirshleifer, D., 2001, "Investor psychology and asset pricing," *Journal of Finance* 56, 1533–1597. Also see Peters, E., and P. Slovic, 1996, "The role of affect and world-views as orienting dispositions in the perception and acceptance of nuclear war," *Journal of Applied Social Psychology* 26, 1427–1453.

23 In a similar vein, when choices are mutually exclusive, often an "avoid extremes" stance is taken.

24 Simonson, I., 1990, "The effect of purchase quantity and timing on variety-seeking behavior," *Journal of Marketing Research* 27, 150–162.

25 This is related to sensation seeking, which is partly about seeking novelty. See Grinblatt, M., and M. Keloharju, 2006, "Sensation seeking, overconfidence and trading activity," Working paper.

26 Kahneman, D., J. L. Knetsch, and R. H. Thaler, 1991, "The endowment effect, loss aversion, and status quo bias," *Journal of Economic Perspectives* 5 (no. 1), 193–206.

27 Samuelson, W., and R. Zeckhauser, 1988, "Status quo bias in decision making," *Journal of Risk and Uncertainty* 1, 7–59.

28 Kahneman, D., P. Slovic, and A. Tversky, eds., 1982, *Judgment under Uncertainty: Heuristics and Biases* (Cambridge University Press, Cambridge, U.K.). The introductory chapter is reproduced from Tversky, A., and D. Kahneman, 1974, "Judgment under uncertainty: Heuristics and biases," *Science* 185, 1124–1131.

29 Ibid.

30 Tversky, A., and D. Kahneman, 1982, "Judgments of and by representativeness," in D. Kahneman, P. Slovic, and A. Tversky, eds., *Judgment under Uncertainty: Heuristics and Biases* (Cambridge University Press, Cambridge, U.K.).

31 Kahneman, D., and A. Tversky, 1973, "On the psychology of prediction," *Psychological Review* 80, 237–251.

32 If we rearrange we have $pr(B \mid A) = pr(B) * [pr(A \mid B) / pr(A)]$, which says that the optimal way to update the probability of B, based on knowing that A is true, is to multiply it by the factor $[pr(A \mid B) / pr(A)]$.

33 Note that the barometer has an indeterminate range: 5% of the time it predicts neither rain nor dry weather.

34 Gilovich, T. R., R. Vallone, and A. Tversky, 1985, "The hot hand in basketball: On the misperception of random sequences," *Cognitive Psychology* 17, 592–596.

35 In general, people don't seem to understand the role of sample size. See Kahneman, D., and A. Tversky, 1972, "Subjective probability: A judgment of representativeness," *Cognitive Psychology* 3, 430–454.

36 How Susan *plays* the cards is quite another matter.

37 Kahneman, D., and A. Tversky, 1972, "Subjective probability: A judgment of representativeness," *Cognitive Psychology* 3, 430–454.

38 Kahneman, D., and A. Tversky, 1973, "On the psychology of prediction," *Psychological Review* 80, 237–251.

39 Shefrin, H., 2000, *Beyond Greed and Fear: Understanding Behavioral Finance and the Psychology of Investing* (Harvard Business School Press, Boston, Massachusetts).

40 In the case of the stronger student there was less of a gap: the prediction was 3.46 and the actual result was 3.30.

41 Tversky, A., and D. Kahneman, 1973, "Availability: A heuristic for judging frequency and probability," *Cognitive Psychology* 4, 207–232.

42 Ross, M., and F. Sicoly, 1979, "Egocentric biases in availability and attribution," *Journal of Personality and Social Psychology* 37, 322–336.

43 Kahneman, D., and A. Tversky, 1973, "On the psychology of prediction," *Psychological Review* 80, 237–251.

44 Again, see Miller, N., and D. T. Campbell, 1959, "Recency and primacy in persuasion as a function of the timing of speeches and measurements," *Journal of Abnormal and Social Psychology* 59, 1–9.

45 Taylor, S. E., 1982, "The availability bias in social perception and interaction," in D. Kahneman, P. Slovic, and A. Tversky, eds., *Judgment under Uncertainty: Heuristics and Biases* (Cambridge University Press, Cambridge, U.K.).

46 Tversky, A., and D. Kahneman, 1974, "Judgment under uncertainty: Heuristics and biases," *Science* 185, 1124–1131.

47 Ibid.

48 Epley, N., and T. Gilovich, 2001, "Putting adjustment back in the anchoring and adjustment heuristic," *Psychological Science* 12, 391–396.

49 Chapman, G. B., and E. J. Johnson, 2002, "Incorporating the irrelevant: Anchors in judgments of belief and value," in T. Gilovich, D. Griffin, and D. Kahneman, eds., *Heuristics and Biases: The Psychology of Intuitive Judgment* (Cambridge University Press, Cambridge, U.K.).

50 Gigerenzer, G., P. M. Todd, and ABC Research Group, eds., 1999, *Simple Heuristics That Make Us Smart* (Oxford University Press, Oxford, U.K.).

51 Simon, H. A., 1992, *Economics, Bounded Rationality, and the Cognitive Revolution* (Elgar, Aldershot Hants, England).

52 Gigerenzer, G., J. Czerlinski, and L. Martignon, 2002, "How good are fast and frugal heuristics?" in T. Gilovich, D. Griffin, and D. Kahneman, eds., *Heuristics and Biases: The Psychology of Intuitive Judgment* (Cambridge University Press, Cambridge, U.K.).

53 Gilovich, T., and D. Griffin, 2002, "Heuristics and biases: Then and now," in *Heuristics and Biases: The Psychology of Intuitive Judgment* (Cambridge University Press, Cambridge, U.K.).

54 See Lo, A. W., 2004, "The adaptive markets hypothesis: Market efficiency from an evolutionary perspective," Working paper; and Lo, A. W., 2005, "Reconciling efficient markets with behavioral finance: The adaptive markets hypothesis," Working paper.

55 Barberis, N., A. Shleifer, and R. Vishny, 1998, "A model of investor sentiment," *Journal of Financial Economics* 49, 307–344.

OVERCONFIDENCE

CHAPTER **6**

6.1 INTRODUCTION

Overconfidence is the tendency for people to overestimate their knowledge, abilities, and the precision of their information, or to be overly sanguine of the future and their ability to control it.[1] That most people most of the time are overconfident is well documented by researchers in the psychology literature. This chapter will survey some of the more important results. Later, in Chapters 9 and 16, we will see that the financial economics literature also provides abundant evidence that people are often overconfident in the realm of financial decision-making.

Overconfidence comes in different forms. We begin this chapter by describing miscalibration, the tendency to believe that your knowledge is more precise than it really is. Then in Section 6.3 we go on to describe other forms of overconfidence: the better-than-average effect, illusion of control, and excessive optimism. We also learn that it is not clear that these different manifestations of overconfidence are even measuring the same thing, since the same individual can be both overconfident and underconfident, depending on the test. Moreover, these tests are prone to the criticism of framing. In Section 6.4, we also discuss the various biases that abet overconfidence formation and durability. We end by asking ourselves whether overconfidence is an unmitigated evil.

6.2 MISCALIBRATION

WHAT IS IT?

In a research setting, overconfidence can be measured in several ways. We begin with **miscalibration**.[2] As stated before, miscalibration is the tendency for people to overestimate the precision of their knowledge.[3] A calibration test often works in the following fashion. In a controlled environment, individuals are asked to construct (say) 90% confidence intervals for currently (or soon) knowable magnitudes (such as the height of Mount Everest, or the level of the Dow in a month). Typically, they are found to be miscalibrated, which means their intervals are too narrow.

More precisely, if people are asked a large number of (say) $x\%$ confidence interval questions—sampling error is reduced by asking a sufficiently large number of questions—then proper calibration implies that about $x\%$ of their confidence intervals should contain correct answers to the questions. Or, focusing on a particular question that is asked of a large number of respondents, if the group as a whole is properly calibrated, $x\%$ of these individuals should have confidence intervals bracketing the correct answer.

The reality turns out to be quite different. A percentage of individuals usually markedly below $x\%$ produces intervals that bracket the true answer. The same holds at the level of the individual. If someone is asked a series of such questions, as is shown in the calibration test described in the next section, it is commonplace for substantially fewer than $x\%$ of her intervals to be "right." In sum, calibration studies find that the confidence intervals that individuals provide are too narrow, resulting in correct answers lying within the confidence ranges less often than an accurate sense of one's limitations would imply.

Calibration tests are also operationalized in other ways. For example, sometimes respondents are asked a question and then provided with a menu of answers. This could be a simple true or false option, or a series of multiple choices. In a second stage, people are then asked how sure they are in the correctness of their answers. If someone has (say) an average certainty level of 70%, but she only gets 55% of the questions right, this implies overconfidence. Sometimes people say they are absolutely certain of their answers. In one study, events that individuals believed to be certain to occur actually occurred only about 80% of the time, while events that they considered impossible occurred about 20% of the time.[4]

EXAMPLE OF A CALIBRATION TEST

We report one study documenting overconfidence via a calibration test. Marc Alpert and Howard Raiffa surveyed 800 students enrolled in the Harvard MBA program during the 1968–1969 academic year.[5] Specifically, the students were asked three either/or questions where opinions or preferences were elicited, followed by 10 questions whose answers were unknown quantities. The first three of the latter 10 questions were based on average responses to the three opinion/preference questions. Table 6.1 provides a full list of the questions, as well as the correct answers. Notice the questions run the gamut from knowledge of peer opinions and tastes to somewhat obscure factual information.

For all 10 of the uncertain-quantity questions, students were asked to provide .01, .25, .50, .75, and .99 percentiles. Note that the difference between one's .75 percentile and .25 percentile is both an interquartile range and also a 50% confidence interval. This is true because one would expect the true answer to fall between these bounds half the time. Similarly, the difference between one's .99 percentile and .01 percentile is a 98% confidence interval, consistent with the expectation that the true answer will fall between these bounds 98% of the time.

Table 6.2 provides the distribution of subjects' answers by question and percentile range. First, notice that there are six percentile ranges (PRs), two open and four closed. Let's label them as: PR1: below .01; PR2: between .01 and .25; PR3: between .25 and .50; PR4: between .50 and .75; PR5: between .75 and .99; and

TABLE 6.1	QUESTIONS ASKED IN ALPERT & RAIFFA CALIBRATION STUDY

Opinion/preference questions

A. Do you prefer bourbon or scotch?

B. Do you favor draft deferments for all graduate students while in school regardless of concentration?

C. Would you accept a 50-50 gamble where you could lose $50 or win $100?

Uncertain quantity questions: Provide .01, .25, .50, .75, and .99 percentile ranges for ...	True value
1. The percentage of first-year students responding, excluding those who never drink, who prefer bourbon to scotch.	42.5
2. The percentage of first-year students responding who favor draft deferments for all graduate students while in school regardless of field of concentration.	65.5
3. The percentage of first-year students responding who would accept the gamble in question C above.	55.2
4. The percentage of respondents expressing an opinion to a July, 1968, Gallup Poll surveying a representative sample of adult Americans who felt that if a full-scale war were to start in the Middle East, the United States should send troops to help Israel.	10.4
5. The percentage of respondents expressing an opinion to a March, 1968, Gallup Poll surveying a representative sample of adult Americans who felt that public school teachers should be permitted to join unions.	63.5
6. The number of "Physicians and Surgeons" listed in the 1968 yellow pages of the phone directory for Boston and vicinity.	2,600
7. The total number of students currently enrolled in the doctoral program at the Harvard Business School.	235
8. The total egg production in millions in the United States in 1965.	64,588
9. The number of foreign automobiles imported into the United States in 1967 in thousands.	697
10. The toll collections of the Panama Canal in fiscal 1967 in millions of dollars.	82.3

Source: Alpert, M. and H. Raiffa, 1982, "A progress report on the training of probability assessors," in D. Kahneman, P. Slovic, and A. Tversky, eds., *Judgment under Uncertainty: Heuristics and Biases* (Cambridge University Press, Cambridge, U.K.).

PR6: above .99. To interpret, let us use the sixth question (from Table 6.1). Students were asked for "the number of 'Physicians and Surgeons' listed in the 1968 Yellow Pages of the phone directory for Boston and vicinity." The correct answer (at the time) was 2,600. Let's say someone's .25 and .50 percentiles were 1,500 and 3,000, respectively. Since the true answer is between these two percentile values, she would be assigned to range 3. Those belonging to this range numbered 12%. Since as many people were in ranges 1–3 (those overestimating the answer) as were in ranges 4–6 (those underestimating), the inference to be drawn is that in

TABLE 6.2 | DISTRIBUTION (IN PERCENT) OF SUBJECTS' ANSWERS BY QUESTION AND PERCENTILE RANGE IN ALPERT & RAIFFA CALIBRATION STUDY

QN	Topic	PR1: Below .01	PR2: .01 to .25	PR3: .25 to .50	PR4: .50 to .75	PR5: .75 to .99	PR6: Above .99	Total
1	Bourbon	3	16	20	40	11	10	100
2	Draft	15	12	35	19	10	9	100
3	Gamble	11	8	28	29	13	11	100
4	Mid-East	51	41	6	1	1	0	100
5	Union	1	1	13	28	29	28	100
6	Doctors	24	14	12	13	10	27	100
7	Grad students	1	3	11	9	15	61	100
8	Eggs	9	2	13	10	8	58	100
9	Cars	25	15	18	9	7	26	100
10	Revenue	18	8	8	12	16	38	100
Total		158	120	164	170	120	268	1,000
Exp. freq.		10	240	250	250	240	10	1,000

the case of this particular question, there was no persistent bias in terms of point estimate (50th percentile). Note that not all questions could safely make this same claim: for example, in the case of question 4, many people overestimated, while in the case of question 8, many people underestimated.

It is more relevant for our purposes to focus on interquartile ranges (PR3 and PR4) and all ranges save the two extreme (open) intervals (PR1 and PR6). Again, if people are properly calibrated, 50% of the time correct answers should be within their interquartile ranges. Expected frequencies are shown in the last row of Table 6.2, which shows the expected number of times (out of 1,000—since for each question we are working in terms of percentages, and there are 10 questions) a particular range should contain the correct answers. The two middle ranges should each contain 250 correct answers (i.e., 25% of the time), and summing these gives us 500 for the 10 interquartile ranges. In reality, only 334 interquartile ranges contained correct answers, versus the expectation of 500. On this basis, one can conclude a moderate level of overconfidence.

It is worth noting that the percentage falling within the interquartile range is very much question-specific. On questions 1–3, most of the time correct answers fell in ranges 3 and 4, which reflects mild underconfidence. In all other cases, less than half the time answers fell in ranges 3 and 4, signifying overconfidence. In a certain sense, questions 1–3 were "easy" questions, since they were all first asked of individual subjects, which gave people the opportunity to mull them over, perhaps even guess how others might answer. Moreover, to some extent they all involve personal experience and opinions. On the other hand, the remaining questions were "hard" questions—they were more factual in nature, and in some cases downright obscure.

The reason this observation is important is because it implies that, while overconfidence is observed for most individuals most of the time, it is not universal. There is the tendency for underconfidence to be detected in certain situations. This is often so for easy questions as opposed to hard questions.[6] This is called the **hard-easy effect**. It is appropriate to note here that there is also evidence that underconfidence may arise when the strength of the evidence is low while the credibility of the source is high.[7] For example, a moderately positive reference letter from a very credible source may lead to underconfidence in the candidate's potential, unlike the case of a strong reference letter originating from a dubious source, which is more likely to lead to overconfidence.

Returning to the Alpert and Raiffa study, and in particular focusing on the two extreme ranges (ranges 1 and 6), whereas for a given question correct answers should fall in these ranges 2% of the time, now we witness much starker evidence of calibration difficulties. Take question 6 for example, where we earlier said on average people seemed to have it right. Unfortunately, respondents were too sure of their views: 51% (24+27) of the time answers were located in these two extreme ranges instead of the 2% that proper calibration requires. In the case of all 10 questions, well in excess of 2% of the time answers were located in the two extreme ranges. While this was true to a lesser extent for the "easy" questions 1–3, nonetheless, even these questions reflected marked overconfidence in the extreme ranges.

6.3   OTHER STRAINS OF OVERCONFIDENCE

Overconfidence manifests itself in other ways in addition to faulty precision of knowledge. Many people unrealistically have the tendency to think that their abilities and knowledge are better than average. Illusion of control causes people to believe that they have more power to exert control over events than is logical. Excessive optimism reflects the feeling that things will be rosier than objective analysis suggests.

BETTER-THAN-AVERAGE EFFECT

Some studies have asked people to rate themselves relative to average on certain positive personal attributes such as athletic skill or driving ability, and, consistent with a **better-than-average effect**, many rate themselves as above average on those attributes. But, of course, only (slightly fewer than) 50% of the people in any pool can truly be superior. One researcher surveyed a sample of students, reporting that 82% rated themselves in the top 30% of their group on driving safety.[8]

One factor that facilitates a better-than-average belief is that often the exact definition of excellence or competence is unclear.[9] Naturally enough, people have in the backs of their minds the definition that will make them look best. Take driving. Some might see "best" as most adept at steering; others might see it as most competent at anticipating hazard; while still others might see it as being most skillful at weaving back and forth while speeding down the interstate. Both motivational and cognitive mechanisms are likely behind the better-than-average effect. On the motivational side, thinking that you are better than average enhances self-esteem. On the cognitive side, the performance criteria that most easily come to mind are often those that you are best at.

ILLUSION OF CONTROL

Another strain of overconfidence is called **illusion of control**. This reveals itself when people think that they have more control over events than objectively can be true. For example, one sees dice players acting as if they can control the outcome of the dice roll, and people actually believe that the risk of infection is partly a function of the character of the person that they are coming into contact with.[10]

In one experiment, students were enrolled to participate in a gambling contest.[11] When subjects entered the room individually, they faced another student who was also to participate, but the latter student was actually a confederate who had been instructed to role play as either "dapper" or a "schnook." The experimenter shuffled cards and gave both the subject and the confederate a card face down. Each was allowed to bet (privately) up to 25 cents per round that his card was higher than his opponent's. Clearly, this is a pure game of chance, with no skill whatsoever involved. Nevertheless, subjects made significantly higher bets (16.25 cents vs. 11.04 cents) when they were facing the "schnook." Perhaps subjects' feelings of superiority induced a mindset that they could influence chance events.

EXCESSIVE OPTIMISM

Related to illusion of control is **excessive optimism**. Abundant empirical investigation has corroborated the existence of this manifestation of overconfidence.[12] Excessive optimism is present when people assign probabilities to favorable/unfavorable outcomes that are just too high/low given historical experience or reasoned analysis. Examples of such very positive events or very negative events are winning the lottery or dying of cancer.[13] Further, students expect to receive higher marks than they actually do receive, and they overestimate the number of job offers that they will receive.[14] Despite high divorce rates, newlyweds almost universally expect that their marriages will succeed.[15]

Subject to so-called **planning fallacy**, people often think that they can accomplish more than they actually end up accomplishing, and that any costs incurred will be as expected. In reality, many of us fall short of our work goals on a regular basis. And, budget overruns are a common feature of large public projects. The Sydney Opera House, for instance, was supposed to be completed in 1963 at a cost of $7 million. Instead, it was finished 10 years later at a cost of $102 million.[16]

Such lack of realism is not without cost.[17] The inability to meet one's goals can lead to disappointment, loss of self-esteem, and reduced social regard. Also, time and money can be wasted pursuing goals that are unrealistic. Think of someone enrolling in a program of study that to neutral observers is beyond his capability.

Should he fail, a significant amount of time and money will have been wasted, and, because of disappointment, he might be hesitant in the future to strive for other goals that are truly within his grasp.

BEING OVERCONFIDENT IN MORE THAN ONE SENSE

Optimism and miscalibration can easily go hand in hand. Let's suppose you are about to bowl with your friends. In standard 10-pin bowling, 300 is the maximum score, and 200 is an excellent one. You are feeling buoyant today and boldly predict 225 as your score, with a 90% confidence range of between 200 and 250. Over the year, you have averaged 175, with 90% of your results falling within 50 points of this magnitude (i.e., between 125 and 225). On the basis of your season record, you are excessively optimistic (by 50 points). Moreover, you are miscalibrated, with your confidence interval being only 50% as wide as it should be.

Though separating out excessive optimism and miscalibration in this case was straightforward, in reality it is not always easy to tease out the different strains of overconfidence. Returning to the example of someone enrolling in a program of study that is to neutral observers beyond his capability, previously we argued that excessive optimism was the culprit. It may be that the individual knows his limitations, but is confident that he can pull it off this time. On the other hand, he might not know his true level, attributing past failures to factors beyond his control. Indeed, the better-than-average effect might be the problem, as he truly believes that he is sufficiently capable to perform well.

ARE PEOPLE EQUALLY OVERCONFIDENT?

While it may be natural to be unsure of your knowledge in the case of general knowledge, studies have also shown that people can be quite overconfident in their fields of expertise. This has been shown for such occupations as market forecasters, investment bankers, business managers, lawyers, and medical professionals.[18] Thus, overconfidence afflicts experts as well as amateurs.

There is also evidence that the extent of overconfidence may be a function of demographics. Most reliable is the difference in the degree of overconfidence between men and women, with men tending to be more overconfident than women.[19] Interestingly, the magnitude of the difference depends to a great extent on the tasks that they are asked to perform, with the difference being greater for tasks that are perceived to be "masculine."[20]

While we would all like to think that education is an unmitigated good, it appears to have its downside. In a Canadian survey, more educated people were not only more *confident* than less educated people in their investment knowledge (which is natural enough), but they were also more *overconfident*, which means that the gap between their knowledge perception and actual knowledge was greater.[21] Perhaps people should take to heart the words of the Greek philosopher Socrates, who is reputed to have once said, "I know nothing except the fact of my ignorance."[22]

ARE PEOPLE CONSISTENTLY OVERCONFIDENT?

The fact that overconfidence has a number of manifestations, and that there are different ways to measure it, begs the following questions. Are these same metrics getting at the same psychological tendency? Are people consistently overconfident? Is overconfidence, however measured, even a stable psychological construct?

Ideally, one might hope that, whatever the actual numerical results of particular tests, if one is overconfident using one test, one should also be overconfident using another approach. This turns out to be not necessarily so, as people have been shown to be sometimes overconfident and sometimes underconfident, depending on the test.[23]

If individuals' overconfidence metrics are correlated—in other words, an individual, who is shown to have a high overconfidence rating relative to her peers on one test, is also likely be quite overconfident relative to her peers on another test—this should provide comfort. Research has shown that this is not necessarily the case, either. In fact, sometimes such correlations are very low.[24]

Gerd Gigerenzer even argues that overconfidence as demonstrated by calibration tests may be an illusion.[25] His point is that overconfidence can be made to disappear if the questions are reframed. In several experiments, he and collaborators asked respondents a number of either/or questions. For example, which city has more inhabitants, Hyderabad or Islamabad? Then subjects were asked how confident they were in their answer: 50% (a guess), 60%, 70%, 80%, 90%, or 100% (I am sure). Referring to the two numerical columns on the left of Table 6.3, while people were right 52%–56% of the time, when averaging over their confidence assessments was done, their judgment was they would be right 67%–72% of the time. This reflects mild overconfidence. In addition, at the end of all questions, subjects were asked how many questions they thought they had successfully answered. In this case, pure frequency judgments could be compared to actual frequencies. The two numerical columns on the right of the table show that, given this apples-to-apples comparison, overconfidence seems to disappear. Certainly one must conclude that the manner in which questions are asked, that is, the frame of the experiment, will have an impact on results.

TABLE 6.3 | CONFIDENCE JUDGMENTS, ESTIMATED FREQUENCIES AND DISAPPEARING OVERCONFIDENCE

	Comparing confidence judgments with frequencies		Comparing frequency judgments with frequencies	
	Exp. 1 ($n = 80$)	Exp. 2 ($n = 97$)	Exp. 1 ($n = 80$)	Exp. 2 ($n = 97$)
Judgment	0.67	0.72	0.52	0.52
Relative frequency	0.52	0.56	0.53	0.56
Difference	0.15	0.16	−0.01	−0.04

Source: How to make cognitive illusions disappear: Beyond 'heuristics and biases', Gigerenzer, G., *European Review of Social Psychology* Volume 2, 1991, pp. 83–115, reprinted by permission of the Taylor & Francis Group, http://www.informaworld.com.

6.4   FACTORS IMPEDING CORRECTION

Researchers have tried to explain why overconfidence is so prevalent among people, and, more puzzlingly, why people fail to learn from past mistakes. It is believed that three behavioral biases may contribute to the durability of overconfidence. These are self-attribution bias, hindsight bias, and confirmation bias.

Biases Interfering with Learning

In social psychology, **attribution theory** investigates how people make causal attributions, that is, how they come up with explanations for the causes of actions and outcomes.[26] Certain persistent errors occur. For example, people, when observing others, tend to over-attribute behavior to dispositional (as opposed to situational) factors. If someone seems to be behaving badly, we naturally believe them to be of bad character, rather than searching out environmental details that may be explanatory.

Another manifestation of attribution bias appears to contribute to overconfidence. **Self-attribution bias**, the tendency for people to attribute successes or good outcomes to their own abilities, while blaming failures on circumstances beyond their control, can lead to an increase in overconfidence.[27] Suppose an overconfident individual observes personal performance outcomes that are logically a combination of external and internal (to the individual) forces. If things go well, the thinking will be that this is because of great ability, skill, or knowledge (much more so than an objective consideration of circumstances would warrant), and the result will be an increase in overconfidence. On the other hand, adverse events, being only moderately ascribed to personal forces, will not lead to symmetric (but of opposite sign) revisions in overconfidence. As it were, people "learn" to be overconfident.[28]

Closely related to self-attribution bias is **hindsight bias**, which pushes people into thinking that "they knew it all along." This bias appears to be especially prevalent when the focal event has well-defined alternative outcomes (e.g., an election or the World Cup final); when the event in question has emotional or moral overtones; or when the event is subject to the process of imagination before its outcome is known.[29]

Going hand in hand with hindsight bias is **confirmation bias**, the tendency to search out evidence consistent with one's prior beliefs and to ignore conflicting data. For example, in one experimental study where both proponents and opponents of capital punishment were exposed to evidence of a mixed nature, belief polarization occurred, with those on each side sifting through the evidence to find support for their prior view.[30]

Is Overconfidence an Unmitigated Flaw?

Overconfidence, particularly excessive optimism, may not be an unmitigated flaw.[31] Research has shown that predictions about the future tend to be more optimistic when there is a low degree of temporal proximity (that is, when one's goal is far off), and when a course of action has been committed to as opposed to the situation where several options are being contemplated. When these conditions are met, being overly optimistic may enhance performance, and studies corroborate this.[32]

Still, while performance may sometimes be enhanced, it generally falls short of predictions. Certain defense mechanisms, however, are in place to alleviate disappointment.[33] Specifically, there can be bias in either performance evaluation or in prediction recall, and convenient excuses may suggest themselves. Take a student whose performance on a test has fallen short of personal expectations. He might say to himself: "Well, I did better than the class average anyway (shifting benchmark)"; "My expectation was ridiculously high given the difficulty of the material: I couldn't have been serious (questioning of prediction)"; or "Considering I had a splitting headache from lack of sleep, I think I did amazingly well (convenient excuse)." These defense mechanisms, by assuaging disappointment, allow one to go forward with minimal damage to self-esteem and be just as optimistic the next time round.

6.5 LOOKING AHEAD TO FINANCIAL APPLICATIONS

Overconfidence is prevalent in many realms, not the least of which is financial decision-making. For example, in 15 surveys (each with approximately 1,000 respondents) conducted between 1998 and 2000 by the Gallup Organization for UBS PaineWebber, respondents were asked what they expected the rates of return on the stock market and on their portfolios to be in the following 12 months.[34] On average, respondents expected their portfolios to outperform the market—that is, they were excessively optimistic. Interestingly, consistent with the gender effect discussed earlier, men expected their portfolios to outperform by a higher margin than did women. Women, while overconfident, were less so than men.

In Chapter 9 we will discuss how overconfidence impacts the financial decision-making of investors. Evidence will be presented that it leads people to trade too much, underdiversify, and take on too much risk. Miscalibration, or believing that one's information and analysis is more precise than it really is, can lead people into a false notion that they can time the market or pick the next hot stock. We also discussed in this chapter several forces that work against people learning their true abilities. Consider how self-attribution bias might work in an investment context. When the market is rising, most stocks will do well, including those that investors select for their portfolios, and most people will take that as an affirmation of their acumen. On the other hand, when their stocks drop in price, they will generally blame it on circumstances over which they had no control— such as the general condition of the market or the economy.

Overconfidence may have an impact at the level of markets. In Chapter 13, we will discuss behavioral explanations of anomalies. A number of models have been formulated that account for such anomalies as momentum and reversal. Some of these models accord an important role to overconfidence and related biases.

In Chapter 16, we will discuss how overconfidence can afflict managers and entrepreneurs. Evidence will be presented that they are too ready to enter markets, allow cash flows to dictate investment, invest excessively, acquire other companies too readily, and take on too much debt because of excessive optimism and other strains of overconfidence.

Finally, we argued that overconfidence may not be an unmitigated negative in the sense that it can lead to performance enhancement. Consider the case of market entry. An individual has decided to start up a small business, and has made commitments in this regard. While excessive optimism may have been a negative in the sense that too many people pursue this particular goal given the evidence on small business failure rates, it is helpful in another sense. The belief that success is likely can foster effort and motivation, actually increasing one's probability of success.

CHAPTER HIGHLIGHTS

1. Overconfidence is the tendency for people to overestimate their knowledge, abilities, and the precision of their information, or to be overly sanguine of the future and their ability to control it.
2. The calibration approach is often based on asking people to provide $x\%$ confidence intervals. Miscalibration is present when the correct answer falls inside the confidence intervals a percentage of the time markedly different from $x\%$.
3. Most people are overconfident most of the time, in the sense that their confidence intervals are too narrow.
4. But sometimes underconfidence occurs, especially for easy questions.
5. Other strains of overconfidence exist as well. Consistent with the better-than-average effect, many people unrealistically have the tendency to think that their abilities and knowledge are better than average.
6. Illusion of control causes people to believe that they have more power to exert control over events than is logical.
7. Excessive optimism reflects the feeling that things will be rosier than objective analysis suggests.
8. Not everyone is equally overconfident. Overconfidence is most prevalent in well-educated males.
9. Some have criticized the ways in which overconfidence has been measured, pointing out that someone can be overconfident using one test, but underconfident using another. Others have argued that overconfidence can disappear if the question is reframed.
10. Various biases impede the elimination of overconfidence. These are self-attribution bias, hindsight bias, and confirmation bias.
11. Overconfidence may not be an unmitigated flaw. For example, under certain conditions, it may enhance performance.

DISCUSSION QUESTIONS AND PROBLEMS

1. Differentiate the following terms/concepts:

   a. Miscalibration and excessive optimism
   b. Better-than-average effect and illusion of control
   c. Self-attribution bias and confirmation bias
   d. Pros and cons of overconfidence

2. Is miscalibration greater for easy questions or hard questions? Is it greater when we look at 50% confidence ranges or 98% confidence ranges?

3. Provide an example where someone can be both excessively optimistic and miscalibrated at the same time.

4. Overconfidence does not quickly dissipate via learning because of the existence of contributing biases. Explain.

5. In 2007, the New England Patriots (an American football team) had a banner year, winning all 16 regular season games. In these 16 games, their points were: 38, 38, 38, 34, 34, 48, 49, 52, 24, 56, 31, 27, 34, 20, 28, and 38. Despite this obvious success, their fans were still a bit overconfident going into the playoffs. The consensus among fans was that they would average 50 points per game in the playoffs. Plus, their fans were 95% sure that they would be within five points of this number (45 to 55). Illustrate the dimensions of their overconfidence. (For the purposes of this question, assume the Patriots participated in four playoff games.)

ENDNOTES

1 Some people use overconfidence in the sense that we use miscalibration (to be described), an example being Hirshleifer, D., 2001, "Investor psychology and asset pricing," *Journal of Finance* 56, 1533–1597. Others use it in the broader sense that we use it here. Examples are Camerer, C. F., and D. Lovallo, 1999, "Overconfidence and excess entry: An experimental approach," *American Economic Review* 89, 306–318; and Glaser, M., and M. Weber, 2007, "Overconfidence and trading volume," *Geneva Risk and Insurance Review* 32, 1–36.

2 See Lichtenstein, S., B. Fischhoff, and L. D. Phillips, 1982, "Calibration of probabilities: The state of the art to 1980," in D. Kahneman, P. Slovic, and A. Tversky, eds., *Judgment under Uncertainty: Heuristics and Biases* (Cambridge University Press, Cambridge, U.K.), for a full description.

3 One can also be underconfident and miscalibrated, but the norm is overconfidence and miscalibration.

4 Fischhoff, B., P. Slovic, and S. Lichtenstein, 1977, "Knowing with certainty: The appropriateness of extreme confidence," *Journal of Experimental Psychology: Human Perception and Performance* 3, 552–564.

5 Alpert, M., and H. Raiffa, 1982, "A progress report on the training of probability assessors," in D. Kahneman, P. Slovic, and A. Tversky, eds.: *Judgment under Uncertainty: Heuristics and Biases* (Cambridge University Press, Cambridge, U.K.). Note that this group had been exposed to decisions trees, probability distributions, and utility theory.

6 Fischhoff, B., 1982, "For those condemned to study the past: Heuristics and biases in hindsight," in D. Kahneman, P. Slovic, and A. Tversky, eds., *Judgment under Uncertainty: Heuristics and Biases* (Cambridge University Press, Cambridge, U.K.).

7 Griffin, D., and A. Tversky, 1992, "The weighing of evidence and the determinants of confidence," *Cognitive Psychology* 24, 411–435.

8 Svenson, O., 1981, "Are we all less risky and more skilful than our fellow drivers?" *Acta Psychologica* 47, 143–148.

9 See Dunning, D., J. A. Meyerowitz, and A. D. Holzberg, 1978, "Ambiguity and self-evaluation: The role of idiosyncratic trait definitions in self-serving assessments of ability," *Journal of Personality and Social Psychology* 57, 1082–1090, for a discussion.

10 For example, see Nemeroff, C., 1995, "Magical thinking about illness virulence: Conceptions of germs from "safe" versus "dangerous" others," *Health Psychology* 14, 147–151.

11 Langer, E. J., 1975, "The illusion of control," *Journal of Personality and Social Psychology* 32, 311–328.

12 See Armor, D. A., and S. E. Taylor, 2002, "When predictions fail: The dilemma of unrealistic optimism," in T. Gilovich, D. Griffin, and D. Kahneman, eds., *Heuristics and Biases: The Psychology of Intuitive Judgment* (Cambridge University Press, Cambridge, U.K.), for a full review of the excessive optimism literature.

13 Weinstein, N., 1980, "Unrealistic optimism about future life events," *Journal of Personality and Social Psychology* 39, 806–820.

14 See Hoch, S. J., 1985, "Counterfactual reasoning and accuracy in predicting personal events," *Journal of Experimental Psychology: Learning, Memory, and Cognition* 11, 719–731; and Shepperd, J. A., J. A. Ouellette, and J. K. Fernandez, 1996, "Abandoning unrealistic optimism: Performance estimates and the temporal proximity of self-relevant feedback," *Journal of Personality and Social Psychology* 70, 844–855.

15 Baker, L. A., and R. E. Emery, 1993, "When every relationship is above average: Perceptions and expectations of divorce at the time of marriage," *Law and Human Behavior* 17, 439–450.

16 Buehler, R., D. Griffin, and M. Ross, 2002, "Inside the planning fallacy: The causes and consequences of optimistic time predictions," in T. Gilovich, D. Griffin, and D. Kahneman, eds., *Heuristics and Biases: The Psychology of Intuitive Judgment* (Cambridge University Press, Cambridge, U.K.).

17 Again, see Armor, D. A., and S. E. Taylor, 2002, "When predictions fail: The dilemma of unrealistic optimism," in T. Gilovich, D. Griffin, and D. Kahneman, eds., *Heuristics and Biases: The Psychology of Intuitive Judgment* (Cambridge University Press, Cambridge, U.K.), for a discussion.

18 See Barber, B., and T. Odean, 1999, "The courage of misguided convictions," *Financial Analysts Journal* (Special Issue on Behavioral Finance), 41–55; and Deaves, R., E. Lüders, and M. Schröder, 2007, "The dynamics of overconfidence: Evidence from stock market forecasters," Working paper.

19 Lundeberg, M. A., P. W. Fox, and J. Punccohar, 1994, "Highly confident but wrong: Gender differences and similarities in confidence judgments," *Journal of Educational Psychology* 86, 114–121.

20 Beyer, S., and E. M. Bowden, 1997, "Gender difference in self-perception: Convergence evidence from three measures of accuracy and bias," *Personality and Social Psychology Bulletin* 23, 157–172.

21 Bhandari, G., and R. Deaves, 2006, "The demographics of overconfidence," *Journal of Behavioral Finance* 7(1), 5–11.

22 Laertius, Diogenes, 1938. *Lives of the Eminent Philosophers* (Harvard University Press., Cambridge, Massachusetts).

23 The previously discussed hard-easy effect is an example. Also see, Kirchler, E., and B. Maciejovsky, 2002, "Simultaneous over- and under-confidence: Evidence from experimental asset markets," *Journal of Risk and Uncertainty* 25, 65–85.

24 Glaser, M., T. Langer, and M. Weber, 2005, "Overconfidence of professionals and laymen: Individual differences within and between tasks?" Working paper.

25 Gigerenzer, G., 1991, "How to make cognitive illusions disappear: Beyond 'heuristics and biases,'" *European Review of Social Psychology* 2, 83–115.

26 See Plous, S., 1993, *The Psychology of Judgment and Decision-making* (McGraw-Hill, New York), for a full discussion.

27 See, for example, Miller, D. T., and M. Ross, 1975, "Self-serving biases in the attribution of causality: Fact or fiction?" *Psychological Bulletin* 82, 213–225. Their review of the evidence strongly supports the self-enhancing side of self-attribution bias (i.e., attributing success to personal factors), but finds only minimal evidence for the self-protective side of self-attribution bias (i.e., attributing failure to external forces).

28 See Gervais, S., and T. Odean, 2001, "Learning to be overconfident," *Review of Financial Studies* 14, 1–27; and Deaves, R., E. Lüders, and M. Schröder, 2007, "The dynamics of overconfidence: Evidence from stock market forecasters," Working paper.

29 Hawkins, S. A, and R. Hastie, 1990, "Hindsight: Biased judgments of past events after the outcomes are known," *Psychological Bulletin* 107, 311–327.

30 See Lord, C. G., L. Ross, and M. R. Lepper, 1979, "Biased assimilation and attitude polarization: The effects of prior theories on subsequently considered evidence," *Journal of Personality and Social Psychology* 37, 2098–2109, for this experimental evidence.

31 See Armor, D. A., and S. E. Taylor, 2002, "When predictions fail: The dilemma of unrealistic optimism," in T. Gilovich, D. Griffin, and D. Kahneman, eds., *Heuristics and Biases: The Psychology of Intuitive Judgment* (Cambridge University Press, Cambridge, U.K.), for a discussion of the evidence.

32 Campbell, J. D., and P. J. Fairey, 1985, "Effects of self-esteem, hypothetical explanations, and verbalization of expectancies on future performance," *Journal of Personality and Social Psychology* 48, 1097–1111.

33 Again, see Armor, D. A., and S. E. Taylor, 2002, "When predictions fail: The dilemma of unrealistic optimism," in T. Gilovich, D. Griffin, and D. Kahneman, eds., *Heuristics and Biases: The Psychology of Intuitive Judgment* (Cambridge University Press, Cambridge, U.K.), for a discussion.

34 This story is recounted in Barber, B., and T. Odean, 2001, "Boys will be boys: Gender, overconfidence, and common stock investment," *Quarterly Journal of Economics* 116, 261–292.

EMOTIONAL FOUNDATIONS

CHAPTER 7

7.1 INTRODUCTION

Television and print reporters commonly attribute the decisions people make to emotions. The financial press, in particular, relies on emotion to explain the movements of financial markets, both up and down. But, we really do not know that much about how emotions interact with behavioral influences and other emotions to produce human actions and decisions. Even less is known about how the interactions of innately emotional people produce market outcomes. To provide a basis for our exploration of the role of emotion in financial decision-making, this chapter reviews some of the pertinent psychological findings on emotion.

The chapter begins with defining what an emotion is. Six observable features allow us to differentiate emotions from other mental states people experience, like moods. Next, Section 7.3 reviews psychologists' views on how we experience emotions. Whether our brain controls our emotions, or vice versa, is important for us to understand because as financial decision-makers we want to know how to control (or even put to good use) our emotional responses. Sections 7.4 and 7.5 consider evolutionary theory and the structure of the brain. The human brain has undergone great changes through evolution. Progress scientists have made in learning about the evolution of the structure of the brain and the functions of particular parts of the brain will allow us to use our brains to become better decision-makers. In addition, studies of patients with damage to particular parts of the brain have provided significant insights into decision-making. Importantly, the evidence presented in Section 7.6 suggests that decision-making actually suffers when emotional responses are lacking. Finally, after a section that recaps the relationship between our minds and our bodies, Section 7.8 previews how emotion impacts financial decision-making.

7.2 THE SUBSTANCE OF EMOTION

Psychologists generally agree that such states as happiness, sadness, anger, interest, contempt, disgust, pride, fear, surprise, and regret are emotions. We can each create our own list of emotions, but we begin by asking: What exactly is an emotion? And how do emotions differ from other mental states? Although no features are unique to emotions, Jon Elster argues that six observable features allow us to define an emotion:[1]

1. **Cognitive antecedents**. In most cases, beliefs trigger an emotional response. For example, you become angry when another driver runs a red light and almost causes a collision because you believe the other driver is driving carelessly and has endangered your life. Notice how this emotion differs from hunger, another bodily state that arises because your stomach is empty. Though hunger may be triggered by a belief (such as "it is noon so I must be hungry for lunch"), it is generally triggered by a sensory signal (such as an empty feeling or growling), rather than a thought. Of course the distinction is not perfect, but it is generally understood that beliefs are important in the generation of emotions.

2. **Intentional objects**. Emotions are about something like a person or situation. For example, you are angry with the driver who ran the light. In most cases, the object of the emotion is closely related to the belief that triggered the emotion. You are angry with the driver of the other car because he is reckless. Also note that the distinction between an emotion and a mood is important. An emotion is about something, whereas a **mood** is a general feeling that does not focus on anything in particular. You are angry with the reckless driver, but you may also have been in a melancholy mood, in general, if you suffered from depression.

3. **Physiological arousal**. Hormonal and nervous system changes accompany emotional responses. Your body actually goes through hormonal changes when you experience an emotion. During the near collision, you might feel your blood pressure rising.

4. **Physiological expressions**. Emotions can be characterized by observable expressions that are associated with how a person functions. You may express your anger at the other driver by raising your voice or shaking your fist in his direction. Though some physiological responses are functional, others simply result from the situation. For example, an angry person's red face results from increased blood flow, but does not necessarily assist the person in resolving the problem. Many physical expressions associated with emotions are consistently observed characteristics. For example, if you saw a person with a red face and clenched fists, you might guess that he was angry. Notice, also, that the expressions are not necessarily unique and can result from very different emotions. A red face is also associated with embarrassment or feelings of shame. In addition to an angry reaction, a person might also clench his fists in a time of celebration or joy.

5. **Valence**. Emotions can be rated on a scale with a neutral point in the center and positive and negative feelings on the endpoints.[2] Valence is a psychological term that is used to rate feelings of pleasure and pain or happiness and unhappiness. You are feeling very negative toward the other driver. In many cases, emotions that are highly stimulating are also at the positive or negative endpoints for feelings. Notice that we can't always assume

that strong emotions are at the endpoints (or vice versa). For example, one author's teenage daughter sometimes reports very strong feelings of boredom, an emotion low on valence.

6. **Action tendencies.** Emotions are linked to action tendencies. When you experience an emotion, you often feel an urge to act a certain way. In some cases, you might even feel compelled to take action. You may have an impulse to follow the reckless driver and give him a piece of your mind. Or, you might modify the initial urge to action and simply drive away, while carefully watching other drivers on your way home. This regulation of your action tendency can result with or without conscious choice.[3] Your body might actually automatically inhibit your reaction. At the same time, social forces rein you in.[4] For example, you might decide against chasing the reckless driver and telling him exactly what you think of him because you realize that others will see a seemingly out-of-control response.

Together, the six features just described help us define what an emotion is and differentiate emotions from other mental states.

Notice that many emotions can be regarded as negative (anger, contempt, disgust, fear, and sadness). Historically, researchers in psychology have focused on negative emotions. Positive emotions, such as happiness, have received much less attention. This differential attention may have resulted from a desire to prevent mental illness and make the world a better place. Recently, though, some psychologists argue that positive psychology has more promise in improving the quality of life and alleviating suffering.[5] According to this new branch of the discipline, a focus on positive functioning will allow psychologists to develop a science that promotes positive growth in people and society.

It is equally important to understand what an emotion is not. As mentioned previously, mood is distinct from emotion. Like emotions, moods usually have positive or negative valence, but, unlike emotions, moods tend to persist for long periods of time. In addition, emotions and moods are distinct in that emotions arise in relation to an object or stimulus, whereas a mood is a general feeling not focusing on any particular item. In contrast to emotions and moods is **affect**, or how a person experiences a feeling. A person's **affective assessment** is the experience a person has in response to a stimulus. Affect is evaluative in that a person can say whether a stimulus is good or bad, positive or negative. Note that although affect reflects an evaluation, it does not require (or preclude) a cognitive response. For example, you might think that a rose smells good but not really be able to cognitively evaluate *why* it smells good to you. We think of emotional processes as including affective reactions.[6] Now that we know something about how emotions are characterized, we turn to theories developed by psychologists to describe how emotions are experienced.

7.3   A SHORT HISTORY OF EMOTION THEORY

If we understand where emotions come from and how they impact our behavior, we will become better financial decision-makers. Can we control our emotions, or do they control us? Though sometimes emotions are characterized as simply irrational responses to a situation, psychologists do not regard thought processes and emotions as separate, opposing influences. Psychologists recognize that emotions include cognitive, physiological, and overt behavioral elements.

Cognitive psychologists focus on specific mental processes, including conscious mental processes like thinking, speaking, problem solving, and learning. Early work on emotions explained emotions in terms of cognitive processes so that an emotion is simply what we *think* about a situation. Taking a different perspective, in 1884, William James developed a prominent theory of emotion that remains influential today.[7] This theory suggested that an emotion is a feeling resulting from an autonomic response. The **autonomic nervous system** governs our bodies' involuntary actions, such as sweating, shaking, and even fleeing. According to James, if you see a bear in the woods, you respond by freezing in your tracks and (initially) without emotion appraising the situation, and *then* you have the conscious feeling of fear. Notice that this differs from the simple explanation that when you see a bear in the woods you feel fear and then you respond (see Figure 7.1). According to James, "we feel sorry because we cry, angry because we strike, afraid because we tremble, and not that we cry, strike, or tremble, because we are sorry, angry, or fearful, as the case may be."[8]

James's theory was dominant until another influential study by Walter Cannon.[9] Cannon argued that physiological responses sometimes occur without emotion (e.g., sweaty palms). Although he agreed with James that emotions are different from other states of the mind because of how the body responds, Cannon did not agree that autonomic responses differentiated emotions because we can observe very similar responses with very different emotions (e.g., you might clench your fists in joy or anger). Cannon also argued that people's brains respond to a stimulus *before* their body takes action. According to his theory, when you see a bear in the woods, your brain and nervous system simultaneously receive signals. You then experience the conscious feeling of fear and autonomic arousal at the same time (you are probably sweating when faced with a large bear).

Until the 1960s, emotions were used to *describe* how people behaved. Many psychologists were behaviorists and believed that their work should focus on observed behavior, rather than mental processes. In other words, emotions were simply descriptions of observed behavior, and psychologists devoted little attention to understanding the source of emotion[10]—that is, until Stanley Schachter and Jerome Singer again raised the question of where emotions come from.[11] They concluded that emotions are our brain's interpretation of a situation. Like James, they believed that autonomic responses are important, but at the same time, they questioned, as Cannon did, whether emotions can be differentiated simply by autonomic responses. Their solution was a model that included a cognitive appraisal of the situation. When you see a bear in the woods, your body responds. Then your brain searches for an explanation to the arousal. Your brain recognizes that your body is responding to the bear, and you feel fear. You may want to run, but your emotions exert control, allowing you to remain calm and leave the area as quickly as possible. If you run, the bear will chase, which does not lead to the best outcome.

Though Schachter and Singer's model and appraisal theories remain powerful, in 1980, Robert Zajonc noted that an important piece was missing.[12] He showed that sometimes people experience emotion without any cognitive recognition of the stimulus. In experiments in which he used subliminal exposure to stimuli,

FIGURE 7.1 Theories of Emotional Response – I See a Bear[33]

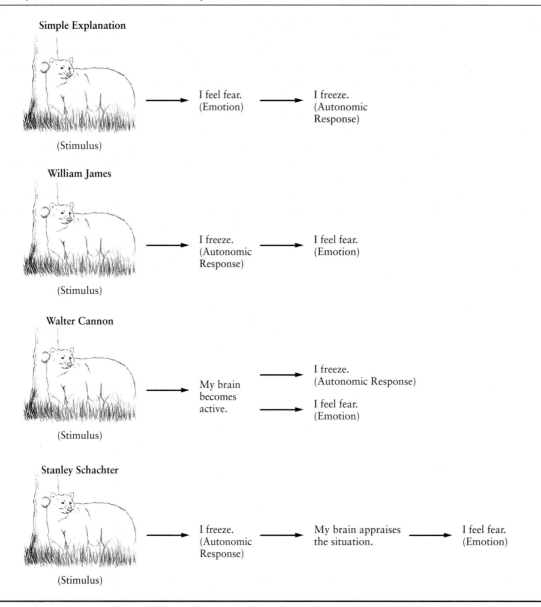

Simple Explanation

(Stimulus) → I feel fear. (Emotion) → I freeze. (Autonomic Response)

William James

(Stimulus) → I freeze. (Autonomic Response) → I feel fear. (Emotion)

Walter Cannon

(Stimulus) → My brain becomes active. → I freeze. (Autonomic Response) / I feel fear. (Emotion)

Stanley Schachter

(Stimulus) → I freeze. (Autonomic Response) → My brain appraises the situation. → I feel fear. (Emotion)

Zajonc found that people seemed to like patterns they were previously exposed to but they could not reliably recognize. This finding is important because it suggests that emotions can develop independent of cognition.

7.4   EVOLUTIONARY THEORY

In Chapter 3, we presented evidence that prospect theory has an evolutionary aspect to it. Emotions are no different. Recently, some psychologists have returned to the contributions of Charles Darwin, which were made more than a hundred years ago. Darwin is best known for his theory of evolution and natural selection.[13] According to this theory, traits that contribute to the survival of a species become characteristics of the species in the long run. Less fit individuals do not survive, and fit parents pass their characteristics on to their offspring. Species that do not adapt this way become extinct. Darwin later argued that emotions, as well as physical traits, are inherited and have become innate.[14]

Following Darwin, evolutionary theorists have also argued that our basic emotions have evolved to promote the survival of the species.[15] At times, a situation demands a quick response and there is no time for deliberation. Indeed, many emotions are explained as rapid-fire innate responses to a stimulus, with cognition taking a smaller role. An adaptive role is served because emotions lead to appropriate action and communication. Consider the fearful animals in Figure 7.2. Though cats and dogs are very different species, notice how similar their facial responses are. In addition, you might have noticed how their hair becomes erect in a dangerous situation. They are on the defensive, and if you came across either of them, the message would be clear. Get away as quickly as possible! It is the emotional expression that communicates this.

Importantly, not only do emotions serve as communicating mechanisms, they also serve as infectious mechanisms, that is, emotions can create analogous emotions

FIGURE 7.2 Similar Responses to a Dangerous Situation[34]

in the observer, and this often occurs in a subliminal, noncognitive fashion.[16] In one study, merely seeing the *picture* of another person smiling led to the observer smiling in concert.[17] People observing emotions in a movie felt the same emotions as the ones portrayed.[18] People acting tensely transmitted tension to those watching.[19] The ability of emotions to be "transmitted" is potentially important in the context of social forces—a snowball effect occurs, with many people feeling the same way at the time, not only because the original stimulus acts on different people, but also because of the infectiousness of emotion.

While in a previous example we have observed commonality in emotional expression among animal species, does the same hold for people in different cultures? It is interesting to note that similar facial and bodily expressions usually communicate the same emotions in people of different cultures. Facial expressions appear to define a set of emotions, though the elements of this set are not fully agreed upon. Generally, the set of basic emotions defined by facial manifestations includes anger, disgust, fear, interest, joy, and surprise.[20] In addition, although there has been some debate about whether there exists a universality of emotional facial expressions, recent cross-cultural studies provide support for the notion that there are strong similarities in facial expressions across distinct cultures.[21]

For evolutionary psychologists, it is no surprise that emotions are similar across cultures because animals display facial expressions that are consistent with analogous human emotions. Though animals are not capable of complex reasoning, their facial expressions are similar to the human facial expressions commonly associated with certain emotional responses. Certain emotions, generally called **primary emotions**, are hardwired into our brains because they evolved before other mental systems.[22] Evolutionary psychologists believe that the higher brain areas that govern our complex mental processes evolved after primary emotions were already in place. Vertebrate animals have similar brain structures, although with one very important difference: the size of the forebrain. In the following section, we consider the anatomy of the human brain to better understand the source of emotion.

7.5   THE BRAIN

An understanding of the brain is important when we study emotion. Scientists have devoted a lot of attention to mapping the brain and associating functions with parts of the brain. In this regard, modern technology has been very helpful to scientists in moving forward. **PET (positron emission tomography)** scans use harmless radioactive substances to map brain activity. The radioactive substances tend to accumulate in active areas of the brain, giving colored maps of brain activity. Another very useful tool to scientists is **fMRI (functional magnetic resonance imaging)**, which is much less invasive because it does not require injection of any substances. Using fMRI, scientists can monitor blood and oxygen flow in the brain and locate active areas.[23]

Scientists have been able to associate human functions with parts of the brain. Figure 7.3 illustrates the anatomy of the brain, which we will briefly review starting at the bottom. The picture on the left shows the brain stem structures and major lobes of the brain. The brain stem structures include the medulla, pons, and cerebellum. The medulla connects the rest of the brain to the spinal cord and regu-

FIGURE 7.3 Anatomy of the Brain

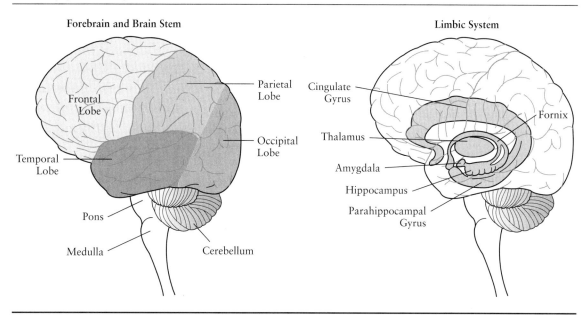

The limbic system is deeper in the brain and scientists have not fully defined its boundaries. This system borders the upper and lower parts of the brain. It is particularly important to us because it regulates instinct and some believe it to be the center of much emotional activity. The thalamus is in the middle of the limbic system and most sensory information passes through it. The thalamus integrates this information and sends it on to other parts of the brain. The **amygdala** evaluates sensory information and is important in the evaluation of primary emotions such as anger and fear. These responses can be characterized as automatic, rather than resulting from controlled evaluation. The hippocampus is important for the storage of long-term memory and allows us to access facts and events to assess new situations. The cingulate gyrus is thought to be important in evaluating emotional experiences. The two remaining structures of the limbic system are the fornix and parahippocampal gyrus, which connect parts of the brain.

The **forebrain** includes the cerebrum, the largest part of the brain. The cerebrum can be divided into two hemispheres, each consisting of four parts: the temporal, occipital, parietal, and frontal lobes. Scientists have had some success in identifying the purpose of each lobe. The temporal lobe governs speech, language, and memory. The occipital lobe is the center of vision functions. The parietal lobe is our center of sensory feeling, including skin response and temperature. The **frontal lobe** is the largest lobe in our brain and regulates motor abilities, memory, judgment, decision-making, and the ability to plan for the future.

In the last few million years, the human brain has experienced remarkable changes. The human brain grew quickly and doubled in mass. As we will now discuss, the cerebrum gives humans a decided advantage over other animals—the ability to plan.

7.6   EMOTION AND REASONING

Scientists have discovered a lot about the structure of the brain, though they are not all in agreement about the functions of each part. Many important emotions appear to be centered in the amygdala, but as we will see, the frontal lobe is also important. We will also now see that we cannot separate emotion and cognition when we consider whether emotions are good or bad in the context of decision-making.

Antonio Damasio provides remarkable evidence that decision-making suffers *without* emotion.[24] His behavioral and physiological evidence indicates that the neural systems for reason and emotion cannot be separated. Thus, decision-making and emotion are intertwined. Damasio closely studied the behavior of brain-damaged patients who were emotionally flat because of frontal lobe brain damage. These patients had average or above-average cognitive abilities though their emotional responses were abnormal. Damasio evaluated the patients' abstract problem solving, attention, knowledge, language, and memory and found no deficiencies. Yet, his patients had difficulty making decisions. They were not able to plan a future course of action. This evidence led Damasio to hypothesize that flawed reason and impaired feelings were related.

The experience of an individual who lived in the nineteenth century heavily influences Damasio's thinking. In 1848, a 25-year-old construction foreman named Phineas Gage was involved in a catastrophic construction accident. Phineas was considered to be a successful and capable railroad construction manager, and was known to show good character and be able-bodied—that is, until a distracted Phineas inadvertently discharged an explosion that sent an iron bar through his left cheek, exiting the top of his head. Figure 7.4 illustrates the nature of his injury.

FIGURE 7.4 Phineas Gage

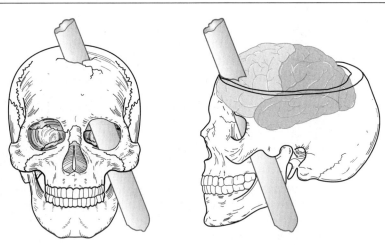

Remarkably, the iron bar used to explode rock was three-feet, seven-inches long and one and one-quarter inches in diameter, while weighing thirteen and one-quarter pounds. Even more remarkable is the fact that Phineas survived!

Phineas eventually regained physical strength and had no speech or language problems. Yet, all who knew him observed a severe change in personality. The change was so extreme that his former employers would not allow him to return to his construction job. Though he worked odd jobs, Phineas was never able to land a stable position. He no longer seemed to have concern for his future. Damasio connects Phineas's change of character to frontal lobe damage. Other researchers have also noted that patients with frontal lobe damage are severely restricted in their ability to plan for the future.[25] Though they appear to be very calm, these patients are also unable to plan.

Another more recent case, referred to as Elliot, provides additional support for this conclusion. Elliot had an acute change in personality following the removal of a brain tumor in his frontal lobe while in his thirties. Elliot had been a thriving member of the community and was known as a good husband, father, and businessman. After surgery to remove the tumor, Elliot was no longer productive. He could not hold a job or maintain social relationships. His family and friends could not understand his foolish behavior. At the same time, his intelligence quotient (IQ) continued to indicate superior intelligence. Elliot had no apparent damage to his memory, perceptual ability, language, arithmetic ability, or comprehension of new material. Yet, Elliot was completely incapable of making a decision, particularly if it was of a personal or social nature. He could reason through a problem, but he could not select a future course of action. Even Elliot, himself, realized that he no longer had the same response to emotional stimuli. Things that once made him strongly react, now had no effect on him whatsoever. Elliot's experience exemplifies the link between planning and emotion. With impaired emotional responses, Elliot did not seem to think about how his choices impacted his life going forward.

Based on Phineas's and Elliot's experiences, as well as those of other brain-damaged patients, and extensive study of the brain, Damasio concludes that emotion has an important influence on reasoning. Reason and emotion are integral parts of a human being, and the brain and body are interconnected. We cannot understand human behavior if we don't recognize the connections between the mind and body. Damasio's research suggests that emotion and rational decision-making are complementary.

Other neuroscience studies provide support for Damasio's claims. **Neuroscience** is the science that studies the brain and nervous system. Neuro scientists have concluded that emotion enhances decision-making in two ways.[26] First, when making a decision is critical, emotion pushes us to make one. Sometimes there are so many options to consider that if we evaluated each one we would spend absurd amounts of time making a decision. Emotion allows us to focus on the critical aspects of a decision so we don't get tangled up in all the details. Our emotions help us to optimize because the cost of processing all information can be overly burdensome. Second, our emotions can help us make better decisions. Psychology studies show that emotions have an important influence on decision-making.[27] Although suboptimal decisions are often attributed to emotions, poor decisions can result when emotions are missing. Positive emotions may actually facilitate access to information in the brain, creativity, problem solving, and negotiation, thus building a better decision-making process. In addition, when we are provided with many courses of action, our emotions promote the choice of the best path.[28]

As discussed previously, after millions of years of natural selection, the human brain has had an astonishing transformation. Unlike other vertebrate animals, we can reason and plan for the future. These abilities are critical for the survival of the human species. It has even been argued that a person's ability to succeed greatly depends on his **emotional intelligence** as measured by his **emotional quotient (EQ)**.[29] Analogous to a measure of a person's cognitive intelligence using an IQ test, EQ tests attempt to measure a person's ability to identify and manage their own emotional responses, as well as those of others. Emotions allow us to make quick, appropriate, and rational responses to stimuli, including such divergent situations as a dangerous encounter or a financial decision.

7.7   OUR MINDS, BODIES, AND EMOTION

We have learned a lot about emotions and the brain in this chapter, but central questions remain. What is the source of emotions? We know that emotions are part of the human experience, but how do they arise?

The source of emotion includes cognitive, physiological, and evolutionary aspects. Thought processes and emotion should not be viewed as separate, opposing influences. Psychologists recognize that emotions include cognitive, physiological, and overt behavioral elements. The reasoning of a person is the result of a complex interaction of the mind and body, and an understanding of the process must include all aspects of the being.[30]

Evolutionary theories of emotion suggest that emotions are responses resulting from evolutionary conditioning.[31] Though these responses may be useful, do we choose them or are they simply thrust upon us in response to a situation? Strictly speaking, we cannot choose our emotional response if an emotion is an innate response to a stimulus. Even if our emotions are not consciously chosen, we all have the ability to control the degree of an emotional response, at least to some extent.[32] In the case of extreme emotional response, whether positive or negative, we are all better off if we take a step back and attempt to carefully consider the best response.

7.8   LOOKING AHEAD

Later in the book, particularly in Chapters 10, 14, 16 and 20, we discuss how emotion (along with mood and brain architecture) impacts financial decision-making. Before looking ahead, let's look back—to prospect theory. In Chapter 3 we discussed prospect theory and made the point that prospect theory is sometimes argued to have a strong emotional basis.

By way of motivation, recall the fact that many people buy lottery tickets, which runs counter to loss aversion in the domain of gains. At the same time, many of these same people are buying insurance, which runs counter to risk seeking in the domain of losses. Two common emotions that are often associated with financial markets are fear and greed. Buying a lottery ticket has an expected negative return, so it can hardly be viewed as an investment. It is natural to associate such behavior with a desire to get rich quick. Is this greed? On the other hand, buying insurance, again a negative-return investment, is all about fear, the fear of catastrophe and ruin. In prospect theory, the inverse-S shape of the weighting function explains the purchase of lottery tickets and insurance. This suggests that the nonlinearity of the weighting function may arise from emotion.

If activities such as purchasing lottery tickets and insurance have a strong emotional component, in emotion-rich situations one might expect the weighting function to be more inverse-S shaped (that is, farther from linear) than in situations with less emotional resonance. In one novel experiment, Yuval Rottenstreich and Christopher Hsee found evidence that this was so. Half of the students who participated were told to hypothetically choose between meeting and kissing their favorite movie star (with certainty) versus $50 (also with certainty). A second group of students were offered the choice between a lottery offering a 1% chance of winning $50 in cash versus a 1% chance of meeting and kissing their favorite movie star. In the certainty condition, 70% preferred the cash, while in the lottery condition, 65% preferred the chance of a kiss. This result can be explained by the inverse-S shaped weighting function being less linear (more "bent") in the case of emotion-laden situations (such as the star kiss prize). In effect, the greater bend in the weighting function, implying greater weights for very low-probability events, pushes some people into preferring the chance of the kiss prize. Marketers of lottery tickets seem to sense this as they don't tend to show winners in advertisements with suitcases of money. Rather, they show them with sports cars and sunning in the South Seas.

In Chapter 10, the focus will be on the manner in which emotion impacts how individual investors make financial decisions. Two behaviors will be stressed. The first is the disposition effect, the tendency to hold losing investments longer than winning investments. The second is really two related behaviors, one being the house money effect, which is the tendency to take on more risk after investment success; and the other being the break even effect, the tendency to take on more risk after poor investment results. What the house money effect and the break even effect clearly have in common is that they imply that changing fortunes lead to increased risk taking. Notably, both the disposition effect and the house money/break even effects have competing prospect theory and emotion explanations. This perhaps should not be surprising given the relationship between emotion and prospect theory. Also in Chapter 10, we consider whether market mood may have an impact on prices. When a person has a positive disposition (perhaps because of national sporting success or because the weather is agreeable), is there a tendency to be more open to risk taking? Can lower aggregate risk aversion push prices up? A house money effect at the level of the stock market may operate in a similar fashion: high prices create euphoria, reducing risk aversion, leading to still higher prices. In an analogous fashion, systematic pessimism (for related, but opposite, reasons) may push aggregate stock prices down.

Looking even further ahead, in Chapter 14 we look at certain puzzles at the level of aggregate stock prices. One puzzle is the equity premium puzzle, namely the finding that equities have earned even more than they should have versus fixed-income investments such as bonds, when one objectively considers the differential risk. One explanation that has been proposed is based on loss aversion. Emotion suggests a possible basis for loss aversion in that people may strongly fear the unknown. In Chapter 16 we consider whether corporate managers are influenced by emotion. Indeed there seems to be some evidence that affect impacts the adoption of investment projects. Finally, in Chapter 20 we focus on the trader who, through experience, has honed his trading skills. **Neurofinance** provides new insight into how skills, like trading, are developed. Neurofinance is a new and rapidly growing field that uses neurotechnology to examine how the brain behaves while a person is making financial decisions.

CHAPTER HIGHLIGHTS

1. Examples of common emotions are anger, contempt, disgust, fear, happiness, sadness, regret, and surprise.
2. Six observable features differentiate emotions from other mental states: cognitive antecedents, intentional objects, physiological arousal, physiological expressions, valence, and action tendencies.
3. Early theories of emotion focused on whether autonomic responses defined emotions and how the brain processes information.
4. More recently, theorists recognize that evolution is an important determinant of emotions. Emotions promote communication both within and across cultures and species.
5. Scientists have been able to associate human functions with specific parts of the brain.
6. The cerebrum is what distinguishes the human brain from those of other vertebrate animals. The ability to plan for the future is critical to the advancement of the human species.
7. Decision-making actually suffers without emotion. The case of Phineas Gage provides a striking historical example.
8. Emotions push us to make a decision when timing is critical.
9. Emotions help us to make better decisions because they allow us to better evaluate information.
10. A person's success is dependent on his emotional intelligence, in addition to his intelligence quotient.
11. Emotions and cognition are intertwined, just as the mind and body interact.
12. Although we might not always choose our emotions, we can regulate their intensity.

DISCUSSION QUESTIONS AND PROBLEMS

1. Differentiate the following terms/concepts/individuals:

   a. IQ and EQ
   b. Mood and emotion
   c. Human brain and the brain of other animals
   d. Phineas Gage and Elliot

2. You are considering managing your own money rather than trusting in an investment advisor. Some argue that emotional intelligence may be just as important as investment knowledge. Do you agree? Discuss.

3. Imagine you just won a lottery with a $10 million prize. What primary emotions might you feel? (Note that the seven primary emotions generally include anger, contempt, disgust, fear, happiness, sadness, and surprise.) Describe their features, including the six used to define an emotion. Be sure to include observables.

4. Your colleague argues that emotion and reasoning are completely separate influences on decision-making. Do you agree? Discuss.

5. Put yourself in the place of an equity mutual fund manager. Think of all the stocks you might select for inclusion in the portfolio. How would emotions enhance your decision-making process?

ENDNOTES

1 Elster, J., 1998, "Emotions and economic theory," *Journal of Economic Literature* 36 (1), 47–74.

2 The structure of this bipolar scale is disputed by psychologists. For example, some argue that positive and negative feelings are reciprocal, so an increase in positivity is a decrease in negativity. See Russell, J. A., 1979, "Affective space is bipolar," *Journal of Personality and Social Psychology* 37, 345–356. Others, however, argue that positive and negative feelings are independent factors. See Diener, E. and R. A. Emmons, "The independence of positive and negative affect," *Journal of Personality and Social Psychology* 47, 1105–1117. Despite the continued debate over the structure of experiences, the bipolar characterization is generally accepted.

3 Frijda, N. H., 1986, *The Emotions* (Cambridge University Press, Cambridge).

4 In Chapters 11 and 12 we will consider social forces in depth.

5 Seligman, M. E. P., and M. Csikszentmihalyi, 2000, "Positive psychology: An introduction," *American Psychologist* 55, 5–14.

6 Frijda, N. H., 2000, "The psychologists' point of view," in M. Lewis, and J. M. Haviland-Jones, eds., *Handbook of Emotions* (Guilford Press, New York).

7 James, W., 1884, "What is an emotion?" *Mind* 9, 188–205.

8 Ibid., p. 190.

9 Cannon, W. B., 1927, "The James-Lange theory of emotions: A critical examination and alternative theory," *American Journal of Psychology* 39, 106–124.

10 LeDoux, J., 1996, *The Emotional Brain* (Simon and Schuster, New York).

11 Schachter, S., and J. E. Singer, 1962, "Cognitive, social, and physiological determinants of emotional state," *Psychological Review* 69, 379–399; and Schachter, S., and J. E. Singer, 1979, "Comments on the Maslach and Marshall-Zimbardo experiments," *Journal of Personality and Social Psychology* 17, 989–995.

12 Zajonc, R., 1980, "Feeling and thinking: Preferences need no inferences," *American Psychologist* 35, 151–175.

13 Darwin, C., 1859, *The Origin of Species by Means of Natural Selection; Or, the Preservation of Favored Races in the Struggle for Life* (Collier, New York).

14 Darwin, C., 1872, *The Expression of the Emotions in Man and Animals*, (University of Chicago Press, Chicago).

15 Plutchik, R., 1980, *Emotion: A Psychoevolutionary Synthesis* (Harper and Row, New York).

16 See Goleman, D., 2006, *Social Intelligence* (Bantam Books, New York), for a good review.

17 Dimburg, U., and M. Thunberg, 2000, "Rapid facial reactions to emotional facial expression," *Scandinavian Journal of Psychology* 39, 39–46.

18 Hasson, U., Y. Nir, I. Levy, G. Fuhrmann, and R. Malach, 2004, "Intersubject synchronization of cortical activity during natural vision," *Science* 303(5664), 1634–1640.

19 Butler, E. A., B. Egloff, F. H. Wilhelm, N. C. Smith, E. A. Erickson, and J. J. Gross, 2003, "The social consequences of expressive suppression," *Emotion* 3, 48–67.

20 Weiten, W., 2005, *Psychology: Themes and Variations*, 6th ed. (Wadsworth/Thomson Learning, Belmont, California).

21 Ekman, P., et al., 1987, "Universal and cultural differences in the judgments of facial expressions of emotion," *Journal of Personality and Social Psychology* 53(4), 712–717.

22 According to Elster, J., 1998, "Emotions and economic theory," *Journal of Economic Literature* 36(1), 47–74, the seven primary emotions include anger, contempt, disgust, fear, happiness, sadness, and surprise.

23 As we will discuss elsewhere in the book, fMRI technology is now being used to provide insight into economic and financial decision-making.

24 Damasio, A. R., 1994, *Descartes' Error: Emotion, Reason, and the Human Brain* (Putnam, New York).

25 Gilbert, D., 2006, *Stumbling on Happiness* (Knopf Canada, Toronto).

26 See Damasio, A. R., 1994, *Descartes' Error: Emotion, Reason, and the Human Brain* (Putnam, New York); and LeDoux, J., 1996, *The Emotional Brain: The Mysterious Underpinnings of Emotional Life* (Simon & Schuster, New York).

27 For additional discussion of emotion and decision-making, see Elster, J., 1998, "Emotions and economic theory," *Journal of Economic Literature* 36(1), 47–74; and Hermalin, B., and A. M. Isen, 2000, "The effect of affect on economic and strategic decision making," Johnson Graduate School of Management, Working paper.

28 Rolls, E. T., 1980, *The Brain and Emotion* (Oxford University, Oxford).

29 For a good review of emotional intelligence, see Goleman, D., 1995, *Emotional Intelligence* (Bantam, New York). It is possible to argue that EQ is as important as (financial) IQ when it comes to the decision whether one is better off managing one's money or enlisting the (costly) aid of experts. See Deaves, R., 2006, *What Kind of an Investor Are You?* (Insomniac Press, Toronto, Canada.)

30 For additional discussion of how psychologists and economists think about emotion and decision-making, see Ackert, L. F., B. K. Church, and R. Deaves, 2003, "Emotion and financial markets," *Federal Reserve Bank of Atlanta Economic Review*, Second Quarter, 33–41.

31 See Frank, R. H., 1988, *Passions within Reason* (Norton, New York); and LeDoux, J., 1996, *The Emotional Brain: The Mysterious Underpinnings of Emotional Life* (Simon & Schuster, New York).

32 Wade, C., and C. Tavris, 2006, *Psychology*, 8th ed. (Pearson Prentice Hall, Upper Saddle River, New Jersey).

33 The bear picture is an original drawing by Moira M. Church.

34 The pictures are original drawings by Moira M. Church.

INVESTOR BEHAVIOR

PART III

CHAPTER 8   Implications of Heuristics and Biases
             for Financial Decision-Making

CHAPTER 9   Implications of Overconfidence
             for Financial Decision-Making

CHAPTER 10   Individual Investors and the Force of Emotion

IMPLICATIONS OF HEURISTICS AND BIASES FOR FINANCIAL DECISION-MAKING

8.1 INTRODUCTION

As we saw in Chapter 5, while heuristics are usually excellent time- and effort-saving decision-making mechanisms, they sometimes appear to lead investors in unfortunate directions. In this and later chapters, we return to these heuristics when we investigate their potential impact on the behavior of investors, future retirees, analysts, and managers, and how they may potentially impact market outcomes. The focus of this chapter is how heuristics influence investor financial decision-making, with the investment decisions of future retirees reserved for Chapter 17.

Section 8.2 deals with financial behaviors stemming from familiarity. One aspect of familiarity is home bias, the tendency to overinvest domestically and locally. While investment close to home can stem from an informational advantage, this is probably not the whole answer. Related to home bias is the tendency to invest in companies you work for or brands you know. In Section 8.3, we turn to behaviors stemming from representativeness and related biases. The tendency to overestimate predictability likely induces investors to believe that good companies are good investments. This, coupled with recency, persuades people to believe that good recent stock market performers are good buys. And the availability bias pushes people into concentrating on investments in securities for which information is freely available. In Section 8.4, we show that anchoring causes people to be excessively influenced by suggested or available cues, instead of relying on their own opinion or expertise. This is demonstrated in the context of expert views of real estate value.

8.2   FINANCIAL BEHAVIORS STEMMING FROM FAMILIARITY

Home Bias

Though preferences are slowly changing in this regard, it continues to be true that domestic investors hold mostly domestic securities—that is, American investors hold mostly U.S. securities; Japanese investors hold mostly Japanese securities; British investors hold mostly U.K. securities; and so on. Kenneth French and James Poterba documented this tendency.[1] Referring to the first numerical column of Table 8.1, we see displayed the aggregate market values of the six biggest stock markets in the world. The United States, as of 1989, had 47.8% of world market capitalization, Japan 26.5%, the U.K. 13.8%, France 4.3%, Germany 3.8%, and Canada 3.8%.[2] Nevertheless, a typical U.S. investor held 93.8% in U.S. stocks; a typical Japanese investor held 98.1% in Japanese stocks; and a typical U.K. investor held 82.0% in U.K. stocks.[3] Thus, domestic investors overweight domestic stocks. This behavior is called **home bias**.

Bias toward the home country flies in the face of evidence indicating that diversifying internationally allows investors to reduce risk without surrendering return.[4] This is particularly true since stock markets in different countries are not highly correlated.[5] The average pairwise correlation coefficient for the countries listed in the previous paragraph during 1975–1989 was 0.502, which attests to the gains from diversification.

One reason why investors might hold more domestic securities is because they are optimistic about their markets relative to foreign markets. Using an expected utility maximization approach and historical correlations between markets, French and Poterba estimated what expected returns would have to be in order to justify the observed asset allocation, and Table 8.2 reports their results. To justify their overweighted U.S. holdings, American investors would have to believe that their market would beat the second-best market (Canada) by 80 basis points; Japanese investors would have to believe their market would outperform by at least 280 basis points; and in the United Kingdom, the comparable figure was a whopping 430 basis points. Obviously this set of beliefs is contradictory and implies excessive

TABLE 8.1 | Estimated Country Weights (%) among International Investors

	Market value weights	U.S. investors	Japanese investors	U.K. investors
U.S.	47.8	93.8	1.3	5.9
Japan	26.5	3.1	98.1	4.8
U.K.	13.8	1.1	0.2	82.0
France	4.3	0.5	0.1	3.2
Germany	3.8	0.5	0.1	3.5
Canada	3.8	0.1	0.1	0.6

Source: French, K. R., and J. M. Poterba, 1991, "Investor diversification and international equity markets," *American Economic Review* 81, 222–226.

TABLE 8.2	EXPECTED RETURNS (%) IMPLIED BY ACTUAL PORTFOLIO HOLDINGS		
	U.S. investors	Japanese investors	U.K. investors
U.S.	5.5	3.1	4.4
Japan	3.2	6.6	3.8
U.K.	4.5	3.8	9.6
France	4.3	3.4	5.3
Germany	3.6	3.0	4.8
Canada	4.7	3.0	4.0

Source: French, K. R., and J. M. Poterba, 1991, "Investor diversification and international equity markets," *American Economic Review* 81, 222–226.

optimism—at least on the part of two of the three sets of investors. The next chapter will focus on excessive optimism in financial decision-making.

Another behavioral explanation is along the lines of comfort-seeking and familiarity. As we discussed in Chapter 5, people tend to favor that which is familiar. U.S. investors are more familiar with U.S. stocks and markets, and so they are more comfortable investing in U.S. securities. The same holds equally for foreign investors.[6]

As is so often true where behavioral explanations have been advanced to explain apparently anomalous behavior, rational explanations are also put forward. International investment may be less attractive because of institutional barriers, examples of which are capital movement restrictions, differential trading costs, and differential tax rates. French and Poterba downplay these arguments, however. While at one time there were significant capital movement restrictions, at the time of their work, they were not in effect. As for differential trading costs, if costs in one country are lower than in other countries, this is a reason for *all* investors to favor the low-cost country, but we do not see this type of behavior. Additionally, especially with the international system of dividend withholding taxes and counterbalancing tax credits, there is little difference between domestic and foreign tax burdens for most investors.

DISTANCE, CULTURE, AND LANGUAGE

The argument that institutional considerations cause investors to shy away from foreign investments becomes weak if it can be demonstrated that people prefer to invest locally, even within their own country. Gur Huberman reports on a case of such "intra-national" home bias."[7] In 1984, AT&T was forced by the court into a divestiture whereby seven "Baby Bells" were created. These companies were created along regional lines. An example is BellSouth serving the southeastern United States. If people like familiarity, then we would expect a disproportionate number of a Baby Bell's customers to hold a disproportionate number of shares in the same Baby Bell. Indeed, that is exactly what happened after the divestiture. While we often hear that we should buy locally, from a diversification standpoint, if anything, you are wise to *underweight* (not overweight) local companies. If the economy of your region fares poorly, this will be bad both for the stock market performance of local companies and the employment prospects of local workers (yourself included). If you work and invest locally, technically speaking, your two income sources are highly correlated. Diversification theory says you should look for income streams that are weakly correlated. For this reason, it would have been better for investors to buy stock in Baby Bells *outside* their region.

In a related study, Mark Grinblatt and Matti Keloharju demonstrate that the preference for familiarity extends to language and culture.[8] In Finland, there are two official languages, Finnish and Swedish.[9] Annual reports are normally published in Finnish or in both official languages, but in a few cases reports are only published in Swedish. It turns out that, after controlling for other relevant factors, Finnish investors prefer companies whose language of publication is Finnish, and Swedish investors prefer companies whose language is Swedish—with bilingual companies being mid-ranked by both groups of investors. Interestingly, culture matters as well. These authors took note of whether CEOs were Finnish or Swedish. Controlling for the language of the company, Finnish speakers prefer Finnish CEOs, and Swedish speakers prefer Swedish CEOs. The lesson seems clear: familiarity, on all levels, "breeds" investment.[10] Moreover, there is evidence that even institutional investors may not be immune from this tendency.[11]

LOCAL INVESTING AND INFORMATIONAL ADVANTAGES

One reason why investors may favor local markets—where local is interpreted as either domestic or close-to-home, but within the same country—is because they may possess, or may feel that they possess, **informational advantages**. Gains from being geographically close to a company may appear in improved monitoring capability and access to private information. Joshua Coval and Tobias Moskowitz investigated this issue in the context of mutual fund managerial performance.[12] They first established that mutual fund managers, consistent with familiarity bias, tend to favor local investments, that is, they tend to buy firms headquartered within a 100-mile (or 161-kilometer) radius of their head office. Specifically, they conclude that the average manager invests in companies that are located about 10% closer to her than the average firm she could have held. Further, local equity preference is related to firm size, leverage and output tradability, with small, levered firms producing goods that are not traded internationally tending to be the ones where local preference comes through strongest.

Consider rational motivations for investing locally. One is hedging demand. If you consume local goods at local prices, it can make sense to hedge by investing locally. If locally produced goods are not traded outside the local region, then it is reasonable to talk about local prices. Take haircuts, which are as non-tradable as one gets.[13] If you buy the stock of a local haircutting company, your future haircut consumption, which must be local, is well hedged. The finding that local equity preference is more pronounced among companies whose goods are not traded internationally is consistent with hedging demand.

Size and leverage, on the other hand, suggest an information differential explanation, as smaller, levered firms are likely to be ones for which local informational advantage may be stronger. To test this, Coval and Moskowitz investigate whether local preference can generate a boost to performance. As has been discussed previously, most studies indicate that the average actively managed mutual fund has been unable to consistently outperform its benchmark on a risk-adjusted basis.[14] Notably though, Coval and Moskowitz demonstrate a significant payoff to local investing. Fund managers on average earn 2.67% per year more on local investments, while local stocks avoided by managers underperform by 3% per year. Moreover, they find that those better able to select local stocks tend to concentrate their holdings more locally. Are retail investors also able to exploit this? The evidence points in this direction as stocks with high levels of local ownership tend to outperform, and this effect lasts for several months, suggesting those with access to such data could earn excess returns. In other research, there is evidence that retail investors take advantage of the opportunity.[15] Reminiscent of the money manager finding, based on a dataset of retail investors, local investments outperform remote investments by 3.2% per year.

INVESTING IN YOUR EMPLOYER OR BRANDS THAT YOU KNOW

There is also abundant evidence that investors overweight the stocks of companies whose brands are familiar or that they work for. As for the first, Laura Frieder and Avanidhar Subrahmanyam looked at survey data on perceived brand quality and brand familiarity (recognition) and asked whether these attributes impacted investor preferences.[16] To answer this question, they correlated institutional holdings with these factors. Note that high institutional holding in a stock implies low retail holding in that same stock. These researchers found that institutional holdings are significantly and negatively related to brand recognition, but no discernible impact was present for brand quality. The former implies that retail investors have a higher demand for firms with brand recognition, which is consistent with comfort-seeking and familiarity.

Still, Frieder and Subrahmanyam argue that recognizable brands are associated with companies with more readily accessible information for average investors. They provide a model that shows that investors will, ceteris paribus, demand more of a stock when they have more precise information about the stock. Therefore, in this context as in others, a natural informational advantage may stem from familiarity.

As for overweighting companies that one works for, while the same sort of familiarity versus informational advantage debate is possible, the extent to which some investors invest in these companies seems to transcend an informational explanation. Many "employee-investors" put a very high percentage of their investible wealth in their employer's stock, thus foregoing a significant amount of possible diversification.[17] This will be discussed in more detail in Chapter 17.

8.3   FINANCIAL BEHAVIORS STEMMING FROM REPRESENTATIVENESS

There is evidence that representativeness and related biases induce inappropriate investment decisions. To casual observers it seems obvious that if a company has high-quality management, a strong image, and consistent growth in earnings, it must be a good investment. Students of finance, of course, know better. In valuation, future cash flows are forecasted and discounted back to the present using an appropriate risk-adjusted discount rate. All the aforementioned attributes that make a company a good company should theoretically be reflected in these estimates of future cash flows (including the growth in cash flows) and the risk-adjusted discount rate—that is, they should already be impounded in price. Loosely speaking, good companies will sell at high prices, and bad companies will sell at low prices. But, once the market has adjusted, there is no reason to favor a good company over a bad company, or, for that matter, a bad company over a good company. Quite simply, it is a mistake to think that a good company is representative of a good investment, and yet, that is exactly what people often seem to believe. Further, according to market efficiency, excess returns should be unpredictable. Nevertheless, as we have noted, there is a tendency to overestimate predictability. In this context then, there may be a tendency to associate past success (which led to high *past* returns) with likely future returns.

GOOD COMPANIES VS. GOOD INVESTMENTS

Hersh Shefrin and Meir Statman provide some very revealing evidence.[18] As they report, *Fortune* magazine has been surveying senior executives on company attributes for a number of years.[19] Executives are asked to assign values between "0" (poor) and "10" (excellent) to each company in their industry for the following items: quality of management; quality of products/services; innovativeness; long-term investment value; financial soundness; ability to attract, develop, and keep talented people; responsibility to the community and environment; and wise use of corporate assets. While *Fortune* reports average scores on all attributes as a proxy for company quality, because 82% of respondents consider quality of management as the most important attribute of a company's quality, these researchers use it as their proxy for company quality.

In Table 8.3 we report some regressions from Shefrin and Statman. From the first panel, we see that management quality (i.e., good company measure) and value as a long-term investment (i.e., good stock measure) are very highly correlated: the R^2 value from the first regression suggests a correlation (take the square root of R^2) of 0.93—that is, executives believe that good companies are good stocks. As discussed before, it is important to understand that no company attribute *should* be associated with investment value: all information on company quality should already be embedded in stock prices so that all companies (good ones and bad ones) are equally good investments (on an *ex ante* basis).

The bottom three regressions (i.e., those in the lower panel) reveal that two firm characteristics, size and the book-to-market ratio, are strongly associated with perceived management quality. Specifically, big companies and those that have low book-to-market ratios (where the latter are considered growth companies) are seen to be good companies. This is not overly surprising. Big companies have often become big because they are good (i.e., well managed), and growth should come from quality.

Turn to the last regression in the upper panel. In this regression, value as a long-term investment is regressed on size, book-to-market, and management quality. As before, the latter strongly impacts perceived investment value. Additionally,

TABLE 8.3 | INVESTMENT VALUE AND MANAGEMENT QUALITY REGRESSIONS

Constant	Log(Size)	Log(B/M)	Management Quality	N	Adj. R^2
Dependent variable: Value as a long-term investment					
−0.79			1.03	311	0.86
(5.13)			(43.95)		
−0.86	0.15	−0.11	0.85	257	0.89
(4.48)	(7.53)	(2.63)	(31.69)		
Dependent variable: Management quality					
3.71	0.36			270	0.23
(11.32)	(9.02)				
6.16		−0.75		257	0.26
(79.02)		(9.46)			
4.64	0.21	−0.57		257	0.31
(13.72)	(4.60)	(6.60)			

Source: Shefrin, H., and M. Statman, 1995, "Making sense of beta, size, and book-to market," *Journal of Portfolio Management* 21(2), 26–34.

however, size and book-to-market, even after accounting for their impact on management quality, *independently* influence investment value. Big firms are viewed as good investments, and growth companies are viewed as good investments. In other words, big high-growth firms are representative of good investments. Interestingly, as was discussed in Chapter 4, the empirical evidence points in the exact opposite direction. It is small-cap value firms that have historically outperformed. Indeed, the tendency for individuals to use representativeness in this context may have contributed to the small-firm and value anomalies.[20]

In related research, there is evidence that firm image impacts the perception of investment attractiveness. As argued previously, while a positive firm image can only be seen as a good attribute, its ability to generate cash flows and growth should have already been capitalized in the price of the stock. In one experiment, disclosures related to image that are not value-relevant are released to participants.[21] Subjects are more likely to invest in firms with a positive image than those with a negative image, even controlling for such value-relevant attributes as industry membership and financial data.[22] If firm image has such impact, one might expect the same would be true for perception of brand quality. Nevertheless, in one previously discussed study, there was no evidence that perception of brand quality, once brand recognition was controlled for, led to retail investors increasing their demand for a stock.[23]

CHASING WINNERS

Research has also shown that investors choose securities and investment funds based on past performance. To those with this view, investment performance in the recent past is representative of future investment performance. This form of representativeness is often called recency. Such **trend-following**, or **momentum-chasing**, has long been a popular strategy, and, coupled with detecting turning points, is at the heart of technical analysis.[24] A survey of individuals from the *American Association of Individual Investors* reports that more people become bullish if the market has recently turned up.[25] In the context of mutual funds, strong past performance leads to abnormally high inflows of investor money.[26]

Trend-following is an international phenomenon. From Japan, the evidence is that stocks that experience increases in individual ownership were past winners.[27] In Canada, a survey of workers managing their own retirement money indicates they are momentum-chasers, rather than contrarians.[28] More specifically, respondents were asked to start their pensions from scratch and allocate money between two stocks, one with an "average return over the last 5 years of 5%," and a second with an "average return over the last 5 years of 15%." Further, they were told that "analysts forecast that both stocks should earn about 10% per year over the next 5 years." Those neutral on future direction would go 50/50 in order to maximize diversification. Momentum-chasers would put more than 50% in the second stock, while contrarians would put more than 50% of their money in the first stock. Figure 8.1 shows the frequency distribution of the percentage difference between investment in the "loser" stock and the "winner" stock. A high percentage of respondents (63.8%) were momentum-chasers, while far fewer (11.6%) were contrarians.

Shlomo Benartzi evaluates investment in company stock in 401(k)s in relation to momentum-chasing.[29] When he divides plans into quintiles based on company stock performance over the previous 10 years, he finds that employees of the top-performing companies contribute 40% of their discretionary money into company stock versus 10% for the bottom-performing quintile. Did momentum-chasing work for these investors? Unfortunately not, as in the year after portfolio formation employees who allocated the most to company stock earned 6.77% *less* than did those who allocated the least.

FIGURE 8.1 Frequency Distribution of Loser vs. Winner Stock Percentages among Canadian DC Investors

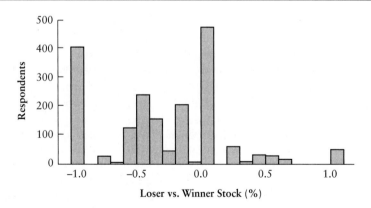

Source: Deaves, R., 2005, "Flawed self-directed retirement account decision-making and its implications," *Canadian Investment Review* (Spring), 6–15.

So is there any evidence in favor of the popular notion that momentum-chasing is profitable? The answer is both yes and no. There *is* evidence that risk-adjusted returns are positively serially correlated for 3- to 12-month return intervals.[30] For longer periods of three years or more (as in both the Benartzi paper and in the Canadian survey), the evidence favors reversals or negative serial correlation.[31] Later, in Chapter 13, we will present behavioral models that seek to account for this pattern of intermediate-term momentum followed by long-term reversal.

AVAILABILITY AND ATTENTION-GRABBING

In Chapter 5 we saw that when information on certain types of events is freely available, people often get the impression that such events are more likely. For example, news reports of violent crime may induce people to revise upward their subjective probabilities of such violent attacks. Brad Barber and Terrance Odean investigated whether information availability impacts the trading behavior of investors.[32] They argue that since attention is a scarce resource and there is a plethora of possible investment opportunities, the transactions of retail investors are likely to be concentrated in stocks where information is freely available. "Attention-grabbing" is proxied in three ways: news reports on a stock, unusually high trading volume, and extreme returns. The latter two factors control for impact since sometimes news might be neutral. While news can be of a positive or negative nature, since individual investors rarely short-sell and normally own only a small subset of stocks, negative news is likely to be ignored, while positive news may attract purchases. On this basis, these researchers suggest that news is likely to lead to net *purchases* for retail investors. On the other hand, institutional investors are much less likely to be so affected, because in their work they typically consider all the securities in their universe, without requiring any external prompt. Indeed, the empirical evidence is in line with the expectations of Barber and Odean.

8.4   ANCHORING TO AVAILABLE ECONOMIC CUES

In Chapter 5 we provided an example where experimental subjects, when asked to estimate an uncertain magnitude, anchored their estimates on obviously meaningless red herrings. Anchoring is even more likely to occur when the potential anchor appears prima facie to have economic content.

AN EXPERIMENTAL STUDY OF REAL ESTATE APPRAISALS

Gregory Northcraft and Margaret Neale investigated whether anchoring might occur in the context of real estate appraisals.[33] Two randomly selected groups of real estate agents were taken to a house and asked to appraise it. They were given the same tour and identical packages of information, which included the house's (purported) list price. The only difference between the two groups was that the first group was given a list price of $65,900, while the second group was given a list price of $83,900—$18,000 more. Put yourself in the place of the agents. There is always some uncertainty in an appraisal. While you can exclusively use your own expertise and totally ignore the list price, perhaps it should not be surprising that agents were influenced by the list price. Yet, list prices are quite variable and often have a strategic component.

The average appraisal price of the first group came in at $67,811, and that of the second group was $75,190. These dollar figures are summarized in Table 8.4. If we take the mid-point of these values ($71,500.50) as our best estimate of the true appraisal value, the gaps between the two appraisal averages was a full 10%. Clearly, the real estate agents were anchored on the list prices that they were exposed to—despite the fact that only 25% mentioned the list price as one of the factors that they considered. One can think of the agents as using the following appraisal estimate mechanism:

8.1   *Appraisal estimate* = a * *Personal appraisal estimate* + (1 − a) * *List price*

Only those ignoring the list price would set $a = 1$. For the first group of real estate agents, it turned out that $a = .34$, suggesting that the list price was very influential; for the second group, $a = .70$. We can also calculate the appraisal price that sets a equal for the two groups. One can show that this is $69,136.43, at $a = .59$, still suggesting significant influence of the list price on the real estate agents' appraisals.

There is no reason to think that the tendency to anchor is not present in other economic and financial situations. The reality is that anchors in such contexts are likely to be common. All of us anchor on market prices. There is a rational side to this, though, because market prices are consensus estimates of value. But unfortunately this implies some circularity—if *everyone* is anchored on market price. Any initial value, however "off," would have an influence on the eventual market price. Consider the high valuations of Internet stocks in 1999. Quite a few observers had misgivings about their levels, but many were clever in their ability to justify them. Were they heavily influenced by the anchor of the current market price? Was this anchor "dropped" by the irrationality of a subset of traders who had little idea of fundamental value? In retrospect, this seems to be a valid view.

TABLE 8.4 | LIST PRICES AND APPRAISALS BY REAL ESTATE AGENTS

List prices and appraisals	Dollar figures
List price LOW	$65,900.00
Appraisal LOW	$67,811.00
Price	$71,500.50
Appraisal HIGH	$75,190.00
List price HIGH	$83,900.00

Source: Northcraft, G. B., and M. A. Neale, 1987, "Experts, amateurs and real estate: An anchoring-and-adjustment perspective on property pricing decisions," *Organizational Behavior and Human Decision Processes* 39, 84–97.

ANCHORING VS. HERDING AND ANALYSTS

Since anchoring and **herding** are closely related, it makes sense at this point to say a few words about herding. There is a social component to herding behavior, so we will mostly leave it to Chapter 12. In the real estate appraisal experiment, if an agent had been told that a second agent had come up with a certain appraisal, and the first agent's appraisal was pulled toward this value (even taking into account the influence of the list price), this would be an example of herding or following the crowd.

Professional financial analysts who publicly estimate value, forecast earnings, and make buy/sell recommendations, are often said to anchor or herd. Let us briefly consider whether analysts exhibit anchoring and/or herding behavior. One way in which anchoring can be exhibited by analysts is if they are slow to change their initial opinion. In Chapter 13 we argue that this behavior may be the source of certain anomalies. Analysts may herd if some analysts are influenced by the recommendations or earnings estimates of other analysts. There is research indicating that analysts go with the crowd when it comes to recommendation revisions.[34] The evidence for earnings estimates is more mixed, with some of it pointing in the direction of herding and other research suggesting "anti-herding" (i.e., running contrary to the crowd).[35] For example, a recent study using U.K. data on earnings forecasts is consistent with herding behavior, while another, using German data, is consistent with anti-herding behavior.[36] Note that while herding makes sense because going with the crowd is easy and safe, anti-herding can make sense if you believe you have private information and you *want* to make yourself visible for the purpose of career advancement.

CHAPTER HIGHLIGHTS

1. There is a preference for investing close to home. This manifests itself in home-country bias, investing locally within the domestic market, and preferring one's own language and culture.
2. One explanation for home bias is the comfort-seeking associated with familiarity.
3. Another explanation for home bias is informational advantage, a view reinforced by evidence on the efficacy of local investment on the part of money managers and retail investors.
4. Representativeness causes investors to think that good companies are good investments, whereas known positive characteristics should already be impounded in the price of a stock.
5. Because of recency, investors are prone to chasing winning stocks and funds. While there is some evidence of medium-term (3–12 months) momentum, in the longer-term (3–5 years), reversal is the order of the day.
6. Availability bias is evidenced when investors tend to buy stocks that are in the news.
7. Anchoring appears in research showing that real estate appraisals are anchored to list prices.

DISCUSSION QUESTIONS AND PROBLEMS

1. Differentiate the following terms/concepts:

   a. Good company and good stock
   b. Momentum-chaser and contrarian
   c. International diversification and domestic diversification
   d. Anchoring and herding

2. In a regression of perceived long-term investment value (LTIV) on size (S), book-to-market (B/M), and management quality (MQ), the following coefficients (all significant) were estimated:

$$LTIV = -.86 + .15\log(S) - .11\log(B/M) + .85MQ$$

   Discuss what can be learned from this regression (which appears in Shefrin, H., and M. Statman, 1995, "Making sense of beta, size, and book-to-market," *Journal of Portfolio Management* 21 (no. 2), 26–34).

3. Home bias has a potential information-based explanation. Discuss.

4. In Canada there are two official languages, French and English. Some Canadian corporations are headquartered in Quebec where French is the official language. Most, however, are headquartered outside Quebec where English is dominant. Would you expect Quebecers to invest more in Quebec companies, and non-Quebecers to invest more in companies based outside Quebec? Also, do you think the first language of the CEO might matter in accounting for investor preferences? Explain.

5. Anchors are ubiquitous in financial markets. Give some examples.

ENDNOTES

1 French, K. R., and J. M. Poterba, 1991, "Investor diversification and international equity markets," *American Economic Review* 81, 222–226.

2 In this context, the "world" is comprised of these six countries.

3 French and Poterba report that the domestic ownership share of the U.S. market was 92.2%; the domestic ownership share of the Japanese market was 95.7%; and the domestic ownership share of the U.K. market was 92.0%. See French, K. R., and J. M. Poterba, 1991, "Investor diversification and international equity markets," *American Economic Review* 81, 222–226.

4 See, for example, Solnik, B., 1974, "An equilibrium model of the international capital market," *Journal of Economic Theory* 8, 500–524.

5 Correlations between national markets have been rising as the world's economy becomes more integrated. Moreover, in times of rising global volatility, correlations rise. See Longin, F., and B. Solnik, 1995, "Is the correlation in international equity returns constant: 1960-1990?" *Journal of International Money and Finance* 14(1), 3–26; and Karolyi, G. A., and R. M. Stulz, 1996, "Why do markets move together? An investigation of U.S.-Japan stock return comovements," *Journal of Finance* 51(3), 951–986.

6 Experimental evidence corroborates the importance of familiarity in decision-making. Home bias may arise because individuals are more comfortable with domestic companies, regardless of differences in information or knowledge. See Ackert, L. F., B. K. Church, J. Tompkins, and P. Zhang, 2005, "What's in a name? An experimental examination of investment behavior," *Review of Finance* 9, 281–304; and Ackert, L. F., and B. K. Church, 2009,

"Home bias: Taking comfort in what you know?" *International Journal of Behavioural Accounting and Finance*, forthcoming.

7 Huberman, G., 2001, "Familiarity breeds investment," *Review of Financial Studies* 14, 659–680.

8 Grinblatt, M., and M. Keloharju, 2001, "How distance, language, and culture influence stockholdings and trades," *Journal of Finance* 56, 1053–1073.

9 While Finnish speakers make up 93% of the population versus 6% for Swedish speakers, Swedish speakers hold 23% of household shareowner wealth.

10 This play on words is from the title of Huberman, G., 2001, "Familiarity breeds investment," *Review of Financial Studies* 14, 659–680.

11 Visibility, proxied by media coverage (Falkenstein, E. G., 1996, "Preferences for stock characteristics as revealed by mutual fund portfolio holdings," *Journal of Finance* 51, 111–135) or analyst coverage (Ackert, L. F., and G. Athanassakos, 2001, "Visibility, institutional preferences and agency considerations," *Journal of Psychology and Financial Markets* 2(4), 201–209), leads to increased levels of institutional investment.

12 See Coval, J. D., and T. J. Moskowitz, 1999, "Home bias at home: Local equity preference in domestic portfolios," *Journal of Finance* 54, 145–166; and Coval, J. D., and T. J. Moskowitz, 2001, "The geography of investment: Informed trading and asset prices," *Journal of Political Economy* 109, 811–841.

13 One way to "import" haircuts is to have a haircut while traveling in a low-wage country.

14 See, for example, Malkiel, B. G., 1995, "Returns from investing in equity mutual funds 1971 to 1991," *Journal of Finance* 50, 549–572.

15 See Ivkovic, Z., and S. Weisbenner, 2005, "Local does as local is: Information content of the geography of individual investors'

common stock investments," *Journal of Finance* 60, 267–306.

16 Frieder, L., and A. Subrahmanyam, 2005, "Brand perceptions and the market for common stock," *Journal of Financial and Quantitative Analysis* 40, 57–85.

17 Benartzi, S., 2001, "Excessive extrapolation and the allocation of 401(k) accounts to company stock," *Journal of Finance* 56, 1747–1764.

18 Shefrin, H., and M. Statman, 1995, "Making sense of beta, size, and book-to-market," *Journal of Portfolio Management* 21(2), 26–34.

19 While we have said that we will look at the behavior of corporate managers later in the book, here we examine their views as *investors*.

20 Many would argue that this is true on a risk-adjusted basis, while others would counter that these factors are in fact risk factors (more on this debate later in the book).

21 Ackert, L. F., and B. K. Church, 2006, "Firm image and individual investment decisions," *Journal of Behavioral Finance* 7(3), 155–167.

22 Firm image is associated with positive affect, which is discussed in Chapter 10.

23 See Frieder, L., and A. Subrahmanyam, 2005, "Brand perceptions and the market for common stock," *Journal of Financial and Quantitative Analysis* 40, 57–85, for details.

24 See, for example, Covel, M., 2004. *Trend Following: How Great Traders Make Millions in Up and Down Markets* (Financial Times Prentice Hall, London, U.K.).

25 See De Bondt, W. F. M., 1998, "A portrait of the individual investor," *European Economic Review* 42, 831–844, for details.

26 See, for example, Sirri, E. R., and P. Tufano, 1998, "Costly search and mutual fund flows," *Journal of Finance* 53, 1589–1622.

27 Kim, K. A., and J. R. Nofsinger, 2002, "The behavior and performance of individual investors in Japan," Working paper.

28 These workers have "defined contribution" (DC) pensions. See Deaves, R., 2005, "Flawed self-directed retirement account decision-making and its implications," *Canadian Investment Review* (Spring), 6–15.

29 Benartzi, S., 2001, "Excessive extrapolation and the allocation of 401(k) accounts to company stock," *Journal of Finance* 56, 1747–1764.

30 Jegadeesh, N., and S. Titman, 1993, "Returns to buying winners and selling losers: Implications for stock market efficiency," *Journal of Finance* 48, 65–91. On long-term returns and the joint hypothesis problem, see Loughran, T., and J. R. Ritter, 2000, "Uniformly least powerful tests of market efficiency," *Journal of Financial Economics* 55, 361–389.

31 De Bondt, W. F. M., and R. Thaler, 1985, "Does the stock market overreact?" *Journal of Finance* 40, 793–807.

32 Barber, B., and T. Odean, 2008, "All that glitters: The effect of attention and news on the buying behavior of individual and institutional investors," *Review of Financial Studies* 21(2), 785–818.

33 Northcraft, G. B., and M. A. Neale, 1987, "Experts, amateurs and real estate: An anchoring-and-adjustment perspective on property pricing decisions," *Organizational Behavior and Human Decision Processes* 39, 84–97.

34 Welch, I., 2000, "Herding among security analysts," *Journal of Financial Economics* 58, 369–396; and Jegadeesh, N., and W. Kim, 2007, "Do analysts herd? An analysis of recommendations and market reactions," Working paper.

35 See, for example, Chen, Q., and W. Jiang, 2006, "Analysts' weighting of private and public information," *Review of Financial Studies* 19, 319–355.

36 De Bondt, W. F. M., and W. P. Forbes, 1999, "Herding in analyst earnings forecasts: Evidence from the United Kingdom," *European Financial Management* 5, 143–163; and Aretz, K., M. Naujoks, A. Kerl, and A. Walter, 2007, "Do German security analysts herd?" Working paper.

IMPLICATIONS OF OVERCONFIDENCE FOR FINANCIAL DECISION-MAKING

9.1 INTRODUCTION

As we saw in Chapter 5, overconfidence is pandemic in society. In this chapter, we address the extent to which this behavioral tendency impacts financial decision-making. As in the previous chapter, our focus will be on investors and other market practitioners. Later, in Chapter 16, we will consider how entrepreneurs and corporate managers might be affected. In Chapter 13, overconfidence will be seen to play a central role in models that seek to explain various market anomalies.

In Section 9.2, the various manifestations of overconfidence and excessive trading are related. We begin with a simple model illustrating the relationship between overconfidence and trading, and then move to evidence from naturally occurring markets, surveys, and experiments. We turn to the demographics and dynamics of overconfidence in a financial setting in Section 9.3. Some groups (e.g., men) tend to display greater overconfidence. Moreover, we investigate whether overconfidence can be "learned" by past experience in markets. In Section 9.4, evidence that relates overconfidence to underdiversification and excessive risk taking is explored. Finally, in Section 9.5, we briefly present evidence that analysts exhibit excessive optimism. This is likely due to more than psychology, as will be discussed in Chapter 12 when we revisit the financial behavior of this group of practitioners.

9.2 OVERCONFIDENCE AND EXCESSIVE TRADING

There is evidence that the overconfidence of investors leads to excessive trading. Theoretical models have been constructed that yield this result. To illustrate the insights provided by these models, we begin with a simple illustrative model that relates overconfidence and trading activity.

OVERCONFIDENT TRADERS: A SIMPLE MODEL

Consider the demand for a particular security. At the level of the individual, demand will be a function of the investor's estimate of the security's (intrinsic) value. If the investor believes that the value exceeds the market price, he will wish to hold more of the security than if the security was perceived to be fairly priced. Let q_n equal the (neutral) number of shares that an investor would hold if price and value were equivalent.[1] If the value exceeds the price, the investor will want to hold more than q_n shares. On the other hand, if value falls short of price, the investor will want to hold less than q_n shares.

The difference between investors is that they respond differently to prices that deviate from their value estimates. In order to understand how different prices affect desired holdings, we begin with a mechanism for value estimation. First assume that since there are many investors, all are price-takers.[2] Further, we will assume that when estimating value, an investor uses two items of information, his own opinion (prior value) and the market price (which is the weighted average of all investors' opinions), as follows:

9.1
$$v_i = a_i v_i^* + (1 - a_i)\, p, \quad 0 \le a_i \le 1$$

where v_i is the (posterior) estimate of value of investor i; v_i^* is the same investor's prior estimate of value; p is the market price; and a_i is the weight investor i puts on his prior relative to the market price. The higher a_i is, the higher is the weight an investor puts on his own opinion. Since there is a very large number of investor views determining p, any value of a_i more than slightly above zero suggests some overconfidence, with higher values suggesting more overconfidence than lower values. Here, by *overconfident* we primarily mean miscalibrated, which implies an inflated view of the precision of one's information (or opinion). The better-than-average effect, here the feeling that one is better at estimating value than other market participants, also likely plays a role.

Consider how 9.1 feeds into demand for the stock. Suppose that the demand curve can be written as:

9.2
$$q_i = q_n + \theta(v_i - p), \quad \theta > 0$$

where q_i is investor i's demand and θ is the sensitivity of demand to a divergence between the posterior value estimate and price.[3] Substitute 9.1 into 9.2 and simplify to arrive at:

9.3
$$q_i = q_n + \theta a_i (v_i^* - p)$$

Next take the partial derivative of q_i with respect to p:

9.4
$$\partial q_i / \partial p = -\theta a_i$$

The higher the investor's level of overconfidence (a_i), the more responsive demand is to changes in price. As a_i approaches one, which means market price has no influence, the closer $\partial q_i/\partial p$ is to $-\theta$. On the other hand, as a_i moves toward zero, the demand changes little when the price changes.

It is conventional to write demand curves with p on the y-axis and q on the x-axis. Using this approach, the higher the investor's level of overconfidence (a_i) is, the *flatter* is the demand curve. And as a_i moves toward zero, the demand curve becomes close to *vertical*. Figure 9.1 illustrates graphically the situation for three investors. On this graph, their demand curves for a given security are depicted. These are labeled $D1_{PC}$, $D2_{LOC}$, and $D3_{HOC}$, where "PC" refers to "proper calibration," "LOC" refers to "low overconfidence," and "HOC" refers to "high overconfidence." As has been discussed, a more overconfident investor in this context is one who more strongly believes in his ability to appropriately value the security. The three investors are similar in some respects. They all analyze the security in question and arrive at the same prior value estimate, which is designated as in the v_0 graph. For this reason the equilibrium price (and all posterior value estimates) is also equal to v_0. This is why the three individual demand curves intersect at (q_n, v_0).

One investor (the one whose demand curve is $D1_{PC}$) has a vertical demand curve. For him, $a_1 = 0$. The other two investors have negatively sloped demand curves, implying that lower prices increase demand, and higher prices decrease demand. For both investors, a_i is positive, but note that $a_3 > a_2$. While the second investor pays some attention to her own opinion, the third investor pays the most attention to his own opinion. Since Investor 3 is more influenced by prior value-price discrepancies than is Investor 2, Investor 3 is relatively more overconfident. Investor 3 puts less weight on the market price and more credence in his own prior estimate. Thus, when the market price increases, he responds by adjusting demand further down relative to Investor 2. Similarly, when the market price adjusts

---

FIGURE 9.1 Demand for a Security as a Function of Overconfidence

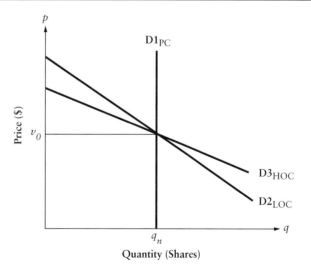

down, Investor 3 responds more strongly than Investor 2 by demanding relatively more shares.

Let us use this framework to elucidate the role of overconfidence on trading and volatility. To do so, we will assume that there are 300 shares outstanding ($Q = 300$). For this illustration, we will assume that the demand curves of the three investors are as follows:

9.5 $\qquad\qquad\qquad q_1 = 100\ (Investor\ 1)$

9.6 $\qquad\qquad\qquad p = 20 - 0.1 * q_2\ (Investor\ 2)$

9.7 $\qquad\qquad\qquad p = 15 - 0.05 * q_3\ (Investor\ 3)$

Notice that the more overconfident trader has a flatter, more price-responsive demand curve (i.e., the slope for 9.6 is less than the slope for 9.7). Figure 9.2 shows the aggregate supply and aggregate demand curves on a single graph. The aggregate supply for shares is 300. The aggregate demand curve is a horizontal summation of all individual investors' demand curves. At $20 or more, Investor 1 demands 100 shares and no other investors express interest; between $20 and $15, Investor 1 continues to demand 100 shares and Investor 2 now demands a positive amount that declines with price; at lower prices, all investors have positive demands. Aggregate supply and aggregate demand intersect at $10, which is where $v_o = p$ and $q_n = q_1 = q_2 = q_3 = 100$.

Periodically, investors reassess their prior value estimates. Many will do so when material news arrives. To keep this example simple, let's suppose that one

---

FIGURE 9.2 Aggregate Demand and Aggregate Supply

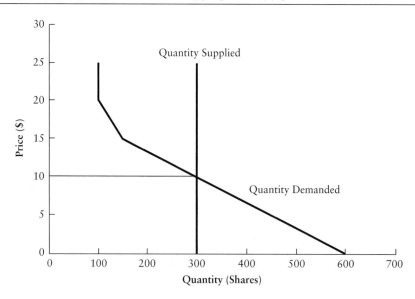

investor alters her value estimate after a thorough (second) analysis of the stock. Specifically, suppose Investor 2 believes that the security has become more valuable. We operationalize this by a $5 parallel shift in the demand curve of Investor 2. The new demand curve for this investor is:

9.8 $p = 25 - 0.1 * q_2$ (*Investor 2 – Scenario 1*)

Note that we call the environment as specified Scenario 1. Figure 9.3 shows how the aggregate demand curve looks after this revision. Not surprisingly, the aggregate demand curve has shifted up. The new equilibrium price is $11.67. This illustrates that price is a weighted average of the three value estimates—while the other two investors still believe the stock should sell for $10, the third thinks $15 is right.

To investigate the role of overconfidence, we will alter the situation again by increasing the overconfidence level of one of the traders (while returning to the initial situation where for all traders $v_0 = 10), thus generating Scenario 2. We do so as follows:

9.9 $p = 15 - 0.05 * q_2$ (*Investor 2 – Scenario 2*)

Investor 2 now has the same demand curve as Investor 3, which implies that they both now have the same (high) level of overconfidence. Figure 9.4 illustrates that the initial equilibrium price, $10, is the same as before, since all investors still initially believe that the value of the security is $10.

FIGURE 9.3 Market Equilibrium after Value Revision (Scenario 1)

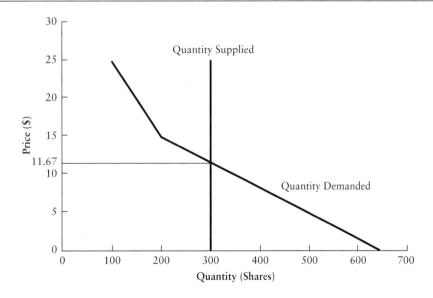

FIGURE 9.4 Aggregate Demand and Aggregate Supply (Scenario 2)

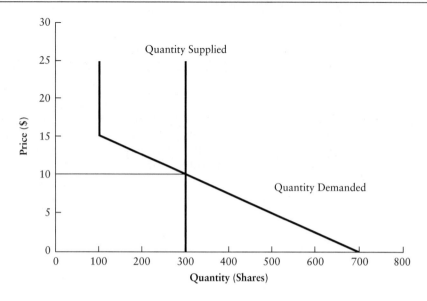

The difference, though, is apparent if we consider Scenario 3, which combines Scenarios 1 and 2 in the sense that Investor 2 is both more overconfident than before and she also increases her estimate of value by $5. Her new demand curve is:

9.10 $$p = 20 - 0.05 * q_2 \ (\textit{Investor 2 – Scenario 3})$$

Figure 9.5 shows that, once again, not surprisingly, the price rises, this time to $12.50. Note that the price rise is higher than before since the investor with the extreme view, being more overconfident than before, is more willing to trust her opinion and transact on this basis. The price is still a weighted average of the three value estimates, but the investor with the extreme view exerts a greater influence on it because of her willingness to trade more.

It is straightforward to show that a value revision in the negative direction will work the same but in reverse. The first lesson is that volatility increases with overconfidence. The same value revision led to a greater price change when one of the traders was more overconfident.

The second lesson is that overconfidence induces greater trading activity—as well as higher levels of volume at the level of the market. Assuming that all investors begin with 100 shares (the initial situation), in Scenario 1, Investor 2, who has become more optimistic, increases her holding to 133.33 shares. This is accommodated by a 33.33 sale by Investor 3. Contrast that to Scenario 3. In this case, Investor 2 increases her holding to 150 shares, for a net purchase of 50 shares. This is accommodated by a 50 share sale by Investor 3. Thus higher overconfidence is associated with more trading.

While this example is merely suggestive, it is consistent with rigorous theoretical models. For example, Terrance Odean formulates a model where investors

FIGURE 9.5 Market Equilibrium after Value Revision (Scenario 3)

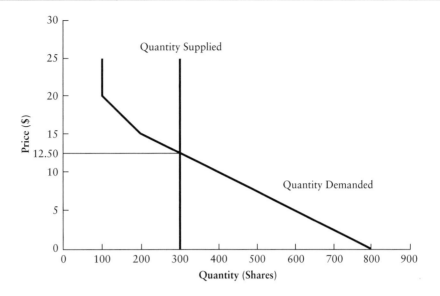

receive noisy signals on the future value of a stock.[4] While investors realize their information and opinions are imperfect, they believe them to be more precise than they really are. In other words, they are overconfident in the sense of being miscalibrated. Several predictions are derived from Odean's model. Consistent with the overconfidence example presented here, it is demonstrated that: 1) expected trading volume increases as overconfidence increases; and 2) price volatility increases with overconfidence. Several other notable results emerge as well: 3) overconfidence worsens the quality of prices, which means they are less likely to be accurate estimates of value; and 4) overconfident traders have lower expected utility than do those who are properly calibrated. The third prediction follows from the fact that divergent views sometimes receive a lot of weight if the trader in question is well-capitalized and egregiously overconfident. The fourth follows from the fact that investors take on excess risk relative to those who are well calibrated.

EVIDENCE FROM THE FIELD

Are these predictions corroborated by evidence from the field? Brad Barber and Terrance Odean investigated the performance of individual investors by examining the trading histories of more than 60,000 U.S. discount brokerage investors between 1991 and 1996.[5] Their goal was to see if the trades of these investors were justified in the sense that they led to improvements in portfolio performance. Think about why a market transaction would make sense. Suppose, for example, you sell one stock and use the proceeds to buy another, and in doing so incur $200 in transaction costs. This transaction is only logical if you expect to generate a higher portfolio return—high enough to at least offset the transaction cost. To be sure, individual investors do a lot of trading. In their study, Barber and Odean found that, on average, investors turn over 75% of their portfolios annually. This means that, for a typical investor who holds a $100,000 portfolio, in a given year she trades $75,000 worth of stock.

Barber and Odean divided their sample of individual investors into five equal groups (quintiles), where the groups were formed on the basis of portfolio turnover. Specifically, the 20% of investors who traded the least were assigned to the lowest turnover quintile (no. 1), the 20% of investors who traded the next least were assigned to quintile 2, and so on—all the way to quintile 5, which was reserved for those investors trading the most. To put all this into perspective, those trading the least only turned over 0.19% of their portfolio per month—less than 3% per year. Those trading the most turned over 21.49% of their portfolio per month—more than 300% per year. Referring to Figure 9.6, we see for each quintile the gross average monthly return and the net (after transaction costs) average monthly return. The returns for all quintiles (both gross and net) were fairly high during this period (even for those trading excessively) because the overall stock market was performing quite well.

Was all this trading worthwhile? Was it based on superior information, or was it based on the *perception* of superior information (i.e., misinformation)? An inspection of the figure reveals that while the additional trading did lead to a very slight improvement in gross performance, net performance suffered. In other words, most of the trading was not helpful. The evidence reported by Barber and Odean suggests that the trades were not based on superior information, but rather were often conducted because of misinformation. While it is impossible to prove without a doubt that overconfidence was the culprit, this view appears to be a reasonable one.

FIGURE 9.6 Gross and Net Returns for Groups with Different Trading Intensities

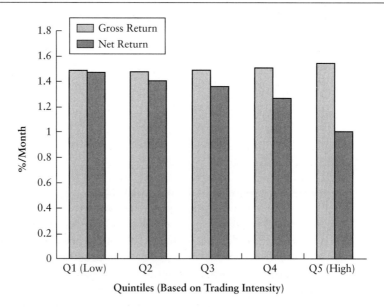

Source: Barber, B., and T. Odean, 2000, "Trading is hazardous to your wealth: The common stock investment performance of individual investors," *Journal of Finance* 55, 773–806.

While Figure 9.6 is in terms of raw returns, sometimes returns are high because greater risk is taken and investors are merely being properly rewarded for the risk borne. If an investor earns high average returns only because high risk has been borne, this does not imply any sort of stock-picking skill. After risk-adjusting returns, Barber and Odean found that their results were quite similar to those displayed in Figure 9.6. For all investors, the net risk-adjusted annual return (after taking into account transaction costs, bid-ask spreads, and differential risk) was below the market return by well over 3.00%. The 20% of investors who traded the most underperformed the market (again on a net risk-adjusted basis) by about 10% per year.

EVIDENCE FROM SURVEYS AND THE LAB

While the previous study by Barber and Odean is an important one, it does have one unavoidable drawback. It is difficult to unambiguously explore the potential nexus between overconfidence and trading activity using market data, since normally no psychometric data on individuals (or markets) exist.

New research seeks to overcome this problem. For example, Markus Glaser and Martin Weber combined naturally occurring data with information elicited from a survey.[6] Using trading data from online brokerage accounts and psychometric data obtained from the same group of investors who responded to an online questionnaire, they correlate various measures of trading activity with a number of metrics of overconfidence. While there was solid evidence that those who are most subject to the better-than-average effect trade more, there was little such corresponding evidence for those who were most overconfident based on calibration tests.[7]

In a similar vein, Mark Grinblatt and Matti Keloharju investigate whether trading activity, based on a comprehensive dataset of equity trading data in Finland, is related to overconfidence and **sensation seeking**.[8] Sensation seeking is a personality trait whose four dimensions are thrill and adventure seeking (i.e., a desire to engage in thrilling and even dangerous activities); experience seeking (i.e., the desire to have new and exciting experiences, even if illegal); disinhibition (i.e., behaviors associated with a loss of social inhibitions); and boredom susceptibility (i.e., dislike of repetition of experience).[9] We might reasonably expect those with a high degree of sensation seeking to be prone to excessive trading because of the novelty derived from the experience of the trade and new stock in their portfolio. In the Grinblatt-Keloharju paper sensation seeking is proxied by the number of speeding tickets obtained by an individual. Arguably, this only captures the thrill and adventure-seeking dimension of sensation seeking. A measure of overconfidence is obtained from a mandatory psychological profile given to all Finnish males upon entry into military service. While precise details are not publicly available, this overconfidence measure appears to be closest to the better-than-average effect. The authors conclude that trading activity is positively related to both overconfidence and sensation seeking in their sample.

In an experimental setting, Bruno Biais, Denis Hilton, Karine Mazurier and Sébastien Pouget considered the impact of two psychological traits, overconfidence, based on calibration tests, and **self-monitoring**, namely the disposition to attend to social cues and appropriately adjust behavior.[10] Both measures were taken prior to the participation of students in a series of trading sessions. They found that while overconfidence did not lead to a significant increase in trading intensity, it did serve to significantly reduce profits. High self-monitors, on the other hand, earned relatively greater trading profits.

In another experiment, researchers explored the relationship between trading activity (number of transactions) and their miscalibration-based proxy for overconfidence, the better-than-average effect, and illusion of control.[11] Their approach was novel in that their experimental design induced overconfident traders to believe that their signals were more informative than those of others. In previous experimental work, when private information was provided there was either no difference in signal quality or, when differences in quality existed, signals were randomly assigned. They took their cue from naturally occurring markets where many, through some form of analysis, habitually generate their own information.

Referring to Table 9.1, Specification (1), they found that both miscalibration and the better-than-average effect led to more trading. No significant effect was found for illusion of control. Specification (2) explored additional determinants of trading activity beyond overconfidence measures. Older subjects (p-value = 0.016) with more

Table 9.1	REGRESSIONS OF TRADING ACTIVITY ON OVERCONFIDENCE METRICS AND DEMOGRAPHIC VARIABLES	
Independent variable	Specification 1	Specification 2
Constant	−8.854 (0.509)	43.908 (0.026)
CBO	49.673 (0.008)	40.499 (0.023)
BTA	1.008 (0.027)	0.700 (0.164)
IoC	−2.611 (0.152)	
AGE		−1.818 (0.016)
EDUC		−0.794 (0.003)
EXP		16.454 (0.023)
Adjusted R^2	13.8% (9.5%)	27.5% (18.5%)

Source: Deaves, R., E. Lüders, and G. Y. Luo, 2008, "An experimental test of the impact of overconfidence and gender on trading activity," Forthcoming in *Review of Finance*.

Note: This table displays the coefficients and p-values from regressions when individual-specific trading activity is regressed on calibration-based overconfidence (CBO), better-than-average effect-based overconfidence (BTA), illusion of control (IoC), age (AGE), financial education (EDUC), and trading experience (EXP).

financial education (p-value = 0.003) traded less. On the other hand, those with real-world trading experience felt more comfortable "pulling the trigger" and hence traded more (p-value = 0.023).[12]

9.3 DEMOGRAPHICS AND DYNAMICS

GENDER AND OVERCONFIDENCE IN THE FINANCIAL REALM

Recall from Chapter 5 that men tend to be more overconfident than women. Does this translate into the financial realm? The answer appears to be yes. Barber and Odean, using the dataset discussed previously in this chapter, explored the role of gender in the context of investment decision-making.[13] They reported that, on average, men traded 45% more than did women, thus incurring higher trading costs. While both genders reduce their net returns by trading, men do so by 0.94% more than women. The difference between single men and single women is starker, with single men trading 67% more, thus reducing their returns by 1.44% more than women.

Other studies comparing the activity of male and female portfolio managers and male and female business students find little difference between the genders and trading activity and overconfidence.[14] One possible reason is that the finance and business professions, being often viewed as male activities, attract women who are relatively more overconfident.[15]

DYNAMICS OF OVERCONFIDENCE AMONG MARKET PRACTITIONERS

While most of the preceding discussion has focused on retail investors, there is no reason to think that sophisticated investors, even those whose success relies on having a good sense of the limits of their knowledge, are immune. In the realm of financial markets, market practitioners are often called on to generate forecasts. Analysts and portfolio managers, for example, forecast revenues and earnings, and economists forecast GDP and the level of the stock market. In the case of analysts who suffer from conflicts of interest, as discussed later in the chapter, there are reasons to take their prognostications with a grain of salt. This argument, however, does not hold for money managers who are seeking to capture alpha (excess returns) and who have no such conflicts of interest. Nor does it obviously hold for macroeconomic or market forecasters.

One advantage to looking at professionals is that they often make public forecasts. This begs the question: Do professionals learn by their mistakes and over time develop a good sense of their knowledge? The dynamics of overconfidence is clearly an important issue. It seems logical to think that if people recall their successes and failures equally clearly, they should move toward an accurate view over time. Experience should engender wisdom. On the other hand, the prevalence and persistence of overconfidence suggest that forces able to eliminate it are weak. Cognitive dissonance sometimes induces us to forget what is unpleasant or did not go our way.[16] Moreover, as discussed earlier, self-attribution bias leads us to remember our successes with great clarity, if not embellishment; hindsight bias induces us to idealize our memory of what we believe or forecasted in the past; and confirmation bias, the tendency to search out evidence consistent with one's prior beliefs and to ignore conflicting data, also contribute.[17] A strict efficient markets view of the world would seem to argue that those fooling themselves in this way will be driven from the marketplace, but some have called this into question.[18]

The dynamic nature of overconfidence is stressed in a number of theoretical models. In the multi-period of setting of Simon Gervais and Odean, past successes, through the mechanism of self-attribution bias, exacerbate overconfidence, while past failures tend to be downplayed.[19] The inference is that those who have had the good fortune of being successful in their fields might for a time be more overconfident than those who have just entered the market. Eventually, however, experience should reveal to people their true knowledge level.

The evidence on whether professionals are overconfident is mixed. One study examined a dataset of futures market traders and was unable to find any costs associated with their trading activity.[20] From this the authors inferred that these traders were not overconfident. On the other hand, they found that less-disciplined traders were less successful than other traders, arguing that a lack of discipline can stem from overconfidently ignoring new public information.

In another study, the forecasts of a group of German market practitioners were examined.[21] These individuals were asked to provide both forecasts for the future level of the DAX (the German counterpart to the Dow) and 90% confidence bounds. This respondent group was egregiously overconfident. Their dynamic behavior, however, seemed more in line with rational learning than self-attribution bias because respondents narrowed their intervals after successes as much as they widened them after failures. At the same time, this research found that market experience made overconfidence worse, which is more consistent with a "learning to be overconfident" view and self-attribution. A likely reason for this is that experience is a double-edged sword. While we learn about our abilities (or lack thereof) from experience, those surviving in financial markets often have done so because of a run of success (good luck?), which has reinforced overconfidence through self-attribution bias.

The latter research also provided evidence that overconfidence can increase even at the level of the entire market, which was apparent from the correlation of past returns and changes in overconfidence. This is in accord with what would be expected since high past returns are likely to make many in the market feel successful. Previously, this tendency had been shown *indirectly,* in that lagged market returns were correlated with increases in trading activity (which proxied for increases in overconfidence).[22]

9.4   UNDERDIVERSIFICATION AND EXCESSIVE RISK TAKING

Another investor error likely related to overconfidence is the tendency to be underdiversified. This is suggested by the illustrative model previously presented—**underdiversified** people are too quick to overweight/underweight securities when they receive a positive/negative signal, and insufficient diversification results. Another factor is that most retail investors, lacking the time to analyze a large set of securities, will stop after several. As long as they believe they have identified a few "winners" in this group, they are content. After all, if they are so sure that certain stocks are good buys, why dilute their portfolios with stocks that they have not studied?

In one study, the portfolio composition of more than 3,000 U.S. individuals was examined.[23] Most held no stocks at all. Of those households that did hold stocks (more than 600), he found that the median number of stocks in their portfolios was only *one*. And only about 5% of stock-holding households held 10 or more stocks. Most evidence says that to achieve a reasonable level of diversification, one has to hold more than 10 different stocks (preferably in different sectors of the economy). Thus it seems clear that many individual investors are quite underdiversified.

William Goetzmann and Alok Kumar sought to ascertain who were most prone to being underdiversified.[24] Not surprisingly, they found that underdiversification was less severe among people who were financially sophisticated. Moreover, diversification increased with income, wealth, and age. Those who traded the most also tended to be the least diversified. This is likely because overconfidence is the driving force behind both excessive trading and underdiversification. Also less diversified were those people who were sensitive to price trends and those who were influenced by home bias. Once again, these are likely markers of a lack of sophistication.

Related to underdiversification is excessive risk taking. This is actually tautological, in that underdiversification is tantamount to taking on risk for which there is no apparent reward. It is done, of course, in the hope of finding undervalued securities.

The disposition effect, the tendency to hold on to losers too long with deleterious consequences for performance, while often linked to regret, is also sometimes associated with overconfidence. An overconfident trader, overly wedded to prior beliefs, may discount negative public information that pushes down prices, thus holding on to losers and taking on excessive risk. Indeed, there is evidence that futures traders exhibit this behavior. Traders with mid-day losses increase their risk and perform poorly subsequently.[25]

9.5 EXCESSIVE OPTIMISM AND ANALYSTS

Abundant research has established that analysts tend to be excessively optimistic about the prospects of the companies that they are following.[26] This is true both in the United States and internationally. While this issue will be revisited in Chapter 12, in order to set the stage, consider Table 9.2 that shows the distribution of analyst recommendations among strong buy, buy, hold, sell, and strong sell for G7 countries.[27] It is clear that analysts are much more likely to recommend a purchase than a sale. In the United States, where this tendency was most pronounced, buys/sells were observed 52%/3% of the time. In Germany, where this tendency was least pronounced, the buy/sell ratio was 39%/20%. As will be made clear in our later discussion, while excessive optimism is one interpretation, another is a conflict of interest induced by a perceived need to keep prospective issuers happy.

| **TABLE** 9.2 | RECOMMENDATION DISTRIBUTIONS (%) IN G7 COUNTRIES DURING 1993–2002 |

	Strong buy	Buy	Hold	Sell/strong sell
U.S.	28.6	33.6	34.5	3.3
Britain	24.3	22.3	41.7	11.8
Canada	29.4	28.6	29.9	12.1
France	24.7	28.3	31.1	15.9
Germany	18.3	20.3	41.5	19.9
Italy	19.2	20.0	47.1	13.6
Japan	23.6	22.4	35.7	18.3

Source: Jegadeesh, N., and W. Kim, 2006, "Value of analyst recommendations: International evidence," *Journal of Financial Markets* 9, 274–309.

CHAPTER HIGHLIGHTS

1. Overconfident investors are more certain of their value estimates than others and for this reason trade excessively.
2. This relationship is evidenced by the fact that inferior performance net of transaction costs is associated with high levels of trading, and by survey and experimental work that directly associates overconfidence and high levels of trading.
3. While experience and performance feedback should allow a person to learn his true ability, self-attribution bias, hindsight bias, and confirmation bias exacerbate overconfidence. The evidence is mixed on whether overconfidence eventually dissipates, and how long it takes.
4. Overconfident investors underdiversify.
5. In large part because of underdiversification, overconfident traders also tend to take on too much risk.
6. Analysts are excessively optimistic. Their overoptimism is likely not entirely due to psychology.

DISCUSSION QUESTIONS AND PROBLEMS

1. Differentiate the following terms/concepts:

   a. Indirect and direct tests of relationship between overconfidence and trading activity
   b. Sensation seeking and overconfidence
   c. Underdiversification and excessive trading
   d. Statics and dynamics of overconfidence

2. Consider two investors (A and B) with the following demand curves for a stock:

$$A : p = 100 - q$$
$$B : p = 150 - 2q$$

   a. At a price of $50, how much will A and B purchase?

b. If the price falls to $30, who will increase their holdings more? Explain.

c. On this basis, which investor seems to be more overconfident?

3. Discuss what the evidence (using naturally occurring data, survey data, and experimental data) suggests about the relationship among overconfidence, trading activity, and portfolio performance.

4. What evidence is there that people do not diversify enough? Why is it that this occurs? What is the simplest way to "buy" a high level of diversification in an equity portfolio?

5. Research indicates that stock market forecasters are also overconfident. Do they learn from their mistakes? Discuss.

ENDNOTES

1 To simplify the presentation, we are assuming that all investors have the same net wealth and are equally well diversified.

2 While in the example that follows there are only three investors, this is done to keep the calculations simple.

3 Assumed to be equal across investors, θ will be higher the greater an investor's willingness to expose himself to diversifiable risk to pursue excess returns.

4 See Odean, T., 1998, "Volume, volatility, price and profit when all traders are above average," *Journal of Finance* 53, 1887–1934. Some other key theoretical papers include Daniel, K., D. Hirshleifer, and A. Subrahmanyam, 1998, "Investor psychology and security market under- and overreactions," *Journal of Finance* 53, 1839–85; Daniel, K., D. Hirshleifer, and A. Subrahmanyam, 2001, "Overconfidence, arbitrage, and equilibrium asset pricing," *Journal of Finance* 56, 921–965; Benos, A. V., 1998, "Aggressiveness and survival of overconfident traders," *Journal of Financial Markets* 1, 353–383; and Kyle, A. S., and F. A. Wang, 1997, "Speculation duopoly with agreement to disagree: Can overconfidence survive the market test?" *Journal of Finance* 55, 2073–2090.

5 Barber, B., and T. Odean, 2000, "Trading is hazardous to your wealth: The common stock investment performance of individual investors," *Journal of Finance* 55, 773–806.

6 Glaser, M., and M. Weber, 2007, "Overconfidence and trading volume," *Geneva Risk and Insurance Review* 32, 1–36.

7 Their overconfidence measures were in fact weakly correlated, suggesting that different constructs were perhaps being measured. For corroborating evidence, see Kirchler, E., and B. Maciejovsky, 2002, "Simultaneous over- and under-confidence: Evidence from experimental asset markets," *Journal of Risk and Uncertainty* 25, 65–85. It has also been found that sensation seekers trade more often (Grinblatt, M., and M. Keloharju, 2008, "Sensation seeking, overconfidence, and trading activity," Working paper). Other work relates trading activity to a feeling of "competence," which is argued to be tantamount to a feeling of being better than average (Graham, J. R., C. R. Harvey, and H. Huang, 2006, "Investor competence, trading frequency, and home bias," Working paper).

8 Grinblatt, M., and M. Keloharju, 2008, "Sensation seeking, overconfidence and trading activity," Working paper.

9 For sensation seeking, see Zuckerman, M., 1971, "Dimensions of sensation seeking," *Journal of Consulting and Clinical Psychology* 36, 45–52.

10 Biais, B., D. Hilton, K. Mazurier, and S. Pouget, 2005, "Judgemental overconfidence, self-monitoring, and trading performance in an experimental financial market," *Review of Economic Studies* 72, 287–312.

11 See Deaves, R., E. Lüders, and G. Y. Luo, 2008, "An experimental test of the impact of overconfidence and gender on trading activity," *Review of Finance,* forthcoming. Recall that illusion of control is the belief that people have more control over events (like picking the right stock) than can objectively be true.

12 This could be related to the finding that investors who feel more competent trade more often. See Graham, J. R., C. R. Harvey, and H. Huang, 2006, "Investor competence, trading frequency, and home bias," Working paper.

13 Barber, B., and T. Odean, 2001, "Boys will be boys: Gender, overconfidence, and common stock investment," *Quarterly Journal of Economics* 116, 261–292.

14 See Atkinson, S. M., S. B. Baird, and M. B. Frye, 2001, "Do female mutual fund managers manage differently?" *Journal of Financial Research* 26, 1–18; and Deaves, R., E. Lüders, and G. Y. Luo, 2008, "An experimental test of the impact of overconfidence and gender on trading activity," *Review of Finance,* forthcoming.

15 See Nekby, L., P. S. Thoursie, and L. Vahtrik, 2007, "Gender and self-selection into a competitive environment: Are women more overconfident than men?" Working paper.

16 See Plous, S., 1993, *The Psychology of Judgment and Decision-making* (McGraw-Hill, New York).

17 Forsythe, R., F. Nelson, G. Neumann, and J. Wright, 1992, "Anatomy of an experimental political stock market," *American Economic Review* 82, 1142–1161.

18 Hirshleifer, D., and G. Y. Luo, 2001, "On the survival of overconfident traders in a competitive security market," *Journal of Financial Markets* 4, 73–84.

19 Gervais, S., and T. Odean, 2001, "Learning to be overconfident," *Review of Financial Studies* 14, 1–27. Also see the models of Daniel, K., D. Hirshleifer, and A. Subrahmanyam, 1998, "Investor psychology and security market under- and overreactions," *Journal of Finance* 53, 1839–1885; and Daniel, K., D. Hirshleifer, and A. Subrahmanyam, 2001, "Overconfidence, arbitrage, and equilibrium asset pricing," *Journal of Finance* 56, 921–965.

20 Locke, P. R., and S. C. Mann, 2005, "Professional trader discipline and trade disposition," *Journal of Financial Economics* 76, 401–444.

21 Deaves, R., E. Lüders, and M. Schröder, 2008, "The dynamics of overconfidence: Evidence from stock market forecasters," Working paper.

22 See Statman, M., S. Thorley, and K. Vorkink, 2006, "Investor overconfidence and trading volume," *Review of Financial Studies* 19, 1531–1565. As for whether individual investors adjust volume more in response to market returns or own-portfolio returns, the evidence is that those who keep track of their own portfolios are more influenced by the latter, while those less aware are more likely to be influenced by market returns. For details, see Glaser, M., and M. Weber, 2009, "Which past returns affect trading volume?" *Journal of Financial Markets* 12(1), 1–31.

23 Kelly, M., 1995, "All their eggs in one basket: Portfolio diversification of U.S. households," *Journal of Economic Behavior and Organization* 27, 87–96.

24 Goetzmann, W. N., and A. Kumar, 2005, "Equity portfolio diversification," *Review of Finance* 12, 433–463.

25 See Coval, J. D., and T. Shumway, 2005, "Do behavioral biases affect prices?" *Journal of Finance* 60, 1–34; and Locke, P. R., and S. C. Mann, 2005, "Professional trader discipline and trade disposition," *Journal of Financial Economics* 76, 401–444.

26 See, for example, Carleton, W. T., C. R. Chen, and T. L. Steiner, 1998, "Optimism biases among brokerage and non-brokerage firms' equity recommendations: Agency costs in the investment industry," *Financial Management* 27, 17–30.

27 See Jegadeesh, N., and "Value of analyst recommenda national evidence," *Journal of Markets* 9, 274–309.

INDIVIDUAL INVESTORS AND THE FORCE OF EMOTION

CHAPTER 1

10.1   INTRODUCTION

Market movements are commonly attributed to the emotions of investors. Yet it is not obvious how to separate the role of emotions from that of fundamentals in producing market outcomes. In Chapter 7 we considered the foundations of emotion. We learned that emotion includes cognitive, physiological, and evolutionary aspects. It was argued that emotions, when in balance, can facilitate decision-making, rather than hinder it. In this chapter, we will consider the extent to which the various aspects of emotion influence observed individual behavior in the financial realm.

The chapter begins, in Section 10.2, with a discussion of how mood impacts the decisions of individual investors. We will see that it is not easy to characterize the interaction between an investor's mood and risk attitude. Next, Section 10.3 considers two emotions that have received a lot of attention: pride and regret. Researchers have shown that these two emotions have very important effects on investor behavior. Section 10.4 focuses on the disposition effect, one investor behavior that can be explained by emotion. The empirical evidence indicates that people tend to sell stocks that have performed well too soon, while holding on to poorly performing stocks too long. Though traditionally this behavior has been rationalized using prospect theory, theoretical and experimental evidence suggest that emotions may provide a better explanation. Next, Section 10.5 discusses the house money effect, so-named from the observation that gamblers take increased risks after winning because they feel they are betting with the house's money. A house money effect has been documented even for very large gambles, as research of game show contestant behavior shows. Finally, Section 10.6 considers how a person's assessment of a situation or impression of another, referred to as affect, shapes financial decision-making.

10.2 IS THE MOOD OF THE INVESTOR THE MOOD OF THE MARKET?

In his best-selling book *Irrational Exuberance*, economist Robert Shiller argues that "the emotional state of investors when they decide on their investments is no doubt one of the most important factors causing the bull market" experienced around the world in the 1990s.[1] Do traders' emotional dispositions translate into a market mood that, in turn, moves the market? This is a very interesting question. Some recent research concludes that what appears to be anomalous financial behavior can be explained by emotion.

Here are some examples of this work. One study using data from 26 international stock exchanges argues that good moods resulting from morning sunshine lead to higher stock returns.[2] A sunny day might make people more optimistic so that, in turn, they are more likely to buy stocks. Other researchers report that stock markets fall when traders' sleep patterns are disrupted due to clock changes with daylight savings time.[3] A third recent study suggests that the outcomes of soccer games are strongly correlated with the mood of investors.[4] After a loss in a World Cup elimination game, significant market declines are reported in the losing country's market.

Whether these aggregate studies of the effect of mood on stock market pricing provide clear evidence on how individual behavior translates into market outcomes is debatable. For example, even if people were irrationally optimistic on a sunny day, does it necessarily mean that they run out and buy stocks? Would you? Even if some people do rush to buy stocks on sunny days, market behavior can be consistent with rational pricing when individual behavior is characterized as irrational, as theoretical and experimental evidence suggests.[5]

At a more fundamental level, though, it is not clear that there is a simple way to characterize the relationship between mood and risk attitude. As we discussed in Chapter 1, risk attitude is important because it affects how a person values an asset. If risk aversion changes in response to changes in mood, how much a person is willing to pay for a stock will change. When someone is in a poor mood, does he take more risks or fewer? The answer probably depends on the context and the individual's personality. For example, one person who is in a very sour mood may engage in risky behavior like driving recklessly or drinking too much alcohol. Another person who is not having a good day may shy away from risk more than usual and simply withdraw from others. The evidence does not provide compelling evidence that a buoyant mood consistently leads to lower risk aversion or that a poor mood consistently leads to increased risk aversion, particularly in a financial context.

Some research suggests that happier people are more optimistic and assign higher probabilities to positive events.[6] But at the same time, other decision-making research indicates that even though people may be more optimistic about their likelihood of winning a gamble when they are happy, the same people are much *less* willing to actually take the gamble.[7] In other words, they are more risk averse when they are happy. When you are in a good mood you are less likely to gamble because you do not want to jeopardize the good mood. Thus, taken together, it is unclear how positive and negative emotional states translate into changes in risk attitude and, in turn, market pricing.

In addition to the studies that tie market movements to changes in mood, some researchers link depression induced by reduced daylight to stock market cycles.[8] As with the evidence on the effect of mood on risk choices, evidence on the relationship between risk attitude and depression does not provide a clear picture. Clinical depression is clearly different from a simple bad mood—depression has a biochemical basis and can occur with no cognitive appraisals. The current view of depression by psychologists recognizes that it may involve altered brain circuitry.[9] A person with no chemical imbalances will naturally experience anxiety in some situations (e.g., a job interview) but a depressed person can feel chronically anxious. Some researchers question the importance of anxiety or depression in explaining choices across risky alternatives.[10] Others conclude that risk aversion is correlated with depressive tendencies, but the correlation between depressive symptoms and risk aversion may arise from the correlation between anxiety and depression.[11] Thus, the fundamental issue of how depression and risk attitude are linked remains unresolved.[12] While a depressed person who shies away from risk with no apparent basis may seem to be irrational, an anxious person may be completely rational when he decides to move toward safer alternatives. Further research is needed before we can move toward definitive conclusions. Neuroscience research, as will be discussed in Chapter 20, is making inroads into the workings of the human brain.

10.3   PRIDE AND REGRET

While it may be premature to assert that we understand every factor that affects decision-making, some emotions have proven to be useful in understanding the financial choices people make, perhaps most notably, pride and regret. **Regret** is obviously a negative emotion. You might regret a bad investment decision and wish you had made a different choice. Your negative feelings are only amplified if you have to report a loss to your spouse, friends, or colleagues. **Pride** is the flip side of regret. You probably would not mind too much if it just slipped out in conversation that you made a good profit on a trade.

Psychologists and economists recognize the important impact regret and pride have on financial decision-making. Researchers believe that people are strongly motivated to avoid the feeling of regret.[13] Importantly, the effects of pride and regret are asymmetric. It seems that the negative emotion, regret, is felt more strongly by people.

Researchers found that a number of the implications of expected utility theory are not corroborated by experimental evidence. This led to the development of alternative models of decision-making under uncertainty, prospect theory being the most popular of these. As was discussed in Chapter 3, central to prospect theory is that people are sometimes risk seeking. This occurs in the domain of losses and in the domain of gains for lottery-type prospects. Is it possible that regret and pride are behind these two tendencies to be risk seeking?

In the case of risk seeking in the domain of losses, it may be that people want to avoid the negative feeling of regret that would occur if they had to recognize a loss, and so they gravitate away from their natural tendency to be risk averse. As for the lottery effect, a big low-probability gain, whether from picking a long shot at the track or from undertaking some research to find a "diamond in the rough" stock that you think is about to take off against all odds, may lead to anticipated pride and even risk seeking as you can just see yourself telling your friends about your acumen. Whatever the reality, it is clear that pride and regret are powerful emotions that impact the decisions people make. Now we will consider a specific financial behavior and investigate whether emotion explains observed choices.

10.4   THE DISPOSITION EFFECT

Researchers have recognized the tendency of investors to sell superior-performing stocks too early while holding on to losing stocks too long.[14] Perhaps you have observed this behavior in others, or even experienced it yourself. Have you ever heard someone express a sentiment such as, "This stock has really shot up so I better sell now and realize the gain?" Or, can you imagine yourself thinking, "I have lost a lot of money on this stock already, but I can't sell it now because it *has* to turn around some day?" The tendency to sell winners and hold losers is called the disposition effect.

EMPIRICAL EVIDENCE

We begin with some recent empirical evidence documenting the existence of the disposition effect. For example, Terrance Odean, using a database that included trading records for 10,000 discount brokerage accounts with almost 100,000 transactions during 1987–1993, carefully documented the tendency of individual investors to sell winners and hold on to losers.[15] To distinguish between winners and losers we need a reference point. Consistent with prospect theory, Odean used the purchase price of each security (or average purchase price in the case of multiple transactions). One issue that had to be confronted is that in an up market many stocks will be winners, so it is natural that more winners than losers will be sold. Odean dealt with this by focusing on the frequency of winner/loser sales relative to the opportunities for winner/loser sales. Specifically, he calculated the proportion of gains realized (PGR) as:

10.1
$$PGR = \frac{Realized\ gains}{Realized\ gains + Paper\ gains}$$

For example, when the sale of a winner occurs in an account, you compare this to all winners that could have been sold. Paper gains include any sales that could have been made at a gain. Similarly, the proportion of losses realized (PLR) was calculated as follows:

10.2
$$PLR = \frac{Realized\ losses}{Realized\ losses + Paper\ losses}$$

To provide insight into the tendency of these individual investors to sell winners while holding losers, Odean tested the hypothesis that the proportion of gains realized exceeded the proportion of losses realized.

TABLE 10.1	AGGREGATE PROPORTION OF GAINS (PGR) AND LOSSES (PLR) REALIZED		
	Entire Year	December	January–November
PLR	0.098	0.128	0.094
PGR	0.148	0.108	0.152
Difference in proportions	–0.050	0.020	–0.058
t-statistic	–35	4.3	–38

Source: Odean, T., 1998, "Are investors reluctant to realize their losses?" in *Journal of Finance* 53(5), 1775–1798. © 1998 Wiley Publishing, Inc. This material is used by permission of John Wiley & Sons, Inc.

From Table 10.1, which aggregates over all investor accounts, there is a clear tendency to sell winners over losers (PGR > PLR) over the entire year. It is important to note that for tax reasons investors should prefer to sell losers, not winners. An investor with a positive tax rate should put off realizing gains on winners because of the tax liability generated, but should recognize losses sooner in order to reduce current tax liability. The second numerical column in the table shows that the disposition effect operates *despite* the fact that some investors understand this tax issue and act accordingly. In the month of December, when investors are most likely to transact for tax reasons, there is actually a greater tendency to sell losers rather than winners. It is in the other 11 months (the third numerical column) where the disposition effect dominates.

To explain these observations, Odean considers several possibilities related to rationality. First, portfolio rebalancing suggests that losers, whose aggregate value is now lower than winners, need to have their positions increased relative to winners in order restore desired portfolio allocations. Odean investigated this and found it did not matter appreciably. Second, perhaps investors anticipate that losers will outperform winners looking forward. This is symptomatic of the tendency for long-term reversal discussed in Chapter 4. Unfortunately, investors have their timing wrong, as they are selling medium-term (not long-term) winners and holding on to medium-term (not long-term) losers. This is exactly the opposite of what they should do. Indeed, looking ahead over the next year, Odean finds that winners sold outperform losers held by 3.41% on a risk-adjusted basis. It is for this reason that researchers sometimes speak of the disposition effect as selling winners too soon and holding on to losers too long.

PROSPECT THEORY AS AN EXPLANATION FOR THE DISPOSITION EFFECT

Hersh Shefrin and Meir Statman were the first to try to explain why the disposition effect is observed.[16] Their explanations fall into two categories: prospect theory (coupled with mental accounting) and regret aversion (coupled with self-control problems). While nothing precludes the possibility of a role for both behavioral explanations, Shefrin and Statman emphasize prospect theory over the emotion of regret, and many commentators since then have followed this cue. Based on recent research described next, however, emotion may be the more important factor.

First we begin with the prospect theory explanation. Consider Figure 10.1, which shows how gains and losses appear according to prospect theory, provided that prior outcomes are integrated. Stocks A and B have suffered losses, while C and D have experienced gains. How would these gains and losses affect your behavior as an investor? After a large gain (D), you have moved to the risk-averse segment of the value function. Only major reversals of fortune are likely to move you back to the origin. On the other hand, after a large loss (A) you have moved to the risk-seeking segment of the value function and, again, you are unlikely to move quickly back to your reference point. The implication is that since you are less risk averse for losers than winners, you are more likely to hold on to them.

Still, why not engage in a tax swap (the simultaneous purchase and sale of two similar securities for tax reasons) in order to reduce tax payments? With a tax swap, an investor sells a losing stock and buys another stock with similar risk in order to realize a loss for tax purposes without changing the risk exposure in her portfolio. Though this strategy seems to make sense, if the investor uses mental accounting and evaluates the stocks separately, a tax swap would entail closing one account at a loss. As we have seen, many have difficulty doing so.

Closing an account at a loss is difficult because of regret aversion. Shefrin and Statman argue that the fear of triggering regret leads an investor to postpone losses, whereas on the other side, the desire for pride (and/or rejoicing) leads to the realization of gains. An investor feels regretful when closing a position with a loss because of the (ex post) poor investment decision that was made, but feels pride when closing a position with a gain because the financial decision resulted in a profit. As for self-control, it is argued that even though investors often know they are doing the wrong thing, they have difficulty controlling the impulse to hold on to losers.

FIGURE 10.1 Gains, Losses, and the Prospect Theory Value Function

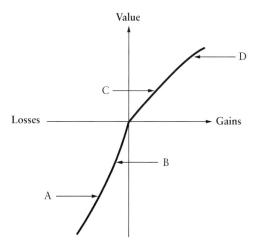

ANOTHER POSSIBLE EXPLANATION

Nicholas Barberis and Wei Xiong have recently revisited the prospect theory explanation of the disposition effect.[17] Noting that previous justifications have been informal at best, they adopt a rigorous theoretical perspective. These researchers conclude that depending on the assumed parameters of the model, the implied behavior of investors can easily be the very *opposite* of what prospect theory would suggest. They argue that the problem with prospect theory is that it does not take account of the initial decision to purchase the stock.

In the two-period version of the Barberis-Xiong model, the parameterization of prospect theory preferences put forth by Kahneman and Tversky *always* predicts behavior opposite of what prospect theory calls for. The following simple example is provided. Given loss aversion, the expected return on the stock must be high. Otherwise, investors would not hold it to start with. Say a stock is priced at $50 and can go up or down next period with equal probability. If it goes up, it rises to $60 for a $10 gain. A loss aversion coefficient of two ($\lambda = 2$), which is in the neighborhood of the Tversky-Kahneman value, implies that an investor would have only been willing to acquire the stock in the first place if the possible loss next period were $5 or less. Let's assume $5. Now consider what happens after the stock is acquired and either a loss or gain has been experienced.

In their model, if a stock has initially done well, an investor will take a position in a stock that leads to breaking even if, in the worst-case scenario, the stock falls the following period. On the other hand, if a stock has initially done poorly, the position taken will be one that will lead to their breaking even in the best-case scenario. Suppose the stock initially did well and increased in value to $60. Since after a gain of $10 a subsequent loss will only take away half of this, the investor doubles the number of shares. This is because the value function is mildly concave in the gain domain so the investor is close to risk neutral. Conversely, suppose the stock fell to $45 the first period. With a loss of $5, only a half a share is required to get the investor back to square one if the stock increases in value. This suggests a partial liquidation, with the investor selling half a share. In short, the exact opposite of the disposition effect is implied. The investor with prospect theory preferences buys after a gain and sells after a loss.

EXPERIMENTAL EVIDENCE

A recent experiment by Barbara Summers and Darren Duxbury also favors emotions over prospect theory in explaining the disposition effect.[18] Their experimental design is predicated on whether or not individuals have chosen their investments. Suppose, contrary to what generally occurs in reality, there is no choice and you merely have to sit back and observe how your stocks are performing. When a stock you own fares poorly, you experience disappointment, and when your stock performs well you experience elation. If you actually selected these stocks yourself, arguably you will experience emotions with higher valence—in the face of a loss, you will experience regret (which is stronger than disappointment), and in the face of a gain, you will experience rejoicing (which is stronger than elation). Summers and Duxbury hypothesize that anticipated regret and rejoicing are necessary to generate behavior that is consistent with the disposition effect.

In order to separate the emotional responses, Summers and Duxbury manipulated choice and responsibility regarding participants' current stock positions. Each participant was shown a graph of a single stock, with some groups given a winning stock and others a losing stock. Participants were then allowed to sell some or all of their stock. In the first treatment, there was no initial choice—subjects were told that they had inherited the stock from a relative. In the second treatment, there was an earlier stage where subjects could freely decide how much (if any) of the stock to hold. If prospect theory without emotion explains the disposition effect, the mere experience of a gain or loss without personal responsibility for the choice of investments (first treatment) should induce the disposition effect. It did not. The second treatment where choice was given did, however, reveal a disposition effect, with the proportion of gains realized greater than the proportion of losses realized (with statistical significance at less than 1%). Summers and Duxbury concluded that responsibility for an outcome is a prerequisite for the disposition effect, which highlights the importance of emotions in understanding the choices of investors.

The disposition effect has been documented in another experimental study by Martin Weber and Colin Camerer.[19] Interestingly, in one condition, participants' stock holdings were sold at the end of each period, regardless of their preferences. When shares were automatically sold, the disposition effect was moderated. This finding is consistent with a role for emotion in traders' choices, because when they begin anew each period, the negative feelings of regret and rejoicing are suppressed.

10.5 HOUSE MONEY

Next, we turn to another example of path-dependent behavior. Path-dependent behavior means that people's decisions are influenced by what has previously transpired. Richard Thaler and Eric Johnson provide evidence regarding how individual behavior is affected by prior gains and losses.[20] After a prior gain, people become more open to assuming risk. This observed behavior is referred to as the house money effect, alluding to casino gamblers who are more willing to risk money that was recently won. After a prior loss, matters are not so clear-cut. On the one hand, people seem to value breaking even, so a person with a prior loss may take a risky gamble in order to try to break even. This observed behavior is referred to as the break even effect. On the other hand, an initial loss can cause an increase in risk aversion in what has been called the **snake-bit effect**.

EVIDENCE OF A HOUSE MONEY EFFECT ON A LARGE SCALE

The first evidence of path-dependence in decision-making came from hypothetical surveys or experiments conducted using student subjects, so whether the findings would carry over to high-stakes financial decisions was always open to challenge. To obviate this concern, some researchers turned to consideration of the decisions of game show contestants to provide insight into behavior when the stakes are large.

One recent study by Thierry Post, Martijn J. van den Assem, Guido Baltussen, and Richard Thaler examined the choices made on the popular game show "Deal or No Deal?" This show first aired in the Netherlands in 2002 and has since been broadcast in numerous countries including Germany, Mexico, Spain, and the United States. Indeed, the stakes are large, with possible payouts in the Netherlands ranging from 0.01 to 5,000,000 euros. Though the rules of the game vary across countries, here is the basic setup. A contestant is presented with 26 suitcases each containing a hidden payout. The contestant selects one of the 26 as her own. This suitcase remains closed as she selects six others and views their contents. Next, a "bank offer" is made to the contestant, and, if she accepts it, she walks away with the offer with certainty. Otherwise, there is "no deal" between the contestant and the bank. She holds on to her suitcase, selects five more, and views their contents. The bank offers another deal, and the game continues until a deal is accepted or the contestant walks away with the contents of her suitcase. While the bank offers are not perfectly predictable, they typically begin low, rise over time, and increase (or decrease) when low- (or high-) value suitcases are opened.

The researchers find that contestants' decisions are strongly influenced by what has happened before. When suitcases with low values are opened, contestants take on more risk. This is consistent with a house money effect because when low payoffs are eliminated, expected winnings are higher and a contestant experiences a gain. On the other hand, when high-value suitcases are opened, a contestant experiences a loss in terms of expected winnings. Consistent with a break-even effect, contestants' decisions reflect decreased risk aversion, and they take risky gambles that give them the opportunity to break even. Importantly, the bottom line is that significant changes in expected wealth *regardless of the sign* lead to more risk taking.

PROSPECT THEORY AND SEQUENTIAL DECISIONS

Some of the findings on behavior following gains and losses appear to contradict prospect theory. The house money effect suggests reduced risk aversion after an initial gain, whereas prospect theory makes no such prediction. It is notable, though, that a house money effect is not inconsistent with prospect theory because prospect theory was developed to describe one-shot gambles. Recall our discussion of integration versus segregation in Chapter 3. Under integration, an investor combines the results of successive gambles, whereas, under segregation, each gamble is viewed separately. Instead of presenting a challenge to prospect theory, the house money effect is best seen as evidence that sequential gambles are sometimes integrated rather than segregated. If one integrates after a large gain, one has moved safely away from the value function loss aversion kink, serving to lessen risk aversion. Thinking in terms of emotions, how emotions like pride and regret are felt depends on how experiences are classified, as incremental or grouped together.

The evidence provided by Thaler and Johnson provides important insight into how individuals make sequential decisions. People do not necessarily combine the outcomes of different gambles. Other researchers also document a house money effect on individual behavior.[21] Financial theory is increasingly incorporating insights on individual behavior provided by psychology and decision-making research. For example, in the model of Nicholas Barberis, Ming Huang, and Tano Santos, investors receive utility from consumption and changes in wealth. In traditional models, people value only consumption.[22] In this extension, investors are loss averse so that they are more sensitive to decreases than to increases in wealth, and, thus, prior outcomes affect subsequent behavior. After a stock price increase, people are less risk averse because prior gains cushion subsequent losses, whereas after a decline in stock prices, people are concerned about further losses and risk aversion increases. Therefore, Barberis, Huang, and Santos's model predicts that the existence of the house money effect in financial markets leads to greater volatility in stock prices. After prices rise, investors have a cushion of gains and are less averse to the risks involved in owning stock. Indeed, as in this model, aspects of prospect theory are increasingly being embedded in financial models.

Despite progress, it does not seem that our understanding of sequential behavior in a market setting is complete. How does individual behavior translate to a market setting? A recent experimental study that includes a market with sequential decision-making provides some insight.[23] Traders who are given a greater windfall of income before trading begins bid higher to acquire the asset, and, thus, the market prices are significantly higher. In fact, prices remain higher over the entirety of the three-period markets. As the house money effect would predict, people seem to be less risk averse after a windfall of money, as if the earlier gain cushions subsequent losses. Observed behavior does not always suggest that traders will pay more to acquire stock after further increases in wealth. There is no evidence that traders become more risk taking if additional profits are generated by good trades when the market is open. The results indicate that the absolute level of wealth has a dominating influence on subsequent behavior so that changes in wealth are less important. This observed behavior among traders could be because professional traders are trained to act in a more normative (i.e., less prospect theory-like, less emotional) fashion. Indeed, more work is required to allow us to better understand the dynamics of markets and whether individual behavior adapts to or influences market outcomes.[24]

10.6   AFFECT

Thus far we have argued that emotions, particularly regret, can impact financial decision-making. Emotional responses are also caused by the many stimuli we experience continuously every day. A person's affective assessment is the sentiment that arises from a stimulus. For instance, imagine yourself negotiating a contract for your firm. Then imagine you had an immediate dislike for the other negotiator. Would you guess that the outcome is probably affected by your sentiment? Affect refers to the quality of a stimulus and reflects a person's impression or assessment. Cognitively, a person's perception includes affective reactions and, thus, judgment and decision-making are tied to the particular reactions the person has.

Some psychologists have argued that peoples' thoughts are made up of images that include perceptual and symbolic representations.[25] The images are marked by positive or negative feelings that are linked to somatic (or body) states. At the neural level, somatic markers arising from experience establish a connection between an experience and a body state (such as pleasant or unpleasant). In effect, affective reactions are cognitive representations of distinct body states, and the brain uses an emotion to interpret a situation. People are attracted to a stimulus linked with a positive somatic marker and avoid those associated with negative somatic markers.

Affective reactions that are easy for a person to access provide convenient and efficient means for decision making because the reactions allow a far easier way to evaluate the plusses and minuses of a stimulus.[26]

Some research has examined the role of affect in financial decision-making. In Chapter 16, we discuss how managers might be influenced. Affect also plays a role in markets. For example, some argue that a relationship exists between the image of a market and what has occurred in the market.[27] This conclusion is based on the observation that experimental participants' willingness to invest in a firm is influenced by the subjects' affective reaction to the firm's industry membership. Other experiments also indicate that firm image has a significant effect on the portfolio allocation decisions of participants.[28]

In the future, we will likely see more research on the role of affect in financial decisions. Psychologists believe that affective reactions influence judgment and decision making, even without cognitive evaluations, but we do not have a full understanding of how the influences mesh into outcomes.[29] In addition, psychologists suggest that when affective reactions and cognitive evaluations suggest different courses of action, the emotional aspects can be the dominating influence on behavior.[30] But again, we have a lot to learn if we are to understand when a particular force is likely to dominate.

CHAPTER HIGHLIGHTS

1. Some researchers suggest that the mood of the investor translates into the mood of the market and, in turn, impacts market outcomes. These conclusions should be interpreted with caution because we do not fully understand the relationship between emotion and risk attitude.

2. Much evidence suggests that two emotions, pride and regret, have significant effects on individual financial decision-making.

3. According to the disposition effect, people sell winners too soon and hold on to losers too long. Empirical evidence documents this tendency.

4. The disposition effect has traditionally been explained by prospect theory. Because of the shape of the value function, investors are less risk averse for losers, so they are more likely to hold on to them.

5. Recent theoretical arguments and experimental evidence suggest that loss aversion resulting from a fear of regret may provide a better account of the disposition effect.

6. According to the house money effect, after a prior gain, investors become less risk averse.

7. After losses, the snake-bit effect (whereby people are less likely to take on risk), and the break-even effect (whereby people are more likely to take on risk) operate in opposite directions. The latter seems to usually dominate.

8. Path-dependence in decisions, which suggests that people sometimes integrate sequential gambles, is corroborated for large-scale gambles by considering the choices made by game show contestants.

9. Affect reflects a person's impression or assessment of a stimulus. Because a person's perception is tied to the affective reaction, decisions are impacted by affect.

DISCUSSION QUESTIONS AND PROBLEMS

1. Differentiate the following terms/concepts:

   a. Regret and disappointment
   b. House money and break-even effects
   c. Affect (noun) and affect (verb)
   d. Bad mood and depression

2. In housing markets, there is a positive correlation between prices and trading volume. When there is a housing boom, many houses sell at, or even above, the prices asked by sellers. In times of bust, homes sit on the market for a long time with asking prices that exceed the prices that can reasonably be expected. How can this be explained?

3. Some investment banks engage in proprietary trading, which means that the firm's traders actively trade financial securities using the bank's money, in order to generate a profit. To offset a slowdown in one division, traders in a profitable division might more actively engage in proprietary trading. Do you think this practice is wise?

4. This morning I woke up in a sour mood because my favorite team lost its game yesterday. Then I had to wait an extra-long time in line for coffee. It started to rain, and I forgot my umbrella in the car. When I arrived at my office (finally), I found that a stock I held in my portfolio was falling in value, so I sold. Is this evidence that mood moves markets?

5. What does research based on the game show *Deal or No Deal* tell us about path-dependence and integration versus segregation of gambles?

ENDNOTES

1 Shiller, R. J., 2000, *Irrational Exuberance* (Princeton University Press, Princeton, New Jersey), p. 57.

2 Hirshleifer, D., and T. Shumway, 2003, "Good day sunshine: Stock returns and the weather," *Journal of Finance* 58(3), 1009–1032.

3 Kamstra, M. J., L. A. Kramer, and M. D. Levi, 2002, "Losing sleep at the market: The daylight saving anomaly," *American Economic Review* 90(4), 1005–1011.

4 Edmans, A., D. Garcia, and O. Norli, 2007, "Sports sentiment and stock returns," *Journal of Finance* 62(4), 1967–1998.

5 Ackert, L. F., and B. K. Church, 2001, "The effects of subject pool and design experience on rationality in experimental asset markets," *Journal of Psychology and Financial Markets* 2(1), 6–28; Jamal, K., and S. Sunder, 1996, "Bayesian equilibrium in double auctions populated by biased heuristic traders," *Journal of Economic Behavior and Organization* 31(2), 273–291; Jamal, K., and S. Sunder, 2001, "Why do biased heuristics approximate Bayes' rule in double auctions?" *Journal of Economic Behavior and Organization* 46(4), 431–435; and Chen, S.-H., and C.-H. Yeh, 2002, "On the emergent properties of artificial stock markets: The efficient markets hypothesis and the rational expectations hypothesis," *Journal of Economic Behavior and Organization* 49(2), 217–239.

6 Wright, W. F., and G. H. Bower, 1992, "Mood effects on subjective probability assessment," *Organizational Behavior and Human Decision Processes* 52, 276–291.

7 Isen, A. M., T. E. Nygren, and F. G. Ashby, 1988, "Influence of positive affect on the subjective utility of gains and losses: It is just not worth the risk," *Journal of Personality and Social Psychology* 55, 710–717.

8 Kamstra, M. J., L. A. Kramer, and M. D. Levi, 2003, "Winter blues: A SAD stock

market cycle," *American Economic Review* 93(1), 324–343.

9 LeDoux, J., 2002, *Synaptic Self: How Our Brains Become Who We Are* (Simon & Schuster, New York).

10 Hockey, G. R. J., A. J. Maule, P. J. Clough, and L. Bdzola, 2000, "Effects of negative mood states on risk in everyday decision making," *Cognition and Emotion* 14(6), 823–856.

11 Eisenberg, A. E., J. Baron, and M. E. P. Seligman, 1998, "Individual differences in risk aversion and anxiety," University of Pennsylvania working paper.

12 Note that many decision-making studies are based on hypothetical questions and decisions are not motivated financially. In some cases, measures of depressive symptoms are based on student surveys given in a college course. The actual incidence of clinically diagnosed depression in a sample may be unknown. Interpretation of the results becomes even more difficult because some researchers find that anxiety and sadness have distinct influences on behavior. In one study, gamblers who are sad prefer high-risk options, whereas gamblers who are anxious prefer low-risk options. See Raghunathan, R., and M. T. Pham, 1999, "All negative moods are not equal: Motivational influences of anxiety and sadness on decision making," *Organizational Behavior and Human Decision Processes* 79(1), 56–77.

13 See Kahneman, D., and A. Tversky, 1979, "Prospect theory: An analysis of decision under risk," *Econometrica* 47(2), 263–291; and Thaler, R., 1980, "Toward a positive theory of consumer choice," *Journal of Economic Behavior and Organization* 1(1), 39–60.

14 See, for example, Ferris, S. P., R. A. Haugen, and A. K. Makhija, 1988, "Predicting contemporary volume with historic volume at differential price levels: Evidence supporting the disposition effect," *Journal of Finance* 43(3), 677–697.

15 Odean, T., 1998, "Are investors reluctant to realize their losses?" *Journal of Finance* 53(5), 1775–1798.

16 Shefrin, H., and M. Statman, 1985, "The disposition to sell winners too early and ride losers too long: Theory and evidence," *Journal of Finance* 40(3), 777–792.

17 Barberis, N., and W. Xiong, 2006, "What drives the disposition effect? An analysis of a long-standing preference-based explanation," NBER Working paper number 12397.

18 Summers, B., and D. Duxbury, 2007, "Unraveling the disposition effect: The role of prospect theory and emotions," Working paper.

19 Weber, M., and C. F. Camerer, 1998, "The disposition effect in securities trading: An experimental analysis," *Journal of Economic Behavior and Organization* 33(2), 167–184.

20 Thaler, R. H., and E. J. Johnson, 1990, "Gambling with the house money and trying to break even: The effects of prior outcomes on risky choice," *Management Science* 36(6), 643–660.

21 Battalio, R. C., J. H. Kagel, and K. Jiranyakul, 1990, "Testing between alternative models of choice under uncertainty: Some initial results," *Journal of Risk and Uncertainty* 3(1), 25–50; and Gertner, R., 1993, "Game shows and economic behavior: Risk-taking on 'Card sharks'," *Quarterly Journal of Economics* 108(2), 507–521.

22 Barberis, N., M. Huang, and T. Santos, 2001, "Prospect theory and asset prices," *Quarterly Journal of Economics* 116(1), 1–53.

23 Ackert, L. F., N. Charupat, B. K. Church, and R. Deaves, 2006, "An experimental examination of the house money effect in a multi-period setting," *Experimental Economics* 9, 5–16.

24 One recent study suggests that the house money effect may explain observed patterns in index option implied volatilities. The author reports that prior gains may mitigate fear of loss. See Low, C., 2004, "The fear

and exuberance from implied volatility of S&P 100 index options," *Journal of Business* 77(3), 527–546.

25 Damasio, A. R., 1994, *Descartes' Error: Emotion, Reason, and the Human Brain* (Putnam, New York); and Charlton, B., 2000, *Psychiatry and the Human Condition* (Radcliffe Medical Press, Oxford).

26 Finucane, M. L., A. Alhakami, P. Slovic, and S. M. Johnson, 2000, "The affect heuristic in judgments of risks and benefits," *Journal of Behavioral Decision Making* 13(1), 1–17.

27 MacGregor, D. G., P. Slovic, D. Dreman, and M. Berry, 2000, "Imagery, affect, and financial judgment," *Journal of Psychology and Financial Markets* 1(2), 104–110.

28 Ackert, L. F., and B. K. Church, 2006, "Firm image and individual investments decisions," *Journal of Behavioral Finance* 7(3), 155–167.

29 See Zajonc, R. B., 1980, "Feeling and thinking; Preferences need no inferences," *American Psychologist* 35(2), 151–175; and Zajonc, R. B., 1984, "On the primacy of affect," *American Psychologist* 39, 117–123.

30 Nesse, R. M., and R. Klaas, 1994, "Risk perception by patients with anxiety disorders," *Journal of Nervous and Mental Disease* 182(8), 465–470; and Rolls, E. T., 1999, *The Brain and Emotion* (Oxford University Press, Oxford).

SOCIAL FORCES

PART **IV**

CHAPTER 11   Social Forces: Selfishness or Altruism?

CHAPTER 12   Social Forces at Work: The Collapse
of an American Corporation

SOCIAL FORCES: SELFISHNESS OR ALTRUISM?

11.1 INTRODUCTION

Homo economicus, or the "economic man," is a rational, self-interested decision-maker. Earlier chapters in this book have described what it means in finance to be a rational decision-maker and presented some evidence suggesting that rationality might not always be the best assumption. Recent important contributions to how we think about decision-making focus on another quality of economic man—human beings sometimes choose actions that are not in their material self-interest. This chapter will consider evidence that social interests influence how people make decisions. We focus on what we call **other-regarding preferences**, like fairness and reciprocity, because self-interested people are at the heart of most finance theory and practice.

This chapter begins in Section 11.2 with a clarification of the concept of the economic man. Then in Section 11.3, we describe experiments that measure peoples' tendencies toward fairness, reciprocity, and trust. The section also reports evidence of social influences across a wide variety of cultures. People often behave reciprocally, even when there is no role for reputation and no opportunity for retaliation by others. After reviewing the evidence in support of the notion that people have other-regarding preferences, in Section 11.4 we provide two examples to illustrate how ignoring social influences can lead to incorrect conclusions about important finance issues. In particular, we consider the relationship between social forces and competition in markets and the optimal design of contracts. Next, in Section 11.5, we consider conformity to social pressure. In Section 11.6, we see that emotion and social behavior are linked. The chapter concludes in Section 11.7 with a consideration of the argument that our reaction to social forces is "hardwired" in our brains through the forces of evolution.

11.2 *HOMO ECONOMICUS*

The decision-makers portrayed in the bulk of finance theory are rational and self-interested. This *homo economicus* view of man's behavior is generally attributed to nineteenth-century economist John Stuart Mill, though he did not actually use this wording.[1] As Mill argues, economics[2]

> ... does not treat the whole of man's nature as modified by the social state, nor of the whole conduct of man in society. It is concerned with him solely as a being who desires to possess wealth, and who is capable of judging of the comparative efficacy of means for obtaining that end. It predicts only such of the phenomena of the social state as take place in consequence of the pursuit of wealth. It makes entire abstraction of every other human passion or motive; except those which may be regarded as perpetually antagonizing principles to the desire of wealth, namely, aversion to labour, and desire of the present enjoyment of costly indulgences.

Notice that while people want to accumulate wealth, Mill argued that labor is minimized. Mill also recognized that other motives might be important, but at the same time he wanted to include only those that were "perpetually antagonizing." In developing theories, Mill realized that including a wide range of factors would lead to models that were indeterminate. If a model cannot provide predictions or directions for practical decision-making, it is not useful. In Mill's words, if economics is going to be a science "... practical rules must be capable of being founded upon it."[3]

While Mill excluded the "whole conduct of man in society" in his definition of economic man, he did not rule out any role for society. Much of his work centered on the important role of institutions. For example, he was critical of the system of tenant farming in Ireland because he argued that it gave the farmer no incentive to exert effort.

Recent evidence suggests that monetary incentives are not the only thing people care about. Thus, the view that our theory appropriately "... considers mankind as occupied solely in acquiring and consuming wealth" may be too narrow.[4] A wider range of human motivations is important for understanding financial decision-making.

11.3 FAIRNESS, RECIPROCITY, AND TRUST

Most people would accept with little argument the claim that fairness is valued in our society. At the same time, though, fewer people would accept the argument that fairness is important for financial decision-making. Nevertheless, in recent years some researchers contend that fairness, reciprocity, and trust are critical for business transactions. At a basic level, trust is a prerequisite for an efficiently functioning economy. We could write contracts specifying every single detail of every single business and personal transaction, but think of the cost! If we trust that other people will act fairly, the costs of transacting are reduced enormously. In fact, research shows that a large number of people treat fairly and trust others, even those whom they do not know and will likely never meet again.[5] An everyday example of fairness and trust is the practice of tipping servers in restaurants.

As long as the service is reasonably good, we normally tip the staff. The tip is not required, but most of us who eat out would consider it to be fair, and, on the other side, servers who are conscientious trust that patrons will recognize their efforts.[6]

ULTIMATUM AND DICTATOR GAMES

Consider a hypothetical experiment in which you and another student are anonymously paired. You two will split a sum of money. Though the situation is hypothetical, try to answer the following question as if real dollars were at stake:

Game 1:

One-half of the participants are completing the experiment in Room A and the other half in Room B. Each participant in Room A will be randomly paired with someone in Room B. Neither will ever learn the identity of the other. Participants in Room A (proposers) have been given $10 and the opportunity to send any portion of their $10 to a randomly assigned participant in Room B (responders). Participants in Room A can send any dollar amount—$0, $1, $2, $3, $4, $5, $6, $7, $8, $9, or $10. Participants in Room B can choose to keep the amount sent, in which case the division proposed by A is final. Or, participants in Room B can reject the amount sent, in which case both individuals receive nothing.

You are a proposer in Room A. How much do you send to your paired participant in Room B? Remember you can send any dollar amount from $0 to $10 and the participant in Room B can accept this offer, or reject it, in which case you both receive nothing. If the other participant accepts and you send $x, you keep $10 – $x.

Amount Sent to Room B: _____

This is called the **ultimatum game**, and traditional economic theory predicts that a self-interested responder will accept any positive amount.[7] A proposer who realizes this should make the smallest possible offer, $1 in the previous example.

Is your choice similar to those of other students? On average, proposers send more than the minimum possible offer. Perhaps this is because they anticipate that responders will retaliate against offers they perceive to be unfair by rejecting them. Across many experiments in many different countries with different types of participants, responders reject offers that are less than 20% of the proposer's endowment ($2 in our example) about half of the time.[8]

The results of the ultimatum game seem to be inconsistent with pure self-interest in two respects. First, contrary to the maximization of their self-interest, responders reject positive offers. Second, proposers' behavior may indicate a taste for fairness as they, on average, send more than the minimum offer. This second conclusion could be premature because proposers may behave strategically and offer more than the minimum if they anticipate the retaliation of the responders.

Another game was proposed to separate fairness and strategy. Again, consider a hypothetical experiment in which you and another student are anonymously paired. You two will split a sum of money. Though the situation is still hypothetical, try to answer the following question as if real money were at stake:

Game 2:

One-half of the participants are completing the experiment in Room A and the other half in Room B. Each participant in Room A will be randomly paired with someone in Room B. Neither will ever learn the identity of the other. Participants in Room A (proposers) have been given $10 and the opportunity to send any portion of their $10 to a randomly assigned participant in Room B (receivers). Participants in Room A can send any dollar amount—$0, $1, $2, $3, $4, $5, $6, $7, $8, $9, or $10. The division proposed by A is final.

You are a proposer in Room A. How much do you send to your paired participant in Room B? Remember, you can send any dollar amount from $0 to $10. If you send x, you keep $10 − x.

Amount Sent to Room B: _____

This is called the **dictator game** because the receivers in Room B have no decision to make. Here it seems clear that the proposer should send nothing at all unless he cares about fairness. Remember that the players' identities are closely guarded so that reputation plays no role.[9]

Figure 11.1 illustrates the typical results and compares the ultimatum and dictator games. The proposers' endowment in this particular game was $5, unlike the

---

FIGURE 11.1 Offers by Proposers in Ultimatum and Dictator Games

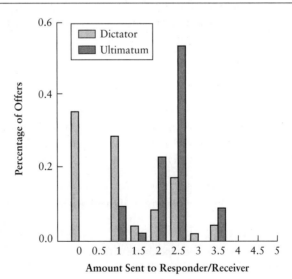

Notes: The proposers' endowment in the game was $5. The horizontal axis indicates the amount sent to the responder/receiver in dollars and the vertical axis shows the percentage of offers at each dollar amount.

Reprinted from Games and Economic Behavior, Vol 6, Issue 3, Forsythe, R., J. L. Horowitz, N. E. Savin, and M. Sefton, "Fairness in simple bargaining experiments," 347–369. © May 1994. With permission from Elsevier.

game described before in which the endowment was $10. The horizontal axis in the figure indicates the amount sent to the responder/receiver in dollars, and the vertical axis shows the percentage of offers at each dollar amount. If fairness was the only factor driving proposers' behavior in the ultimatum game, the distributions should be similar. The figure indicates this is not the case. The distribution of offers for the ultimatum game is clearly centered further to the right than the distribution for the dictator game. Participants in the ultimatum game are more generous. In this dictator game, 36% of the players offer nothing, whereas in the ultimatum game, all players make positive offers.

While the dictator game results indicate that fairness alone does not drive the generosity observed in the ultimatum game, we continue to conclude that many people value fairness. Note that if 36% of the dictators gave nothing, 64% gave something to a person they did not know and would not knowingly interact with in the future. This is real money the proposers could have easily kept. There was no opportunity for retaliation, punishment, or reputation formation. Remember also that about 20% of the responders in ultimatum games are willing to sacrifice their own income to retaliate against a player they perceive to be unfair.

THE TRUST GAME

A dictator game can be thought of as measuring pure altruism. Another game, known as the **trust game**, measures trust and reciprocity.[10] As before, try to answer the following hypothetical question as if real money were at stake:

Game 3:
One-half of the participants are completing the experiment in Room A and the other half in Room B. Each participant in Room A (investors) will be randomly paired with someone in Room B (trustees). Participants in each room are given $10. Investors then have the opportunity to send any portion of their $10 to a randomly assigned participant in Room B. Participants in Room A can send any dollar amount—$0, $1, $2, $3, $4, $5, $6, $7, $8, $9, or $10.

Each dollar sent to Room B is increased *three* times. Participants in Room B decide how much money to send back to Room A and how much money to keep. Participants in Room B can send back any dollar amount—ranging from $0 to three times the amount received from Room A.

You are an investor in Room A. How much do you send to your paired participant in Room B? Remember you can send any dollar amount from $0 to $10. If you send $x, the trustee receives $3x$ and you keep $10 - x. The trustee then decides the dollar amount to return to you (y). The trustee can return any dollar amount from $0 to $3x$. Your total earnings will be what you initially keep, plus what the trustee returns or ($10 - x) + y.

Amount Sent to Room B: _____

This is called the trust game because it measures how much the investors in Room A trust the trustees in Room B. It is also referred to as the investment game because the participants in Room A are "investing" the amount $x in participants in Room B.

In theory, the trustees in Room B should return nothing at all if they are purely self-interested ($y = 0$). The investors in Room A will anticipate the motivations of those in Room B and send nothing to begin with ($x = 0$). But notice that if the investors trust the trustees, there is a lot to be gained. With no trust, the total gain in the game is $20 ($10 + $10) because each participant keeps the $10 he is given. With complete trust, the total gain is $40 ($10 times 3 + $10) because the trustor sends his $10 endowment, which is then multiplied by 3. If there is trust, all players can potentially be better off.

Typically, investors send about half of their endowment to trustees, though there is a lot of variation across people. The amount sent represents the trust exhibited by subjects in Room A. The trustees in Room B typically return less than what they receive from the investors ($y < $x). Thus, trust does not pay for many investors.

Figure 11.2 illustrates the results of a trust game. In this game, both players initially received $10 and the amount sent by investors was multiplied by 3 in

---

FIGURE 11.2 The Behavior of Investors and Responders in Trust Games

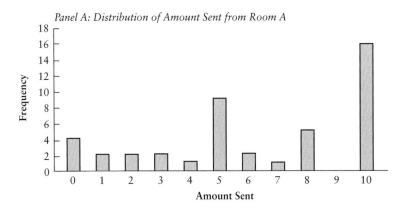

Panel A: Distribution of Amount Sent from Room A

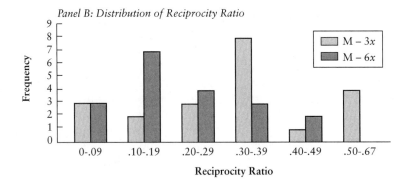

Panel B: Distribution of Reciprocity Ratio

Notes: Both players were endowed with $10. The top panel shows the frequency that each dollar amount was sent by investors. The bottom panel shows the distribution of reciprocity.
Source: Ackert, L. F., B. K. Church, and S. Davis, 2006, "Social distance and reciprocity," Working paper, Kennesaw State University.

some cases $(M - 3x)$ and 6 in others $(M - 6x)$. The majority of the investors in Room A (33 of 44 subjects) sent at least one-half of their initial endowment to Room B. The mean amount sent is more than $6, but variation across people is clear from the graph. Reciprocity is defined as the amount returned to investors divided by the amount available to students in Room B (i.e., the multiplier times the amount received). The reciprocity ratio is less than 50% most of the time, implying that participants in Room B kept *more* than they returned. In fact, many investors received less than they sent so that trust did not necessarily pay in this game.

Trust and reciprocity have important implications for business transactions. As in this game, without trust a great deal of the potential benefit of a transaction may be lost.

WHO IS MORE FAIR?

The evidence provided in this chapter indicates that some people are fair, behave reciprocally, and trust others. We also saw, though, that there is great variation in these traits across people. Can we say anything about the characteristics of people who are fairer?

Many studies have examined whether certain people are more prone to pro-social behavior, and the conclusions are quite mixed. Consideration of culture, gender, or academic background does not lead to reliable conclusions. One factor that does seem to have a consistent effect is age, at least for very young children. Young children tend to be more self-interested, and as they grow older, they become more socially minded.[11]

Though individual characteristics do not seem to matter much, the results of cross-cultural experiments indicate that there are important ties between social behavior and the economic organization of a culture. Experiments with the Machiguenga people who live in the Peruvian Amazon provided some startling results.[12] The Machiguenga live in single-family or small extended-family groups. They live by hunting and fishing and practice slash-and-burn horticulture. Exchange is within the family unit, and outside cooperation is extremely rare. Thus, you can imagine that their culture and daily lives are quite different from those of the typical urban college student. In experiments, the Machiguenga were much less generous than reported elsewhere in the literature.

Was this an outlier, or did it indicate a strong cultural difference? A team of researchers set out to answer this question.[13] They identified a variety of groups with different cultures and sent researchers to conduct games, including the ultimatum game. While student proposers typically offered between 42% and 48% of their endowments to responders, the proposers in the cross-cultural experiments had much more dispersed offers of from 25% to 57% of their endowments. The behavior of responders was also more variable than observed previously. As Figure 11.3 shows, rejections of offers are rare in some groups but common in others. Low offers, defined as less than 20% of the endowment, were not rejected at all in some populations. Even offers of more than 50% of the endowment (which most would consider quite fair) were rejected in other groups like the Gnau of Papua New Guinea.

Though this work continues, it seems that pro-social behavior is related to how people lead their daily lives. While individual demographic differences did not seem

FIGURE 11.3 Responders' Rejections of Offers in Ultimatum Games

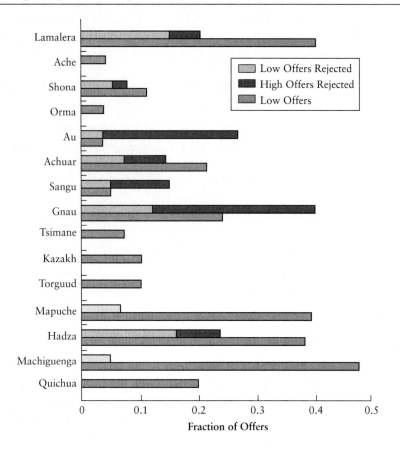

Henrich, J., 2000, "Does culture matter in economic behavior? Ultimatum game bargaining among the Machiguenga of the Peruvian Amazon," *American Economic Review* 90(4), 973–979. © 2000 American Economic Review. Reproduced with the permission of the publisher and the author.

to matter much, the economic organization of the group and the degree of market integration had important effects. In finance we usually think that markets function better when people are self-interested. Cross-cultural research finds the opposite. In cultures with more active exchange, experimental participants made more generous offers. In the future, additional investigation might help us to better understand the direction of the effect. In other words, are people more pro-social because they are accustomed to interpersonal exchange, or are they more prone to exchange because they are pro-social? This research will provide important implications for how we think about the functioning of financial markets.

11.4   SOCIAL INFLUENCES MATTER

Earlier in this chapter we presented evidence indicating that people are not purely motivated by self-interest. At this point, you might be wondering why we care.

Later, in Chapter 12, we provide additional examples of how social forces matter in finance. In order to convince you that we should care, we provide two examples here of how fairness and social preferences can be important in the finance realm. We will first consider how social preferences might impact market competition and then optimal contract design. In Chapter 2, we saw that the efficient functioning of markets and the alignment of incentives across principals and agents are critical issues in finance.[14]

COMPETITION IN MARKETS

Some people can be classified as selfish according to the games described here. Others behave reciprocally and seem to care about fairness. Recent research shows that we cannot understand how competition impacts market prices if we ignore the effect of fairness. In fact, research reported by Urs Fischbacher, Christina Fong, and Ernst Fehr indicates that changing the number of competitors *by only one* can have a significant effect on market outcomes.[15]

To see this, consider the following modification of the ultimatum game. Start with the ultimatum game, but increase the number of responders from one to two or five who are in competition with one another. The proposer makes his offer and then the responders simultaneously decide whether to accept or reject the offer. If more than one responder accepts, one is randomly chosen to get the amount offered by the proposer. If only one responder accepts, he gets the offered amount, and if all responders reject, all receive nothing.

This modified ultimatum game is analogous to a goods market with one seller (the proposer) and multiple competing buyers (the responders). Everyone in the market knows the value of the good to everyone else, so the seller should set the price at the buyers' maximum willingness to pay (which is the same for all buyers). In this game with purely self-interested sellers and buyers, the seller should take all the gains in a transaction. To understand this, think about a two-person game. If both are self-interested, the seller will set the price exactly equal to the maximum amount the buyer will pay because if the price is one cent less, the buyer is better off. If the seller sets the price one cent higher than the maximum amount the buyer will pay, the buyer would reject the offer.

Adding competition to the game should have no effect because the proposer is already reaping all the gains from the transaction. In other words, competition among the buyers is not expected to change the price because with self-interested buyers and sellers, the seller is already setting the highest price possible. Competition among the buyers does not give the seller more power.

Yet, Fischbacher, Fong, and Fehr find that competition has a large effect on the market. They report that with one buyer, the buyer received about 41% of the gains from the transaction, but with two buyers, the trading buyer received only 19% of the gain. Recall that with multiple buyers only one is randomly selected for the transaction. With five buyers, the trading buyer receives about 14% of the gains from trade. Figure 11.4 illustrates the average accepted offers across the 20 periods played in the game for three groups: BG (bilateral or two-person game), RC2 (two competing responders), and RC5 (five competing responders). The average offers do not seem to change that much over time and the ordering remains the same.

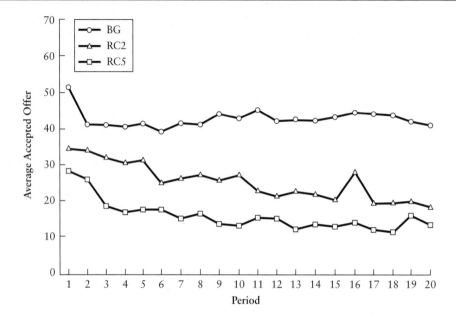

FIGURE 11.4 Average Accepted Offer Across 20 Trading Periods for Three Groups: BG (Bilateral or Two-Person Game), RC2 (Two Competing Responders), and RC5 (Five Competing Responders)

Source: Fischbacher, U., C. M. Fong and E. Fehr. 2003, "Fairness, errors and the power of competition," in Institute for Empirical Research in Economics, University of Zurich, Working paper number 133. © 2003 University of Zurich.

Although the results are not consistent with purely self-interested traders, fairness and reciprocity can explain why the responders' share decreases with competition. Think back to the two-person ultimatum gain. The proposer should set an offer that is as small as possible, but not very close to zero because proposers anticipate that responders will reject low offers.[16] Responders know they can punish a proposer who is viewed as unfair by rejecting the offer. With more than one responder, a player who retaliates against an unfair proposer may not be successful because he cannot be assured that the other responders will reject the low offer. With more competitors, it is more likely that at least one of the responders is selfish and will accept any positive offer. Even responders who would normally behave reciprocally may accept low offers because they recognize that other responders may be selfish.

These results indicate that competition has important effects on market outcomes when some people care about fairness. Other research by Fehr and Fischbacher shows that fairness concerns define competitive market outcomes under certain conditions.[17] Thus, we cannot rule out fairness as a potentially important factor in markets.

INCENTIVES AND CONTRACT DESIGN

In Chapter 2 we recognized the importance of contract design in aligning the incentives of principals and agents. Owners of a firm want to provide incentives for workers to expend high effort. Stockholders want to design contracts to give managers motivation to act in the owners' best interest and avoid shirking. Experimental studies show that workers respond to wage offers that are viewed as generous or fair by working harder than predicted by models of self-interested agents. As we saw with the ultimatum game, however, there is a great deal of variation across people. Some make purely selfish choices and expend the smallest amount of effort, while a large fraction behaves reciprocally.

A natural question that arises is: Can we provide better incentives for those who are self-interested by designing contracts with explicit incentives? For example, workers could be penalized if a minimum level of effort is not met. These material incentives might lead to extra effort above and beyond the effort level driven by reciprocity. On the other hand, workers may negatively perceive these explicit incentives as indicative of distrust.

Fehr and Simon Gächter designed an experiment to examine these questions.[18] In their game, employers offered workers wages and stated a desired effort level. In one group (TT or trust group), the desired effort level was stated but not binding, and in another group (IT or incentive group), employers were able to fine shirking workers so there were explicit performance incentives.

Figure 11.5 shows the average actual effort level chosen for offered "rent" categories. Here rent measures the workers' payoff by taking the offered wage and subtracting the cost of effort. The number above each bar in the figure indicates the percentage of contracts in each interval for each group. For example, 21% of the contracts in the IT group offered rents between 0% and 5%. With the exception of the lowest offered wages, the average effort level chosen by workers is *lower* with explicit incentives. The results indicate that there is a tension between

FIGURE 11.5 Average Actual Effort Level Chosen Across Rent Categories

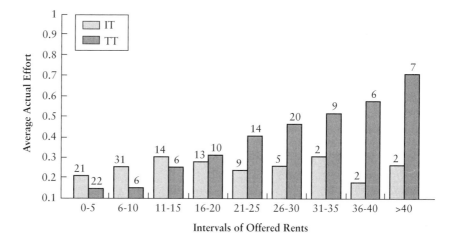

Fehr, E. and S. Gächter. 2001, "Do incentive contracts crowd out voluntary cooperation?" in University of Southern California Law School, Center in Law, Economics and Organization Research Paper Series Number C01–3, 2001, 23. © 2001 USC Gould School of Law.

motives generated by fairness and reciprocity and those generated by material incentives. Workers may respond to explicit incentives with hostility.

Typically, principal-agent models suggest that the best contracts should include
all verifiable performance measures. This research provides insight into why we
might optimally observe incomplete employment contracts. Explicit performance
incentives can actually have an effect that is opposite to the desired direction.[19]

11.5   CONFORMITY

In this chapter we have presented evidence that social interests influence how people make decisions. We focused on preferences like fairness and reciprocity, because self-interested people are at the center of most finance theory. Of course,
other social forces affect human behavior and here we will focus on **conformity**,
one aspect of human behavior with which we are all familiar. When people conform they give in to real or imagined social pressure. Later in Chapter 12, we consider some empirical evidence concerning how conformity affects two questions
that have received significant attention: herding by professional financial analysts
and the optimal composition of corporate boards.

TESTING CONFORMITY

Psychologists have studied conformity for some time. Here is a classic example of
the power of conformity:

> **Game 4:**
> Consider the lines in Figure 11.6 and decide which of the lines A, B, or C is
> identical in length to the first line.
>
> The line identical to the first one is _____.

It seems obvious that the answer is line C, doesn't it? What if you were in a room
with eight other university students who all said the answer was line A? Researcher
Solomon Asch found that student participants conformed to an incorrect majority
about one-third of the time. Three-fourths of the students conformed at least one

---

FIGURE 11.6 Asch's Lines

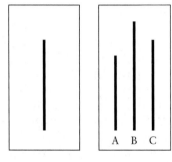

time.[20] Asch's experiment has been replicated many times, and because the level of conformity changes over time, psychologists believe that conformity reflects social norms and culture.[21]

An extreme form of conformity is **groupthink**.[22] Groupthink can take hold in a small group of individuals who are insulated from outside influences. Group members may begin to think alike, while stressing loyalty and suppressing dissent. The group may ignore relevant information and believe they are invulnerable. One recent example of disastrous consequences attributed to groupthink was the Columbia explosion.[23] NASA was warned by a panel that the shuttle had safety problems. Yet, NASA removed five of the nine members on the panel and went ahead with its plan to launch the shuttle. All seven crew members perished.

Fortunately, groupthink has warning signs and can be prevented. If you are a member of a group that ignores warnings, punishes dissenters, or seems invulnerable, remember that you are not. It is actually a good idea to encourage people to express their opinions, particularly opinions that are not consistent with the majority.

Though we may not normally face groupthink in our day-to-day lives, we all observe some degree of conforming behavior among ourselves and others with whom we interact. People tend to evaluate themselves in comparison to others who are close to them.[24] So, for example, a professional financial analyst considers his choices in relation to other analysts in his reference group. If financial decision-makers consider the behavior of others before making a choice, we may observe herd behavior. In the financial press, herding has a negative connotation, but herding might not be such a bad thing if you believe others have better information.[25]

OBEDIENCE TO AUTHORITY

Psychologist Stanley Milgram conducted some startling experiments of obedience in the 1960s that have become famous around the world. In his experiments, Milgram created a box with levers that purportedly delivered electric shock from 0 to 450 volts. The voltages were labeled from "slight shock" to a final designation of "XXX." The final, ominous designation was two switches after "danger: severe shock." Subjects thought they were participating in an experiment on punishment and learning, but instead Milgram was examining obedience to authority. Each participant was assigned the role of the "teacher," and the "learner" was actually an actor. Wires connected the electric box to the learner, but in actuality, the learner only acted as if an electric shock was transmitted. When the teacher administered shock, the learner feigned a painful response.

How many people do you think would administer a shock when a learner answered a question incorrectly? Does your answer change if the experimenter was viewed as an authority because of his title and lab coat, and if you know that participants received financial compensation?

Every subject in Milgram's original study administered some shock to the learner. Several variations of the experiment were conducted to examine how behavior changed. In the first variant, the teacher (the participant) could not see the learner or hear the learner's (actor's) verbal responses to the shock. The learner's responses appeared on a signal box. But, at 300 volts, the teacher could hear the learner pounding on the wall in protest. At 315 volts, no answers appear on the box and the pounding stopped. Astoundingly, 26 of 40 subjects administered the maximum possible shock. Though many of the teachers were obviously agitated, they continued to administer the shock. Here are comments made by one participant when he declined to administer additional shock:[26]

> I think he's trying to communicate, he's knocking … Well it's not fair to shock the guy … these are terrific volts. I don't think this is very humane … Oh, I can't go on with this; no, this isn't right. It's a hell of an experiment. The guy is suffering in there. No, I don't want to go on. This is crazy.

Milgram's experiment and results have been replicated many times with diverse subject pools. Many subjects suggested that loyalty drove their behavior. Participants were more likely to disobey the experimenter when other subjects in the room also disobeyed, the experimenter left the room, the learner and teacher were in the same room, or there were two experimenters giving conflicting direction.

11.6   SOCIAL BEHAVIOR AND EMOTION

In Chapter 7 we discussed emotion and brain circuitry. Also, recall that fMRI technology allows us to see which parts of the brain are operating at different times. Through research using fMRI, there is increasing evidence that emotions and social interaction are inextricably linked. Much of this research is slotted under **social neuroscience**, which investigates the "social brain," the neural circuitry that operates when we deal with other people.[27]

As an example, fMRI technology was used to investigate cognitive and emotional processes during the ultimatum game.[28] As we discussed earlier in this chapter, results of the ultimatum game sometimes seem to be inconsistent with pure self-interest, in the sense that positive offers are rejected to the detriment of both parties. This may be because of the perception that fairness has been breached. Naturally enough, when we feel that we are being treated unfairly, anger is triggered. In Chapter 7 we saw that the forebrain is critical for rational thought, while the limbic system is the primary seat of emotion. When ultimatum game participants were scanned using fMRIs, it was apparent that unfair offers triggered activity in both the forebrain (rational thought: "should I accept this offer since it is in my self-interest?") and the limbic system (emotion: "I'm getting even with this guy, even though it will cost me"). When unfair offers were rejected, heightened activity was observed in the limbic system, making it clear which part of the brain won the argument.

11.7   SOCIAL BEHAVIOR AND EVOLUTION

What is the source of the human desire to conform? Why are many people willing to be fair when they really don't have to be? It is possible that evolution favored people who were cooperative and equitable in exchanges.[29] Perhaps we are actually "hardwired" to behave socially. Evolution may favor reciprocal behavior because groups that are pro-social will outperform groups that are not. Imagine our society if everyone always acted in terms of their own, narrow self-interest. Conformity may encourage cooperative behavior.

Evidence supports the argument that other-regarding preferences influence human behavior. But, many things influence behavior and we cannot include everything in our model when we want to make inferences and policy recommendations. As Mill put it, "... because, as no two individual cases are exactly alike, no *general* maxims could ever be laid down unless *some* of the circumstances of the particular case were left out of consideration."[30] Researchers are today making the case that social influences are so important that their impact must be considered. In the next chapter, we will see how social forces were of great consequence in the fall of a large American corporation, the Enron Corporation.

CHAPTER HIGHLIGHTS

1. *Homo economicus* or economic man makes rational decisions that are in his best interest.
2. Real people are often generous, fair, and cooperative in exchanges.
3. Reciprocity and trust are important for business transactions because they reduce costs.
4. Pro-social behavior varies quite a lot across people, and while some people are fairness-minded, others seem to be driven by self-interest.
5. We cannot predict who will behave pro-socially based on observable characteristics, but significant differences across cultures are observed.
6. Even if only a subset of people exhibits fairness-minded behavior, market prices can be influenced.
7. Explicit performance incentives in labor contracts can have an effect opposite to that intended because some people react negatively if they think that others believe they are not trustworthy.
8. People often succumb to social pressures and conform to the majority of a group.
9. Some people will obey an authority figure even when the actions that are demanded conflict with their personal conscience.
10. Researchers look at the parts of the brain that are activated when decisions are made and conclude that emotions and social behavior are linked.
11. Evolution may favor pro-social behavior because, when members of a group cooperate, the group will perform better.

DISCUSSION QUESTIONS AND PROBLEMS

1. Differentiate the following terms/concepts:

    a. Dictator and ultimatum games
    b. Trust and reciprocity
    c. Conformity and groupthink
    d. Economic man and real people

2. Discuss the merits of the following statement: The evidence clearly indicates that proposers in dictator games care about fairness because they send responders more money than they have to.

3. In 1962, U.S. President John F. Kennedy took specific actions to avoid the pitfalls of groupthink in deciding how to proceed during the Cuban Missile Crisis. Conduct your own research, and write a few paragraphs evaluating the steps taken and their effectiveness.

4. Your firm has built a manufacturing plant not too far from a large European city. You are a member of a management team that is charged with designing employment contracts that promote high effort among the employees. What factors might you bring to the attention of the team? Would your answer change if the manufacturing plant is located near a fairly isolated village in a developing nation?

5. The highly successful online auction site eBay has attracted millions of buyers and sellers. In these faceless exchanges, trust on both sides of a transaction could be of concern. One action eBay has taken to promote trust in exchanges is to allow feedback. Why is this so important and effective?

ENDNOTES

1 For a more detailed review of the origin and meaning of the term *homo economicus*, see Persky, J., 1995, "Retrospectives: The ethology of *homo economicus*," *Journal of Economic Perspectives* 9(2) (Spring), 221–231.

2 Mill, J. S., 1874, *Essays on Some Unsettled Questions of Political Economy*, 2nd ed. reprinted 1968 (Augustus M. Kelley Publishers, New York), pp. 137–138.

3 Ibid., p. 124.

4 Ibid., p. 138.

5 For one of the early arguments that fairness is an important consideration in economic decision-making, see Kahneman, D., J. L. Knetsch, and R. H. Thaler, 1986, "Fairness and the assumptions of economics," *Journal of Business* 59(4), S285–S300.

6 Many researchers have examined why tipping is common practice. See, for example, Azar, O. H., 2007, "The social norm of tipping: A review," *Journal of Applied Social Psychology* 37(2), 380–402.

7 Early ultimatum games were reported by Guth, W., R. Schmittberger, and B. Schwarze, 1982, "An experimental analysis of ultimatum bargaining," *Journal of Economic Behavior and Organization* 3(4), 367–388.

8 For in-depth results regarding cross-cultural tests of fairness, see Henrich, J., R. Boyd, S. Bowles, C. Camerer, E. Fehr, and H. Gintis, eds., 2004, *Foundations of Human Sociality* (Oxford University Press, Oxford, UK).

9 Forsythe, R., J. L. Horowitz, N.E. Savin, and M. Sefton, 1994, "Fairness in simple bargaining experiments," *Games and Economic Behavior* 6, 347–369.

10 For an experiment that separates trust from altruism and reciprocity, see Cox, J. C., 2004, "How to identify trust and reciprocity," *Games and Economic Behavior* 46, 260–281.

11 A comprehensive review of the literature is presented by Camerer, C. F., 2003, *Behavioral Game Theory: Experiments in Strategic Interaction* (Russell Sage Foundation, New York).

12 See Henrich, J., R. Boyd, S. Bowles, C. Camerer, E. Fehr, and H. Gintis, eds., 2004, *Foundations of Human Sociality* (Oxford University Press, Oxford, UK), p. 21.

13 Ibid.

14 These two examples are adapted from Fehr, E., and U. Fischbacher, 2002, "Why social preferences matter—The impact of nonselfish motives on competition, cooperation, and incentives," *The Economic Journal* 112, C1–C33.

15 See Fischbacher, U., C. M. Fong, and E. Fehr, 2003, "Fairness, errors, and the power of competition," Institute for Empirical Research in Economics, University of Zurich, Working paper no. 133.

16 Notice in the example that the price is the proposer's endowment less that amount offered (i.e., it is what the responder gets to keep).

17 See Fehr, E., and U. Fischbacher, 2002, "Why social preferences matter—The impact of non-selfish motives on competition, cooperation, and incentives," *The Economic Journal* 112, C1–C33. In their example, the enforceability of contracts is critical.

18 Fehr, E., and S. Gächter, 2001, "Do incentive contracts crowd out voluntary cooperation?" University of Southern California Law School, Center for Law, Economics and Organization Research Paper Series No. C01-3.

19 Others have also argued that close supervision of employees can lead to resentment and hostility toward the employer. See Akerlof, G. A., and R. E. Kranton, 2008, "Identity, supervision, and work groups," *American Economic Review* 98(2), 212–217.

20 Asch, S., 1955, "Opinions and social pressure," *Scientific American*, 31–35; and Asch, S., 1956, "Studies of independence and conformity: A minority of one against a unanimous majority," *Psychological Monographs* 70(9).

21 Bond, R., and P. B. Smith, 1996, "Culture and conformity: A meta-analysis of studies using Asch's line judgment task," *Psychological Bulletin* 119, 111–137.

22 Janis, I. L., 1982, *Groupthink: Psychological Studies of Policy Decisions and Fiascoes*, 2nd ed. (Houghton-Mifflin, Boston).

23 Ferraris, C., and R. Carveth, 2003, "NASA and the Columbia disaster: Decision-making by Groupthink?" Proceedings of the 2003 Association for Business Communication Annual Convention.

24 Psychologist Leon Festinger proposed social comparison theory in which people look outside themselves to evaluate their worth. See Festinger, L., 1954, "A theory of social comparison processes," *Human Relations* 7 (2), 117–140.

25 A model of rational herding behavior is proposed by Banerjee, A. V., "A simple model of herd behavior," *Quarterly Journal of Economics* 107(3), 797–817.

26 Milgram, S., 1974, *Obedience to Authority: An Experimental View* (Harper & Row, New York), p. 32.

27 Goleman, D., 2006, *Social Intelligence: The New Science of Human Relationships* (Bantam Books, New York).

28 Sanfey, A. G., J. K. Rilling, J. A. Aronson, L. E. Nystrom, and J. D. Cohen, 2003, "The neural basis of economic decision-making in the ultimatum game," *Science* 300, 1755–1758.

29 See Gintis, H., S. Bowles, R. Boyd, and E. Fehr, 2005, *Moral Sentiments and Material Interests: The Foundations of Cooperation in Economic Life* (MIT Press, Cambridge, Massachusetts).

30 Mill, J. S., 1874, *Essays on Some Unsettled Questions of Political Economy*, 2nd ed. reprinted 1968 (Augustus M. Kelley Publishers, New York), p. 146.

SOCIAL FORCES AT WORK: THE COLLAPSE OF AN AMERICAN CORPORATION

CHAPTER 12

12.1 INTRODUCTION

During the 1990s, investors witnessed soaring stock prices for some corporations. While valuations seemed to be disconnected from underlying fundamentals, many argued they were warranted because it was a "new economy." Here is how the argument went. The structure of the world economy was fundamentally changed by the Internet revolution so that long periods of growth were to be expected. As so often occurs when it seems too good to be true, a downturn in the economy beginning in 2000 led to more realistic expectations.

Some of the firms that experienced the most astounding growth later experienced even more astounding falls. One particularly notorious rise and fall was that of Enron. In December 2000, Enron's market capitalization was more than $60 billion, and *Fortune* magazine rated it the most innovative large company in the United States.[1] Just one year later in December of 2001, the firm filed for bankruptcy. This chapter focuses on the social forces that impacted the behavior of two groups of very important players in the collapse of Enron: the corporation's board and the financial analysts who followed the firm.

The chapter begins in Section 12.2 with a discussion of why the corporate form of ownership is prevalent around the world. Optimal board size and composition, as well as directors' incentive structure and compensation, are examined. Next, in Section 12.3, we consider financial analysts' role as information intermediaries, their performance, and behavior. Section 12.4 focuses on the rise and fall of Enron. The behavior of its directors, financial analysts, and other players are examined. The final section notes the importance of retaining a personal identity in any organization and being aware of the potentially mesmerizing effect of social influences.

12.2   CORPORATE BOARDS

In terms of size, the corporate form of ownership is dominant. What is so good about the corporation? The **corporation** is a legal entity separate from its founders or owners. A corporation's life is not limited and its ownership shares can be easily transferred. Though a corporation can be sued, the shareholders have limited liability and can only lose their investment. In 1819, Chief Justice John Marshall described a corporation as follows:[2]

> A corporation is an artificial being, invisible, intangible, and existing only in contemplation of law. Being the mere creature of law, it possesses only those properties which the charter of its creation confers upon it, either expressly, or as incidental to its very existence. These are such as are supposed best calculated to effect the object for which it was created. Among the most important are immortality, and, if the expression may be allowed, individuality; properties, by which a perpetual succession of many persons are considered as the same, and may act as a single individual. They enable a corporation to manage its own affairs, and to hold property, without the perplexing intricacies, the hazardous and endless necessity, of perpetual conveyances for the purpose of transmitting it from hand to hand. It is chiefly for the purpose of clothing bodies of men, in succession, with these qualities and capacities, that corporations were invented, and are in use. By these means, a perpetual succession of individuals are capable of acting for the promotion of the particular object, like one immortal being.

The potential for an unlimited life is an important benefit of incorporation, though, as we all know, no corporation is truly immortal. Even though it is nearly 200 years old, the justice's opinion remains important because it limits the ability of a state to interfere with the business of a corporation.

Of course, while there are limits on state interference, corporations have external and internal constraints. Perhaps the most notable external force in the United States is the **Securities and Exchange Commission** (SEC). The SEC was created under the Securities and Exchange Act of 1934, and its mission "is to protect investors, maintain fair, orderly, and efficient markets, and facilitate capital formation."[3] Internally, corporations are governed by a board of directors. In fact, a board is a legal requirement for incorporation. Before we turn to the social forces affecting the decisions of board members, we will consider why a board of directors is desirable, as well as the optimal structure of the board.

Benefits of a Corporate Board

Ideally, corporate boards advise and counsel executives and provide discipline to managers. Boards of directors are common throughout the world and are not merely an American phenomenon. Though boards are mandated by regulation, many were in existence *before* these regulations were in place. Thus, there must be some economic reason for corporate boards. In Chapter 2, we considered the agency problem that exists between managers (agents) and shareholders (principals). A corporate board may be one way to mitigate the conflicts of interest between managers and shareholders.[4]

Because many of today's corporations are very large and have many share-holders, it is often difficult to monitor managers directly. Some shareholders may even shirk their responsibility to monitor, assuming others will monitor managers. This shirking is often referred to as the **free rider problem**. In addition, the average shareholder may lack the knowledge, skills, and information necessary to fully understand complicated business transactions. A board of directors that is responsible for monitoring management may be an efficient solution to the agency problem.[5] If shareholders trust the board, they may indicate their trust by investing in the firm.

Researchers have investigated whether there is an optimal board size and composition that promotes efficient monitoring and engenders the trust of shareholders in a board. Some argue that small boards are better than large boards. When boards are large, the directors tend to be less involved with the management of the firm and agency problems can increase. For example, some directors may free ride on others. The empirical evidence is consistent with the theory that small boards are more effective and increase the value of the firm, as compared to large boards.[6] Recent theoretical evidence, however, suggests that the optimal board size depends on the firm's individual characteristics, including the level of shareholder activism.[7]

What about the composition of the board? Most boards are combinations of **insiders** and **outsiders**. Inside directors are managers or executives of the company, whereas outside directors are not employees. Advantages of inside directors include their privileged access to firm-specific information, dedication to the firm, and better expertise relating to the firm's activities. Advantages of outside directors include their broad backgrounds, independent evaluations, and shareholder orientation.[8] Research into the link between firm performance and the proportion of outside directors finds little evidence that board composition is related to the performance of a corporation in cross-sectional analyses of actual firm data.

OUTSIDE DIRECTORS

Particularly after the corporate scandals of recent years, a policy of ensuring that boards have a majority of outside directors has been advocated. Yet, there was little basis for believing this was advisable until recently. Empirical examination of the relationship between board composition and firm performance is challenging because independence is fundamentally unobservable. Is any individual who is not an employee of the firm truly independent from the firm's managers and executives? What if our CEO and "independent" board member were college roommates at Princeton? What if they play tennis on the same doubles team on weekends? What if the "independent" board member is also a CEO and our CEO is an "independent" board member on the other board?

In cases in which researchers have difficulties isolating the variables of interest, investigations using an experimental method are particularly useful. A recent study examines voting behavior in an experimental setting in which the board is faced with conflicts of interest between insiders and shareholders.[9] The board consists of uninformed outsiders whose incentives are aligned with owners and informed insiders whose incentives are not so aligned. The evidence suggests that outsider-dominated boards more often produce outcomes consistent with the interests of owners. In addition, this research suggests that decision-making may be more efficient with small boards.

IT'S A SMALL WORLD

Today the common view is that corporate boards should have a majority of outside directors. While, as noted before, experimental evidence supports this view, even boards with a majority of outside directors sometimes seem to disregard the interests of the firm's owners. This may be because board members that are classified as independent really are not. After all, it really is a small world.

You have probably heard the common legend that any two people can be connected by a chain of six links or "six degrees of separation."[10] This legend is not purely myth. Psychologist Stanley Milgram conducted field experiments and concluded that two randomly chosen individuals can be connected by surprisingly short chains.[11] He found that any two Americans are likely tied by chains of five or six.

The world of corporate directors is even smaller. Many boards are *interlocked*, meaning that there are overlapping board memberships. A recent study of several thousand directors serving on several hundred of the largest U.S. companies found that the directors could be connected by only 4.3 links.[12] A link means that two individuals serve on the same board. If boards met once per month, then an idea (or rumor) discussed at one board meeting would be transmitted to 97% of the boards of large U.S. corporations *in only six months*!

It is natural to wonder at this point whether the connections across board members may be related to social ties, such as clubs and schooling. For example, do we observe short chains among directors because a large proportion of them graduated from Ivy League institutions? And even if the directors are closely connected, it is important to consider whether firm performance suffers. It could be the case that a social network allows better identification of highly qualified directors. Recent research examines how social networks impact corporate governance.[13] The study is based on a unique dataset of executives and directors in France during 1992–2003. In France there are readily identified business elites, which allow better measurement of the social networks. The authors conclude that connected CEOs appoint friendly directors, and, as a result, inefficient executives tend to remain in power longer.

DIRECTORS, COMPENSATION, AND SELF-INTEREST

The small world of corporate directors means that managerial innovations can spread rapidly. It also means that managers may be particularly susceptible to contagion, regardless of whether the behavior increases or decreases the value of the enterprise.

One of the most important decisions a corporate board makes is the CEO's compensation. The task of a corporate board is to monitor managers and one way to do so is to align managers' incentives with shareholder interests. The popular press and shareholders have expressed concern that top executives' earnings are going through the roof and reducing shareholder welfare. In 2006, the CEOs of the 500 largest U.S. companies earned an average of $15.2 million, up 38% from 2005.[14] Could social forces play a role in skyrocketing executive compensation?

Imagine this situation. You are on the board of a company and your friend, Susan, is the CEO. The boards are interlocked, and Susan also happens to be on the board of the company for which you are CEO. Will you be thinking of the stockholders of Susan's company when you consider her compensation package, or will you be thinking about maximizing her income because next week your board will evaluate your compensation package?

Also, consider this situation. Your acquaintance, Keith, is CEO of a third company. He is currently putting together a slate of nominations for his board to replace individuals who have completed their terms. Do you think Keith is more likely to include your name on the slate if he thinks you are likely to be agreeable to his point of view? Keep in mind that this directorship is highly desirable both from a reputation standpoint and in monetary terms. Membership on the board of a highly visible company is a nice line item for your resume and provides good conversation at social gatherings. Directors of large corporations can make hundreds of thousands of dollars.[15]

In some cases, it may be that directors who put their interests ahead of shareholders are purely self-interested, in blatant disregard of their duty. It is also possible, however, that many of these individuals see themselves as simply trying to be cooperative. They may realize they are not being completely honest in their assessments of performance or appropriate compensation level, but at the same time, they do not view themselves as dishonest. Research shows that people quite often tell "little white lies" that they view as harmless.[16] People sometimes tell white lies in order to mold the impressions others have of them. These white lies may actually be viewed as beneficial if they smooth social situations. The problem is that little lies often lead down a slippery slope to harmful deception.

DIRECTORS AND LOYALTY

It is also possible that directors are prone to misplaced loyalty. Loyalty is valued by people and may be particularly valuable in business relationships. Directors might go along with a CEO because of a predisposition to obedience.[17] Recall the experiments conducted by Stanley Milgram, which were reported in Chapter 11.[18] In the experiments, subjects were asked to deliver electric shocks to others when they answered a question incorrectly. Amazingly, every participant administered some shock. These experiments provide compelling evidence on the power of authority. People will sometimes disregard their conscience when a person of authority calls for action.

Loyalty might have important consequences in the boardroom if directors are prone to blindly follow the CEO. From research we know that the impact of loyalty can be mitigated by encouraging dissenting opinions, a diverse board, and truly independent directors. In addition, the board can be encouraged to meet without the CEO. Notice that these practices may also allow the board to avoid the pitfalls of groupthink, discussed in Chapter 11.

12.3   ANALYSTS

As we will discuss in the following section, the behavior of corporate boards came under much scrutiny after recent corporate scandals. Financial analysts also received a great deal of attention. In this section, we consider the important role of financial analysts in our financial system and the social forces they may be susceptible to. In Chapters 8 and 9 we briefly mentioned that analysts tend to herd (while sometimes exhibiting anti-herding behavior), and that their earnings forecasts and recommendations are often excessively optimistic. In this section, we elaborate on the role and behavior of analysts.

WHAT DO PROFESSIONAL SECURITY ANALYSTS DO?

Security analysts are information intermediaries. They are valuable to investors because, through their expertise, they assimilate a great deal of information and provide recommendations concerning investment opportunities. Analysts consider information from financial statements, trade shows, the press, conversations with corporate executives, and other insiders. In some cases they make recommendations regarding whether a stock should be purchased, with recommendations being discrete. For example, their recommendation might follow these lines: strong buy, buy, hold, sell, strong sell. Analysts also provide forecasts of future performance, including earnings and growth rates. These forecasts help investors better evaluate the future prospects of a firm.

There are three types of professional analysts. **Sell-side analysts** are typically employed by brokers, dealers, and investment banks. Often their reports are used to attract investment banking business to the firm. **Buy-side analysts** are usually employed by large money management firms, including mutual and hedge funds and insurance companies. These reports are usually generated for internal purposes. Finally, there are **independent analysts**. These analysts are not associated with any large investment or money management firm. They provide independent research, and their firms generate earnings through subscriptions or fee-based research.

THE PERFORMANCE OF SECURITY ANALYSTS

Much academic research has investigated the properties of analysts' earnings forecasts and recommendations. As discussed earlier, the evidence indicates that analysts are too optimistic.[19] The focus has been on sell-side and independent analysts because the reports of buy-side analysts are generally not available to the public. Shouldn't the goal of professional analysts be to provide the most accurate forecasts possible? If their only concern was providing forecasts with minimum error, the answer seems straightforward. Their incentives, however, are much more complicated.

A clear conflict of interest provides a likely source of optimism for sell-side analysts. Analysts in research units may want to assist their corporate finance arms by providing optimistic forecasts, particularly because they do not directly contribute to the firm's revenues. Not only does optimism help to sell stock that the investment bank is currently offering, it also attracts firms who might need investment banking services in the future. The empirical evidence is consistent with the idea that these conflicts of interest have real effects. An analyst whose firm also has an investment banking relationship with a firm the analyst is following is more optimistic than an analyst whose firm does not have a relationship with the firm.[20] In addition, stocks that are recommended as investments by affiliated underwriter analysts perform worse than those recommended by unaffiliated analysts.[21] Even analysts employed by independent research firms may suffer from conflicts of interest. Management is an important source of information about a covered firm.[22] A low earnings forecast or sell recommendation could close the channels of information flow.[23]

DO ANALYSTS HERD?

In addition to the conflicts of interest just described, analysts' decisions may be affected by social forces. As with people in general, security analysts may not like standing out in a crowd, particularly when there is little uncertainty about a covered firm's performance. Research shows that when the uncertainty surrounding a firm they follow is low, analysts tend not to be too optimistic. When uncertainty is high, however, analysts are less concerned about harming their reputations and are not so afraid to issue optimistic forecasts.[24]

If analysts avoid standing out in a crowd, does this mean they also tend to follow the crowd? Herding, or convergence in behavior, among investors is often proposed as an explanation for large swings in market prices. Because professional financial analysts are important information intermediaries, irrational herding among them would raise concern.

People, in general, are subject to the force of the herd. Though we might want to dismiss the tendency to herd as a force influencing only the young or inexperienced, few could seriously contend that they have never succumbed to imitation of another. Of course, what appears to be herding might simply be the result of people having similar information. If everyone knows a certain restaurant is better then others in the neighborhood, a queue will soon result.

Or, herding could result because information acquisition is costly. People often have different information, and it is not costless to determine which alternative is the best. So, if you are in a new city for a day and you see a lot of people going to a restaurant, you might join the queue even if you heard that the one down the street is better. Most people can eat only one dinner. It can be rational to disregard your information and follow the behavior of others. This is referred to as **social learning**.[25]

As are people in general, analysts are social learners, which may explain the finding that analysts' forecasts are biased. In one recent theoretical model, analysts with lower ability release forecasts that do not completely reflect their private information.[26] In this model, when analysts of high and low ability release forecasts simultaneously, the forecasts of low ability analysts are less extreme than their private information suggests. When analysts release forecasts sequentially, analysts of low ability ignore their private information and mimic the behavior of others. With either simultaneous or sequential forecast release, analysts of low ability block private information to favorably affect investors' assessment of their ability. Analysts with low ability want to be perceived as high ability. This is a case of *rational* herding.

As discussed in Chapter 8, while much of the empirical evidence is consistent with herding among analysts, still other evidence suggests that analysts sometimes anti-herd (when, for career concerns, they desire to stick out). In the next section, we turn to Enron. As will be seen, directors and analysts played a leading role in this debacle.

12.4   ENRON

The bankruptcy of Enron was the largest U.S. bankruptcy at the time, now second only to the failure of Worldcom. In Chapter 9 we discussed how overconfidence can have significant deleterious effects on decision-making. The leaders of the Enron Corporation were known for their hubris and perhaps unparalleled arrogance. Certainly the executives of the firm are culpable, but what about the other players? In this section, we will consider how social forces may have influenced the behavior of the board of directors and financial analysts. First, we provide some background on the company.[27]

THE PERFORMANCE AND BUSINESS OF ENRON

Enron was formed in 1985 by Kenneth Lay through the merger of natural gas pipeline companies. Around that time, the natural gas market was deregulated and with its large pipeline network, Enron benefited. In order to continue along a growth path, the firm diversified into natural gas trading and later applied its trading model to other markets. The model allowed buyers and sellers of energy to manage risks and appeared to be phenomenally successful. Few seemed to ask questions or probe into the transactions fueling the firm's growth.

At its peak in 2000, Enron stock traded at $90.75 per share. At the time of the firm's bankruptcy filing at the end of 2001, the stock was worth $0.25. Shareholders faced massive losses. Employees, many of whom had invested heavily in Enron stock in their retirement accounts, were devastated.

Enron's stock price experience from 1990 through 2001, compared to the S&P 500 stock index, is shown in Figure 12.1. To promote comparison, the S&P 500 index value is divided by 10 in the figure. The figure does not seem to suggest that Enron's price experience prior to 2001 was particularly out of the ordinary. The market as a whole was bullish, though, as we will discuss in Chapter 14, this bullishness seems, at least in retrospect, to have been unwarranted.

Other measures of performance might have tipped investors off that something was out of the ordinary for Enron. In addition to the stock price, a commonly reported performance measure is the price-to-earnings (P/E) ratio. Figure 12.2 shows Enron's P/E, compared to the P/E for the S&P 500. At the end of 2000, Enron's P/E ratio was a whopping 68. Even the P/E for the S&P was quite high at 37, but still paled in comparison to Enron's. Clearly, investors were willing to pay a high price per dollar of current earnings to acquire Enron's stock. Was this because the future prospects of the firm were outstanding? Or, was it because of the way they chose to manage earnings and report financial information? Transparency in reporting is very important if markets are to properly evaluate the prospects of a firm. The evidence suggests that Enron's management engaged in numerous questionable accounting practices. We will describe two of these questionable practices to illustrate how investors were duped.

FIGURE 12.1 Enron's Stock Performance in Comparison to the S&P 500

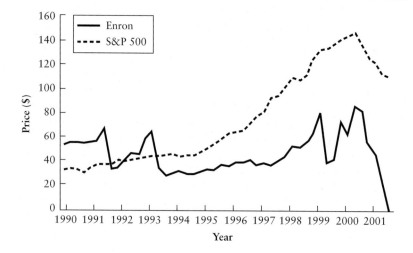

Source: Enron data are from the *Standard and Poor's Stock Guide*. Data for the S&P 500 index are from Shiller's Web site: http://www.econ.yale.edu/~shiller/data.htm. All data are end of quarter.

Enron created literally hundreds of special purpose entities (SPEs). Some were used to hide foreign income from U.S. taxation and others to hide huge amounts of debt financing. An SPE is basically a shell created by a sponsor (Enron) and

FIGURE 12.2 Enron's Price-to-Earnings Ratio in Comparison to that of the S&P 500

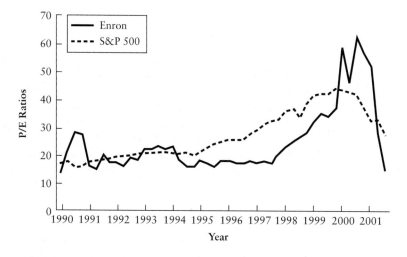

Source: Enron data are from the *Standard and Poor's Stock Guide*. Data for the S&P 500 index are from Shiller's Web site: http://www.econ.yale.edu/~shiller/data.htm. All data are end of quarter.

financed by independent third parties. Under current accounting rules, Enron was not required to consolidate their financial statements as long as an independent party had an equity stake of 3% of the SPE's assets. Enron used large amounts of debt to finance the activities of the SPEs, and their principal asset was Enron stock. When the stock price was increasing, all seemed fine. But, notice that shareholders may not have understood that Enron had taken on huge amounts of debt. When the stock price fell, the assets of the SPEs could not cover the debt, and Enron was then forced to take over the debt.

The structure of an SPE is really quite complicated. Consider this simplified example to better understand the game executives were playing.[28] Suppose that you bought a sports car and your spouse was not happy about it. Not only is driving the car risky because it is so fast, but it is also a money pit. There always seems to be something wrong with it. To make your spouse happy, you tell her you sold it to your friend John for $60,000, twice what you paid for it. You convinced John that the car was a great buy and John has never really been known to make good financial decisions. Somehow you forget to mention to your spouse the fact that you lent John the $60,000 to buy the car. Unless by some miracle the car increases in value, you are probably going to be forced to cover a big loss. Think of your spouse as a shareholder. Do you think she/he would be happy about this business decision if all the details were transparent? Notice that most would agree that your omission of information was not exactly the right thing to do, but you did not lie or break any law.

Another noteworthy practice followed at Enron involves fair value accounting. With mark-to-market accounting, the value of a position is fairly easy to estimate if market values are observable. In some cases, asset values could be based on a model when market valuations are not available. Of course all models need inputs and though managers are expected to make reasonable estimates, it seems that Enron executives picked those that painted the rosiest picture. For example, when the firm entered into a long-term contract, the present value of future cash flows was estimated and recognized as current revenues.

A deal with Blockbuster Video provides an illustration. On July 19, 2000, Enron and Blockbuster announced that they had entered into a 20-year agreement to deliver video on demand (VOD) through the Enron Intelligent Network. They set their goals quite high. Their announcement indicated that they would introduce entertainment on demand in multiple U.S. markets by the end of the year, later expanding domestically and internationally. Enron recognized $110 million in profits even though there were serious concerns about the potential of the project. Interestingly, Blockbuster did not recognize any profits from the deal. In March 2001, the agreement between Blockbuster and Enron was officially terminated. In October 2001, Enron had to reverse the profits it had taken earlier.

Ex post, it seems easy to see that the financial reporting of Enron was questionable, to say the least. Why didn't the directors or professional financial analysts following the firm notice?

THE DIRECTORS

The directors of Enron seemed to rubber-stamp anything management brought before them. They were a highly paid group. In 2000, their average compensation for serving on the board was $380,000, among the highest in the U.S.[29] Did the Enron board monitor or strive to please management?

What could have gone wrong with the board? Earlier in the chapter we argued that a majority of board members should be outsiders. Along with the two CEOs of Enron during this time, 15 external directors served. We know that these external board members had much experience and significant expertise and though they were classified as external, we do not know for sure that they were truly independent. With this caveat, it appears that the standard that the board should have a majority of outsiders was satisfied.[30]

Another feature of the board's structure stands out. The board was relatively large, and research suggests that in many cases small boards are better because the directors are more involved. In hindsight, these board members did not seem to be particularly involved or question information brought forth by executives. For example, Enron's audit committee, which included a subset of outside directors, once met for only 85 minutes despite a long agenda that included many important items.[31]

In the end, the directors did not get away without penalty. Their reputations were tarnished and, perhaps, can never be reclaimed. In 2005, 10 of the directors agreed to a settlement in litigation brought by shareholders.[32] Though board members are normally protected by insurance paid for by the firm, in this case they actually had to pay $13 million out of their own pockets. As outsiders ourselves to the board room, it is difficult to assess the extent to which self-interest, loyalty, and groupthink affected directors' behavior, but it certainly seems likely that these behavioral forces played a role. It is a challenge for future research to isolate and measure the impact of these effects on decision-making.

THE ANALYSTS

Should analysts have warned investors of the problems at Enron? During the time leading up to Enron's bankruptcy, analysts continued to be optimistic about the firm. They either accepted managerial projections, or they did not question them. In fact, even after the SEC began inquiring about conflicts of interest at Enron, the average analyst recommendation was buy or 1.9, where 1 = strong buy and 5 = strong sell.[33] Though we cannot directly test this, the evidence is consistent with conflicts of interest among analysts. They may have been optimistic because of the large investment banking fees generated by Enron. Even analysts that were employed with an investment banking firm that did not currently do business with Enron would have been subject to these conflicts of interest because there was always concern about future business relationships. In addition, analysts would have wanted to keep open the channels of information with management.

Since the dot-com boom of the 1990s, sell-side analysts have received a great deal of attention. The SEC implemented **Regulation Fair Disclosure (Reg FD)** in an attempt to thwart selective disclosure by publicly traded firms to large investors. According to the regulation, firms must disclose material information to all investors, large and small, simultaneously. Later in 2002, the **Sarbanes-Oxley Act (SOX)** was signed in response to corporate scandals such as the Enron bankruptcy. Included in SOX was a requirement that walls be established between analysts in research and a firm's investment banking arm. The goal was to promote increased public confidence in the research reported by analysts.

OTHER PLAYERS IN ENRON'S DOWNFALL

The directors and analysts are not the only players who have received blame in the fall of Enron. In the mania of the dot-com run-up in stock prices, investors seemed to focus entirely on short-term gains. Executives seemed also to care a great deal about the short run, possibly because a significant amount of their compensation package was in terms of stock options. As we will discuss in Chapter 15, if investors are irrational, managers may be in a position to benefit from temporary gains in stock prices and can pursue actions that cater to the desires of such investors.

In addition, Enron's auditor, Arthur Anderson, too readily accepted Enron's business model and method of accounting. The financial transactions were quite complicated, but even so, it is an auditor's responsibility to gain the necessary level of expertise and exercise skepticism. Perhaps Anderson's partners were blinded by the huge fees earned.[34] In 2000, Anderson earned $25 million in audit fees and $27 million in consulting fees from Enron.[35] In 2002, Anderson officials were found guilty of obstructing justice based on its shredding of Enron documents, and the firm voluntarily gave up its licenses to practice accounting. Despite the fact that the Supreme Court overturned the conviction of Anderson in 2005, the firm is highly unlikely to become a viable entity.

ORGANIZATIONAL CULTURE AND PERSONAL IDENTITY

Everyone loved Enron, including its employees, the investors, board members, and analysts.[36] Even as losses mounted, many analysts and investors remained optimistic about the firm. Consider the following newspaper account published in October 2001:[37]

> CSFB's Mr. [Curt Launer] also has been a longtime defender of the company, occasionally issuing research reports to rebut critical stories about Enron in the financial press. On Monday, he wrote that he expects questions about Enron's partnerships and accounting disclosure to continue, but that he remains "confident in the business and operating growth prospects for [Enron] and an ultimate recovery in the share price."

> In recent years, Wall Street researchers have been overwhelmingly—critics would say blindly—enthusiastic about Enron, even as they acknowledge not understanding the complex financial transactions that accounted for its soaring profits. Now, Enron is reporting steep losses from some of its most complicated transactions, which many on Wall Street still can't figure out.

The firm had a unique corporate culture. Employees of Enron were very loyal to the firm. They thought their firm was invincible. Earlier in this chapter we discussed the perils of loyalty. Loyalty to an organization can be even more dangerous than loyalty to a person. According to Milgram:

> Each individual possesses a conscience which to a greater or lesser degree serves to restrain the unimpeded flow of impulses destructive to others. But when he merges his person into an organizational structure, a new creature replaces autonomous man, unhindered by the limitation of individual morality, freed of human inhibition, mindful only of the sanctions of authority.[38]

One crucial lesson exemplified by the fall of Enron is that it is important for any person in any organization to keep a separate identity. Whether a member of a board, an analyst providing information about a firm, an employee, or a stockholder, it is important to take a step back and make an independent evaluation of the situation at hand to avoid being pulled by social forces.

CHAPTER HIGHLIGHTS

1. A corporation's board of directors serves as an internal monitor, advising executives and providing discipline to managers.
2. A smaller board with a majority of outside directors is thought to perform decision-making tasks more efficiently.
3. Problems can arise when board members are self-interested or fall prey to misplaced loyalty.
4. Financial analysts are important players in our financial markets because they are information intermediaries.
5. Financial analysts can be affected by conflicts of interest in that what is in their best interest may not be best for investors.
6. The bankruptcy of Enron illustrates some of the social forces that are important in understanding the scandalous downfall of a large American corporation.

DISCUSSION QUESTIONS AND PROBLEMS

1. Differentiate the following terms/concepts:

   a. Obedience and loyalty
   b. Little white lies and cooperation
   c. Herding and social learning
   d. Outside director and independent board member

2. Discuss the merits of the following statement: Inside directors should constitute the majority of a corporate board because insiders have superior understanding of the firm's business operations.

3. Your firm, which specializes in complex electronic products, has grown rapidly and you are now incorporating. Even after incorporation, a large percentage of the stock will be held by the founders, including you. Your colleague recommends a large corporate board made up exclusively of outsiders. She is very concerned about the sensationalized corporate scandals in recent years. Do you agree with her recommendation? Explain.

4. Describe the three types of professional financial analysts and identify actual firms that employ each type.

5. The largest U.S. bankruptcy occurred in 2002 with the fall of Worldcom, Inc. Its outside directors paid out of their own pockets to settle securities lawsuits, as did Enron directors. While the Worldcom directors may not have played an active role in the flagrant accounting fraud, they were criticized for other choices they made. Research the events surrounding Worldcom and the role played by its board. What do you think their biggest mistakes were?

ENDNOTES

1 Stein, N., October 2, 2000, "Global most admired: The world's most admired companies," *Fortune* 142(7), pp. 182–186.

2 *Trustees of Dartmouth College v. Woodward,* 17 U.S. 518 (1819), p. 636.

3 See http://www.sec.gov/about/whatwedo.shtml (accessed on November 25, 2008).

4 For an examination of corporate governance from an agency perspective, see Marnet, O., 2005, "Behavior and rationality in corporate governance," *Journal of Economic Issues* 39 (3), 613–632.

5 It is argued that boards are a market solution to the agency problem between managers and shareholders that has arisen endogenously. See Hermalin, B. E., and M. S. Weisbach, 2003, "Boards of directors as an endogenously determined institution: A survey of the economic literature," *Federal Reserve Bank of New York Economic Policy Review* (April), 7–26.

6 Yermack, D., 1996, "Higher market valuations of companies with a small board of directors," *Journal of Financial Economics* 40(2), 185–211.

7 Noe, T. H., M. J. Rebello, and R. Sonti, 2007, "Activists, raiders, and directors: Opportunism and the balance of corporate power," Social Science Research Network working paper 1102902.

8 For an in-depth discussion of corporate boards, see Vance, S. C., 1983, *Corporate Leadership: Boards, Directors, and Strategy* (McGraw-Hill, New York).

9 See Gillette, A. B., T. H. Noe, and M. J. Rebello, 2003, "Corporate board composition, protocols, and voting behavior: Experimental evidence," *Journal of Finance* 58(5), 1997–2032.

10 You may have heard of the game "Six Degrees of Kevin Bacon" in which players attempt to link actors by six or fewer links.

11 Milgram, S., 1967, "The small world problem," *Psychology Today* 1, 60–67.

12 Davis, G. F., M. Yoo, and W. E. Baker, 2003, "The small world of the American corporate elite, 1982–2001," *Strategic Organization* 1(3) (August), 301–326.

13 Kramarz, F., and D. Thesmar, 2006, "Social networks in the boardroom," IZA Discussion Paper No. 1940 (January).

14 Forbes.com, May 3, 2007, "Special report: CEO compensation."

15 Estimates of median compensation for board members of the top 100 NYSE and NASDAQ firms as of March 31, 2006 were $199,448 and $232,035. See Frederic W., Cook & Co., Inc., 2006, "Director compensation: NASDAQ 100 vs. NYSE 100," October.

16 Experimental research suggests that people tell lies to impact the impressions others have of them. See Ackert, L. F., B. K. Church, X. J. Kuang, and L. Qi, 2007, "White lies: Why bother?" Georgia Tech working paper.

17 Morck, R., 2004, "Behavioral finance in corporate governance—Independent directors and non-executive chairs," National Bureau of Economic Research working paper 10644.

18 Milgram, S., 1974, *Obedience to Authority: An Experimental View* (Harper & Row, New York).

19 Schipper, K., 1991, "Commentary on analysts' forecasts," *Accounting Horizons* 5 (December), 105–121.

20 Dugar, A., and S. Nathan, 1995, "The effect of investment banking relationships on financial analysts' earnings forecasts and investment recommendations," *Contemporary Accounting Research* 12(1), 131–160.

21 Michaely, R., and K. L. Womack, 1999, "Conflict of interest and the credibility of underwriter analyst recommendations," *Review of Financial Studies* 12(4) (July), 653–686.

22 Access to management may not be as important as it was in the past due to the passage of Regulation FD, which is discussed later in this chapter.

23 Francis, J., and D. Philbrick, 1993, "Analysts' decisions as products of a multi-task environment," *Journal of Accounting Research* 31(2), 216–230.

24 Ackert, L. F., and G. Athanassakos, 1997, "Prior uncertainty, analyst bias, and subsequent abnormal returns," *Journal of Financial Research* 20(2), 263–273.

25 Bikhchandani, S., D. Hirshleifer, and I. Welch, 1998, "Learning from the behavior of others: Conformity, fads, and informational cascades," *Journal of Economic Perspectives* 12(3) (Summer), 151–170.

26 See Trueman, B., 1994, "Analyst forecasts and herding behavior," *Review of Financial Studies* 7(1), 97–124. For an experimental examination of herding among analysts, see Ackert, L. F., B. K. Church, and K. Ely, 2009, "Biases in individual forecasts: Experimental evidence," *Journal of Behavioral Finance* 9(2), 53–61; and for a comprehensive review of the literature, see Hirshleifer, D., and S. H. Teoh, 2003, "Herd behavior and cascading in capital markets: A review and synthesis," *European Financial Management* 9(1), 25–66.

27 For a comprehensive discussion of the Enron bankruptcy, see Benston, G. J., and A. L. Hartgraves, 2002, "Enron: What happened and what we can learn from it," *Journal of Accounting and Public Policy* 21(2), 105–127; and Healy, P. M., and K. G. Palepu, 2003, "The fall of Enron," *Journal of Economic Perspectives* 17(2) (Spring), 3–26.

28 This example was suggested in the following editorial: *Wall Street Journal Europe*, August 23, 2002, "The Enron and Tyco Cleanups," Review and Outlook (editorial), p. A8.

29 Abelson, R., December 16, 2001, "Enron board comes under a storm of criticism," *New York Times*, p. BU4.

30 On the qualifications of the boards, see Zandstra, G., 2002, "Enron, board governance, and moral failings," *Corporate Governance* 2(2), 16–19.

31 Healy, P. M., and K. G. Palepu, 2003, "The fall of Enron," *Journal of Economic Perspectives* 17(2) (Spring), 3–26.

32 Smith, R. and J. Weil, January 10, 2005, "Ex-Enron directors reach settlement," *Wall Street Journal*, WSJ.com.

33 Healy, P. M., and K. G. Palepu, 2003, "The fall of Enron," *Journal of Economic Perspectives* 17(2) (Spring), 3–26.

34 Of course, many factors influence auditors' decisions. For example, auditors with longer tenure are better able to detect fraud. See Fairchild, R. J., 2007, "Does audit tenure lead to more fraud? A game-theoretic approach," Social Science Research Network working paper 993400.

35 Benston, G. J., and A. L. Hartgraves, 2002, "Enron: What happened and what we can learn from it," *Journal of Accounting and Public Policy* 21(2), 105–127; and Healy, P. M., and K. G. Palepu, 2003, "The fall of Enron," *Journal of Economic Perspectives* 17(2) (Spring), 3–26.

36 Compelling accounts of the Enron story are provided by Eichenwald, K., 2005, *Conspiracy of Fools: A True Story* (Broadway Books, New York); and McLean, B., and P. Elkind, 2004, *The Smartest Guys in the Room: The Amazing Rise and Scandalous Fall of Enron* (Penguin Books, New York).

37 Craig, S., and J. Weil, October 26, 2001, "Most analysts remain plugged in to Enron," Heard on the Street, *Wall Street Journal*, page C1.

38 Milgram S., 1974, *Obedience to Authority: An Experimental View* (Harper & Row, New York), page 188.

MARKET OUTCOMES

PART | V

CHAPTER 13   Behavioral Explanations for Anomalies

CHAPTER 14   Do Behavioral Factors Explain Stock Market Puzzles?

BEHAVIORAL EXPLANATIONS FOR ANOMALIES

13.1 INTRODUCTION

In Chapter 4, we reviewed some key anomalies. Recall that anomalies are defined as empirical results that, unless adequately explained, seem to run counter to market efficiency. These key anomalies reviewed were: 1) the small-firm effect; 2) lagged reactions to earnings announcements; 3) value versus growth; and 4) momentum and reversal. In this chapter we discuss possible explanations for the last three anomalies. The small-firm effect is not usually attributed to behavioral factors. Yet, it is included in the group of key anomalies because it plays a central role in the Fama-French three-factor model, which has become a conventional risk-adjustment technique.

We begin, in Section 13.2, with a discussion of lagged earnings announcements and of the tendency for value to outperform growth. In Section 13.3, we turn to momentum and reversal. Three alternative behavioral models for momentum and/or reversal are sketched out. As discussed in Chapter 4, tests of market efficiency are by their very nature joint hypothesis tests, with rejection implying *either* inefficiency or an inappropriate risk-adjustment method (or perhaps both). With this perspective in mind, in Section 13.4, we consider whether appropriate risk adjustment can account for apparent anomalies.

13.2 EARNINGS ANNOUNCEMENTS AND VALUE VS. GROWTH

What is Behind Lagged Reactions to Earnings Announcements?

Recall that extreme earnings announcements, whether very positive or very negative, are only incompletely reflected in prices, leading to a period of delayed reaction. What may partly explain this evidence of post-announcement drift is that it seems that both analysts and investors anchor on recent earnings, implying that they underreact to new information. For example, Value Line analysts' quarterly earnings forecast errors (or surprises) are positively correlated over the first three lags, which means they predictably have the same sign because of underreaction.[1] Consistent with a behavioral explanation is evidence showing that among investors it is primarily small (unsophisticated) traders who exhibit the type of behavior that leads to post-earnings announcement drift.[2]

Concurrent with underreaction in the short term may be overreaction in the long term. One common measure of expected earnings growth is the P/E ratio, with high P/Es reflecting a perception of high future growth and low P/Es reflecting a perception of low future growth. P/Es in the United States at the end of 1999 were quite dispersed, with a 10th percentile of 7.4 and a 90th percentile of 53.9.[3] Similar disparity existed at the same time among analysts, with their forecasts of five-year earnings growth rates having a 10th to 90th percentile range of 8.9% to 40%. Yet, the evidence is that few firms grow rapidly for long periods and mean reversion is the order of the day.[4]

Aside from being too dispersed, analysts' forecasts also tend to be too optimistic.[5] While earlier we discussed psychological reasons for optimism, there are also agency explanations. Prior to Regulation FD (Fair Disclosure), the management of companies had some discretion in the process of information flow, and sometimes favored analysts would get information sooner.[6] In this environment, it may have been optimal (in the sense of minimizing expected squared error of forecasts) for analysts to issue biased forecasts while at the same time receiving preferential information.[7] Also suggestive of an agency motivation is the finding that analysts are more likely to weight information optimistically if their firms are about to underwrite for the rated firms.[8]

WHAT IS BEHIND THE VALUE ADVANTAGE?

As we have seen, historically value stocks have outperformed growth stocks. Aside from risk considerations (to which we will turn later in the chapter), Josef Lakonishok, Andrei Shleifer, and Robert Vishny speculated on potential reasons for the value advantage.[9] They suggest four reasons why retail and institutional investors may become too excited about glamour (or growth) stocks versus value stocks. The first two reasons are mistakes in judgment, and one might guess that individual investors are more prone to committing them than are institutional investors:

1. They are committing judgment errors in extrapolating past growth rates too far into the future, and are thus surprised when value stocks shine and glamour stocks disappoint. This is the so-called expectational error hypothesis.
2. Because of representativeness, investors may assume that good companies are good investments.[10]

The next two reasons are due to agency considerations. They both suggest that, while institutional investors may know better, because of career concerns, they may avoid value stocks:

3. Because sponsors view companies with steady earnings and buoyant growth as prudent investments, so as to *appear* to be following their fiduciary obligation

to act prudently, institutional investors may shy away from hard-to-defend out-of-favor value stocks.[11]

4. Because of career concerns, institutional investors, who are evaluated over short horizons, may be nervous about tilting too far in any direction, thus incurring tracking error. A value strategy would require such a tilt and may take some time to pay off, so it is in this sense risky.

While likely all the above are contributing factors, most attention has been accorded to the first, the expectational error hypothesis. Looking at it from the perspective of growth stocks, the intuition is that markets have overreacted to good news (perhaps after first underreacting to it). While prices have logically risen in response to the good news, they have gone too far (relative to fundamentals), and thus must fall back down to some extent. This leads to weak returns from growth stocks going forward. From the perspective of value stocks that have witnessed price declines after bad news, prices have fallen too far, and thus must rise back up. This leads to strong returns from growth stocks in the future.

Circumstantial evidence has been provided in support of the value advantage being an anomaly, in general, and in support of the expectational error hypothesis, in particular. For example, when portfolios are formed *merely* on the basis of analysts' earnings growth estimates, those portfolios with high growth estimates substantially underperform those with low growth estimates.[12] Further, high expected growth stocks experience returns around earnings-announcement (three-day) windows well below those of low expected growth stocks. Viewed another way, stocks ranked by book-to-market value (B/P) also have predictable returns around earnings announcement windows.[13] More specifically, the highest B/P decile outperforms the lowest B/P during subsequent earnings-announcement windows for a number of years after portfolio formation. While the value-growth return gap dissipates somewhat, it is still significant in both an economic and statistical sense five years on.

Further, if we presume that insiders have better information than outsiders, it is revealing that insider buying frequency tends to rise as stocks increasingly move into the value territory.[14] One reason why opportunities are not easily eliminated is because of noise trader risk, namely the risk that mispricing could get worse.[15] In this regard, consistent with a behavioral explanation for the value advantage is the fact that the B/P effect is greater for stocks that have higher volatility (and thus a higher probability that mispricing could get worse).[16] The same research finds that stocks with lower investor sophistication also have a stronger B/P effect.

13.3   WHAT IS BEHIND MOMENTUM AND REVERSAL?

Recall the existence of intermediate-term momentum and long-term reversal. Putting these results together suggests that investors first underreact and then overreact. In essence we have a combination of the underreaction seen in the earnings announcement literature and the overreaction requiring reversal that we see in the value literature. In the next section of the chapter, several alternative behavioral models that account for momentum and reversal are presented.

The first model, formulated by Kent Daniel, David Hirshleifer, and Avanidhar Subrahmanyam, in its simplest form explains reversal by incorporating overconfidence.[17] The second, by Mark Grinblatt and Bing Han, explains momentum using prospect theory, mental accounting, and the disposition effect.[18] And the third, by Nicholas Barberis, Andrei Shleifer, and Robert Vishny, which accounts for both momentum and reversal, is based on the anchoring and representativeness heuristics.[19]

DANIEL-HIRSHLEIFER-SUBRAHMANYAM MODEL AND EXPLAINING REVERSAL

The Daniel-Hirshleifer-Subrahmanyam model (hereafter DHS) is based on overconfident investors overestimating the precision of their own private signals. This leads to negative serial correlation in prices, or reversal. Here we present a scaled-down version of their simplest model.[20] Consider a world where one class of traders, assumed to be risk neutral, is informed in the sense that it generates its own information about the value of a security. These traders, however, are overconfident about the accuracy of this information. In this model there may also be traders who are unbiased. If so, they are price-takers.

Suppose we begin in equilibrium at $t = 0$; at $t = 1$ a private noisy signal appears (one can assume informed investors undertake some analysis generating some imperfect insights on the true value of the security); and at $t = 2$ the true value of the security is revealed. Formally, the private signal at $t = 1$ is:

13.1
$$s_1 = \theta + \varepsilon$$

where θ is a mean-zero random variable with variance σ_θ^2 that represents the change in the true value of the security. It is observed imperfectly because of a mean-zero noise term with variance σ_ε^2. Overconfidence is a factor because informed traders exaggerate in their own minds the accuracy of their private signal, using σ_C^2 instead of σ_ε^2, where $\sigma_C^2 < \sigma_\varepsilon^2$. Given the risk neutrality of the informed traders, the price at $t = 1$ settles at the expected value of θ conditional on s_1. At $t = 2$, the price reaches the true value of the security.

Consider the price at $t = 1$. The challenge is to separate the information from the noise. Intuitively, if σ_ε^2 is low relative to σ_θ^2, it will be rational to believe that the signal is primarily the true change in value. On the other hand, if σ_ε^2 is high relative to σ_θ^2, it will be rational to believe that the signal is primarily noise. In the former case, it will be rational to alter valuations almost as much as s_1. In the latter case, prices should not move much. More formally, it can be shown that:

13.2
$$p_1 = \frac{\sigma_\theta^2}{(\sigma_\theta^2 + \sigma_\varepsilon^2)} (\theta + \varepsilon)$$

where p_1 is the value of the security at $t = 1$. Overconfident investors, on the other hand, believe that their error is less than is objectively the case. For this reason, their perception of value at $t = 1$ is:

13.3

$$p_1 = \frac{\sigma_\theta^2}{(\sigma_\theta^2 + \sigma_C^2)}(\theta + \varepsilon)$$

Since $\sigma_\varepsilon^2 > \sigma_C^2$, prices are more influenced by the signal than is rational.

An example, illustrated in Figure 13.1, shows what this means for prices. Suppose that $\theta = 2$; $\sigma_\theta^2 = \sigma_\varepsilon^2 = 1$; and $\sigma_C^2 = 0.5$. We will consider two cases: $\varepsilon = 2.5$ (Case 1) and $\varepsilon = 1.5$ (Case 2). The solid lines show price paths assuming that overconfident traders drive prices. The broken lines shows price paths assuming no overconfidence.

Begin with Case 1. Even the rational price goes to $2.25—a little above its equilibrium value. The reason is that, since $\sigma_\theta^2 = \sigma_\varepsilon^2$, it is logical, according to 13.2, to believe that half of the signal ($s_1/2 = (2 + 2.5)/2 = 2.25$) is true information. The overconfident investors, however, believe that an even greater proportion of s_1 is information and push up prices even higher, to $3. Consider Case 2. Now the rational price goes to $1.75—a little below its equilibrium value. The reader will notice that when half of the signal is true information and half error, as will be true on average, the rational price will immediately go to equilibrium. Overreaction again occurs for the overconfident investors under Case 2. They will push prices up to $2.33. While given a low enough error relative to the information even the overconfident investors will set prices below equilibrium, on average, they will overreact, necessitating reversal.

The DHS model offers a number of testable implications. For example, managers should issue shares when they believe their stocks to be undervalued, and buy them back when they believe them to be undervalued. Indeed, as will be seen in Chapter 15, the evidence points in this direction.

FIGURE 13.1 Simulation Based on DHS Model

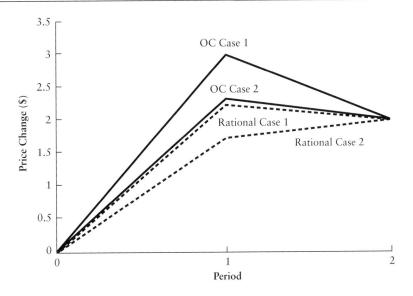

Grinblatt-Han Model and Explaining Momentum

As stated before, the Grinblatt-Han model (hereafter GH), is based on prospect theory, mental accounting, and the disposition effect. In brief, the tendency for winners/losers to be sold too quickly/slowly suggests a delayed reaction to good/bad news, because reference-point-influenced investors have demand curves that reflect recent performance.

To motivate their model, refer to Figure 13.2, which displays a standard prospect theory value function. Recall the concavity of the function in the gains domain (consistent with risk aversion), convexity in the losses domain (consistent with risk seeking), and the kink at the reference point. Further, recall the integration versus segregation discussion, which is related to mental accounting and closing accounts. Let's suppose that investors segregate gambles on different securities (which means they don't think in portfolio terms, instead looking at securities one at a time), but they integrate gambles on the *same* security (which means their reference point, most logically the purchase price of the security, only slowly changes). So if a security has made money from the original date of purchase, it moves up along the prospect theory value function (to points C and D), while, if a security has lost money, it moves down along the same function (to A and B). The argument is that the farther you are away from the risk-seeking domain, the less a particular gamble is likely to enter this domain, so risk aversion is higher for gambles beginning at D versus C, or C versus B, or B versus A. This suggests that demand will be greater for securities that have suffered capital losses (the higher the loss, the greater the demand), and lower for securities that have experienced gains (with higher gains leading to lower demands). This is one potential explanation behind the disposition effect, and is a key element of the GH model.

Figure 13.2 Prospect Theory Value Function and Disposition Effect

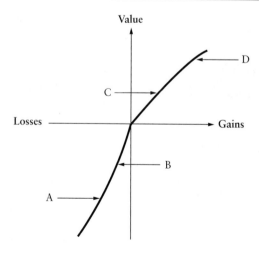

Consider the (intrinsic) value (f_t) of a security in the GH model. It follows a random walk, only changing as relevant news (ε_t) arrives:

13.4 $$f_{t+1} = f_t + \varepsilon_{t+1}$$

Demand comes from two groups of investors: rational investors (R) and those who are influenced by prospect theory and mental accounting (PT/MA). The first group has the following demand function:

13.5 $$D(R)_t = 1 + b(f_t - p_t)$$

where $D(R)_t$ is demand coming from rational investors at t; and p_t is the share price at t. Note that $b > 0$ reflects the slope of the rational demand curve. To the extent that value exceeds price, rational investors will demand more units.[21] PT/MA investors account for the second component of overall market demand:

13.6 $$D(PT/MA)_t = 1 + b(f_t - p_t) + \lambda(ref_t - p_t)$$

where $D(PT/MA)_t$ is demand at t arising from those investors who are influenced by prospect theory and mental accounting. Here, ref_t is the reference point and λ (>0) denotes the relative importance of the capital gain component to PT/MA investors. Note that, if $ref_t > p_t$, demand is higher since the price is in the risk-seeking domain. If PT/MA investors; are $\mu\%$ of all investors; we aggregate demand over the two groups; normalize supply at one unit; and clear the market; the resulting equilibrium price is:

13.7 $$p_t = wf_t + (1 - w)ref_t, \qquad w = \frac{1}{1 + \mu\lambda}$$

To interpret, market price is a weighted average of value and the reference point. Underreaction to news is clear. Say, beginning from a steady state (where $f_t = p_t = ref_t$), positive news pushes up value. Price will react in the same direction, but it will be held back somewhat by the reference point (which, as will be shown, moves more slowly). Only over time will price reach the right level. Because this takes time, we have momentum. Further, the more PT/MA investors there are (higher μ), and the more important is the capital gain component to them (higher λ), the more influential is the reference point and the greater is the underreaction.

We need to think of the reference point as the average reference point for all PT/MA investors. It will vary over time as trading occurs. For example, assume that a particular PT/MA investor bought shares at $5 (so her reference point is $5). The price now rises to $7 for a capital gain of $2, but her reference point remains at $5. Suppose she needs cash and sells her shares to another PT/MA investor for $7. His reference point will be $7, which is his purchase price (not hers). Therefore, over time because of trading, the reference point moves toward the market price. This enters the model in the following reference point adjustment equation, where the speed of adjustment is v:

13.8
$$ref_{t+1} = vp_t + (1 - v)ref_t$$

Clearly v will be related to turnover.

An example might be instructive. Suppose we begin at $t = 0$ in a steady state where $f_t = p_t = ref_t = \$1$, and then extremely positive news (at $t = 1$) causes value to double to 2. Letting $\mu = .5$ and $\lambda = 2$, Figure 13.3 shows the evolution of prices and reference points over the next 24 months (to $t = 25$). Price moves toward value, but it does so gradually because PT/MA investors fixate on the reference point, which moves more slowly. The reader will of course realize that real-world securities never exhibit momentum as "clean" as in this example. The reason is that new additional information (affecting f_t) is often arriving.

It is straightforward to show that the expected return (R_t) at any point in time is equal to:

13.9
$$E_t(R_{t+1}) = (1 - w)v\frac{p_t - ref_t}{p_t}$$

Note that we are assuming no dividends, so the expected return is entirely a capital gain. Expected returns are high if v is high because rapid adjustment of the

---

FIGURE 13.3 Simulation Based on GH Model

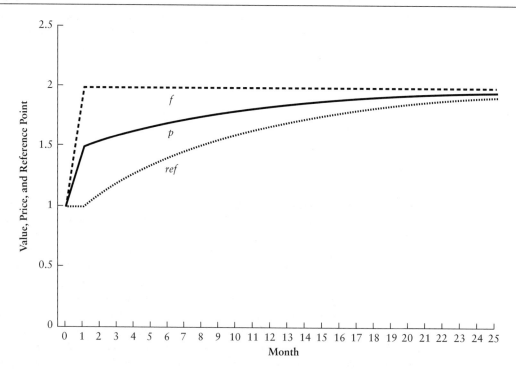

reference point means that price can move now as opposed to later. Low w (high μ and high λ) also implies that prices will move more, because a low w suggests that prices have farther to move. Most notably, we expect higher returns the greater is the average investor's unrealized capital gain $((p_t - ref_t)/p_t)$. In the figure, we see this as the narrowing gap between p_t and ref_t, which occurs at the same time that positive returns taper off.[22]

It is important to note that Equation 13.9 does not relate future expected returns to past returns (momentum) *directly*. Nevertheless, a stock's unrealized capital gain is likely to be highly correlated with past returns, so standard momentum is easily implied by the model. Yet, this capital gain should be a better predictor of future returns than past returns. Indeed, Grinblatt and Han find this to be true: the return-based momentum effect disappears once the PT/MA disposition effect is controlled for. Still, one weakness of the GH model is that it only explains momentum, not reversal. For this reason, we turn to the final model, which explains both momentum and reversal.

BARBERIS-SHLEIFER-VISHNY MODEL AND EXPLAINING MOMENTUM AND REVERSAL

Recall in Chapter 5 where we told the story of the couple heading out for a picnic. They were initially overly anchored in their belief that it was not going to rain, but later, when new evidence (dark clouds) began to arrive, they changed tack and became convinced that rain was at hand. Initially, they exhibited anchoring, while later they were subject to the base rate underweighting variant of representativeness. The Barberis-Shleifer-Vishny model (hereafter BSV) is driven by the tendency for individuals to be coarsely calibrated in the sense of this example, that is, to either believe that things are black or white. Their model leads to a world where investors at first underreact, and then overreact to salient news. Or, one can say that investors "overreact slowly."[23]

There is evidence that earnings follow something very close to a random walk, which is another way of saying that past earnings growth is not particularly helpful in predicting future earnings growth.[24] Suppose we assume that a random walk holds for earnings (n_t):

13.10
$$n_{t+1} = n_t + \varepsilon_{t+1}$$

For simplicity, changes in earnings, $\varepsilon_{t+1} = n_{t+1} - n_t$, are assumed to be either $+y$ or $-y$, with equal probability. Investors, however, being coarsely calibrated, believe that stocks switch between two regimes. Under regime 1, it is believed that earnings mean-revert. This means that a positive/negative earnings change is likely to be followed by a negative/positive earnings change in the next period. More formally, given a positive/negative earnings change, there is a low probability (p^k_L) of another positive/negative earnings change in the next period. On the other hand, under regime 2, given a positive/negative earnings change, there is a high probability (p^k_H) of another positive/negative earnings change in the next period. In other words, it is believed that there is continuation in earnings. Note that $p^k_H > p^k_L$. The model also requires probabilities of switching between perceived regimes. We assume that, given that we are in regime 1 ($s_t = 1$), there is a λ_1 probability of switching to regime 2; and, if we are in regime 2 ($s_t = 2$), there is a λ_2 probability of switching to regime 1. At all points in time, individuals must guess whether the world is in regime 1 or 2. Their estimated probabilities will rise and fall as events unfold. A sequence of alternating changes (e.g., +y, −y, +y, −y) will lead people to believe that regime 1 is in effect, while a sequence of like earnings changes (e.g., +y, +y, +y, +y; or −y, −y, −y, −y) will lead people to believe that regime 2 is in effect.

It can be shown that if earnings changes are the same at both t and $t + 1$, the perceived probability that regime 1 is in place is the following function of the parameters of the model:

13.11
$$q_{t+1} = \frac{[(1-\lambda_1)q_t + \lambda_2(1-q_t)]p^t_L}{[(1-\lambda_1)q_t + \lambda_2(1-q_t)]p^t_L + [\lambda_1 q_t + (1-\lambda_2)(1-q_t)]p^t_H}$$

It is possible to prove that $q_{t+1} < q_t$. In other words, after continuation it is less likely than before that we are in regime 1. If on the other hand the earnings changes at both t and $t + 1$ have been different, then the perceived probability that regime 1 is in place is:

13.12
$$q_{t+1} = \frac{[(1-\lambda_1)q_t + \lambda_2(1-q_t)](1-p^t_L)}{[(1-\lambda_1)q_t + \lambda_2(1-q_t)](1-p^t_L) + [\lambda_1 q_t + (1-\lambda_2)(1-q_t)](1-p^t_H)}$$

This time it is possible to prove that $q_{t+1} > q_t$. In other words, after reversal it is more likely that we are in regime 1. To see how the model works in terms of the revision over time of the probability that the world is in regime 1, refer to Figure 13.4. Here it is assumed that $p^t_H = 3/4$; $p^t_L = 1/3$; $\lambda_1 = 0.1$; and $\lambda_2 = 0.3$. Note that q_t rises after a sign switch, but falls after a sign continuation.

Turning to valuation, it is assumed that all earnings are returned to investors in the form of dividends. Using a standard dividend discount model, value is:

13.13
$$p_t = \frac{E_t d_{t+1}}{(1+R)^1} + \frac{E_t d_{t+2}}{(1+R)^2} + \frac{E_t d_{t+3}}{(1+R)^3} + \dots$$

where p_t is the time-t price, d_t is the time-t dividend and R is the discount rate. If investors correctly perceive a random walk, 13.13 is simply a perpetuity and reduces to:

13.14
$$p_t = n_t / R$$

It can be shown that the nature of investor beliefs about regimes and switching between them is such that the actual price will be:

13.15
$$p_t = n_t / R + k_t \varepsilon_t$$

While the factor k_t is a complicated function of q_t, it can be shown that it is negative when q_t is fairly high, which means that after a positive/negative earnings change, while prices react in the right direction, they do not react enough—underreaction. When q_t reaches a low enough level, the second term is positive/negative after a positive/negative earnings change—overreaction. So we see that this

FIGURE 13.4 Simulation Based on BSV Model

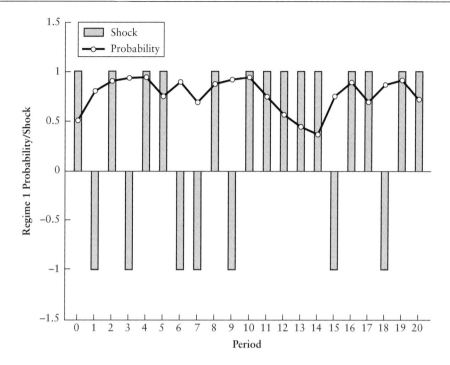

Source: Barberis, N., A. Shleifer, and R. Vishny, 1998, "A model of investor sentiment," *Journal of Financial Economics* 49, 307–344.

model is capable of generating the sort of underreaction and overreaction that we witness empirically.

The authors then go on to perform a simulation to see if the model is capable of producing more precisely the sort of patterns that we observe in historical data. Using the same parameters that were assumed earlier, artificial datasets of earnings and prices for 2,000 firms over a six-year period were generated.[25] What we need to see is underreaction after news, followed by overreaction after a series of similar news events. For each *n*-year period in the sample (*n* = 1, 2, 3, 4), portfolios are formed of all firms with positive/negative earnings announcements over *n* consecutive years. In Table 13.1 in the first numerical column, we show the differences between the positive earnings change and negative earnings change portfolios. The results are as expected: initially prices continue to drift upward/downward, but eventually they correct themselves.

Recall that the momentum and reversal results in the literature are in terms of past returns, not in terms of the history of earnings. To see if the model was capable of explaining these results, the authors also simulate portfolio return differences on the basis of past returns. Deciles are formed each year on the basis of returns. In the second numerical column of Table 13.1, best and worst decile differences for

TABLE 13.1	SIMULATED RETURNS FROM EARNINGS AND RETURNS SORTS BASED ON BSV MODEL	
Holding Period	Earnings Sort	Returns Sort
1 year	0.0391	0.0280
2 years	0.0131	0.0102
3 years	−0.0072	−0.0094
4 years	−0.0309	−0.0181

Source: Reprinted from the Journal of Financial Economics, Vol 49, Issue 3, Barberis, N., A. Shleifer, and R. Vishny, "A model of investor sentiment," pp. 307–44, © September 1998. With permission from Elsevier.

the following year are shown. As in previously cited momentum papers, we see persistence when we condition on intermediate-term intervals (one and two years) and reversal conditioning on longer-term intervals (three and four years).

The model was able to produce results consistent with the value versus growth phenomenon as well. Since there were no accounting numbers for the simulated firms (and hence no book values), the authors worked in terms of P/E ratios, which, given the assumptions of the model, were the same as prices over dividends. Deciles were also formed on P/E and the authors calculated the average difference in returns going forward between the lowest P/E firms and the highest P/E firms. They found this value to be 4.35%. Thus, by and large, the model was able to account for the evidence on earnings drift, momentum, and reversal, and value versus growth.

13.4   RATIONAL EXPLANATIONS

One should not immediately declare that markets are inefficient because anomalies have been detected. There are, in fact, a number of explanations that are perfectly consistent with rationality and efficiency. We have already discussed data snooping, the likelihood that if one looks long enough, "the data will surrender."[26] Nevertheless, the consistency of some anomalies, especially momentum and the value premium, over different time periods and in different markets, weakens this criticism considerably. Another possibility is that the methodology that has established a particular anomaly is flawed, thus making the finding of inefficiency an illusion. This debate is technical and won't concern us here, but for the most part, the major anomalies have withstood this particular criticism.[27] The main attack is in the form of inappropriate risk adjustments.

INAPPROPRIATE RISK ADJUSTMENT

As mentioned earlier, all tests of efficiency are by their very nature joint hypothesis tests. In particular, the null hypothesis requires: 1) efficiency, and 2) a particular model of risk adjustment. Early tests of market efficiency assumed that appropriate risk adjustment only required the consideration of market or beta risk (as in CAPM). Suppose that a particular study rejects market efficiency. The problem is that a rejection of the null hypothesis is a rejection of the joint hypothesis. This means that either markets are inefficient; we are using the wrong asset pricing model (that is, we are assuming an incorrect risk-adjustment mechanism), or both. Thus, rejection is never clear-cut, since we might just be ignoring additional components of risk.

Consider the following gambling example. This example involves no pricing or markets, but it does illustrate the joint-hypothesis problem. People go to play the slot machines at a particular casino where the advertised "return" is –2%. This means that for every $1 gambled, *on average* 98 cents will come back. No doubt this is a poor investment, and most gamblers know this, but the non-pecuniary side benefits (an outing with friends? dreams of wealth?) make it all worthwhile. Of course most people are losing, but the occasional jackpot may seem to justify the gamble. On this basis, the consensus belief of customers is that they will enter the casino expecting to lose 2%. Suppose, in fact, the (true) average loss is higher, 5%. This is perhaps because the machines have been incorrectly set, or management is acting fraudulently.

If a test of market efficiency were done, the hypothesis would likely be rejected. The implicit "pricing model," that the return is –2% (as advertised), would be inconsistent with the observed loss of 5%. But suppose that over time people learn. They learn from personal experience and talk to enough of their fellow players to form fairly accurate views. On this basis, they adjust their expectations, in fact coming to expect a 5% loss (regardless of what the management of the casino advertises). This "return" is still competitive with other casinos (the advertised return of –2% would have been a great deal), and perhaps customers like the casino's ambience, so most of the original customers continue to come. Then "markets" will *become* efficient in that gamblers expect to lose 5%, and that is, in fact, what happens. This illustrates the possibility that deviations from efficiency can be temporary.

But now a clever financial economist comes along and decides to see if casino "markets" are efficient, and uses this particular casino's payout experience as her sample. She notices that the advertised "return" is –2% and decides this is the appropriate benchmark. If her sample of payout experience is sufficiently large, she will reject market efficiency. But the problem is not that markets are inefficient—she has simply used the wrong model of equilibrium.

In a well-known paper published in 1992 that shook up the academic finance community, Eugene Fama and Kenneth French found that, based on the latest data (1963–1990), CAPM did not seem to be working any more.[28] Recall that CAPM says that only a security's exposure to market risk, that is, its beta, should be priced. Nothing else should have an impact on expected returns. And yet these authors were able to conclude that:

> In short, our tests do not support the most basic prediction of the ... [CAPM] model, that average stock returns are positively related to market betas.

They go on to say that the combination of size and book-to-market equity explains stock returns during their sample. Then they argue:

> If assets are priced rationally, our results suggest that stock risks are multidimensional. One dimension of risk is proxied by size ... Another dimension of risk is proxied by ... the ratio of the book value of common equity to its market value.

This is the crux of the matter. Statistical issues aside, anomalies either reflect investor error of some sort or inappropriate risk adjustment. In follow-up work, Fama and French demonstrated that, if mimicking portfolios for size and book-to-market are constructed, they do a good job, along with the excess market return, of explaining variation in stock returns. On this basis, they suggest (page 452) that "size and book-to-market equity proxy for risk factors in stock returns." The result of this is the well-known Fama-French three-factor model.

FAMA-FRENCH THREE-FACTOR MODEL

According to the **Fama-French three-factor model**, excess returns are calculated not just after accounting for market risk, but also after adjusting for risk factors associated with size and book-to-market. If a particular stock or portfolio i has no excess return, its alpha (α^i) in the following regression will be zero:

13.16
$$R_t^i - R_{f,t} = \alpha^i + \beta_1^i(R_{m,t} - R_{f,t}) + \beta_2^i SML_t + \beta_3^i HML_t + \varepsilon_t^i$$

where the return on security or portfolio i at t is R_t^i, the risk-free rate at t is $R_{f,t}$, the market return at t is $R_{m,t}$, the size factor at t is SML_t, the book-to-market factor at t is HML_t, and the three sensitivities to the risk factors are β_1^i, β_2^i, and β_3^i.[29]

This is a hotly debated model, with some arguing that it appropriately captures known sources of risk, with others counteracting that it is contrived and is only converting investor error into risk factors.[30] The debate can become quite technical, and will not be resolved here. One issue is what underlies the second and third Fama-French risk factors. Fama and French suggest that different aspects of so-called "distress risk" are being captured. But, these distressed stocks do not perform appreciably worse in bad times.[31] In any case, even those who believe that irrationality rather than rationality is behind the risk factors often find the Fama-French three-factor model useful because it is a useful style-control technique in the evaluation of professional investors. This is a topic that we will return to in Chapter 19.

EXPLAINING MOMENTUM

The Fama-French three-factor model is not able to account for momentum, a point that even Fama and French concede.[32] But other risk-based explanations for momentum have been proposed. For example, some research relates momentum to the business cycle and the state of the market, arguing that (non-diversifiable) macroeconomic instruments account for a large portion of momentum profits.[33] If indeed these are risk proxies, then a proper adjustment for risk would seriously reduce the efficacy of trading on prior returns.[34]

Another recent rational justification for momentum argues that a simple time-varying CAPM with beta uncertainty can contribute to an explanation of momentum.[35] When the market is doing well, investors, using Bayesian learning, will revise upward the betas of stocks experiencing positive shocks, and revise downward those of stocks that have negative shocks. So subsequent momentum "profit" can be largely risk that has not been accounted for.

TEMPORARY DEVIATIONS FROM EFFICIENCY AND THE ADAPTIVE MARKETS HYPOTHESIS

It is possible that markets are sometimes *temporarily* inefficient, but when a sufficient number of arbitrageurs figure out how to capitalize on an inefficiency, mispricing gradually disappears. Along these lines, as will be discussed in Chapter 19, there is evidence that the small-firm effect has been declining. Josef Lakonishok, Andrei Shleifer, and Robert Vishny, when in 1994 posing the question whether the value advantage was likely to eventually disappear, wrote:[36]

> Perhaps the recent move into disciplined quantitative investment strategies, evaluated based only on performance and not on individual stock picks, will increase the demand for value stocks and reduce the agency problems that result in picking glamour stocks. Such sea changes rarely occur overnight, however. The time-series and cross-country evidence support the idea that the behavioral and institutional factors underlying the higher returns to value stocks have been pervasive and enduring features of equity markets.

Indeed, shortly after these words were written, for a number of years growth dramatically outperformed value—before strongly rebounding at the beginning of the millennium.[37] The fact that the value advantage seems to be in great part behaviorally based, and people likely change slowly in this regard, allows one to argue that value will have more staying power (than, for instance, the small-firm effect, which does not have any obvious behavioral interpretation). These issues will be picked up again in Chapter 19.

The rise and fall (followed by recurrences) of anomalies is consistent with the **adaptive markets hypothesis** of Andrew Lo, who has recently suggested that this cyclicality is to be expected in a world where markets are subject to evolutionary forces.[38] Opportunities that exist because of faulty heuristics and limits to arbitrage may evaporate since with sufficient time and given the existence of competitive forces, any counterproductive heuristic can be adapted for the current environment. On the other hand, if some of those exploiting particular opportunities leave the market, profitability may be rekindled as human nature reasserts itself.

CHAPTER HIGHLIGHTS

1. Post-announcement earnings drift appears to be driven by anchoring on the part of investors and analysts.
2. The value premium is likely due to both behavioral and agency-related institutional factors.
3. A number of theoretical models have been formulated to account for momentum and reversal.
4. The DHS model explains reversal using overconfidence; the GH model explains momentum using prospect theory, mental accounting, and the disposition effect; and the BSV model accounts for both momentum and reversal and is based on the anchoring and representativeness heuristics.
5. Much of the empirical evidence is consistent with the implications of these models.

6. Another view is that risk has been improperly accounted for in the research that has identified these anomalies, and a proper treatment of risk will render these anomalies as merely risk premiums.
7. The Fama-French three-factor model has value and small cap as risk factors over and above market risk.
8. Under Fama-French, value is a risk factor, not an anomaly. Some have questioned whether greater exposure to the value factor really does entail additional risk.
9. Momentum is not credibly accounted for by any risk-adjustment technique.

DISCUSSION QUESTIONS AND PROBLEMS

1. Differentiate the following terms/concepts:

    a. Momentum and reversal
    b. Mean-reversion and continuation scenarios in BSV model
    c. Size factor and book-to-market factor
    d. Risk-based and behavioral explanations (for anomalies)

2. In the context of the BSV model, explain intuitively (nontechnically) why two consecutive earnings changes in the same direction make investors less likely to think that they are in regime 1 (mean-reversion) versus the case of two earnings changes in alternate directions.

3. In the chapter example of the DHS model, in one of the two cases even rational investors overreacted. This implies that overreaction is rational. Comment.

4. Again using the DHS model, suppose that $\theta = 1$; $\sigma_\theta^2 = 1$; $\sigma_\varepsilon^2 = 2$; $\sigma_C^2 = 1$; and $s_1 = 2$. Describe and comment on the path of prices when overconfident investors determine prices versus the rational path of prices.

5. Momentum is the anomaly that gives those subscribing to efficient markets the most trouble. Explain.

ENDNOTES

1 Abarbanell, J. S., and V. L. Bernard, 1992, "Tests of analysts' overreaction/underreaction to earnings information as an explanation for anomalous stock price behavior," *Journal of Finance* 47, 1181–1207.
2 Battalio, R. H, and R. R. Mendenhall, 2005, "Earnings expectations, investor trade size, and anomalous returns around earnings announcements," *Journal of Financial Economics* 77, 289–319.
3 Chan, L. K. C., J. Karceski, and J. Lakonishok, 2003, "The level and persistence of growth rates," *Journal of Finance* 58, 643–684.
4 Ibid.
5 As an example, see ibid.
6 On August 15, 2000, the U.S. Securities and Exchange Commission (SEC) adopted Regulation FD (Fair Disclosure) to address the selective disclosure of information by publicly traded companies and other issuers. Regulation FD stipulates that when an issuer discloses material nonpublic information to certain individuals or entities (e.g., securities market professionals, such as stock analysts, or holders of the issuer's securities who may well trade on the basis of the information), the issuer must make public the disclosure of that information. In this way, the new rule aims to promote full and fair disclosure.
7 Lim, T., 2001, "Rationality and analysts' forecast bias," *Journal of Finance* 56, 369–385.

8 Chen, Q., and W. Jiang, 2006, "Analysts' weighting of private and public information," *Review of Financial Studies* 19, 319–355.

9 Lakonishok, J., A. Shleifer, and R. Vishny, 1994, "Contrarian investment, extrapolation and risk," *Journal of Finance* 49, 1541–1578.

10 Related to this is the positive affect generated by successful growth companies that was discussed in Chapter 10. See MacGregor, D. G., P. Slovic, D. Dreman, and M. Berry, 2000, "Imagery, affect, and financial judgment," *Journal of Psychology and Financial Markets* 1 (no. 2), 104–110.

11 See Lakonishok, J., A. Shleifer, and R. W. Vishny, 1992, "The structure and performance of the money management industry," *Brookings Papers on Economic Activity: Microeconomics* 339–391; and Del Guercio, D., 1996, "The distorting effects of the prudent-man laws on institutional equity investments," *Journal of Financial Economics* 40, 31–62.

12 LaPorta, R., 1996, "Expectations and the cross-section of stock returns," *Journal of Finance* 51, 1715–1742.

13 LaPorta, R., J. Lakonishok, A. Shleifer, and R. Vishny, 1997, "Good news for value stocks: Further evidence on market efficiency," *Journal of Finance* 52, 859–874.

14 Rozeff, M. S., and M. A. Zaman, 1998, "Overreaction and insider trading: Evidence from growth and value portfolios," *Journal of Finance* 53, 701–716.

15 See Shleifer, A., and R. Vishny, 1997, "The limits of arbitrage," *Journal of Finance* 52, 35–55, for a discussion.

16 Ali, A., L.-S. Hwang, and M. A. Trombley, 2003, "Arbitrage risk and the book-to-market anomaly," *Journal of Financial Economics* 69, 355–373.

17 Daniel, K., D. Hirshleifer, and A. Subrahmanyam, 1998, "Investor psychology and security market under- and overreactions," *Journal of Finance* 53, 1839–1885.

18 Grinblatt, M., and B. Han, 2004, "Prospect theory, mental accounting and momentum," *Journal of Financial Economics* 78, 311–339.

19 Barberis, N., A. Shleifer, and R. Vishny, 1998, "A model of investor sentiment," *Journal of Financial Economics* 49, 307–344.

20 In the same paper, Daniel, Hirshleifer and Subrahmanyam extend their model by recognizing self-attribution bias. This induces momentum in addition to reversal. The model we present is a scaled-down version of their simple model (without self-attribution bias).

21 It is also necessary to assume limits to arbitrage.

22 In the steady state the expected return is zero.

23 This phrase appears in Haugen, R. A., 1999, *The New Finance: The Case against Efficient Markets*, 2nd ed. (Prentice Hall, Upper Saddle River, New Jersey).

24 See Chan, L. K. C., J. Karceski, and J. Lakonishok, 2003, "The level and persistence of growth rates," *Journal of Finance* 58, 643–684, for a discussion.

25 The authors acknowledge certain limitations in their simulation. For example, for tractability, earnings and prices can go negative (but only the range where this is impossible is allowed).

26 See Conrad, J., M. Cooper, and G. Kaul, 2003, "Value vs. glamour," *Journal of Finance* 58, 1969–1996, who attempt to quantify the potential impact of data snooping.

27 See Kothari, S. P., J. Shanken, and R. G. Sloan, 1995, "Another look at the cross-section of expected stock returns," *Journal of Finance* 50, 157–184; Chan, L. K. C., N. Jegadeesh, and J. Lakonishok, 1995, "Evaluating the performance of value vs. glamour stocks: The impact of selection bias," *Journal of Financial Economics* 38, 269–296; Conrad, J., and G. Kaul, 1993, "Long-term market overreaction or biases in computed

returns?" *Journal of Finance* 48, 39–63; Conrad, J., and G. Kaul, 1998, "An anatomy of trading strategies," *Review of Financial Studies* 11, 489–519; and Jegadeesh, N., and S. Titman, 2002, "Cross-sectional and time-series determinants of momentum returns," *Review of Financial Studies* 15, 143–157.

28 Fama, E. F., and K. R. French, 1992, "The cross-section of expected stock returns," *Journal of Finance* 47, 427–465.

29 See Fama, E. F., and K. R. French, 1993, "Common risk factors in the returns on stocks and bonds," *Journal of Financial Economics* 33, 3–56; and Fama, E. F., and K. R. French, 1996, "Multifactor explanations of asset pricing anomalies," *Journal of Finance* 51, 55–84.

30 For two takes on the debate, see chapter 1 of Shleifer, A., 2000, *Inefficient Markets: An Introduction to Behavioral Finance* (Oxford University Press, Oxford, U.K.); and Brav, A., J. B. Heaton, and A. Rosenberg, 2004, "The rational-behavioral debate in financial economics," *Journal of Economic Methodology* 11, 393–409.

31 See Lakonishok, J., A. Shleifer, and R. Vishny, 1994, "Contrarian investment, extrapolation and risk," *Journal of Finance* 49, 1541–1578; and Chan, K. C., and N. Chen, 1991, "Structural and return characteristics of small and large firms," *Journal of Finance* 46, 1467–1484.

32 Note that many momentum studies use the three-factor model as a risk-adjustment model and it has no appreciable impact on results. See, for example, Cooper, M., Jr., R. C. Gutierrez, and A. Hameed, 2004, "Market states and momentum," *Journal of Finance* 59, 1345–1365. Without any real backing for momentum being a risk factor, one can tack on momentum as a fourth factor, as in Carhart, M. M., 1997, "On persistence in mutual fund performance," *Journal of Finance* 52, 57–82.

33 Chordia, T., and L. Shivakumar, 2002, "Momentum, business cycle, and time-varying expected returns," *Journal of Finance* 57, 985–1020.

34 Nevertheless, Cooper, M., Jr., R. C. Gutierrez, and A. Hameed, 2004, "Market states and momentum," *Journal of Finance* 59, 1345–1365, counter that the Chordia and Shivakumar results do not survive common screens to control for microstructure-induced biases. Cooper, Gutierrez, and Hameed also show that momentum profits exist exclusively after up-market states. They argue that this finding is consistent with the model of Daniel, K., D. Hirshleifer, and A. Subrahmanyam, 1998, "Investor psychology and security market under- and overreactions," *Journal of Finance* 53, 1839–1885, because overconfidence is positively correlated with market performance. See Statman, M., S. Thorley, and K. Vorkink, 2006, "Investor overconfidence and trading volume," *Review of Financial Studies* 19, 1531–1565; and Deaves, R., E. Lüders, and M. Schröder, 2008, "The dynamics of overconfidence: Evidence from stock market forecasters," Working paper.

35 Wang, K. Q., 2005, "Why does the CAPM fail to explain momentum?" Working paper.

36 Lakonishok, J., A. Shleifer, and R. Vishny, 1994, "Contrarian investment, extrapolation and risk," *Journal of Finance* 49, 1541–1578.

37 Chan, L. K. C., and J. Lakonishok, 2004, "Value and growth investing: A review and update," *Financial Analysts Journal* 60 (Jan/Feb), 71 (16 pages).

38 See Lo, A. W., 2004, "The adaptive markets hypothesis: Market efficiency from an evolutionary perspective," Working paper; and Lo, A. W., 2005, "Reconciling efficient markets with behavioral finance: The adaptive markets hypothesis," Working paper.

DO BEHAVIORAL FACTORS EXPLAIN STOCK MARKET PUZZLES?

CHAPTER 14

14.1 INTRODUCTION

In the previous chapter, we argued that behavioral considerations can contribute to an understanding of certain anomalies in the pricing of individual stocks. There we took a cross-sectional (or individual stock) approach. If we aggregate the market values of all stocks in the market, we have the aggregate value of the stock market. It turns out that, just as there are cross-sectional anomalies, there are also aggregate stock market puzzles. In this chapter, we consider whether behavioral factors can help us account for these puzzles.

The focus will be on three puzzles: the equity premium puzzle; bubbles; and excessive volatility. We begin in Section 14.2 with the equity premium puzzle, namely the observation that, while equities are riskier than fixed-income securities and as a result should earn higher average returns in compensation for the additional risk borne, it is apparent that the historical gap between stock and bond returns is implausibly high from the standpoint of expected utility theory. Next we turn to overvaluation and bubbles, beginning in Section 14.3 with two famous overvaluation episodes, the tulip mania, which occurred in Europe close to 400 years ago, and the tech/Internet bubble that occurred in world stock markets in the late 1990s. Focusing on the United States, while the entire stock market likely deviated far from valuations based on economic fundamentals, much of the overvaluation was concentrated in tech and Internet stocks. One problem with looking at real-world data is that it is always difficult to categorically say that an episode of overvaluation is occurring. Because of the ability to carefully control the environment, experimental asset markets, as reported in Section 14.4, provide insight into the conditions under which asset price bubbles are generated. In Section 14.5, we consider whether behavioral finance can contribute to an understanding of overvaluation episodes, including asset price bubbles. Finally, in Section 14.6, we turn to the puzzle that stock market prices seem to exhibit too much volatility. This has long been a contentious point, but as of early 2009 has taken on even greater resonance as amazingly high levels of volatility have been observed along with dramatic declines in asset values. The chapter concludes, in Section 14.7, with a tentative interpretation of events that roiled markets in 2008.

14.2   THE EQUITY PREMIUM PUZZLE

THE EQUITY PREMIUM

Much research has examined the **equity premium puzzle**, which was forcefully brought to light by Rajinish Mehra and Edward Prescott.[1] The equity premium is defined to be the gap between the expected return on the aggregate stock market and a portfolio of fixed-income securities. Since no one can easily observe expected returns, we approximate the equity premium using historical average returns. On this basis, the equity premium can be calculated in a number of ways: it depends on whether you use arithmetic versus geometric average returns, the sample you employ, and what your market and fixed-income proxies are.[2] There is no right answer, so it is useful to calculate the equity premium in different ways.

Jeremy Siegel in his best-selling book *Stocks for the Long Run* provides a wealth of data on the equity premium.[3] What is very nice about his dataset is that it goes all the way back to 1802. While the sample ends in 1997, given its long history, it is still quite useful today. Figure 14.1 asks the following question: If you began with $1 invested in a particular asset class and "let it ride," how much would you (or, more accurately, your heirs) have by 1997? The asset classes examined are U.S. stocks, bonds, Treasury bills, and gold. Incredibly, your $1 investment in stocks would have surpassed $7 million—not bad for the patient investor. Bonds would be worth over $10,500 and T-bills over $3,500. Of course, $1 in 1802 bought a lot more than it does today. For reference purposes, the figure also shows the rise in prices (as proxied by the Consumer Price Index, or CPI).

To control for price changes, Figure 14.2 restates Figure 14.1, but now all returns are on a real (or constant-dollar) basis. Stocks are tamed to some extent, but a $1 investment still grows to over $550,000, versus less than $1,000 for bonds and bills, and (perhaps surprisingly to some) less than $1 for gold.

In Table 14.1, we convert everything into average (annual) returns. Real returns are presented both for the full sample and for three roughly equal subperiods. Beginning with stocks, the average returns on stocks have been fairly stable. Using the more conservative geometric average measure, long-term averages have ranged from 6.6% to 7.2%. The comparable numbers for bonds and bills have been 2%–4.8% and 0.6%–5.1%. If we choose the lowest full-sample equity premium, it is 3.5% (stocks vs. bonds using the geometric average). For the most recent subperiod, which begins in 1926, this same gap is 5.2%.

WHY IS THE EQUITY PREMIUM A PUZZLE?

Is the equity premium really a puzzle? Stocks after all are riskier, so they should earn higher returns. The reason a puzzle exists is that, assuming expected utility

FIGURE 14.1 The Future Value of an 1802 Dollar Invested in Different Asset Classes (in nominal terms)

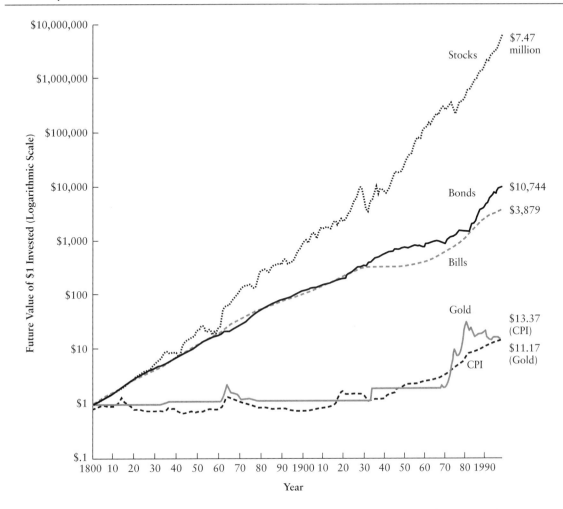

theory applies, an implausibly high level of risk aversion would have to be assumed to rationalize these numbers. This can be seen in a number of ways. First, Mehra and Prescott argue that a reasonable level of risk aversion would lead to an equity premium of 0.1%. Second, recalling from Chapter 1 the discussion of utility functions and again using the popular logarithmic function, the **coefficient of relative risk aversion,** one measure of distaste for risk, is 1.0.[4] Higher numbers indicate more risk aversion. The coefficient of relative risk aversion needed to justify the observed equity premium would have to be a whopping 30 in order to explain observed returns! Third, recalling prospects and certainty equivalents, consider the

FIGURE 14.2 The Future Value of an 1802 Dollar Invested in Different Asset Classes (in real terms)

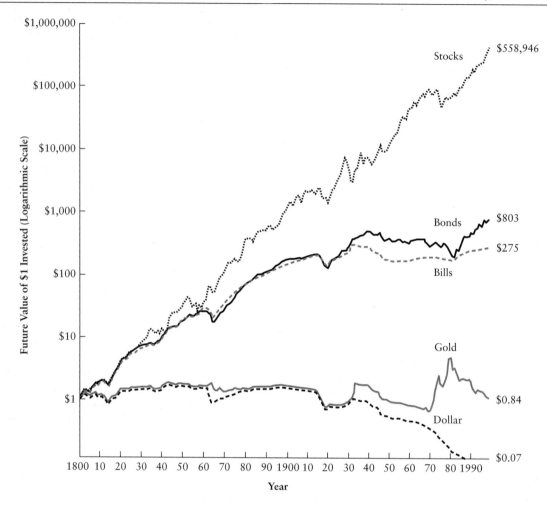

Source: Siegel, J. J. From "The Future Value of an 1802 Dollar Invested in Different Assett Classes (in nominal terms)," in *Stocks for the Long Run* 2nd Edition, 1998 (McGraw Hill, New York, New York), 1998. © 1998 by McGraw-Hill, Inc. All rights reserved. Reproduced by permission.

following prospect: P1(0.50, $50,000, $100,000). What certainty equivalent, $x, would make someone indifferent between P1 and this certain amount of money? For someone with a coefficient of relative risk aversion of 30, $x would need to be $51,209.[5] It seems unlikely that people are that afraid of risk.

WHAT CAN EXPLAIN THIS PUZZLE?

There is much debate on what accounts for observed equity premiums. Some explanations are based on rationality, and some take a more behavioral approach. As an example of the former, it has been suggested that survivorship bias may

TABLE 14.1 | Average Real Returns (in %) on Stocks, Bonds, and Bills

	1802–1997	1802–1870	1871–1925	1926–1997
Stocks (Geometric)	7.0	7.0	6.6	7.2
Stocks (Arithmetic)	8.5	8.3	7.9	9.2
Bonds (Geometric)	3.5	4.8	3.7	2.0
Bonds (Arithmetic)	3.8	5.1	3.9	2.6
Bills (Geometric)	2.9	5.1	3.2	0.6
Bills (Arithmetic)	3.1	5.4	3.3	0.7

Source: Siegel, J. J. From "Average Real Returns (in %) on Stocks, Bonds and Bills," in *Stocks for the Long Run* 2nd Edition, 1998 (McGraw Hill, New York, New York), 1998. © 1998 by McGraw-Hill, Inc. All rights reserved. Reproduced by permission.

contribute to an understanding of the puzzle.[6] To put this explanation into perspective, consider the following sports example. In golf tournaments, typically a group of players shoots two rounds. All players in the group with the lowest cumulative score (up to some predetermined number of players) continue on to play the third and fourth rounds.[7] The surviving player with the lowest four-round total wins the tournament. Let's say a statistician comes along and wants to estimate the average performance of all golfers. He shows up at the end of the tournament and calculates the average score per round of all surviving golfers. Clearly this would be biased downward. As an illustration, we conducted the following simple experiment. We simulated a hypothetical tournament with 100 players, using the assumptions that all players have equal skill and there is independence among rounds. The latter is tantamount to the non-existence of a "hot hand effect." A distributional mean of 71 and a standard deviation of 3 were assumed. Then, after two rounds we took the top half (and ties) of all golfers and let them continue on to play the last two rounds. The rest of the golfers did not make the cut. The average score per round for all surviving golfers was 70.1—about a stroke below the distributional mean. In contrast, the average score over the first two rounds for all 100 golfers was 70.9—very close to the distributional mean. A researcher does not want to make the mistake of only looking at survivors.

In the context of the equity premium puzzle, Stephen Brown, William Goetzmann, and Stephen Ross looked at performance histories of national stock markets around the world.[8] As of the beginning of the twentieth century, 36 national stock markets existed. More than half of these, either due to wars or nationalizations, have suffered at least one major break in trading. These events often result in very large losses in wealth for investors. But if we only look at the roughly half of all national markets with continuous trading histories, the golf example makes it clear that the average market return will be upward-biased because of survivorship bias.

On the behavioral side, there are two main explanations. One is based on ambiguity aversion. The equity premium puzzle suggests that required risk aversion is simply too high to be credible. But what if people are both risk averse and ambiguity averse? Not only do investors, naturally enough, not know what the random draw from the return distribution will be, but they also do not know what the distributional parameters themselves are. This is consistent with survey evidence showing wide disagreement on the level of the ex ante equity premium, which means that we don't know the mean of the return distribution.[9] Under such circumstances, "effective risk aversion" increases.[10] Assuming plausible values for risk aversion and ambiguity aversion (or uncertainty aversion), an equity premium in the neighborhood of 5% turns out to be quite reasonable.

A second behavioral explanation for the equity premium puzzle, as proposed by Shlomo Benartzi and Richard Thaler, is based on loss aversion and mental accounting.[11] Recall that people who are loss averse feel losses much more than gains of equivalent size. The two-part power function described in Chapter 3 is a popular prospect theory value function. It is reproduced here, where v is value and z is change in wealth:

14.1
$$v(z) = \begin{array}{ll} z^\alpha & 0 < \alpha < 1 & \text{if } z \geq 0 \\ -\lambda(-z)^\beta & \lambda > 1,\, 0 < \beta < 1 & \text{if } z < 0 \end{array}$$

This function exhibits risk aversion in the positive domain ($0 < \alpha < 1$), risk seeking in the negative domain ($0 < \beta < 1$) and loss aversion ($\lambda > 1$). All we need, however, for present purposes is loss aversion, so, if we set $\alpha = \beta = 1$, we have the following "kinked" linear function:

14.2
$$v(w) = \begin{array}{ll} z & \text{if } z \geq 0 \\ \lambda z & \lambda > 1 & \text{if } z < 0 \end{array}$$

This function says that people are risk neutral once they are away from the reference point. In the equation below we will assume $\lambda = 2.5$.[12] Another complication of prospect theory is the weighting function, but once again we can keep matters simple and assume that, as in the case of expected utility, weights and probabilities are equivalent.

Mental accounting is also assumed. Recall that mental accounting involves separating blocks of information into more manageable pieces. This concept is significant because how people aggregate information has an effect on how the information is evaluated. When people hold portfolios, it is natural that for a while they do not monitor things too carefully. By this we mean that they do not pay too much attention to precise losses or gains. For this reason, short-term market value changes are effectively integrated. Periodically, however, people will look at their portfolios more carefully. They will note whether they have made gains or losses. At this point, in the parlance of mental accounting, they will "book their losses." In this sense, they are segregating the past from the future. Since people don't like losses, they are likely ex ante to avoid investments that have an uncomfortably high probability of ending up in negative territory when it is time for portfolios to be evaluated.

Consider the following prospect: P2(0.50, $200, -$100). Would someone with the previous value function accept this prospect or prefer to do nothing? Think of this prospect as an investment where one can make $200 or lose $100. In other words, noting that the expected gain is $50, is the risk of the investment worth the potential gain? On a one-shot basis, the answer is no, since, as shown in this example, the value of this prospect is zero:

14.3
$$V(P2) = 0.50(200) + 0.50(2.5(-100)) = -25$$

What if the prospect is allowed to be run twice before the investor carefully notes the result? In other words, she integrates two prospects until she looks closely at the result, at which point segregation occurs. In this case, this investor would take two of these gambles. The possible outcomes after two gambles are $400 with a probability 25%, $100 with a probability of 50%, and –$200 with a probability of 25%. First note that two runs of P2 lead to: P3(0.25, .50; $400, $100, –$200). In this straightforward extension of the previous prospect notation, the first two numbers are probabilities that should be associated with the first two wealth outcomes (to the right of the semicolon), while the residual probability should be associated with the third wealth outcome. The value of P3 is:

14.4 $$V(P3) = 0.25(400) + 0.50(100) + .25(2.5(-200)) = 25$$

Note that now a loss is only half as likely (25% vs. 50%) to occur. While this person remains loss averse, she is now more willing to take the risk of the investment as long as she evaluates the outcomes two prospects at a time. This is tantamount to looking at one's portfolio every two periods.

Returning to the equity premium puzzle, Benartzi and Thaler argue that the observed level of the equity premium follows from people being loss averse and fairly frequently evaluating their wealth position. How frequently? It turns out that the answer is in the neighborhood of one year, which is about how often many people carefully look at their portfolios. Most people are investing for the long term, for retirement. This implies losses are only truly losses if they exist as of the end of the (long-term for most) horizon, but investors can't help but look at their portfolios earlier than the end of the horizon and they hate to see losses. In essence, they are unwilling to accept the short-run variability of stock returns even if this variability will not hurt them in the long run. This less-than-optimal behavior is called **myopic loss aversion**. While Benartzi and Thaler cannot *prove* that myopic loss aversion explains the equity premium, there is evidence that people are subject to it. For example, recent evidence suggests that professional traders at the Chicago Board of Trade show signs of myopic loss aversion—to an even greater extent than students![13]

14.3   REAL-WORLD BUBBLES

Stock valuations sometimes seem to be completely disconnected from the forecasted or observed performance of a corporation. In Chapter 12, we discussed the bankruptcy of Enron in the context of the influences of social forces, particularly the corporate board and financial analysts. Investors, through the high price they were willing to pay for the company, also played a role in this episode. Enron was certainly not the only corporation that was overvalued during the 1990s. The Nasdaq Composite Index, which is heavily weighted in technology firms, closed at 2,406.00 on March 10, 1999.[14] One year later, on March 10, 2000, the index had more than doubled, reaching a maximum of 5,048.62. Precipitous price declines followed, with the index reaching a low point of 1,114.11 on October 9, 2002. Since that time, the index has experienced periods of increase, but has yet to recross

3,000. Most neutral observers would agree that many tech/Internet stocks were egregiously overvalued in early 2000. If so, how could the market make such a big mistake?

TULIP MANIA

The tech/Internet bubble is certainly not the first price bubble ever observed. A **bubble** (or speculative bubble) is said to exist when high prices seem to be generated more by traders' enthusiasm than by economic fundamentals. Notice that a bubble must be defined ex post—at some point the bubble bursts and prices adjust downward, sometimes very quickly. Interestingly, hindsight bias often kicks in. Many investors can be heard saying that they knew it along, but then why did they participate and, in some cases, lose vast sums of money?

Extreme prices that seem to be at odds with rational explanations have occurred repeatedly throughout history. One of the most remarkable examples is the tulip bubble, or tulip mania, of the 1630s. The tulip first appeared in Western Europe in the sixteenth century.[15] First the wealthy, and then the middle class, became quite avid about the tulip, and soon high prices were paid for rare tulip bulbs. Tulip demand seemed to escalate each year, particularly in Holland and Germany. By the 1630s, tulip markets sprang up in numerous cities with the sole purpose of facilitating tulip trade. Gambling and speculation seemed to be taking hold, and many fortunes were made and then lost. Amazing stories of what goods people were willing to trade for tulips have been recorded. For example, one person traded everything on the following list for *one* rare tulip bulb:[16]

Two lasts of wheat[17]	448
Four lasts of rye	558
Four fat oxen	480
Eight fat swine	240
Twelve fat sheep	120
Two hogsheads of wine	70
Four tuns of beer[18]	32
Two tuns of butter	192
One thousand lbs. of cheese	120
A complete bed	100
A suit of clothes	80
A silver drinking cup	60
Total	**2,500 florins**

Note that the value of each item above is in florins, the currency of the Netherlands until 2002 when the euro became the official currency.

This amount of goods seems like a great deal to trade for a single tulip bulb. Was the tulip mania a speculative bubble? In hindsight, most would agree that people acted irrationally. What were they thinking? We may never know for sure, but one popular explanation is that people bought tulips because they believed that others would pay even more. According to the **greater fool theory**, you buy an asset that you realize is overvalued because you think there is a foolish individual out there who will pay even more—maybe you are unwise, but there is a "greater fool" somewhere. Thus, you might really know the tulip bulb is not worth anywhere near 2,500 florins, but you think someone else will pay more to get it.

We should not assume irrationality too quickly. Perhaps there is another interpretation for the tulip mania.[19] Tulips come in many varieties and color patterns and many are truly rare. Is a tulip fancier who pays a high price for a bulb any more irrational that an art collector who pays millions of dollars for a painting?[20] As odd as it might seem to us today, the high values associated with tulip bulbs could have been rationally based on people's preferences at that time in history. The bubble bursting could have been due to a sudden change in preferences— unlikely perhaps, but not impossible.

THE TECH/INTERNET BUBBLE

Let us return to the tech/Internet bubble. While technology and Internet stocks were notorious for their excessive valuations, stocks across the board were caught up in the excitement. It is now widely believed that the level of the U.S. stock market by early 2000 reflected irrationality on the part of investors.[21] Some of the most persuasive evidence was provided before the correction by Robert Shiller. He argued that "irrational exuberance" was a good way to describe the psychology of the market in the late 1990s.[22] This term was first used by Federal Reserve Chairman Alan Greenspan in a speech on December 5, 1996. Stock markets seemed to drop in response to Greenspan's remarks, perhaps because people thought the market might be overvalued. The reaction was short-lived however: U.S. markets continued to rise, reaching a peak early in 2000.[23]

Figure 14.3 shows monthly real stock price and earnings experience in the United States for January 1871 through August 2008 using the Standard and Poor's 500 Composite Stock Price Index (S&P 500). The S&P 500, a widely followed benchmark for the U.S. market, is a stock basket that includes 500 large stocks weighted by market capitalization. Nominal series are adjusted for inflation using the consumer price index (CPI) because we want to control for the general level of price increase in the economy. Before proceeding with our discussion, note the graph shows that a precipitous market decline in U.S. markets occurred in 2008. While some of this decline is apparent in the figure, most of it occurred after August 2008. We will say more about this late 2008 decline toward the end of the chapter.

The figure gives us a snapshot of how stock prices have moved over long periods of time. While on the surface price levels in the late 1990s were unprecedented, it is important to control for earnings. A close look at Figure 14.3 shows a contemporaneous rise in earnings, but was it enough? To get a fix on this, we turn to Figure 14.4, which shows the S&P 500 price-to-earnings (P/E) ratio. This measure gives us insight into how the market values stock because it tells us how much investors are willing to pay per dollar of earnings. Recall that in Chapter 12 we used the P/E ratio to provide perspective on Enron's stock price performance. We observe some notable peaks in the P/E ratio including a value of 32.6 in September

FIGURE 14.3 Real S&P 500 Stock Prices and Earnings

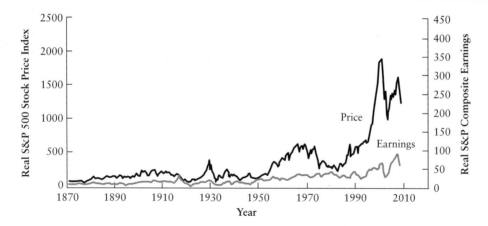

Source: Shiller, Robert. From "Figure 1: Real S&P 500 Stock Prices and Earnings," in http://www.econ.yale.edu/~shiller/data.htm © 2008 International Center for Finance at Yale School of Management. Reproduced by permission.

FIGURE 14.4 Real S&P 500 Price-to-Earnings Ratio

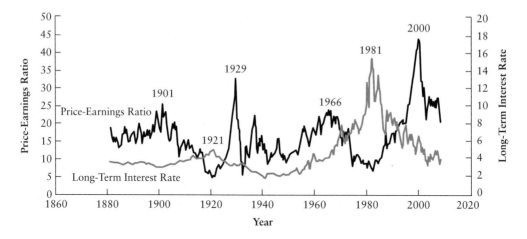

Source: Shiller, Robert. From "Figure 3: Real S&P 500 Stock Prices and Earnings," in http://www.econ.yale.edu/~shiller/data.htm © 2008 International Center for Finance at Yale School of Management. Reproduced by permission.

of 1929. This was the high point of the 1920s bull market and was followed by a startling decline in the market of over 80% by 1932. Also looking into the past, two other notable peaks were 1901 and 1966. In each case, the market declined after the peaks. Nevertheless, the peak of 44.2 in December 1999 was unparalleled.

How could investors have believed in 1999 that they were paying reasonable prices for stocks? Many argued it was a "new era" hailing the computer (especially through the Internet) as a new source of impressive future earnings and efficiency gains. In Chapter 4 we discussed the effects that investor sentiment can have in driving stock valuations. Though firms' current earnings did not seem to be a valid basis for high stock prices, investors thought that because of advances in technology that came with the Internet, future earnings would grow at rapid rates. Shiller argued that the Internet and the increased ease of trading generated by online and 24-hour trading were important factors in explaining the bubble.[24]

As always, we should be careful not to close the door on rationality too quickly. One research paper published in 2000 concludes: "… depending on the parameters chosen and *given high enough growth rates of revenues*, the value of an Internet stock may be rational."[25] In other words, perhaps the "new era" view was a credible one *at the time*.

Were Greenspan and Shiller the only observers who suspected overvaluation in the late 1990s? Measuring investor confidence in the valuation of the market is a tricky matter. Given our previous discussion of framing, it will not be surprising to hear that how the question is asked will have a significant impact on how investors answer it. Since 1989, Shiller and The Investor Behavior Project at Yale University have conducted surveys to appraise investor attitudes.[26] One question asks the following:

> Stock prices in the United States, when compared with measures of true fundamental value or sensible investment value, are:
>
> [CIRCLE ONE NUMBER]
>
> 1. Too low.   2. Too high.   3. About right.   4. Do not know.

The confidence index is a percentage computed by dividing the number of responses of 1. or 3. (too low or about right) by the number who respond 1., 2., or 3. Confidence is measured for individual as well as institutional investors.

As Figure 14.5 illustrates, confidence in the market declined for both individual and institutional investors from 1989 through 1999. Interestingly, the low point in confidence occurred in 1999, with only 31% of individual investors and 29% of institutional investors confident that the market was not overvalued. This means that 69% (71%) of individual (institutional) investors thought that stock prices were too high, so evidently many suspected overvaluation! The decline in confidence was reversed after the peak in stock prices in early 2000, and confidence soon returned to levels observed in the early 1990s. Though ups and downs in confidence are reported, from about 2003 to mid-2008 confidence, both for individuals and institutions, has been fairly stable.

The evidence suggests that many people thought valuations were too high at the end of the 1990s. Perhaps those who continued to buy at ever-increasing prices believed in the greater fool theory. They were willing to pay more than they thought a stock was worth because they believed someone else would pay an even higher price. We now turn to the experimental finance literature that has identified factors that are important in understanding why bubbles form.

14.4 EXPERIMENTAL BUBBLES MARKETS

Throughout this book we have discussed how the results of experiments have changed the way many people think about financial decision-making. Experimental

Figure 14.5 Shiller's Valuation Confidence Index

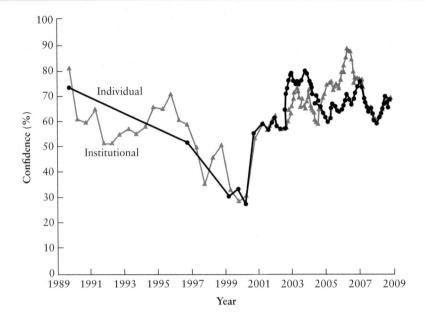

Source: Shiller, Robert. From "Valuation Confidence Index," in http://icf.som.yale.edu/Confidence.Index/ValueIndex. shtml. © 2008 International Center for Finance at Yale School of Management. Reproduced by permission.

asset markets have provided new insights into how markets work. One of the most perplexing findings from this research is the tendency of prices to rise far above fundamental value and then later crash in a particular, simple market structure. In this section, we describe these so-called experimental bubbles markets and review the results of this large literature.

Design of Bubbles Markets

The first study to report bubbles in experimental asset markets was published in 1988 by Vernon Smith, Gerry Suchanek, and Arlington Williams.[27] What is most surprising is that it was clear that bubbles were often being created in markets where the experimental design was such that the intrinsic value of securities was trivial to calculate at all points in time. This is of course totally unlike the real world where we can never be sure about beliefs about asset characteristics. Since then, many studies have duplicated these results and have gone on to investigate factors that both mitigate and promote bubble formation.

In a typical **bubbles market design**, subjects trade an asset over a fixed number of periods. The asset has a common dividend that is earned on all units and determined at the end of a trading period using a known probability distribution. If risk neutrality is assumed, we can easily compute the fundamental value of the asset by multiplying the number of trading periods by the expected dividend each period.

Let's consider an example using the dividend distributions from one bubbles experiment, as provided in Table 14.2.[28] For now, we will focus on the standard asset, leaving the lottery asset for later. The asset trades for 12 five-minute periods, so if you buy one unit in Period 1 and hold it until the end of the experiment, you would earn 12 dividends. The expected value of the dividend each period is simply computed as the sum of the probability of each dollar dividend multiplied by the amount of the dividend or:

14.5 $0.48 * 0.50 + .048 * 0.90 + 0.04 * 1.20 = 0.72$ or 72 cents

Given that you do not know the outcomes of future dividend draws in Period 1, how much would you be willing to pay for a unit of the asset? If you are risk neutral, you will pay the expected dividend per period (0.72) times 12 periods, or $8.64. This is the fundamental value of the asset in Period 1, and fundamental values in all subsequent periods can be computed just as easily by multiplying the number of periods remaining times the expected value of $0.72. For a trader who is risk averse, the fundamental value is lower because he must be compensated for taking on risk.

Figure 14.6 illustrates the typical price pattern in bubbles markets. The solid line indicates the fundamental value each period, beginning at $8.64 in Period 1 and falling by $0.72 each period. The dashed lines show median transactions prices per period for four different bubbles markets. Notice that the patterns are similar. Usually the price in Period 1 is below fundamental value but quickly rises high above the value warranted by expected dividends. The price in the first period may be low due to subjects' initial risk aversion because they are trading in an environment in which they are inexperienced. Some of the bubbles in this figure are quite persistent, but all eventually crash back to fundamental value as fewer trading periods remain.

What Can We Learn From These Experiments?

Though experimental bubbles markets are rather simple and obviously do not include all the important features of complex markets like the Tokyo, London, and

TABLE 14.2 | Distribution of Dividends

	Asset Dividend Distributions			Expected Value of Dividends	Fund. Value in Period 1
Probability	0.48	0.48	0.04		
Standard asset's dividends	0.50	0.90	1.20	0.72	8.64
Lottery asset's dividends	0.00	0.00	18.00		

Note: The fundamental value in Period 1 is the expected dividend per period multiplied by the number of trading periods (12).

Source: This is Panel B of Table 1 from Ackert, L. F., N. Charupat, B. K. Church, and R. Deaves, 2006, "Margin, short selling, and lotteries in experimental asset markets," *Southern Economic Journal* 73(2), p. 424.

FIGURE 14.6 Bubbles in Experimental Asset Markets

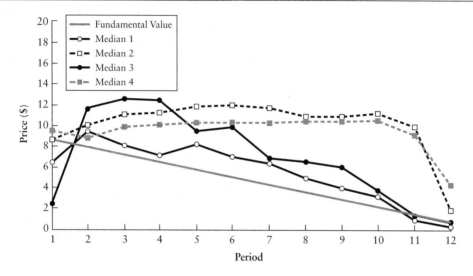

Source: Ackert, L. F., N. Charupat, B. K. Church, and R. Deaves, 2006, "Margin, short selling, and lotteries in experimental asset markets," *Southern Economic Journal* 73(2), p. 427.

New York Stock Exchanges, we have learned a lot about how bubbles form. Importantly, price bubbles are more moderate and disappear faster when traders are experienced both in terms of their knowledge of financial markets and with previous experience in an experimental bubbles market.[29] This probably does not surprise you. As we will discuss further in Chapter 20, expertise comes with experience and knowledge in most domains. Traders with financial knowledge and experience in trading will price the asset closer to its economic value. Importantly, price deviations above fundamental value are small even when only a subset of the traders is knowledgeable and experienced.[30] So, we do not need *all* traders to be knowledgeable and experienced for a market to price securities efficiently.

In some experiments, two assets are traded in order to investigate whether pricing differs across the assets. As Table 14.2 indicates, one study allowed trading of two assets: a standard asset and a **lottery asset**. The second asset is referred to as the lottery asset because its payoffs are similar to a small-scale lottery. In most cases the payoff is zero, but 4% of the time the asset receives a large dividend payment of $18.00. Although the standard and lottery assets have identical expected values, in experimental markets traders were willing to pay *more* for the lottery asset. This suggests that traders may be subject to probability judgment error. Consistent with the prospect theory weighting function, people overweight low probabilities.[31] Another possible explanation is that speculation or gambling plays into how people determine what they will pay to acquire an asset. They are willing to pay more for the lottery asset because they become more risk taking as they get caught up in the excitement of trading.

Speculation and bubbles formation seem to be fueled by a great deal of cash in a market.[32] This is reminiscent of the house money effect. To investigate the role of gambling or speculation in bubbles generation, one experiment restricted traders to act as either buyers *or* sellers of the asset.[33] Even though this design eliminates the opportunity to speculate, frequent bubbles are reported. This led the researchers to conclude that speculation is not necessary for bubble formation, with the key ingredient being irrational behavior. Other research investigates specific forms of irrationality. One paper, for example, that investigated pricing in bubbles markets reports a relationship between the frequency (and magnitude) of bubbles and the presence of probability judgment error.[34] At the same time, it is reported that speculation appears to play a role in pricing.

In addition to expertise, probability weighting, and speculation, research has shown that regulation of a market can have important effects on pricing. For example, restrictions on short selling promote bubble formation because those who are optimistic about an asset's value drive pricing.[35] A pessimistic trader who already owns the asset can simply sell. But others who do not currently hold the asset and are pessimistic may not be able to take an action that reflects their view of the asset's value when they cannot short sell. Without short selling, the market may be driven to high levels that are not really warranted by the view of the entire market. Thus, policymakers are cautioned against increasing trading restrictions that can, in the end, undermine market efficiency.

14.5   BEHAVIORAL FINANCE AND MARKET VALUATIONS

Behavioral finance has contributed to our understanding of how people value assets in a variety of markets, from tulips, to stocks, to experimental assets. Investors and academics alike strive to quantify asset values based on observable factors, but experience clearly indicates that the human side has very real effects. As Shiller points out, "[i]nvesting in speculative assets is a social activity."[36] In Chapters 11 and 12 we considered how social forces impact the behavior of investors, managers, and others. In this chapter, we have seen that asset values may be impacted by a number of behavioral influences, including fashions, changes in tastes (including risk attitude), and what appears in hindsight to be simple irrationality.

A challenge for behavioral finance is to bring what we have learned about how people make decisions to markets. In Chapter 10, we considered one such model. Recall that in Barberis, Huang, and Santos's model, investors are loss averse so that prior outcomes affect subsequent behavior.[37] After stock prices increase, the investor is less risk averse because prior gains cushion subsequent losses, while after stock prices decrease, the investor is concerned about further losses and risk aversion increases. The result is higher volatility in stock prices. Changes in attitudes toward risk can have important effects on both asset valuations and price changes. In the following section, we turn to the issue of market volatility.

14.6   EXCESSIVE VOLATILITY

DO PRICES MOVE TOO MUCH?

In addition to valuations that sometimes seem puzzling, the stock market appears to be much too volatile. Researchers have shown that while some variation in stock return volatility can be attributed to news, a large portion cannot. In other words, **excessive volatility** exists. David Cutler, James Poterba, and Larry Summers provide some compelling evidence.[38] They examined news events and major stock price movements over a 50-year period ending in the late 1980s. First, they looked at major news events (as reported in the *New York Times*) and considered whether market movements resulted from them. For example, when the Japanese attacked Pearl Harbor on December 8, 1941, the U.S. market dropped by 4.37%. That makes perfect sense. We also might expect significant market reactions to presidential elections, which are also major news events, because of perceived differences in economic policy between candidates. But when Johnson defeated Goldwater in 1964, the market didn't move (it went up by 0.05%) because Johnson was widely anticipated to win by a landslide.

Cutler, Porterba, and Summers also looked at the 50 biggest price moves and tried to relate them to material information. While in many instances this task was easy, in other cases there seemed to be no compelling reason for a market reaction. For example, on September 3, 1946, the market dropped by 6.73% (this was the fourth biggest price change) and the *New York Times* wrote that there was "no basic reason for the assault on prices."

DEMONSTRATING EXCESSIVE VOLATILITY

An innovative inequality relationship introduced by Shiller changed the way that many think about efficiency at the level of aggregate stock markets.[39] Recall from Chapter 2 the present value model of stock prices, which says that a stock's current value should equal the present value of expected future dividends. While we have to form expectations of dividends, what if we actually know the dividends that will eventually be paid? Shiller called the present value of actual (rather than expected) dividends the "ex post rational stock price," because it is the price if you know all future dividends. According to theory, the price today is the best forecast of the ex post rational stock price based on all currently available information. Using this insight, Shiller derived an inequality that he argued should not be violated if market efficiency holds. Shiller's inequality says that the standard deviation of the stock price is bounded above by the standard deviation of the ex post rational stock price. The price should be the expectation of the ex post rational stock price, and, because the latter will move based on unexpected information (that is, information available to investors when the actual price is set), the volatility of the price should be lower.

Shiller tested his inequality using the real S&P 500 stock price index, shown earlier in Figure 14.3. To compute the ex post rational stock price, he assumed a long-run growth rate in dividends. Figure 14.7 shows a rather striking result. The solid line is the observed value of the S&P 500 index (p) and the broken line is the ex post rational stock price (p*). As the figure unmistakably illustrates, stock prices are much too volatile to be justified by the present value of future dividends. Recall that Shiller's inequality says that the volatility of p should be smaller than the volatility of p*. Depending on the parameters used in estimation, the volatility of stock prices over the last century is *5 to 13 times* too large! How can stock prices be so volatile when dividends are so smooth?

Figure 14.7 Shiller's Volatility Comparisons

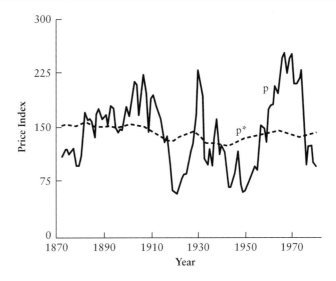

Source: Shiller, Robert J. "Do stock prices move too much to be justified by subsequent changes in dividends?" American Economic Review 71(3), p. 422. © American Economic Review. Reproduced with permission of the publisher and the author.

Explaining Excessive Volatility

While research has allowed us to gain some key insights into how markets value risky assets like stocks, to many people the stock market became even more puzzling following the publication of Shiller's work. While possible explanations for high stock market volatility have been proposed by researchers,[40] the prevailing view is that the stock market is overly volatile.

Researchers have devoted great effort to understanding patterns in volatility. One observation is that stock volatility tends to increase after a market crash. In addition, it seems that Nasdaq volatility in recent years is unusually high in comparison to the volatility of the S&P 500. In addition to jumps in the volatilities of S&P 500 and Nasdaq indexes after the 1987 crash and during the tech/Internet bubble and readjustment in 1998–2001, researchers report that the ratio of Nasdaq to S&P 500 volatility indicates an upward trend over time.[41] This is not surprising since the factor that seems to best explain high stock volatility over this time period is membership in the technology industry.

Volatility Forecasts and the Spike of 2008

A popular measure of investors' view of market conditions is the **implied volatility index (VIX)** provided by the Chicago Board Options Exchange (or CBOE).[42] The VIX, commonly referred to as the fear index, gauges investors' expectations of future stock market volatility using current option prices. This volatility measure is referred to as "implied" because it is derived from the prices of traded options on

FIGURE 14.8 The Volatility Index

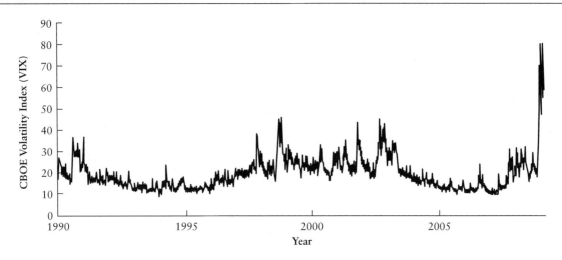

the S&P 500. In periods of uncertainty when investors are wary of market declines, the VIX tends to rise.

As Figure 14.8 illustrates, the VIX has historically varied around its long-term average of about 20. Prior to 2008, the maximum value of the VIX was 46, reached on October 8, 1998. At that time, the Asian financial crisis of 1997 had spread to Russia and impacted many large hedge funds, including Long Term Capital Management, which suffered large losses in 1998. In the late months of 1998, there was a great deal of uncertainty regarding how far the financial crisis would spread. While the level of uncertainty was high in 1998, it pales in comparison to late 2008. In the fall of 2008, the VIX rose to unprecedented levels, reaching its peak on November 20, 2008 at 81. We next turn to market conditions in the fall of 2008.

14.7   MARKETS IN 2008

What could have led to such unprecedented volatility? We begin with a review of economic and market events leading up to this volatility spike. In the summer of 2007, a liquidity crisis gripped financial markets leading to injections of capital by both the U.S. Federal Reserve and the European Central Bank. Many large institutions that had huge investments in securitized mortgage obligations misjudged the risks they were taking and subsequently ran into financial difficulty. Some contend that a contributing factor to the crisis was liberalization of mortgage terms in the United States and increased prevalence of zero-down mortgage loans. In addition, it has been argued that little or no due diligence was conducted of the likelihood that the borrowers would be able to make payments.[43] Many of these loans were pooled, securitized, and sold off to investors (or kept by banks and investment banks). These innovations had the capacity to imperil the financial institutions or investors holding them if their values were based on incorrect assumptions, including the risk of default. After the U.S. housing market turned down in 2006, increases in delinquencies and foreclosures were observed.[44] Suddenly the market values of these mortgage-backed securities declined dramatically. Further, institutions with significant exposures to these products saw their market values drop dramatically to the point where solvency became an issue.

In September 2008, things came to a head. Consider the following events that occurred during a single week in September 2008 (September 15 to 19):

- Two of America's biggest investment banks essentially disappeared on the same day, with Lehman Brothers filing for bankruptcy protection and Merrill Lynch agreeing to be acquired by the Bank of America.
- AIG, a short time before the world's largest insurance company by market value, also on the brink of collapse, was forced to accept a deal offered by the U.S. government giving up a majority stake in return for an injection of cash.
- The last two major independent U.S. investment banks, Morgan Stanley and Goldman Sachs, came under fierce attack from short sellers who thought their days were numbered.
- Finally, at the end of the week, the U.S. government announced a $700 billion bailout (the TARP program), whereby many bad loans would be acquired by the government and thus taken off the books of the financial institutions that were exposed to them.

To get a sense of the enormity of all these events, one press article wrote at the time (with some hyperbole):[45]

For a generation, Wall Street was held up as a model for the rest of the world of strength, efficiency and transparency. But now, the country's vaunted banking system lies on the brink of ruin. Only the U.S. Treasury and Federal Reserve Board stand in the way of a total collapse with a $1-trillion (U.S.) bailout ... The price is so steep it could wreck the country's finances.

Amazingly, the market, possibly buoyed by the impending bailout, did not lose ground that week. Things were to get much worse, though. Refer to Figure 14.9, which shows the path of the S&P 500 from the end of 2007 up to November 20, 2008 (the day of the volatility spike). From September 19, 2008 to November 20, 2008, the S&P 500 lost 40% of its market value—trillions of dollars in stock market value disappeared. From the end of 2007, the cumulative loss was 49%!

As Table 14.3 makes clear, comparable declines occurred around the world. For example, markets in local terms declined by 43% in Japan, 65% in China, 33% in the United Kingdom, 38% in Canada, 44% in France, 42% in Germany, 50% in Italy, 67% in Russia, 47% in Australia, 53% in India, 50% in Argentina, 42% in Brazil, and 24% in Mexico. Further, note that the U.S dollar appreciated in comparison to most currencies in 2008, as often happens when nervousness increases. This led to even greater market declines when denominated in U.S. dollars in most countries.

What led to this steep decline? We believe it was a combination of fundamentals and psychology. On the fundamentals side, the failure of Lehman Brothers led

FIGURE 14.9 The S&P 500: December 31, 2007 to November 20, 2008

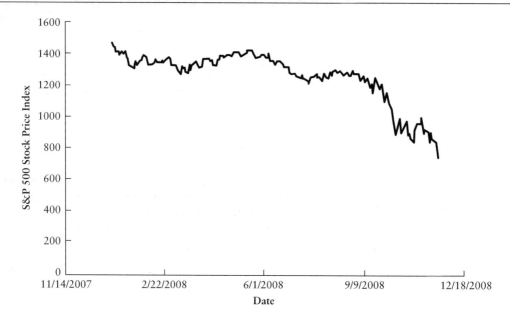

to a lack of trust among financial institutions, which in turn created a calamitous credit crunch. Further, the U.S. Congress at first balked at passing the massive TARP bailout, leading to a "who's in charge?" crisis in confidence. In addition, it soon became clear that the upcoming recession was not going to be short or painless.

As the VIX evidence attests, while markets were declining, dizzying volatility was present. In the 44 trading days during which the S&P 500 dropped 40%, 14 days had absolute price changes of 5% or more. Amazingly, the two biggest price changes were positive—10.8% and 11.6%!

Consider the behavioral influences behind this market downturn. Throughout history we have seen significant price adjustments that did not seem to be in any way justified by fundamentals. Many such moves have taken place during the recent financial crisis. As we discussed earlier in the chapter, in Barberis, Huang, and Santos's model, risk aversion among investors increases after stock prices fall, which reinforces the drop in prices. In addition to higher risk aversion that might have resulted from downward market adjustments, perceptions of elevated risks seem to be widespread in recent months. Some financial institutions were heavily invested in securities that even they could not properly value. In addition, while foreclosure rates had increased, the fear was that the bottom was not yet reached. Was the market reaction due to increased credit default risk or merely perceptions that the risk had increased?

We are perhaps too close to these events to interpret them with clarity. How much of the market decline has been fundamental and how much of it an overreaction? Why has volatility increased so dramatically? And will the higher levels of

TABLE 14.3	Market Index Percentage Declines in Selected Countries for 2008	
Country	In Local Currency	In $US
U.S. (Dow)	36	36
U.S. (S&P 500)	41	41
Japan	43	29
China	65	63
U.K.	33	51
Canada	38	50
France	44	46
Germany	42	43
Italy	50	52
Netherlands	53	55
Spain	42	43
Czech Republic	52	54
Poland	51	59
Russia	67	72
Switzerland	36	30
Turkey	52	63
Australia	47	57
Hong Kong	49	48
India	53	62
Korea	41	56
Thailand	48	50
Argentina	50	54
Brazil	42	57
Mexico	24	39
Egypt	59	59
Israel	53	52
South Africa	27	47

Note: For all countries (except Germany) dividends are excluded.

Source: Data adapted from "Economic and Financial Indicators," in The Economist Magazine, January 3, 2009, p. 76. © 2009 The Economist Magazine.

volatility persist over time? We cannot say with certainty that the recently observed levels of stock prices and volatility are irrational, but it certainly seems difficult to argue that it was a rational response to changing fundamentals. Some have asked whether "40 is the new 20" for the VIX, indicating a permanent upward shift in market volatility.[46] A very important lesson can be learned from this episode, however—financial markets are always capable of surprising us.

CHAPTER HIGHLIGHTS

1. The equity premium is the difference between the expected returns on equity and debt. The high level of the premium is puzzling because it seems to require very high risk aversion.
2. Survivorship bias refers to the tendency to get biased results because failed observations are excluded from the sample over time. This may explain the equity premium.
3. Loss aversion, combined with mental accounting and so-called myopic loss aversion, can explain why investors require a large premium on equity.
4. A speculative bubble is present in a market when high prices seem to be generated more by traders' enthusiasm than by economic fundamentals.
5. Price bubbles are observed in diverse markets. For example, during the tulip mania, people traded large sums of money and goods for tulip bulbs.
6. According to the greater fool theory, a person buys an asset because he believes another will pay even more to acquire it.
7. In the 1990s, the entire U.S. market seems to have deviated far from valuations based on economic fundamentals. The technology sector was affected most dramatically.
8. "Irrational exuberance" is a term used to describe the U.S. stock market by Federal Reserve Chairman Greenspan in the 1990s.
9. Extremely high price-to-earnings ratios were explained by "new era" arguments.
10. Survey data indicate that a majority of individual and institutional investors thought the market was overvalued in 1999.
11. In experimental bubbles markets, assets are traded over a fixed number of periods and traders can easily compute expected fundamental values.
12. Prices in experiments typically bubble high above the fundamental value, crashing down as the end of trading approaches.
13. Bubbles moderate when a subset of traders is knowledgeable and experienced, there is not too much cash in the market, and short sales are permitted.
14. The generation of price bubbles is encouraged by probability judgment error and speculation.
15. Stock prices are too volatile to be explained by future dividends.
16. Volatility is higher for technology firms and the level of volatility is increasing, as is the difference in volatility across the S&P 500 and Nasdaq.
17. The VIX, or fear index, gauges investors' expectations of future stock market volatility using current option prices. In recent months, the VIX rose to unprecedented levels.
18. Beginning in 2007, markets were gripped by a liquidity crisis. Potential contributing factors included the large risky positions taken by financial institutions, easy lending practices, and the perception that credit default risk was high.

DISCUSSION QUESTIONS AND PROBLEMS

1. Differentiate the following terms/concepts:

    a. Certainty equivalent and a gamble
    b. Loss aversion and myopic loss aversion
    c. Speculative price bubble and ex post rational stock price
    d. Greater fool theory and speculation

2. In a Ponzi scheme, named after Charles Ponzi, investors are paid profits out of money paid by subsequent investors, instead of from revenues generated by a real business operation. Unless an ever-increasing flow of money from investors is available, a Ponzi scheme is doomed to failure. What's the difference between a Ponzi scheme and an asset price bubble?

3. An individual with cash to invest has two investment choices:

    Buy a stock fund that every year either earns 40% or -20% with a 50/50 probability.
    Buy a bond fund that every year returns either 5% or 0% also with a 50/50 probability.

Assume that the returns on the two funds are independent, and that returns from year to year are also independent. Also assume an initial portfolio value of $1. (The answers, however, will be unaffected if you use a different initial portfolio value.)

In addition, suppose the value function is linear and is specified as:

$$v(z) = z \text{ for } z > 0$$
$$v(z) = 3z \text{ for } z < 0$$

    a. Which fund does the investor prefer if he looks at his portfolio i) once a year; or ii) once every two years?
    b. How does your answer to part a. help us understand the equity premium puzzle?

4. What do experimental bubble markets teach us about the likelihood of bubbles in the real world? In what sense does this research have its limitations?

5. Do you believe that stock prices are too volatile? Be sure to explain what you mean when you say "volatility" and "too much."

ENDNOTES

1 Mehra, R., and E. C. Prescott, 1985, "The equity premium: A puzzle," *Journal of Monetary Economics* 15(2), 145–161.

2 The arithmetic average return is the simple average over a period of time, whereas the geometric average return is the average compounded return.

3 Siegel, J. J., 1998, *Stocks for the Long Run*, 2nd ed. (McGraw Hill, New York).

4 The coefficient of relative risk aversion ($R(w)$) is calculated as $-wu''(w)/u'(w)$. For the logarithmic utility function, $R(w) = -w$ $(-w^{-2})/w^{-1} = 1.0$. See Hirshleifer, J., and J. G. Riley, 1992, *The Analytics of Uncertainty and Information* (Cambridge University Press, Cambridge), p. 86.

5 This example is provided by Mankiw, N. G., and S. P. Zeldes, 1991, "The consumption of stockholders and nonstockholders," *Journal of Financial Economics* 29(1), 97–112.

6 For other possible explanations, see Cornell, B., 1999, *The Equity Risk Premium: The Long-run Future of the Stock Market* (John Wiley & Sons, New York).

7 For example, in the U.S. Open, the top 60 players (plus ties, plus those within 10 shots of the lead) continue on to play rounds 3 and 4.

8 Brown, S. J., W. N. Goetzmann, and S. A. Ross, 1995, "Survival," *Journal of Finance* 50, 853–873.

9 A survey among financial economists reported a high level of variability in estimates of the equity premium. See Welch, I., 2000, "Views of financial economists on the equity premium and on professional controversies," *Journal of Business* 73, 501–538.

10 Maenhout, P, 2004, "Robust portfolio rules and asset pricing," *Review of Financial Studies* 17, 951–983.

11 Benartzi, S., and R. H. Thaler, 1995, "Myopic loss aversion and the equity premium puzzle," *Quarterly Journal of Economics* 110(1), 73–92.

12 This example is provided by Benartzi, S., and R. H. Thaler, 1995, "Myopic loss aversion and the equity premium puzzle," *Quarterly Journal of Economics* 110(1) 73–92.

13 Haigh, M. S., and J. A. List, 2005, "Do professional traders exhibit myopic loss aversion? An experimental analysis," *Journal of Finance* 60(1), 523–534.

14 Nasdaq index data is available at: http://finance.yahoo.com (accessed on December 5, 2008).

15 For a detailed account of the tulip and other manias, see Mackay, C., 1841, *Extraordinary Popular Delusions and the Madness of Crowds* (Bentley, London).

16 Ibid., p. 91. Florins are commonly called guilders.

17 A "last" is a unit of capacity for grain equivalent to 80 bushels.

18 A "tun" is a large cask holding in volume the equivalent of 252 gallons.

19 This interpretation is suggested in Shiller, R. J., 2000, *Irrational Exuberance* (Princeton University Press, Princeton, New Jersey), p. 178.

20 For example, a painting by Henri Matisse recently sold for $33.6 million, significantly higher that its highest value estimate of $20 million. See Crow, K., and L. A. E. Schuker, "Best of the art blog: Auctions," *Wall Street Journal*, November 10, 2007, p. W2.

21 Stock prices can also experience periods of undervaluation. For example, investors may undervalue stocks when inflation is high. See Ritter, J. R., and R. S. Warr, 2002, "The decline of inflation and the bull markets of 1982–1999," *Journal of Financial and Quantitative Analysis* 37(1), 29–61.

22 See Shiller, R. J., 1990, *Market Volatility* (MIT Press, Cambridge, Massachusetts); and Shiller, R. J., 2000, *Irrational Exuberance* (Princeton University Press, Princeton, New Jersey); and Shiller's Web site at: http://www.econ.yale.edu/~shiller (accessed on December 5, 2008).

23 The Dow reached its 2000 high on January 14, 2000; the Nasdaq on March 10, 2000; and the S&P 500 on March 24, 2000.

24 Shiller, R. J., 2000, *Irrational Exuberance* (Princeton University Press, Princeton, New Jersey).

25 See Schwartz, E. S., and M. Moon, 2000, "Rational pricing of Internet companies," *Financial Analysts Journal* 56(3), 62–75.

26 See http://icf.som.yale.edu/Confidence.Index/ (accessed on December 5, 2008).

27 Smith, V. L., G. L. Suchanek, and A. W. Williams, 1988, "Bubbles, crashes, and endogenous expectations in experimental spot asset markets," *Econometrica* 56(5), 1119–1151.

28 These dividend distributions are from Ackert, L. F., N. Charupat, B. K. Church, and R. Deaves, 2006, "Margin, short selling, and lotteries in experimental asset markets," *Southern Economic Journal* 73(2), 419–436.

29 Ackert, L. F., and B. K. Church, 2001, "The effects of subject pool and design experience on rationality in experimental asset markets," *The Journal of Psychology and Financial Markets* 2(1), 6–28.

30 Ibid.; and Dufwenberg, M., T. Lindqvist, and E. Moore, 2005, "Bubbles and experience: An experiment," *American Economic Review* 95(5), 1731–1737.

31 In a recent model of security pricing, investors who can be described using cumulative prospect theory overprice an asset whose returns are positively skewed (like the lottery asset described in the chapter), as compared to the price suggested under expected utility theory. See Barberis, N., and M. Huang, 2008, "Stocks as lotteries: The implications of probability weighting for security prices," *American Economic Review* 98(5), 2066–2100.

32 Caginalp, G., D. Porter, and V. Smith, 2001, "Financial bubbles: Excess cash, momentum, and incomplete information," *Journal of Psychology and Financial Markets* 2(2), 80–99.

33 Lei, V., C. Noussair, and C. Plott, 2001, "Nonspeculative bubbles in experimental asset markets: Lack of common knowledge of rationality vs. actual irrationality," *Econometrica* 69(4), 831–859.

34 Ackert, L. F., N. Charupat, R. Deaves, and B. D. Kluger, "Probability judgment error and speculation in laboratory asset market bubbles," *Journal of Financial and Quantitative Analysis*, forthcoming.

35 Ackert, L. F., N. Charupat, B. K. Church, and R. Deaves, 2006, "Margin, short selling, and lotteries in experimental asset markets," *Southern Economic Journal* 73(2), 419–436; and Haruvy, E. and C. Noussair, 2006, "The effect of short selling on bubbles and crashes in experimental spot asset markets," *Journal of Finance* 61(3), 1119–1157.

36 Shiller, R. J., 1984, "Stock prices and social dynamics," *Brookings Papers on Economic Activity* 2, 457–498.

37 Barberis, N., M. Huang, and T. Santos, 2001, "Prospect theory and asset prices," *Quarterly Journal of Economics* 116(1), 1–53.

38 Cutler, D. M., J. M. Poterba, and L. H. Summers, 1989, "What moves stock prices?" *Journal of Portfolio Management* 15(3), 4–12.

39 Shiller, R. J., 1981, "Do stock prices move too much to be justified by subsequent changes in dividends?" *American Economic Review* 71(3), 421–436.

40 See Ackert, L. F., and B. F. Smith, 1993, "Stock price volatility, ordinary dividends, and other cash flows to shareholders," *Journal of Finance* 48(4), 1147–1160. This research shows that stock prices are not too volatile when cash flows to shareholders are defined broadly to include cash distributions through share repurchases and takeovers.

41 Schwert, G. W., 1990, "Stock volatility and the crash of '87," *Review of Financial Studies* 3(1), 77–102; and Schwert, G. W., 2002, "Stock volatility in the new millennium: How wacky is the Nasdaq?" *Journal of Monetary Economics* 49(1), 3–26.

42 For details on the construction of the VIX, see Whaley, R. E., 2000, "The investor fear gauge," *Journal of Portfolio Management* 26(3), 12–17.

43 On the effect of liberal lending practices and failure of due diligence, see Bajaj, V., and L. Story, February 12, 2008, "Mortgage crisis spreads past subprime loans," *New York Times*.

44 On the increases in foreclosures, see Mortgage Bankers Association, December 6, 2007, "Delinquencies and foreclosures increase in latest MBA national delinquency survey."

45 *Report on Business, Globe and Mail*, September 20, 2008.

46 Gongloff, M., December 1, 2008, "For the VIX, 40 looks like it's the new 20," *Wall Street Journal*, C1.

CORPORATE FINANCE

CHAPTER 15 Rational Managers and Irrational Investors

CHAPTER 16 Behavioral Corporate Finance and
Managerial Decision-Making

PART | VI

RATIONAL MANAGERS AND IRRATIONAL INVESTORS

15.1 INTRODUCTION

In a corporate finance setting, behavioral factors may matter for two reasons. First, managers, like investors and other financial market participants (as described in Chapters 8–10), appear to sometimes act in a less than fully rational fashion due to cognitive limitations, overconfidence, and the force of emotion. This is the topic of the next chapter. Second, rational managers may at times take advantage of the valuation mistakes made by irrational investors. This is the topic of the present chapter.

Before proceeding, it should be noted that the latter "rational managers with irrational investors approach" is predicated on the following: 1) irrational investors impact prices because arbitrage is limited; and 2) managers have the ability to detect when valuations are wrong and they act on mispricing. While we have reviewed the relevant arguments for the first at length elsewhere, the second requires comment.[1] Logically, information asymmetry exists between investors and managers. After all, managers are insiders. In addition, managers are less constrained than other investors. For example, if an investor believes a firm is overvalued but does not own the stock, short sales constraints may limit his opportunities. A manager, in contrast, can issue more shares when the market highly values her company's stock.

In Section 15.2, we begin with a heuristic model showing that predominantly rational managers operating in a world with sometimes irrational investors are conflicted between short-run and long-run goals, between looking out for themselves and the interests of their shareholders, and between maximizing intrinsic value and catering to irrational investor preferences. As a result, managers maximize price rather than value, either in pursuit of their own narrow interests or in the interests of their shareholders. Managers maximize price by catering to investor perceptions and desires. In Section 15.3, several examples of catering are described, such as changing the company name to something more appealing to investors, and responding to dividend payout preferences. Interests of long-run shareholders can be accommodated by issuing stock when it is expensive (as well as buying it back when it is cheap), and undertaking stock acquisitions of relatively less overvalued targets. Empirical evidence consistent with these tendencies will be cited. Finally, in Section 15.4, we consider the policy implications of irrational investors, as compared to irrational managers.

15.2   MISPRICING AND THE GOALS OF MANAGERS

A SIMPLE HEURISTIC MODEL

Malcolm Baker, Richard Ruback, and Jeffrey Wurgler formulate a heuristic model of how managers balance three conflicting goals in the presence of potential mispricing.[2] In our simplified version of their model, managers, as is conventional, first wish to maximize the rationally calculated present value of future cash flows. Fundamental value is:

15.1
$$f(K, d) - K$$

where K is investment, d the dividend, and f a standard production function that is concave and increasing in K.[3] For simplicity, the cost of capital is normalized at one. Dividends may enter because of their non-neutrality in the tax system.

Managers' second goal is to maximize the *current* share price relative to value. This goal can be pursued by undertaking various actions that **cater** to a range of investor desires unrelated to (rational) value enhancement. Temporary mispricing (price minus value) is denoted as δ, which in our treatment is a function of the same two arguments as f (plus two additional ones):

15.2
$$\delta(K, d, e, x)$$

K may matter if investors believe that certain kinds of investment (e.g., in computer technology in the 1990s) create more value than should really be the case.[4] Since ill-founded investment is patently costly, it is natural that managers may be torn between maximizing rational value ($f - K$) and catering (by maximizing δ). As for dividends, as will be discussed more fully later, if certain investor groups with particular dividend preferences (e.g., those desiring high, low, or no payout) exist, and if not enough firms currently satisfy the desires of these investor groups, catering may operate as firms alter their dividend payout in response. The third argument, e, is the fraction of the firm potentially sold off in a share issue. This stems from the idea that a share issue designed to take advantage of mispricing is likely to impact δ because the act of issuing shares should partly correct mispricing. For example, if the firm is overvalued, managers sell shares at a high price, and the selling pressure may reduce the level of mispricing. Finally, x is an indicator variable that equals one if management undertakes a particular action designed to appeal to investors.[5] For simplicity, we will assume that such actions entail negligible cost. Examples are accounting changes, earnings management, and name changes (the latter of which is discussed later).[6]

A third goal of managers is to take advantage of current mispricing so as to benefit existing long-term shareholders. This is done by issuing stock when it is overvalued and buying it back when it is undervalued.[7] Doing so of course benefits existing (and continuing) shareholders at the expense of new shareholders.[8] By selling a fraction of the firm, e, current shareholders gain by:

15.3
$$e\delta(K, e, d, x)$$

Putting these three goals together leads to the following optimization problem:

15.4
$$\max_{K, e, d, x} \lambda[f(K, d) - K + e\delta(K, e, d, x)] + (1 - \lambda)\delta(K, e, d, x)$$

where $0 < \lambda < 1$ is the manager's horizon.[9] With a very short-term horizon ($\lambda \to 0$), the previous problem reduces to:

15.5
$$\max_{K, e, d, x} \delta(K, e, d, x)$$

In this case, managers only worry about short-term catering and have a "take the money and run" attitude. Hopefully, for a variety of reasons, not the least of which are reputation concerns and judicious contracting, this will be the less usual case.[10] On the other hand, with a very long-term horizon ($\lambda \to 1$) the previous problem converges to:

15.6
$$\max_{K, e, d, x} f(K, d) - K + e\delta(K, e, d, x)$$

Here managers are sensitive to catering only in so far as it can benefit the current shareholders of the firm when shares are issued or bought back, and catering does not enter as an argument other than through this channel.

First Order Conditions

First order conditions for the continuous control variables (K, e, d) are as follows:

15.7
$$f_K = 1 - \left(e + \frac{1 - \lambda}{\lambda}\right)\delta_K$$

15.8
$$\delta = -\left(e + \frac{1 - \lambda}{\lambda}\right)\delta_e$$

15.9
$$-f_d = \left(e + \frac{1 - \lambda}{\lambda}\right)\delta_d$$

Condition 15.7 pertains to investment policy, 15.8 to financing policy, and 15.9 to dividend policy. To interpret, the first says that investment should continue to the point where the payoff falls to the level of the cost of capital, subject to any bene-fits from catering, which can occur both through its potential to lead to market timing of financing and as a short-term goal unto itself. The second condition re-lates to financing and the ability of managers to time security issues. Here two goals are in conflict. Issuing shares when they are overvalued is desirable from a long-term shareholder standpoint, but, since doing so will cause mispricing to de-cline, this is undesirable from the point of short-term mispricing maximization. Op-timal share issuance weighs these two factors against each other. And finally, the third condition concerns dividends. Because of tax reasons, the impact of dividends on true value is unambiguously detrimental. Stockholders must pay personal taxes on dividends received. To the extent that investors want to see payout changed, the gains from catering, both through an effort to time markets and as a goal unto itself, have to be weighed against their value-reducing aspect.

Consider the case where managers have very short-term horizons. Investment should continue, without regard to true NPV, up to the point where price (relative to value) is pushed up as far as possible. Additionally, dividend policy should be completely at the service of short-term investor preferences.[11]

As for the indicator variable, x, mispricing levels with and without the action in question being taken are compared. If the following condition is met, managers should proceed with the action:

15.10
$$\delta(K, e, d, x = 1) > \delta(K, e, d, x = 0)$$

Making such choices is beneficial both from the standpoint of short-term catering and in order to undertake share issues that will benefit long-term shareholders.

In what follows, we look more closely at what the evidence tells us about whether managers can and do take advantage of investor irrationality both for the benefit of long-term shareholders and for their own personal (short-term) gains. In the next section, we begin with a rather remarkable and entertaining example of an action designed to take advantage of investor irrationality.

15.3 EXAMPLES OF MANAGERIAL ACTIONS TAKING ADVANTAGE OF MISPRICING

COMPANY NAME CHANGES

One example of a simple catering strategy at negligible cost is to change the com-pany name to something with greater appeal to investors. While marketers know the value of the right product name, here we present evidence that investors, de-spite the fact that they would seem to have more at stake and should thus employ clearer thinking than consumers, may be affected as well. To understand why a name change might matter, recall our discussion of positive affect in Chapter 10, where evidence was presented that certain industries induce more favorable emo-tional stimuli than others, thus encouraging investment in the former and not in the latter. While the actual industry of operations is probably not at the discretion of current managers—presumably the founders made this choice for reasons having little to do with positive affect, and it's hard to see current managers moving into an entirely new industry to induce emotional stimuli—the *name* of the company itself is clearly something more at their discretion.

Michael Cooper, Orlin Dimitrov, and Raghavendra Rau address this issue in the context of companies that changed their names to "dotcom" names during the Internet craze of the late 1990s. Their sample included 147 firms that changed their names in this fashion from June 1998 to July 1998. Amazingly, these firms saw their shares appreciate (and often dramatically so), even when their underlying business had little or nothing to do with the Internet.[12] One striking example was Computer Literacy, Inc., which argued that it changed its name to fatbrain.com because customers had difficulty remembering the Web site address. The share price went up by 33% the day before the announcement when news of the impending move leaked to Internet chat forums. Anecdote aside, these researchers found that the dotcom affect led to average cumulative excess returns of 74% during a 10-day announcement window.

Perhaps even more remarkably, after Internet-oriented firms started to see major price declines, companies also profited by eliminating the negative effect associated with an Internet name.[13] Between August 2000 and September 2001, firms that *dropped* their dotcom names saw a positive announcement effect of about 70%.

EXPLAINING DIVIDEND PATTERNS

In a world of perfect markets, dividend payout should be irrelevant. More specifically, the Modigliani-Miller dividend irrelevance theorem states that, if there are no taxes, transaction costs and information asymmetries, and holding constant a firm's financing and investment policy, a firm's dividend payout should be irrelevant—that is to say, it should have no impact on firm value.[14]

Let's consider why this is so. Suppose that a firm currently pays out all of its free cash flows in the form of a dividend, but it is now considering eliminating its payout.[15] If a particular investor actually desires the (say) 10% cash flow yield that currently comes in the form of a dividend, assuming the company goes ahead with its plan, she could employ a process known as **home-made dividends**. This involves selling off shares in lieu of receiving a cash dividend and using the proceeds to "pay" herself an amount of cash equivalent to the former dividend. Conversely, if an investor holds a dividend-paying stock but does not desire cash flow, an automatic dividend reinvestment program will serve to negate payout. In essence, abstracting from transaction costs and taxes, an investor can seamlessly "set" his own dividend yield.

For a number of reasons, however, the real world is much more complicated than this. Frictions like taxes and transaction costs exist. It is partly because of these frictions that managers accommodate the dividend stability that investors seem to desire, and only as a last resort cut dividends.[16]

There is evidence that managers use dividends as a catering tool.[17] To put this possibility into perspective, let us first consider the extent to which dividend payout patterns have been changing over time. Eugene Fama and Kenneth French, focusing on NYSE, AMEX, and NASDAQ firms from 1972 to 1999, document that for much of this period the percentage of firms paying dividends was on the decline.[18]

In 1973, 52.8% of publicly traded nonfinancial nonutility firms paid dividends. This percentage rose until 1978, by which time it hit 66.5%, before falling to 20.8% by 1999. One reason why the number of dividend payers in percentage terms may change is that the characteristics of firms may change, tilting toward the characteristics that nonpayers embody. Indeed, Fama and French conclude this is about half of the explanation for the declining propensity to pay dividends. Larger, more profitable firms with fewer investment opportunities tend to be payers, and it turned out that many of the newly listed firms were smaller and less profitable with an array of investment opportunities. For example, many of the new listers in the 1970s tended to be quite profitable (with the earnings of new lists averaging in at 17.8% of book value vs. 13.7% for all firms), whereas the earnings of new lists during 1993–1998 averaged in at 2.1% (vs. 11.3% for all firms).

It is the unexplained half, reflecting a reduced propensity to pay dividends while holding firm characteristics constant, that is of most interest here. Malcolm Baker and Jeffrey Wurgler suggest that the catering motive is the best explanation.[19] Their evidence is based on time-variation in the so-called **dividend premium**. One way in which they proxy this premium is the difference between the average market-to-book ratio of dividend payers and nonpayers. They investigate whether dividend initiations and omissions are related to time-variation in this premium. Indeed, Figure 15.1 shows that the dividend premium predicts the rate of dividend initiation. When the dividend premium rises, reflecting increased investor preference for dividends, initiations subsequently rise. On the other hand, when the dividend premium falls, reflecting decreased investor preference for dividends, initiations soon fall.

Further, these researchers show that there have actually been four distinct recent trends in the propensity to pay dividends. These were an increasing trend in the mid-1960s; then a decline falling into negative territory through 1969; next a positive trend in 1970 staying in positive territory until 1977; and finally the well-known **disappearing dividends** period ensuing after that. Notably, each of these trends lines up with a corresponding fluctuation in the dividend premium.[20]

On the surface, there are two salient possibilities that may explain patterns in the propensity to pay dividends: 1) firms are accommodating *rational* investor preferences for dividends (or the lack thereof); or 2) firms are catering to changing investor sentiment for dividends. Earlier work by Fischer Black and Myron Scholes, of option-pricing theory fame, is along the lines of the first possibility.[21] They argue for the existence of dividend clienteles related to market imperfections such as taxes, transaction costs, and the institutional environment. It is worthwhile noting that their clientele story is more consistent with an equilibrium view of the world with unsatisfied clienteles being accommodated fairly quickly by firms, after which there are no further incentives to change dividend policy. The Baker-Wurgler view, on the other hand, is more consistent with a disequilibrium state, as any benefits from changing policy seem to exist for prolonged periods.

Baker and Wurgler contend that the evidence is better explained by catering to irrational investor preferences rather than accommodating rational clienteles. First, rational clienteles would be more concerned with the overall *level* of payout, not the percentage of firms paying dividends, but the dividend premium does not explain the aggregate level of dividends. Second, tax changes impacting dividends (proxied by the relative tax advantage of dividends vs. capital gains) seem to have

FIGURE 15.1 Dividend Premium and Initiation Rate over Time

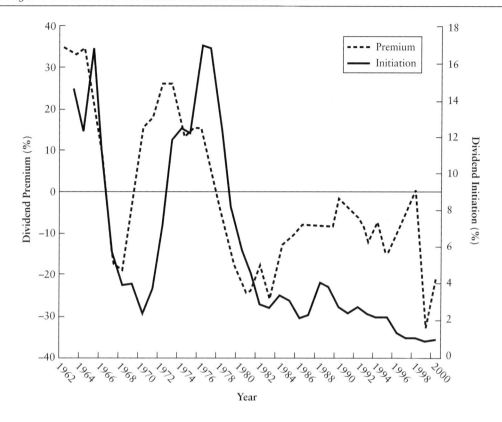

Source: Baker, M., and J. Wurgler, 2004, "Appearing and disappearing dividends," *Journal of Financial Economics* 73, 271–288.

had little impact on the dividend premium. Third, while the secular decline in transaction costs beginning in the mid-1970s is consistent with a reduction in dividend payers (as it is became less expensive to take the "home-made" route), the dividend premium continues to be the most important driver of initiations. Fourth, though the 1974 passage in the United States of the Employee Retirement Income Security Act (ERISA) and its 1979 revision may have first favored dividends and then caused a movement away from them, this factor seems at best to be a partial explanation of the stylized facts.

Taken together, these arguments seem to leave investor sentiment as the most important factor.[22] Further suggestive evidence that sentiment is at least partly behind the dividend premium is the fact that the average closed-end fund discount (another proxy for investor sentiment) is correlated with the dividend premium.[23] Another factor that favors a sentiment-leading-to-mispricing story is the finding that an increase in the rate of initiation forecasts a decrease in the average return of payers versus that of nonpayers (suggesting that the overvaluation of payers leads to the increase in initiation).[24]

SHARE ISSUES AND REPURCHASES

When shares are overvalued, current long-run shareholders benefit when management issues shares. Conversely, when shares are undervalued, holding shareholders benefit when managers repurchase stock. In this sense, managers seek to employ market timing. Issuing stock can either be effected via an IPO (in the case of a private company) or via an SEO (in the case of a publicly traded company). While evidence on the ability to market time is controversial, it is clear from the survey evidence that managers at least *believe* that they are often issuing shares to take advantage of misvaluation.[25]

Much evidence from around the world indicates a correlation between (ex ante and ex post) measures of mispricing and issuance. For example, in Italy during 1982–1992, the main factor influencing an IPO was the average price-to-book in the industry: a one standard deviation increase in price-to-book led to a 25% increase in the probability of an IPO.[26] While this could be because such firms are more likely in need of financing for investment prospects, the fact that post-issuance investment and profitability both fell suggests that timing was playing at least a partial role.

After-market performance of IPOs elsewhere points in the same direction. One study, using U.S. data from 1935–1972, documents five-year returns that are below market returns by 21%–35%.[27] Market timing in this realm also seems to exist at the level of national markets. In the United States, equity issuance as a percentage of total financing (debt and equity) predicts market returns, with high equity-issuance years preceding weak markets.[28] International evidence is along the same lines, with high issuance activity leading to low future returns in 12 out of 13 major markets.[29]

As for repurchases, the evidence is also consistent with the existence of private information that allows managers to time such activity for the benefit of long-term shareholders. An empirical study of 5,111 repurchases from the Hong Kong stock market reveals substantial timing ability.[30] While investors bidding up firms after repurchases is consistent with rationality, market underreaction to share repurchases leading to long-run excess returns is not consistent with full efficiency.[31]

Dividends and repurchases are two ways of returning money to shareholders. Survey and empirical evidence shows that managers view repurchases as the more flexible alternative—firms wish to avoid dividend instability, but view repurchase volatility as acceptable.[32] While the role of dividends can be viewed as a short-run catering mechanism (as was discussed in the previous section), it is possible to view repurchases in this light as well. The model of Richard Fairchild and Ganggang Zhang takes this tack.[33] Just as in the case of dividends, repurchases designed for catering purposes are inefficient when profitable investment opportunities are foregone.

MERGERS AND ACQUISITIONS

Potential misvaluation adds an additional dimension to the theory of mergers and acquisitions. Under the standard theory, it makes sense for even correctly priced firms to combine when synergies exist, with both firms sharing in the spoils.

In the model of Andrei Shleifer and Robert Vishny, acquiring firms are mispriced (especially overvalued).[34] While synergies may be *perceived* by the market, in their model the reality is that they do not truly exist. While no one would claim that such conditions always hold, it is interesting to note that this model explains a good number of stylized facts, such as who acquires whom; the cash versus stock choice; the valuation consequences of mergers; and merger waves.

Suppose there are two firms, 0 and 1, whose capital stocks, K and K_1, are valued by the market at Q and Q_1 per unit of capital. Assume that $Q < Q_1$, that is, firm 1 is more overvalued. Suppose in the event of a merger the market values a unit of capital of the combined firm at S. In this case, the total market value of the combined firm is $S(K + K_1)$, where S is the market's perceived value of a unit of capital of the combined firm. Typically, the market would value a unit of capital of the combined firm at somewhere between Q and Q_1, so $Q < S < Q_1$.[35] The short-run gain from merging is:

15.11
$$S(K + K_1) - KQ - K_1Q_1$$

If the market sets S high enough, so that the latter expression is positive, then this implies that it perceives synergies.[36]

Since in this model synergies are apparent rather than real, if we assume that in the long run the market eventually "gets it right," there are no long-run gains from merging. Further, both bidder and target managers know this. They also know how short-run valuations will, because of misvaluation, differ from long-term valuations, implying that they understand the market's error. The goal of all managers is to maximize personal wealth subject to the constraints they face (including personal horizons). Given agency costs and the nature of compensation contracts, this may not be the same as maximizing the wealth of their shareholders.

Assume that the price offered to the target is P, where, logically, P is above Q (the no-takeover-premium level) and below S (the level at which price would reach the short-run merged value per unit of capital). It is easy to see that both bidder and target can gain in the short run as long as there are perceived synergies. The immediate gain in the short-run value of the target (i.e., firm 0) is:

15.12
$$(P - Q)K > 0$$

On the other hand, the immediate gain in the short-run value of the bidder (i.e., firm 1) is:

15.13
$$(S - P)K + (S - Q_1)K_1 > 0$$

Since the second term in 15.12 (the dilution effect) is negative, if P is too close to S, then the short-run change in the value of the bidder can actually be negative.

It would seem that in this latter case mergers will not occur, but this is not necessarily so. In fact, it still may be in the interest of the bidder to go ahead even if their shareholders see a negative short-run return. To see why, we need to distinguish between cash and stock acquisitions. It turns out that the extent to which bidders and targets gain or lose in the long run partly depends on whether the medium of exchange is cash or stock. Recalling that in the long run capital is correctly valued (let us say at q per unit), in the following table we illustrate the long-run possibilities:

	Cash acquisition	Stock acquisition
Target gain	$K(P - q)$	$qK(P/S - 1)$
Bidder gain	$K(q - P)$	$qK(1 - P/S)$

In the case of a cash acquisition, the only reason for a merger from the standpoint of the bidder is to acquire undervalued assets. But managers of targets in such cases, despite any short-run gains, are right to claim that such a deal is not in the interest of long-term shareholders. This is the reason why often there is keen resistance to such takeovers.

Stock acquisitions are quite different. Bidding shareholders gain in the long run if $P < S$. This can still be consistent with the target shareholders experiencing a positive price boost in the short-run. Target management, even though they understand that their shareholders will lose in the long run, may still be amenable to merger. There are a couple of reasons why this is so. First, their horizon may be short. Since they plan to get out before the long run comes, their only concern is the short run. Managers who want to sell out (perhaps because they are nearing retirement) would fit the bill. The acquisition allows them to cash out overvalued equity.[37] Second, target managers may expect to be paid for their acquiescence. This could be in the form of acceleration in the exercise of stock options, generous severance pay, or retaining management positions.

It is interesting to note that stock acquisitions may be advantageous for bidders even if they lead to negative short-run and long-run returns. For managers and shareholders with a long-run perspective, the short-run is immaterial, while the long-run return, even if it is negative, may still be *higher* than what it would have been in the absence of the acquisition as the market eventually revalues appropriately. The stock acquisition, as it were, has cushioned the fall.

The evidence seems to be largely in line with the predictions of the model. Long-run returns to acquirers are positive after cash acquisitions, but negative after stock acquisitions.[38] Glamour bidders (which tend to be more overvalued) are more likely to pay with (overvalued) stock than are value bidders.[39] Mergers waves line up as expected.[40] They tend to cluster around periods of high valuations. The conglomerate merger wave of the 1960s along with the tech mergers of the 1990s were both based on popular synergy stories: the first was about efficiency gains through better management, while the second was about tech complementarities, with neither for the most part panning out. Stock acquisitions were common in both cases, and acquirers, in light of later developments, were often egregiously overvalued. On the other hand, mergers in the 1980s often involved undervalued firms, were profitable (especially after subsequent bust-ups), and tended to be accomplished by cash.

15.4   IRRATIONAL MANAGERS OR IRRATIONAL INVESTORS?

In this chapter, we have focused on how managers make rational decisions when investors behave less than optimally. In the following chapter, we consider the mistakes managers make because they are subject to behavioral influences. It is important to note that the two approaches have very different policy implications. If managers are rationally making decisions in a world with irrational investors, they should be protected from the short-run influences of markets and unrealistic pressures from stockholders. If, on the other hand, managers are subject to behavioral biases that negatively impact shareholder value, managerial decisions must be closely scrutinized by owners and regulators.

CHAPTER HIGHLIGHTS

1. There is evidence that predominantly rational managers sometimes capitalize on the pricing errors of irrational investors.
2. In one model, managers' objectives include maximization of fundamental value, catering to investors, and market timing.
3. Catering operates when management undertakes actions designed to appeal to investors and lead to price exceeding value in the short run.
4. Examples of catering are company name changes and accommodating dividend payout preferences.
5. To serve long-run shareholders (including perhaps themselves), managers appear to try to time share issues and buybacks.
6. A behavioral theory of mergers that abstracts from synergies explains many of the stylized facts. For example, overvalued acquirers tend to pursue (less) overvalued targets with stock.
7. Cash acquisitions make sense when undervalued assets can be acquired. The hostility of target management in such cases serves the interests of their own shareholders.

DISCUSSION QUESTIONS AND PROBLEMS

1. Differentiate the following terms/concepts:

   a. Clienteles and catering
   b. Dividend payment and home-made dividend
   c. Investor sentiment and irrationality
   d. Synergy and valuation consequences of a merger

2. One of John Lintner's conclusions in his classic study of dividend policy is that managers do not seem to change dividend payment in response to capital requirements for new investment (Lintner, J., 1956, "Distributions of incomes of corporations among dividends, retained earnings and taxes," *American Economic Review* 46, 97–113).

Consider this finding in light of the chapter discussion.

3. You work for Toxic Waste, Inc. Given the evidence that the market can respond well to a company name change, suggest a new company name to the CEO, and explain why you think it might positively impact the share price.

4. Suppose a particular investment is believed by management to be a negative-NPV undertaking, but many shareholders believe otherwise, holding the view that investments of this type are value-creating. What should be done? Discuss in the context of the heuristic model presented in the chapter.

5. A company has 1,000,000 shares outstanding trading at $15 apiece. Managers believe that the discount rate appropriate for the risk borne is 15% and total cash flows, expected to be $1 million next year, will rise by 5% per year indefinitely. Discuss a strategy that is beneficial to the current shareholders.

ENDNOTES

1 See Baker, M., R. S. Ruback, and J. Wurgler, 2004, "Behavioral corporate finance: A survey," Working paper, for details.

2 This model requires various simplifications. See Baker, M., R. S. Ruback, and J. Wurgler, 2004, "Behavioral corporate finance: A survey," Working paper, for details. This section (and chapter) benefited greatly from this review paper.

3 Production is a function of the capital stock, so, technically, K should be viewed as changes in the capital stock.

4 Chirinko, R. S., and H. Schaller, 2001, "Business fixed investment and 'bubbles': The Japanese case," *American Economic Review* 91, 663–680.

5 Since many such actions can be undertaken, x should be viewed as a vector of potential actions.

6 In reality, such actions may be costly in the sense that they impact the long-run credibility of management and the firm. We will, however, ignore this issue.

7 A similar argument holds for issuing overvalued debt. Since the degree of overvaluation is likely to be less severe for debt, we focus on equity.

8 Those holding overvalued shares can of course personally benefit by selling them off whenever they like. The advantage of the act of issuing shares when they are overvalued is it locks in a gain for the current shareholders.

9 Logically, horizon would be a function of such factors as age and the nature of compensation contracts.

10 Of course reputation matters since managers likely wish to remain attractive in the labor market. Reputation is of more concern for those in early or mid-career.

11 As for e, it is not likely that managers will buy back shares to increase mispricing since this effect is likely to be minimal.

12 Cooper, M., O. Dimitrov, and P. R. Rau, 2001, "A Rose.com by any other name," *Journal of Finance* 56, 2371–2388.

13 Cooper, M. J., A. Khorana, I. Osobov, A. Patel, and P. R. Rau, 2004, "Managerial actions in response to a market downturn: Valuation effects of name changes in the dot.com decline," *Journal of Corporate Finance*, forthcoming. Note that some companies were "double dippers," that is, companies that changed their names to dot com names on the way up, and away from dot com names on the way down.

14 "Perfect markets" require such assumptions as no taxes, transaction costs, or information asymmetries. For a proof of this proposition, see Miller, M. H., and F. Modilgiani, 1961, "Dividend policy, growth, and the valuation of shares," *Journal of Business* 34(4), 411–433.

15 Since the cash must go somewhere and we are assuming no change in investment policy (where it should be noted that holding back cash, even if only for the use of buying short-term securities, of necessity entails investment), then it must be the case that shares are repurchased with the loose cash.

16 See Lintner, J., 1956, "Distributions of incomes of corporations among dividends, retained earnings and taxes," *American Economic Review* 46, 97–113, for the classic treatment; and Brav, A., J. Graham, C. R. Harvey, and R. Michaely, 2005,

"Payout policy in the 21st century," *Journal of Financial Economics* 77, 483–527, for more recent evidence.

17 See Baker, M., and J. Wurgler, 2004, "Appearing and disappearing dividends," *Journal of Financial Economics* 73, 271–288; and Baker, M., and J. Wurgler, 2004, "A catering theory of dividends," *Journal of Finance* 59, 1125–1166.

18 Fama, E. F., and K. R. French, 2001, "Disappearing dividends: Changing firm characteristics or lower propensity to pay?" *Journal of Financial Economics* 60, 3–43.

19 Baker, M., and J. Wurgler, 2004, "A catering theory of dividends," *Journal of Finance* 59, 1125–1166.

20 The lone disconnect can be attributed to Nixon-era controls.

21 Black, F., and M. S. Scholes, 1974, "The effects of dividend yield and dividend policy on common stock prices and returns," *Journal of Financial Economics* 1, 1–22.

22 One possible driver behind a sentiment-based preference for dividends is that investor desire for imposed discipline ("preserve capital by only spending cash flows") might vary over time. See Shefrin, H., and M. Statman, 1984, "Explaining investor preference for cash dividends," *Journal of Financial Economics* 13, 253–282.

23 See Baker, M., and J. Wurgler, 2004, "A catering theory of dividends," *Journal of Finance* 59, 1125–1166. Closed-end funds issue a fixed number of shares that are then traded on a stock exchange. Investors close positions by selling their shares, rather than closing at net asset value as with an open-end fund. Closed-end funds often trade at prices that deviate from the underlying asset value, with the difference providing a measure of investor sentiment referred to as the fund discount. See Lee, C. M. C., A. Shleifer, and R. H. Thaler, 1991, "Investor sentiment and the closed-end fund puzzle," *Journal of Finance* 46(1), 75–109.

24 Ibid.

25 For survey evidence on managerial behavior, see Graham, J. R., and C. R. Harvey, 2001, "The theory and practice of corporate finance: Evidence from the field," *Journal of Financial Economics* 60, 187–243. For evidence that managers actively attempt to time the market when making decisions for the firm and their own portfolios, see Jeter, D., 2005, "Market timing and managerial portfolio decisions," *Journal of Finance* 60 (4), 1903–1949. In addition, for evidence showing that managers use external equity financing when their cost of equity is low, see Huang, R., and J. R. Ritter, "Testing theories of capital structure and estimating the speed of adjustment," *Journal of Financial and Quantitative Analysis*, forthcoming.

26 Pagano, M., F. Panetta, and L. Zingales, 1998, "Why do companies go public? An empirical analysis," *Journal of Finance* 53, 27–64.

27 Gompers, P. A., and J. Lerner, 2003, "The really long-run performance of initial public offerings: The pre-Nasdaq evidence," *Journal of Finance* 58, 1355–1392.

28 Baker, M., and J. Wurgler, 2000, "The equity share in new issues and aggregate stock returns," *Journal of Finance* 55, 2219–2257.

29 Henderson, B. J., N. Jegadeesh, and M. S. Weisbach, 2003, "World markets for raising new capital," Working paper.

30 Brockman, P., and D. Y. Chung, 2001, "Managerial timing and corporate liquidity: Evidence from actual share repurchases," *Journal of Financial Economics* 61, 417–448.

31 Ikenberry, D., J. Lakonishok, and T. Vermaelen, 1995, "Market underreaction to open market share repurchases, *Journal of Financial Economics* 39, 181–208.

32 See, for example, Graham, J. R., and C. R. Harvey, 2001, "The theory and practice of corporate finance: Evidence from the field," *Journal of Financial Economics* 60, 187–243.

33 Fairchild, R., and G. Zhang, 2005, "Repurchase and dividend catering, managerial myopia, and long-run value-destruction," Working paper.

34 Shleifer, A., and R. W. Vishny, 2003, "Stock market driven acquisitions," *Journal of Financial Economics* 70, 295–311.

35 Shleifer and Vishny note that it is possible that $S > Q_1$ in a "euphoric" market. While it is also possible that $Q > S$, a merger would not be likely under these circumstances.

36 See Shleifer, A., and R. W. Vishny, 2003, "Stock market driven acquisitions," *Journal of Financial Economics* 70, 295–311, for details.

37 The same incentive does not exist with cash acquisitions of undervalued assets.

38 Rau, P. R., and T. Vermaelen, 1998, "Glamour, value and the post-acquisition performance of acquiring firms," *Journal of Financial Economics* 49, 223–253.

39 Ibid.

40 See Shleifer, A., and R. W. Vishny, 2003, "Stock market driven acquisitions," *Journal of Financial Economics* 70, 295–311, for details.

BEHAVIORAL CORPORATE FINANCE AND MANAGERIAL DECISION-MAKING

16.1 INTRODUCTION

Initial interest in behavioral explanations of financial decisions was primarily in the realm of choices made by investors. Of late, more attention has been paid to sub-optimal decisions made by firms' managers and entrepreneurs.[1] The stress has been the extent to which overconfidence impacts the decisions of these individuals.[2] In the following section, we begin with possible mistakes in the capital budgeting process potentially caused by cognitive and emotional forces. Next, in Section 16.3, after citing some evidence that managers are no different from the rest of the population in terms of their overconfidence, we turn to the consequences. Much research has been devoted to the impact of overconfidence on various forms of investment. In Section 16.4, we will focus on overinvestment, investment sensitivity to cash flows, mergers and acquisitions (M&As), and start-ups.[3] Finally, we briefly consider whether managerial overconfidence has a positive role to play.

16.2 CAPITAL BUDGETING: EASE OF PROCESSING, LOSS AVERSION AND AFFECT

It is likely that behavioral flaws impact capital budgeting decisions. Specifically, we consider the still wide-spread use of (patently inferior) payback as a project selection technique, the tendency to throw good money after bad (sunk costs), and the proclivity to allow irrelevant information to influence project adoption.

Payback and Ease of Processing

Conventional finance theory demonstrates that, when properly applied, net present value (NPV) is the optimal decision rule for capital budgeting purposes.[4] Yet a number of surveys show that managers often utilize less-than-ideal techniques, such as the internal rate of return (IRR) and, even worse, payback.[5] It has been suggested that one reason for the durability of such rules is that they are easier to process and are more salient.[6] The desirability of getting your money back quickly (as reflected in payback) is obvious to even the most unsophisticated observer, though many do not realize that any payback benchmark can only be arbitrary. Somewhat less intuitive is IRR, but a comparison between the project's estimated return and its cost of capital is still quite compelling. NPV, which is all about value creation, is perhaps a harder concept to grasp. So it is possible that psychology is playing a role in the sometimes weak capital budgeting technique choices that are made.

Allowing Sunk Costs to Influence the Abandonment Decision

Due to loss aversion, people will take steps to avoid "booking" a loss. Managers are no different. There is evidence, for example, that slightly negative earnings announcements are rare.[7] This is likely because they are, if possible, "managed away."[8]

Mental accounting suggests that if an account can be kept open in the hope of eventually turning things around, this will often be done. In the context of capital budgeting, suppose a prior investment has not gone as well as anticipated. Proper capital budgeting practice is to periodically assess the viability of all current investments, even proceeding with their abandonment when this is a value-enhancing course of action. The problem with abandonment, however, is that it forces recognition of an ex post mistake.[9] But because of loss aversion, it may happen that managers foolishly hang on, throwing good money after bad.

The market seems to sense the problem. One study indicates that announcements of project terminations are usually well received.[10] One well-known example of a company hanging on too long is Lockheed (which the government ended up bailing out) and its L-1011 airplane project. When the firm eventually announced abandonment, the market pushed up its stock price by 18%.

High personal responsibility in the original investment decision increases the resistance to project abandonment.[11] This seems to be due to the greater regret that would be induced by "admitting defeat," as compared to the feeling of cutting losses and getting back on track that a new manager without the same level of emotional commitment to the project would feel. A takeover can facilitate such fresh thinking.[12]

Allowing Affect to Influence Choices

Is it possible that emotion impacts capital budgeting decisions? Since emotion plays a role in so many other realms, financial and otherwise, it would not be surprising to see it wield influence here. Direct evidence is likely to be anecdotal at best, since it is not clear how to calibrate a manager's emotional state.[13]

Experimental treatments, despite some limitations, can thus be helpful in filling the gap. Thomas Kida, Kimberley Moreno, and James Smith performed such an exercise.[14] A total of 114 managers (or individuals with similar responsibilities) served as subjects. They were presented with one of five treatments where they had to make a choice between two internal investment opportunities. In four of the treatments, the choice was between one alternative with a higher NPV and a description inducing negative affect, and a second alternative with a lower NPV but a neutral description.

As an example, in scenario 1, participants were told that they were divisional managers deciding between two product investments, each of which would require working with a different sister division run by two different managers. While the description clearly stated that both managers had strong reputations for performance, in one case the manager in question was characterized as being arrogant and condescending in interactions with people. Nevertheless, financial information was provided indicating that the project, if done with this individual, would generate a set of cash flows leading to a higher NPV than the other project. The other three negative affect scenarios were similar in their attempt to elicit a negative mood or emotion. The final treatment had neutral descriptions attached to both investment projects.

Table 16.1 shows what occurred. While in the control group the majority of subjects chose the higher-yielding project, in all four negative treatments the

TABLE 16.1 | CAPITAL BUDGETING CHOICES IN AN EXPERIMENTAL CONTEXT

Experimental scenarios	Negative affect choice	Neutral alternative
Scenario 1		
Number	6	21
Percentage	22.2%	77.8%
Scenario 2		
Number	2	15
Percentage	11.8%	88.2%
Scenario 3		
Number	6	28
Percentage	17.6%	82.4%
Scenario 4		
Number	3	12
Percentage	20.0%	80.0%
Control group		
Number	16	5
Percentage	76.2%	23.8%

Source: Kida, T. E., K. K. Moreno, and J. F. Smith, 2001, "The influence of affect on managers' capital-budgeting decisions," *Contemporary Accounting Research* Volume 18 Issue (3), 477–494. © The Canadian Academic Accounting Association.

opposite happened: situations associated with negative affect were avoided to the point of accepting value destruction.

16.3   MANAGERIAL OVERCONFIDENCE

It would be surprising if managers of corporations were markedly different from the rest of the population in terms of their overconfidence. Indeed, there is abundant evidence that managers, like investors, are egregiously overconfident. One study found that managers tended to predict stronger performance for their operations than actually occurred.[15] Excessive optimism in project cost forecasts is endemic.[16] When CFOs predict market movements, only 40% of realizations fall within 80% confidence intervals.[17]

The process of CEO selection and monitoring also likely rewards and encourages overconfidence.[18] For one thing, CEOs are "tournament winners," and often such winners only become winners because they take chances. Additionally, it can be argued that normal corporate governance exacerbates any latent tendencies in this direction. There are two forces here. First, generous executive compensation (often only weakly related to firm performance) signals success. Greater overconfidence can result because of associated self-attribution bias. Second, the tendency for boards to be overly deferential and for investors to employ the "Wall Street rule" (sell if unhappy with management) also plays to managerial overconfidence.

Various managerial behaviors have been attributed to overconfidence. For example, research indicates that overconfident managers tend to miss earnings targets in voluntary forecasts, and, as a result, display a greater proclivity to manage earnings.[19] In the next section, we turn to the impact of overconfidence on investment behavior.

16.4   INVESTMENT AND OVERCONFIDENCE

OVERINVESTMENT

Itzhak Ben-David, John Graham, and Campbell Harvey utilized an extensive quarterly survey of CFOs over a six-year period, which, among other things, asked for 90% confidence intervals for 1-year-ahead and 10-year-ahead market returns, as well as respondents' optimism levels for the economy and prospects for their own companies.[20] The advantage of this survey is that it elicited two separate overconfidence metrics: one based on miscalibration (which they call overconfidence) and the other based on excessive optimism. These researchers then acquired data on the companies for which these CFOs were employed so as to be able to correlate overconfidence metrics with firm-level behavior. While CFOs do not make unilateral decisions, it is logical to believe that they will have a major say in decisions of a financial nature. It was possible to conclude that overconfident managers invest more. In the next section, evidence is presented that the investment strategy of overconfident managers can be suboptimal.

INVESTMENT SENSITIVITY TO CASH FLOWS

Empirically, it has been established that there is a positive relationship between corporate investment and cash flow.[21] Under perfect markets and market efficiency, this should not be observed. If a positive-NPV project is identified, investment should proceed whether or not internal funds are available.

Two traditional explanations for such investment distortions have been put forth. First, it has been suggested that the potential misalignment of managerial and shareholder interests induces overinvestment when free cash is available, as managers are keen to empire build and provide themselves perks.[22] Second, an asymmetric information view purports that the firm's managers, acting in the best interests of shareholders and noticing that the company's shares are undervalued, will not issue new shares to undertake investment projects.[23] In both cases, investment and cash flows will be positively correlated.

An overconfidence "story" has also been suggested for this stylized fact by Ulrike Malmendier and Geoffrey Tate.[24] Excessively optimistic managers often overestimate the returns to investment projects. As a result, if they have excess internal funds, they will tend to overinvest. If they lack internal funds, however, perceiving that the market is undervaluing the firm's stock, they will not invest. Thus excessive optimism may be able to explain the cash flow-investment relationship. Malmendier and Tate empirically explored this possibility using naturally occurring data. Of course, the difficulty in operating in the field is that agents' levels of overconfidence are not readily observed. Thus, they must be inferred. Recall, for example, that Barber and Odean proxied overconfidence by trading activity.[25]

Malmendier and Tate accomplish the task of generating reasonable proxies for overconfidence in several clever ways. They argue that overconfident managers, thinking that their firms will perform well in the future, are happy to expose themselves to own-firm-specific risk even when diversification gains are available. CEOs often receive stock and option grants as compensation. This is done so that shareholders' and managers' interests are aligned. While there are limitations as to when options can be exercised, at some point managers do have the ability to exercise them. One metric these researchers use for overconfidence is the tendency to voluntarily hold a large number of in-the-money options (that optimally from the standpoint of diversification gains should be exercised, but that are still being held).[26]

The empirical results turned out to be consistent with the predictions of these researchers. Table 16.2 provides several key regression results illustrating this.[27] Firm-level investment is regressed on the following: cash flows; the market value of the assets over the book value of the assets, or Tobin's Q (which is a standard performance measure); overconfidence (as proxied by the tendency to hold options longer than optimal); and the interaction of the latter and cash flows. The first displayed regression excludes the overconfidence variable and its interactive term. As previous work has indicated, investment increases with cash flows and Tobin's Q.[28] The second regression incorporates overconfidence and the interaction of overconfidence and cash flows. To interpret, the coefficient on cash flows provides the sensitivity of investment to cash flows, and the latter plus the coefficient on the interactive term provides the comparable sensitivity for overconfident managers. Since the coefficient on the interactive term is significantly positive, it is clear

TABLE 16.2 | REGRESSIONS OF INVESTMENT ON CASH FLOWS AND OVERCONFIDENCE

	Coefficient estimates and t-statistics	
Independent variable	Regression (1)	Regression (2)
Cash flows	0.6419 (7.19)	0.6729 (7.56)
Q	0.0635 (6.54)	0.0656 (6.79)
Overconfidence	—	–0.0351 (1.35)
Overconfidence * cash flows	—	0.1648 (3.39)
R^2	0.56	0.56

Source: Malmendier, U., and G. Tate, 2005, "CEO overconfidence and corporate investment," *Journal of Finance* 60, 2661–2700. © Wiley Publishing, Inc. This material is used by permission of john Wiley & Sons, Inc.

that the sensitivity of investment to cash flows is higher for overconfident managers. This is consistent with the hypothesis that overconfident managers, despite what theory suggests, are more influenced by cash flows than less overconfident managers.

MERGERS AND ACQUISITIONS

Survey evidence documents that overconfident managers appear to be more active on the M&A front.[29] Malmendier and Tate, in related research, investigate whether naturally occurring data support this, and, if so, whether success results from this heightened activity.[30] To be sure, as a group, acquiring firms do not appear to serve their shareholders: during 1980–2001, $220 billion was lost immediately after bid announcements.[31]

At the outset, it needs to be noted that it is not obvious that overconfidence should lead to more mergers. The reason is that there are two conflicting motivations. First, most obviously, managers embodying this tendency will overestimate synergies and their ability to stickhandle problems. This encourages merger attempts. Second, discouraging mergers, because overconfident managers see their firms as undervalued, they are *less* likely to engage in such activity if transactions must be externally financed. It is not clear on balance which force predominates.

Using the same proxy for overconfidence as in their earlier study, Malmendier and Tate document that the former force has the greater impact.[32] Referring to Figure 16.1, we see that in all but two years of their sample overconfident managers engage in more M&A activity. Consistent with their previous study, the impact of overconfidence is greater for firms with abundant internal resources.

The market has a sense of the value destruction wrought by overconfident managers. While the typical market response to an announcement of a merger attempt engineered by a less overconfident manager is a drop of 12 basis points, managers subject to an inflated sense of their ability witness a (much larger) 90-basis point drop.

Various alternative explanations for these findings are considered. The same behavior could result from greater risk-seeking or agency (empire-building) considerations. The authors, however, argue that the first is difficult to reconcile with an

FIGURE 16.1 Merger Activity by Overconfident and Other Managers

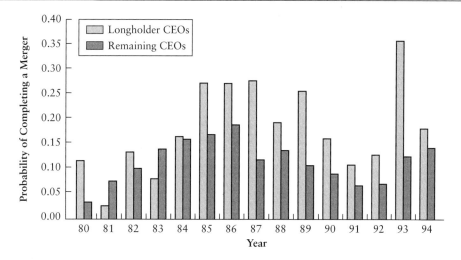

Source: Malmendier, U., and G. Tate, 2008, "Faimess Who makes acquisitions? CEO overconfidence and the market's reactions," *Reprinted from the Journal of Financial Economics,* Vol 89, Issue 1, 20–43. © July 2008. With permission from Elsevier.

observed preference for cash acquisitions; and the second is not easy to tally with CEOs' personal overinvestment.

John Doukas and Dimitris Petmezas provide robustness checks along several dimensions.[33] First, they investigate U.K. merger activity between 1980 and 2004, concentrating on the acquisition of private firms.[34] The United Kingdom is an appropriate market to investigate since it has, after the United States, the most merger activity: indeed, 65% of European transactions occur there. Second, they utilize alternative proxies for overconfidence. One is based on the argument that only egregiously overconfident managers engage in a spate of deals within a short period of time. On this basis, they classify managers as overconfident if they complete at least five deals within three years.[35] They are able to conclude that overconfident bidders realize lower announcement returns than their counterparts. Further, poorer long-term performance results.

START-UPS

It is well known that businesses, especially small ones, fail at an alarmingly high rate. One study reports that 81% believe their chance of success is 70% or better, while 33% are *sure* (as incredible as this may seem) that they will succeed.[36] It turns out though that 75% of new businesses fail within five years. A likely reason for such misguided expectations is overconfidence. Excessive optimism may mistakenly lead people to think that the market is crying out for their goods and services, and a better-than-average effect may lead entrepreneurs to think that, even if industry-wide opportunities are limited, they will still beat the odds. Venture capitalists, whose expertise is in the realm of identifying profitable opportunities, are also subject to overconfidence.[37]

As we have discussed before, overconfidence requires a proxy, and indeed several clever ones have been used. But these require a track record or visibility, which many entrepreneurs do not possess. While it can be observed that entry seems to be excessive, it is not clear what the characteristics of the entrepreneurs are who are entering an industry, and how they compare to those who are staying out. So field tests are problematic. As we have mentioned previously, an experimental setting, in allowing for environmental control, allows us to isolate factors of potential importance. Colin Camerer and Dan Lovallo performed an experiment, where subjects had to choose, over multiple rounds (periods), whether or not to enter markets.[38] Payoffs to participants were dependent on the number of entrants in a given period. This is realistic since, in naturally occurring markets, payoffs are higher when fewer people (or businesses) enter an industry. While the rules were known, the task was not easy since, given the noncommunicative nature of the environment, no one knew how many competitors would also enter in a given round.

Previous experiments of this type had been conducted with the following setup. An appearance fee was received by all participants. Suppose this value is $10. In the event of non-entry into the market, participants keep the fee. Entry, on the other hand, risks losing some of (or all of) this fee. At the same time, a positive profit is possible as a result of entry. N players choose whether to enter a market in a given round; c is the market capacity; and E the number of players who actually choose to enter. Then the profit function is specified as follows:

16.1
$$Profit = [\$10/(N - c)] * (c - E)$$

In these earlier formulations of the experiment, all of the "E" entrants earned the same payoff. Suppose $c = 8$ and $N = 16$. If $E = 4$, then the four entrants earn $5 each (taking home $15). Industry profit is $20 (4 * $5). On the other hand, if $E = 12$, then the 12 entrants lose $5 each, implying that industry profit is –$60 (12 * (–$5)). Industry profit is zero if $c = E$. When such experiments were run, E was typically close to c, implying the familiar zero-profit condition of microeconomics.

Camerer and Lovallo made the following key adjustments to incorporate overconfidence into this setting:

1. Profit depended on subjects' ranks (r) in the following fashion:
   a) the first c entrants in rank received:

16.2 $Profit = \$50 * [(c + 1 - r)/(1 + 2 + ... + c)]$, where $r = 1, 2, 3...c$

   b) all entrants with rank lower than c received:

16.3
$$Profit = -\$10$$

For example, given $c = 3$ and $E = 12$, we have:

16.4 $r = 1: Profit = \$25; r = 2: Profit = \$17; r = 3: Profit = \$8; r = 4, 5...12:$
$Profit = -\$10$

Note that if, as here, $E > c+5$, the industry profit is negative (here it is –$40).

2. Subjects' ranks depended on either a random device or skill, where skill was assessed after the completion of the experiment using either brain teasers or trivia quizzes (involving current events and sports).
3. Subjects in some experiments (but not all) were told in advance that the experiment depended on skill. When told, subjects were consciously "self-selecting" into this environment.
4. Subjects forecast the number of entrants in each period.
5. Entry decisions were made in two rounds of 12 periods each, with ranking being skill-based in one round and random in the other.
6. Market capacity was as follows: c = 2, 4, 6, and 8.

Only at the end of the experimental sessions did subjects do their skill-testing puzzles and trivia quizzes, after which one period (out of the 24) was randomly chosen as the payoff period. The only feedback subjects received during the course of the experiment was the number of entrants after each period. Assuming risk neutrality and no feelings of skill (or good luck) on the part of participants, the mixed-strategy equilibrium is to enter a market randomly $[(c + 5)/N]$% of the time (which implies an expected overall profit of zero).

Table 16.3 provides the key results. The main issue under investigation is whether or not there is a tendency to enter a round more freely when one's profit is determined by skill. If people had a true picture of their skill relative to the skill of others, there would be no impact. The reason is that, while those more skillful (and in knowledge of this) would be more likely to enter, those less skillful (and in knowledge of this) would be less likely to enter. On balance, these tendencies should cancel out. Focusing on the column on the right, when regular instructions were used, the random-versus-skilled differential profit was 8.96 (or 19.79 – 10.83), suggesting additional entry when the payoff was to be determined by skill. The differential was even greater when self-selection instructions were used. In this case, the random-versus-skilled differential profit was 27.92 (or 13.96 – (–13.96)). The overall

TABLE 16.3 | AVERAGE INDUSTRY PROFIT BY ROUND AND CONDITION

| Rank condition | Round | | | | | | | | | | | | |
	1	2	3	4	5	6	7	8	9	10	11	12	Avg.
Regular instructions													
Random	15	25	15	27.5	12.5	12.5	17.5	27.5	17.5	22.5	20	25	19.79
Skill	15	2.5	15	17.5	7.5	0	17.5	5	10	12.5	10	15	10.83
Self-selection instructions													
Random	20	15	15	15	12.5	17.5	7.5	20	7.5	10	7.5	20	13.96
Skill	–12.5	–20	–15	–12.5	–22.5	–17.5	–25	–5	–17.5	–2.5	–12.5	–5	–13.96

Source: Camerer, C. F., and D. Lovallo, 1999, "Overconfidence and excess entry: An experimental approach," *American Economic Review* 89, 306–318. © 1999 American Economic Review. Reproduced with the permission of the publisher and the authors.

average differential was a highly significant 18.43 (or 16.87 − (−1.56)), consistent with the main hypothesis tested in the paper.

The fact that the differential was significantly higher under the self-selection treatment was argued to be consistent with a **reference group neglect** effect. Though this particular design was likely to lead to a more highly skilled group volunteering to participate, this same group seemed to forget the fact that others in the group were also more likely to be superior in terms of skill and, for this reason, keen to "play the game."

One possible non-behavioral reason for excessive entry into markets that the authors were able to eliminate is "competitive blind spots," that is, the tendency to enter a market and then be surprised by the amount of competition—without any feeling of great personal skill. Such a view would lead to a prediction of positive profit in the skill treatments, implying that the actual negative or low profits came as a surprise. The reality proved to be otherwise, as subjects consistently predicted higher profits for the random periods than for the skill periods. Thus, while people expected low (or negative) *aggregate* profits in the skill rounds, they expected that they themselves would do well.

16.5   CAN MANAGERIAL OVERCONFIDENCE HAVE A POSITIVE SIDE?

As we have suggested elsewhere, overconfidence may have a positive aspect. A moderate level of overconfidence could have a salutary side, if it leads to elevated, concentrated effort.[39] In the context of principal-agent theory, this can alleviate the moral hazard problem due to the non-observability of the agent's effort.[40]

Further, since managers can be more risk averse than shareholders might like, overconfidence can counteract this tendency, moving the firm toward what is desirable.[41] Aside from obvious potential impacts on investment, capital structure may also be affected. Dirk Hackbarth has formulated a model where otherwise rational managers are not only excessively optimistic about their firm's prospects, but also overly sure about their views.[42] This model suggests that managerial overconfidence is positively correlated with debt issuance, because optimism about future cash flows leads to a belief that there will be little problem in covering interest payments. Ironically, the natural tendency to shy away from debt because of job concerns (which is value-destroying because the benefits of debt are not exhausted) is counteracted by overconfidence.

Finally, it has even been suggested that overconfidence among entrepreneurs, even if *personally* deleterious, might be *socially* beneficial, because entrepreneurial activity can provide valuable information to society (unlike herders, who provide no information).[43] In this sense, it serves a valuable evolutionary purpose.

CHAPTER HIGHLIGHTS

1. Because of ease of processing, inappropriate capital budgeting techniques may be favored. Because of loss aversion, managers may throw good money after bad. And because of affect, emotion sometimes gets in the way of optimal managerial decision-making.

2. There are many markers of managerial overconfidence. One is the tendency to hold on to in-the-money options too long.
3. Managerial overconfidence likely leads to various forms of investment distortions or overinvestment.
4. Aside from too much capital spending, overinvestment manifests itself in tendencies toward excessive M&A activity and to be too quick to undertake start-ups.
5. An example of an investment distortion is allowing the availability of internal funds to dictate whether investment should go ahead.
6. Overconfidence may have a bright side, though, in particular because it "corrects" excessive managerial risk aversion.

DISCUSSION QUESTIONS AND PROBLEMS

1. Differentiate the following terms/concepts:

   a. Payback and NPV
   b. Holding in-the-money options too long and engaging in frequent acquisitions
   c. Random treatment and self-selection treatment in Camerer and Lovallo experiment
   d. Risk aversion and overconfidence in debt issuance

2. Investment activity is driven by both rational value maximization and behavioral influences on the part of managers. Discuss.

3. In the Camerer and Lovallo experiment, let $N = 10$ and $c = 2$. Specify the number of entrants that maximizes industry profit. What will this industry profit be? Specify the number of entrants that minimizes industry profits. What will this industry profit be? What number of entrants leads to zero industry profits?

4. In the Camerer and Lovallo experiment, overconfidence leads to excessive entry into markets. Do you believe that if a prospective entrepreneur read this research she would be more or less likely to undertake a start-up? Explain.

5. You are a divisional manager. Currently you are a member of a committee that is considering two product investments proposed by two other divisional managers, Joe and John. While walking over to the presentations, Joe seems rather arrogant. He mentions that he golfs with the CEO, is a key player in the firm, and that you could really learn a lot from him. In thinking over the projects after the presentations, you find that you are really leaning toward John's proposal even though the projects are quite similar in terms of estimated cash flows and risks. How can you explain this?

ENDNOTES

1 As suggested by Fairchild, R., 2007, "Behavioral corporate finance: Existing research and future decisions," Working paper, combining irrational investors and irrational managers is a fruitful area for future research.

2 It is also assumed that corporate governance is limited in its ability to constrain the behavior of managers. See Baker, M., R. S. Ruback, and J. Wurgler, 2004, "Behavioral corporate finance: A survey," Working paper, for details.

3 Managerial overconfidence seems to matter for other decisions as well. For example, Fairchild, R., 2005, "The effect of managerial overconfidence, asymmetric information, and moral hazard on capital structure decisions," Working paper, shows that overconfidence may lead to excessive use of welfare-reducing debt.

4 Certain caveats, such as equalization of project lives and consideration of real options, must be accounted for. See, for example, Ross, S. A., J. Jaffe, and R. A. Westerfield, 2006, *Corporate Finance* (McGraw-Hill, New York).

5 See, for example, Graham, J. R., and C. R. Harvey, 2001, "The theory and practice of corporate finance: Evidence from the field," *Journal of Financial Economics* 60, 187–243.

6 Shefrin, H., 2007, *Behavioral Corporate Finance: Decisions That Create Value* (McGraw-Hill Irwin, Boston, Massachusetts).

7 Burgstahler, D., and I. Dichev, 1997, "Earnings management to avoid earnings increases and losses," *Journal of Accounting and Economics* 24, 99–126.

8 If this isn't feasible, the tendency is to "take a bath," thus increasing the probability of a positive earnings number next time round.

9 Of course the investment might have been the best move ex ante.

10 Statman, M., and D. Caldwell, 1987, "Applying behavioral finance to capital budgeting: Project terminations," *Financial Management* 16 (no. 4), 7–15.

11 Staw, B., 1976, "Knee-deep in the big muddy: A study of escalating commitment toward a chosen course of action," *Organizational Behavior and Human Decision Processes* 20, 27–44.

12 Jensen, M. C., 1987, "The takeover controversy: Analysis and evidence," in Coffee, J. C., L. Lowenstein, and S. Rose-Ackerman, eds., 1987, *Knights, Raiders and Targets: The Impact of the Hostile Takeover* (Oxford University Press, Oxford, U. K.).

13 As will be discussed in Chapter 20, however, new research in neuroeconomics and neurofinance is making strides in this regard.

14 Kida, T. E., K. K. Moreno, and J. F. Smith, 2001, "The influence of affect on managers' capital-budgeting decisions," *Contemporary Accounting Research* 18, 477–494.

15 Kidd, J. B., and J. R. Morgan, 1969, "A predictive information system for management," *Operational Research Quarterly* 20, 149–170.

16 Statman, M., and T. T. Tyebjee, 1985, "Optimistic capital budgeting forecasts: An experiment," *Financial Management* 14, 27–33.

17 Ben-David, I., J. R. Graham, and C. Harvey, 2007, "Managerial overconfidence and corporate policies," Working paper.

18 See Paredes, T. A., 2004, "Too much pay, too much deference: Is CEO overconfidence the product of corporate governance?" Working paper, for a discussion.

19 Hribar, P., and H. Yang, 2006, "CEO overconfidence, management earnings forecasts, and earnings management," Working paper.

20 Ben-David, I., J. R. Graham, and C. Harvey, 2007, "Managerial overconfidence and corporate policies," Working paper.

21 Fazzari, S., R. G. Hubbard, and B. Peterson, 1988, "Financing constraints and corporate investment," *Brookings Papers on Economic Activity*, 141–195.

22 Jensen, M. C., and W. Meckling, 1976, "The theory of the firm: Managerial behavior, agency costs, and ownership structure," *Journal of Financial Economics* 3, 305–360.

23 This view of the world of course is along the lines of the previous chapter.

24 Malmendier, U., and G. Tate, 2005, "CEO overconfidence and corporate investment," *Journal of Finance* 60, 2661–2700. Also, see Heaton, J. B., 2002, "Managerial optimism and corporate finance," *Financial Management* 31 (no. 2), 33–45.

25 Barber, B., and T. Odean, 2000, "Trading is hazardous to your wealth: The common

stock investment performance of individual investors," *Journal of Finance* 55, 773–806.

26 A related proxy is that a manager is overconfident if she holds options all the way to expiration. A third is that a manager is judged to be overconfident if he, contrary to the tenets of diversification, continues to increase his holdings in the company's stock.

27 These regressions come from Table V of Malmendier, U., and G. Tate, 2005, "CEO overconfidence and corporate investment," *Journal of Finance* 60, 2661–2700.

28 When Tobin's q is equal to one, the market value of a company is equal to the replacement value of its assets. Researchers have documented that in takeovers with bidders which have q-ratios greater than one and targets with q-ratios less than one, the total returns to the takeover are larger. Thus, better-performing firms make better investment decisions and create more value. See, for example, Servaes, H., 1991, "Tobin's q and the gains from takeovers," *Journal of Finance* 46(1), 409–419.

29 Ben-David, I., J. R. Graham, and C. Harvey, 2007, "Managerial overconfidence and corporate policies," Working paper.

30 Malmendier, U., and G. Tate, 2008, "Who makes acquisitions? CEO overconfidence and the market's reaction," *Journal of Financial Economics, forthcoming.*

31 Moeller, S., F. Schlingemann, and R. Stulz, 2004, "Wealth destruction on a massive scale? A study of acquiring-firm returns in the recent merger wave," Working paper.

32 Their results are robust to using a press-based proxy for overconfidence, where a manager is judged to be overconfident if he/she is often described as "confident" or "optimistic."

33 Doukas, J. A., and D. Petmezas, 2007, "Acquisitions, overconfident managers and self-attribution bias," *European Financial Management, forthcoming.*

34 Public firms are acquired far less often: private acquisitions in the U.K. market account for about 90% of all M&As.

35 They obtain similar results when they use, as an alternative proxy, insiders' net purchases (more specifically, the ratio of purchases to sales).

36 Cooper, A. C., C. Y. Woo, and W. C. Dunkelberg, 1988, "Entrepreneurs' perceived chances of success," *Journal of Business Venturing* 3, 97–108.

37 Zacharakis, A. L., and D. A. Shepherd, 2001, "The nature of information and overconfidence on venture capitalists' decision making," *Journal of Business Venturing* 16, 311–332.

38 Camerer, C. F., and D. Lovallo, 1999, "Overconfidence and excess entry: An experimental approach," *American Economic Review* 89, 306–318.

39 Larwood, L., and W. Whittaker, 1977, "Managerial myopia: Self-serving biases in organizational planning," *Journal of Applied Psychology* 62, 194–198.

40 Keiber, K. L., 2002, "Managerial compensation contracts and overconfidence," Working paper.

41 Goel, A. M., and A. V. Thakor, 2000, "Rationality, overconfidence and leadership," Working paper.

42 Hackbarth, D., 2007, "Managerial optimism, overconfidence, and capital structure decisions," Working paper.

43 Bernardo, A. E., and I. Welch, 2001, "On the evolution of overconfidence and entrepreneurs," Working paper.

RETIREMENT, PENSIONS, EDUCATION, DEBIASING, AND CLIENT MANAGEMENT

PART

CHAPTER 17   Understanding Retirement Saving Behavior
             and Improving DC Pensions

CHAPTER 18   Debiasing, Education, and Client Management

UNDERSTANDING RETIREMENT SAVING BEHAVIOR AND IMPROVING DC PENSIONS

17.1 INTRODUCTION

One area where the lessons of behavioral finance are being employed to great effect is understanding retirement saving behavior and improving pensions. This chapter will help us understand some of the key issues. We begin in Section 17.2 by describing an international movement toward pensions where employees are also investors in the sense that they must monitor and control their own retirement accounts. Unfortunately, employee-investors are often ill equipped for the task. The problem facing them is a very difficult one. How much should be saved? What asset classes should be invested in, and in what proportions? What specific investment vehicles should be used? In Section 17.3, we address the issue of how much one should save to be prepared for retirement. Unfortunately, saving can be hampered by the fact that we are all subject to limited self-control and procrastination, even though the consequences can be quite damaging in this realm. In Section 17.4, we turn to one of the most important decisions that all investors need to make, the asset allocation decision. Nevertheless, many are confused by this decision, suggesting the need for education. While education can help unsophisticated investors make more informed decisions, pension design improvements, especially those capitalizing on such behavioral tendencies as procrastination and loss aversion, seem to hold greater promise. The final section of the chapter discusses pension design innovations.

17.2   THE WORLD-WIDE MOVE TO DC PENSIONS AND ITS CONSEQUENCES

DBs vs. DCs

Over the last number of years, the pension environment around the world has been evolving. Most notably, many developed countries have been moving from employer-invested **defined benefit (DB) pensions** to employee-invested **defined contribution (DC) pensions**. In a DB, the employer normally promises, according to a formula, periodic payments subsequent to retirement, whereas, in a DC, the employer along with the employee normally makes contributions into a retirement account whose accumulation is a function of investment returns, without any guarantee as to what will be available after retirement. The United States has been a leader in DC pensions, spurred by the passage of the Employment Retirement Income Security Act (ERISA) in 1974 and changes to the Internal Revenue Code (taking effect in 1980), which led to the burgeoning DC-like 401(k) market. Other countries are now moving in the direction of DCs, including the United Kingdom, Australia, Canada, the Netherlands, Sweden, and Chile.[1]

To get a sense of the shift, in the United States between 1975 and 2003 the number of private defined benefit pension plans declined from 100,000 to less than 31,000.[2] Of those with pension coverage, 58% rely exclusively on 401(k)s or comparable plans. About half of the rest rely just on a DB, with the other half having both a DB and a DC.[3] Those DBs that remain in existence are increasingly being frozen to new hires or hard-frozen, in the sense that current members are not able to accrue additional benefits.[4]

Before moving forward, some additional background on the nature of DBs versus DCs is in order. Suppose you are a DB member and your pension formula specifies that you are to receive 1.5% of the average of your salary over the last five years times the number of years of service up to a maximum of 35 years. So, if you earn $60,000 per year on average over the last five years of your employment, and you were with the firm for 20 years, then your pension would be $18,000 per year as long as you live. How does a firm manage this? Companies have a fiduciary responsibility to set aside in a dedicated pension fund an amount sufficient to pay future retirees what they have been promised. The managers of these pension funds in turn invest the money in stocks, bonds, and other appropriate assets, so that the required growth can be achieved.

A DC is much simpler. Normally the employee and her firm make contributions into a pension account that is managed by the employee. Money can be invested among a menu of professionally managed funds. Typically, a match will be in effect. For example, if the employee sets aside 5% each payday, a 50% match would entail the company supplying an additional 2.5% of salary. The amount of money in the account at retirement is entirely a function of how much is contributed by both parties, and how successfully the money is invested. One option for a worker on retirement is to take the lump sum in the account and to purchase an annuity whose term corresponds to the worker's expected remaining life span (plus a few years as a hedge).

What are the pros and cons of DB versus DC pensions? From the standpoint of the worker, DB pensions are beneficial in that two important sources of risk are avoided: market risk and longevity risk. First, because the benefit is defined, there is certainty as to what lump sum or life annuity payment will be received on retirement—regardless of how markets fare.[5] Second, if one opts for the annuity, on retirement the worker is certain that he will receive his pension payment until his eventual death.[6] If market risk and longevity risk are not borne by the worker, they must be borne by the firm. Although longevity risk, assuming actuaries are coming up with reliable mortality tables, can be diversified away fairly easily, market risk cannot be. Time diversification can help with alleviating market risk, as good and bad markets tend to average out. But persistent bear markets are not so easy to deal with—poor markets in 2000–2002 and 2008–2009 have served to send many DBs into underfunded status, the solution to which may require years of good markets and higher contributions.

On the other side of the coin, DC pensions may be preferred by workers in that they are more portable. This is important for the increasingly large cohort of mobile workers, especially in the United States. Some also like the greater tangibility occasioned by periodic statements and control over risk and investments. Moreover, if investors believe that good markets are likely to follow good markets (and we saw evidence of this in Chapter 8), then DCs can *appear* attractive in bull markets—as was the case during the 1990s. For this reason, some of the shift to DC (especially early on) came in response to worker preferences.

What about from the standpoint of the company? It is not hard to understand the growing popularity of DCs in the corporate world. Pension contributions are predictable and market fluctuations do not seriously impact the bottom line.

With the increasing popularity of DCs among employees and employers, are savers better off with this type of plan? DCs can create serious difficulties for some workers. First of all, if an employee has not deferred enough of her income, or if investment returns have been below expectations, she may have insufficient funds for retirement purposes. Moreover, on retirement, unless the worker purchases a life annuity, there will always be the possibility of running out of money (which means relying solely on government benefits or other external assistance).

Another concern is that investors may not design their portfolios in the best manner to achieve their goals. If employees are insufficiently sophisticated to handle their own retirement accounts, the result will be a cohort of employees reaching retirement financially unprepared. There is some evidence that money managed by investor-employees does not grow as much as money managed by the pros. One U.S. study estimated that DB-invested money has outperformed DC-invested money net of all fees by about 2% per year.[7] In part this gap stems from DC money being more actively managed, but without the performance to offset the fees. DBs are sometimes indexed in those sectors where it is believed that risk-adjusted returns sufficiently high to offset fees are unlikely. Also, mutual funds in the United States form the basis of practically all DC investing, and such funds tend to have fee structures higher than comparable institutional funds. Finally, some DC members appear to take inappropriate amounts of risk or select portfolios that are not optimally diversified. Let us look at problems faced by employee-investors in more detail.

Problems Faced by Employee-Investors

Future retirees who manage their pension accounts act in most respects like other retail investors, except in one regard: they are "drafted" for the job, as compared to the willing cohort of amateur investors. For this reason, retirement account investors are likely to have lower levels of investment knowledge than those actively choosing to invest on their own account. As evidence of this, the basics of risk and diversification may not be understood: it is common to believe that an individual security is less risky than a diversified equity fund market.[8] As a result, the investment decisions that these employee-investors make are often suboptimal, and, interestingly, the investors themselves realize this.[9]

There is another respect in which this group of investors is likely to be different from their more willing counterparts. As our discussion of overconfidence in Chapter 9 revealed, while willing investors often take too many actions, employee-investors can become increasingly hesitant and even paralyzed when offered more than a few asset choices.[10] The result is not taking any action at all.[11] And if they do get around to investing, often they will rarely, if ever, adjust their holdings over time.[12]

Two areas where employee-investors arguably have the most serious problems will be stressed here. First, some in this group are not saving enough (with a smaller group not saving at all). Second, employee-investors often have difficulty with the fundamental investment decision, asset allocation. In the following section, we document and discuss these problems. Later in the chapter, we will consider how the lessons of behavioral finance can be utilized to ameliorate the problem.

17.3   SAVING WITH LIMITED SELF-CONTROL AND PROCRASTINATION

Why is it that many people are not saving enough? It comes down to those most human of traits: **limited self-control** and **procrastination**. Classical economics makes two assumptions that the behavioral sciences question. First, it is assumed that agents make economically optimal choices.[13] And, second, it is assumed that they follow through and implement those choices. In the realm of saving for retirement, both of these assumptions are tenuous. We begin by considering the first assumption.

How Much Needs to be Saved?

We have previously met *homo economicus*. This rational being has foresight and plans for his retirement. Therefore, he needs to decide how much to set aside from his pay each month in order to properly provide for his golden years. Let's consider how to approach the problem. It makes sense to work backward. How much annual income is needed during retirement years? Normally, experts do not answer this question by providing a dollar amount. Rather, they answer it on an **income replacement ratio** basis. The latter is defined to be retirement income as a percentage of working (or employment) income. The reason this approach makes sense is that, if your working income is $25,000, you have become accustomed to a certain standard of living. And, if your working income is $100,000, you have become accustomed to another, much higher, standard of living. For most people, a reasonable goal is to roughly maintain what they are used to. A common rule of thumb is about 70% as an income replacement ratio. Why can you get by with less than 100% during your retirement years? For one thing, you will be moving from a period of saving (to one of dissaving). Also, your children will be grown up so it is likely you will have no one dependent on you. You won't face work travel, work dining, and work clothing expenses. For some people, 70% might be appropriate, but in other cases it could be that higher (or lower) percentages are called for.

Let's try a concrete example. Wendy Chan is 30 years of age, and she plans to work until age 60. Her income is $50,000. To her credit, she has already amassed $40,000 in retirement savings. She estimates that on retirement she will have $8,000/year from external sources (e.g., subsidized public services for seniors, government health-care assistance such as Medicare, any DB pension payments, etc.). So, as of right now, she can replace 16% of her income with these external sources. The $40,000 of retirement savings when invested over time will help as well. But, she will need to set aside additional funds on a regular basis to reach her goals. The problem is to arrive at the percentage of her income that she needs to set aside on a regular basis in order to have 70% replacement at retirement. Note that this percentage can be a blend of employer/employee contributions. When she retires, her plan is to buy an annuity that will make equal periodic payments until the end of its term. She believes that a 30-year annuity is very likely to hold out until her demise (estimated to be at age 90 or less).

To calculate what percentage of her pay she needs to set aside, that is, her required **deferral rate**, we need to assume values for the following variables: 1) required income replacement ratio (70%); 2) working years (30 years); 3) years of annuity (30 years); 4) wage growth (0%); 5) investment return on retirement savings (5%); and 6) annuity interest rate (2%). Given all these values, we can arrive at a required deferral rate of approximately 13%. Certain assumptions were made to get to the answer. Indeed, a lot of uncertainty has been buried. For example, because of health issues, she may not be able to work for 30 more years. On the other hand, with good fortune, she may have more than 30 years in retirement. What about wage growth, investment returns, and the annuity interest rate? Don't they seem on the low side? The answer here is that all our values (dollar figures and returns) are in real (inflation-adjusted) terms. It is assumed that she has reached the top of her career path and future pay increases will only occur due to inflation, which explains the 0% wage growth. What about the investment return of 5%? If we (reasonably) assume a 50/50 average stock-bond investment portfolio mix, a real risk-free return of 2% and a 6% equity premium, then this 5% value seems reasonable. And, the annuity interest rate comes directly from the (assumed) risk-free rate of interest.

In Table 17.1 we show some additional deferral rate/income replacement ratio combinations. Note that, even saving as early as 30, if she only saves 5%–6% of her income, her income will be more than cut in half at retirement!

Now, while it is true that readers of this book will find such assumptions heroic, you will not find the actual time value calculations to be overly challenging. But many 401(k) plan members will have severe difficulties with the latter. Fortunately, though, financial planners can be of assistance. Often one hears

| TABLE 17.1 | DEFERRAL RATES VS. INCOME REPLACEMENT RATIOS |

Deferral rate	Income replacement ratio
5%	46%
6%	49%
7%	52%
8%	55%
9%	58%
10%	61%
11%	64%
12%	67%
13%	70%
14%	73%
15%	76%

Source: Calculations are based on assumptions in example in Section 17.3.

rules-of-thumb such as 10%–15% of pay, and in Wendy's case, the midpoint of this range will be about right. The bigger problem is described next.

LIMITED SELF-CONTROL

What about the assumption that people will follow through on their commitments? There is abundant evidence that many people have problems. For example, after the holiday season becomes a memory, many of us realize it would be nice to shed a few pounds. Still, if the choice is between a piece of pie for dessert or pushing the plate away, that is, between current gratification and deferred gratification, many of us will opt for the former. After all, nobody likes to give up what is pleasant to him. We know what the right choice is, but sometimes we can't follow through.

People realize that they sometimes need self-imposed discipline and rules. They also recognize that controlling their environment can be helpful. Continuing our weight loss analogy, a diet is a set of rules. For example, one diet might specify that one is not supposed to eat more than a certain number of calories per day, or one is not allowed any dessert. Environmental control is important. If you are on a no-dessert diet, it is probably not wise to accompany your friends to a dessert restaurant.

There are many examples of self-control difficulties and associated commitment devices. Can't save enough for that vacation? Join a vacation club. Can't maintain a regular exercise program? Join a health club that insists on a long-term contract. Can't stop impulse spending? Cut up those credit cards. In the realm of saving for retirement, planners have come up with the mantra "pay yourself first." For those who buy in, the money is taken off the top before temptation rears its ugly head. The best way to operationalize such a saving program is to obviate the need to resist paycheck temptation by automatic withdrawals at the source. This is one reason for the automatic withdrawal mechanism commonly used for 401(k)s.

EXPONENTIAL AND HYPERBOLIC DISCOUNT FUNCTIONS

Numerous experiments have shown that people (and animals) often act as if they are using a hyperbolic discount function rather than an exponential one.[14] To understand this, consider the following scenario. People are given a choice between two payments: a small one at time t and a larger one at $t+1$. When t is far off, people may prefer the bigger reward. But as t gets close to zero (now), the decision is often reversed. For concreteness, many of us will choose $115 in two years over $100 in a year, but at the same time will choose $100 today versus $115 in a year. This is reflective of preferences that are dynamically inconsistent. In the context of saving, many people will be keen to start a strict saving program next year. "Just not today," they will say.

Let us define ∂ as the *subjective* present value of a $1. This is the amount that would make somebody indifferent between saving another dollar or spending another dollar. The value ∂ is related to the individual's **rate of time preference**, with the relationship being:

17.1
$$\partial = \frac{1}{1 + \rho}$$

where ρ is the rate of time preference, and $\partial < 1$. If we use the interest rate (or, more generally, the discount rate) in this formula instead of the rate of time preference, we have the *objective* present value of $1. The difference is that, while the interest rate is market-determined, in 17.1 the rate of time preference is subjective and individual-specific. It expresses preferences, not market outcomes. Say, for example, that a particular individual would be indifferent between $10 now and $11 next year. This implies that $\rho = 10\%$ and ∂ is 0.909 ($1/(1 + 10\%)$). If this individual at the present time has an extra dollar to either spend or save, she would save if the interest rate were greater than 10%. On the other hand, if the interest rate were less than 10%, she would spend the dollar.

What if the comparison were between $10 next year and $11 in two years? Then we would need to know her subjective discount function. Classical economics, in comparing the perceived value of a dollar at different points in time, has typically used an **exponential discount function**. For an individual with such a function, the subjective present value of a dollar received in one year is ∂; in two years ∂^2; in three years ∂^3; and so on. The ratio of the subjective value of a dollar at some point in time (say t) to its value one period further in the future is as follows:

17.2
$$\partial = \frac{\partial^t}{\partial^{t+1}} = \partial^{-1} = 1 + \rho, \qquad t \geq 0$$

Notice that this ratio is the same at all points in time. In this sense, preferences are dynamically consistent. If you like the idea now of saving a dollar in a year, you will also like the idea now of saving a dollar now.

Somebody who likes the idea of saving a dollar in a year, but is not keen to do it now, is said to have a **hyperbolic discount function**. Refer to Figure 17.1 where both exponential and hyperbolic discount functions are displayed. To arrive at the exponential discount function in the figure, we have set ∂ equal to .951. The

FIGURE 17.1 Hyperbolic vs. Exponential Discount Functions

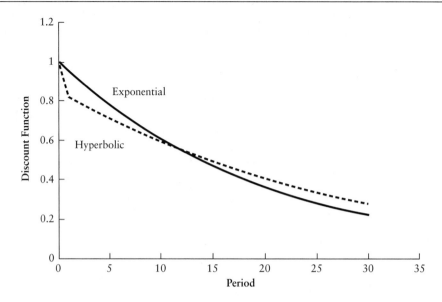

Note: Parameter values come from Section 17.3.

hyperbolic function has values $\{\beta, \beta\partial_H, \beta\partial_H{}^2, \beta\partial_H{}^3, ...\}$ where we have used $\beta = .85$ and $\partial_H = .964$.[15] Notice the initial steep decline in the hyperbolic discount function, followed by something that looks a lot like the exponential function. Hyperbolic discounters exhibit standard preferences when comparing money at two different *future* points in time, but they have problems when one of the sums to be compared is immediate. This is because the ratio of the subjective value of a dollar at t to its value one period further in the future is β for $t = 0$ and ∂_H^{-1} for $t \geq 1$. In other words, it is not constant. If $\beta < \partial_H$, at interest rates implying intermediate values only postponed saving will occur.

This is the self-control problem writ large: sure, a diet is no problem—as long as I can start tomorrow. By the way, returning to our $115 versus $100 choice, notice that using the exponential function leads to a consistent choice of the higher sum of money. On the other hand, using the hyperbolic function leads to deferred gratification—but only if the deferral is deferred.

PROCRASTINATION

Procrastination is closely linked to self-control. As we have seen, often financial decisions require careful analysis. It is not just a matter of exerting self-control in saving, but we also must decide how much to save and which savings vehicles to utilize. We have already mentioned that 401(k)s often provide a very wide choice of funds. With procrastination, even though people realize that postponing investment decisions can be costly, decision-postponement or procrastination might still occur because there is an *immediate* cost to be incurred in terms of time and effort. In fact, it has been suggested that the bigger the stakes, the worse the procrastination.[16] Intuitively, big decisions are more complex, and the immediate cost of confronting them may encourage ongoing procrastination.

EVIDENCE ON RETIREMENT PREPAREDNESS

The evidence is fairly strong that most people are not saving enough—and they know it. For example, in one survey, 76% of respondents believed they should be saving more for retirement.[17] When retirement occurs there is often a dramatic decline in income. Of course, one must be careful to not too quickly attribute this to irrationality. Theory, after all, does not say that consumption should be smoothed. Rather, it says that the marginal utility of consumption should be smoothed. Retirement may lead to a change in circumstances and tastes: for example, there might be a reduced desire for expensive leisure activities and travel. Such a possibility has been investigated, but, since no rational reason for such a large consumption drop could be unearthed, the logical inference to be drawn was that an *unexpected* decline in consumption occurred for many people.[18]

One can question whether substantial drops in consumption actually make retirees less happy.[19] It turns out that once health-related issues are controlled for, despite the hefty declines in income that occur, there is no discernible difference in reported well-being. The explanation may be that people overestimate their retirement needs. Alternatively, resilience to changing circumstances may be underestimated, and the correlation between consumption and happiness is overestimated by many people.[20] This caveat notwithstanding, a precipitous drop in income (as opposed to a moderate drop) is not a fate that would be welcomed by many.

17.4 ASSET ALLOCATION CONFUSION

DOCUMENTING THE PROBLEM

One finding that has been particularly troubling is that many future retirees do not seem to understand **asset allocation**. In other words, they do not understand how to select assets whose aggregate risk lines up with their risk tolerance. What makes this confusion potentially damaging is that it is often observed that the asset allocation decision is the most important one for an investor's long-term portfolio performance.[21]

One way to ascertain whether people are having problems in this regard is to see if they exhibit consistency in their choices when they are forced to make their opinions known. As we have seen, when individuals are unsure, they often rely on heuristics that allow them to make what to them seems a reasonable choice. The **diversification heuristic**, whereby people when unsure automatically choose "a bit of everything," has been documented.[22] Shlomo Benartzi and Richard Thaler have provided evidence that this heuristic also appears to come into play for decisions as important as asset allocation.[23] University of California employees participating in a survey, when told to allocate their money among five funds, of which four were fixed-income and one equity, did so in a manner suggesting a 43% equity share.

While there is nothing wrong with this in and of itself, in a second treatment, employees were told to allocate their money among five other funds, of which, this time, four out of five were equity. This time the asset allocation suggested a (much higher) 68% equity share. The obvious inference is that confused respondents allowed the menu of options to have a major impact on their choice. Indeed, there was the tendency on the part of some to put *1/nth* of available money into all *n* funds. For this reason, in this context, the diversification heuristic is sometimes called the *1/n* **heuristic**.

Behavioral regularities are observed across borders. In a Canadian survey of DC plan members, respondents were asked to hypothetically allocate their pension money among a "government bond fund," a "corporate bond fund," and a "stock fund."[24] A second question was identical, except that the three choices were a "bond fund," a "growth stock fund," and a "value stock fund."

Figures 17.2 and 17.3 show the frequency distributions for these two questions. On the first question, when one of the three funds was an equity fund, the mean equity share was 43%. On the other hand, on the second question, when two of the three funds were equity funds, the mean equity share was a much higher 69%. Thus, based on survey evidence, it seems that many future retirees, both in the United States and elsewhere, are confused by asset allocation decisions and seem to be swayed by whatever fund menu is available to them. As we have discussed previously, the frame of the problem can affect the decision made, particularly, as here, when knowledge levels are low.

But are *actual* asset allocation decisions made in a manner consistent with the *survey* evidence? One reason to think that the problem should not be so severe is

FIGURE 17.2 Frequency Distribution of Equity Allocation When One Out of Three Choices is an Equity Fund

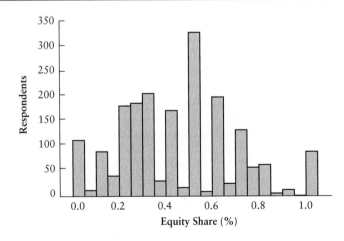

Source: Deaves, R., 2005, "Flawed self-directed retirement account decision-making and its implications," *Canadian Investment Review* (Spring), 6–15.

FIGURE 17.3 Frequency Distribution of Equity Allocation When Two Out of Three Choices are Equity Funds

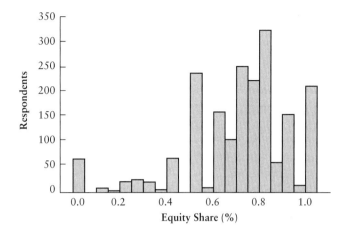

Source: Deaves, R., 2005, "Flawed self-directed retirement account decision-making and its implications," *Canadian Investment Review* (Spring), 6–15.

that actual decisions are "salient," because they involve real money. For this reason, people are liable to take greater care and even utilize informed advice.

The evidence is mixed. Benartzi and Thaler analyzed a database of the actual decisions made by 1.5 million members across 170 plans, concluding that there is solid evidence that the available choices affect allocations—when there are a lot of equity funds, people tend to put more of their money into equities.[25] On the other hand, Gur Huberman and Wei Jiang show that greater precision is obtained (and bias reduced) by examining individual versus plan-level data.[26] They show that the *1/n* heuristic holds in the sense that many people spread their money evenly among all funds chosen—not over all available funds. Note that this version of the heuristic can be quite rational. If someone's correct asset allocation is two-thirds equity, this can be accomplished by choosing two equity funds and one fixed-income fund and then using the *1/n* heuristic. They also show that menu effects are weak in the sense that so-called plan-level equity exposure (the percentage of funds that are equity funds) and individual-level equity allocation (the percentage of money invested in equity funds) are only weakly correlated. Notably, and consistent with surveys, menu effects seem much stronger when there are 10 or fewer funds available, versus when 11 or more are offered.

ARE THERE "CORRECT" ASSET ALLOCATIONS?

If one wishes to encourage employee-investors to develop plans that will help them achieve their goals, it is necessary to have some sense of what is best. The reality is that there is no known exact allocation for any given individual that can be theoretically defended. In practice there can be substantial disagreement. While DB pension funds have historically opted for a 60/40 stock-bond mix, some commentators argue for a much higher (or lower) equity share.[27]

What does theory say? It is clear that the two principal normative demographic factors are risk attitude and age. First, highly risk-averse individuals, purely because of personal preferences, will naturally choose a higher fixed-income exposure in their portfolios. There is evidence that one proxy for risk attitude is gender, with women being more risk averse than men.[28] Second, as an individual ages and approaches retirement, her stock of relatively safe human capital declines, requiring a lower equity exposure to maintain a fairly stable risk stance.[29] Indeed, it is typical for financial planners to recommend an equity share that not only conforms to an investor's risk attitude, but also declines one for one (1%/year) as people approach retirement.[30]

According to the empirical evidence, some seem to act in a manner consistent with theory.[31] As expected, younger, more risk-tolerant males hold more stock.[32] Additionally, higher-earning people hold more equity. This is logical in that income should be correlated with one's stock of human capital. Married individuals also tilt toward stocks. One possible reason for this is that two-income families can afford to take on more risk because of their greater ability to diversify labor-market shocks. Those with high net worth lean toward equities. The causality is ambiguous: are people wealthier because they have in the past been risk takers, or do they favor stocks because they can withstand adverse market movements? Finally, seniority (which is logically related to job security) is associated with risk taking.

Evidence has also been presented that risk taking versus age is a humped function.[33] At first, people increase risk taking as they age, and, only later, after a maximum is achieved, does equity exposure begin to decline. This non-monotonicity is consistent with recent theoretical advancements. If one's income and stock returns are positively correlated to a sufficient degree, then risk taking should *increase* with time because of reduced hedging demand.[34] Because of this, it is even possible that on retirement an individual could increase equity exposure.[35] Moreover, exposure to nondiversifiable entrepreneurial risk is often more prevalent among the relatively young.[36] The same is true of leveraged real estate purchases and personal illiquid projects such as private business start-ups.[37]

In sum, while it seems that some investors are acting according to normative theory, the behavior of a large number of investors is inconsistent with predictions. Sometimes it appears that they are putting far too much of their money in highly risky asset classes (such as company stock). Sometimes it seems that they are putting far too much of their money into low-risk investments (such as government bond funds). In the next chapter, we review the traditional process of asset allocation determination, which attempts to get people to take on the amount of risk that is right for them. In the next section of this chapter, we consider how changes to pension design can be made that will give future retirees a better chance of meeting their goals.

MOVING TOWARD A SOLUTION

Let us assume that people, whether because of a lack of attention or knowledge, or even irrationality, are not acting in an optimal fashion when it comes to retirement and pensions. One approach is to simply argue that as long as there is full information disclosure, there need not be any further intervention. Some would counter that this approach is problematic because if participants lack understanding, information provision will not be enough and intervention is warranted. Admittedly, there is a paternalistic slant to this latter view.[38] Assuming we go beyond mere information provision, there are two principal ways to ameliorate the situation. The first approach is to provide the sort of education and advice that will allow people to make judicious decisions on their own. The second is to redesign DC pensions to allow savers to make good decisions with minimal intervention.

Is Education the Answer?

While education in a broader context will be revisited in the next chapter, a few words are in order now. Surely if future retirees receive some remedial education they will be better prepared to take care of their retirement accounts. While the evidence is weak and open to interpretation, researchers have documented a small payoff to financial education among DC plan members. The key question is: Does education cause behavior to change? Promisingly, some research documents that workplace financial education increases saving.[39]

Nevertheless, interpreting the evidence can be problematic for several reasons. For example, those attending educational seminars tend to save more—but where is the causality? Maybe savers are more likely to go to seminars. Also, when people attend seminars and fill out surveys of future intentions, afterward, while they may *say* they will change behavior—for example, an increase in deferrals—it is important to follow up and see that their procrastination has been successfully fought off and there is indeed a change.

There are a priori reasons to believe that education will be a tough sell. To see the problem, consider why university business students are normally quite receptive to education. For one thing, they have consciously elected to obtain an education. Also, persistent procrastination is not really an option for them, as exams loom on the horizon. Many DC plan members are not equally receptive to education. As was discussed in the previous chapter (in the context of investor types), many have little or no interest in personal finance. Also, the prod of a deadline does not exist for them—the deadline of interest to them, retirement, is quite far off to most of them. Now, this is less true for those approaching retirement, but if such individuals are just beginning to consider the matter carefully at this juncture, in most cases they have left it until too late—just like a university student in a corporate finance principles course "cracking open" the text for the first time the night before the exam.[40]

17.5   IMPROVEMENTS IN DC PENSION DESIGN

A number of commentators have suggested pension design mechanisms to steer individuals in the direction suggested by normative theory. Automatic enrollment is helpful in getting people to save. A program whereby people lock themselves into scheduled deferral increases is effective in inducing people to save more. To encourage people to save with appropriate risk exposure, one strategy is to utilize asset allocation-type funds, especially those designed to dynamically adjust asset allocation as individuals approach retirement.

AUTOMATIC ENROLLMENT

The most fundamental problem afflicting voluntary savings programs like DCs is that they are voluntary. This is why we find that older households (whose heads were born between 1931 and 1941) with DB pensions seem to have adequate income replacement ratios, and why there is now so much hand-wringing about tomorrow's (often DC) pensioners being egregiously ill-equipped for retirement.[41] First things first: it is important that people *begin* to save.

Brigitte Madrian and Dennis Shea have documented that **automatic enrollment**, a situation that exists when employees must *negatively* elect nonparticipation in a company retirement savings plan (as compared to the traditional approach where employees must *positively* elect participation in such a plan), is a powerful mechanism to get people started.[42] A Fortune 500 company decided to switch to automatic enrollment as of April 1, 1998. No other salient features were altered in its 401(k). Prior to the change, participation in the plan was limited to employees with at least one year of tenure. While 15% of pay could be contributed, the first 6% was eligible for a 50% company match. After April 1, 1998, two changes were made: first, all current employees were made immediately eligible, although they still required a year of tenure to qualify for the match; and, second, all new employees were immediately enrolled (unless they took active steps to do otherwise). For this latter group, the deferral rate was set at 3%. Additionally, though the company offered nine investment choices (which included a money market fund, a bond fund, a balanced fund, and several stock funds), the fund that received the money unless workers stated otherwise, that is, the default fund, was the money market fund.

As shown in Figure 17.4, the participation rate skyrocketed. To interpret, "NEW" workers were those hired in the first year under the auto-enrollment scheme. The "WINDOW" employees were current employees who became immediately eligible to join as of April 1, 1998, but without the required one-year tenure to receive the company match. And, finally, the "OLD" group had between one and two years of experience, which means they were already eligible and already receiving the company match if participating. Notice the stark differences in participation between the NEW and WINDOW groups: 86% versus 49%.[43] Clearly, auto-enrollment is effective in getting people to begin saving. The figure is also useful for illustrating a service effect. Even without auto-enrollment, most workers will eventually enroll, since, over time, they will realize the wisdom of retirement saving. By 20 years or more of service, 83% had joined, notably though a percentage still a little less than the NEW auto-enrolled group. So, for many, the advantages of auto-enrollment are confined to the early years of their career, but time compounding makes clear that these are important years for asset accumulation.

Despite the obvious advantages, there is an important problem with an auto-enrollment arrangement. Many of those so enrolled exhibit, through their inertia, "default" behavior—that is, they tend to stick with the default deferral rate and the default asset allocation. If the defaults are not chosen carefully, this can lead to insufficient saving and inappropriate risk taking. In the case of the company under study, a 3% deferral rate, though a start, will hardly lead to a well-funded

FIGURE 17.4 401(k) Participation by Tenure Subsequent to a Move to Auto-enrollment

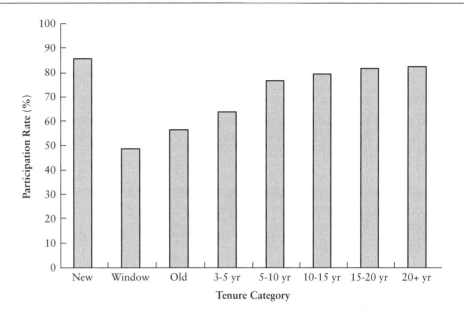

Source: Madrian, B. C., and D. F. Shea, 2001, "The power of suggestion: Inertia in 401(k) participation and savings behavior," *Quarterly Journal of Economics* 116, 1149–1187.

retirement. And an account fully invested in a money market account will not have the sort of risk profile needed to take advantage of time diversification and to move people to reasonable income replacement ratios. Further, note that to fully take advantage of the company match, 6% saving is required, so defaulters will only achieve half of the maximum match.[44] While those who would not have otherwise joined are still better off, worse off are those who would have joined anyway, but at a higher deferral rate and with more appropriate asset allocation. While some do get around to changing their behavior, endowment and endorsement effects pull in the other direction. Endowment effects may lead someone to think that her original (default) asset allocation is somehow ideal. And **endorsement effects** are present when an employee believes that the company itself is making an implicit recommendation in setting up the default in this particular fashion. Interestingly, Madrian and Shea note a kind of herding as well. Those plan participants hired before the switch, but who only become participants after the switch, are more likely to choose the money market account.

So, automatic enrollment does not seem to be the entire solution. As Madrian and Shea note, "to turn automatic enrollment from a win-lose proposition to a win-win proposition, employers must find ways to move employees into higher contribution rates and more aggressive strategies."[45] The next two sections address these two issues.

SCHEDULED DEFERRAL INCREASE PROGRAMS

As we have said, while automatic enrollment may be a step forward, there is a salient disadvantage—those auto-enrolled often do not alter their deferral rate. If the auto-rate is low (say 3%), the same inertia and procrastination that induce individuals to never join, or take their time in joining, a plan is likely to leave people at this low deferral rate indefinitely.

Richard Thaler and Shlomo Benartzi have argued for the use of **scheduled deferral increase programs (SDIPs)** to remedy this defect.[46] The goal of such programs is to not only convince people to save, but also to convince them to save a sufficient amount for a properly funded retirement. In a nutshell, firms employ financial counselors who endeavor to persuade workers to sign up for a program of deferral increases, which only begin to kick in at a future date. The essential ingredient is the sort of commitment mechanism that we have discussed previously. Recall, for example, that one way to lock oneself into exercising is to join a health club. Here the twist would be to sign a contract to join a health club that is only opening in (say) three months.

SDIPs are designed to capitalize on (rather than battle) the behavioral biases that exist in this area. Typically they have four features. First, employees are approached to consider signing on well in advance of the commitment device taking effect. Since people like to postpone unpleasantness (I will start exercising next week), this strategy plays into people's predisposition to do the right thing—just not right now. Second, the commitment device is designed to take effect with the employee's next pay raise. This plays on loss aversion and money illusion. We have discussed the former already. Those subject to the latter will think they are better off if their pay rises purely because of inflation—in fact, they will be confusing *nominal* and *real* (that is, inflation-adjusted) magnitudes. Since loss aversion is likely to make a cut in take-home pay because of a deferral increase appear unattractive, the trick is to match the deferral increase and a pay hike. For example, a 3.5% pay increase may occur at the same time as a 3% deferral increase. The take-home pay will go up slightly. In reality, if (say) 2% of the pay hike is to offset inflation (while the other 1.5% is productivity-based), then in actual fact there has been a 1.5% *real* pay cut. Some people miss this because of "money illusion," the tendency to confound nominal and real wage (and price) changes.[47] Third, deferral rate increases are scheduled to continue to occur on subsequent pay increase dates—until a preset maximum is reached. Inertia is the program's friend, as riders on the train are unlikely to actively ask to get off—especially when they can gradually see the benefits of participation in their growing account balances. Fourth, as is standard with 401(k)s, employees can change their minds at any time. While legally nothing else would be feasible, this feature does have the advantage of making it easier to convince people to sign up in the first place.

Thaler and Benartzi report on the use of SDIPs in several pilots. In one at a "midsize manufacturing company," an investment consultant was hired to advise 315 employees eligible for the retirement savings plan. Of these, 286 agreed to meet with him. Using commercial software designed to indicate what savings rate was required to get people on target, he advised people to move to this deferral rate. The one exception was when people seemed quite reluctant. In such cases, he

TABLE 17.2	AVERAGE SAVINGS RATES FROM AN SDIP PILOT				
	Those not contacting financial consultant	Those accepting recommended savings rate	Those joining SDIP	Those rejecting SDIP	All
No.	29	79	162	45	315
Pre-advice	6.6%	4.4%	3.5%	6.1%	4.4%
1st pay hike	6.5%	9.1%	6.5%	6.3%	7.1%
2nd pay hike	6.8%	8.9%	9.4%	6.2%	8.6%
3rd pay hike	6.6%	8.7%	11.6%	6.1%	9.8%
4th pay hike	6.2%	8.8%	13.6%	5.9%	10.6%

Thaler, R. H., and S. Benartzi. From "Save more tomorrow: Using behavioral economics to increase employee saving," in *Journal of Political Economy*, 2004, vol. 112, no. S1. © 2004 by The University of Chicago. All rights reserved.

suggested a deferral increase of no more than 5%. The advice of the investment consultant was accepted by 28% of the employees. The rest were then offered the chance to join the SDIP with deferral rate increases of 3% at every pay hike until the preset limit was reached. Of these people, 78% opted to try the SDIP.

The program worked as planned. Table 17.2 tells the story.[48] Those who were convinced to join the program went from a pre-advice savings rate of 3.5% to 6.5% after the first pay hike, 9.4% after the second pay hike, 11.6% after the third, and 13.6% after the fourth. These increments are less than 3% for two reasons. First, some were reaching the preset maximum. Second, some decided to opt out of the program mid-course. Nevertheless, they did not cut deferrals back to original levels, so they were still better off. Gratifyingly, though, 80% remained in the program through four pay raises. It is interesting to compare deferral profiles of those accepting the financial consultant's advice with those of individuals on the program. Initially, the former save much more, but, from this point on, inertia kicks in—negative inertia for those accepting the advice, because they never move beyond their initial deferral increase (recall that for many the recommendation was capped at 5%), and positive inertia for those on the SDIP, since to take no action was to passively accept future deferral increases.

ASSET ALLOCATION FUNDS

We have seen that employee-investors often do not seem to understand asset allocation. Moreover, they are prone to inertia. The first flaw implies that in the absence of advice they may choose a degree of risk taking that is very much inappropriate for their circumstances. The reason that inertia is problematic is that the appropriate degree of risk taking normally declines with age and proximity to retirement. To use the conventional wisdom often cited by financial planners, one should have an equity exposure equal to 100 minus one's age. As Figure 17.5 illustrates, this implies something very different for a 65-year-old than a 20-year-old.

FIGURE 17.5 Recommended Equity Exposure as a Function of Age

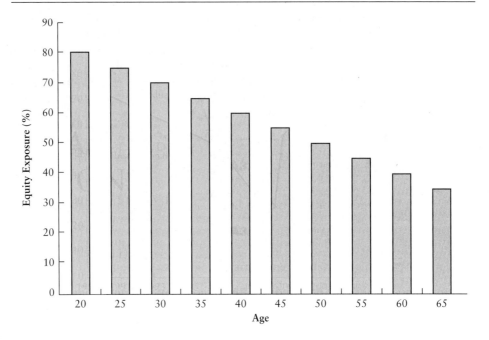

Note: Above is calculated as 100 minus age.

Let's say that a 30-year-old begins employment and is sophisticated enough to begin an adequate saving program with her 401(k). She receives good advice and chooses a set of funds aggregating to 70% equity exposure and 30% fixed-income exposure. Many providers offer a ladder of balanced funds that allow her to just select a single fund—here a 70/30 fund—that will provide her the risk taking that she is looking for. Other balanced funds in such menus could fall in equity-exposure increments of 10, yielding 100/0, 90/10, 80/20, ..., 20/80, 10/90, and 0/100 funds. Such funds are commonly called **lifestyle funds**.

Initially, all would be well and good. But with the passage of time, this investor's asset allocation would tend to stray from target for two reasons. First, after five years have passed, assuming no reallocation of assets and no asset growth, her equity exposure would be 5% too low. Second, exacerbating the latter is the fact that equity funds *on average* achieve higher growth than fixed-income funds due to the reward that markets offer investors for risk taking. So, in reality, after five years her equity exposure could easily be much more than 5% out of line. Now, historically, it has been left up to plan members (and sponsors through communication and education) to monitor portfolios and to effect appropriate asset allocation adjustments. The problem, of course, is inertia. Evidence of this is that the median number of asset allocation changes among DC plan members reported in one study was zero.[49]

One solution that the market has started to adopt is the so-called **life-cycle (or target date) funds.** The idea is quite simple. A single fund is chosen by the employee-investor, which is not only appropriate initially in its risk-taking stance, but which also *dynamically* adjusts its equity exposure with the passage of time. One company, for example, cleverly markets these funds using target retirement dates.[50] For example, a 2025 fund could have been purchased by someone in 2005 who was planning on retiring in 20 years. Initially, the equity exposure would have been in the neighborhood of 60%. After five years, it would drop to 55%, and so on, ending in 2025 with an equity exposure of about 40%. Such products are increasingly being offered by the industry.[51]

Moving toward the Ideal 401(k)

Of course no one really knows what the ideal 401(k) would look like. But, arguably, it would incorporate lessons from the previous three sections. We have seen the importance of defaults. Since many never stray from default behavior, the default should induce sufficient saving at an appropriate level of risk taking. Therefore, the default should be one of automatic enrollment (to get people started saving), graduated deferral increases up to a preset maximum (low enough at first to convince people to stay the course, but moving over time to a deferral rate sufficient to fund a reasonable income replacement ratio), and a suitable asset allocation fund as the investment vehicle. This way, those who never lift a finger would end up with a retirement plan that is roughly appropriate for them to reach their goals.

Of course one of the great advantages of 401(k)s is individual choice. An ideal 401(k) would create sufficient opportunity for such choice. Those wishing to take more active control over their retirement planning should be offered a menu of funds—both actively managed and indexed—which cover all asset allocation classes. This is especially important for those whose individual circumstances are such that the defaults are not necessarily optimal for their circumstances.

CHAPTER HIGHLIGHTS

1. In large part spurred by a corporate desire to control benefit costs, there has been a move in many countries to DC pensions where employee-investors must manage their own pension accounts.
2. The rise of the 401(k) in the United States is a prime example.
3. Classical economics assumes that people make good choices and follow through with them.
4. The first assumption is open to question given the great difficulty of the retirement saving problem.
5. The second assumption is also debatable because of such human traits as limited self-control and procrastination.

6. Many people seem to have time preferences described by a hyperbolic discount function, where the relative value of money today versus money in one period (whatever its length) is greater than the relative value of future money versus future money one period beyond.

7. Some employee-investors do not have a firm grasp of asset allocation, which is especially worrisome since this is likely the most important investment decision that future retirees have to make.

8. Education can help people make better decisions, but there are reasons to be skeptical about its effectiveness. For one thing, those having the most problems are often the ones least likely to participate.

9. Auto-enrollment has proven to be effective in getting people to begin a regular retirement savings program.

10. Scheduled deferral increase programs have also been useful in encouraging people to save an amount sufficient to move them toward their retirement goals.

11. Lifestyle and life-cycle funds are a good fit for many in that complicated asset allocation decisions can be painlessly avoided.

12. An ideal 401(k) would include both appropriate defaults and a selection of building block funds for those who want themselves to assemble their own portfolios.

DISCUSSION QUESTIONS AND PROBLEMS

1. Differentiate the following terms/concepts:

   a. DCs and DBs
   b. Auto-enrollment and SDIP programs
   c. Exponential and hyperbolic discount functions
   d. Deferral rate and income replacement rate

2. Sue is an exponential discounter. Her discount function which illustrates her preference for money at various points in time is characterized as follows:

$$\partial(t) = 1/(1.07)^t \text{ for } t = 0,1,2, \ldots$$

Bob on the other hand is a hyperbolic discounter. His discount function is:

$$\partial(t) = 1 \qquad\qquad \text{for } t = 0$$
$$= .8/(1.03)^{t-1} \quad \text{for } t = 1, 2, \ldots$$

a. What would Sue/Bob rather have: $1 today or $1.10 next year? Explain.
b. What would Sue/Bob rather have: $1 next year or $1.10 the year after that? Explain.

3. If employee-investors are unsophisticated and unlikely to be materially influenced by educational efforts, the best way to improve the welfare of employee-investors is pension design. Discuss.

4. Would you rather have had a DB or a DC in the summer of 2008? Explain.

5. Using the saving example in the text (Wendy Chan), calculate the income replacement ratio based on a deferral rate of 10% and an investment return on retirement savings of 3.5%. (All other assumed values remain the same.)

ENDNOTES

1 See Munnell, A. H., and A. Sunden, 2004, *Coming Up Short: The Challenge of 401(k) Plans*, (Brookings Institution Press, Washington, D.C.) for historical background. Most, but not all, DC-type pensions are 401(k)s, which, technically, are prescribed under clause 401(k) of the Internal Revenue Code. ERISA was primarily designed to strengthen workers' claims on benefits after several high-profile DB defaults. For international evidence, see Nyce, S. A., and S. J. Schieber, 2005, *The Economic Implications of Aging Societies: The Costs of Living Happily Ever After* (Cambridge University Press, Cambridge, U.K.); and *Financial Times*, 2003, *Defined Contributions: A Lot at Stake When the Switch Comes*, May 21. In some cases (e.g., Australia, Chile, and Sweden), DCs are important components of the *public* tier of pensions.

2 VanDerhei, J., and C. Copeland, 2004, "ERISA at 30: The decline of private-sector defined benefit promises and annuity payments? What will it mean?" *EBRI Issue Brief* (269).

3 Munnell, A. H., and A. Sunden, 2004, *Coming Up Short: The Challenge of 401(k) Plans* (Brookings Institution Press, Washington, D.C.).

4 VanDerhei, J., 2006, "Defined benefit plan freezes: Who's affected, how much, and replacing lost accruals," *EBRI Issue Brief* (291).

5 The number of DBs offering a lump sum on retirement is on the rise. As of 1995, 85% of workers in medium and large establishments who participated in a DB were not offered a lump sum distribution. By 2000, 43% were offered this opportunity. See VanDerhei, J., and C. Copeland, 2004, "ERISA at 30: The decline of private-sector defined benefit promises and annuity payments? What will it mean?" *EBRI Issue Brief* (269).

6 Pension payment "certainty" is not necessarily ironclad, only existing when government guarantees are in place. In the United States, private pension benefits are guaranteed by the Pension Benefits Guaranty Corporation. Companies must pay premiums for this insurance.

7 Waring, M. B., L. D. Harbert, and L. B. Siegel, 2000, "Mind the gap! Why DC plans underperform DB plans, and how to fix them," *Investment Insights (Barclays Global Investors)* 3 (no. 1, April).

8 Mitchell, O. S., and S. P. Utkus, 2003, "Company stock and retirement plan diversification," in O. S. Mitchell, and K. Smetters, eds., *The Pension Challenge: Risk Transfers and Retirement Income* (Oxford University Press, Oxford).

9 Benartzi, S., and R. H. Thaler, 2002, "How much is investor autonomy worth?" *Journal of Finance* 57, 1593–1616.

10 Sethi-Iyengar, S., G. Huberman, and W. Jiang, 2004, "How much choice is too much? Contributions to 401(k) retirement plans," in O. S. Mitchell, and S. P. Utkus, eds.: *Pension Design and Structure: New Lessons from Behavioral Finance* (Oxford University Press, New York).

11 When companies offer a match, not taking full advantage of it is tantamount to "leaving money on the table."

12 Ameriks, J., and S. P. Zeldes, 2001, "How do household portfolio shares vary with age?" Working paper (Columbia University).

13 Of course, it is difficult to say with certainty what the optimal or right choice is for an individual because we all have different preferences. In our discussion we presume that encouraging saving for retirement is the goal, though we recognize that not all would agree that this should be the goal.

14 See Laibson, D. I., A. Repetto, and J. Tobacman, 1998, "Self control and saving for

retirement," *Brookings Papers on Economic Activity* 1, 91–196 for numerous citations.

15　Beta is a constant factor needed to create two sections to the function. These functions and the parameter values are from Laibson, D. I., A. Repetto, and J. Tobacman, 1998, "Self control and saving for retirement," *Brookings Papers on Economic Activity* 1, 91–196. More technically, the second function is a quasi-hyperbolic function in that it only approximates a hyperbolic function. (It is used because it is more tractable.)

16　O'Donoghue, T., and M. Rabin, 1999, "Procrastination in preparing for retirement," in H. J. Aaron, ed., *Behavioral Dimensions of Retirement Economics* (Brookings Institution Press & Russell Sage Foundation, Washington, D.C. and New York).

17　See Laibson, D. I., A. Repetto, and J. Tobacman, 1998, "Self control and saving for retirement," *Brookings Papers on Economic Activity* 1, 91–196. Note that those with a predisposition to plan tend to be good savers (as reported by Ameriks, J., A. Caplin, and J. Leahy, 2003, "Wealth accumulation and the propensity to plan," *Quarterly Journal of Economics* 68, 1007–1048).

18　For the United Kingdom, see Banks, J., R. Blundell, and S. Tanner, 1998, "Is there a retirement-savings puzzle?" *American Economic Review* 88, 769–788. And for the United States, see Bernheim, B. D., J. Skinner, and S. Weinberg, 2001, "What accounts for the variation in retirement wealth among U.S. households?" *American Economic Review* 91, 832–857.

19　Loewenstein, G. F., D. Prelec, and R. Weber, 1999, "What, me worry? A psychological perspective on the economic aspects of retirement," in H. J. Aaron, ed., *Behavioral Dimensions of Retirement Economics* (Brookings Institution Press & Russell Sage Foundation, Washington, D.C. and New York).

20　Gilbert, D. T., 2006, *Stumbling on Happiness* (Alfred A. Knopf, New York).

21　See Brinson, G. P., L. R. Hood, and G. R. Beebower, 1986, "Determinants of portfolio performance," *Financial Analysts Journal* (July/August), 39–44; and Brinson, G. P., B. D. Singer, and G. R. Beebower, 1991, "Determinants of portfolio performance II: An update," *Financial Analysts Journal* (May/June), 40–48.

22　See Read, D., and G. Loewenstein, 1995, "Diversification bias: Explaining the discrepancy in variety seeking between combined and separated choices," *Journal of Experimental Psychology: Applied* 1, 34–49; and Simonson, I., 1990, "The effect of purchase quantity and timing on variety-seeking behavior," *Journal of Marketing Research* 27, 150–162.

23　Benartzi, S., and R. Thaler, 2001, "Naïve diversification strategies in defined contribution saving plans," *American Economic Review* 91, 79–98.

24　Deaves, R., 2005, "Flawed self-directed retirement account decision-making and its implications," *Canadian Investment Review* (Spring), 6–15.

25　Benartzi, S., and R. Thaler, 2001, "Naïve diversification strategies in defined contribution saving plans," *American Economic Review* 91, 79–98.

26　Huberman, G., and W. Jiang, 2006, "Offering vs. choice in 401(k) plans: Equity exposure and number of funds," *Journal of Finance* 61, 763–801.

27　See Bodie, Z., and M. J. Clowes, 2003, *Worry-free Investing: A Safe Approach to Achieving Your Lifetime Goals* (Pearson Education, Upper Saddle River, New Jersey); and Thaler, R. H., and J. P. Williamson, 1994, "College and endowment equity funds: Why not 100% equities?" *Journal of Portfolio Management* (Fall), 27–37.

28　Barsky, R. B., F. T. Juster, M. S. Kimball, and M. D. Shapiro, 1997, "Preference parameters and behavioral heterogeneity: An experimental approach in the Health and Retirement Study," *Quarterly Journal of Economics* 112, 537–579.

29 Bodie, Z., R. C. Merton, and W. F. Samuelson, 1992, "Labor supply flexibility and portfolio choice in a life-cycle model," *Journal of Economic Dynamics and Control* 16, 427–449.

30 To state the obvious, there is nothing "perfect" about this rule. Still, it is probably *reasonable* for *many* people.

31 See Ackert, L. F., B. K. Church, and B. Englis, 2002, "The asset allocation decision and investor heterogeneity: A puzzle?" *Journal of Economic Behavior and Organization* 47, 423–433; Agnew, J., P. Balduzzi, and A. Sundén, 2003, "Portfolio choice and trading in a large 401(k) plan," *American Economic Review* 93, 193–215; Ameriks, J., and S. P. Zeldes, 2001, "How do household portfolio shares vary with age?" Working paper (Columbia University); Bodie, Z., and D. B. Crane, 1997, "Personal investing: Advice, theory and evidence," *Financial Analysts Journal* 53 (Nov/Dec), 13–23; Faig, M., and P. M. Shum, 2004, "What explains household stock holdings?" Working paper; and Sundén, A. E., and B. J. Surette, 1998, "Gender differences in the allocation of assets in retirement savings plans," *American Economic Review* 88, 207–211. Ackert, Church, and Englis (2002) investigate a survey conducted by the Stanford Research Institute. Sundén and Surette (1998) and Faig and Shum (2004) explore the *Survey of Consumer Finances*. Bodie and Crane (1997), Ameriks and Zeldes (2001) and Agnew, Balduzzi, and Sundén (2003) perform clinical studies of actual asset allocation choices in 403(b)s or 401(k)s, with the first two papers focusing on TIAA-CREF plan participants and the latter on a company pension plan.

32 See Bhandari, G., and R. Deaves, 2006, "Misinformed and informed asset allocation decisions of self-directed retirement plan members," *Journal of Economic Psychology* 29, 473–490. This paper finds that those who signal lack of understanding by exhibiting asset allocation confusion are less likely to adjust their equity exposure as they move through their careers.

33 Ameriks, J., and S. P. Zeldes, 2001, "How do household portfolio shares vary with age?" Working paper (Columbia University).

34 Jagannathan, R., and N. R. Kocherlakota, 1996, "Why should older people invest less in stocks than younger people?" *Federal Reserve Bank of Minneapolis Quarterly Review* 20 (no. 3), 11–23.

35 Viceira, L. M., 2001, "Optimal portfolio choice for long-horizon investors with non-tradable labor income," *Journal of Finance* 56, 433–470.

36 Heaton, J., and D. Lucas, 2000, "Portfolio choice and asset prices: The importance of entrepreneurial risk," *Journal of Finance* 55, 1163–1198.

37 See Flavin, M., and T. Yamashita, 2002, "Owner-occupied housing and the composition of the household portfolio," *American Economic Review* 92, 345–362; and Faig, M., and P. M. Shum, 2002, "Portfolio choice in the presence of personal illiquid projects," *Journal of Finance* 57, 303–328.

38 Thaler, R. H., and C. R. Sunstein, 2003, "Libertarian paternalism," *American Economic Review* 93 (Papers & Proceedings), 175–179.

39 See Bernheim, B. D., and D. M. Garrett, 2003, "The effects of financial education in the workplace: Evidence from a survey of households," *Journal of Public Economics* 87, 1487–1519; and Lusardi, A., 2004, "Saving and the effectiveness of financial education," in O. S. Mitchell, and S. P. Utkus, eds., *Pension Design and Structure: New Lessons from Behavioral Finance* (Oxford University Press, New York).

40 Since education will be a hard sell, it is important to try to "optimize" it. See Chapter 18 for a discussion.

41 Gustman, A. L., and T. L. Steinmeier, 1998, "Effects of pensions on savings: Analysis with data from the Health and Retirement Study," Working paper (NBER).

42 See Madrian, B. C., and D. F. Shea, 2001, "The power of suggestion: Inertia in 401(k)

participation and savings behavior," *Quarterly Journal of Economics* 116, 1149–1187. This paper reports that as of 1999, only about 7% of 401(k) sponsors had automatic enrollment.

43 Actually, if one controls for tenure (which matters since people are more likely to join as they accumulate service), the WINDOW group had only 37% participation at the same point in their service.

44 While the match does not kick in until a year has elapsed, many will not get around to changing their deferral rate appropriately.

45 Ibid, p. 1185.

46 See Thaler, R. H., and S. Benartzi, 2004, "Save more tomorrow: Using behavioral economics to increase employee saving," *Journal of Political Economy* 112, S164–187. This paper coins the term SMarT ("save more tomorrow") for such SDIPs.

47 Shafir, E., P. Diamond, and A. Tversky, 1997, "Money illusion," *Quarterly Journal of Economics* 112, 341–374.

48 This table is reproduced from Thaler, R. H., and S. Benartzi, 2004, "Save more tomorrow: Using behavioral economics to increase employee saving," *Journal of Political Economy* 112, S164–187.

49 Ameriks, J., and S. P. Zeldes, 2001, "How do household portfolio shares vary with age?" Working paper (Columbia University).

50 Fidelity offers target date funds branded in this fashion.

51 Holden, S., and J. VanDerhei, 2005, "401(k) plan asset allocation, account balances, and loan activity in 2004," *EBRI Issue Brief* (269).

DEBIASING, EDUCATION, AND CLIENT MANAGEMENT

18.1   INTRODUCTION

Throughout this book we have seen that individual investors (not to mention more sophisticated ones) are subject to bias and emotion. The result can be portfolios that are not assembled optimally. In the last chapter we saw that employee-investors are perhaps in the most precarious position.

This chapter begins in Section 18.2 by looking at various debiasing strategies discussed in the psychology literature. These strategies can also be applied in the context of financial decision-making. One obvious strategy with some evidence of a payoff is education. In Section 18.3, we discuss how education can be enhanced if we have knowledge of the psychological mindset of the investor. The last section operationalizes this discussion for wealth managers whose clients may be subject to bias and emotion. This is particularly important for the asset allocation problem.

18.2   CAN BIAS BE ELIMINATED?

The psychology literature addresses the problem of bias and explores potential remedies. Let us begin by considering what is needed to eliminate bias.

STEPS REQUIRED TO ELIMINATE BIAS

Once people become "contaminated" by bias, that is, once their cognitive process has been influenced by less than rational factors, a number of steps must occur before the bias is successfully expunged. These steps are:

1. Awareness of bias
2. Motivation to eliminate bias
3. Direction and magnitude awareness of bias
4. Ability to eliminate bias.

Timothy Wilson, David Centerbar, and Nancy Brekke give an example of an interviewer who forms a negative impression of a minority job applicant.[1] While not certain, the interviewer suspects that part of this negative view might have been induced by past exposure to racial prejudice. Let's apply the paradigm. First, awareness of bias: the interviewer must become aware that unwanted processing has occurred. This can happen due to introspection or because of a credible "lay theory." An example of the latter could be: "It is well known that this group has suffered persistent racial prejudice, and many people not from this group are susceptible to it." Note that, if the bias is more subtle and cannot easily be ascribed to such a theory—say the interviewer has subconscious negative feelings toward left-handed individuals and the interviewee, rather than being from a racial minority, is from a "manual" minority—then it is unlikely to be detected.

Second, motivation: the interviewer must be motivated to correct the bias. This could be because the individual is a decent person who wants to do the right thing, or there could be fears of job dismissal or litigation if persistent improper patterns are uncovered.

Third, there needs to be awareness of the direction and magnitude of the bias. Since racial prejudice can cause one to harbor negative impressions, the direction is obvious, but the magnitude is not so easy to determine. It could be that the candidate was weak and his race had at most a slight negative impact on the interviewer's rating. Or, it could be that the candidate was quite good and bias materially damaged his prospects. The problem in the former case is that corrective matters might make the situation worse. Let's say that on a 10-point scale the applicant deserved a 5. There was, however, minor impact from bias that pushed the score down to 4.5. If the interviewer suspects significant bias and adjusts all the way up to 8, then overreaction has occurred, and the "corrected" score is even farther from the truth.

Fourth, ability: the interviewer has to be able to adjust his response, that is, he must have mental control. It is always possible that even though bias is suspected, the interviewer might not be able to disregard the negative impression so induced.

In the realm of financial markets, some of these conditions are easily met, others less so. Take the example of someone who slavishly chases past results at the cost of lost diversification. The first requirement, awareness, is a major hurdle. Many people are simply not aware of the power of the recency bias to influence their thinking. The second requirement, motivation, should be less of a problem. Obviously with money on the line people should be easily able to rouse themselves to action. The third requirement, direction and magnitude, is also problematic. The direction is obvious, but the magnitude less obvious. As we have discussed, it *does* make sense to look at (without being driven by) past performance, since it is a weak predictor of future performance. But subtlety must be exerted: while momentum has historically been a valid strategy, one must be careful to condition on the correct past return interval. The fourth requirement, ability, should be a fairly easy hurdle. One simply has to make the appropriate portfolio adjustments. The only difficulty is if the account is managed by an external party (e.g., a broker) who is part of the problem—this individual may attempt to provide counterarguments.

From this discussion, we see that bias elimination is a tricky process.[2] For this reason, exposure control, that is, managing one's environment so that the bias takes hold only with great difficulty, may be the best solution. In the context of the potential racial prejudice case, if the interviewer had never been exposed to statements or actions reflecting bias, then it is unlikely that any contamination would have occurred. The problem, though, is that such prejudice is often "learned" as a child. Still, as an adult, the interviewer can avoid listening to those who espouse biased views.

What about the investor subject to recency? The problem is that he is paying far too much attention to the recent past. The appropriate advice—counterintuitive, since it is wrong in most other domains, such as driving—is to pay less attention. He shouldn't check his stocks and brokerage accounts on a daily basis: well-spaced periodic intervals are better. In what follows, we discuss environmental control further.

STRATEGIES FOR HELPING THOSE AFFECTED BY BIAS

When we detect that somebody else is affected by bias, how can we help? Baruch Fischhoff suggests a taxonomy of **debiasing** strategies depending on the distinction between "perfectible judges" and "incorrigible judges."[3] The former can learn to overcome their biases, so for this group various remedial and educational measures are called for.

To eliminate unwanted behavior in the perfectible, the following means, in increasing order of intervention, are available:

1. Warn of problem
2. Describe problem
3. Provide personalized feedback
4. Train extensively.

Consider the ubiquitous problem of the miscalibration variant of overconfidence. One could first warn those required to make judgments that many people have difficulty coming up with confidence intervals of the appropriate width, without indicating the precise nature of the typical error. This sort of alert might lead to a concentration of mind. The next step is to directly state that most people tend to come up with intervals that are too narrow—in this sense, the mean member of the population is overconfident. Still, some will merely think that it is only *others* who are afflicted. Thus, the provision of personalized **feedback**, where people are tested and shown to be miscalibrated, is a good next step.[4] Finally, extensive training can move people in the direction of proper calibration. A number of studies have validated the efficacy of the latter approach.[5] One training technique that has been demonstrated to be useful is having people list reasons why their preferred answers might be wrong.[6]

How should we deal with incorrigible judges? To eliminate unwanted behavior in this group, the following means are available:

1. Replace them
2. Recalibrate their responses
3. Build error into your planning.

As an example of the second, researchers have proposed a technique to externally debias the predictions of overconfident forecasters, provided one has a history of their answers.[7] Suppose overconfidence manifests itself in potential excessive optimism (or, perhaps, pessimism) and miscalibration. Suppose you have a time series of some-body's forecasts of quarterly GDP growth over the previous 10 years. In addition to providing point estimates, the individual has also been required to provide 90% con-fidence intervals. Say for next month the expert predicts L, X, and U, which are the 90% lower bound, the point estimate, and the 90% upper bound for the change in interest rates over the next month. How might we change these numbers to reflect past experience? Let's assume that on average the true value (X^*) has been different from the point estimate (X) by a factor β. Then the "debiased" point estimate, X^*, is:

18.1
$$X^* = \beta X$$

As an example, suppose average GDP growth has been 2% (annualized), but the forecaster has on average predicted 2.5%. This implies $\beta = 0.8$. If for the next quarter the prediction is 1%, it should be adjusted as follows:

18.2
$$X^* = 0.8 * 1\% = 0.8\%$$

Further, the upper interval (the upper bound minus the point estimate) historically has been too narrow by a factor of $\alpha(U)$. Then the debiased upper interval would be:

18.3
$$U^* - X^* = \alpha(U) * (U - X)$$

Similarly, the appropriately debiased lower interval would be:

18.4
$$L^* - X^* = \alpha(L) * (L - X)$$

Say $\alpha(U) = \alpha(L) = 1.5$. This means that both the upper part of the confidence inter-val and the lower part would both have to be expanded by 50%, which in turn means that the entire confidence interval would have to be expanded by 50%. Assume U = 2% and L = 0%, so U − L = 2%. The adjusted interval would have to be increased to 3%. This means that the **debiased confidence interval** would now be $U^* = 2.3\%$ and $L^* = -0.7\%$.

With these adjustments, while the expert will still make mistakes, her adjusted forecasts will at least have the appropriate amount of optimism/pessimism and be properly calibrated. While recalibration can in principle be effective in such circum-stances, if one lacks the required information to perform it and yet is aware that significant error is likely to occur, then mistakes have to be planned for. One approach could be to solicit alternate views or forecasts.

18.3   DEBIASING THROUGH EDUCATION

We now turn to how education can be used to debias people as they make finan-cial decisions. We will see that psychology continues to be useful in this regard.

Psychographic Profiling, Personality Types, and Money Attitudes

Some important questions in the context of financial educational design are the following. Which people are having the most difficulty? Who are those most subject to behavioral bias? Do they have a specific demographic profile? Do they fall into certain personality groups? **Psychographic profiling**, a common marketing technique, is the process of assigning individuals to groups based on personality, attitudes, values, and beliefs. It is of use in this context because, if we know what types of people are susceptible to what types of problems, we can channel our energies appropriately.

Probably the best-known psychographic profiling technique is the Myers-Briggs Type Indicator personality assessment.[8] According to Myers-Briggs, after filling out a questionnaire, people can be slotted into one of 16 **personality types.** This is operationalized by determining where people fall on the following four key attribute scales:

1. E vs. I (Extrovert vs. Introvert): How do you interact with the world?
2. S vs. N (Sensing vs. Intuitive): What kind of information do you notice?
3. T vs. F (Thinking vs. Feeling): How do you make decisions?
4. J vs. P (Judging vs. Perceiving): Do you act in a structured fashion or spontaneously?

Where people are situated across these types has been shown to be a useful predictor of such behavioral flaws as overconfidence and optimism, and may be more revealing of true risk tolerance than standard risk tolerance questionnaires.[9] The ESTP (extroverted-sensing-thinking-perceiving) personality type tends to be the least risk averse and most overconfident (with ENTP, ESTJ, ISTP, and ESFP coming in somewhat behind). On the other hand, the INFJ (introverted-intuitive-feeling-judging) personality type tends to be the most risk averse and least overconfident (again with ENFJ, INFP, INTJ, and ISFJ tending to a lesser extent in those directions).

Other personality tests have been investigated in a financial context. One example is the Keirsey Temperament Sorter, which classifies people into four basic temperament groups: guardians, artisans, rationals, and idealists.[10] Guardians tend to be cautious, rule-oriented managers; artisans are compulsive and competitive; idealists are quite concerned with growth and personal development; and rationals are scientifically inclined problem-solvers. Research has shown that one's Keirsey Temperament is a useful predictor of risk tolerance and the preference for domestic versus international securities.[11]

Psychographic procedures have been designed specifically for a financial setting. The main approach is to attitudinally segment respondents based on measurable attributes according to their **money attitude.** Value added is available to the extent that money personality can explain investor behavior over and above pure demographics. A good example is research conducted by money management company Vanguard using a statistical technique known as cluster analysis to assign DC plan members to different money personality groups.[12]

The Vanguard study uses a series of questions that focus on factors relating to interest in retirement and financial planning, savings behavior, optimism, and risk taking. The end result is the following five segments (with sample percentages indicated in brackets):

1. Successful planners (21%)
2. Up-and-coming planners (26%)
3. Secure doers (20%)
4. Stressed avoiders (19%)
5. Live-for-today avoiders (14%)

Successful planners are older and wealthier. Possessing a vision of retirement, they have clear goals and an interest in retirement planning. They enjoy dealing with finances, and are optimistic that they will meet their retirement goals. Disciplined savers, they are comfortable with equity risk taking, and are willing to take on significant risk for higher return.

Up-and-coming planners could be viewed as successful planners in training. Younger and a little more uncertain than successful planners, they still enjoy planning and dealing with finances. They are not quite ready to meet retirement goals, but are optimistic they will eventually be able to do so. Disciplined savers, they are willing to assume some risk for higher return.

The next segment, the secure doers, tend to be older and wealthier than average. Their vision of retirement is less goal focused than either shade of planner, nor do they really enjoy financial planning and dealing with finances. Optimistic that they will meet their retirement goals, they are willing savers. They are more reluctant to take on risk for higher return than planners.

Stressed avoiders tend to be subject to regret. Most of their information tends to come from the plan provider and employer. Worried about the future and not very goal oriented, they are confused about financial planning and dealing with finances in general. Pessimistic about whether they will successfully meet retirement goals, their savings behavior is characterized by confusion and worry. Also, they tend to lack confidence in their investment skills.

Finally, live-for-today avoiders, who tend to be younger than the other groups, are not focused on the future. They have little interest in financial planning and dealing with finances. For them retirement is off the radar screen. They derive little intrinsic satisfaction from saving. As far as risk taking goes, they have a middle-of-the-road attitude. As Figure 18.1 shows, these groups can be put on a **planner-avoider continuum,** with successful **planners** and live-for-today **avoiders** occupying the poles. For most of our remaining discussion, a coarse distinction between planners and avoiders will suffice.

FIGURE 18.1 Planner-Avoider Continuum

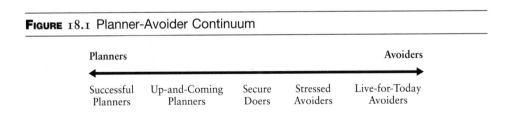

Supporting this attitudinal segmentation work is recent evidence that planners behave differently from avoiders in their savings and investment behavior. If planners actively consider their financial future and the adequacy of their current state of preparedness, they are likely to take steps when any deficiency is detected. Indeed, research has shown that those with a planner mindset tend to be much better at wealth accumulation.[13] Additionally, planners are more comfortable taking on risk than avoiders.[14] Who are the planners? As suggested by the work by Vanguard and corroborated elsewhere, older, wealthier males (especially those owning a home) are more likely to be planners.[15]

OPTIMIZING EDUCATION

We have seen that people are subject to behavioral bias and this bias can lead them astray. As suggested before, for those open to improvement (and it is to be hoped that most are in this category), education may be a useful strategy. One form of education is simply communicating to individuals that they are prone to certain types of bias, and suggesting where these biases are likely to lead them. The idea is that if forewarned, people will adjust.

Books on behavioral finance designed for the mass audience, a good example being John Nofsinger's *Investment Madness: How Psychology Affects Your Investing and What to Do About It*, sometimes try to accomplish this task.[16] In his chapter "Battling your biases," a checklist of major biases is given, along with the likely effect on investment behavior and consequences. The reader is also presented with a series of strategies, such as utilizing quantitative screens and controlling the investment environment. It is argued that such strategies may be helpful in minimizing the problem. As an example of the latter, the reader is instructed to check and trade stocks no more often than once per month and to review the entire portfolio no more than annually. This will mitigate the effect of short-term fluctuations in price, which, since many of these will be downward, can trigger loss aversion, regret and fleeing to safety.

Professional providers of financial education want their product to be as effective as possible. One way in which education can be made more effective is through **customization** for the relevant audience. This is an especially important issue for those designing educational materials for the quickly growing DC pension plan marketplace. As the previous chapter made clear, many members of these plans are quite unsophisticated employee-investors. Still, within this group, planners tend to be on fairly solid ground. Their level of preparedness will likely be little impacted by the education that they are (or are not) exposed to. Avoiders on the other hand are the group that needs to be reached out to. For this reason, education in DC plans should cater to avoiders.

If education is to have any impact for avoiders, it must play to their strengths. Avoiders are more likely to be influenced by what is known as an "adult-based learning approach."[17] The idea is that education works better if the focus is on the learner, not the information. The intention is to engage members as goal-directed and self-regulated learners, not fact digesters, and to connect principles to personal perceptions and experience. Avoiders may not have much in the way of financial acumen or interest, but, like the rest of us, they are armed with rich histories.

In one test of this approach, performed at CIGNA Retirement and Investment Services, call-in agents, who normally answered fairly mundane questions about member DC pensions, were trained to engage callers in a discussion of the benefits of saving and the current deferral rate of the caller.[18] This was not done in a lecturing mode, but, rather, in an experiential approach. They became "educators in disguise," as it were. Deferrals increased dramatically.

Another realm where customization can be used is retirement planning Web sites.[19] First, it is important to get avoiders to visit the sites. Barriers should be minimized. For example, given the inertia and procrastination of avoiders, it is better to have an active link in an e-mail informing participants about a Web site than to inform people of this by surface mail. Once there, it is important to keep avoiders there so they actually use the available tools. Whereas planners are comfortable with a Web site replete with data, such an approach is likely to turn off many avoiders. How can avoiders be encouraged to make use of such facilities? To appeal to an avoider, the front end of a Web site should be kept simple, appealing, and directive. Complexities appealing to planners can be placed one or more levels down.

Can avoiders be made into planners through financial education? To some extent, it is likely you are either born a planner or an avoider—that is, such a tendency may in large part be hardwired and personality-based. But it is also likely that planning may be somewhat amenable to educational effort. For example, one study found that participants in a workshop to improve decision-making skills showed a significant increase in planning attributes.[20] Other researchers document that financial education at the high school level can foster the ability to develop the saving habit. This suggests that the teaching of planning tools, such as budgeting, can change behavior.[21] To conclude this section, those employers and pension providers who are providing education and advice through seminars and Web sites while trying to cater to the avoider clientele are likely assisting their employees, though there is certainly scope for improvement in the latter regard.

18.4   CLIENT MANAGEMENT USING BEHAVIORAL FINANCE

In this section the focus is on how a financial advisor can use behavioral finance to facilitate the asset allocation decision for a client. The other important functions that a good advisor manages are not addressed. We begin with the traditional approach to the asset allocation decision in order to see why change may be in order.

TRADITIONAL PROCESS OF ASSET ALLOCATION DETERMINATION

The previous chapter reviewed the normative determinants of asset allocation, and the fact that unsophisticated investors, if left to their own devices, sometimes take on an inappropriate amount of risk. It was argued that model portfolios, appropriate defaults, and asset allocation funds can serve to channel people into appropriate risk stances. Often the first step will be for an individual to fill out a questionnaire to measure how much risk should be assumed. Questionnaires are designed to ascertain an investor's **risk tolerance**, which is a function of both **risk capacity** and **risk attitude**. To clarify the difference, risk capacity referes to the amount of risk that is appropriate for an *average* individual with the same age, retirement plans, income, liquidity needs, and so on, as the respondent. Risk attitude, on the other hand, is best viewed as an adjustment factor, reflecting to what extent the *specific* individual wishes to deviate from capacity because of personal preference and psychological factors.[22] The end result is a risk score that can be mapped on to a suggested asset allocation. Thinking in terms of the stock-bond mix, those with higher scores are able to withstand higher levels of equity exposure.[23]

Let's call the asset allocation solution coming from such questionnaires **subjective risk**, since it is based in part on individuals' attitudes and beliefs toward risk. This can be distinguished from **objective risk**, which is derived from *actual* investment decisions as reflected in the percentage of risky assets in overall portfolios.[24] While the two forms often give similar results, there are frequent divergences, leading to the question of which is better. In fact, both forms have potential problems.[25] While it is natural to prefer what is actually done to statements made (actions speak louder than words), objective risk is flawed, principally by ignorance and inertia. Ignorance can lead to investment choices whose risk is out of line with preferences. And the lack of rebalancing induced by inertia can cause allocations to differ from intentions as markets move up and down.

So, maybe subjective risk is better. How comfortable should we be with answers from these risk questionnaires? Problematically, the results can err either because the respondent is flawed or because the instrument is flawed. First, focusing on the former, people often have difficulty understanding risk, and hence they don't really know how to answer the scoring questions. Most commonly, people have great difficulty in seeing that risk is very much horizon-specific. In one experimental study, employees at a firm offering a defined contribution pension were asked to allocate their money between two funds, labeled "A" and "B."[26] Despite the neutrality of the language, the information presented for these funds was based on historical data for a broad U.S. stock market index and 5-year Treasury bonds. The experimental treatment was to display to one group a return distribution for each asset class in terms of 1-year returns, and, to the second group, return distributions in terms of 30-year returns. The authors of the study conjectured that, because of loss aversion, the average allocation going to the stock fund would be much higher when people were shown 30-year return distributions compared to the case where people saw distributions for a 1-year horizon. The experimental evidence proved them right.

Is this study merely an academic curiosity? Far from it. One common type of question seen in many risk questionnaires asks people how they would feel about and react to significant short-term portfolio losses. Something like the following is commonly asked: "Your stock portfolio has lost $x\%$ of its value over the past year. How would you act (with choices ranging from "sell everything" to "buy more stock")?" The problem with such questions is that they validate in the investor's mind that it is appropriate to fixate on short-term volatility when the real concern should be horizon-specific risk versus return. Admittedly, one can argue that such questions have to be asked, because, if those who are excessively nervous about volatility are corralled into serpentine investments, their tendency to feel snake-bit when the market inevitably moves south may cause them to radically and permanently adjust their equity exposure. This is a valid concern.

Questionnaires can also produce poor results because the instrument is flawed. Principally, they may lack validity and reliability.[27] Validity is the extent to which a questionnaire actually measures what it claims to measure, while reliability is an indication of how consistent its results are. To attain validity, the right questions must be asked. So since we need to explore capacity, in a good questionnaire, age and proximity to retirement will play a leading role. For example, a typical question is: "In how many years do you plan to retire?" Space permitting, it may also be judicious to bring in such factors as income and other investments. After such capacity issues are covered, normally a good portion of the questions will attempt to uncover the respondent's personal risk attitude, with a view to adjusting upward or downward the amount of risk taking that an examination of capacity alone would suggest. To strive for reliability, the trick is to ask appropriate questions in sufficient quantity. Quantity matters since the impact of a misunderstood question will be magnified if it is only one of a few.

USING BEHAVIORAL FINANCE TO REFINE PROCESS

Given all the problems alluded to in the previous section, it is natural to look for help. Some suggest that behavioral finance can be utilized by financial advisors not only to enhance the relationship between the client and the advisor but also to improve the process of portfolio selection. To the extent that a particular client's biases are known to the advisor, the advisor can react accordingly. As a leading example of this approach, Daniel Kahneman and Mark Riepe have come up with a series of questions that can be assembled as a kind of behavioral test to be given to clients in order to tease out the particular biases to which the client in question is most prone.[28] They can also first be used by the advisor to see if she herself is biased. One example from their article is:

> Which of the following sequences is more likely to occur when a coin is tossed —HHHTTT or HTHTTH?

The answer is both are equally likely. But to those who might be prone to over-react to chance events (such as recent performance), the first will *seem* less likely. Kahneman and Riepe advise people who are prone to this blind spot to:

- Ask yourself whether you have real reasons to believe that you know more than the market.
- Before making an active decision, consider the possibility that the trade is based on random factors. List the reasons why it isn't before making the trade.

Notice that the last sentence uses the disconfirming evidence debiasing strategy described earlier.

Michael Pompian argues that the main result of learning about how a client's psychological constitution and biases should be to use this enhanced understanding to improve the asset allocation process.[29] Suppose that there is divergence between subjective risk (obtained from the client filling out a questionnaire) and objective risk, either based on the current portfolio composition, or based on what the client wants the current portfolio to look like. For concreteness, let us work in terms of the stock-bond mix, and assume that, while the client's subjective risk stance calls for a 60% equity exposure, she actually desires only a 30% allocation. The question is, what should the wealth manager do about this? Pompian poses the following questions: When should biases be moderated (i.e., counteracted), and when should they be adapted to (i.e., accommodated)? His solution is to espouse two principles:

> Principle 1: Moderate biases in less wealthy clients. And adapt to biases in wealthier clients.
>
> Principle 2: Moderate cognitive biases. And adapt to emotional biases.

Consider the thinking behind the first principle. A big risk for the less wealthy in investing for retirement is outliving one's assets—not short-term volatility. If, for example, loss aversion is causing an investor to shy away too much from equity risk, while a wealthier investor with the same bias would still have sufficient resources in retirement, the same is not necessarily true in the case of a less wealthy investor. For this reason, it is better to try to convince the less wealthy investor to adjust his thinking. Educating him on the fact that many are subject to loss aversion, but that over the long run poor markets tend to be moderated by good markets, is a step in the right direction.

As for the second principle, the thinking here is that biases (both cognitive and judgmental) are more easily thwarted by appropriate education than emotion. Emotion, deep-seated in the limbic system, is a much tougher nut to crack. If it is emotional considerations that have caused an inappropriate view on risk taking, it is often best for the advisor to adapt to these views. Assuming that lower risk than is normatively called for is desired by the client, if he is pushed into riskier investments against his emotional predisposition, he will be more likely to change course (and even fire the advisor despite good advice) when markets inevitably turn sour.

Using these principles, the advisor channels her client into the "best practical allocation." This is the allocation that, while perhaps suboptimal, is as close to optimal as one can get without running the risk of the client "changing horses" halfway through the race.

While Pompian's approach has some strengths, it does embody one salient weakness. This is its embedded assumption that the "best" asset allocation is the one coming from a risk questionnaire. Previously we discussed the pitfalls of such questionnaires. We also made the point that normative theory, while helpful, does not necessarily yield the perfect answer. Perhaps the "second best" solution is to utilize a weighted average of subjective and normative (with the weights a function of the confidence one has in these methods).

While the use of behavioral finance in client management is in its infancy, many in the wealth management industry are coming around to the view that an understanding of the biases and emotions that their clients—not to mention they themselves—are subject to can only lead to improved advisor-investor relationships and managed portfolios that better suit clients' goals while, when necessary, adapting to particular preferences and psychology.

CHAPTER HIGHLIGHTS

1. Successful debiasing requires awareness of bias, motivation, awareness of direction and magnitude of bias, and the ability to do what is needed.
2. Since debiasing is a difficult process, environmental control designed to prevent a bias from ever taking root is wise whenever possible.
3. To perfect judges, the following steps can be effective: warning of the problem, describing the problem, providing personalized feedback, and undertaking extensive training.
4. There is abundant evidence that people can be grouped by personality type. Well-known examples are Myers-Briggs and the planner-avoider continuum.
5. Education can be improved by adapting it to the personality types and money attitudes of the individual to be educated.
6. Traditional asset allocation is operationalized by the "know your client" strategy of having the client fill out a risk questionnaire.
7. Risk attitude is one's attitude with respect to risk taking. Risk capacity measures one's ability to withstand market shocks, and is largely a function of age and proximity to retirement. Putting them together, we have risk tolerance.
8. The appropriate asset allocation is a function of both risk attitude and risk capacity.
9. Neither subjective risk nor objective risk (based on actual allocations) is an ideal indicator of the appropriate asset allocation.
10. Knowing clients' personality types, money attitudes, and the biases that they are most susceptible to can lead to improved advisor-investor relationships and managed portfolios that better suit goals to outcomes.

DISCUSSION QUESTIONS AND PROBLEMS

1. Differentiate the following terms/concepts:

    a. Personality types and money attitudes
    b. Planners and avoiders
    c. Moderating and adapting to biases
    d. "Perfectible judges" and "incorrigible judges"

2. Say the level of the market as measured by the Dow Jones Industrial Average is currently at 12,000. A forecaster has made a prediction of 13,300 for the level of the market in one year, along with a 95% confidence interval whose lower bound is 12,500 and whose upper bound is 14,500. You know from experience that this particular forecaster tends to be both excessively optimistic and miscalibrated. Describe how you might debias this individual. Give a numerical example (making up relevant numbers as appropriate).

3. What steps must occur before bias can be successfully expunged? Describe the process.

4. Risk tolerance comes from risk capacity and risk attitude. What are the major determinants of risk capacity and risk attitude?

5. Describe how educational efforts should be directed towards avoiders.

ENDNOTES

1 Wilson, T. D., D. B. Centerbar, and N. Brekke, 2002, "Mental contamination and the debiasing problem," in T. Gilovich, D. Griffin, and D. Kahneman, eds., *Heuristics and Biases: The Psychology of Intuitive Judgment* (Cambridge University Press, Cambridge, U.K.).

2 Sometimes one hears the term "decontamination."

3 Fischhoff, B., 1982, "Debiasing," in D. Kahneman, P. Slovic, and A. Tversky, eds., *Judgment under Uncertainty: Heuristics and Biases* (Cambridge University Press, Cambridge, U.K.).

4 In one exercise, a decision support system is formulated to provide remedial feedback to investors exhibiting bias. See Bhandari, G., R. Deaves, and K. Hassanein, 2007, "Using decision support systems to debias investors," *Decision Support Systems* 46, 399–410.

5 See Fischhoff, B., 1982, "Debiasing," in D. Kahneman, P. Slovic, and A. Tversky, eds., *Judgment under Uncertainty: Heuristics and Biases* (Cambridge University Press, Cambridge, U.K.), for numerous references.

6 Koriat, A., S. Lichtenstein, and B. Fischhoff, 1980, "Reasons for confidence," *Journal of Experimental Psychology: Human Learning and Memory* 6, 107–118.

7 Clemen, R. T., and K. C. Lichtendahl Jr., 2002, "Debiasing expert overconfidence: A Bayesian calibration model," Working paper.

8 For a discussion of Myers-Briggs, see Larsen, R. J., and D. M. Buss, 2008, *Personality Psychology*, 3rd ed. (McGraw-Hill, New York).

9 Pompian, M. M., and J. M. Longo, 2004, "A new paradigm for practical application of behavioral finance: Creating investment programs based on personality type and gender to produce better investment results," *Journal of Wealth Management* (Fall), 1–7.

10 Keirsey, D., 1998, *Please Understand Me II: Temperament, Character and Intelligence* (Prometheus Nemesis Book Company, Del Mar, California).

11 See Statman, M., and V. Wood, 2004, "Investment temperament," Working paper. Aside from Myers-Briggs and Keirsey, another example is the Values and Lifestyles system developed by the Stanford Research Institute; and Ackert, L. F., B. K. Church, and B. Englis, 2002, "The asset allocation decision and investor heterogeneity: A puzzle?" *Journal of Economic Behavior and Organization* 47, 423–433.

12 See Marconi, C. M., and S. P. Utkus, 2002, "Using 'money attitudes' to enhance retirement communications," Working paper (Vanguard Center for Retirement Research); and MacFarland, D. M., C. D. Marconi, and S. P. Utkus, 2004, "'Money attitudes' and retirement plan design: One size does not fit all," in O. S. Mitchell and S. P. Utkus, eds., *Pension Design and Structure: New Lessons from Behavioral Finance* (Oxford University Press, New York).

13 Ameriks, J., A. Caplin, and J. Leahy, 2003, "Wealth accumulation and the propensity to plan," *Quarterly Journal of Economics* 68, 1007–1048.

14 Deaves, R., T. Veit, G. Bhandari, and J. Cheney 2007, "The savings and investment decisions of planners: An exploratory study of college employees," *Financial Services Review* 16, 117–33.

15 Ibid.

16 Nofsinger, J., 2001, *Investment Madness: How Psychology Affects Your Investing and What to Do About It* (Prentice Hall, Upper Saddle River, New Jersey).

17 Saliterman, V., and B. G. Sheckley, 2004, "Adult learning principles and pension participant behavior," in O. S. Mitchell and S. P. Utkus, eds., *Pension Design and Structure: New Lessons from Behavioral Finance* (Oxford University Press, New York).

18 Ibid.

19 Scott, J., and G. Stein, 2004, "Retirement security in a DC world: Using behavioral finance to bridge the expertise gap," in O. S. Mitchell and S. P. Utkus, eds., *Pension Design and Structure: New Lessons from Behavioral Finance* (Oxford University Press, New York).

20 See Mann, L., G. Beswick, P. Allouache, and M. Ivey, 1989, "Decision workshops for the improvement of decision making skills and confidence," *Journal of Counseling and Development* 67, 478–481, for details.

21 Bernheim, D., D. Garrett, and D. Maki, 2001, "Education and saving: The long-term effects of high school curriculum mandates," *Journal of Public Economics* 80, 435–465.

22 Some argue that the two risk metrics should not be combined on the same questionnaire. See Roszkowski, M. J., G. Davey, and J. E. Grable, 2005, "Insights from psychology and psychometrics on measuring risk tolerance," *Journal of Financial Planning* (April), 66–77. As for using risk attitude for the psychological construct and risk tolerance as an amalgam of risk attitude and risk capacity. Roszkowski, Davey, and Grable state that the majority of planners and their clients use risk tolerance as it is used in the chapter.

23 Typically, different answers to the questions are assigned points, and the resultant sum is mapped on to a particular asset allocation. For example, just thinking in terms of the stock-bond mix, a "75" might be mapped on to a 60–80% equity share.

24 See Hallahan, T. A., R. W. Faff, and M. D. McKenzie, 2004, "An empirical investigation of personal financial risk tolerance," *Financial Services Review* 13, 57–78, who compare subjective and objective risk tolerance. Regardless of the type of risk tolerance assessed, it seems that researchers do not necessarily have a consensus regarding the fundamental nature of humans' risk-taking behavior. Some consider an individual's risk tolerance as a stable personality trait—see Hanna, S., and P. Chen, 1997, "Subjective and objective risk tolerance: Implications for optimal portfolios," *Financial Counseling and Planning* 8(2), 17–26; whereas others view it as dynamic and underscore the potential influences of such factors as experiences, knowledge, and social interaction in changing its level—see Baker, H. K., and J. R. Nofsinger, 2002, "Psychological biases of investors," *Financial Services Review* 11, 97–116.

25 One could say that a third variety of risk tolerance is "normative" risk tolerance, namely the risk taking that an individual *should* take on as function of his/her stage of life, preferences, and other considerations. While normative risk tolerance is on the surface the ideal, it does not provide complete and definitive answers. It is incomplete because, while we need both an investor's risk capacity and her risk attitude, it only speaks to the former. And normative risk tolerance is not definitive simply because, as the previous chapter made clear, while researchers have been devoting great attention to the problem during the last number of years, there appears to be as yet no clear consensus.

26 Benartzi, S., and R. H. Thaler, 2002, "How much is investor autonomy worth?" *Journal of Finance* 57, 1593–1616.

27 See Roszkowski, M. J., G. Davey, and J. E. Grable, 2005, "Insights from psychology and psychometrics on measuring risk tolerance," *Journal of Financial Planning* (April), 66–77, for a discussion.

28 See Kahneman, D., and M. Riepe, 1998, "Aspects of investor psychology," *Journal of Portfolio Management* 24 (Summer), 52–65. Another lengthy exercise in this vein is Pompian, M., 2006, *Behavioral Finance and Wealth Management: How to Build Optimal Portfolios That Account for Investor Biases* (John Wiley & Sons, Hoboken, New Jersey).

29 Pompian, M., 2006, *Behavioral Finance and Wealth Management: How to Build Optimal Portfolios That Account for Investor Biases* (John Wiley & Sons, Hoboken, New Jersey).

MONEY MANAGEMENT

PART VIII

CHAPTER 19   Behavioral Investing

CHAPTER 20   Neurofinance and the Trader's Brain

BEHAVIORAL INVESTING | CHAPTER 19

19.1 INTRODUCTION

In this chapter we consider **behavioral investing**, the attempt to enhance portfolio performance by applying lessons learned from behavioral finance. Based on Chapter 13, it might seem that the process is an easy one. There we discussed evidence that momentum and reversal, as well as the value advantage, were well supported empirically, both in different sample periods and in different national stock markets. Moreover, these anomalies also had a firm behavioral foundation based on theoretical models. Improving portfolio performance by tilting toward stocks embodying these attributes seems appropriate based on this evidence.

We begin in Section 19.2 by looking at several reasons why matters are not as simple as one might initially believe: anomaly attenuation, style peer groups, and style investing. In the following section, we discuss how investors can further improve performance, not just by capitalizing on anomalies in isolation, but by both combining them and by incorporating other screens. In Section 19.4, we move beyond this to explore multiple screens. In the penultimate section, we consider style rotation, the attempt to time style returns. Finally, in Section 19.6, we ask whether there is any evidence that behavioral investing can lead to return enhancement.

19.2 ANOMALY ATTENUATION, STYLE PEER GROUPS, AND STYLE INVESTING

William Schwert, writing in 2002, showed that a number of **anomalies**, once reported in the academic literature, either **attenuated** or fully disappeared afterward.[1] He cited as examples the small-firm effect, the January effect (the tendency for returns to be higher in the month of January), the weekend effect (the tendency for returns to be lower on Monday), and the value advantage.

Does that mean that managers should never expect persistence in anomalies? Anomaly dissipation is exactly what we expect to happen in a world that, though not always perfectly efficient, has a tendency to move in that direction via remedial arbitrage activity once information is disseminated. Anomalies, however, that have been argued to be risk factors, in particular value and firm size, should *not* disappear, because, under a risk story, they are not anomalies at all but rather fair compensation for risk borne. In addition, it should be noted that while the value advantage declined in the late 1990s, it came back with a vengeance with the bursting of the tech bubble beginning in 2000.[2] These issues notwithstanding, the lesson is clear. Just because an anomaly has been detected using past data, there is no reason to *assume* that capitalizing on it will be easy in the future.

Even if an anomaly is persistent, this is not the end of the story for portfolio managers seeking to capitalize on it. It is becoming common practice for managers to be evaluated relative to their size/value peer group, that is to say, relative to their **style peer group**. Style is usually defined in terms of firm size and growth versus value. For example, Morningstar sorts domestic mutual fund managers into nine groups based on a three-by-three matrix, where size ranges from small-cap to mid-cap to large-cap, and value versus growth ranges from value to blend to growth.[3] So, if a manager tilts toward small-cap value because historically small-cap value has outperformed other market segments, she will be compared against other managers doing the exact same thing. To rise above the crowd, she must do more! This could be done by stock selection of a fundamental nature, by employing additional screens, or a combination of both. The next section provides some additional guidance in this regard.

Before moving forward, a few words on **style investing** are in order. Consideration of style in portfolio formation can mean different things. First, given the evidence that style returns are cyclical, with sometimes small-cap outperforming large-cap and vice versa, and sometimes value outperforming growth and vice versa, gains in risk reduction can be obtained by consciously diversifying over different styles. Second, within this diversification approach, because value has historically outperformed growth, and small-cap has outperformed large-cap, it may be advisable to tilt towards small-cap and value, while still investing in different styles. If a manager operates exclusively in a particular style segment, then in effect the tilt is 100%. This could make sense if a manager has expertise in stock picking in this segment and is part of a style-diversified team (implying the overall portfolio is style diversified). Third, if it is possible to predict when styles will be favored by investors, there may be scope for style rotation, depending on what a manager's predictive model is calling for.

To provide a simple example in terms of the value-growth choice, say a neutral value-growth allocation would be 50%/50%. If you consciously style diversify, you would hold 50% in growth and 50% in value. If you believe that value is more often than not better, you might tilt toward value by investing 60% of your portfolio in value stocks. If you believe you have a predictive model that allows you to time style returns, you might be willing to toggle back and forth, 80% or 40% in value, depending on what your model is presently calling for.

Nicholas Barberis and Andrei Shleifer have constructed a model of style investing, based on style rotation in the aggregate. They show that a number of interesting implications arise from making the following two assumptions: first, investors chase with their dollars past relative style performance; and, second, flows affect prices.[4] The latter is appropriate if many are trying to chase the same style, and, given that arbitrage is limited, prices must adjust. Among other things, their model explains both the existence of style factors that are divorced from the nature of underlying cash flows and the tendency for style returns to phase over time.

19.3   REFINING ANOMALY CAPTURE

In this section we begin by examining research that shows how simplistic value investing can be refined by looking at financial statement information. Then we describe how simplistic momentum investing can be refined by further conditioning on volume.

REFINING VALUE INVESTING USING ACCOUNTING DATA

Research shows that value investing can be enhanced by conditioning on volatility and investor sophistication.[5] Taking a different tack, Joseph Piotroski has shown that financial statement information can also be useful.[6] It turns out that the effectiveness of value investing relies on a small number of firms—using a simple book-to-market approach, less than 44% of high book-to-market firms earn positive market-adjusted returns in the two years following portfolio formation. Piotroski's contribution is to use financial statement information to separate the wheat from the chaff. Specifically, nine fundamental signals are used to measure three areas of a firm's financial condition: profitability, financial leverage/liquidity, and operating efficiency. On the basis of these signals, an F-score (financial soundness) is calculated, where higher/lower values are more/less likely to be exhibited by firms due for a turnaround. F-scores take on integer values and range from 0 (least sound) to 9 (most sound). An investment strategy based on buying value firms with very high (8–9) F-scores and shorting those with very low (0–1) F-scores generates a 23% excess return between 1976 and 1996. An even more conservative cut where an F-score is designated as high if it is 5 or more (while low F-scores are 4 or less) yields a return difference of 9.7%/year. Moreover, as shown in Figure 19.1, such a strategy proved quite dependable on a year-to-year basis. In only three of the 21 years of the sample does a long-short strategy earn negative risk-adjusted returns—and in two of these years the return is close to zero.[7]

REFINING MOMENTUM-INVESTING USING VOLUME

There is evidence that momentum-investing can also be refined by the incorporation of additional screens. In particular, the strength of momentum covaries with market state, with negative market states causing momentum dissipation.[8] Volume is another possible screen. Technical analysts, as well as focusing on past returns, have for a long time considered volume to be an important indicator.[9] Charles Lee and Bhaskaran Swaminathan document a relationship between volume and momentum, showing that volume predicts both the magnitude and persistence of momentum.[10] Table 19.1 shows a two-way sort on momentum and volume. As well as creating 10 past-return deciles (R1 to R10, with R10 indicating highest past returns), these researchers form three volume deciles, with V1 indicating low volume and V3 indicating high volume. Thus we have 30 momentum-volume portfolios. They find that low-volume firms earn higher returns, so the best mixed momentum-volume strategy is to go long low volume-high momentum firms and short high volume-low momentum firms. The former group earns 1.67%/month, while the latter earns 0.09%/month, for a spread of 1.56%/month.

Lee and Swaminathan also document the tendency for momentum returns to eventually reverse, suggesting that momentum is partly a case of overreaction, and

FIGURE 19.1 One-year Returns to a Long-short Value Strategy where Additional Financial Statement Information is Used to Differentiate Predicted Winners and Losers

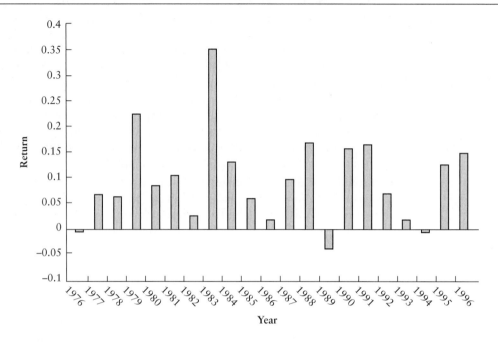

Source: Piotroski, J. D.. From "Value investing: The use of historical financial statement information to separate winners from losers," *Journal of Accounting Research* 38, (Supplement), 2000, pp. 1–41. Reproduced by permission of Blackwell Publishers

TABLE 19.1 | TWO-WAY SORT OF MOMENTUM AND VOLUME

	V1	V2	V3	V3–V1
R1	1.12	0.67	0.09	–1.04
	(2.74)	(1.61)	(0.20)	(2.74)
R5	1.36	1.34	1.15	–0.21
	(5.37)	(4.63)	(3.28)	(1.33)
R10	1.67	1.78	1.55	–0.12
	(5.30)	(5.41)	(4.16)	(0.67)
R10–R1	0.54	1.11	1.46	0.91
	(2.07)	(4.46)	(5.93)	(4.61)

Source: Lee, C. M. C. and B. Swaminathan. From "Price momentum and trading volume," in *Journal of Finance* 55, pp. 2017–69. © 2000 Wiley Publishing, Inc. This material is used by permission of John Wiley & Sons, Inc.
Note: Table shows returns/month and t-statistics in parentheses.

that momentum and reversal are linked. Further, they show that volume is a noisy proxy for value, with low volume being associated with high book-to-market, lower analyst following, lower long-term earnings growth forecasts, lower past-five-year stock returns, and future positive earnings surprises. They argue that a "momentum life cycle" captures some of the patterns in the data. Referring to Figure 19.2, stocks tend to phase, and momentum and volume are two of the key markers. Stocks with good past returns are on the left, and stocks with high volume are in the upper half. Take a stock that peaks, and then encounters a string of bad news. It loses ground, and investors dump it at high volume. Moving out of favor, and continuing to decline, volume dries up. But eventually the stock may be set for a turnaround. When it finally starts to climb, initially volume remains low, as it takes some time for investors and analysts to put it back on their radar screen. But, as the turnaround continues, it becomes increasingly noticed, and volume eventually rises.

The next contributions that we review pick up some of these threads, with the first examining the term structure of past returns, thus simultaneously considering momentum and reversal, and the second relating momentum and value.

MOMENTUM AND REVERSAL

Mark Grinblatt and Tobias Moskowitz documented the gains available if one conditions on the entire term structure of past returns.[11] As we have seen earlier, there is negative serial correlation using both short-term (one-month) returns and long-term (3–5 year) returns, while positive serial correlation is present for medium-term (6–12 month) returns. In their approach they allow for asymmetries between

---

FIGURE 19.2 Momentum Life Cycle

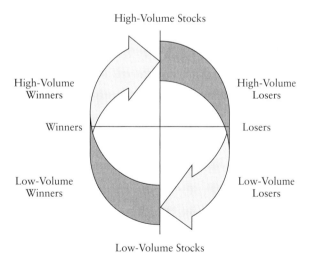

Source: Lee, C. M. C. and B. Swaminathan. From "Price momentum and trading volume," in *Journal of Finance* 55, pp. 2017–69. © 2000 Wiley Publishing, Inc. This material is used by permission of John Wiley & Sons, Inc.

past gains and losses, and also take into consideration the consistency of past gains and losses. Why might consistency matter? Recall the Grinblatt-Han model of Chapter 13. In this model it is the capital gains overhang rather than the past return that drives the future return. Stocks that are consistent winners are more likely to have larger unrealized capital gains than stocks whose identical past return was achieved by a dramatic month or two of price jumps. Table 19.2 shows a regression of hedged monthly security returns on a set of term structure variables.[12]

To interpret, let's focus on the four –12 to –2 variables and estimated coefficients. As expected, we observe significant positive serial correlation based on the return from 12 months back to one month back ("Return from –12 to –2"). The next variable down ("Return from –12 to –2 (L)") is defined as min(0, Return from –12 to –2), which means it only comes into play for negative returns over this span and its coefficient measures the *incremental impact* of negative returns. The fact that the coefficient is also (significantly) positive suggests *greater* persistence in the case of loser firms. The next variable is an indicator variable that equals one if at least 8 of the 11 months (from –12 to –2) witnessed positive returns: in other words, positive consistency. The variable below that, the consistent loser variable, is an indicator variable equaling one if at least 8 of the 11 months from –12 to –2 have witnessed negative returns.[13] We see that being a consistent winner enhances momentum, while being a consistent loser has no effect. In general, the results at other term structure segments are quite similar. The extent of the serial correlation (whether positive or negative) is amplified for losers relative to winners; consistency for winners increases returns (enhancing momentum and diminishing reversal); and consistency for losers never has any impact.

TABLE 19.2 | REGRESSION OF HEDGED MONTHLY STOCK RETURNS ON A SET OF TERM STRUCTURE VARIABLES

Independent variables	Coefficient	Abs. t-stats
Previous month's return	–0.0472	11.39
Previous month's return (L)	–0.0764	9.63
Previous month's return consistency indicator (W)	0.0051	8.79
Return from –12 to –2	0.0028	2.50
Return from –12 to –2 (L)	0.0113	2.97
Return from –12 to –2 consistency indicator (W)	0.0046	5.80
Return from –12 to –2 consistency indicator (L)	–0.0007	0.76
Return from –36 to –13	–0.0015	3.47
Return from –36 to –13 (L)	–0.0052	2.04
Return from –36 to –13 consistency indicator (W)	0.0014	2.73
Return from –36 to –13 consistency indicator (L)	–0.0007	0.80

Source: Reprinted from the *Journal of Financial Economics*, Vol 71, Issue 3, Grinblatt, M., and T. J. Moskowitz., "Predicting stock price movements from past returns: The role of consistency and tax-loss selling," pp. 541–79, © 2004. With permission from Elsevier.

Grinblatt and Moskowitz next examine the economic relevance of these patterns in the data: can they be used to enhance portfolio performance? Stocks are ranked into deciles from lowest expected return to highest, depending on beginning-of-period regressor values and coefficients estimated using available information. Figure 19.3 shows average returns by decile for these zero-cost portfolios. Notice that they line up in order, with decile 10 earning the highest average returns and decile 1 earning the lowest. The decile 10 versus decile 1 gap is an impressive (and highly significant) 1.68%/month. Indeed, conditioning on the term structure of past returns seems a wise strategy. This is of course what technical analysts have always done, though likely not with the same statistical rigor.

MOMENTUM AND VALUE

What happens when we attempt to form portfolios where both value and momentum screens are used at the same time? A study by Clifford Asness documented that

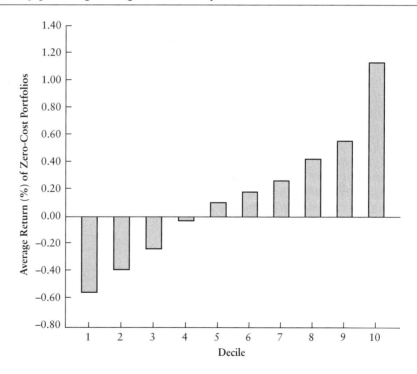

FIGURE 19.3 Average Hedged Returns by Deciles

Source: Reprinted from the *Journal of Financial Economics*, Vol 71, Issue 3, Grinblatt, M. and T. J. Moskowitz, "Predicting stock price movements from past returns: The role of consistency and tax-loss selling," pp. 541–79, © March 2004. With permission from Elsevier.

the gains are not as great as one might imagine.[14] U.S. stocks were first sorted into both value and momentum quintiles. Then intersection portfolios were formed, leading to 25 (five times five) distinct groups of stocks. As shown in Table 19.3, a portfolio of high momentum-high value stocks averaged a return of 1.62%/month versus a low momentum-low value portfolio that averaged 0.03%/month. The implication is that a long-short portfolio would have generated a return of 1.59%. What reduces the benefit of simultaneously conditioning on both value and momentum is that value works best for low-momentum stocks, and momentum works best for low-value stocks. For example, in the case of low-value stocks, the momentum differential is 1.47%, a figure that is very close to the differential for high momentum-high value stocks versus low momentum-low value stocks.

19.4 MULTIVARIATE APPROACHES

In the previous section, we examined research that explored the impact of value and momentum simultaneously. But why stop at two factors? Here we report two studies that have taken a **multivariate approach**. We begin with early work by Marc Reinganum.[15] In order to investigate whether "winners" tended to share certain common characteristics, he employed a sample of 222 firms whose stocks had at least doubled in price during one year between 1970 and 1983. The issue was, after identification of these characteristics, whether a successful trading strategy could be developed focusing on these characteristics. Reinganum identified the following four key commonalities:

1. A price-to-book ratio less than one
2. Acceleration in quarterly earnings growth
3. Fewer than 20 million common shares outstanding
4. High relative strength[16]

The first (value) and fourth (momentum) should look familiar. The second may be a means of extracting the diamonds in the rough (as in Piotroski), and the third may be proxying for market capitalization. To perform an out-of-sample test,

TABLE 19.3 | AVERAGE ONE-MONTH RETURNS (IN PERCENT) BASED ON A TWO-WAY SORT OF VALUE AND MOMENTUM

		Value					
		Low	2	3	4	High	Average
	Low	0.03	0.49	0.80	0.83	1.00	0.63
	2	0.61	0.59	0.90	1.25	1.35	0.94
Momentum	3	0.52	0.93	0.80	1.19	1.44	0.98
	4	0.99	0.97	1.17	1.45	1.68	1.25
	High	1.50	1.44	1.49	1.60	1.62	1.53
	Average	0.73	0.88	1.03	1.26	1.42	

Source: Data adapted from Asness, C. S., 1997, "The interaction of value and momentum strategies," in *Financial Analysts Journal* vol. 53, No. 2, (March/Apr 1997), p. 29. With permission from CFA Institute. Copyright 1997. All rights reserved.
Note: Marginal values are averages of internal two-way sort returns.

Reinganum omitted the 222 firms that he had used to come up with the commonalities, and then applied these four commonalities as screens over all AMEX and NYSE firms over the same 1970–1983 period.[17] A buy signal was triggered by all of the relevant characteristics holding simultaneously for a firm. After a buy signal, the security was arbitrarily held for a two-year period and then sold off. Cumulative excess returns were calculated through each of the eight quarters that a stock was held. The results were impressive, outperforming the S&P 500 by 37.14% (at a comparable risk level).

Following this approach, Robert Haugen and Nardin Baker investigated the predictive contribution of a large selection of factors grouped into five categories: risk, liquidity, price level, growth potential, and technical.[18] Risk factors include such standard risk factors as beta and sensitivities to macroeconomic variables. Illiquid stocks need to have higher returns to compensate traders who must face higher transaction costs, so such logical factors as price per share and volume were included. Price level factors essentially capture value strategies, as this category includes share price relative to various accounting magnitudes. Growth potential factors point to the likelihood of higher growth in earnings and dividends, with various profitability measures being used as proxies in this regard. The idea here is that, for a given price relative to accounting measures, indicators suggesting higher future growth might point to diamonds in the rough. And finally, technical factors include standard momentum and reversal measures.

The following regression was then run using all these independent variables:

19.1
$$R_{j,t} = \Sigma_i\, \beta_{t,i} F_{j,i,t-1} + u_{j,t}$$

where $R_{j,t}$ is the return on stock j at month t; $\beta_{t,i}$ is the regression coefficient or payoff to factor i at month t; and $F_{j,i,t-1}$ is the exposure to factor i of stock j at month t. These researchers first estimated this regression cross-sectionally (at a single point in time) for all 180 months during 1979–1993. For the first half of the sample, the average factor payoffs for the 12 most important factors are shown in Table 19.4 (along with associated absolute t-statistics). The coefficients can be interpreted as the change in the stock's monthly expected return associated with a one standard deviation change in the stock's exposure to a factor in the cross-section. To check for robustness, the last two columns of the table repeat the exercise for the second half of the sample. Several points are salient. First, the impact of the factors is remarkably consistent. Second, no risk measures appear. Third, not surprisingly, what dominate are technical factors, price level factors, and liquidity.

As an out-of-sample test, the following procedure was employed. Factor sensitivities were estimated using the 12 months prior to the beginning of 1993, and then expected returns for each stock were fitted for January 1993 using these sensitivities and each stock's exposure to these factors. Next, stocks were ranked from highest expected return to lowest and 10 deciles were formed, with decile 10 representing the 10% of stocks with the highest expected return down to decile 1 comprised of stocks with the lowest expected return.[19] This procedure was repeated for the 180 months of the sample. Figure 19.4 shows the average returns to the 10 deciles during this sample period. The Haugen and Baker expected return approach

TABLE 19.4 | Factor Coefficients and T-statistics

	1979/2001 to 1986/2006		1986/2007 to 1993/2012	
	Mean	Abs. t-stat.	Mean	Abs. t-stat.
One-month excess return	−0.97%	17.04	−0.72%	11.04
12-month excess return	0.52%	7.09	0.52%	7.09
Volume/market cap	−0.35%	5.28	−0.20%	2.33
2-month excess return	−0.20%	4.97	−0.11%	2.37
E/P	0.27%	4.56	0.26%	4.42
ROE	0.24%	4.34	0.13%	2.06
Book-to-price	0.35%	3.90	0.39%	6.72
Volume trend	−0.10%	3.17	−0.09%	2.58
6-month excess return	0.24%	3.01	0.19%	2.55
CF/P	0.13%	2.64	0.26%	4.42
Variability in CF/P	−0.11%	2.55	−0.15%	3.38

Source: Reprinted from the *Journal of Financial Economics*, Vol 41, Issue 3, Haugen, R. A., and N. L. Baker, "Commonality in the determinants of expected stock returns," pp. 401–39, © July 1996. With permission from Elsevier.

FIGURE 19.4 Average Decile Returns to Expected Return Portfolios

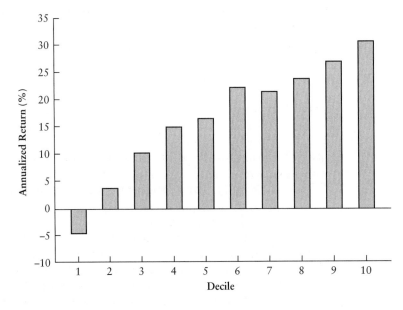

Source: Reprinted from the *Journal of Financial Economics*, Vol 41, Issue 3, Haugen, R. A., and N. L. Baker, "Commonality in the determinants of expected stock returns," pp. 401–39, © July 1996. With permission from Elsevier.

appears to be quite successful in predicting which stocks will outperform going forward.

While momentum and value seem to be the heart of it, other factors apparently matter as well. Nevertheless, recent work casts doubt on the contribution of factors over and above momentum and value.[20] When transaction costs are factored into the analysis—and it should be noted that the Haugen and Baker strategy entails monthly rebalancing—there appears to be no value added beyond momentum and value.[21]

19.5   STYLE ROTATION

Style rotation is the act of moving from style to style in the attempt to time aggregate style preference shifts. Of course one must have a predictive model with some reliability in order to make the exercise a feasible one. Typically, studies along these lines have employed such macroeconomic factors as the default premium, the term structure slope, and the aggregate dividend yield. There is evidence of return enhancement using such an approach for the United States, United Kingdom, and Japan.[22]

To illustrate the use of style rotation, we turn to research at the level of country stock markets. Stéphanie Desrosiers, Jean-Francois L'Her, and Jean-Francois Plante show that just as it is possible to move among stocks in a domestic portfolio based on momentum and value, one can also move among national stock markets in an international portfolio based on momentum and value signals.[23] MSCI country indexes in U.S. dollars for the United States, Canada, Australia, Hong Kong, Japan, Singapore, and 12 major European markets from 1975 to 2003 were used. Under a relative-value strategy, a one-month portfolio was formed, which was long the four markets with the highest book-to-market and short the four markets with the lowest book-to-market. Such a portfolio generated a raw return of 0.32%/month. Under a relative-strength (momentum) strategy, a one-month portfolio was formed that was long the four markets with the highest past annual returns and short the four markets with the lowest past annual returns. In this case the average portfolio return was 0.81%/month. Notably, these portfolios were negatively correlated with each other, with the correlation coefficient averaging in at –.56 on a rolling five-year basis over the sample, suggesting the efficacy of a style-diversified approach. A portfolio half in relative value and half in relative strength earned a return of .86%/month—and at substantially lower risk than either of its two constituents.

These researchers also investigate whether style rotation can do even better. Switching between strategies requires a decision rule. They argue that as the market falls/rises, a relative-value/relative-strength approach enjoys greater success. The former is due to the house money effect, which purports that risk aversion increases with market failure, while the latter is due to the greater aggregate overconfidence that arises when market returns are high (where we recall that one model of momentum relates it to the extent of overconfidence).[24]

Indeed, as shown in Table 19.5, style rotation pays off. Of the 203 months where the signal calls for a relative-value tilt, while it pays off only during 100 months, the payoff is 0.93%/month on a weighted-average basis (vs. the

Table 19.5	Average One-Month Returns for Relative-Value Tilt, Relative-Strength Tilt, and Style Rotation Using Country Indexes

	Relative-value Tilt	Relative-strength Tilt	Style Rotation
Correct prediction months	3.32%	5.18%	4.20%
Incorrect prediction months	−1.38%	−4.12%	−2.29%
Weighted average of all prediction months	0.93%	1.81%	1.30%
Single-style approach	0.32%	0.81%	

0.32%/month for the all relative-value strategy) because the successful-month average return is 3.32% versus the -1.38% earned during unsuccessful months. On the other hand, of the 141 months where the signal calls for a relative-strength tilt, now a good majority (90) witness success. Coupled with the fact that successful months generate 5.18%/month compared to −4.12%/month for unsuccessful months, on a weighted-average basis the payoff is 1.81% (vs. the .81%/month for the all relative-strength strategy). Overall, style rotation generates a return of 1.30%/month.[25] To conclude, while diversification over styles pays off at the level of country indexes, even greater gains can be garnered by style rotation based on prior year returns.

19.6   IS IT POSSIBLE TO ENHANCE PORTFOLIO PERFORMANCE USING BEHAVIORAL FINANCE?

Early Evidence

In a recent study addressing whether it is possible to enhance portfolio performance using behavioral finance, the performance of 16 self-proclaimed or media-identified behavioral mutual funds was evaluated.[26] These funds claim to base their investment strategies in whole or in part on the principles of behavioral finance. Of course one of the weaknesses of the paper, as acknowledged by the authors, is the sparseness of the sample. Other funds not included in the sample may be following behavioral precepts as well, but their identity is unknown. Moreover, there is no guarantee that behavioral investing is really being followed by the funds in the sample. There is after all evidence that changing your name or professed strategy to what might be viewed as the flavor of the month is successful at attracting flows of funds.[27] Indeed, it turns out that the behavioral funds in the study are luring investor money, and their name or professed investment strategy may be one reason.

Still, likely the main reason that these funds have been able to attract investors is that they, as a group, have outperformed the S&P 500. Nevertheless, when the

Fama-French three-factor model is supplemented with an additional factor for momentum, the behavioral funds are not able to earn excess returns. Mostly they seem to have capitalized on the value advantage. So in this sense, the authors conclude, there is no evidence that behavioral investing has paid off up to now. A few points suggest themselves. First, few observers would claim that momentum is a risk factor, so including it as an additional factor can be called into question. And yet, the use of such a risk-adjustment mechanism requires that funds do better than just simply capitalizing on the well-known small-firm, value, and momentum anomalies. Since this seems a reasonable requirement, the finding that these funds as a group are not adding value seems valid. Second, even if we grant the latter, sample limitations and test power are salient issues. As for the latter, while it may be difficult to reject deviations from market efficiency, it is also difficult to reject small deviations. In other words, these funds may be providing some value added, but statistical tests are not able to conclude this.

What is Behavioral Investing?

We introduced this chapter by defining behavioral investing as the attempt to enhance portfolio performance by applying lessons learned from behavioral finance. But what does this really mean? To call your fund (say) the "Behavioral Value Fund," for example, or to espouse behavioral principles in the prospectus, doesn't seem quite enough.

The collection of anomalies described in Chapter 4 and elsewhere in this book is common knowledge, having been published in many of the best journals and reported in the popular press. As was discussed in Chapter 13, some of them have been shown to be implications of an array of behavioral models. Is the utilization of this knowledge in portfolio construction tantamount to behavioral investing? We believe another element is required. One can always find a set of selection screens that would have worked well in the past. The big question for managers is which of these are likely to be operative going forward. Some of these are patently spurious: hemlines and who wins the Super Bowl spring to mind as obvious examples. Judicious managers can safely ignore them. Others, while logical, may not have legs going forward. In our view, one of the main determinants of whether a pattern in the data has usefulness for the future is whether or not it is behaviorally based. Such anomalies are in some sense "natural," and while they can potentially be arbitraged away, given the limits to arbitrage and human nature, this is not necessarily easy to do, especially when selection screens are refined by the inclusion of additional supporting variables, as discussed in this chapter. In this regard, one can compare the value advantage and the small-firm effect. The former is central to behavioral models; the latter is not. The former seems to be alive and well (despite cyclicality), while many have called the continued existence of the latter into question. In our view, behavioral investing should be more than "kitchen-sink" empirics, with a preference being shown to behaviorally based factors.[28]

So notwithstanding the aforementioned performance study, should we expect behavioral investing to provide a payoff? While there is no evidence of this as yet, given the limitations of the extant evidence and the currently amorphous nature of behavioral investing, we believe that the jury is still out on this important question.

CHAPTER HIGHLIGHTS

1. Momentum and value investing have shown themselves to be robust over different samples and markets. But the forces of arbitrage-driven anomaly attenuation are always present.
2. The fact that managers are compared to others in their style peer group makes it vital to look for an additional edge.
3. Value can be enhanced by utilizing financial statement information. Momentum can be enhanced by taking volume into consideration. Looking at the entire term structure of past returns, and consistency of return, also leads to a payoff.
4. Multivariate approaches seek to utilize all relevant factors, but it is not clear if there is any value added beyond momentum or value.
5. Style rotation seeks to time style shifts. Preliminary research both within countries and using national markets suggests promise.
6. There is no evidence that behavioral investing leads to any return boost. Given the paucity of funds espousing a behavioral bent, however, and the lack of clarity on what behavioral investing really is, the jury is still out on this question.

DISCUSSION QUESTIONS AND PROBLEMS

1. Differentiate the following terms/concepts:

    a. Style peer groups and style investing
    b. Style tilting and style rotation
    c. Financial soundness and financial statements
    d. Univariate and multivariate approaches

2. Describe how momentum can be refined by conditioning on the entire term structure of interest rates in the manner of the Grinblatt and Moskowitz regression model.

3. Describe how value investing can be refined by paying close attention to a company's financial statements.

4. What does the early evidence on the ability of behavioral investing to enhance performance tell us?

5. What is an example of an anomaly that once reported in research studies has attenuated? Is this positive or negative from the standpoint of market efficiency?

ENDNOTES

1 Schwert, G. W., 2002, "Anomalies and market efficiency," Working paper.
2 Chan, L. K. C., and J. Lakonishok, 2004, "Value and growth investing: A review and update," *Financial Analysts Journal* 60 (Jan/Feb), 71–86.
3 See Benz, C., P. Di Teresa, and R. Kinnel, 2003, *Morningstar Guide to Mutual Funds: 5-Star Strategies for Success* (John Wiley & Sons, Hoboken, New Jersey), for a discussion.
4 Barberis, N., and A. Shleifer, 2003, "Style investing," *Journal of Financial Economics* 68, 161–199.
5 Ali, A., L. S. Hwang, and M. A. Trombley, 2003, "Arbitrage risk and the book-to-market anomaly," *Journal of Financial Economics* 69, 355–373.

6 Piotroski, J. D., 2000, "Value investing: The use of historical financial statement information to separate winners from losers," *Journal of Accounting Research* 38 (Supplement), 1–41.

7 This graph is based on the more conservative cut.

8 See Cooper, M., Jr., R. C. Gutierrez, and A. Hameed, 2004, "Market states and momentum," *Journal of Finance* 59, 1345–1365; and, for Canada, Deaves, R., and P. Miu, 2007, "Momentum, reversal and market state," *Canadian Investment Review* 20 (no. 4), 8–14.

9 See, for example, Thomsett, M. C., 1999, *Mastering Technical Analysis* (Dearborn Financial Publishing, Chicago, Illinois).

10 Lee, C. M. C., and B. Swaminathan, 2000, "Price momentum and trading volume," *Journal of Finance* 55, 2017–2069.

11 Grinblatt, M., and T. J. Moskowitz, 2004, "Predicting stock price movements from past returns: The role of consistency and tax-loss selling," *Journal of Financial Economics* 71, 541–579.

12 The hedged return is defined to be the return on the stock for the month in question minus the return on a hedge portfolio of similar size, value, and industry attributes.

13 It is not clear if consistent winners (or losers) can actually be losers (or winners). For example, a stock could have eight positive returns and three large negative returns.

14 Asness, C. S., 1997, "The interaction of value and momentum strategies," *Financial Analysts Journal* 53 (March/Apr), 29–36.

15 Reinganum, M. R., 1988, "The anatomy of a stock market winner," *Financial Analysts Journal* 44 (March/April), 16–28.

16 Reinganum defines relative strength as the weighted average of quarterly price changes during the year. Despite the fact that momentum is in terms of returns, which include dividends, relative strength and momentum are closely related. Note that Reinganum also investigated a broader group of nine commonalities, but argued that these four were the most important.

17 To be sure, a pure out-of-sample test (using a different time period or sample) would be preferable.

18 Haugen, R. A., and N. L. Baker, 1996, "Commonality in the determinants of expected stock returns," *Journal of Financial Economics* 41, 401–439.

19 This ranking procedure is similar to that of Grinblatt, M., and T. J. Moskowitz, 2004, "Predicting stock price movements from past returns: The role of consistency and tax-loss selling," *Journal of Financial Economics* 71, 541–579.

20 Hanna, J. D., and M. J. Ready, 2005, "Profitable predictability in the cross section of stock returns," *Journal of Financial Economics* 78, 463–505.

21 Whether Haugen and Baker's results could be resurrected by holding positions longer than a month is a matter of conjecture.

22 See, for the United States, Cooper, M., H. Gulen, and M. Vassalou, 2001, "Investing in size and book-to-market portfolios using information about the macroeconomy: Some new trading rules," Working paper; for Japan, Bauer, R., J. Derwall, and R. Molenaar, 2002, "The real-time predictability of the size and value premium in Japan," Working paper; and for the United Kingdom, Levis, M., and N. Tessaromatis, 2003, "Style rotation strategies: Issues of implementation," Working paper. Also, see Montier, J., 2002, *Behavioral Finance: Insights into Irrational Minds and Markets* (John Wiley & Sons, Chichester, England), who suggests IPO activity and the equity premium as additional screens. Finally, see Avramov, D., and T. Chordia, 2006, "Predicting stock returns," *Journal of Financial Economics* 82, 387–415, who have documented the predictability of *individual* stock returns using macroeconomic variables.

23 DesRosiers, S., J. F. L'Her, and J. F. Plante, 2004, "Style management in equity country

allocation," *Financial Analysts Journal* 60 (Nov-Dec), 40–54.

24 See Barberis, N., M. Huang, and T. Santos, 2001, "Prospect theory and asset prices," *Quarterly Journal of Economics* 116, 1–53; and Daniel, K., D. Hirshleifer, and A. Subrahmanyam, 1998, "Investor psychology and security market under- and overreactions," *Journal of Finance* 53, 1839–1885.

25 The results weaken only a little on a risk-adjusted basis.

26 Wright, C., P. Banerjee, and V. Boney, 2006, "Behavioral finance: Are the disciples profiting from the doctrine?" Working paper.

27 Cooper, M. J., H. Gulen, and P. R. Rau, 2005, "Changing names with style: Mutual fund name changes and their effects on fund flows," *Journal of Finance* 60, 2825–2858.

28 See Scott, J., M. Stumpp, and P. Xu, 1999, "Behavioral bias, valuation and active management," *Financial Analysts Journal* 55 (July/Aug), 49–57, for a discussion of using behavioral finance in portfolio management.

NEUROFINANCE AND THE TRADER'S BRAIN

20.1 INTRODUCTION

In this book we have argued that cognition and emotion are powerful influences on people's decisions. Traders are, of course, no different. This chapter begins by considering what we know about what sets a successful trader apart from other people. We have all contemplated the oft-debated question of nature versus nurture in explaining whether a person thrives or fails. In this final chapter, we further investigate where choices come from. The evidence suggests that there are both environmental and biological foundations.

The chapter begins in Section 20.2 with a discussion of expertise, namely, what makes a skillful trader? Cognitive skills are honed through practice and repetition, but emotion also has a significant role. Next, in Section 20.3, we turn to the emerging field of neurofinance. Using imaging technology, researchers are contributing to our understanding of how people make decisions. In Section 20.4, we describe some of the insights recently provided by neurofinance researchers. These researchers have found that cognition and emotion have complementary effects. Traders whose emotions appear to be in balance perform the best. Uncertainty and risk are experienced differently by our brains, as are gains versus losses and risk versus return. The chapter concludes in Section 20.5 with some practical advice.

20.2 EXPERTISE AND IMPLICIT LEARNING

Consider the following situation. You are at a large concert and run into a good friend, Molly. Of course, you recognize her face immediately. Now think about this. What if, instead, you know Molly is at the concert but is seated across the venue. The friend you came to the concert with, Amy, is going to look for Molly, but the two have never met. You do your best at describing Molly to Amy. What's the chance that Amy will be able to identify Molly among thousands of concert goers? Not too likely.

Much of what we know we cannot describe in words. A face is a very complex thing, and we simply do not have enough words to explicitly describe one particular person very accurately. Language is categorical, whereas the distinguishing features of two similar faces may be fuzzy. Some cognitive scientists assert that people have knowledge that they cannot verbalize, referred to as **implicit learning** or **tacit knowledge**.[1]

Brett Steenbarger argues that traders also have information about markets that they cannot adequately describe in words.[2] Like a human face, markets are probably more complex than the language we have to describe them. Does this mean we need a finer grid with which to describe markets? Or, does this view suggest that we need to better understand how traders make decisions?

Excellence in most fields requires expertise. How do we define **expertise**? Usually we think in terms of relative performance so that those at the top of their game are considered to be the experts. Because of tacit knowledge, an expert chess player or pro football player often knows instinctively what the best move is, perhaps without any cognitive evaluation whatsoever. Recall in our discussion of the foundations of emotion in Chapter 7 that psychologists believe that emotions can develop completely independently from cognition. In other words, you can feel fear without first cognitively recognizing what is making you fearful.

While observing a market, a trader may instinctively know the move he wants to make. Steenbarger notes that in many instances traders will make similar buy or sell decisions and then, ex post, provide very different descriptions of the information that led to the decision. The traders saw the same information, acted the same way, but understood their behavior quite differently. Perhaps a trader makes a decision based on instinct with no preceding cognitive evaluation.[3] Afterward, the trader generates an explanation that is cognitively consistent with his expectations. Steenbarger argues that "the successful trader feels the market *but does not become lost in those feelings*."[4] Studies of expert athletic performers have reached similar conclusions. For example, one study argues that "emotions, and the capability to regulate them effectively, arguably account for a large portion of the variance in athletic performance."[5] In the trading domain, an expert trader often has a gut feeling about a particular situation but remains in control by taking careful, deliberate action.

Does this mean that trading expertise is innate and cannot be learned? Reading the information in a market could be like understanding a social interaction. Some people are just better at it than others. While some level of innate ability is probably requisite, the evidence suggests that expertise is finely honed. Not too many of us would believe that a professional quarterback spent his teen and early adult years watching football on television while sitting on the couch eating chips. Knowing the rules of a game does not make you good at the game. Practice and repetition are common ingredients across successful experts. For example, accomplished violinists spend, on average, 10,000 hours practicing.[6]

Successful traders also devote a lot of time to practice. This practice gives them the ability to connect what they know about a market to the action they should take. Through implicit learning they are able to make better and more efficient decisions. A day trader who spends hours, or even minutes, evaluating a current market circumstance before making a trading decision will certainly find it difficult to succeed.

20.3   NEUROFINANCE

While we know that practice is necessary to hone any skill, unlocking the mysteries of the brain is an important key to understanding how to promote the development of expertise in any realm, including investing. Are evolutionary theorists correct in their contention that our basic emotions have evolved to promote the survival of the species as we discussed in Chapter 7? Do expert performers have innate characteristics, or can anyone develop expertise in trading?

Neurofinance and neuroeconomics use neurotechnology to examine how the brain behaves while a person is making financial and economic decisions. In these new and growing fields, results from economics, finance, psychology, and neuroscience provide the basis for further investigation. Neuroscience uses brain imaging, as we described in Chapter 7, to understand brain activity and how the brain works.[7] With this technology, scientists can actually measure emotional response. The potential of the technology has not gone unnoticed by practitioners. In fact, Jason Zweig, senior writer for *Money* magazine and guest columnist for *Time* magazine and cnn.com writes:[8]

> I've been a financial journalist since 1987, and nothing I've ever learned about investing has excited me more than the spectacular findings emerging form the study of "neuroeconomics." Thanks to this newborn field ... we can begin to understand what drives investing behavior not only on the theoretical or practical level, but as a basic biological function. These flashes of fundamental insight will enable you to see as never before what makes you tick as an investor.

Investors who better understand "what makes them tick" will be better prepared to make good investment decisions.

It is important to understand that neuroscience is not simply interested in mapping out parts of the brain. Instead, by looking at how the brain reacts during various activities, scientists can understand how the brain functions and solves problems.[9] We will better understand the mix of cognitive processing and emotional responses. Which responses are controlled and which are automatic responses? These insights will allow economic theorists to improve models of decision-making, as well as investor education efforts.

Recall from our earlier discussion of the brain that automatic and controlled responses are associated with different parts of the brain. Automatic responses often stimulate the amygdala, whereas controlled responses activate the forebrain (or prefrontal cortex). Using imaging technology, scientists can observe the areas of the brain that are activated during a task. In Chapter 7 we also talked about Damasio's studies of the behavior of brain-damaged patients.[10] The patients were emotionally flat due to frontal brain lobe damage, and Damasio concluded that decision-making and emotion are intertwined. Though studies of brain-damaged patients can be informative, brain imaging technology allows more control so that research can be conducted with greater precision. Neuroscientists are making great progress on brain function, and, as a result, researchers are proposing new models and theories that better incorporate aspects of psychology, including emotion.[11]

20.4   INSIGHTS FROM NEUROFINANCE

Neuroscientists have investigated a variety of questions related to financial decision-making. Several studies have lent insight into the forces of emotion on trading by studying the physiological characteristics of professional securities traders while they were actively engaged in live trading. In one study significant correlations between market movements and physiological characteristics such as skin conductance and cardiovascular data were reported.[12] Differences were also detected across traders, perhaps related to trading experience. Another study looked at whether emotion was found to be an important determinant of a trader's ability to succeed in financial markets.[13] It was found that those whose reaction to gains and losses was most intense had the worst trading performance, suggesting the obvious need for balanced emotions.

Brain imaging has been used as experimental participants have made risky choices.[14] This research indicates that how gains and losses are both anticipated and realized is likely to differ inasmuch as different regions of the brain are activated. When gains are anticipated, a subcortical region known as the nucleus accumbens (NAcc) becomes active. This region is rich in dopamine, a substance that has been associated with both the positive affect of monetary rewards and addictive drug use. The fact that this region is only active during anticipated gains (but not losses) lends plausibility to the differential experiencing of gains and losses in prospect theory.

Other brain imaging research indicates that what might lie behind ambiguity aversion is the fact that risk and uncertainty are experienced in different ways.[15] Recall in Chapter 1 where we discussed the distinction between risk and uncertainty. With a risky choice, the person can assess the probability of the outcomes, but under uncertainty the probabilities are unknown. The distinction is important here because the brain may evaluate a choice in a risky situation differently from a choice when one faces uncertainty. Research indicates that when facing uncertainty the most active regions were the orbitofrontal cortex (a region integrating emotion and cognition) and the amygdala (a region central to emotional reaction).[16] In contrast, when facing risk, the brain areas that responded during their task were typically in the parietal lobes so that the researchers concluded that choices in this setting were driven by cognitive factors.[17] In sum, uncertainty appears to be more strongly associated with an emotional response, while risk leads to a cognitive reaction.

It has been suggested that when times becomes more uncertain (for example in 2008, as was described in Chapter 14), the inability of investors to properly assess the distribution of future returns leads to their moving from rational deliberation to a primarily emotional response.[18] The result could be widespread unwillingness to hold risky assets in turbulent markets, a tendency that can only exacerbate market declines.

A neural test of myopic loss aversion has also been conducted.[19] A group of patients with brain lesions on areas known to be associated with the processing of emotions were compared to a control group. The former group was significantly more likely to take on risk than the control group. Further, the lesion group exhibited greater consistency in their levels of risk aversion. In other words, those with a reduced capacity for fearful responses behaved in a manner more in line with expected utility theory.

Another study focused on how decision-makers' brains reacted to varying levels of risk, rather than on learning or expected values.[20] Using a gambling game, expected values and risk were varied while participants' brain activation was monitored. As is typical in finance, rewards were measured using expected payoffs and risk using the variance of payoffs. Interestingly, the researchers report that brain activation varied in both time and location for reward and risk. Brain activation in response to rewards was immediate, whereas brain activation in response to risk was delayed. Time and location of activation is important because if we can separate the effects of risk and reward in the brain, researchers can further investigate how changes in risk perception affect decision-making. For example, they could examine how misperception of risk and cognitive difficulties contribute to less-than-optimal behavior.

20.5 EXPERTISE AND EMOTION

Research indicates that understanding neural responses will help us to gain insight into some of the puzzles we have talked about in this book. In addition, there are important implications for trader education. We are all familiar with the old adage that "practice makes perfect." In order to gain expertise, it is important to know the rules of the game, so reading up on investing is not a bad idea. But, at the same time, much practice through many simulations under divergent market conditions will promote better decision-making while trading.

But, does it pay to become an expert? While we know that many long hours of studying and practice are required, is this effort sufficiently rewarded? There is evidence that this question can be answered in the affirmative for financial practitioners. One researcher constructed a "differential reward index" as the income for a specified percentile divided by the median income for each occupation.[21] This measure allows us to differentiate high average income from high income for those whose expertise is greatest in a particular profession. For financial and business advisors, including stock brokers, earnings are related closely to achievement. At the 90th percentile the differential reward index was 3.5, indicating that the top 10% earned 3.5 times more than the median income level. In fact, this was the largest observed value for the differential reward index across all occupations studied!

Thus the evidence suggests that the benefit of becoming a skilled financial advisor may far exceed the cost. So how can one become an expert? Researchers have concluded that tacit knowledge is an important predictor of success in business as measured by salary, rank, and the level of one's company (e.g., whether it is among the top 500 in the *Fortune* rankings).[22] **Practical knowledge**, or the ability to gain tacit knowledge and turn it into a good strategy, is a function of a person's environment and ability. Thus, with a certain level of competence, hard work can be translated into success.

A successful trader, nonetheless, should always remember that emotion is critical to the outcome. We have argued throughout this book that emotion can enhance decision-making. Previously cited evidence suggested, however, that traders are advised to be wary of intense emotional reactions.[23] Another recent study used neuroimaging to examine how decision-makers' brains responded while playing the ultimatum game described in Chapter 11.[24] When unfair offers were rejected by the responders, the investigators reported significant increases in brain activity in the anterior insula, a brain area associated with emotion. Recall that even offers that are viewed as unfair should be accepted by a responder who cares only about increasing her earnings. Thus, traders are advised to exert their cognitive skills when experiencing a strong emotional reaction in order to overcome the tendency to react emotionally, just as a responder in the ultimatum game who is aware of his emotional response is well advised to accept an offer even if it seems unfair. Emotional responses and cognitive evaluations of risk can be quite different. Think about how many people perceive the risks of automobile and airplane accidents. Though riding in an automobile has been shown to be the less safe alternative, often an emotional response plays the dominant role, which may keep some people off airplanes.

CHAPTER HIGHLIGHTS

1. Expertise is defined in terms of relative performance so that those at the top of their game are considered to be the experts.
2. Implicit learning reflects knowledge that cannot be described using language.
3. Experts have developed implicit knowledge that enhances performance in their particular domain.
4. Neurofinance uses brain imaging technology and results from economics, finance, and psychology to better understand how the brain works.
5. Physiological differences exist across professional traders, and emotion is an important determinant of a trader's ability.
6. Measured brain responses to changes in risk and reward vary in both location and time of activation.
7. Practice is necessary to excel in trading, and good traders may make decisions based on gut feelings, while at the same time ensuring that they control their emotional responses.

DISCUSSION QUESTIONS AND PROBLEMS

1. Differentiate the following terms/concepts:

   a. Implicit learning and practice
   b. Practical knowledge and tacit knowledge
   c. Expertise and ability
   d. Brain function and brain part

2. The fact that uncertainty and risk are experienced differently might matter in times of financial crisis. Discuss.

3. Emotional balance is desirable for financial traders. Discuss.

4. Since graduation from college, your friend William has become a highly paid and successful financial advisor. His list of clients is long, and his advice is sought by many. Discuss the merits of the following statement: William's success is primarily driven by luck.

5. The evidence suggests that the benefit of becoming a skilled financial advisor may far exceed the cost. Discuss why this would be true.

ENDNOTES

1 See Steenbarger, B. N., 2003, *The Psychology of Trading* (Wiley, Hoboken, New Jersey); and Steenbarger, B. N., 2007, *Enhancing Trader Performance: Proven Strategies from the Cutting Edge of Trading Psychology* (Wiley, Hoboken, New Jersey).

2 Steenbarger, B. N., 2003, *The Psychology of Trading* (Wiley, Hoboken, New Jersey).

3 Zajonc, R., 1980, "Feeling and thinking: Preferences need no inferences," *American Psychologist* 35, 151–175.

4 Steenbarger, B. N., 2003, *The Psychology of Trading* (Wiley, Hoboken, New Jersey), p. 48.

5 Janelle, C. M., and C. H. Hillman, 2003, "Expert performance in sport: Current perspectives and critical issues," in J. L. Starkes and K.A. Ericsson, eds., *Expert Performance in Sports* (Champaign, Illinois, Human Kinetics), p. 24.

6 Ibid., pp. 19–47.

7 Neuroscience studies use brain imaging to study a wide variety of issues. Recent work even uses brain imaging to lend insight into social and moral issues. See, for example, Glannon, W., 2007, *Defining Right and Wrong in Brain Science: Essential Readings in Neuroethics* (Dana Press, New York).

8 Zweig, J., 2007, *Your Money and Your Brain: How the New Science of Neuroeconomics Can Help Make You Rich* (Simon and Schuster, New York), p. 1.

9 See Camerer, C., G. Loewenstein, and D. Prelec, 2005, "Neuroeconomics: How neuroscience can inform economics," *Journal of Economic Literature* 43, 9–64; and Camerer, C. F., 2007, "Neuroeconomics: Using neuroscience to make economic predictions," *The Economic Journal* 117, C26–C42.

10 Damasio, A. R., 1994, *Descartes' Error: Emotion, Reason, and the Human Brain* (Putnam, New York).

11 Loewenstein, G. F., C. K. Hsee, E. U. Weber, and N. Welch, 2001, "Risk as feelings," *Psychological Bulletin* 127(2), 267–286.

12 Lo, A. W., and D. V. Repin, 2002, "The psychophysiology of real-time financial risk processing, *Journal of Cognitive Neuroscience* 14(3), 323–339.

13 Lo, A. V., D. V. Repin, and B. N. Steenbarger, 2005, "Fear and greed in financial markets: A clinical study of day traders," Working paper.

14 Knutson, B., C. Adams, G. Fong, and D. Hommer, 2001, "Anticipation of increasing monetary reward selectively recruits nucleus accumbens," *Journal of Neuroscience* 21, 1–5.

15 Rustichini, A., J. Dickhaut, P. Ghirardato, K. Smith, and J. V. Pardo, 2005, "A brain imaging study of the choice procedure," *Games and Economic Behavior* 52(2), 257–282.

16 Hsu, M., M. Bhatt, R. Adolphs, D. Tranel, and C. Camerer, 2005, "Neural systems responding to degrees of uncertainty in human decision-making," *Science* 310, 1680–1683.

17 See Bechara, A., and A. R. Damasio, 2005, "The somatic marker hypothesis: A neural theory of economic decision," *Games and Economic Behavior* 52(2), 336–372; and Spencer, J., July 21, 2005, "Lessons from the brain-damaged investor; Unusual study explores links between emotion and results; 'Neuroeconomics' on Wall Street," *Wall Street Journal*, p. D1.

18 Sapra, S. G., and P. J. Zak, 2008, "Neurofinance: Bridging psychology, neurology and investor behavior," Working paper.

19 Shiv, B., G. Loewenstein, A. Bechara, A. Damasio, and H. Damasio, 2005, "Investment behavior and the dark side of emotion," *Psychological Science* 16, 435–439.

20 Preuschoff, K., P. Bossaerts, and S. R. Quartz, 2006, "Neural differentiation of expected reward and risk in human subcortical structures," *Neuron* 51, 381–390.

21 Hunt, E., 2006, "Expertise, talent, and social encouragement," in K. A. Ericsson,

N. Charness, P. J. Feltovich, and R. R. Hoffman, eds., *The Cambridge Handbook of Expertise and Expert Performance* (Cambridge University Press, New York), 31–38.

22 Cianciolo, A. T., C. Matthew, R. J. Strenberg, and R. K. Wagner, 2006, "Tacit knowledge, practical intelligence, and expertise," in K. A. Ericsson, N. Charness, P. J. Feltovich, and R. R. Hoffman, eds., *The Cambridge Handbook of Expertise and Expert Performance* (Cambridge University Press, New York), 613–632.

23 Lo, A. V., D. V. Repin, and B. N. Steenbarger, 2005, "Fear and greed in financial markets: A clinical study of day traders," Working paper.

24 Sanfrey, A. G., J. K. Rilling, J. A. Aronson, L. E., Nystrom, and J. D. Cohen, 2003, "The neural basis of economic decision-making in the ultimatum game," *Science* 300, 1755–1758.

GLOSSARY

1/n heuristic the tendency to put *1/nth* of money in a retirement savings account into all available *(n)* funds *(Chapter 17)*

abnormal returns see **excess returns**

action tendencies urges to act in a certain way *(Chapter 7)*

adaptive markets hypothesis a hypothesis explaining the cyclical rise and fall of anomalies based on evolutionary forces *(Chapter 13)*

affect how a person experiences a feeling *(Chapter 7)*

affective assessment the experience a person has in response to a stimulus *(Chapter 7)*

agency problem a potential problem existing in an agency relationship when the incentives of an agent and a principal are not aligned *(Chapter 2)*

agency relationship a relationship where someone (the principal) contracts with someone else (the agent) to take actions on behalf of the principal and represent the principal's interests *(Chapter 2)*

Allais paradox a well-known contradiction of expected utility theory *(Chapter 1)*

ambiguity aversion the tendency to prefer risk (with a known probability distribution over outcomes) over uncertainty *(Chapter 5)*

amygdala part of the human brain that evaluates sensory information, and which is important in the evaluation of primary emotions such as anger and fear *(Chapter 7)*

anchoring the tendency to adhere to prior beliefs longer than one should *(Chapter 5)*

anomalies empirical results that appear to run counter to market efficiency *(Chapter 4)*

anomaly attenuation the tendency for anomalies to weaken after public awareness and remedial arbitrage activity *(Chapter 19)*

arbitrage the simultaneous purchase and sale (or short-sale) of securities in order to lock in a risk-free profit *(Chapter 4)*

asset allocation the process of partitioning investments among different asset classes such as stocks and bonds so as to take on the appropriate amount of risk *(Chapter 17)*

attribution theory theory investigating how people make causal attributions, that is, how they come up with explanations for the causes of actions and outcomes *(Chapter 6)*

automatic enrollment a company retirement savings plan design in which employees on being hired are enrolled in the plan unless they take active steps otherwise *(Chapter 17)*

autonomic nervous system the system that governs a body's involuntary actions, such as sweating and shaking *(Chapter 7)*

availability the tendency to find information that is easy to obtain and process more compelling *(Chapter 5)*

avoiders those who avoid planning for their financial futures, with those who are most deficient in this regard being termed "live-for-today avoiders" *(Chapter 18)*

base rate neglect the tendency to ignore or downplay distributional information while paying too much attention to the sample *(Chapter 5)*

Bayes' rule a formula to update probability based on new information *(Chapter 5)*

behavioral investing the attempt to enhance portfolio performance by applying lessons learned from behavioral finance *(Chapter 19)*

beta a measure of risk that takes into account an asset's sensitivity to the market, thus only measuring nondiversifiable risk *(Chapter 2)*

better-than-average effect the tendency for a person to rate himself as above average in knowledge or skills *(Chapter 6)*

bounded rationality a view that posits that people satisfice or do the best that they can under the circumstances *(Chapter 5)*

break even effect an increase in risk taking after a prior loss in an attempt to break even *(Chapter 3)*

bubble an observed price pattern in which high prices seem to be generated more by traders' enthusiasm than by economic fundamentals *(Chapter 14)*

bubbles market design an experimental design normally characterized by subjects trading over a fixed number of periods an asset, whose dividend payout is determined by a known probability distribution common to all participants *(Chapter 14)*

buy-side analysts financial analysts, employed by large money management firms, whose reports are usually generated for internal purposes *(Chapter 12)*

capital asset pricing model (CAPM) a model of how asset prices are determined in which expected returns are linearly related to beta *(Chapter 2)*

capital market line (CML) a line depicting all combinations of the risk-free asset and the market portfolio *(Chapter 2)*

catering a managerial strategy designed to push up the share price (but not the share value) in the short run *(Chapter 15)*

certainty effect overweighting of outcomes that are certain as compared to those that are merely probable *(Chapter 3)*

certainty equivalent the wealth level that leads a decision-maker to be indifferent between a particular prospect and a given wealth level *(Chapter 1)*

coefficient of relative risk aversion a measure of distaste for risk *(Chapter 14)*

cognitive antecedent a belief that triggers an emotional response *(Chapter 7)*

cognitive dissonance a feeling that motivates people to reduce or avoid psychological inconsistencies *(Chapter 5)*

complete preferences preferences such that one can assess all possible pairwise choices and specify either preference of one over the other or indifference *(Chapter 1)*

confirmation bias the tendency to search out evidence consistent with prior beliefs and ignore conflicting data *(Chapter 6)*

conformity the tendency to give in to real or imagined social pressure *(Chapter 11)*

conjunction fallacy a probability mistake that occurs when one believes that a joint probability is higher than one of the simple probabilities *(Chapter 5)*

corporation a legal entity separate from its founders or owners, with unlimited life and limited liability *(Chapter 12)*

correlation a statistical measure of how the movements of two variables are related, which is bounded by -1 and +1, with zero indicating no relationship *(Chapter 2)*

covariance a statistical measure of how the movements of two variables are related with a positive (negative) value indicating that the two variables move together (apart) *(Chapter 2)*

cumulative prospect theory extension of prospect theory in which mathematical specifications for both the value function and the weighting function are presented and estimated *(Chapter 3)*

customization the strategy of adapting educational material to the relevant audience *(Chapter 18)*

data snooping analyzing a dataset exhaustively in an effort to detect apparent anomalies *(Chapter 4)*

debiasing attempting to overcome behavioral bias *(Chapter 18)*

debiased confidence interval a confidence interval that has been adjusted for excessive optimism and miscalibration *(Chapter 18)*

decision weights under prospect theory, weights that are a function of probabilities and that replace probabilities in the calculation of the value of prospects *(Chapter 3)*

deferral rate the percentage of pay set aside for retirement *(Chapter 17)*

defined benefit (DB) pension a pension in which the employer normally promises, according to a formula, periodic payments after retirement *(Chapter 17)*

defined contribution (DC) pension a retirement savings plan in which normally both the employer and employee make contributions into a retirement account whose accumulation is a function of investment returns, without any guarantee as to what will be available after retirement *(Chapter 17)*

dictator game an experiment in which the first player (the proposer) decides how to split an endowment and the second player (the responder) takes a passive role *(Chapter 11)*

disappearing dividends period a period beginning in the late 1970s over which the percentage of firms paying dividends gradually declined *(Chapter 15)*

disposition effect the tendency to sell winners and hold losers *(Chapter 3)*

diversifiable risk that component of total risk, specific to the asset in question, that can be diversified away *(Chapter 2)*

diversification combining assets in a portfolio with the purpose of reducing diversifiable risk *(Chapter 2)*

diversification heuristic the tendency to choose "a bit of everything" *(Chapter 5)*

dividend premium a measure of the value of dividend-paying stocks relative to non-dividend-paying stocks holding all else equal *(Chapter 15)*

ease of processing ready understanding of information *(Chapter 5)*

efficient frontier the set of portfolios that maximize expected return for a given level of risk *(Chapter 2)*

efficient market a market consistent with efficiency, which implies that no investor can consistently earn excess returns after all costs are considered *(Chapter 2)*

efficient markets hypothesis (EMH) see **efficient market**

efficient set see **efficient frontier**

emotion a mental and physiological state defined by observable features *(Chapter 7)*

emotional intelligence (EI) the ability to identify and manage emotional responses, both those of oneself and others *(Chapter 7)*

emotional quotient (EQ) a measure of emotional intelligence, analogous to a measure of intelligence using an IQ test *(Chapter 7)*

endorsement effects effects whereby an employee believes that the company itself is making an implicit recommendation in setting up the default *(Chapter 17)*

endowment effect the observation that the value of a good seems to increase once a person owns it *(Chapter 3)*

equity premium see **market risk premium**

equity premium puzzle the observation that the level of the equity premium implies, under expected utility theory, an implausibly high level of risk aversion *(Chapter 14)*

event study a research study investigating a large number of similar events in a sample of data, which, in terms of event time, computes and accumulates excess returns in order to assess the market's typical reaction to a particular type of event *(Chapter 4)*

excess returns returns, after adjusting for all costs, that exceed those that are fair based on the risk borne *(Chapter 2)*

excessive optimism the tendency to be more optimistic about one's prospects than is objectively warranted *(Chapter 6)*

excessive volatility the tendency for asset price changes to be driven in large part by factors irrelevant for valuation *(Chapter 14)*

expected utility theory a normative theory contending that individuals *should* act in a particular way when undertaking decision-making under uncertainty *(Chapter 1)*

expected value a distributional average such that, as the sample of observations becomes very large, the sample average value converges to the expected value *(Chapter 2)*

expertise the skill of an expert usually defined in terms of relative performance *(Chapter 20)*

exponential discount function a function often used in classical economics when comparing the perceived value of a dollar at different points in time, such that the intertemporal rate of substitution between two equally

spaced points in time is constant *(Chapter 17)*

Fama-French three-factor model a model of security return generation whose risk factors are the market, firm size, and the book-to-market ratio *(Chapter 13)*

familiarity comfort in what is known *(Chapter 5)*

fast and frugal heuristics the view that heuristics almost always lead to reasonable decisions while conserving on time, information requirements, and computation in real-world environments *(Chapter 5)*

feedback the attempt to provide guidance on decision-making in order to debias an individual *(Chapter 18)*

forebrain the outer portion of the brain that is the primary locus of cognition *(Chapter 7)*

fourfold pattern of risk attitudes risk aversion for gains and risk seeking for losses when the outcome probability is high, coupled with risk seeking for gains and risk aversion for losses when the outcome probability is low *(Chapter 3)*

frame a decision-maker's view of a problem and its possible outcomes *(Chapter 1)*

free rider problem a problem resulting from shirking where the free rider bears no cost in relying on others to take responsibility (such as in the case of monitoring) *(Chapter 12)*

frontal lobe the largest lobe in the human brain, which regulates motor abilities, memory, judgment, decision-making, and the ability to plan for the future *(Chapter 7)*

functional magnetic resonance imaging (fMRI) a device that maps brain activity using blood and oxygen flow *(Chapter 7)*

fundamental risk risk that arises because of the potential for rational revaluation as new information arrives *(Chapter 4)*

gambler's fallacy the *erroneous* belief that additional observations should be such that a sample will closely resemble the underlying distribution (*Chapter 5*)

glamour stocks see **growth stocks**

greater fool theory a theory that postulates that people buy an asset that they realize is overvalued because they think there is a foolish individual out there who will pay even more for it (*Chapter 14*)

groupthink an extreme form of conformity where group members begin to think alike, stress loyalty, and discourage dissent (*Chapter 11*)

growth stocks stocks with prices that are low relative to earnings, cash flow, and book value (*Chapter 4*)

halo effect the tendency to base an assessment on earlier impressions or salient characteristics (*Chapter 5*)

hard-easy effect the tendency to be less overconfident on easy questions, even to the point of underconfidence (*Chapter 6*)

herding the tendency to use the behavior of others as an input into one's decisions, which, on a large scale, can lead to a multitude of correlated financial decisions (*Chapter 8*)

heuristics decision rules that utilize a subset of the information set and that sometimes lead to bias (*Chapter 5*)

hindsight bias the tendency to believe that things that have happened were more predictable at the time than they actually were (*Chapter 6*)

home bias the tendency to invest in local securities (*Chapter 8*)

home-made dividends the strategy of selling off shares when received dividends are too low, or buying new shares when received dividends are too high, so as to set one's own payout (*Chapter 15*)

hot hand phenomenon the belief, often coupled with base rate

neglect, that recent events are more likely to occur in the future than history might warrant (*Chapter 5*)

house money effect the willingness to take greater risk with money that was recently won (*Chapter 3*)

hyperbolic discount function a function comparing the perceived value of a dollar at different points in time, such that the preference for a current dollar versus a dollar received one period in the future is greater than the preference for a future dollar versus a dollar received one period after that future date (*Chapter 17*)

illusion of control the tendency to think that there is more control over events than can objectively be true (*Chapter 6*)

implicit learning information acquired without the ability to verbally express what was learned (*Chapter 20*)

implied volatility index (VIX) the Chicago Board Options Exchange measure of fear based on investors' expectations of future stock market volatility using current option prices (*Chapter 14*)

income replacement ratio retirement income as a percentage of working (or employment) income (*Chapter 17*)

independent analysts professional financial analysts who provide independent research and are not associated with a large investment firm (*Chapter 12*)

informational advantages various benefits gained from knowing more about local companies and thus having a more accurate view of value (*Chapter 8*)

information overload a state of confusion and decision avoidance induced by a large amount of information that is difficult to assimilate (*Chapter 5*)

insiders corporate directors who are managers or executives of the company (*Chapter 12*)

integration in the context of prospect theory and mental accounting, the act of moving away from the reference point because of past outcomes and when confronting new choices (*Chapter 3*)

intentional objects objects of emotions, such as persons or situations (*Chapter 7*)

joint-hypothesis problem the unavoidable fact that all tests of market efficiency jointly test efficiency *and* a particular risk-adjustment model (*Chapter 2*)

life-cycle funds a single fund that is not only initially appropriate in its risk-taking stance, but which also *dynamically* adjusts its risk taking so as to be consistent with an average individual's changing risk tolerance (*Chapter 17*)

lifestyle fund a single fund that is initially appropriate in its risk-taking stance for an average individual (*Chapter 17*)

limbic system the inner portion of the brain that is the primary locus of emotional response (*Chapter 7*)

limited self-control the psychological tendency to avoid doing what is rational, especially in terms of saving behavior (*Chapter 17*)

limits to arbitrage the likelihood that mispricing will not be totally eliminated primarily because of the presence of noise-trader risk and career concerns (*Chapter 4*)

loss aversion in prospect theory, the tendency to view a gain as contributing less to utility than an equal-dollar loss subtracts from it (*Chapter 3*)

lottery asset an asset that infrequently pays off, but when it does, the payoff is large (*Chapter 14*)

market efficiency see **efficient market**

market risk premium expected return on the market in excess of the risk-free rate or a fixed-income portfolio (*Chapter 2*)

mean return the sample average *(Chapter 2)*

memory the retrieval of stored information in the brain *(Chapter 5)*

mental accounting a set of often suboptimal cognitive operations that people use to manage and assess financial activities *(Chapter 3)*

miscalibration the tendency to overestimate the precision of knowledge *(Chapter 6)*

modern portfolio theory a practical framework that assumes that investors are risk averse and preferences are defined in terms of the mean and variance of returns *(Chapter 2)*

momentum positive correlation in returns *(Chapter 4)*

momentum-chasing see **trend-following**

money attitude a person's predisposition based on measurable attributes related to financial matters *(Chapter 18)*

mood a general feeling that does not focus on anything in particular *(Chapter 7)*

multivariate approaches attempts to enhance return by conditioning on a multitude of factors *(Chapter 19)*

myopic loss aversion the tendency to be loss averse while frequently evaluating one's wealth position *(Chapter 14)*

neoclassical economics a school of thought that says individuals and firms are self-interested agents who attempt to optimize to the best of their ability in the face of constraints on resources *(Chapter 1)*

neuroeconomics new and rapidly growing field that uses neurotechnology to examine how the brain behaves while a person is making economic decisions *(Chapter 20)*

neurofinance new and rapidly growing field that uses neurotechnology to examine how the brain behaves while a person is making financial decisions *(Chapter 7)*

neuroscience the science that studies the brain and nervous system *(Chapter 7)*

noise misinformation, that is, information not relevant for the valuation of securities, which often leads to noise-trading *(Chapter 4)*

noise-trader risk risk that arises because mispricing induced by noise-traders can become more severe in the short run *(Chapter 4)*

noise-traders individuals who trade based on noise *(Chapter 4)*

nondiversifiable risk the component of total risk that is common to all risky assets in the system and which cannot be diversified away *(Chapter 2)*

nonsystematic risk see **diversifiable risk**

normative theory a theory that describes how people *should* behave *(Chapter 3)*

objective risk risk revealed by actual investment decisions, as reflected in the percentage of risky assets in the overall portfolio *(Chapter 18)*

optimal compensation contract a compensation contract designed to align the interests of shareholders and managers *(Chapter 2)*

other-regarding preferences choices that are inconsistent with pure self-interest, such as fairness and reciprocity *(Chapter 11)*

outsiders corporate directors who are not employees of the company *(Chapter 12)*

overconfidence the tendency to overestimate one's knowledge, abilities, and information precision, or to be overly sanguine about the future and one's ability to control it *(Chapter 6)*

path dependence a state where someone's choice depends on the past rather than only the current situation *(Chapter 3)*

perception the acquisition by the brain of current information *(Chapter 5)*

personality types categories of individuals based on such measurable personality attributes as extroversion versus introversion *(Chapter 18)*

physiological arousal hormonal and nervous system changes associated with emotions *(Chapter 7)*

physiological expressions observable physical expressions associated with emotions *(Chapter 7)*

planner-avoider continuum a scale with successful planners being at one extreme and live-for-today avoiders being at the other *(Chapter 18)*

planners those who plan for their financial futures, with those who are best at it being termed "successful planners" *(Chapter 18)*

planning fallacy the tendency to think that more can be accomplished than is likely *(Chapter 6)*

positive theory a theory that describes how people *actually* behave *(Chapter 3)*

positron emission tomography (PET) scan a device that maps brain activity using harmless radioactive substances *(Chapter 7)*

practical knowledge stored tacit knowledge, which often leads to good strategies *(Chapter 20)*

present value model of stock prices a representation that assumes that a stock price is based on reasonable expectations of its fundamental value *(Chapter 2)*

pride a positive emotion induced by a feeling that one has made a good choice *(Chapter 10)*

primacy effect the tendency to rely on information that comes first when making an assessment *(Chapter 5)*

primary emotions emotions that are hardwired into our brains, and which may include anger, contempt, disgust, fear, happiness, sadness, and surprise (*Chapter 7*)

procrastination a psychological tendency to postpone doing what is rational, especially in the context of savings behavior (*Chapter 17*)

prospect a series of wealth outcomes, each of which is associated with a probability (*Chapter 1*)

prospect theory a positive theory of how individuals make choices when confronted with decisions under risk, whose major features are the four fold pattern of risk attitudes and that individuals consider changes in wealth from a reference point (*Chapter 3*)

psychographic profiling the process of assigning individuals to groups based on personality, attitudes, values, and beliefs (*Chapter 18*)

random walk the theory that the next price change is unpredictable, and the best forecast of the next price is the current price (*Chapter 2*)

rate of time preference the "interest rate" that subjectively converts a future value into a present value (*Chapter 17*)

rational preferences preferences consistent with such reasonable conditions as completeness and transitivity (*Chapter 1*)

recency bias the tendency to more easily recall recent events and to think that such events are more probable than is really the case (*Chapter 5*)

recency effect the tendency to rely on the most recent information when making an assessment (*Chapter 5*)

reference group neglect the tendency for people to be unaware that others in their group, facing the same incentives as themselves, are likely to be comparable in terms of skill (*Chapter 16*)

reference point under prospect theory the point (usually the status quo) from which changes in wealth are considered (*Chapter 3*)

regret a negative emotion induced by a feeling that one has made a poor choice (*Chapter 10*)

Regulation Fair Disclosure (Reg FD) an SEC ruling implemented in 2000 in an attempt to thwart selective disclosure by publicly traded firms to large investors (*Chapter 12*)

representativeness heuristic the tendency to evaluate the probability of an outcome A based on the degree to which A resembles B (*Chapter 5*)

reversal negative correlation in returns (*Chapter 4*)

risk a state that exists when all possible outcomes and their associated probabilities are known (*Chapter 1*)

risk attitude one's personal comfort with risk taking holding all else equal (*Chapter 18*)

risk averse descriptive of a person who prefers the expected value of a prospect to the prospect itself (*Chapter 1*)

risk capacity the amount of risk that is appropriate based on age, retirement plans, income, liquidity needs, and so on, for an individual of average risk attitude (*Chapter 18*)

risk neutral descriptive of a person who is indifferent between the expected value of a prospect and the prospect itself (*Chapter 1*)

risk seeker descriptive of a person who prefers a prospect to its expected value (*Chapter 1*)

risk tolerance the amount of risk that is appropriate for an individual based on both risk capacity and risk attitude (*Chapter 18*)

salience bias the tendency to easily recall salient information when making an assessment, and to think that salient events are more

probable than they really are (*Chapter 5*)

sample standard deviation the positive square root of the sample variance (*Chapter 2*)

sample variance an estimate using a sample of data of the variance (*Chapter 2*)

Sarbanes-Oxley Act (SOX) legislation enacted in 2002 in response to corporate scandals, which included a requirement that walls separating security analysts and the investment banking arm of the same firm be strengthened (*Chapter 12*)

scheduled deferral increase programs (SDIPs) programs based on future deferral increases designed to convince people to save a sufficient amount for a properly funded retirement (*Chapter 17*)

Securities and Exchange Commission (SEC) an entity created in the United States under the Securities and Exchange Act of 1934 with a mission "to protect investors, maintain fair, orderly, and efficient markets, and facilitate capital formation" (*Chapter 12*)

security analysts information intermediaries who provide analysis to investors and firms (*Chapter 12*)

segregation in the context of prospect theory and mental accounting, the act of returning to the reference point after past outcomes and when confronting new choices (*Chapter 3*)

self-attribution bias the tendency to attribute successes to one's own abilities, while blaming failures on circumstances beyond one's control (*Chapter 6*)

self-monitoring the disposition to attend to social cues and appropriately adjust behavior (*Chapter 9*)

sell-side analysts professional financial analysts who are typically employed by brokers, dealers, and investment banks (*Chapter 12*)

semi-strong form market efficiency the version of market efficiency that stipulates that prices reflect all publicly available information (*Chapter 2*)

sensation-seeking a personality trait whose four dimensions are thrill and adventure seeking, experience seeking, disinhibition, and boredom susceptibility (*Chapter 9*)

sentiment the degree to which large numbers of investors simultaneously misvalue some or all securities (*Chapter 4*)

small-firm effect the tendency for firms with low levels of market capitalization to earn excess returns after accounting for market risk (*Chapter 4*)

smart-money traders individuals who trade for purely rational reasons (*Chapter 4*)

snake-bit effect an increase in risk aversion after an initial loss (*Chapter 10*)

social learning learning based on observing the decisions of others (*Chapter 12*)

social neuroscience a science that investigates the neural circuitry that operates when we deal with other people (*Chapter 11*)

standard deviation the positive square root of the variance (*Chapter 2*)

status quo bias see **endowment effect**

strong form market efficiency the version of market efficiency that stipulates that prices reflect all information, both public and private (*Chapter 2*)

style investing consideration of style in portfolio formation (*Chapter 19*)

style peer group a group of investors following the same style, where style is usually defined in terms of firm size and growth versus value (*Chapter 19*)

style rotation act of moving from style to style in an attempt to time aggregate style preference shifts (*Chapter 19*)

subjective risk assessment of risk based in part on individuals' attitudes and beliefs toward risk (*Chapter 18*)

systematic risk see **nondiversifiable risk**

tacit knowledge see **implicit learning**

target date funds see **life-cycle funds**

transitivity a characteristic of preferences such that if *a* is preferred to *b* and *b* is preferred to *c*, then *a* must be preferred to *c* (*Chapter 1*)

trend-following the tendency to purchase securities whose recent performance has been strong (*Chapter 8*)

trust game an experiment in which the amount the first player (the proposer) sends to the second player (the responder) is increased by a multiple, and the second player decides how much to return to the first player (*Chapter 11*)

two-fund separation the theory that says that rational investors maximize utility by combining the risk-free asset with a unique individual-specific risky portfolio (*Chapter 2*)

Type 1 heuristic heuristics appropriate when a very quick decision must be made or when the stakes are low (*Chapter 5*)

Type 2 heuristic heuristics that are more effortful and that are appropriate when the stakes are higher (*Chapter 5*)

ultimatum game an experiment in which the first player (the proposer) decides how to split an endowment and the second player (the responder) can accept or reject the offer (*Chapter 11*)

uncertainty a state that exists when either some possible outcomes and/or their associated probabilities are unknown (*Chapter 1*)

under-diversification the tendency to hold securities in one's portfolio whose number is insufficient to achieve the elimination of most diversifiable risk (*Chapter 9*)

utility function a function that specifies the assignment of numbers to possible outcomes so that preferred choices receive higher numbers (*Chapter 1*)

valence a psychological term used to rate feelings of pleasure and pain or happiness and unhappiness (*Chapter 7*)

value function a function that in prospect theory replaces the utility function in expected utility theory (*Chapter 3*)

value investing the tendency to overweight value stocks (relative to growth stocks) in a portfolio (*Chapter 4*)

value premium average gap between returns on a value portfolio and a growth portfolio (*Chapter 2*)

value stocks stocks with prices that are low relative to accounting measures such as earnings, cash flows, or book value (*Chapter 4*)

variance a statistical measure of the dispersion of a distribution equal to the expected value of the squared deviation from the mean (*Chapter 2*)

weak form market efficiency the version of market efficiency that stipulates that prices reflect all information contained in historical prices and returns (*Chapter 2*)

weighting function a mapping of probabilities on to decision weights (*Chapter 3*)

References

Abarbanell, J. S., and V. L. Bernard, 1992, "Tests of analysts' over-reaction/underreaction to earnings information as an explanation for anomalous stock price behavior," *Journal of Finance* 47, 1181–1207.

Abelson, R., December 16, 2001, "Enron board comes under a storm of criticism," *New York Times*, p. BU4.

Ackert, L. F., and G. Athanassakos, 1997, "Prior uncertainty, analyst bias, and subsequent abnormal returns," *Journal of Financial Research* 20(2), 263–273.

Ackert, L. F., and G. Athanassakos, 2001, "Visibility, institutional preferences and agency considerations," *Journal of Psychology and Financial Markets* 2(4), 201–209.

Ackert, L. F., N. Charupat, B. K. Church, and R. Deaves, 2006, "An experimental examination of the house money effect in a multi-period setting," *Experimental Economics* 9, 5–16.

Ackert, L. F., N. Charupat, B. K. Church, and R. Deaves, 2006, "Margin, short selling, and lotteries in experimental asset markets," *Southern Economic Journal* 73(2), 419–436.

Ackert, L. F., N. Charupat, R. Deaves, and B. D. Kluger, "Probability judgment error and speculation in laboratory asset market bubbles," *Journal of Financial and Quantitative Analysis*, forthcoming.

Ackert, L. F., and B. K. Church, 2001, "The effects of subject pool and design experience on rationality in experimental asset markets," *Journal of Psychology and Financial Markets* 2(1), 6–28.

Ackert, L. F., and B. K. Church, 2006, "Firm image and individual investment decisions," *Journal of Behavioral Finance* 7(3), 155–167.

Ackert, L. F., and B. K. Church, 2009, "Home bias: Taking comfort in what you know?" *International Journal of Behavioural Accounting and Finance*, forthcoming.

Ackert, L. F., B. K. Church, and G. P. Dwyer, Jr., 2007, "When the shoe is on the other foot: Experimental evidence on valuation disparities," *Public Finance Review* 35(2), 199–214.

Ackert, L. F., B. K. Church, and B. Englis, 2002, "The asset allocation decision and investor heterogeneity: A puzzle?" *Journal of Economic Behavior and Organization* 47, 423–433.

Ackert, L. F., B. K. Church, J. Tompkins, and P. Zhang, 2005, "What's in a name? An experimental examination of investment behavior," *Review of Finance* 9, 281–304.

Ackert, L. F., B. K. Church, X. J. Kuang, and L. Qi, 2007, "White lies: Why bother?" Georgia Tech working paper.

Ackert, L. F., B. K. Church, and R. Deaves, 2003, "Emotion and financial markets," *Federal Reserve Bank of Atlanta Economic Review*, 33–41.

Ackert, L. F., B. K. Church, and K. Ely, 2009, "Biases in individual forecasts: Experimental evidence," *Journal of Behavioral Finance* 9(2), 53–61.

Ackert, L. F., and B. F. Smith, 1993, "Stock price volatility, ordinary dividends, and other cash flows to shareholders," *Journal of Finance* 48(4), 1147–1160.

Agnew, J., P. Balduzzi, and A. Sundén, 2003, "Portfolio choice and trading in a large 401(k) plan," *American Economic Review* 93, 193–215.

Akerlof, G. A., and R. E. Kranton, 2008, "Identity, supervision, and work groups," *American Economic Review* 98(2), 212–217.

Ali, A., L.-S. Hwang, and M. A. Trombley, 2003, "Arbitrage risk and the book-to-market anomaly," *Journal of Financial Economics* 69, 355–373.

Allais, M., 1953, "L'Extension des théories de l'équilibre économique général et du rendement social au cas du risque," *Econometrica* 21(2) (April), 269–290.

Alpert, M., and H. Raiffa, 1982, "A progress report on the training of probability assessors," in D. Kahneman, P. Slovic, and A. Tversky, eds.: *Judgment under Uncertainty: Heuristics and Biases* (Cambridge University Press, Cambridge, U.K.).

Ameriks, J., and S. P. Zeldes, 2001, "How do household portfolio shares vary with age?" Columbia University working paper.

Ameriks, J., A. Caplin, and J. Leahy, 2003, "Wealth accumulation and the propensity to plan," *Quarterly Journal of Economics* 68, 1007–1048.

Aretz, K., M. Naujoks, A. Kerl, and A. Walter, 2007, "Do German security analysts herd?" Working paper.

Armor, D. A., and S. E. Taylor, 2002, "When predictions fail: The dilemma of unrealistic optimism," in T. Gilovich, D. Griffin, and D. Kahneman, eds.: *Heuristics and Biases: The Psychology of Intuitive Judgment* (Cambridge University Press, Cambridge, U.K.).

Asch, S., 1955, "Opinions and social pressure," *Scientific American*, 31–35.

Asch, S., 1956, "Studies of independence and conformity: A minority of one against a unanimous majority," *Psychological Monographs* 70(9).

Asness, C. S., 1997, "The interaction of value and momentum strategies," *Financial Analysts Journal* 53 (March/Apr), 29–36.

Atkinson, S. M., S. B. Baird, and M. B. Frye, 2001, "Do female mutual fund managers manage differently?" *Journal of Financial Research* 26, 1–18.

Avramov, D., and T. Chordia, 2006, "Predicting stock returns," *Journal of Financial Economics* 82, 387–415.

Azar, O. H., 2007, "The social norm of tipping: A review," *Journal of Applied Social Psychology* 37(2), 380–402.

Bajaj, V., and L. Story, February 12, 2008, "Mortgage crisis spreads past subprime loans," *New York Times*.

Baker, H. K., and J. R. Nofsinger, 2002, "Psychological biases of investors," *Financial Services Review* 11, 97–116.

Baker, L. A., and R. E. Emery, 1993, "When every relationship is above average: Perceptions and expectations of divorce at the time of marriage," *Law and Human Behavior* 17, 439–450.

Baker, M., and J. Wurgler, 2000, "The equity share in new issues and aggregate stock returns," *Journal of Finance* 55, 2219–2257.

Baker, M., and J. Wurgler, 2004, "A catering theory of dividends," *Journal of Finance* 59, 1125–1166.

Baker, M., and J. Wurgler, 2004, "Appearing and disappearing dividends," *Journal of Financial Economics* 73, 271–288.

Baker, M., R. S. Ruback, and J. Wurgler, 2004, "Behavioral corporate finance: A survey," Working paper.

Ball, R., and P. Brown, 1968, "An empirical evaluation of accounting income numbers," *Journal of Accounting Research* 6, 159–178.

Baltussen, G., T. Post, and P. Van Vliet, 2006, "Violations of cumulative prospect theory in mixed gambles with moderate probabilities," *Management Science* 52(8), 1288–1290.

Banerjee, A. V., "A simple model of herd behavior," *Quarterly Journal of Economics* 107(3), 797–817.

Banks, J., R. Blundell, and S. Tanner, 1998, "Is there a retirement-savings puzzle?" *American Economic Review* 88, 769–788.

Banz, R. W., 1981, "The relationship between return and market value of common stocks," *Journal of Financial Economics* 9, 3–18.

Barber, B., and T. Odean, 1999, "The courage of misguided convictions," *Financial Analysts Journal* (Special Issue on Behavioral Finance), 41–55.

Barber, B., and T. Odean, 2000, "Trading is hazardous to your wealth: The common stock investment performance of individual investors," *Journal of Finance* 55, 773–806.

Barber, B., and T. Odean, 2001, "Boys will be boys: Gender, overconfidence, and common stock investment," *Quarterly Journal of Economics* 116, 261–292.

Barber, B., and T. Odean, 2008, "All that glitters: The effect of attention and news on the buying behavior of individual and institutional investors," *Review of Financial Studies* 21(2), 785–818.

Barberis, N., and A. Shleifer, 2003, "Style investing," *Journal of Financial Economics* 68, 161–199.

Barberis, N., and M. Huang, 2008, "Stocks as lotteries: The implications of probability weighting for security prices," *American Economic Review* 98(5), 2066–2100.

Barberis, N., and W. Xiong, 2006, "What drives the disposition effect? An analysis of a long-standing preference-based explanation," NBER Working paper number 12397.

Barberis, N., A. Shleifer, and R. Vishny, 1998, "A model of investor sentiment," *Journal of Financial Economics* 49, 307–344.

Barberis, N., M. Huang, and T. Santos, 2001, "Prospect theory and asset prices," *Quarterly Journal of Economics* 116(1), 1–53.

Barsky, R. B., F. T. Juster, M. S. Kimball, and M. D. Shapiro, 1997, "Preference parameters and behavioral heterogeneity: An experimental approach in the Health and Retirement Study," *Quarterly Journal of Economics* 112, 537–579.

Basu, S., 1977, "Investment performance of common stocks in relation to their price-earnings ratios: A test of the efficient market hypothesis," *Journal of Finance* 32, 663–682.

Battalio, R. C., J. H. Kagel, and K. Jiranyakul, 1990, "Testing between alternative models of choice under uncertainty: Some initial results," *Journal of Risk and Uncertainty* 3(1), 25–50.

Battalio, R. H, and R. R. Mendenhall, 2005, "Earnings expectations, investor trade size, and anomalous returns around earnings announcements," *Journal of Financial Economics* 77, 289–319.

Bauer, R., J. Derwall, and R. Molenaar, 2002, "The real-time predictability of the size and value premium in Japan," Working paper.

Bechara, A., and A. R. Damasio, 2005, "The somatic marker hypothesis: A neural theory of economic decision," *Games and Economic Behavior* 52(2), 336–372.

Ben-David, I., J. R. Graham, and C. Harvey, 2007, "Managerial overconfidence and corporate policies," Working paper.

Benartzi, S., 2001, "Excessive extrapolation and the allocation of 401(k) accounts to company stock," *Journal of Finance* 56, 1747–1764.

Benartzi, S., and R. H. Thaler, 1995, "Myopic loss aversion and the equity premium puzzle," *Quarterly Journal of Economics* 110(1) 73–92.

Benartzi, S., and R. Thaler, 2001, "Naïve diversification strategies in defined contribution saving plans," *American Economic Review* 91, 79–98.

Benartzi, S., and R. H. Thaler, 2002, "How much is investor autonomy worth?" *Journal of Finance* 57, 1593–1616.

Benos, A. V., 1998, "Aggressiveness and survival of overconfident traders," *Journal of Financial Markets* 1, 353–383.

Benston, G. J., and A. L. Hartgraves, 2002, "Enron: What happened and what we can learn from it," *Journal of Accounting and Public Policy* 21(2), 105–127.

Benz, C., P. Di Teresa, and R. Kinnel, 2003, *Morningstar Guide to Mutual Funds: 5-Star Strategies for Success* (John Wiley & Sons, Hoboken, New Jersey).

Bernardo, A. E., and I. Welch, 2001, "On the evolution of overconfidence and entrepreneurs," Working paper.

Bernheim, B. D., and D. M. Garrett, 2003, "The effects of financial education in the workplace: Evidence from a survey of households," *Journal of Public Economics* 87, 1487–1519.

Bernheim, B. D., J. Skinner, and S. Weinberg, 2001, "What accounts for the variation in retirement wealth among U.S. households?" *American Economic Review* 91, 832–857.

Bernheim, D., D. Garrett, and D. Maki, 2001, "Education and saving: The long-term effects of high school curriculum mandates," *Journal of Public Economics* 80, 435–465.

Beyer, S., and E. M. Bowden, 1997, "Gender difference in self-perception: Convergence evidence from three measures of accuracy and bias," *Personality and Social Psychology Bulletin* 23, 157–172.

Bhandari, G., and R. Deaves, 2006, "Misinformed and informed asset allocation decisions of self-directed retirement plan members," Working paper.

Bhandari, G., and R. Deaves, 2006, "The demographics of overconfidence," *Journal of Behavioral Finance* 7(1), 5–11.

Bhandari, G., R. Deaves, and K. Hassanein, 2007, "Using decision support systems to debias investors," *Decision Support Systems* 46, 399–410.

Biais, B., D. Hilton, K. Mazurier, and S. Pouget, 2005, "Judgemental overconfidence, self-monitoring, and trading performance in an experimental financial market," *Review of Economic Studies* 72, 287–312.

Bikhchandani, S., D. Hirshleifer, and I. Welch, 1998, "Learning from the behavior of others: Conformity, fads, and informational cascades," *Journal of Economic Perspectives* 12(3) (Summer), 151–170.

Black, F., 1972, "Capital market equilibrium with restricted borrowing," *Journal of Business* 45(3), 444–455.

Black, Fischer, 1986, "Noise," *Journal of Finance* 41(3), 529–543.

Black, F., and M. S. Scholes, 1974, "The effects of dividend yield and dividend policy on common stock prices and returns," *Journal of Financial Economics* 1, 1–22.

Bodie, Z., and D. B. Crane, 1997, "Personal investing: Advice, theory and evidence," *Financial Analysts Journal* 53 (Nov/Dec), 13–23.

Bodie, Z., and M. J. Clowes, 2003, *Worry-free Investing: A Safe Approach to Achieving Your Lifetime Goals,* (Pearson Education, Upper Saddle River, New Jersey).

Bodie, Z., R. C. Merton, and W. F. Samuelson, 1992, "Labor supply flexibility and portfolio choice in a life-cycle model," *Journal of Economic Dynamics and Control* 16, 427–449.

Bond, R., and P. B. Smith, 1996, "Culture and conformity: A meta-analysis of studies using Asch's line judgment task," *Psychological Bulletin* 119, 111–137.

Boudoukh, J., M. P. Richardson, and R. F. Whitelaw, 1994, "A tale of three schools: Insights on autocorrelations of short-horizon stock returns," *Review of Financial Studies* 7, 539–573.

Brav, A., J. Graham, C. R. Harvey, and R. Michaely, 2005, "Payout policy in the 21st century," *Journal of Financial Economics* 77, 483–527.

Brav, A., J. B. Heaton, and A. Rosenberg, 2004, "The rational-behavioral debate in financial economics," *Journal of Economic Methodology* 11, 393–409.

Brinson, G. P., L. R. Hood, and G. R. Beebower, 1986, "Determinants of portfolio performance," *Financial Analysts Journal* (July/August), 39–44.

Brinson, G.P., B.D. Singer, and G. R. Beebower, 1991, "Determinants of portfolio performance II: An update," *Financial Analysts Journal* (May/June), 40–48.

Brock, W., J. Lakonishok, and B. LeBaron, 1992, "Simple technical trading rules and the stochastic properties of stock returns," *Journal of Finance* 47, 1731–1764.

Brockman, P., and D. Y. Chung, 2001, "Managerial timing and corporate liquidity: Evidence from actual share repurchases," *Journal of Financial Economics* 61, 417–448.

Brosnan, S. F., O. D. Jones, S. P. Lambeth, M. C. Mareno, A. S. Richardson, and S. J. Schapiro, 2007, "Endowment effects in chimpanzees," *Current Biology* 17(19), 1704–1707.

Brown, S. J., W. N. Goetzmann, and S. A. Ross, 1995, "Survival," *Journal of Finance* 50, 853–873.

Bruner, J. S., and L. J. Postman, 1949, "On the perception of incongruity: A paradigm," *Journal of Personality* 18, 206–223.

Buehler, R., D. Griffin, and M. Ross, 2002, "Inside the planning fallacy: The causes and consequences of optimistic time predictions," in T. Gilovich, D. Griffin, and D. Kahneman, eds.: *Heuristics and Biases: The Psychology of Intuitive Judgment* (Cambridge University Press, Cambridge, U.K.).

Burgstahler, D., and I. Dichev, 1997, "Earnings management to avoid earnings increases and losses," *Journal of Accounting and Economics* 24, 99–126.

Butler, E. A., B. Egloff, F. H. Wilhelm, N. C. Smith, E. A. Erickson, and J. J. Gross, 2003, "The social consequences of expressive suppression," *Emotion* 3, 48–67.

Caginalp, G., D. Porter, and V. Smith, 2001, "Financial bubbles: Excess cash, momentum, and incomplete information," *Journal of Psychology and Financial Markets* 2(2), 80–99.

Camerer, C. F., 2003, *Behavioral Game Theory: Experiments in Strategic Interaction* (Russell Sage Foundation, New York).

Camerer, C. F., 2007, "Neuroeconomics: Using neuroscience to make economic predictions," *The Economic Journal* 117, C26–C42.

Camerer, C., G. Loewenstein, and D. Prelec, 2005, "Neuroeconomics: How neuroscience can inform economics," *Journal of Economic Literature* 43, 9–64.

Camerer, C. F., and D. Lovallo, 1999, "Overconfidence and excess entry: An experimental approach," *American Economic Review* 89, 306–318.

Campbell, J. D., and P. J. Fairey, 1985, "Effects of self-esteem, hypothetical explanations, and verbalization of expectancies on future performance," *Journal of Personality and Social Psychology* 48, 1097–1111.

Cannon, W. B., 1927, "The James-Lange theory of emotions: A critical examination and alternative theory," *American Journal of Psychology* 39, 106–124.

Carhart, M. M., 1997, "On persistence in mutual fund performance," *Journal of Finance* 52, 57–82.

Carleton, W. T., C. R. Chen, and T. L. Steiner, 1998, "Optimism biases among brokerage and non-brokerage firms' equity recommendations: Agency costs in the investment industry," *Financial Management* 27, 17–30.

Chan, K. C., and N. Chen, 1991, "Structural and return characteristics of small and large firms," *Journal of Finance* 46, 1467–1484.

Chan, L. K. C., N. Jegadeesh, and J. Lakonishok, 1995, "Evaluating the performance of value vs. glamour stocks: The impact of selection bias," *Journal of Financial Economics* 38, 269–296.

Chan, L. K. C., N. Jegadeesh, and J. Lakonishok, 1999, "The profitability of momentum strategies," *Financial Analysts Journal* (Special Issue on Behavioral Finance), 80–90.

Chan, L. K. C., J. Karceski, and J. Lakonishok, 2003, "The level and persistence of growth rates," *Journal of Finance* 58, 643–684.

Chan, L. K. C., and J. Lakonishok, 2004, "Value and growth investing: A review and update," *Financial Analysts Journal* 60 (Jan/Feb), 71.

Chan, L. K. C., Y. Hamao, and J. Lakonishok, 1991, "Fundamentals and stock returns in Japan," *Journal of Finance* 46, 1739–1789.

Chapman, G. B., and E. J. Johnson, 2002, "Incorporating the irrelevant: Anchors in judgments of belief and value," in T. Gilovich, D. Griffin, and D. Kahneman, eds.: *Heuristics and Biases: The Psychology of Intuitive Judgment* (Cambridge University Press, Cambridge, U.K.).

Charlton, B., 2000, *Psychiatry and the Human Condition* (Radcliffe Medical Press, Oxford).

Chen, M. K., V. Lakshminarayanan, and L.Santos, 2005, "The evolution of our preferences: Evidence from capuchin-monkey trading behavior," Working paper.

Chen, Q., and W. Jiang, 2006, "Analysts' weighting of private and public information," *Review of Financial Studies* 19, 319–355.

Chen, S.-H., and C.-H. Yeh, 2002, "On the emergent properties of artificial stock markets: The efficient markets hypothesis and the rational expectations hypothesis," *Journal of Economic Behavior and Organization* 49(2), 217–239.

Chew, S. H., L. G. Epstein, and U. Segal, 1991, "Mixture symmetry and quadratic utility," *Econometrica* 59, 139–163.

Chirinko, R. S., and H. Schaller, 2001, "Business fixed investment and 'bubbles': The Japanese case," *American Economic Review* 91, 663–680.

Chordia, T., and L. Shivakumar, 2002,"Momentum, business cycle, and time-varying expected returns," *Journal of Finance* 57, 985–1020.

Chordia, T., and L. Shivakumar, 2006, "Earnings and price momentum," *Journal of Financial Economics* 80, 627–656.

Cianciolo, A. T., C. Matthew, R. J. Strenberg, and R. K. Wagner, 2006, "Tacit knowledge, practical intelligence, and expertise," In *The Cambridge Handbook of Expertise and Expert Performance*, K.A. Ericsson, N.Charness, P. J. Feltovich, and R. R. Hoffman, eds. (Cambridge University Press, New York), 613–632.

Clemen, R. T., and K. C. Lichtendahl Jr., 2002, "Debiasing expert overconfidence: A Bayesian calibration model," Working paper.

Conlisk, J., 1989, "Three variants on the Allais example," *American Economic Review* 79(3) (June), 392–407.

Conrad, J., M. Cooper, and G. Kaul, 2003, "Value vs. glamour," *Journal of Finance* 58, 1969–1996.

Conrad, J., and G. Kaul, 1993, "Long-term market overreaction or biases in computed returns?" *Journal of Finance* 48, 39–63.

Conrad, J., and G. Kaul, 1998, "An anatomy of trading strategies," *Review of Financial Studies* 11, 489–519.

Cooper, A. C., C. Y. Woo, and W. C. Dunkelberg, 1988, "Entrepreneurs' perceived chances of success," *Journal of Business Venturing* 3, 97–108.

Cooper, M. J., H. Gulen, and P. R. Rau, 2005, "Changing names with style: Mutual fund name changes and their effects on fund flows," *Journal of Finance* 60, 2825–2858.

Cooper, M., H. Gulen, and M. Vassalou, 2001, "Investing in size and book-to-market portfolios using information about the macroeconomy: Some new trading rules," Working paper.

Cooper, M., Jr., R. C. Gutierrez, and A. Hameed, 2004, "Market states and momentum," *Journal of Finance* 59, 1345–1365.

Cooper, M., O. Dimitrov, and P. R. Rau, 2001, "A Rose.com by any other name," *Journal of Finance* 56, 2371–2388.

Cooper, M. J., A. Khorana, I. Osobov, A. Patel, and P. R. Rau, 2004, "Managerial actions in response to a market downturn: Valuation effects of name changes in the dot.com decline," *Journal of Corporate Finance*, forthcoming.

Coren, S., and J. Miller, 1974, "Size contrast as a function of figural similarity," *Perception and Psychophysics* 16, 355–357.

Cornell, B., 1999, *The Equity Risk Premium: The Long-run Future of the Stock Market* (John Wiley & Sons, New York).

Coval, J. D., and T. J. Moskowitz, 1999, "Home bias at home: Local equity preference in domestic portfolios," *Journal of Finance* 54, 145–166.

Coval, J. D., and T. J. Moskowitz, 2001, "The geography of investment: Informed trading and asset prices," *Journal of Political Economy* 109, 811–841.

Coval, J. D., and T. Shumway, 2005, "Do behavioral biases affect prices?" *Journal of Finance* 60, 1–34.

Covel, M., 2004. *Trend Following: How Great Traders Make Millions in Up and Down Markets* (Financial Times Prentice Hall, London, U.K.).

Cox, J. C., 2004, "How to identify trust and reciprocity," *Games and Economic Behavior* 46, 260–281.

Craig, S., and J. Weil, October 26, 2001, "Most analysts remain plugged in to Enron," *Heard on the Street, Wall Street Journal*, C1.

Crow, K., and L. A. E. Schuker, "Best of the Art Blog: Auctions," *Wall Street Journal*, November 10, 2007, p. W2.

Cutler, D. M., J. M. Poterba, and L. H. Summers, 1989, "What moves stock prices?" *Journal of Portfolio Management* 15(3), 4–12.

Damasio, Antonio R., 1994, *Descartes' Error: Emotion, Reason, and the Human Brain* (Putnam, New York).

Daniel, K., D. Hirshleifer, and A. Subrahmanyam, 1998, "Investor psychology and security market under- and overreactions," *Journal of Finance* 53, 1839–1885.

Daniel, K., D. Hirshleifer, and A. Subrahmanyam, 2001, "Overconfidence, arbitrage, and equilibrium asset pricing," *Journal of Finance* 56, 921–965.

Darwin, C., 1859, *The Origin of Species by Means of Natural Selection; Or, the Preservation of Favored Races in the Struggle for Life* (Collier, New York).

Darwin, C., 1872, *The Expression of the Emotions in Man and Animals*, (University of Chicago Press, Chicago).

Davis, D. D., and C. A. Holt, 1993, *Experimental Economics* (Princeton University Press, Princeton, New Jersey).

Davis, G. F., M. Yoo, and W. E. Baker, 2003, "The small world of the American corporate elite, 1982–2001," *Strategic Organization* 1(3) (August), 301–326.

De Bondt, W. F. M., 1998, "A portrait of the individual investor," *European Economic Review* 42, 831–844.

De Bondt, W. F. M., and W. P. Forbes, 1999, "Herding in analyst earnings forecasts: Evidence from the United Kingdom," *European Financial Management* 5, 143–163.

De Bondt, W. F. M., and R. Thaler, 1985, "Does the stock market overreact?" *Journal of Finance* 40, 793–807.

De Long, J. B., A. Shleifer, L. H. Summers, and R. Waldmann, 1990, "Noise trader risk in financial markets," *Journal of Political Economy* 98, 703–738.

Deaves, R., 2005, "Flawed self-directed retirement account decision-making and its implications," *Canadian Investment Review* (Spring), 6–15.

Deaves, R., 2006, *What Kind of an Investor Are You?* (Insomniac Press, Toronto, Canada.).

Deaves, R., and P. Miu, 2007, "Momentum, reversal and market state," *Canadian Investment Review*.

Deaves, R., and P. Miu, 2007, "Refining momentum strategies by conditioning on prior long-term returns: Canadian evidence," *Canadian Journal of Administrative Sciences*, 24, 135–145.

Deaves, R., E. Lüders, and G. Y. Luo, 2008, "An experimental test of the impact of overconfidence and gender on trading activity," *Review of Finance*, forthcoming.

Deaves, R., E. Lüders, and M. Schröder, 2008, "The dynamics of overconfidence: Evidence from stock market forecasters," Working paper.

Deaves, R., T. Veit, G. Bhandari, and J. Cheney 2007, "The savings and investment decisions of planners: An exploratory study of college employees," *Financial Services Review* 16, 117–33.

Del Guercio, D., 1996, "The distorting effects of the prudent-man laws on institutional equity investments," *Journal of Financial Economics* 40, 31–62.

DesRosiers, S., J. F. L'Her, and J. F. Plante, 2004, "Style management in equity country allocation," *Financial Analysts Journal* 60 (Nov-Dec), 40–54.

Diener, E. and R. A. Emmons, "The independence of positive and negative affect," *Journal of Personality and Social Psychology* 47, 1105–1117.

Dimburg, U., and M. Thunberg, 2000, "Rapid facial reactions to emotional facial expression," *Scandinavian Journal of Psychology* 39, 39–46.

Doukas, J. A., and D. Petmezas, 2007, "Acquisitions, overconfident managers and self-attribution bias," *European Financial Management*, forthcoming.

Dufwenberg, M., T. Lindqvist, and E. Moore, 2005, "Bubbles and experience: An experiment," *American Economic Review* 95(5), 1731–1737.

Dugar, A., and S. Nathan, 1995, "The effect of investment banking relationships on financial analysts' earnings forecasts and investment recommendations," *Contemporary Accounting Research* 12(1), 131–160.

Dunning, D., J. A. Meyerowitz, and A. D. Holzberg, 1978, "Ambiguity and self-evaluation: The role of idiosyncratic trait definitions in self-serving assessments of ability," *Journal of Personality and Social Psychology* 57, 1082–1090.

Easley, D., and M. O'Hara, 1987, "Price, trade, size, and information in securities markets," *Journal of Financial Economics* 19, 69–90.

Easterday, K. E., P. K. Sen, and J. A. Stephan, 2007, "The small firm/January effect: Is it disappearing in U.S. markets because of investor learning?" Working paper.

Edmans, A., D. Garcia, and O. Norli, 2007, "Sports sentiment and stock returns," *Journal of Finance* 62(4), 1967–1998.

Eichenwald, K., 2005, *Conspiracy of Fools: A True Story* (Broadway Books, New York).

Eisenberg, A. E., J. Baron, and M. E. P. Seligman, 1998, "Individual differences in risk aversion and anxiety," University of Pennsylvania working paper.

Ekman, P., W. V. Friesen, M. O'Sullivan, A. Chan, I. Diacoyanii-Tarlatzis, K. Heider, et al., 1987, "Universal and cultural differences in the judgments of facial expressions of emotion," *Journal of Personality and Social Psychology* 53(4), 712–717.

Ellsberg, D., 1961, "Risk, ambiguity and the Savage axioms," *Quarterly Journal of Economics* 75, 643–669.

Elster, J., 1998, "Emotions and economic theory," *Journal of Economic Literature* 36(1), 47–74.

Epley, N., and T. Gilovich, 2001, "Putting adjustment back in the anchoring and adjustment heuristic," *Psychological Science* 12, 391–396.

Faig, M., and P. M. Shum, 2002, "Portfolio choice in the presence of personal illiquid projects," *Journal of Finance* 57, 303–328.

Faig, M., and P. M. Shum, 2004, "What explains household stock holdings?" Working paper.

Fairchild, R., 2005, "The effect of managerial overconfidence, asymmetric information, and moral hazard on capital structure decisions," Working paper.

Fairchild, R. J., 2007, "Does audit tenure lead to more fraud? A game-theoretic approach," Social Science Research Network working paper 993400.

Fairchild, R., and G. Zhang, 2005, "Repurchase and dividend catering, managerial myopia, and long-run value-destruction," Working paper.

Falkenstein, E. G., 1996, "Preferences for stock characteristics as revealed by mutual fund portfolio holdings," *Journal of Finance* 51, 111–135.

Fama, E. F., 1970, "Efficient capital markets: A review of theory and empirical work," *Journal of Finance* 31(1) (May), 383–417.

Fama, E. F., 1991, "Efficient capital markets: II," *Journal of Finance* 46 (5) (December), 1575–1617.

Fama, E. F., 1998, "Market efficiency, long-term returns and behavioral finance," *Journal of Financial Economics* 49, 283–306.

Fama, E. F, L. Fisher, M. C. Jensen, and R. Roll, 1969, "The adjustment of stock prices to new information," *International Economic Review* 12, 1–21.

Fama, E. F., and K. R. French, 1992, "The cross-section of expected stock returns," *Journal of Finance* 47(2) (June), 427–465.

Fama, E. F., and K. R. French, 1993, "Common risk factors in the returns on stocks and bonds," *Journal of Financial Economics* 33, 3–56.

Fama, E. F., and K. R. French, 1996, "Multifactor explanations of asset pricing anomalies," *Journal of Finance* 51, 55–84.

Fama, E. F., and K. R. French, 1998, "Value vs. growth: The international evidence," *Journal of Finance* 53, 1975–1799.

Fama, E. F., and K. R. French, 2001, "Disappearing dividends: Changing firm characteristics or lower propensity to pay?" *Journal of Financial Economics* 60, 3–43.

Fazzari, S., R. G. Hubbard, and B. Peterson, 1988, "Financing constraints and corporate investment," *Brookings Papers on Economic Activity*, 141–195.

Fehr, E. and U. Fischbacher, 2002, "Why social preferences matter—The impact of non-selfish motives on competition, cooperation, and incentives," *The Economic Journal* 112, C1–C33.

Fehr, E., and S. Gächter, 2001, "Do incentive contracts crowd out voluntary cooperation?" University of Southern California Law School, Center for Law, Economics and Organization Research Paper Series No. C01–3.

Ferraris, C., and R. Carveth, 2003, "NASA and the Columbia disaster: Decision-making by Groupthink?" Proceedings of the 2003 Association for Business Communication Annual Convention.

Ferris, S. P., R. A. Haugen, and A. K. Makhija, 1988, "Predicting contemporary volume with historic volume at differential price levels: Evidence supporting the disposition effect," *Journal of Finance* 43(3), 677–697.

Festinger, L., 1954, "A theory of social comparison processes," *Human Relations* 7(2), 117–140.

Finucane, M. L., A. Alhakami, P. Slovic, and S. M. Johnson, 2000, "The affect heuristic in judgments of risks and benefits," *Journal of Behavioral Decision Making* 13(1), 1–17.

Fischbacher, U., C. M. Fong, and E. Fehr, 2003, "Fairness, errors, and the power of competition," Institute for Empirical Research in Economics, University of Zurich, Working paper no. 133.

Fischhoff, B., 1982, "For those condemned to study the past: Heuristics and biases in hindsight," in D. Kahneman, P.Slovic, and A. Tversky, eds.: *Judgment under Uncertainty: Heuristics and Biases* (Cambridge University Press, Cambridge, U.K.).

Fischhoff, B., P. Slovic, and S. Lichtenstein, 1977, "Knowing with certainty: The appropriateness of extreme confidence," *Journal of Experimental Psychology: Human Perception and Performance* 3, 552–564.

Fishburn, P. C., 1988, "Expected utility: An anniversary and a new era," *Journal of Risk and Uncertainty* 1(3) (September), 267–283.

Flavin, M., and T. Yamashita, 2002, "Owner-occupied housing and the composition of the household portfolio," *American Economic Review* 92, 345–362.

Forsythe, R., J. L. Horowitz, N. E. Savin, and M. Sefton, 1994, "Fairness in simple bargaining experiments," *Games and Economic Behavior* 6, 347–369.

Forsythe, R., F. Nelson, G. Neumann, and J. Wright, 1992, "Anatomy of an experimental political stock market," *American Economic Review* 82, 1142–1161.

Francis, J., and D. Philbrick, 1993, "Analysts' decisions as products of a multi-task environment," *Journal of Accounting Research* 31(2), 216–230.

Frank, R. H., 1988, *Passions within Reason* (Norton, New York).

Frederic W. Cook & Co., Inc., "Director compensation: NASDAQ 100 vs. NYSE 100," October 2006.

French, K. R., and J. M. Poterba, 1991, "Investor diversification and international equity markets," *American Economic Review* 81, 222–226.

Frenkel, O. J., and A. N. Doob, 1976, "Post-decision dissonance at the polling booth," *Canadian Journal of Behavioural Science* 8, 347–350.

Frieder, L., and A. Subrahmanyam, 2005, "Brand perceptions and the market for common stock," *Journal of Financial and Quantitative Analysis* 40, 57–85.

Friedman, M., and L. J. Savage, 1948, "The utility analysis of choices involving risk," *Journal of Political Economy* 56(4), 279–304.

Frijda, N. H., 1986, *The Emotions* (Cambridge University Press, Cambridge).

Frijda, N. H., 2000, "The psychologists' point of view," in Lewis, M., and J. M. Haviland-Jones, eds., *Handbook of Emotions* (Guilford Press, NewYork).

Geczy, C. C., D. K. Musto, and A. V. Reed, 2002, "Stocks are special too: An analysis of the equity lending market," *Journal of Financial Economics* 66, 241–269.

Gertner, R., 1993, "Game shows and economic behavior: Risk-taking on 'card sharks,'" *Quarterly Journal of Economics* 108(2), 507–521.

Gervais, S., and T. Odean, 2001, "Learning to be overconfident," *Review of Financial Studies* 14, 1–27.

Gigerenzer, G., 1991, "How to make cognitive illusions disappear: Beyond 'heuristics and biases,'" *European Review of Social Psychology* 2, 83–115.

Gigerenzer, G., J. Czerlinski, and L.Martignon, 2002, "How good are fast and frugal heuristics?" in T. Gilovich, D. Griffin, and D.Kahneman, eds.: *Heuristics and Biases: The Psychology of Intuitive Judgment* (Cambridge University Press, Cambridge, U.K.).

Gigerenzer, G., P. M. Todd, and ABC Research Group, eds., 1999. *Simple Heuristics That Make Us Smart* (Oxford University Press, Oxford, U.K.).

Gilbert, D.T., 2006, *Stumbling on Happiness,* (Alfred A. Knopf, New York).

Gillette, A. B., T. H. Noe, and M. J. Rebello, 2003, "Corporate board composition, protocols, and voting behavior: Experimental evidence," *Journal of Finance* 58 (5), 1997–2032.

Gilovich, T., D. Griffin, and D. Kahneman, 2002, "Heuristics and biases: Then and now," in *Heuristics and Biases: The Psychology of Intuitive Judgment* (Cambridge University Press, Cambridge, U.K.).

Gilovich, T. R., R. Vallone, and A. Tversky, 1985, "The hot hand in basketball: On the misperception of random sequences," *Cognitive Psychology* 17, 592–596.

Gintis, H., S. Bowles, R. Boyd, and E. Fehr, 2005, *Moral Sentiments and Material Interests: The Foundations of Cooperation in Economic Life* (MIT Press, Cambridge, Massachusetts).

Glannon, Walter, 2007, *Defining Right and Wrong in Brain Science: Essential Readings in Neuroethics* (Dana Press, New York).

Glaser, M., and M. Weber, 2009, "Which past returns affect trading volume?" *Journal of Financial Markets* 12(1), 1–31.

Glaser, M., and M. Weber, 2007, "Overconfidence and trading volume," *Geneva Risk and Insurance Review* 32, 1–36.

Glaser, M., T. Langer, and M. Weber, 2005, "Overconfidence of professionals and laymen: Individual differences within and between tasks?" Working paper.

Goel, A. M., and A. V. Thakor, 2000, "Rationality, overconfidence, and leadership," Working paper.

Goetzmann, W. N., and A. Kumar, 2005, "Equity portfolio diversification," *Review of Finance* 12, 433–463.

Goleman, D., 1995, *Emotional Intelligence* (Bantam, New York).

Goleman, D., 2006, *Social Intelligence: The New Science of Human Relationships* (Bantam Books, New York).

Gompers, P. A., and J. Lerner, 2003, "The really long-run performance of initial public offerings: The pre-Nasdaq evidence," *Journal of Finance* 58, 1355–1392.

Gongloff, M., December 1, 2008, "For the VIX, 40 looks like it's the new 20," *Wall Street Journal*, C1.

Graham, J. R., and C. R. Harvey, 2001, "The theory and practice of corporate finance: Evidence from the field," *Journal of Financial Economics* 60, 187–243.

Graham, J. R., C. R. Harvey, and H. Huang, 2006, "Investor competence, trading frequency, and home bias," Working paper.

Griffin, D., and A. Tversky, 1992, "The weighing of evidence and the determinants of confidence," *Cognitive Psychology* 24, 411–435.

Griffin, J. M., X. Ji, and S. Martin, 2003, "Momentum investing and business cycle risk: Evidence from pole to pole," *Journal of Finance* 63, 2515–2547.

Grinblatt, M., and B. Han, 2004, "Prospect theory, mental accounting and momentum," *Journal of Financial Economics* 78, 311–339.

Grinblatt, M., and M. Keloharju, 2001, "How distance, language, and culture influence stockholdings and trades," *Journal of Finance* 56, 1053–1073.

Grinblatt, M., and M. Keloharju, 2008, "Sensation seeking, overconfidence and trading activity," Working paper.

Grinblatt, M., and T. J. Moskowitz, 2004, "Predicting stock price movements from past returns: The role of consistency and tax-loss selling," *Journal of Financial Economics* 71, 541–579.

Grossman, S. J., and J. E. Stiglitz, 1980, "On the impossibility of informationally efficient markets," *American Economic Review* 70(3), 393–408.

Gul, F., 1991, "A theory of disappointment aversion," *Econometrica* 59, 667–686.

Gustman, A.L., and T. L. Steinmeier, 1998, "Effects of pensions on savings: Analysis with data from the Health and Retirement Study," NBER working paper.

Guth, W., R. Schmittberger, and B. Schwarze, 1982, "An experiment analysis of ultimatum bargaining," *Journal of Economic Behavior and Organization* 3(4), 367–388.

Hackbarth, D., 2007, "Managerial optimism, overconfidence, and capital structure decisions," Working paper.

Haigh, M. S., and J. A. List, 2005, "Do professional traders exhibit myopic loss aversion? An experimental analysis," *Journal of Finance* 60 (1), 523–534.

Hallahan, T.A., R. W. Faff, and M. D. McKenzie, 2004, "An empirical investigation of personal financial risk tolerance," *Financial Services Review* 13, 57–78.

Hanna, J. D., and M. J. Ready, 2005, "Profitable predictability in the cross section of stock returns," *Journal of Financial Economics* 78, 463–505.

Hanna, S., and P. Chen, 1997, "Subjective and objective risk tolerance: Implications for optimal portfolios," *Financial Counseling and Planning* 8(2), 17–26.

Hasson, U., Y. Nir, I. Levy, G. Fuhrmann, and R. Malach, 2004, "Intersubject synchronization of cortical activity during natural vision," *Science* 303 (5664), 1634–1640.

Hastorf, A. H., and H. Cantril, 1954, "They saw a game: A case study," *Journal of Abnormal and Social Psychology* 49, 129–134.

Haugen, R. A., 1999. *The New Finance: The Case against Efficient Markets*, 2nd ed. (Prentice Hall, Upper Saddle River, New Jersey).

Haugen, R. A., and N. L. Baker, 1996, "Commonality in the determinants of expected stock returns," *Journal of Financial Economics* 41, 401–439.

Hawkins, S. A, and R. Hastie, 1990, "Hindsight: Biased judgments of past events after the outcomes are known," *Psychological Bulletin* 107, 311–327.

Haruvy, E. and C. Noussair, 2006, "The effect of short selling on bubbles and crashes in experimental spot asset markets," *Journal of Finance* 61(3), 1119–1157.

Healy, P. M., and K. G. Palepu, 2003, "The fall of Enron," *Journal of Economic Perspectives* 17(2) (Spring), 3–26.

Heath, C., and A. Tversky, 1991, "Preference and belief: Ambiguity and competence in choice under uncertainty," *Journal of Risk and Uncertainty* 4, 5–28.

Heaton, J. B., 2002, "Managerial optimism and corporate finance," *Financial Management* 31 (no. 2), 33–45.

Heaton, J., and D. Lucas, 2000, "Portfolio choice and asset prices: The importance of entrepreneurial risk," *Journal of Finance* 55, 1163–1198.

Henderson, B. J., N. Jegadeesh, and M. S. Weisbach, 2003, "World markets for raising new capital," Working paper.

Hermalin, B., and A. M. Isen, 2000, "The effect of affect on economic- and strategic decision making," Johnson Graduate School of Management Working paper.

Hermalin, B. E., and M. S. Weisbach, 2003, "Boards of directors as an endogenously determined institution: A survey of the economic literature," *Federal Reserve Bank of New York Economic Policy Review* (April), 7–26.

Henrich, J., R. Boyd, S. Bowles, C. Camerer, E. Fehr, and H. Gintis, eds., 2004, *Foundations of Human Sociality* (Oxford University Press, Oxford, UK).

Hirshleifer, D., 2001, "Investor psychology and asset pricing," *Journal of Finance* 56, 1533–1597.

Hirshleifer, D., and G. Y. Luo, 2001, "On the survival of overconfident traders in a competitive security market," *Journal of Financial Markets* 4, 73–84.

Hirshleifer, D., and S. H. Teoh, 2003, "Herd behavior and cascading in capital markets: A review and synthesis," *European Financial Management* 9(1), 25–66.

Hirshleifer, D., and T. Shumway, 2003, "Good day sunshine: Stock returns and the weather," *Journal of Finance* 58(3), 1009–1032.

Hirshleifer, J., and J. G. Riley, 1992, *The Analytics of Uncertainty and Information* (Cambridge University Press, Cambridge).

Hoch, S. J., 1985, "Counterfactual reasoning and accuracy in predicting personal events," *Journal of Experimental Psychology: Learning, Memory, and Cognition* 11, 719–731.

Hockey, G. R. J., A. J. Maule, P. J. Clough, and L. Bdzola, 2000, "Effects of negative mood states on risk in everyday decision making," *Cognition and Emotion* 14(6), 823–856.

Hogarth, R. M., and M. W. Reder, 1986, "Editors' comments: Perspectives from economics and psychology," *Journal of Business* 59(4), S185–S207.

Holden, S., and J. VanDerhei, 2005, "401(k) plan asset allocation, account balances, and loan activity in 2004," *EBRI Issue Brief* (269).

Hribar, P., and H. Yang, 2006, "CEO overconfidence, management earnings forecasts, and earnings management," Working paper.

Hsu, M., M. Bhatt, R. Adolphs, D. Tranel, and C. Camerer, 2005, "Neural systems responding to degrees of uncertainty in human decision-making," *Science* 310, 1680–1683.

Huang, R., and J. R. Ritter, "Testing theories of capital structure and estimating the speed of adjustment," *Journal of Financial and Quantitative Analysis*, forthcoming.

Huberman, G., 2001, "Familiarity breeds investment," *Review of Financial Studies* 14, 659–680.

Huberman, G., and W. Jiang, 2006, "Offering vs. choice in 401(k) plans: Equity exposure and number of funds," *Journal of Finance* 61, 763–801.

Hunt, E., 2006, "Expertise, talent, and social encouragement," In *The Cambridge Handbook of Expertise and Expert Performance*, K. A. Ericsson, N. Charness, P. J. Feltovich, and R. R. Hoffman, eds. (Cambridge University Press, New York), 31–38.

Ikenberry, D., J. Lakonishok, and T. Vermaelen, 1995, "Market underreaction to open market share repurchases, *Journal of Financial Economics* 39, 181–208.

Isen, A. M., T. E. Nygren, and F. G. Ashby, 1988, "Influence of positive affect on the subjective utility of gains and losses: It is just not worth the risk," *Journal of Personality and Social Psychology* 55, 710–717.

Ivkovic, Z., and S. Weisbenner, 2005, "Local does as local is: Information content of the geography of individual investors' common stock investments," *Journal of Finance* 60, 267–306.

Iyengar, S. S., and M. Lepper, 2000, "When choice is demotivating: Can one desire too much of a good thing?" *Journal of Personality and Social Psychology* 76, 995–1006.

Jagannathan, R., and N. R. Kocherlakota, 1996, "Why should older people invest less in stocks than younger people?" *Federal Reserve Bank of Minneapolis Quarterly Review* 20 (no. 3), 11–23.

Jamal, K., and S. Sunder, 1996, "Bayesian equilibrium in double auctions populated by biased heuristic traders," *Journal of Economic Behavior and Organization* 31(2), 273–291.

Jamal, K., and S. Sunder, 2001, "Why do biased heuristics approximate Bayes' rule in double auctions?" *Journal of Economic Behavior and Organization* 46(4), 431–435.

James, W., 1884, "What is an emotion?" *Mind* 9, 188–205.

Janelle, C. M., and C. H. Hillman, 2003, "Expert performance in sport: Current perspectives and critical issues," In J. L. Starkes and K.A. Ericsson, eds., *Expert Performance in Sports* (Champaign, Illinois, Human Kinetics), 19–47.

Janis, I. L., 1982, *Groupthink: Psychological Studies of Policy Decisions and Fiascoes*, 2nd ed. (Houghton-Mifflin, Boston).

Jegadeesh, N., 1990, "Evidence of predictable behavior of security returns," *Journal of Finance* 45, 881–898.

Jegadeesh, N., and W. Kim, 2006, "Value of analyst recommendations: International evidence," *Journal of Financial Markets* 9, 274–309.

Jegadeesh, N., and W. Kim, 2007, "Do analysts herd? An analysis of recommendations and market reactions," Working paper.

Jegadeesh, N., and S. Titman, 1993, "Returns to buying winners and selling losers: Implications for stock market efficiency," *Journal of Finance* 48, 65–91.

Jegadeesh, N., and S. Titman, 2002, "Cross-sectional and time-series determinants of momentum returns," *Review of Financial Studies* 15, 143–157.

Jensen, M. C., 1987, "The takeover controversy: Analysis and evidence," in Coffee, J. C., L. Lowenstein, and S. Rose-Ackerman, eds., 1987, *Knights, Raiders and Targets: The Impact of the Hostile Takeover* (Oxford University Press, Oxford, U. K.).

Jensen, M. C., and W. H. Meckling, 1979, "Theory of the firm: Managerial behavior, agency costs, and ownership structure," *Journal of Financial Economics* 3(4) (October), 305–360.

Jeter, D., 2005, "Market timing and managerial portfolio decisions," *Journal of Finance* 60(4), 1903–1949.

Kagel, J. H., and A. E. Roth, eds., 1995, *Handbook of Experimental Economics* (Princeton University Press, Princeton, New Jersey).

Kahneman, D., J. L. Knetsch, and R. H. Thaler, 1986, "Fairness and the assumptions of economics," *Journal of Business* 59(4), S285–S300.

Kahneman, D., J. L. Knetsch, and R. H. Thaler, 1990, "Experimental tests of the endowment effect and the Coase theorem," *Journal of Political Economy* 98(6), 1325–1348.

Kahneman, D., J. L. Knetsch, and R. H. Thaler, 1991, "The endowment effect, loss aversion, and status quo bias," *Journal of Economic Perspectives* 5 (no. 1), 193–206.

Kahneman, D., and M. Riepe, 1998, "Aspects of investor psychology," *Journal of Portfolio Management* 24 (Summer), 52–65.

Kahneman, D., P. Slovic, and A. Tversky, eds., 1982, *Judgment under Uncertainty: Heuristics and Biases* (Cambridge University Press, Cambridge, U.K.).

Kahneman, D., and A. Tversky, 1972, "Subjective probability: A judgment of representativeness," *Cognitive Psychology* 3, 430–454.

Kahneman, D., and A. Tversky, 1973, "On the psychology of prediction," *Psychological Review* 80, 237–251.

Kahneman, D., and A. Tversky, 1979, "Prospect theory: An analysis of decision under risk," *Econometrica* 47(2), 263–291.

Kamstra, M. J., L. A. Kramer, and M. D. Levi, 2002, "Losing sleep at the market: The daylight saving anomaly," *American Economic Review* 90(4), 1005–1011.

Kamstra, M. J., L. A. Kramer, and M. D. Levi, 2003, "Winter blues: A SAD stock market cycle," *American Economic Review* 93(1), 324–343.

Karolyi, G. A., and R. M. Stulz, 1996, "Why do markets move together? An investigation of U.S.-Japan stock return comovements," *Journal of Finance* 51(3), 951–986.

Keiber, K. L., 2002, "Managerial compensation contracts and over-confidence," Working paper.

Keim, D. B., 1983, "Size-related anomalies and stock return seasonality: Further empirical evidence," *Journal of Financial Economics* 12, 13–32.

Keirsey, D., 1998, *Please Understand Me II: Temperament, Character and Intelligence* (Prometheus Nemesis Book Company, Del Mar, California).

Kelly, M., 1995, "All their eggs in one basket: Portfolio diversification of U.S. households," *Journal of Economic Behavior and Organization* 27, 87–96.

Keynes, J. M., 1964, *The General Theory of Employment, Interest, and Money* (Harcourt, Brace, Jovanovich, New York).

Kida, T. E., K. K. Moreno, and J. F. Smith, 2001, "The influence of affect on managers' capital-budgeting decisions," *Contemporary Accounting Research* 18, 477–494.

Kidd, J. B., and J. R. Morgan, 1969, "A predictive information system for management," *Operational Research Quarterly* 20, 149–170.

Kim, K. A., and J. R. Nofsinger, 2002, "The behavior and performance of individual investors in Japan," Working paper.

Kirchler, E., and B. Maciejovsky, 2002, "Simultaneous over- and under-confidence: Evidence from experimental asset markets," *Journal of Risk and Uncertainty* 25, 65–85.

Knight, F. H., 1921, *Risk, Uncertainty, and Profit* (Houghton Mifflin Company, Boston).

Knutson, B., C. Adams, G. Fong, and D. Hommer, 2001, "Anticipation of increasing monetary reward selectively recruits nucleus accumbens," *Journal of Neuroscience* 21, 1–5.

Korajczyk, R., and R. Sadka, 2004, "Are momentum profits robust to trading costs?" *Journal of Finance* 59, 1039–1082.

Koriat, A., S. Lichtenstein, and B. Fischhoff, 1980, "Reasons for confidence," *Journal of Experimental Psychology: Human Learning and Memory* 6, 107–118.

Kothari, S. P., J. Shanken, and R. G. Sloan, 1995, "Another look at the cross-section of expected stock returns," *Journal of Finance* 50, 157–184.

Kramarz, F., and D. Thesmar, 2006, "Social networks in the boardroom," IZA Discussion Paper No. 1940 (January).

Kyle, A. S., and F. A. Wang, 1997, "Speculation duopoly with agreement to disagree: Can overconfidence survive the market test?" *Journal of Finance* 55, 2073–2090.

Laertius, Diogenes, 1938. *Lives of the Eminent Philosophers* (Harvard University Press., Cambridge, Massachusetts).

Laibson, D.I., A. Repetto, and J. Tobacman, 1998, "Self control and saving for retirement," *Brookings Papers on Economic Activity* 1, 91–196.

Lakonishok, J., A. Shleifer, and R. W. Vishny, 1992, "The structure and performance of the money management industry," *Brookings Papers on Economic Activity: Microeconomics*, 339–391.

Lakonishok, J., A. Shleifer, and R. Vishny, 1994, "Contrarian investment, extrapolation and risk," *Journal of Finance* 49, 1541–1578.

Lamont, O. A., and R. H. Thaler, 2003, "Can the market add and subtract? Mispricing in tech stock carve-outs," *Journal of Political Economy* 111, 227–268.

Landy, D., and H. Sigall, 1974, "Beauty is talent: Task evaluation as a function of the performer's physical attractiveness," *Journal of Personality and Social Psychology* 29, 299–304.

Langer, E. J., 1975, "The illusion of control," *Journal of Personality and Social Psychology* 32, 311–328.

LaPorta, R., 1996, "Expectations and the cross-section of stock returns," *Journal of Finance* 51, 1715–1742.

LaPorta, R., J. Lakonishok, A. Shleifer, and R. Vishny, 1997, "Good news for value stocks: Further evidence on market efficiency," *Journal of Finance* 52, 859–874.

Larsen, R. J., and D. M. Buss, 2008, *Personality Psychology*, 3rd ed. (McGraw-Hill, New York).

Larwood, L., and W. Whittaker, 1977, "Managerial myopia: Self-serving biases in organizational planning," *Journal of Applied Psychology* 62, 194–198.

Laury, S. K., and C. A. Holt, 2005, "Further reflections on prospect theory," Working paper.

LeDoux, J., 1996, *The Emotional Brain: The Mysterious Underpinnings of Emotional Life* (Simon & Schuster, New York).

LeDoux, J., 2002, *Synaptic Self: How Our Brains Become Who We Are* (Simon & Schuster, New York).

Lee, C. M. C., A. Shleifer, and R. H. Thaler, 1988, "Closed-end mutual funds," *Journal of Economic Perspectives* 4, 153–164.

Lee, C. M. C., 2001, "Market efficiency and accounting research: A discussion of 'Capital market research in accounting' by S. P. Kothari," *Journal of Accounting and Economics* 31, 233–253.

Lee, C. M. C., A. Shleifer, and R. H. Thaler, 1991, "Investor sentiment and the closed-end fund puzzle," *Journal of Finance* 46(1), 75–109.

Lee, C. M. C., and B. Swaminathan, 2000, "Price momentum and trading volume," *Journal of Finance* 55, 2017–2069.

Lei, V., C. Noussair, and C. Plott, 2001, "Nonspeculative bubbles in experimental asset markets: Lack of common knowledge of rationality vs. actual irrationality," *Econometrica* 69(4), 831–859.

Levis, M., and N. Tessaromatis, 2003, "Style rotation strategies: Issues of implementation," Working paper.

Levitt, S. D. and S. J. Dubner, 2006, *Freakonomics: A Rogue Economist Exposes the Hidden Side of Everything* (William Morrow: An Imprint of HarperCollins Publishers, New York).

Levy, J. S., 1997, "Prospect theory, rational choice, and international relations," *International Studies Quarterly* 41, 87–112.

Lichtenstein, S., B. Fischhoff, and L. D. Phillips, 1982, "Calibration of probabilities: The state of the art to 1980," in D. Kahneman, P. Slovic, and A. Tversky, eds.: *Judgment under Uncertainty: Heuristics and Biases* (Cambridge University Press, Cambridge, U.K.).

Lim, T., 2001, "Rationality and analysts' forecast bias," *Journal of Finance* 56, 369–385.

Lintner, J., 1956, "Distributions of incomes of corporations among dividends, retained earnings and taxes," *American Economic Review* 46, 97–113.

Lintner, J., 1965, "The valuation of risk assets and the selection of risky investments in stock portfolios and capital budgets," *Review of Economics and Statistics* 47(1), 13–37.

Lo, A. W., 2004, "The adaptive markets hypothesis: Market efficiency from an evolutionary perspective," Working paper.

Lo, A. W., 2005, "Reconciling efficient markets with behavioral finance: The adaptive markets hypothesis," Working paper.

Lo, A. W., and D. V. Repin, 2002, "The psychophysiology of real-time financial risk processing, *Journal of Cognitive Neuroscience* 14(3), 323–339.

Lo, A. V., D. V. Repin, and B. N. Steenbarger, 2005, "Fear and greed in financial markets: A clinical study of day traders," Working paper.

Locke, P. R., and S. C. Mann, 2005, "Professional trader discipline and trade disposition," *Journal of Financial Economics* 76, 401–444.

Loewenstein, G. F., C. K. Hsee, E. U. Weber, and N. Welch, 2001, "Risk as feelings," *Psychological Bulletin* 127(2), 267–286.

Loewenstein, G.F., D. Prelec, and R. Weber, 1999, "What, me worry? A psychological perspective on the economic aspects of retirement," in H. J. Aaron, ed.: *Behavioral Dimensions of Retirement Economics*, (Brookings Institution Press & Russell Sage Foundation, Washington, D.C. and New York).

Loftus, E. F., 2003, "Make-believe memories," *American Psychologist* 58, 867–873.

Longin, F., and B. Solnik, 1995, "Is the correlation in international equity returns constant: 1960-1990?," *Journal of International Money and Finance* 14(1), 3–26.

Loomes, G., and R. Sugden, 1982, "Regret theory: An alternative theory of rational choice under uncertainty," *Economic Journal* 92, 805–824.

Lord, C. G., L. Ross, and M. R. Lepper, 1979, "Biased assimilation and attitude polarization: The effects of prior theories on subsequently considered evidence," *Journal of Personality and Social Psychology* 37, 2098–2109.

Loughran, T., and J. R. Ritter, 2000, "Uniformly least powerful tests of market efficiency," *Journal of Financial Economics* 55, 361–389.

Low, C., 2004, "The fear and exuberance from implied volatility of S&P 100 index options," *Journal of Business* 77(3), 527–546.

Lundeberg, M. A., P. W. Fox, and J. Punccohar, 1994, "Highly confident but wrong: Gender differences and similarities in confidence judgments," *Journal of Educational Psychology* 86, 114–121.

Lusardi, A., 2004, "Saving and the effectiveness of financial education," in O. S. Mitchell, and S. P. Utkus, eds.: *Pension Design and Structure: New Lessons from Behavioral Finance,* (Oxford University Press, New York).

MacFarland, D. M., C. D. Marconi, and S. P. Utkus, 2004, "'Money attitudes' and retirement plan design: One size does not fit all," in O. S. Mitchell, and S. P. Utkus, eds.: *Pension Design and Structure: New Lessons from Behavioral Finance* (Oxford University Press, New York).

MacGregor, D. G., P. Slovic, D. Dreman, and M. Berry, 2000, "Imagery, affect, and financial judgment," *Journal of Psychology and Financial Markets* 1(2), 104–110.

Machina, M. J., 1982, "'Expected utility' theory without the independence axiom," *Econometrica* 50, 277–323.

Mackay, C., 1841, *Extraordinary Popular Delusions and the Madness of Crowds* (Bentley, London).

Madrian, B.C., and D. F. Shea, 2001, "The power of suggestion: Inertia in 401(k) participation and savings behavior," *Quarterly Journal of Economics* 116, 1149–1187.

Maenhout, P., 2004, "Robust portfolio rules and asset pricing," *Review of Financial Studies* 17, 951–983.

Malkiel, B. G., 1995, "Returns from investing in equity mutual funds 1971 to 1991," *Journal of Finance* 50, 549–572.

Malkiel, B. G., 2004, *A Random Walk down Wall Street*, 7th ed. (W.W. Norton & Company, New York).

Malmendier, U., and G. Tate, 2005, "CEO overconfidence and corporate investment," *Journal of Finance* 60, 2661–2700.

Malmendier, U., and G. Tate, 2008, "Who makes acquisitions? CEO overconfidence and the market's reaction," *Journal of Financial Economics*, forthcoming.

Mankiw, N. G., and S. P. Zeldes, 1991, "The consumption of stockholders and nonstockholders," *Journal of Financial Economics* 29(1), 97–112.

Mann, L., G. Beswick, P. Allouache, and M. Ivey, 1989, "Decision workshops for the improvement of decision making skills and confidence," *Journal of Counseling and Development* 67, 478–481.

Marconi, C. M., and S. P. Utkus, 2002, "Using 'money attitudes' to enhance retirement communications," Vanguard Center for Retirement Research working paper.

Markowitz, H., 1952, "Portfolio selection," *Journal of Finance* 7(1), 77–91.

Marnet, O., 2005, "Behavior and rationality in corporate governance," *Journal of Economic Issues* 39(3), 613–632.

McDermott, R., J. H. Fowler, and O. Smirnov, 2008, "On the evolutionary origin of prospect theory preferences," *Journal of Politics* 70(2), 335–350.

McLean, B., and P. Elkind, 2004, *The Smartest Guys in the Room: The Amazing Rise and Scandalous Fall of Enron* (Penguin Books, New York).

Mehra, R., and E. C. Prescott, 1985, "The equity premium: A puzzle," *Journal of Monetary Economics* 15(2), 145–161.

Michaely, R., and K. L. Womack, 1999, "Conflict of interest and the credibility of underwriter analyst recommendations," *Review of Financial Studies* 12(4) (July), 653–686.

Milgram, S., 1967, "The small world problem," *Psychology Today* 1, 60–67.

Milgram, S., 1974, *Obedience to Authority: An Experimental View* (Harper & Row, New York).

Mill, J. S., 1874, *Essays on Some Unsettled Questions of Political Economy*, 2nd ed. reprinted 1968 (Augustus M. Kelley Publishers, New York).

Mill, J. S., 1874, *Essays on Some Unsettled Questions of Political Economy*, 2nd ed. reprinted 1968 (Augustus M. Kelley Publishers, New York).

Miller, D. T., and M. Ross, 1975, "Self-serving biases in the attribution of causality: Fact or fiction?" *Psychological Bulletin* 82, 213–225.

Miller, M. H., and F. Modilgiani, 1961, "Dividend policy, growth, and the valuation of shares," *Journal of Business* 34(4), 411–433.

Miller, N., and D. T. Campbell, 1959, "Recency and primacy in persuasion as a function of the timing of speeches and measurements," *Journal of Abnormal and Social Psychology* 59, 1–9.

Mitchell, O.S., and S. P. Utkus, 2003, "Company stock and retirement plan diversification," in O. S. Mitchell, and K. Smetters, eds.: *The Pension Challenge: Risk Transfers and Retirement Income*, (Oxford University Press, Oxford).

Moeller, S., F. Schlingemann, and R.Stulz, 2004, "Wealth destruction on a massive scale? A study of acquiring-firm returns in the recent merger wave," Working paper.

Montier, J., 2002, *Behavioral Finance: Insights into Irrational Minds and Markets* (John Wiley & Sons, Chichester, England).

Morck, R., 2004, "Behavioral finance—in corporate governance—Independent directors and non-executive chairs," National Bureau of Economic Research working paper 10644.

Moskowitz, T. J., and M. Grinblatt, 1999, "Do industries explain momentum?" *Journal of Finance* 54, 1249–1290.

Munnell, A. H., and A. Sunden, 2004, *Coming Up Short: The Challenge of 401(k) Plans,* (Brookings Institution Press, Washington, D.C.).

Nekby, L., P. S. Thoursie, and L. Vahtrik, 2007, "Gender and self-selection into a competitive environment: Are women more overconfident than men?" Working paper.

Nemeroff, C., 1995, "Magical thinking about illness virulence: Conceptions of germs from "safe" versus "dangerous" others," *Health Psychology* 14, 147–151.

Nesse, R. M., and R. Klaas, 1994, "Risk perception by patients with anxiety disorders," *Journal of Nervous and Mental Disease* 182(8), 465–470.

Noe, T. H., M. J. Rebello, and R.Sonti, 2007, "Activists, raiders, and directors: Opportunism and the balance of corporate power," Social Science Research Network working paper 1102902.

Nofsinger, J., 2001, *Investment Madness: How Psychology Affects Your Investing and What to Do About It* (Prentice Hall, Upper Saddle River, New Jersey).

Northcraft, G. B., and M. A. Neale, 1987, "Experts, amateurs and real estate: An anchoring-and-adjustment perspective on property pricing decisions," *Organizational Behavior and Human Decision Processes* 39, 84–97.

Nyce, S. A., and S. J. Schieber, 2005, *The Economic Implications of Aging Societies: The Costs of Living Happily Ever After,* (Cambridge University Press, Cambridge, U.K.).

O'Donoghue, T., and M. Rabin, 1999, "Procrastination in preparing for retirement," in H. J. Aaron, ed.: *Behavioral Dimensions of Retirement Economics,* (Brookings Institution Press & Russell Sage Foundation, Washington, D.C. and New York).

Odean, T., 1998, "Are investors reluctant to realize their losses?" *Journal of Finance* 53(5), 1775–1798.

Odean, T., 1998, "Volume, volatility, price and profit when all traders are above average," *Journal of Finance* 53, 1887–1934.

Pagano, M., F. Panetta, and L. Zingales, 1998, "Why do companies go public? An empirical analysis," *Journal of Finance* 53, 27–64.

Paredes, T. A., 2004, "Too much pay, too much deference: Is CEO overconfidence the product of corporate governance?" Working paper.

Peters, E., and P. Slovic, 1996, "The role of affect and worldviews as orienting dispositions in the perception and acceptance of nuclear war," *Journal of Applied Social Psychology* 26, 1427–1453.

Piotroski, J. D., 2000, "Value investing: The use of historical financial statement information to separate winners from losers," *Journal of Accounting Research* 38 (Supplement), 1–41.

Plous, S., 1993. *The Psychology of Judgment and Decision-making* (McGraw-Hill, New York).

Plutchik, R., 1980, *Emotion: A Psychoevolutionary Synthesis* (Harper and Row, New York).

Pompian, M., 2006, *Behavioral Finance and Wealth Management: How to Build Optimal Portfolios That Account for Investor Biases* (John Wiley & Sons, Hoboken, New Jersey).

Pompian, M. M., and J. M. Longo, 2004, "A new paradigm for practical application of behavioral finance: Creating investment programs based on personality type and gender to produce better investment results," *Journal of Wealth Management* (Fall), 1–7.

Post, T., M. J. an den Assem, G. Baltussen, and R. H. Thaler, 2008, "Deal or no deal? Decision making under risk in a large-payoff game show," *American Economic Review* 98(1), 38–71.

Preuschoff, K., P. Bossaerts, and S. R. Quartz, 2006, "Neural differentiation of expected reward and risk in human subcortical structures," *Neuron* 51, 381–390.

Raghunathan, R., and M. T. Pham, 1999, "All negative moods are not equal: Motivational influences of anxiety and sadness on decision making," *Organizational Behavior and Human Decision Processes* 79(1), 56–77.

Rau, P. R., and T. Vermaelen, 1998, "Glamour, value and the post-acquisition performance of acquiring firms," *Journal of Financial Economics* 49, 223–253.

Read, D., and G. Loewenstein, 1995, "Diversification bias: Explaining the discrepancy in variety seeking between combined and separated choices," *Journal of Experimental Psychology: Applied* 1, 34–49.

Reber, R., and N. Schwarz, 1999, "Effects of perceptual fluency on judgments of truth," *Consciousness and Cognition* 8, 338–342.

Reinganum, M. R., 1988, "The anatomy of a stock market winner," *Financial Analysts Journal* 44 (March/April), 16–28.

Rendleman, R. J., C. P. Jones, and H. A. Latane, 1982, "Empirical anomalies based on unexpected earnings and the importance of risk adjustments," *Journal of Financial Economics* 10, 269–287.

Ritter, J. R., and R. S. Warr, 2002, "The decline of inflation and the bull markets of 1982–1999," *Journal of Financial and Quantitative Analysis* 37(1), 29–61.

Roll, R., 1981, "A possible explanation of the small firm effect," *Journal of Finance* 36, 879–888.

Rolls, E. T., 1980, *The Brain and Emotion* (Oxford University, Oxford).

Rolls, E. T., 1999, *The Brain and Emotion* (Oxford University Press, Oxford).

Persky, J., 1995, "Retrospectives: The ethology of *homo economicus*," *Journal of Economic Perspectives* 9(2) (Spring), 221–231.

Ross, M., and F. Sicoly, 1979, "Egocentric biases in availability and attribution," *Journal of Personality and Social Psychology* 37, 322–336.

Ross, S. A., J. Jaffe, and R. A. Westerfield, 2006, *Corporate Finance* (McGraw-Hill, New York).

Roszkowski, M. J., G. Davey, and J. E. Grable, 2005, "Insights from psychology and psychometrics on measuring risk tolerance," *Journal of Financial Planning* (April), 66–77.

Rottenstreich, Y., and C. K. Hsee, 2001, "Money, kisses and electric shocks: On the affective psychology of risk," *Psychological Science* 12, 185–190.

Rouwenhorst, K. G., 1998, "International momentum strategies," *Journal of Finance* 53, 267–284.

Rozeff, M. S., and M. A. Zaman, 1998, "Overreaction and insider trading: Evidence from growth and value portfolios," *Journal of Finance* 53, 701–716.

Russell, J. A., 1979, "Affective space is bipolar," *Journal of Personality and Social Psychology* 37, 345–356.

Rustichini, A., J. Dickhaut, P. Ghirardato, Kip Smith, and Jose V. Pardo, 2005, "A brain imaging study of the choice procedure," *Games and Economic Behavior* 52(2), 257–282.

Saliterman, V., and B. G. Sheckley, 2004, "Adult learning principles and pension participant behavior," in O. S. Mitchell and S. P. Utkus, eds.: *Pension Design and Structure: New Lessons from Behavioral Finance* (Oxford University Press, New York).

Samuelson, W., and R. Zeckhauser, 1988, "Status quo bias in decision making," *Journal of Risk and Uncertainty* 1, 7–59.

Sanfey, A. G., J. K. Rilling, J. A. Aronson, L.E. Nystrom, and J. D. Cohen, 2003, "The neural basis of economic decision-making in the ultimatum game," *Science* 300, 1755–1758.

Sapra, S. G., and P. J. Zak, 2008, "Neurofinance: Bridging psychology, neurology and investor behavior," Working paper.

Schachter, S., and J. E. Singer, 1962, "Cognitive, social, and physiological determinants of emotional state," *Psychological Review* 69, 379–399.

Schachter, S., and J. E. Singer, 1979, "Comments on the Maslach and Marshall-Zimbardo experiments," *Journal of Personality and Social Psychology* 17, 989–995.

Schierek, D., W. De Bondt, and M. Weber, 1999, "Contrarian and momentum strategies in Germany," *Financial Analysts Journal* (Special Issue on Behavioral Finance), 104–116.

Schipper, K., 1991, "Commentary on analysts' forecasts," *Accounting Horizons* 5 (December), 105–121.

Schwartz, E. S., and M. Moon, 2000, "Rational pricing of Internet companies," *Financial Analysts Journal* 56(3), 62–75.

Schwert, G. W., 1990, "Stock volatility and the crash of '87," *Review of Financial Studies* 3(1), 77–102.

Schwert, G. W., 2002, "Stock volatility in the new millennium: How wacky is the Nasdaq?" *Journal of Monetary Economics* 49(1), 3–26.

Scott, J., M. Stumpp, and P. Xu, 1999, "Behavioral bias, valuation and active management," *Financial Analysts Journal* 55 (July/Aug), 49–57.

Scott, J., and G. Stein, 2004, "Retirement security in a DC world: Using behavioral finance to bridge the expertise gap," in O. S. Mitchell and S. P. Utkus,

eds.: *Pension Design and Structure: New Lessons from Behavioral Finance* (Oxford University Press, New York).

Seligman, M. E. P., and M. Csikszentmihalyi, 2000, "Positive psychology: An introduction," *American Psychologist* 55, 5–14.

Servaes, H., 1991, "Tobin's q and the gains from takeovers," *Journal of Finance* 46(1), 409–419.

Sethi-Iyengar, S., G. Huberman, and W. Jiang, 2004, "How much choice is too much? Contributions to 401(k) retirement plans," in O. S. Mitchell, and S. P. Utkus, eds.: *Pension Design and Structure: New Lessons from Behavioral Finance* (Oxford University Press, New York).

Shafir, E., P. Diamond, and A. Tversky, 1997, "Money illusion," *Quarterly Journal of Economics* 112, 341–374.

Sharpe, W. F., 1964, "Capital asset prices: A theory of market equilibrium under conditions of risk," *Journal of Finance* 19(3), 425–442.

Shefrin, H., 2000. *Beyond Greed and Fear: Understanding Behavioral Finance and the Psychology of Investing* (Harvard Business School Press, Boston, Massachusetts).

Shefrin, H., 2007, *Behavioral Corporate Finance: Decisions That Create Value* (McGraw-Hill Irwin, Boston, Massachusetts).

Shefrin, H., and M. Statman, 1984, "Explaining investor preference for cash dividends," *Journal of Economics* 13, 253–282.

Shefrin, H., and M. Statman, 1985, "The disposition to sell winners too early and ride losers too long: Theory and evidence," *Journal of Finance* 40(3), 777–792.

Shefrin, H., and M. Statman, 1995, "Making sense of beta, size, and book-to-market," *Journal of Portfolio Management* 21(2), 26–34.

Shepperd, J. A., J. A. Ouellette, and J. K. Fernandez, 1996, "Abandoning unrealistic optimism: Performance estimates and the temporal proximity of self-relevant feedback," *Journal of Personality and Social Psychology* 70, 844–855.

Shiller, R. J., 1981, "Do stock prices move too much to be justified by subsequent changes in dividends?" *American Economic Review* 71(3), 421–436.

Shiller, R. J., 1984, "Stock prices and social dynamics," *Brookings Papers on Economic Activity* 2, 457–498.

Shiller, R. J., 1990, *Market Volatility* (MIT Press, Cambridge Massachusetts).

Shiller, R. J., 2000, *Irrational Exuberance* (Princeton University Press, Princeton, New Jersey).

Shiv, B., G. Loewenstein, A. Bechara, A. Damasio, and H. Damasio, 2005, "Investment behavior and the dark side of emotion," *Psychological Science* 16, 435–439.

Shleifer, A., 2000, *Inefficient Markets: An Introduction to Behavioral Finance* (Oxford University Press, Oxford, U.K.).

Shleifer, A., and L. H. Summers, 1990, "The noise trader approach to finance," *Journal of Finance* 4(2), 19–33.

Shleifer, A., and R. Vishny, 1997, "The limits of arbitrage," *Journal of Finance* 52, 35–55.

Shleifer, A., and R. W. Vishny, 2003, "Stock market driven acquisitions," *Journal of Financial Economics* 70, 295–311.

Siegel, J. J., 1998, *Stocks for the Long Run*, 2nd ed. (McGraw Hill, New York).

Simon, H. A., 1992. *Economics, Bounded Rationality, and the Cognitive Revolution* (Elgar, Aldershot Hants, England).

Simonson, I., 1990, "The effect of purchase quantity and timing on variety-seeking behavior," *Journal of Marketing Research* 27, 150–162.

Sirri, E. R., and P. Tufano, 1998, "Costly search and mutual fund flows," *Journal of Finance* 53, 1589–1622.

Smith, C. W., and J. B. Warner, 1979, "On financial contracting: An analysis of bond covenants," *Journal of Financial Economics* 7(2), 117–161.

Smith, R. and J. Weil, January 10, 2005, "Ex-Enron directors reach settlement," *Wall Street Journal*, WSJ.com.

Smith, V. L. 1994, "Economics in the Laboratory," *Journal of Economic Perspectives* 8(1), 113–131.

Smith, V. L., G. L. Suchanek, and A. W. Williams, 1988, "Bubbles, crashes, and endogenous expectations in experimental spot asset markets," *Econometrica* 56(5), 1119–1151.

Solnik, B., 1974, "An equilibrium model of the international capital market," *Journal of Economic Theory* 8, 500–524.

Spencer, J., July 21, 2005, "Lessons from the brain-damaged investor; Unusual study explores links between emotion and results; 'Neuroeconomics' on Wall Street," *Wall Street Journal*, p. D1.

Starmer, C., 2000, "Developments in non-expected utility theory: The hunt for a descriptive theory of choice under risk," *Journal of Economic Literature* 38, 332–382.

Statman, M., and D. Caldwell, 1987, "Applying behavioral finance to capital budgeting: Project terminations," *Financial Management* 16 (no. 4), 7–15.

Statman, M., S. Thorley, and K. Vorkink, 2006, "Investor overconfidence and trading volume," *Review of Financial Studies* 19, 1531–1565.

Statman, M., and T. T. Tyebjee, 1985, "Optimistic capital budgeting forecasts: An experiment," *Financial Management* 14, 27–33.

Statman, M., and V. Wood, 2004, "Investment temperament," Working paper.

Staw, B., 1976, "Knee-deep in the big muddy: A study of escalating commitment toward a chosen course of action," *Organizational Behavior and Human Decision Processes* 20, 27–44.

Steenbarger, B. N., 2007, *Enhancing Trader Performance: Proven Strategies from the Cutting Edge of Trading Psychology* (Wiley, Hoboken, New Jersey).

Steenbarger, B. N., 2003, *The Psychology of Trading* (Wiley, Hoboken, New Jersey).

Stein, N., October 2, 2000, "Global most admired: The world's most admired companies," *Fortune* 142(7), 182–186.

Summers, B., and D. Duxbury, 2007, "Unraveling the disposition effect: The role of prospect theory and emotions," Working paper.

Sundén, A. E., and B. J. Surette, 1998, "Gender differences in the allocation of assets in retirement savings plans," *American Economic Review* 88, 207–211.

Svenson, O., 1981, "Are we all less risky and more skillful than our fellow drivers?" *Acta Psychologica* 47, 143–148.

Taylor, S. E., 1982, "The availability bias insocial perception and interaction," in D.Kahneman, P.Slovic, and A. Tversky, eds.: *Judgment under Uncertainty: Heuristics and Biases* (CambridgeUniversity Press, Cambridge, U.K.).

Thaler, R. H., 1999, "Mental accounting matters," *Journal of Behavioral Decision Making* 12, 183–206.

Thaler, R. H., 1980, "Toward a positive theory of consumer choice," *Journal of Economic Behavior and Organization* 1(1), 39–60.

Thaler, R. H., and S. Benartzi, 2004, "Save more tomorrow: Using behavioral economics to increase employee saving," *Journal of Political Economy* 112, S164–187.

Thaler, R. H., and E. J. Johnson, 1990, "Gambling with the house money and trying to break even: The effects of prior outcomes on risky choice," *Management Science* 36 (6), 643–660.

Thaler, R. H., and C. R. Sunstein, 2003, "Libertarian paternalism," *American Economic Review* 93 (Papers & Proceedings), 175–179.

Thaler, R. H., and J. P. Williamson, 1994, "College and endowment equity funds: Why not 100% equities?" *Journal of Portfolio Management* (Fall), 27–37.

Thomas, D. L., and E. Diener, 1990, "Memory accuracy in the recall of emotions," *Journal of Personality and Social Psychology* 59, 291–297.

Thomsett, M. C., 1999, *Mastering Technical Analysis* (Dearborn Financial Publishing, Chicago, Illinois).

Treynor, J. L., 1961, "Towards a theory of the market value of risky assets," Unpublished manuscript.

Trueman, B., 1994, "Analyst forecasts and herding behavior," *Review of Financial Studies* 7(1), 97–124.

Tversky, A., and D. Kahneman, 1973, "Availability: A heuristic for judging frequency and probability," *Cognitive Psychology* 4, 207–232.

Tversky, A., and D. Kahneman, 1974, "Judgment under Uncertainty: Heuristics and Biases," *Science* 185, 1124–1131.

Tversky, A., and D. Kahneman, 1981, "The framing of decisions and the psychology of choice," *Science* 211 (January), 453–458.

Tversky, A., and D. Kahneman, 1982, "Judgments of and by representativeness", in D. Kahneman, P. Slovic, and A. Tversky, eds.: *Judgment under Uncertainty: Heuristics and Biases* (Cambridge University Press, Cambridge, U.K.).

Tversky, A., and D. Kahneman, 1986, "Rational choice and the framing of decisions," *Journal of Business* 59(4) (pt. 2), S251–S278.

Tversky, A., and D. Kahneman, 1992, "Advances in prospect theory: Cumulative representation of uncertainty," *Journal of Risk and Uncertainty* 5, 297–323.

Vance, S. C., 1983, *Corporate Leadership: Boards, Directors, and Strategy* (McGraw-Hill, New York).

VanDerhei, J., 2006, "Defined benefit plan freezes: Who's affected, how much, and replacing lost accruals," *EBRI Issue Brief* (291).

VanDerhei, J., and C. Copeland, 2004, "ERISA at 30: The decline of private-sector defined benefit promises and annuity payments? What will it mean?" *EBRI Issue Brief* (269).

Varian, H. R., 2005, *Intermediate Microeconomics: A Modern Approach*, 7th ed. (W. W. Norton, New York).

Viceira, L. M., 2001, "Optimal portfolio choice for long-horizon investors with nontradable labor income," *Journal of Finance* 56, 433–470.

von Neumann, J., and O. Morgenstern, 1944, *Theory of Games and Economic Behavior* (Princeton University Press, Princeton, New Jersey).

Wade, C., and C. Tavris, 2006, *Psychology*, 8th ed. (Pearson Prentice Hall Upper Saddle River, New Jersey).

Wang, K. Q., 2005, "Why does the CAPM fail to explain momentum?" Working paper.

Waring, M. B., L. D. Harbert, and L. B. Siegel, 2000, "Mind the gap! Why DC plans underperform DB plans, and how to fix them," *Investment Insights (Barclays Global Investors)* 3, (no. 1 April).

Weber, M., and C. F. Camerer, 1998, "The disposition effect in securities trading: An experimental analysis," *Journal of Economic Behavior and Organization* 33(2), 167–184.

Weinstein, N., 1980, "Unrealistic optimism about future life events," *Journal of Personality and Social Psychology* 39, 806–820.

Weiten, W., 2005, *Psychology: Themes and Variations*, 6th ed. (Wadsworth/Thomson Learning, Belmont, California).

Welch, I., 2000, "Herding among security analysts," *Journal of Financial Economics* 58, 369–396.

Welch, I., 2000, "Views of financial economists on the equity premium and on professional controversies," *Journal of Business* 73, 501–538.

Whaley, R. E., 2000, "The investor fear gauge," *Journal of Portfolio Management* 26(3), 12–17.

Wilson, T. D., D. B. Centerbar, and N. Brekke, 2002, "Mental contamination and the debiasing problem," in T. Gilovich, D. Griffin, and D. Kahneman, eds.: *Heuristics and Biases: The Psychology of Intuitive Judgment* (Cambridge University Press, Cambridge, U.K.).

Wright, C., P. Banerjee, and V. Boney, 2006, "Behavioral finance: Are the disciples profiting from the doctrine?" Working paper.

Wright, W. F., and G. H. Bower, 1992, "Mood effects on subjective probability assessment," *Organizational Behavior and Human Decision Processes* 52, 276–291.

Yermack, D., 1996, "Higher market valuations of companies with a small board of directors," *Journal of Financial Economics* 40(2), 185–211.

Zacharakis, A. L., and D. A. Shepherd, 2001, "The nature of information and overconfidence on venture capitalists' decision making," *Journal of Business Venturing* 16, 311–332.

Zajonc, R. B., 1980, "Feeling and thinking; Preferences need no inferences," *American Psychologist* 35(2), 151–175.

Zajonc, R. B., 1984, "On the primacy of affect," *American Psychologist* 39, 117–123.

Zandstra, G., 2002, "Enron, board governance, and moral failings," *Corporate Governance* 2(2), 16–19.

Zuckerman, M., "Dimensions of sensation seeking," *Journal of Consulting and Clinical Psychology* 36, 45–52.

Zweig, J., 2007, *Your Money and Your Brain: How the New Science of Neuroeconomics Can Help Make You Rich* (Simon and Schuster, New York).

INDEX

Note: Page numbers referencing figures are followed by an "f". Page numbers referencing tables are followed by a "t".

Numerics

401(k)s, 313

A

Abandonment decision, 280
Accounting
    fair value, 211
    mental, 50–52
Accounts, mental, 50–51
Ackert, L. F., 190, 249–250
Acquisitions, managers taking
    advantage of, 272–274
Action tendencies, in defining
    emotion, 122
Adaptation, irrationality and, 99–
    100
Adaptive markets hypothesis, 233
Advantage, value, 220–221
Affect
    allowing to influence choices,
        280–282
    defined, 122
    emotions of investors and, 177–
        178
Affective assessment, 122
Agency problem, 31
Agency relationship, 31
Agency theory, 31–33
Allais paradox, 11–13, 12t–13t

Alpert, Marc, 107–110
Altruism, selfishness vs., 185–201
Ambiguity aversion, 88–89, 88f,
    356
American Association of Individual
    Investors, 144
American corporations, collapse of,
    202–216. *See also* Enron
    Corporation
American Finance Association
    Presidential Address (1986), 67
Amygdala, 127, 127f
Analysts, 206–209
    buy-side, 207
    Enron Corporation problems
        and, 212
    excessive optimism of, 163, 164t
    herding by, 208–209
    independent, 207
    role of, 207
    security. *See* Security analysts
    sell-side, 207
Anchoring, 97–99
    to available economic cues,
        145–147, 146t
    described, 98
    herding vs., 147
    representativeness vs., 99
Anderson, Arthur, 213

Anomalies
    attenuation, 335–336
    behavioral explanations for,
        219–236
    capture, refining, 337–344
    defined, 60, 219
    earnings announcements, lagged
        reactions to, 61–62, 62f,
        219–220
    key, 61–67, 62f, 64t–65t, 66f,
        67t
    momentum and reversal, 65–67,
        66f, 67t, 221–230
    rational explanations for, 230–
        233
    small-firm effect, 62–63
    value vs. growth, 63–65, 64t–
        65t
Appraisals, real estate, experimental
    study of, 145–146, 146t
Arbitrage
    defined, 60
    limits to, 72–75
    problems associated with, 72–75
    textbook, 71–72
    unlimited, in market efficiency,
        71–72
Artisans, 325
Asch, Solomon, 196–197
Asch's lines, 196–197, 196f

Asness, Clifford, 341–342
Asset allocation-type funds, 307
Assets
  allocation, 303–307
  individual, 20–21
  lottery, 250
  portfolios of, 21–22
Attention-grabbing, in financial
  decision-making, 145
Attitudes
  money, 323–325
  risk, 8–11, 9f–11f, 42, 329
Attribution theory, in durability of
  overconfidence, 114
Authority, obedience to, 197–198
Automatic enrollment, 308–309
Autonomic nervous system, in
  emotional theory, 123
Availability, in financial decision-
  making, 145
Availability heuristic, 96–97
Aversion
  ambiguity, 88–89, 88f, 356
  loss, 39, 45–46, 280–282

B
Baker, Malcolm, 266, 270–271
Baker, Nardin, 343–344
Baltussen, Guido, 175
Barber, Brad, 145, 157–159, 161,
  283
Barberis, Nicholas, 174, 176–177,
  222, 227, 229–230, 251, 256,
  336
Barberis-Shliefer-Vishny (BSV)
  model, 227–230, 229f, 230t
Base rate neglect, 91–95
  Bayesian updating, 92–93
  hot hand phenomenon, 93–95,
    94t
Basu, Sanjoy, 63–64
Bayes' rule, 92
Behavioral biases, durability of
  overconfidence due to, 114–115
Behavioral corporate finance, 279–
  291
  capital budgeting, 279–282
  investment and overconfidence,
    282–288
  managerial overconfidence, 282,
    288
  market valuations and, 251
  overview, 279
Behavioral investing, 335–350
  anomaly attenuation, 335–336

enhancing portfolio
    performance, 346–347
  overview, 335
  refining anomaly capture, 339–
    344
  momentum and reversal, 339–
    341
  momentum and value, 341–342
  multivariate approaches, 342–
    344
  refining momentum-investing
    using volume, 337–339
  refining value investing using
    accounting data, 337
  style peer groups and style
    investing, 336
  style rotation, 344–346
Behavioral science foundations. See
  Biases; entries beginning with
  "Emotion"; Heuristics;
  Overconfidence
Behaviors
  See also Financial decision-
    making
  anomalies, behavioral
    explanations for, 219–236
  familiarity and, 138–141, 138t–
    139t
  observed, key aspects of, 38–40
  path-dependent, example of,
    175
  social, emotion and, 198
  stock market puzzles related to,
    237–261
  in trust games, 190–191, 190f
Benartzi, Shlomo, 144–145, 242–
  243, 303, 305, 310–311
Ben-David, Itzhak, 282
Better-than-average effect, 110–111
Biais, Bruno, 159
Biases
  in durability of overconfidence,
    114–115
  eliminating, steps required, 319–
    321
  future directions in, 100–101
  helping those affected by,
    strategies for, 321–322
  heuristics and, 90
  home, 138–139, 138t–139t
  implications of, 137–150
  recency, 97
  representativeness and related,
    90–97, 91f, 94t
  salience, 97
  status quo, 46, 46f, 89–90

Black, Fischer, 67, 270
Bounded rationality, 99–100
Brain
  anatomy of, 126–127, 127f
  in emotion, 126–128, 127f
  imaging of, 126, 356
  parts of, 126–127
Brands, familiar, investing in, 141
Break even effect, 49–50
Brekke, Nancy, 320
Brown, Stephen, 241
BSV (Barberis-Shliefer-Vishny)
  model, 227–230, 229f, 230t
Bubbles
  defined, 244
  real-world, 243–247, 246f
  tech/Internet, 245–247, 246f
Bubbles markets
  described, 247–248
  design of, 248–249, 249t, 250f
  experimental, 247–251, 248f,
    249t, 250f
Buffett, Warren, 34
Buy-side analysts, 207

C
Calibration tests, 107–110, 108t–
  109t
Camerer, Colin, 175, 286–287
Cannon, Walter, 123–124, 124f
Capital asset pricing model
  (CAPM), 26–28, 27f, 27t
Capital budgeting, 279–282
  ease of processing, 280
  loss aversion and affect, 280–
    282
Capital market line (CML), 26
CAPM (capital asset pricing
  model),
  26–28, 27f, 27t
CARs (cumulative average
  residuals), 61, 62f
CBOE (Chicago Board Options
  Exchange), 253
Centerbar, David, 320
Certainty effect, 42–43
Certainty equivalent, 9–10, 9f
Charupat, N., 249–250
Cheeks, M., 94
Chicago Board Options Exchange
  (CBOE), 253
Church, B. K., 190, 249–250
Client management, using
  behavioral finance in, 326–329
Closure, in mental accounting, 52
CML (capital market line), 26

Cognitive antecedents, in defining emotion, 121
Cognitive dissonance, 84
Companies, good, vs. good investments, 142–143, 143t
Company name, changes in, 268–269
Compensation contract, optimal, 32
Competition, in markets, 193–194, 194f
Competitive blind spots, 288
Compound prospect, 16
Confirmation bias, in durability of overconfidence, 114
Conflicts of interest, for security analysts, 207–208
Conformity, 196–198, 196f
Conjunction fallacy, 91
Conlisk, John, 12
Contract design, incentives and, 194–196, 195f
Contracts, optimal compensation, 32
Contribution pensions, 296
Control, illusion of, 111
Cooper, Michael, 269
Corporate boards, 203–206
    benefits of, 203–204
    insiders and outsiders on, 204–205
Corporate directors
    compensation of, 205–206
    loyalty of, 206
    self-interest of, 205–206
Corporations
    American, collapse of, 202–216
    defined, 203
Correlation, 21
Coval, Joshua, 140–141
Covariance, 21
Cues, economic, 145–147, 146t
Culture, in financial decision-making, 139–140
Cumulative average residuals (CARs), 61, 62f
Cumulative prospect theory, 42
Customization, education, 327
Cutler, David, 252

D
Damasio, Antonio, 128–129
Daniel, Kent, 222
Daniel-Hirshleifer-Subrahmany (DHS) model, 222–223, 223f
Darwin, Charles, 125

Data snooping, 63
Davis, S., 190
Dawkins, Darryl, 94
DB (defined benefit) pensions, 296–297
DC (defined contribution) pensions. See Defined contribution (DC) pensions
De Bondt, Werner, 65–66
De Long, Bradford, 73
Deaves, R., 144, 160, 249–250, 304–305
Debiased confidence interval, 324
Debiasing, 319–332
    overview, 319
    steps required to eliminate bias, 319–321
    strategies for helping those affected by bias, 321–322
    through education, 322–326
Debiasing strategies, 321–322
Debt, overconfidence and, 288
Decision frames, 14, 47
Decision weights, 40
Decision-making, financial. See Financial decision-making
"Default" behavior, 308
Deferral rates, income replacement ratios vs., 300t
Defined benefit (DB) pensions, 296–297
Defined contribution (DC) pensions, 295–318
    asset allocation, 303–307
    defined benefit pensions vs., 296–297
    exponential discount functions, 301–302
    hyperbolic discount functions, 301–302
    improvements in design, 307–313
    limited self-control, 300
    overview, 295
    problems faced by employee-investors, 298
    procrastination, 302–303
    retirement preparedness, 303
    saving needs, determining, 298–300
Demand, aggregate, 154, 154f, 155, 156f
DHS (Daniel-Hirshleifer-Subrahmanyam) model, 222–223, 223f
Dictator game, 188–189, 188f

Differential reward index, 355
Dimitrov, Orlin, 269
Disappearing dividends, 270
Disposition effect, 171–175
    defined, 52, 171
    empirical evidence for, 171–172, 172t
    experimental evidence for, 174–175
    prospect theory as explanation for, 172–174, 173f
Dissonance, cognitive, 84
Distance, in financial decision-making, 139–140
Diversifiable risk, 25
Diversification, principle of, 21
Diversification heuristic, 89, 303
Dividend patterns, explanation of, 269–271, 271f
Dividend premium, 270, 271f
Dividends
    disappearing, 270
    home-made, 269
Dopamine, 354
Doukas, John, 285
Duxbury, Darren, 174–175

E
Earnings, standardized unexpected, 61
Earnings announcements, lagged reactions to, 61–62, 62f, 219–220
Ease of processing, 280
Economic cues, anchoring to, 145–147, 146t
"Economic man", 185–186
Economics, neoclassical. See Neoclassical economics
Education, debiasing through, 322–326
Efficiency, market. See Market efficiency
Elster, Jon, 121
Emotional foundations, 120–134
Emotional intelligence, 130
Emotional quotient (EQ), 130
Emotional response, theories of, 122–124, 124f
Emotions
    affect and, 177–178
    brain, 126–128, 127f
    defining of, 120–122
    disposition effect, 171–175, 172t, 173f

evolutionary theories in, 124–126, 125f, 130
expertise and, 355–356
features of, 121
force of, 168–181
house money, 175–177
mood of market and, 169–170
pride, 170–171
primary, 126
reasoning and, 128–130, 128f
regret, 170–171
source of, 130
substance of, 120–122
Employee Retirement Income Security Act (ERISA) of 1974, 271, 296
Employers, investing in, 141
Endorsement effects, 309
Endowment effect, 46, 46f, 89–90
Enron Corporation
    analysts and, 212
    bankruptcy of, 209
    business of, 209–211, 210f
    collapse of, 202–216
    directors of, 211–212
    fair value accounting at, 211
    Fortune magazine on, 202
    history of, 209
    leaders of, 209
    organizational culture of, 213–214
    performance of, 209–211, 210f
    personal identity of, 213–214
    SPEs of, 210–211
EQ (emotional quotient), 130
Equity allocation, 304f–305f
Equity premium, 27
Equity premium puzzle, 238–243, 239f–240f, 241t
Equivalent, certainty, 9–10, 9f
Equivalent prospect, rational, 16
Equivalent standard prospect, 16
ERISA (Employee Retirement Income Security Act) of 1974, 271, 296
Errors, uncorrelated, 68–70, 70f–71f
Erving, J., 94
ESTP (extroverted-sensing-thinking-perceiving) personality, 323
European Central Bank, 254
Event study methodology, 61
Evolution
    emotion and, 124–126, 125f, 130
    social behavior and, 198–199

Excess returns, 29
Excessive optimism, 111–112, 163, 164t, 282
Excessive risk taking, overconfidence and, 162–163
Excessive volatility, 251–254, 253f–254f. *See also* Volatility
Expected utility
    axioms required to derive, 17
    maximization of, 3
    theory of, 6–8
Expected value, of returns, 20
Experimental bubbles markets, 247–251, 248f, 249t, 250f
Expertise
    emotion and, 355–356
    implicit learning and, 353–354
Exponential discount functions, 301–302
Extroverted-sensing-thinking-perceiving (ESTP) personality, 323

F
Fair value accounting, 211
Fairchild, Richard, 272
Fairness, value of, 186–192, 188f, 190f, 192f
Fallacies
    conjunction, 91
    gambler's, 95
    planning, 111
Fama, Eugene, 28–29, 65, 219, 231–232, 269–270
Fama-French three-factor model, 232, 346
Familiarity
    financial behavior stemming from, 138–141, 138t–139t
    heuristics and, 87–90, 88f
Fast and frugal heuristics, 99–100
Federal Reserve, 254
Feedback, 321
Fehr, Ernst, 193–195
Financial decision-making
    See also Overconfidence
    anchoring to available economic cues in, 145–147, 146t
    availability and attention-grabbing in, 145
    brands, investing in, 141
    chasing winners, 143–145, 144f
    culture, effects of, 139–140
    distance, effects of, 139–140
    employers, investing in, 141

familiarity and, 138t, 139–141, 139t
good companies vs. good investments in, 142–143, 143t
herding in, 147
heuristics and biases and, 100–101, 137–150
home bias in, 138–139, 138t–139t
implications of, 151–167
language, effects of, 139–140
local investing and informational advantages in, 140–141
representativeness and, 141–145, 143t, 144f
First order conditions, 267–268
Fischbacher, Urs, 193–194
Fischhoff, Baruch, 321
fMRI (functional magnetic resonance imaging), 126
Fong, Christina, 193–194
Forebrain, 127, 127f
Forsythe, R., 188
Fortune magazine, 202
401(k)s, 313
Fourfold pattern of risk attitudes, 42
Framing
    defined, 14
    overview, 47–50
    perception and memory effects of, 85–86, 85f
    in processing information, 85–86, 85f
Free rider problems, 204
French, Kenneth, 65, 138–139, 219, 231–232, 269–270
Frieder, Laura, 141
F-scores, 337
Functional magnetic resonance imaging (fMRI), 126
Fundamental risk, arbitrage and, 72

G
Gächter, Simon, 195
Gage, Phineas, 128–129, 128f
Gallup Organization, 115
Gambler's fallacy, 95
Gender, as factor in overconfidence in financial realm, 161
Gervais, Simon, 162
GH (Grinblatt-Han) model, 224–227, 224f–225f
Gigerenzer, Gerd, 99, 102, 113
Gilovich, Thomas, 94, 100

Glamour stocks, value stocks vs., 63–65, 64t–65t
Glaser, Markus, 159
Goetzmann, William, 163, 241
Goldwater, Barry, 252
Graham, John, 282
Greater fool theory, 245
Greenspan, Alan, 245, 247, 258
Griffin, Dale, 100
Grinblatt, Mark, 140, 159, 222, 224, 227, 339–341
Grinblatt-Han (GH) model, 224–227, 224f–225f
Groupthink, 197
Growth potential factors, 343
Growth stocks, value stocks vs., 63–65, 64t–65t
Guardians, 323

H
Hackbarth, Dirk, 288
Halo effect, 86
Han, Bing, 222, 224, 227, 340
Harvey, Campbell, 282
Haugen, Robert, 343–344
Heath, Chip, 87–88
Hedged returns, 340t, 341f
Henrich, J., 192
Herding
    by analysts, 208–209
    anchoring vs., 147
Heuristics, 83–90
    ambiguity aversion in, 88–89, 88f
    availability, 96–97
    biases and, 90
    defined, 86
    described, 86–87
    diversification, 89
    errors induced by, 101
    examples of, 87
    familiarity and, 87–90, 88f
    fast and frugal, 99–100
    future directions in, 100–101
    implications of, 137–150
    in mispricing and managers' goals, 266–267
    representativeness, 91
    Type 1, 86
    Type 2, 86
Hilton, Denis, 159
Hindsight bias, 114
Hirshleifer, David, 222
Hollins, L., 94
Home bias, 138–139, 138t–139t

Home-made dividends, 269
Homo economicus, 185–186, 298
Horowitz, J. L., 188
Hot hand phenomenon, 93–95, 94t
House money effect, 49–50, 175–177
Hsee, Christopher, 131
Huang, Ming, 176–177, 251, 256
Huberman, Gus, 139, 305
Hyperbolic discount functions, 301–302

I
Idealists, 323
Illiquid stocks, 343
Illusion of control, 111
Implementation costs, arbitrage-related, 73–75
Implicit learning, 353–354
Implied volatility index (VIX), 253–254, 254f
Incentives, contract design and, 194–196, 195f
Income replacement ratio, 298–299, 300t
Independent analysts, 207
Individual assets, risk and return for, 20–21
Individual-level equity allocation, 305
Inertia, 311
INFJ (introverted-intuitive-feeling-judging) personality, 323
Information
    market efficiency and, 28–29
    overload of, 86
    relevant, 6
Informational advantages, 140–141
Initiation rate, 270, 271f
Inside directors, 204
Insurance, lottery tickets and, 41–42
Integration
    described, 49, 49f
    in mental accounting, 52
    segregation vs., 48–50, 49f
Intelligence, emotional, 130
Intentional objects, 121
Internal rate of return (IRR), 279
International investors, country weights among, 138, 138t
Internet/tech bubble, 245–247, 246f
Introverted-intuitive-feeling-judging (INFJ) personality, 323

Investment value, management quality regression and, 142, 143t
Investments
    See also Behavioral investing
    in brands, familiar, 141
    in employers, 141
    good, vs. good companies, 142–143, 143t
    local, 140–141
    momentum, 337–339
    overconfidence and, 282–288
    value, 63, 337, 341–342
    winning, 143–145, 144f
The Investor Behavior Project, 247
Investor behaviors. *See* Biases; *entries beginning with "Emotion"*; Financial decision-making; Heuristics; Overconfidence
Investor rationality, 67–68
IRR (internal rate of return), 279
Irrational exuberance, 169
Irrationality, 99–100

J
James, William, 123–124, 124f
Jegadeesh, Narasimhan, 66–67, 164
Jiang, Wei, 305
Johnson, Eric, 175–176
Johnson, Lyndon, 252
Joint hypothesis problem, 30–31
Jones, B., 94
Jones, Charles, 61–62, 94

K
Kahneman, Daniel, 11, 15, 37–38, 42–45, 48–49, 52–55, 90, 108–109, 174, 328
Keirsey Temperament Sorter, 323
Keloharju, Matti, 140, 159
Keynes, John Maynard, 33
Kida, Thomas, 281
Kim, W., 164
Knight, Frank, 7
Kroll, Luisa, 34
Kumar, Alok, 163

L
Lagged reactions to earnings announcements, 61–62, 62f, 219–220
Lakonishok, Josef, 64, 220, 233
Lamont, Owen, 74

Language, in financial decision-making, 139–140
Latane, Henry, 61–62
Launer, Curt, 213
Lay, Kenneth, 209
Learning
    biases interfering with, 114
    social, 208
Lee, Charles, 337–339
Life-cycle (target date) funds, 312–313
Limbic system, 127, 127f
Limited self-control, 300
Lintner, John, 275
Live-for-today avoiders, 324
Lo, Andrew, 233
Local investing, 140–141
Long Term Capital Management, 254
Loss aversion, 39, 45–46, 280–282
Lottery assets, 250
Lottery tickets, 41–42
Lovallo, Dan, 286–287
Low-probability overweighting, 55
Low-risk investments, 306
Lüders, E., 160
Luo, G. Y., 160

M
Madrian, Brigitte, 308–309
Malmendier, Ulrike, 283–285
Management expense ratio (MER), 29
Management quality regression, 142, 143t
Managers, 279–291
    capital budgeting, 279–282
    examples of, 268–274, 271f
    goals of, 266–267, 271f
    irrational, 274–275
    overconfidence, 282–288
    overview, 279
    rational, 265–278
Market efficiency, 28–31
    challenges to, 60–80
    future of, 75
    implications of, 29–30
    information and, 28–29
    joint hypothesis problem in, 30–31
    misconceptions about, 30
    temporary deviations from, 233
    theoretical requirements for, 67–72, 70f–71f

Market equilibrium, 155–156, 155f, 157f
Market outcomes, 217–261
Market practitioners, overconfidence of, 161–162
Market risk premium, 27
Market valuations, 251
Markets
    See also Bubbles markets
    in 2008, 254–257, 256f, 257t
    competition in, 193–194, 194f
    mood of, 169–170
Marshall, John, 203
Maximum wealth level, 16
Mazurier, Karine, 159
Mean return, 20
Mehra, Rajinish, 238–239
Memory
    framing effects of, 85–86, 85f
    in processing information, 84–85
    reconstructiveness of, 84–85
Mental accounts, 50–52
    closing, 50–52
    components of, 51
    described, 50–51
    evaluation of, 51–52
    integration in, 52
    opening, 50–51
    segregation in, 52
MER (management expense ratio), 29
Mergers and acquisitions, 272–274, 284–285
Milgram, Stanley, 197–198, 205–206, 213
Mill, John Stuart, 186, 199
Minimum wealth level, 16
Miscalibration, 106–110, 108t–109t
Mispricing, managers' goals and, 266–274, 271f
Mix, S., 94
Modern portfolio theory, 20
Modigliani-Miller dividend irrelevance theorem, 269
Momentum, 65–67, 66f, 67t
    anomalies due to, 221–230
    BSV model on, 227–230, 229f, 230t
    described, 221–222, 232
    GH model on, 224–227, 224f–225f
    reversal and, 339–341
    value and, 341–342

Momentum (relative-strength) strategy, 345, 347t
Momentum life cycle, 339f
Momentum-chasing, 144
Momentum-investing, 337–339
Money attitudes, 323–325
Moreno, Kimberley, 281
Morgenstern, Oskar, 6
Moskowitz, Tobias, 140–141, 339–341
Multivariate approaches, 342–344

N
NAcc (nucleus accumbens), 354
Neale, Margaret, 145–146
Neglect, base rate. See Base rate neglect
Neoclassical economics
    fundamental assumptions about people in, 4–6
    rational preferences in, 4
    relevant information in, 6
    utility maximization in, 4–5, 5t, 6f
Net present value (NPV), 279
Neurofinance, 353–360
    expertise and emotion, 355–356
    expertise and implicit learning, 353–354
    insights from, 354–355
    overview, 351
Neuroscience, 198, 353
Neutral, risk, 10–11, 11f
New York Stock Exchange (NYSE) Composite Index, 27–28, 27t
Nofsinger, John, 325
Noise-trading, 67–73, 70f–71f
Nondiversifiable risk, 25
Non-expected utility models, 47
Nonsystematic risk, 25
Normative theory, 38
Northcraft, Gregory, 145–146
NPV (net present value), 279
Nucleus accumbens (NAcc), 354
NYSE (New York Stock Exchange) Composite Index, 27–28, 27t

O
Obedience to authority, 197–198
Objective risk, 327
Observed behavior, key aspects of, 38–40
Odean, Terrance, 145, 156–159, 161–162, 171–172, 283
Optimal compensation contract, 32

Optimal portfolio, 22–26, 23t, 24f–25f

Optimism, excessive, 111–112, 163, 164t, 282

Orbitofrontal cortex, 354

Other-regarding preferences, 185

Outside directors, on corporate boards, 204–205

Overconfidence, 106–119, 282–288
 See also Excessive optimism
 better-than-average effect, 110–111
 consistency of, 113, 113t
 defined, 106, 152
 demographics of, 161–162
 durability of, 114–115
 dynamics of, 161–162
 evidence of, 157–159, 158f, 159–161, 160t
 excessive risk taking and, 162–163
 excessive trading related to, 151–161, 153f–158f, 160t
 extent of, 112
 financial applications of, 115–116
 forms of, 106–119
 gender in, 161
 illusion of control, 111, 113
 implications of, 151–167
 managerial, 282
 market practitioners and, 161–162
 miscalibration, 106–110, 108t–109t
 in more than one sense, 112
 security demand as function of, 153, 153f
 underdiversification and, 162–163
 as unmitigated flaw, 114–115

Overinvestment, 282

Overweighting, 55

P

Path dependence, 52, 175

P/E (price-to-earnings) ratio, 209, 210t, 245–246

Perception
 described, 84
 framing effects of, 85–86, 85f
 in processing information, 84

Personality types, 323–325

Personalized feedback, 321

PET (position emission tomography), 126

Petmezas, Dimitris, 285

Physiological arousal, 121

Physiological expressions, 121

Piotroski, Joseph, 337–338, 342

Plan-level equity exposure, 305

Planner-avoider continuum, 324f

Planning fallacy, 111

Pompian, Michael, 328–329

Portfolios
 expected returns implied by, 138, 139t
 optimal, 22–26, 23t, 24f–25f
 risk and return for, 21–22

Position emission tomography (PET), 126

Positive theory, 38

Post, Thierry, 175

Poterba, James, 138–139, 252

Pouget, Sébastien, 159

Practical knowledge, 355

Practicing, 352

Predictability, overestimating, 95–96

Preferences
 other-regarding, 185
 rational, 4

Premiums
 dividend, 270, 271f
 equity, 27
 market risk, 27
 value, 31

Prescott, Edward, 238–239

Present value model of stock prices, 30

Price level factors, 343

Price-to-earnings (P/E) ratio, 209, 210t, 245–246

Pricing
 mispricing, managers' goals and, 266–274, 271f
 of risk, 20–28, 23t, 24f–25f, 27f
 stock, 30

Pride, 170

Primacy effect, 85

Primary emotions, 126

Probability, in risk measurement, 7

Processing information, 83–86
 ease of, 86
 framing effects of, 85–86, 85f
 information overload and, 86
 memory effects on, 84–85
 perception effects on, 84

Procrastination, 302–303

Profit function, 286

Prospect choices, 12, 12t–13t

Prospect theory, 38–47
 competing alternative theories, 47
 cumulative, 42
 described, 38
 endowment effect, 46f
 as explanation for disposition effect, 172–174, 173f
 hypothetical value and weighting functions in, 44–45
 integration vs. segregation, 48–50, 49f
 lottery tickets and insurance, 41–42
 nonmonetary outcomes, 48
 observed behavior in, 38–40
 origins of, 46–47
 to practice, 52–53
 psychology and, 47
 riskless loss aversion in, 45–46
 sequential decisions and, 176–177
 value function in, 40, 41t
 weighting function in, 42–43, 43f, 55–56

Prospects
 compound, 16
 defined, 16
 described, 7–8
 rational equivalent, 16
 standard, 16

Psychographic profiling, 323–325

Psychology
 prospect theory and, 47
 rationality to, 33

Q

Questionnaires, 327–328

R

Raiffa, Howard, 107–110

Random walk, 30

Rate of time preference, 301

Rational equivalent prospect, 16

Rational managers, 265–278

Rational preferences, 4

Rationality
 bounded, 99–100
 to psychology, 33

Rationals, 323

Rau, Raghavendra, 269

Real estate appraisals, experimental study of, 145–146, 146t

Real-world bubbles, 243–247, 246f

Reasoning, emotion and, 128–130, 128f
Recency bias, 97
Recency effect, 85
Reciprocity, value of, 186–192, 188f, 190f, 192f
Reference group neglect effect, 288
Reference points, 39
Reg FD (Regulation Fair Disclosure), 212
Regret, 170
Regulation Fair Disclosure (Reg FD), 212
Reinganum, Marc, 342–343
Relationship, agency, 31
Relative-strength (momentum) strategy, 345, 347t
Relative-value strategy, 345, 347t
Relevant information, 6
Reliability, questionnaire, 328
Rendleman, Richard, 61–62
Representativeness
    anchoring vs., 99
    biases related to, 90–97, 91f, 94t
    financial behaviors stemming from, 141–145, 143t, 144f
Representativeness heuristic, 91
Repurchases, managers taking advantage of, 272
Residuals, cumulative average, 61, 62f
Responders, behavior of, 190–191, 190f
Retirement saving behavior, 295–318
    asset allocation, 303–307
    defined benefit pensions vs. defined contribution pensions, 296–297
    determining saving needs, 298–300
    exponential discount functions, 301–302
    hyperbolic discount functions, 301–302
    improvements in DC pension design, 307–313
    limited self-control, 300
    overview, 295
    problems faced by employee-investors, 298
    procrastination, 302–303
    retirement preparedness, 303
Returns
    excess, 29
    expected value of, 20

for individual assets, 20–21
mean, computation of, 20
for portfolios of assets, 21–22
sample standard deviation of, 21
sample variance of, 20
standard deviation of, 20
variance of, 20
Reversal
    anomalies due to, 221–230
    BSV model on, 227–230, 229f, 230t
    described, 221–222
    DSH model on, 222–223, 223f
    momentum and, 65–67, 66f, 67t, 339–341
Richardson, C., 94
Riepe, Mark, 328
Risk adjustment, inappropriate, 230–232
Risk attitudes, 8–11, 9f–11f, 42, 329
Risk averse, 9, 9f
Risk capacity, 327
Risk neutral, 10–11, 11f
Risk questionnaires, 327–328
Risk seekers, 10, 10f
Risk tolerance, 326
Riskless loss aversion, 45–46
Risk
    diversifiable, 25
    expected utility theory and, 6–7
    fundamental, 72
    for individual assets, 20–21
    noise-trader, 72–73
    nondiversifiable, 25
    nonsystematic, 25
    for portfolios of assets, 21–22
    pricing of, 20–28, 23t, 24f–25f, 27f
    probability in measurement of, 7
    systematic, 25
Risk taking, excessive, 162–163
Ross, Stephen, 241
Rottenstreich, Yuval, 131
Ruback, Richard, 266

S
S&P 500 (Standard and Poor's 500 Composite Stock Price Index), 245
Salience bias, 97
Sample standard deviation, 21
Sample variance, 20
Santos, Tano, 176–177, 251, 256
Sarbanes-Oxley Act (SOX), 212
Savin, N. E., 188

Savings rates, SDIP, 311t
Schachter, Stanley, 123–124, 124f
Scheduled deferral increase programs (SDIPs), 310–311
Scholes, Myron, 270
Schwert, William, 335
SDIPs (scheduled deferral increase programs), 310–311
SEC (Securities and Exchange Commission), 203
Secure doers, 324
Securities and Exchange Act of 1934, 203
Securities and Exchange Commission (SEC), 203
Security demand, as function of overconfidence, 153, 153f
Security analysts
    conflicts of interest for, 207–208
    herding by, 208–209
    performance of, 207–208
    role of, 207
Sefton, M., 188
Segregation
    described, 49, 49f
    integration vs., 48–50, 49f
    in mental accounting, 52
Self-attribution bias, 114
Selfishness, altruism vs., 185–201
Sell-side analysts, 207
Semi-strong form efficiency, 29
Sensation seeking, 159
Sensitivity to cash flows, 283–284
Separation, two-fund, 25
Sequential decisions, 176–177
Shares, issuing of, 272
Sharpe, William, 83
Shea, Dennis, 308–309
Shefrin, Hersh, 142–143, 172–173
Shiller, Robert, 68, 70, 74, 77, 169, 210, 245–248, 251–253
Shiller model, 68–69, 77
Shleifer, Andrei, 64, 72–73, 220–222, 227, 229–230, 233, 272, 336
Siegel, Jeremy, 238–241
Simon, Herbert, 99
Simonson, Itamar, 89
Singer, Jerome, 123
Slovic, P., 108–109
Small-firm effect, 62–63
Smart-money traders, 68
Smith, James, 281
Smith, Vernon, 53, 248
Snake-bit effect, 175

Social behavior
emotion and, 198
evolution and, 198–199
Social forces
conformity, 196–198, 196f
emotion and, 198
fairness, 186–192, 188f, 190f, 192f
homo economicus, 185–186
reciprocity, 186–192, 188f, 190f, 192f
selfishness or altruism, 185–201
social behavior and, 198
social influences and, 192–196, 194f–195f
trust, 186–192, 188f, 190f, 192f
at work, 202–216. *See also* Enron Corporation
Social influences, importance of, 192–196, 194f–195f
Social learning, 208
Social neuroscience, 198
Socrates, 112
SOX (Sarbanes-Oxley Act), 212
Special purpose entities (SPEs), 210–211
Standard and Poor's 500 Composite Stock Price Index (S&P 500), 245
Standard compound prospect, 16
Standard deviation
of returns, 20
sample, 21
Standard prospect, 16
Standard rational equivalent prospect, 16
Standardized unexpected earnings (SUE), 61
Start-ups, 285–288
Statman, Meir, 142–143, 172–173
Status quo bias, 46, 46f, 89–90
Stock market, puzzles of, 237–261
Stock prices, present value of, 30
Stocks
glamour, 63–65, 64t–65t
growth, 63–65, 64t–65t
value, 63–65, 64t–65t
Stressed avoiders, 324
Style investing, 336
Style peer groups, 336
Style rotation, 347t
Subadditivity, 55
Subcertainty, 55–56
Subrahmanyam, Avanidhar, 141, 222

Successful planners, 324
Suchanek, Gerry, 248
SUE (standardized unexpected earnings), 61
Summers, Barbara, 174–175
Summers, Larry, 73, 252
Sunk costs, 279–280
Supply, aggregate, 154, 154f, 155, 156f
Swaminathan, Bhaskaran, 337–339
Systematic risk, 25

T
Tacit knowledge, 352
Target date (life-cycle) funds, 312–313
TARP bailout, 255–256
Tate, Geoffrey, 283–285
Tech/Internet bubble, 245–247, 246f
Technical factors, 343
Textbook arbitrage, 71–72
Thaler, Richard, 50, 65–66, 74, 175–176, 242–243, 303, 305, 310–311
Theories
See also Prospect theory
agency, 31–33
attribution, 114
emotional response, 122–124, 124f
evolutionary, 124–126, 125f, 130
expected utility, 6–8
greater fool, 245
modern portfolio, 20
normative, 38
positive, 38
Titman, Sheridan, 66–67
Tobin's q, 283
Toney, A., 94
Traders
overconfident, 152–157, 153f–157f
smart-money, 68
Trading, excessive, 151–161, 153f–158f, 160t
Transivity, 4
Trend-following, 144
Trust, value of, 186–192, 188f, 190f, 192f
Trust game, 189–191, 190f
Tulip mania, 244–245
Tversky, Amos, 11, 15, 37–38, 42–44, 48–49, 52–55, 87–90, 94, 108–109, 174
Two-fund separation, 25

U
UBS PaineWebber, 115
Ultimatum game, 187–189, 188f, 192f
Uncorrelated errors, in market efficiency, 68–70, 70f–71f
Underdiversification, 162–163
Unexpected earnings, 61
Up-and-coming planners, 324
Utility functions
characteristics of, 18
described, 4–5, 5t, 6f
logarithmic, 5, 6f
Utility maximization, 4–5, 5t, 6f
Utility models, non-expected, 47

V
Valence, 121–122
Validity, questionnaire, 328
Vallone, Robert, 94
Value
expected, 20
of fairness, 186–192, 188f, 190f, 192f
of reciprocity, 186–192, 188f, 190f, 192f
of trust, 186–192, 188f, 190f, 192f
Value advantage, 220–221
Value function, 40, 41t
Value investing
defined, 63
momentum and, 341–342
refining using accounting data, 337
Value Line Investment Survey, 28
Value premium, 31
Value revision, market equilibrium after, 155, 155f, 156, 157f
Value stocks, growth stocks vs., 63–65, 64t–65t
van den Assem, Martijn J., 175
Vanguard study, 323–324
Variance, of returns, 20
Vishny, Robert, 64, 72, 220, 222, 227, 229–230, 233, 272
VIX (implied volatility index), 253–254, 254f
Volatility
excessive, 251–254, 253f–254f
forecasts of, 253–254, 254f
von Neumann, John, 6

W

Waldmann, Robert, 73
"Wall Street rule", 282
Weak form efficiency, 29
Wealth, logarithmic utility of, 5,
   5t, 6f
Weber, Martin, 159, 175
Weighting function, 42–45, 43f
Weights, decision, 40

Williams, Arlington, 248
Wilson, Timothy, 320
Winning investments, 143–145,
   144f
Wurgler, Jeffrey, 266, 270–271

X

Xiong, Wei, 174

Y

Yale University, 247

Z

Zajonc, Robert, 123–124
Zhang, Ganggang, 272